TITO

ARCHITECT
OF
YUGOSLAV
DISINTEGRATION

TITO

ARCHITECT
OF
YUGOSLAV
DISINTEGRATION

by

Bosko S. Vukcevich

RIVERCROSS PUBLISHING, INC.

NEW YORK

ISBN: 0-944957-46-3

Library of Congress Cataloging-in-Publication Data

Vukcevich, Bosko S.
    Tito—architect of Yugoslav disintegration / by Bosko S. Vukcevich. -
- 1st ed.
      p. cm.
    Partly translated from ''Hell or Communism in Montenegro''
originally in Serbo-Croatian (Cyrillic).
    Includes bibliographical references and index.
    ISBN 0-944957-46-3 : $29.95
    1. Yugoslavia—History—1945-1980. 2. Tito, Josip Broz,
1892-1980.   I. Title.
DR1300.V85 1994
949.702′3—dc20   94-25626
                                 CIP

Contents

Original issues of "Hell or Communism in Montenegro."

Foreword

The Serbian people have been condemned to repeat a tragic history because they have relied upon justice, honesty, and fairness to resolve issues, wars, conflicts, in which they have been involved. Unfortunately, they did not, as did the Jews, take their destiny into their own hands throughout history. Instead, though victors, they have been the pawns of Great Power Politics.

In this massive labor of devotion which so meticulously details and documents his every statement, Bosko Vukcevich tells of the events and players that forced the Serbian destiny into their tragic destiny. He shows that the same forces, and some of the same actors, are alive and as determined to demonize and destroy the Serbian people today as they were in WW I and WW II. Perhaps one of the facts he finds hardest to accept in this entire tragedy is that Pope John II urged the bombing of the Serbians and urged Catholics throughout the world to support it. Through the Vatican the Pope pleaded to all important sessions of the EC Security Council Secretary of State, Sodano, to wreak military havoc upon the "Serb aggressors." The Vatican played a major role in the breakup of the former Yugoslavia*, by being the first to recognize Slovenia, Croatia, and Bosnia/Hercegovina. This recognition precluded any consideration of Serbian rights to self-determination, or any civil rights where they were a minority.

Mass media propaganda pushed racial hatred against the Serb "barbarians," painting them as the sole culprits. At the same time the Croats hired the powerful public relations firms like Sachi and Sachi to demonize the Serbs using false information and posters to give their anti-Serb messages visual impact. Also involved were Ruder and Finn and Hill and Knowlton, which staged false bombings and incidents geared toward inciting American involvement or air strikes.

ANTECEDENTS OF THE CIVIL WAR

World War I was forced upon Serbia because of Austro-Hungarian and German ambitions to have an open corridor across Serb lands to gain military and economic control of the wealthy East. Germany tried this four times in preceding decades, but this time, because of US and UN support, might succeed.

World War II began for the Serbs the day World War I ended. Because the German obsession with "drang nach osten" was not fulfilled, Hitler subdued Europe, then turned to Yugoslavia, aiming for that open corridor, and thinking Serbs would surrender. They did not. Despite massive bombing on April 6, 1941, they followed the martyred Serbian General Draza Mihailovich to the mountains, and organized as guerrillas wherever possible, to fight the mighty German war machine. The world was stunned, and praise

---

* Bosnia Hercegovina never before existed as a state in any form.

of Mihailovich and the Serbian Chetniks resounded to the Heaven until, as in the past, the Allies abandoned the Serbians to one of the bloodiest murderers of all time, the Croatian Communist, Tito, to whom they later gave billions of dollars to support his reign.

During Tito's fifty-year reign he used every threat to prohibit one of the most horrible massacres in world history from being known. He forbade any mention, commemoration, or even prayer for the souls of the millions of Serbs, Jews and Gypsies, massacred and thrown into pits by the Axis Allies, the Independent State of Croatia, ruled by Croatian Ustashi. The Serbian people were not then and are not now allowed to mourn this ghastly genocide. We are told what happened fifty years ago is not important. We cannot, like the Jews, ask for justice, properly bury our dead, lay their souls to rest, and proclaim, NEVER AGAIN. This is not being allowed. Tudjman states that genocide is a natural phenomenon. The Holy Monuments at Jasenovac and the Golubarska Pit (uncovered in 1991), and all other signs of the Croat Ustashi genocide, are being bulldozed, blown up or razed, so that no trace remains.

The Holocaust Museum in Washington buries our victims even deeper by inviting Tudjman as a guest, and by refusing to acknowledge this immeasurable tragedy. Today, in the resurrected independent State of Croatia, Serbs are again facing forced conversion, death, or acceptance of the same symbols and some of the same people from the first ISC which carried out the massive genocide against them. The Jews do not have to live under swastikas, but Serbs are expected to live with the checkerboard flag under which they were massacred fifty years ago.

The Serbs have been proclaimed the aggressors in this civil war.

Carefully, with full documentation and primary sources, the author, Vukcevich, proves the catastrophic events which led to the break-up of Yugoslavia were put into motion by the Vatican and Germany. The rest is history, except that it is history that has been convoluted to paint the victims as the culprits. The worst political cynicism is that there was no need for the war in Bosnia/Hercegovina . . that, here too, President Bush succumbed to German and Vatican pressure and to the concept of the New World Order as originally envisioned by Hitler in the 1940's.

Bosko Vukcevich, eye-witness, combatant, painstaking researcher of events in Yugoslavia, has given us a document which has something for everyone who is interested in learning the truth about the Yugoslav conflicts, present and past.

1. Vukcevich traces the origins of the conflict in both the political and media arenas noting especially the horrifying misinformation which is again being used to achieve the same political/military goals as in WW I and II, as best seen in an exposure of the work of public relations firms which are for hire, and which have demonized the Serbian people to make it acceptable for them to be bombed, even annihilated. (Note what happened after the false Kuwaiti Incubator Baby Story was planted on US TV and which

President Bush repeated in ten speeches. He got total approval to bomb the Iraquis who supposedly committed this falsely reported deed.)

2. Vukcevich gives survivors and families of victims from Montenegro an opportunity to learn how and why so many were killed, why the communists ordered fratricide and patricide, and he publishes the orders for the deaths.

3. In this way, he lights a candle in memory of these victims, and allows the survivors to do the same.

For those who wish to understand the worst of all wars, a Civil War, Vukcevich's description and documents will describe the day-by-day events in all their horrible details.

This book provides a valuable resource for research into the entire Yugoslav history, into the "Powder Keg," the "Balkan Question," and any number of topics which can be herein derived.

Vukcevich's use of hitherto hidden archives and untranslated documents, his immense documentation, and his eye-witness testimony make this volume extremely important to those who seek the truth.

Just as the curtain was raised after WW II exposing the incredible deceit and bungling which allowed Tito to become Czar of Yugoslavia, so someday the greatest media hoax and manipulation of this century—the promotion of wars for ratings and self glory—will be exposed. Then the real story of the Serbs will once again emerge. It will be too late for many of us, but at least our children who have been the victims of massive discrimination, prejudice and demonization will again see their people returned to their rightful respected place among the nations for whom they gave their lives and fortunes in the two great wars.

Helen A. Pavichevich, Ph.D.

During WWII and the internal Yugoslav revolution, General Mihailovich was the first guerrilla leader to oppose the Nazis in their occupation of Europe.

His democratic movement was also opposed to Communist Tito and his National Liberation Movement, which was "patriotic in slogans while Communistic in substance."

TITO
ARCHITECT
OF
YUGOSLAV
DISINTEGRATION

PART I

Chapter One

HELL
or
Communism in Montenegro

Volume Number One
An edition of the *Voice of Montenegro*
Publisher, Obod—Cetinje

Preface

With extreme sacrifice, great effort, and at the risk of our very lives we have collected this horrifying material for current and future generations as a vivid picture of an incomprehensible, insane epoch. Unfortunately, all of it is original and true, in word and in photographs. It is excerpted from reports that were attested to and signed by authorities in the localities where the misdeeds were committed. For ethical reasons we have omitted documents of pornographic content, which testified to even more atrocities wreaked on the people of Montenegro by the champions of hell's abyss.

Noted herein are the traitors from all parts of the former Yugoslavia who were educated, supported, and encouraged to betray their faiths and fatherland from early youth. They fully recognized the basic characteristics of Montenegrins: unlimited love of liberty and appreciation of their historical ties with Slavic Russia, from which Montenegrins were accustomed to being blessed with great benefits and vast personal prestige.

Inpenetrable Montenegrin mountains came at just the right time for their dark goals. They had persistently honed their bloody plans and preparations for twenty years. Their fanaticism and good organization brought about their success, especially among the youth. Using the motto "Serbianism, Slavs, Liberty" it was not hard at all to recruit adherents. Who knows how it would have ended and what the destiny of this people would have been if they had not made their fatal mistake, one that dug their common grave.

After they jumped on the backs of their own people, they began to execute their bloody program during the period of foreign occupations.

It is impossible, indeed to explain why they insisted on destroying faith, the nation, and family dignity; why they killed and massacred masses of popular leaders and protectors of the sacredness of their own people, from whom they demanded both property and blood. Whence came their self-confidence and imprudence in the country where ties of fraternity, kinship, and blood were so strong? Why did they cut off the branch on which they sat? Probably only a psychiatrist could explain it. One thing is certain: historians, sociologists, and psychiatrists would never succeed in finding convincing reasons for such a bloody and beastly drama in the glorious land of Njegosh, on the soil of knights with sword, spirit, and dignity. They knew the glory of their tiny country was spread throughout the world, and that she had friendly ties with great and strong nations as an equal.

The Partisans in their nine months' rule [*the last three months in 1941 and the first half of 1942*] left for the people as souvenirs bloody tracks that will never disappear even with seven southern rains. They left the skeletons of their brothers, whom we searched for and found in pits and holes and whom we need to continue to look for during the next decade. The results of their hatred will have pernicious consequences for the next century.

Though the material was ample, we were technically unable to publish one book in coherent, chronological order. Therefore, we divided the book into several volumes. Each volume would deal with one part of the whole story so arranged that they could later be bound into one large book. In each volume would be several lists of Communist leaders: commanders of detachments, battalions, and companies; political commissars; judges, executioners, and their assistants; and pictures and lists of their victims, burned houses, killings, lootings, plunderings, and debaucheries.

These original documents, by their words and pictures, disclose many bloody secrets that were previously covered up and expose many individuals who are today concealing themselves or who are adapting themselves to the new political environment while waiting for the right moment to stab their opponents in the back and continue their bloody job of butchery and debauchery. In our volumes we will gradually publish lists of each person killed, wounded, or victimized by theft or other property damage, large numbers of pictures of live Partisans as well as victims—dug-out corpses, and voluminous Partisan original documents. In a word, nothing will be missing. The lists of casualties and damages will be included in later volumes for all communities. Either we already possess the documents, or we will visit specific locales to uncover the whole grievous story.

It is imperative as a historical necessity that honest and true patriots force themselves, reluctantly and with tears in their eyes, to see the material presented and be repulsed by Tito's Communist massacres.

The effect of these volumes will be the full portrayal of the national movement, its leaders, and all that the victims endured to destroy the tyrannical Partisan regime. In the exposed documents the reader will easily see the unforgivable mistakes of national gravediggers, atheists, and immoral riffraff as well as the brother bloodsuckers who called themselves Partisans.

While collecting our material we found some leaders who were conscientious about their responsibilities to history. They truly understood it; therefore they supported us in our endeavor, which we greatly appreciate. Also, many private individuals helped us, to whom we are also thankful!

READ AND JUDGE FOR YOURSELF

Persons Killed in the Spanish Civil War

MILAN SHARANOVICH
law school student

DJOKO KOVACEVICH
law school student

GOJKO BJEDOV
student of agronomy

MIJAT MASKOVICH
law school student

Mosha Pijade

He was born in Belgrade, on December 22, 1889, of Jewish parents.
Mosha was very intelligent, with a broad education and knowledge of almost

all the world's main languages. He could not have a quiet life with such revolutionary blood. For that very reason he often came in conflict with the law. Therefore he spent almost twenty years in prison.

During the occupation he came to Montenegro, where he became an organizer, spiritual leader, and the father of all evils that happened there while we were living under the tyrannical Partisan regime. It was not hard for him because he was surrounded by half-educated primitives living according to the instincts of their wild ancestors. They saw him as a Messiah and higher being. In spite of his endeavors against our nation, where he found asylum with some of his fellow tribesmen, he nevertheless had a considerable number of sympathizers and protectors in Belgrade society. That society was so deeply rotten, so unconsciously antinational, as to let the impossible be possible.

Mosha Pijade was sentenced to long-term imprisonment in Sremska Mitrovica. Despite this, his artwork and portrait were hung on the wall of the Prince Paul Museum. Furthermore, in prison he had privileges and the opportunity to translate that grandiose work of Marx, *Das Kapital*. He found a publisher to publish it under the pseudonym "Mr. Porobich."

The well-known Belgrade writer Veljko Petrovich felt deeply sorry for Mosha's destiny as a Jew. Mosha was a convict, but Petrovich believed him to be a respected man. He immortalized him in the *People's Encyclopedia*, vol. 3, year 1928, writing about him in an almost tender, brotherly way:

Pijade, Mosha, was an artist and publicist. He completed the fifth grade of gymnasium. Afterward he was admitted to the art vocational school. In 1906 to 1907 he went to Munich to learn drafting and painting. From 1909 to 1910 he studied in La Grande Chamiere. Pijade rarely exhibited his art and he never took part in collective exhibitions. In 1914 most of his art work was gone on the Greek railroad. In 1919 he took up journalism. At first he worked on an art magazine and review. Then in the *Free Word* he began to publicize a study about Meshtrovich. After WWI he joined the revolutionary labor movement. Meanwhile he spent all of his energy writing as an authority on Communist professional and propagandist literature. In 1924 he was jailed for such activities. Pijade was a capable artist, as can be seen in his two self-portraits (1916 and 1919), illustrations, and folksongs about Marko Kraljevich, which were published in 1920 in Belgrade by *Progress* under a pseudonym. In the Mitrovica prison he began to paint again.

V. Petrovich

[*Here is a question: Why did the editor of* Hell or Communism *call Pijade a spiritual leader and the father of all the evils of the tyrannical Partisan regime? Pijade was considered an outstanding scholar among the Yugoslav intelligencia. Before the revolution broke out, Tito and members of the central committee of the Yugoslav Communist party (CPY) decided to send revolutionary party members throughout the country to ignite and coordinate direct actions. Some party members from the towns and cities were ordered to move to the countryside, while others remained as informers in the cities. Tito strongly believed that the French revolution of 1789 failed because it occurred in the city instead of in the countryside. As soon as the people in Montenegro heard that some prominent individuals had been executed by the Communist party, they became suspicious of the influx of city people to the villages. In the people's mind the outsiders were nothing but conspirators bent on carrying out party orders. In that period of mistrust if someone even moved from one village to another he or she came under suspicion. Furthermore, at the beginning the people in Montenegro could not conceive of the rapaciousness and atrocities that could be committed by and among themselves! During the revolution Pijade was sent to the Durmitor area. He supervised a farm of twelve thousand sheep, most of them confiscated from nationalistic families.*

In Embattled Mountain *Deakin mentioned what Pijade had told him about the excessive executions in Montenegro by the Communist party. In addition, Milovan Djilas says Mosha was well known as a vehement defender of the Serbian cause in the central committee of the CPY. Pijade intelligently and without bias quickly realized who was suffering the most in the tragic Yugoslav theater as well as who were being neglected, like the Serbs and Jews. Tito and his entire CPY apparatus had played a deceiving role in the Ustashe genocide and the secret collaboration of Croatian Partisans with them and with Nazis as well. Kardelj quietly protected Slovenes, while Serbian Communists declared themselves as internationalists, cutting their ties to their nationalistic identity.*

In 1943 Pijade presented a proposal for territorial autonomy for Serbs in Croatia. If his proposal had been adopted the ethnic flare-up in Croatia would not have happened. For it, give thanks to Tito and his Serbian cohorts.

Finally, judging from the facts, Pijade was more honest and fair than any other Yugoslav Communist who looked at the heart of Yugoslav events. I am convinced that if the editor of Hell or Communism *had had more facts at the time of his writing he would have judged Pijade differently.*]

Captured Partisan Men and Women

DR. PETAR JOVANOVICH
Communist doctor

LJUBOMIR CUPICH
political commissar

MIHAILO B. POPOVICH
political commissar

NISHA MIHAILOVICH
commandant of Partisan strike battalion

DJURDJINA PANTOVICH
from Gornje Polje

The pit at Kopilje
58 m. deep

BRANKO MILJEVICH
Podgorica

DUSHAN RADONJICH
Jelenak

VUKA ALEKSICH
by birth from Drobnjak

RADE LUCICH
from Kupinovo

Commandants of Partisan Battalions and Their Assistants

Bosko Ostojich, peasant, 50 years old. Community Meljak, district Pljevlja.
Velimir Jakich, forest engineer, 35 years old. Community Ilino Brdo, district Pljevlja.

Dobrica Bakovich, judicial assistant, 30 years old. Community Matarugi, district Pljevlja.

Joko Knezevich, law school student, 32 years old. Community Matarugi, district Pljevlja.

Ilija V. Zecevich, student, 24 years old. Community Ocevinci, district Pljevlja.

Kesha Djurovich, 28 years old. Community Petrushine, district Danilovgrad.

Slobodan Bujishich, professor, 30 years old. Community Prencanci, district Pljevlja.

Slobodan Mikacevich, commandant of Second Battalion. Community Gotovushka, district Pljevlja.

Arso Boskovich, company commander. Community Gotovushka, district Pljevlja.

Gojko Krezovich, railroad employee, 35 years old. Community Bukovica, district Pljevlja.

Mirko J. Krdzich, an active captain, 45 years old. Community Polimlje, district Andrijevica.

Sekula Popovich, company commander, from Lushci. Community Manastir, district Berane.

Vuko Z. Novovich, auditor, 32 years old. Community Trepcha, district Andrijevica.

Ljubomir Bakocevich, peasant, 45 years old. Community Mojkovac, district Bijelo Polje.

Ivan Minjich, battalion commandant. Community Jelenak, district Danilovgrad.

Vlado Raspopovich, political commissar of battalion. Community Jelenak, district Danilovgrad.

Miloje Dobrashinovich, professor, 45 years old. Community Bijelo Polje, district Bijelo Polje.

Shpiro Radulovich, peasant, 40 years old. Community Spuz, district Danilovgrad.

Nesho Joksimovich, forest engineer, 26 years old. Community Pavino Polje, district Bijelo Polje.

Petar Vukovich, law student, 28 years old. Community Pavino Polje, district Bijelo Polje.

Ljuboje Kmajevich, former community president, 45 years old. Community Pavino Polje, district Bijelo Polje.

Dushan Barovich, commandant. Community Komani, district Danilovgrad.

Milan Radulovich, company commander. Community Komani, district Danilovgrad.

Vidoje Djurovich, business student, 26 years old. Community Zagarac, district Danilovgrad.

Dushan S. Barovich, district court employee, 25 years old. com munity Zagarac, district Danilovgrad.

Petar S. Vujovich, judicial assistant, 30 years old. Community Zagarac, district Danilovgrad.
Radomir Janketich, student, 32 years old. Community Shahovici, district Bijelo Polje.
Ljubo Radosavljevich, student, 31 years old. Community Ravna Rijeka, district Bijelo Polje.
Manojlo Bulatovich, reserve lieutenant, 32 years old. Community Ravna Rijeka, district Bijelo Polje.
Shćepan Djukich, auditor, 29 years old. Community Lijeva Rijeka, district Andrijevica.
Vlado F. Abramovich, student, 30 years old. Community Bjelice, district Cetinje.

ASK THE PARTISANS OR THEIR FAMILIES ABOUT THE MISDEEDS AND THE BLOODTHIRSTINESS CARRIED OUT IN MONTENEGRO AND SANDZAK. THEY WILL TELL YOU THEY ARE INNOCENT AS GOD'S LAMBS!

Political Commissars and Their Assistants

Mihailo Aletich, teacher, 40 years old. Community Meljak, district Pljevlja.
Mihailo Zugich, teacher. Community Ilino Brdo, district Pljevlja.
Drago Despotovich, peasant, 20 years old. Community Matarugi, district Pljevlja.
Urosh Golubovich, law student, 34 years old. Community Matarugi, district Pljevlja.
Radosh Kontich, student, 20 years old. Community Ocevinci, district Pljevlja.
Urosh Golubovich, student, 34 years old. Community Prencanci, district Pljevlja.
Marko M. Radonjich, community Petrushine, district Danilovgrad.
Djordjije Rodjen, medical student, 26 years old. Community Bukovica, district Pljevlja.
Vera Crvencanin, law student, 22 years old. Community Bukovica, district Pljevlja.
Radoje Toshich, student, 27 years old. Community Gotovushka, district Pljevlja.
Vido Lj. Shoshkich, law student, reserve officer, 32 years old. Community Polimlje, district Andrijevica.
Djordjije Pajkovich from Lushca. Community Manastir, district Berane.
Ruzica S. Raicevich, teacher, 35 years old. Community Trepcha, district Andrijevica.
Zivko Zizich, law student, 34 years old. Community Mojkovac, district Bijelo Polje.

Rade Kovacevich, community Jelenak, district Danilovgrad.
Tomash Zizich, agronomy engineer, 32 years old. Community Bijelo Polje, district Bijelo Polje.
Adam Lucich, student, 30 years old. Community Spuz, district Danilovgrad.
Rade Bojceta, law student, 20 years old. Community Pavino Polje, district Bijelo Polje.
Milutin Pavicevich, high school senior, 22 years old. Community Pavkovici, district Danilovgrad.
Vuleta Djuranovich, 30 years old. Community Komani, district Danilovgrad.
Milosov Radulovich, 30 years old. Community Komani, district Danilovgrad.
Vuleta Djuranovich, 30 years old. Community Zagarac, district Danilovgrad.
Veljko M. Kekovich, student, 28 years old. Community Zagarac, district Danilovgrad.
Tomash Zizich, agronomy engineer, 32 years old. Community Shahovici, district Bijelo Polje. [duplication in original]
Dragoje Kujovich, graduate of seminary school, 26 years old. Community Ravna Rijeka, district Bijelo Polje.
Mrkoje Markovich, road maintenance worker, 32 years old. Community Ravna Rijeka, district Bijelo Polje.
Mirko Veshovich, lawyer, 35 years old. Community Lijeva Rijeka, district Andrijevica.

The thousands of innocent victims killed and massacred by them, the thousands of burned homes, and the hundreds in millions in damages are of no more concern to the Partisans than a wisp of smoke from a cigarette. The more one is a bloodsucker, the better comrade he is for them.

Partisan Judges and Their Assistants

Djordjije Rocen, medical student, 26 years old. Community Meljak, district Pljevlja.
Djordjije Perunicich from Maoci, military judge, 34 years old. Community Ilino Brdo, district Pljevlja.
Danilo Knezevich, student, 25 years old. Community Ilino Brdo, district Pljevlja.
Velimir Jakich, forestry engineer, 35 years old. Community Gotovushka, district Pljevlja.
Vlado Knezevich, community Gotovushka, district Pljevlja.

Mitar Terzich, peasant, 41 years old, president of Partisan court. Community Ocevinci, district Pljevlja.

Petar Tomcich, peasant, 34 years old, secretary of Partisan court. Community Ocevinci, district Pljevlja.

Radmila Nedich from Berane. Community Manastir, district Berane.

Mihailo T. Lalich, jurist, 30 years old. Community Trepcha, district Andrijevica.

Savo Joksimovich, law student, 32 years old. Community Mojkovac, district Bijelo Polje.

Novak Brajovich, community Jelenak, district Danilovgrad.

Savo Zarich, community Jelenak, district Danilovgrad.

Dushan Korach, teacher, 28 years old. Community Bijelo Polje, district Bijelo Polje.

Nikola Barovich, Partisan delegate from Danilovgrad district. Community Komani, district Danilovgrad.

Mirko I. Stamatovich, peasant, 24 years old. Community Zagarac, district Danilovgrad.

Ilija M. Shcepanovich, peasant, 26 years old. Community Zagarac, district Danilovgrad.

Tomash Zizich, agronomist, 35 years old. Community Shahovici, district Bijelo Polje.

Vasilije Lasica, peasant, 45 years old. Community Ravna Rijeka, district Bijelo Polje.

The Executioners and Their Assistants

Ljubisav Zorich, peasant, 25 years old. Community Meljak, district Pljevlja.

Joko Borota, boxer from Boka Kotorska. Community Ilino Brdo, district Pljevlja.

Olga Jovovich, housewife from Shumani, 25 years old. Community Matarugi, district Pljevlja.

Misho Vranich, community Gotovushka, district Pljevlja.

Bozo Glavonich, community Gotovushka, district Pljevlja.

Avro M. Ivanovich, craftsman, 32 years old. Community Trepcha, district Andrijevica.

Milovan Ulich, peasant, 35 years old. Community Spuz, district Danilovgrad.

Radomir Kmajevich, peasant, 20 years old. Community Pavino Polje, district Bijelo Polje.

Milosh Kmajevich, peasant, 20 years old. Comunity Pavino Polje, district Bijelo Polje.

Milosh M. Jovanovich, peasant, 30 years old. Community Zagarac, district Danilovgrad.

Mirash Zizich, high school student, 20 years old. Community Shahovici, district Bijelo Polje.

Ilija Juskovich, peasant, 28 years old. Community Ravna Rijeka, district Bijelo Polje.

Their law is what their heart yearns for;
What does not yearn in the Koran, it is not written.

Njegosh

Ask any Partisan judge or executioner or their assistants, "From where came the thousands of corpses in various pits and ravines?" They will quickly tell you that the people were tired of their lives and therefore committed suicide by throwing themselves into the pits.

Results of the Partisan Work

Various Verdicts and Crimes

In the Name of the People:

The military court of the Niksic Partisan Detachment met to determine the quilt or innocence of Novica S. Kovacevich, judge from Spile, against whom criminal charges have been brought. He was tried from December 31, 1941 to January 4, 1942. A decision was reached on January 15, 1942.

VERDICT:

Sentenced to be executed by firing squad:

1. Novica S. Kovacevich, judge from Spile, as the agent of the people's treason of Draza Mihailovich against the national liberation struggle, as the main organizer for old Velimski District's so-called people's army of Draza Mihailovich, and as a person highly trusted by the occupier.

2. Djordjije P. Markovich, retired captain from Jabuka, as the main organizer with Novica and Blazo Kovacevich of the so-called people's army of Draza Mihailovich, a breaker of unity in the struggle against the occupier, and his [*the occupier's*] servant.

3. Blazo S. Kovacevich, teacher from Spile, as the main organizer with Novica S. Kovacevich and Djordjije Markovich of the so-called people's army of Draza Mihailovich.

4. Nikola B. Bulajich, peasant from Prisoje, as one of the main propagandists in his neighborhood for the so-called people's army of Draza Mihailovich and breaker of people's unity in the struggle against the occupier.

5. Marko K. Kovacevich, peasant from Spile, as a deserter from the Partisan army, breaker of people's unity in the struggle against the occupier, servant and agent of the occupier, and plunderer and people's oppressor.

6. Mirko J. Kovacevich, peasant from Vilusi, one of the main propagandists in his neighborhood for the so-called people's army of Draza Mihailovich, breaker of people's unity in the struggle against the occupier, and his servant.

7. Marko R. Bulajich, peasant from Jabuka, as one of the main propagandists in his neighborhood for the so-called people's army of Draza Mihailovich, breaker of the people's unity, servant to the occupier and to all former regimes, and a cheater and oppressor of the people.

8. Petar V. Kovacevich, businessman from Spile, as one of the main propagandists in his neighborhood for the so-called people's army of Draza Mihailovich and breaker of the people's unity in the struggle against the occupier.

9. Lazo J. Kovacevich, peasant from Vilusi, as breaker of the people's unity in the struggle against the occupier.

10. Luka S. Kovacevich, peasant from Vilusi, as an active propagandist in his neighborhood and breaker of the people's unity for the so-called people's army of Draza Mihailovich.

11. Novak J. Krivokapich, peasant from Jabuka, as an active propagandist in his neighborhood for the so-called people's army of Draza Mihailovich.

12. Krsto N. Kovacevich, peasant from Vilusi, as an active propagandist in his neighborhood for the so-called people's army of Draza Mihailovich.

13. Ivan Lj. Kovacevich, business manager from Vilusi, as a collaborator during the organization of the Kovacevich Company of the so-called people's army of Draza Mihailovich and a deserter from the Partisan army.

14. Momir N. Bulajich, peasant from Vilusi, as an active propagandist in his neighborhood for the so-called people's army of Draza Mihailovich.

15. Janko B. Kovacevich, peasant from Spile, as a collaborator during the organization of the Kovacevich Sixth Company of the so-called people's army of Draza Mihailovich.

16. Mirko A. Markovich, peasant from Jabuka, as an active propagandist in his neighborhood for the so-called people's army of Draza Mihailovich.

17. Stevo M. Kovacevich, post office employee from Vilusi, as a collaborator during the organization of the Kovacevich Sixth Company of the so-called people's army of Draza Mihailovich.

18. Ivan M. Janicich, former lieutenant from Brocanac, as an active propagandist in his neighborhood for the so-called people's army of Draza Mihailovich.

19. Petar N. Bulajich, peasant from Jabuka, as a propagandist for the so-called people's army of Draza Mihailovich and breaker of people's unity in the struggle against the occupier.

The pronouncement of sentence of the accused from no. 9 to no. 19, inclusively, is conditional for one year. However, if within one year the accused commit the slightest violation against the national liberation movement in the struggle against the occupier, they will be immediately executed.

REASONS:

From documents captured referring to the accused, from their statements, and from interrogation of witnesses it is irrefutably determined: In November of last year in Niksic, where there was a strong occupier garrison, accused No. 1 was visited by a delegate of Draza Mihailovich. He was entrusted to visit two other persons to organize the so-called national army in the old district of Velimlje. Also, the accused admitted that as soon as he came to his native place Spile he began to organize such an army. The other traitors tried to collaborate with the occupier throughout Montenegro. On December 23, 1941, the accused organized a meeting in Podbozur at which time a fourteen-point statute of organization of the former Kovacevich Company of the so-called national army of Draza Mihailovich was proposed to those present. With his personal influence and his clan connections he succeeded in winning over fifty signatories to the bylaws of the national army. Among those signing were some Partisans from the list of Partisan companies. In the meantime, Grahovo was liberated from the occupier and the administration was taken over by the national liberation Partisan army. The accused knew well how Partisans punish adherents of Draza Mihailovich for their treason and action against the national struggle. Therefore, he formally changed the bylaws of his army and omitted one point that was tied for Draza Mihailovich. He did it at a meeting in his home on December 29 of last year. On that evening he received an invitation from Grahovo Partisan headquarters asking him to appear there immediately. He refused to come to Grahovo that night. The next day he appeared with fifty armed men. He was disarmed and jailed.

The fact is the accused had formed units for Draza Mihailovich. There was ample proof that he was actively engaged in undermining the people's unity in the mutual struggle against an occupier. In a word, he betrayed his people, which helped the occupier, according to Partisan accusors.

Draza Mihailovich's treason in negotiating with Nedich and the Germans while at the same time leading the fratricidal struggle against the Partisan army is well known. At the meeting in Podbozur when the Partisan army was organized and at other meetings that followed at his home the accused was opposed to the struggle directed against the occupier under the pretext that it was yet too early. Further, he states that the Partisan movement is led by irresponsible people. In a word, he was trying to sabotage the national liberation struggle, betraying his people at the same time.

In the bylaws of Draza Mihailovich's movement the accused emphasizes the struggle against an enemy. As to the occupier, point four says that toward the occupier we'll act (it does not say we'll fight) according to the order of Draza Mihailovich. The meaning is clear; the enemies are somebody else, not the occupiers. For Draza Mihailovich's main target was the Partisan army. It was characteristic of the treachery and circumstances of the accused, who was not a fighter because he did not take part in the Yugoslav war. He began to organize soldiers at the moment our courageous Partisans spilled blood in Crkvice.

When the Italians were beseiged in Grahovo, they were exhausted and on the brink of surrender. Because he succeeded in causing confusion among the Partisan fighters of the Jabuka Company, they made only weak efforts against the occupier during the burning of Grahovo homes.

After the July uprising the accused had a meeting in Trubjelo with the commandant of the occupation troops in Niksic. He lived freely under occupation control. He obtained a pass that said he had good moral and political behavior. What did that mean? He was greatly trusted by the occupier.

As to organizing a so-called national army, the accused's defense that he had tried to rally fighters from the former Kovacevich Company was inappropriate because to form military units, especially one of Draza Mihailovich's, actually meant breaking up national unity. Also, it was incorrect that he had only heard about the conflict between Draza and the Partisans on December 23 and 29. Meanwhile, everyone had known it much earlier. The Partisan press, as the accused acknowledged, wrote a lot about the conflict caused by Draza's betrayal.

In the case of accused no. 2, it was concluded that on his return from Niksic with no. 1 and no. 3, he became a main collaborator in organizing the so-called national army. He tried to persuade Partisans not to join their ranks at the position near Crkvice but to go on meeting in Podbozur. With such acts he broke up unity in the struggle against the occupier.

In September of last year, under protection of the occupier, he took a job as a community member and became a village judge. He was designated to take arms away from the people as soon as he became a servant to the occupier.

For the same reason as for no. 3, his defense was inappropriate. In defending himself for rendering services to the occupier he maintains he did so to protect the Grahovo tribe from destruction by the occupier. That defense was improper because he could not serve his people's interests on the one hand and on the other hand collaborate with those who were killing, burning, and plundering the same people.

In the case of the accused no. 3, after his return from visiting his brother Novica both men organized the national army of Draza Mihailovich. At all gatherings and meetings in addition to the accused Novica he was the main speaker. He wrote the statutes in his own hand and he was chosen temporary commander in charge of sentries and couriers. In general he was the righthand man to Novica for all his treacherous acts. His defense was as improper as it was for accused no. 1.

In the case of the accused no. 4, it was ascertained that he was working with three others accused of organizing the so-called national army. He threatened the Partisans who had taken positions in front of his village that he would fire at them if they dared to open fire against the occupier. This aggressiveness toward the Partisans meant that he sabotaged them and broke up the people's unity in the struggle against the occupier.

In the case of the accused no. 5, during a requiem mass for his relative Mirko, who had been executed by the occupier, he accused the Partisans of being to blame for Mirko's tragedy. He deliberately went to the occupier despite the Partisan ban. He took part in the meeting in Osjecenica sponsored by the Italians. He met with the traitor Andrija Milovich in an Italian automobile even though that is forbidden by the Partisan army. Also, he was a soldier in the Partisan army, which he deserted to join the Sixth Kovacevich Company. He is known among the people as a plunderer and oppressor. During distribution of the money confiscated during the Yugoslav capitulation he kept some of it himself, setting aside a portion for Spiljani, to whom he gave slightly burned bank notes.

In the case of the accused no. 6, it is ascertained that he was in close cooperation with accused no. 1 and no. 3 in organizing the national army. In September of last year he accepted a job as a community member and village judge under the auspices of the occupier. He was sentry commander. By order of the occupier he guarded roads against the Partisans in the community of Grahovo. After the July actions rumor spread that the Partisans were mercenaries of Ante Pavelich. During the July action he agitated among the Spiljani not to take up arms. With such work he broke up the people's unity in the struggle against the occupier.

In the case of the accused no. 7, it was concluded that he was in close cooperation with the first three accused for participation in the so-called national army. He threatened and menaced Partisans. This accused is known among the people as a thief during the first occupation and as an oppressor and fake.

In the case of the accused no. 8, it is ascertained that he was in very close relations with accused no. 1 and no. 3 during the organization of the so-called national army, for which he was very active while showing animosity toward the Partisans. Among the people he is known as a plunderer and oppressor of the people. As such he distinguished himself during the Yugoslav capitulation.

In the case of the accused no. 9, it was concluded that when the community administration was established under the occupier's auspices he greeted the Italian colonel with a toast, promising him to destroy Communists.

In the case of the accused no. 10, it was found that he was in very close cooperation with accused no. 1 and no. 3 during the organization of the so-called national army. As the village mayor he was endorsed by the occupier; he also organized an Italian gathering in Osjecenica by using threats to force people to attend.

In the case of the accused no. 11, it was found that he was in close cooperation with the first three accused in organizing the so-called national army, as well as being sergeant of the Jabuka Platoon of the same army.

In the case of the accused no. 12, it was concluded that he was in close cooperation with accused no. 1 and no. 3 during organization of the so-called national army. He dissuaded young men from joining the Partisan army.

In the case of the accused no. 13, it was found that he helped write the second statute of the Sixth Kovacevich Company of the so-called national army and he deserted from the Partisan army.

In the case of the accused no. 14, it was found that he was in close cooperation with the first three accused in organizing the so-called national army. He agitated for that organization. He was a commander of that army's Jabuka-Zagorje Company.

In the case of the accused no. 15, it was found that he was in close cooperation with the first three accused in organizing the so-called national army. He agitated for that organization and he was a deserter from the Partisan army as well.

In the case of the accused no. 16, it was found that he was in close cooperation with the first three accused in organizing the so-called national army. He agitated for that organization and he served as courier.

In the case of the accused no. 17, it was found that he was in close cooperation with the first three accused in organizing the so-called national army. He deserted from the Partisan army in which he was commissar for food for the Spile Company, and then he joined Draza's army.

In the case of the accused no. 18, it was found that he agitated for the so-called national army, made a speech at a meeting in Podbozur, and distributed the statutes of that organization.

In the case of the accused no. 19, it was found that he actively agitated for the so-called national army and against the Partisans and that he threatened the Partisan army.

All properties that personally belong to the first eight accused would be confiscated for the benefit of the National Liberation Partisan army.

This sentence can be carried out without right of appeal.

Court Secretary,   Members of the Court:
Marija Kosh (signed)

                                          Milinko Djurovich (signed)
                                          Nikola A. Djurkovich (signed)
President of Military Court,   Dimitrije S. Bulajich (signed)
Sava B. Kovacevich (signed)   Mato Dj. Antunovich (signed)

Grahovljani!

The above sentence of the Niksic Partisan Detachment by military court martial is carried out to destroy the nucleus of fifth-column bandits in the

Grahovo community of Zametkuci. It was necessary to destroy an evil that had contaminated the health of our people and had fractured the people's unity in the struggle against the occupier, as well as those who sowed death and destruction in the fratricidal conflict in Montenegro like what was happening in Serbia led by Draza Mihailovich.

The bloody battle led by our courageous Partisan army against the occupier for national liberation is inseparable from the struggle against the fifth-column elements, against the enemy who was trying from the inside to undermine our struggle.

The past history of Montenegro and other nations shows similar actions. The struggle against the Turks unavoidably demanded the extermination of renegades.

Liberating Grahovo and continuing our national liberation struggle was certainly our goal in exterminating the evil in its core. In this case we carried out our responsibilities before our courageous Partisan army and before the people in order to ensure the successful end of our struggle. In the future we'll act the same, probably even at the least attempt to destroy our achievements or to water down the blood of our brave Partisans.

Our actions were mandated by the many sons of our people who were executed, the many homes burned and looted, and the many victims throughout the whole world who would fall down against fascism. It is our duty to carry on without any excuse or sentimentality; to do otherwise would be a betrayal today of the Partisan liberation struggle. If the former Spanish republic had acted decisively toward Gen. Franco and his accomplices the Spanish people would not have spilled so much blood in the vain struggle for their freedom.

Our Partisans are aware of the danger of the internal evil. We have received confirmations from many annals with hundreds of signatures from Montenegro, Hercegovina, and Boka, where they asked us to stop the actions of those contemporary renegades.

DEATH TO TRAITORS! DEATH TO FASCISM!
FREEDOM TO THE PEOPLE!

January 19, 1942
Headquarters of the National Liberation Partisan Battalion
(five-pointed star)
Headquarters of First Battalion
Montengrin-Sandzak Detachment
January 10, 1942
Kamena Gora

Obrad Jevtovich from the village of Zabr. Toca was accused by the peasants of his community of the following: (1) he was on the Chetnik list, recruited by a monk from Priboj under the auspices of the occupier and against the struggle of the national liberation fighters; (2) he formerly served as an agent of the enemy; (3) in the community he tried to forcibly organize Chetnik bands; (4) he forced eleven peasants to go to Priboj to take an oath.

During his interrogation the accused acknowledged that he was with Chetniks in the district of Priboj. He came later to his village, in which a large number of Chetniks were enrolled, although the initiative for it did not come from him. He did not admit to spying for the enemy or to forcing the peasants to take the Chetniks' oath.

For that reason the accused was an occupier's Chetnik, that is, one of the bands that mistreated Partisans. Therefore, for his suspicious behavior toward the occupier and his attempt to organize Chetnik bands in Toci,

THIS HEADQUARTERS
SENTENCES TO DEATH

Obrad Jevtovich as a traitor to the people and servant to the occupier
DEATH TO FASCISM—FREEDOM TO THE PEOPLE!

Assistant Commandant,
Vel. Knezevich (signed)
assistant to political commissar

Commandant,
Spiro Mugosa (signed)

Political Commissar,
Perisa Vujosevich (signed)

Headquarters of First Battalion
Montenegro-Sandzak Detachment
January 8, 1942
Kamena Gora

Jovan Ducich from the village of Karosevina was accused by the peasants of Karosevina and of other villages as follows:

He was a spy in the service of the occupier. He was unfriendly toward the Partisans. He tried to persuade the peasants to bring charges against Partisans.

During an interrogation he acknowledged he had a hostile attitude toward Partisans. He ran away from the Partisans in order not to offend the Italians. On the day of fighting in Savin Lakat he was in Prijepolje. He told Rajko Bakovich, "Don't play with your head to bring Montenegrins here." During Partisan appearances he ran away toward Prijepolje shouting, "Loot and you'll pay for it." He defended himself unskillfully, avoiding replying to specific questions. He said what was on his mind because he was drunk.

According to the opinion of the peasants and the impression obtained during the interrogation of the accused, he spied for the benefit of the enemy and he was hostile toward the national liberation struggle.

According to what was found out and in accordance with directives [*Note: The headquarters had already received directives and were forced to fulfill their share of liquidations.*]

DEATH TO SPIES! JOVAN DUCICH SENTENCED TO DEATH.

DEATH TO FASCISM—FREEDOM TO THE PEOPLE!

The sentence was carried out the same day.

Political Commissar,	Commandant,
Perisa Vujosevich (signed)	Spiro Mugosa (signed)
Assistant,	Assistant,
Danilo Knezevich (signed)	Vel. M. Knezevich (signed)

Risto Golubovich, former president of Vrbovo
Milojica Zarkovich
Vule Brasanac, Babinje Toci
Done at the Hall—December 16, 1941

The peasants from Vrbovo charged that farmer woman Stana Koruc deals in espionage and steadily goes to Prijepolje to the Italians to report the arrival of Partisans in this village. The general opinion of all peasants from that village is that she deserves death.

During the interrogation the accused skillfully pulled herself out, shrewdly acknowledging that she carried a letter from the president of the Bobinje community to a major of the Prijepolje district.

General opinion: She is guilty

UNANIMOUS DECISION: DEATH

in Kadin Do, December 16, 1941

The members of the court:

(1) Commandant of Combined Battalion, Spiro Mugosa (signed)	(3) Milosav Cerovich (sg.)
(2) Commander of Zeta Company, Perisa Velj. I. Terzich (signed)	(4) Political Commissar of Zeta Company, Perisa Vujoshevich (signed)
	(5) D. Dj. Uskokovich (sg.)

The death penalty was immediately carried out.

Milovan Joksimovich, Mica Zejak, Zivko Zejak, from Pavino Polje, Milosh Boshkovich, Jevto Radovich, Grujo Mrdan, Savo Zejak, from Barice. [*Original does not say why these names are listed.*]

Our good and honest Dr. Milo. We knew him for thirty years when he, as a young man, gave up a prosperous and comfortable life in Great Russia and rushed back to his native region in our Cetinje with his Russian wife, Mrs. Klaudija. As a true Samaritan he helped all patients with equal love whether they were rich or poor. As an outstanding doctor he quickly acquired the universal love and respect of the people. In his career he advanced to the highest level—to general and medical army chief.

After his children were educated he retreated as a retired general to his birthplace, Brcele. There he built a small house where he could live near his relatives for the rest of his life. In the later years of his life his great knowledge and tremendous experience were used for the benefit of the

DOCTOR MILO ILICKOVICH
Retired Medical General

people. In his professional mission he did not differentiate red [*Communists*] from white [*non-Communists*], honest from dishonest. He gave medical treatment to everyone who needed it.

It was certain that he could not adjust his life's views to agree with the Partisans. As an independent thinker he disturbed them. No one could conceive of the murder of him and his wife Klaudija, as older people could not be a danger to anyone. To the contrary, they could be very helpful, even to the Partisans. It reeked of the greediness and looting that are clearly evidenced in the following Communist document:

Headquarters
National Liberation Partisan Battalion
Jovan Tomasevich
No. 46 Field Position, April 4, 1942
To the Headquarters of the National Liberation Partisan Detachment, in the Field
We sent you a report referring to the theft of belongings from Dr. Gen. Ilickovich and his wife.

On the 19th of last month we escorted Gen. Ilickovich and his wife to your headquarters via the Partisan detachment of July 13. He was totally convinced he had been invited to detachment headquarters to work in one of our Partisan hospitals. With him was conveyed what is enclosed now. In the meantime, the Partisan company from Gradjani told us there was fighting in your sector, so he could not be escorted. We immediately ordered the Gradjani Partisan company of the July 13th Battalion to liquidate Ilickovich and his wife. They refused to do it. They said we should get him and execute him ourselves if we wanted to. Afterward men were sent to liquidate him. In addition we asked the headquarters of the Partisan company from Gradjani to return the belongings of Dr. Ilickovich and his wife. There were three large suitcases full. We received the following reply from company headquarters:

The Headquarters of Battalion Jovan Tomasevich. We sent you a list of the contents of Dr. Ilickovich's suitcases. We gave the list to July 13th Battalion. We were of the opinion we had the right to keep the suitcases and to return them after we found out what would be our share. We think we should get as much as the Second Company from Dupilo that took part in that fighting. We just got 300 bullets. We demand you send us two pillows that were taken from Joko M. Popovich by Dr. Milo. During the murder the pillows went into the ground along with the victims

Political Commissar in the Field,
Assistant Commissar,
Djuro J. Petrovich (signed)

We further insisted on the return of Dr. Milo's belongings. We received two suitcases, one completely empty, things for which we returned a receipt in the other: cash 7,300 dinars in silver and paper, 7,497 Italian lire; two gold watches, four gold rings, one silver ring, one silver pin, one cigarette case, two eyeglasses with cases, one big silver eating spoon, four smaller spoons, one round spoon; one short coat, one scarf, one lady's overcoat, one dress, one sweater, two undergarments, one apron, one silk shawl, one sleeping cap, one pants, four white handkerchiefs, one pair lady's boots, one pair slippers, one hair net, one pair man's socks and one lady's stockings; shaving equipment, one brush, one towel; two small wallets, one man's and one lady's handbag; two large and one small suitcase; one bigger metal plate; two smaller boxes for medical equipment, one medical container; and one revolver.

There was no authorization to open the suitcases, though they must have known they had to be sent to the Lovcen Detachment or returned to our headquarters. These are logical conclusions. According to the evidence, about a hundred thousand dinars' worth of items were stolen. This was proven by the following facts:

They sent us only one suitcase of belongings instead of all three. One suitcase was sent empty and the third one, according to them, was empty also. They kept one for themselves as well as one revolver. In addition, fifteen days later they sent us 4,700 dinars, 2,400 lire, and one raincoat. With that additional parcel they tried to minimize their looting, while in their earlier report they told us they had kept nothing.

We are informed that the general took with him various items of his wife's jewelry, gold chains, watches, and gloves as well as his valuable gold things, silver utensils weighing about four kilograms. He took with him all metal valuables. In one case were eighteen silver spoons and forks that were not returned from the company headquarters. The general also took with him some medicine, extra underwear, suits, socks, and shoes. All of that was in case it was necessary to stay longer at some hospital. His wife took with her necessary goods. Furthermore, the destiny of his fountain pen is unknown.

(1) Now the question is who at company headquarters emptied the two suitcases and where are the items they contained? (2) A strict investigation must be conducted to search without warning very carefully through their homes to compel them to return everything. We will investigate this matter further and we will send you word of what we discover.

The Red Army is with us—victory is ours!

DEATH TO FASCISM—FREEDOM TO THE PEOPLE!

Political Commissar, (seal)
Velimir Lekovich (signed)
For Commandant,
Danilo Sorovich (signed)

As a postscript, we are informed he had only 17,000 lire.

FATHER PETAR VUJOVICH
from Zupa Dobrska

MILOVAN DJ. BESICH
former district head of Savnik

Father Vujovich was an honest Serb, a devoted and faithful servant of Christ's church, good shepherd of his flock, an exemplary father, and the pride of his clan and tribe. He met a martyr's death at the hands of the Partisans in the notorious Kunovo Prisoje. He was thrown into a 17-meter pit. According to herdsmen his voice was heard from the pit for five days.

The following Partisans abducted him: Milutin Pejanovich, teacher; Zarko Vukich, dropout student; and Nikola-Kole Jablan, post office employee.

The court that sentenced him to death at the Partisan battalion was composed of: Andrija Pejovich, battalion commandant; Mican Petricevich, political commissar; Milo Jovicevich, professor; and Danica Marinovich.

After the death sentence was pronounced he was taken to the headquarters of the Lovcen Detachment, which had approved the verdict of battalion headquarters through the word of Mihailo Vickovich, commissar of the Lovcen Detachment.

The actual executioners were: Mihailo, son of Filip M. Pejovich, a teacher who is now in apostasy; Andro B. Lopichich from Ceklin; and Krsto Djurovich from Orasi.

All necessary data we obtained from his uncle, Jovan B. Vujovich.

Milovan Dj. Beshich, former district head of Savnik

While the national resistance was being organized Besich fell into the hands of Communist criminals and was sentenced to death. After the announcement of his death sentence in the headquarters of the Zeta Detachment Besich grabbed the head of one Partisan executioner and threw him to the floor. Then he took another's rifle and wounded one of the Communists. The frightened Communist thugs rushed to their comrades' aid and shot Besich dead with a revolver. They took his clothes off and left him naked. They cut off his nose and plucked out his eyes. Afterward he was thrown into one of the many holes dug by bombs during the air raid of Radovce. So in his forty-fourth year he was deprived of his life. He was an excellent and responsible civil servant, an exemplary patriot, a courageous man, and a benefactor of the people.

Pesho (Petar) Celovich, long-term president of the Risan community, president of the church organization in Risan, member of the committee of the Montenegrin-Littoral-Skenderijski diocese, a well-known national tribunal, eminent member of many national and cultural societies, and descendant of the well-known patriotic family Celovich. He was born in 1882 in Risan.

By the order of Partisan leader Nikola Djurkovich, political commissar for Boka Kotorska, Petar was killed cruelly by two young men.

On March 7, on the way to Herceg Novi, Petar was ambushed by two young men on the road to Baosic. He was taken a few meters above the road, where he was hit by a blunt object. He was horribly tortured and then riddled with bullets from a revolver. He was left half dead where he fell.

The executioners plundered his gold wrist watch, wallet, and rings. Pesho died after three days of unbearable suffering. An investigation was carried out. The names of the murderers were discovered. They were local executioners who had the assignment to carry out orders for executions in their locales for those sentenced by the notorious "headquarters from Orjen."

Petar was buried in Risan. As expected, his funeral was attended by many people, including representatives of authority from Kotor and Risan.

On August 5, by verdict of the military court in Kotor, the murderers of Petar Celovich were executed in Baosic. They were Vaso Kamilich and S. Cvjetkovich, young men from Baosic.

PETAR (PESHO) CELOVICH
businessman from Risan

MILUTIN V. VUKOVICH
former court employee
from the village Lushac
near Berane

MITAR T. MAKOCEVICH
peasant from Crnci,
community Piperi

On December 25, 1941, Milutin V. Vukovich was killed at his home by Partisans who came to disarm him as suspicious and dangerous to their movement. He refused to give up his weapon. It looked as if the encounter would end without incident. However, a Partisan shot him in the back at the moment that he entered his house.

Milutin was a conscientious employee and good patriot, an honest and respected citizen welcome in any society. He left behind four daughters and one son.

———————

On March 25, 1942, Mitar T. Makocevich was taken away from his home and was executed at Radovce. His corpse along with three other naked, unidentified bodies was discovered in a hole dug by airplane bombs.

The Partisans who took him away were: Milovan Matich, commander of Strike Company, former sergeant and pilot from Stijena, Piperi: Djordjije N. Shcepanovich, political commissar of the Partisan Crnci Company, from Crnci, by profession a shepherd, and Nikola T. Vukashinovich, secretary of the Piperi community from the village Kopilje.

At Radovce he was investigated for several days and tortured. They were willing to let him go free, until a written statement was submitted by Blazo R. Dzankich, commissar for division of Celija Monastery property, which addressed the investigators thusly:

I call headquarters' attention to the following:

If you let Mitar T. Makocevich go free he will join Mijovich, with the nationalists who are entrenched in the Turkish watchtower Pazarishte above Spuz, from where they'll fight against us.

In my opinion he should be liquidated quickly on my responsibility.

Blazo R. Dzankich
(signed)
Commissar for division of Celija Monastery property, Saint Stevan Piperski.

Until the Partisans took over, half the peasants from the village Crnci did not know that the signatory, Blazo Dzankich, was a 25-year-old mental incompetent. For the headquarters at Radovce his opinion was authoritative enough to behead a fair and honest host, good soldier, and outstanding tribesman.

ROSE M. KUSOVAC
from Ljubotinj over 70 years old

MILAN V. ADZOVICH
junior police sergeant in Podgorica

She was the wife of a well-known hero, Markisha S. Kusovac, and mother of Blazo Kusovac, who was also severely wounded in the conflict against the Partisans. She disagreed with Partisan activities.

Mere criticism from someone was enough to make them take offense. While she lay in bed alone at home, ill and tired from old age, there came into her house three murderers:

Vaso Markov Prlja, dropout student, and two Partisan spinsters, Danica Kolinovich and Rose Kaludjerovich. They fired three rifle rounds into the sick old woman. Then they stole everything from the house and went away happy, feeling that they had carried out an "honest and courageous" act.

We received all the information from her son, Blazo M. Kusovac.

Milan B. Adzovich was an exemplary patriot who joined the national ranks of Col. Bajo Stanishich on March 3, 1942 and remained until April 10. That day he was killed in Zagarac by a Partisan troika composed of: Ilija B. Martinovich, Tomashevich, and Vukadinovich.

Milan was born December 15, 1912, in the village of Petrovici, community Hum, district Trebinje-Hercegovina.

Abyss and Hell
People Killed by Partisans

Suljo Cosovich, peasant, 20 years old. Community Meljak, district Pljevlja.
Milun Cosovich, peasant, 19 years old. Community Meljak, district Pljevlja.

Salkan Cosovich, peasant, 35 years old. Community Meljak, district Pljevlja.

Zivko Golshcan, community Ilino Brdo, district Pljevlja. They abducted him and killed him with a blunt object and then by rifle shot. The following Partisans were involved: Vidak Vukovich, Milivoje Djakovich, and Milivoje Zarubica. The body was discovered in Ivanovo Polje.

Vasilije Djurovich, peasant, 50 years old. Community Ilino Brdo, district Pljevlja. Wounded by Partisans: Vidak Vukovich, Milivoje Djakovich, and Milivoje Zarubica. He died from the wounds in a hospital.

Milosh S. Knezevich, peasant, 35 years old. Community Ilino Brdo, district Pljevlja. He was killed by the Partisan Milosh Perunicich and others.

Danilo M. Borovich, accountant, 28 years old. Community Boljanici, district Pljevlja. Abducted and killed by Partisans: Milutin Jelovac, commandant of the Eleventh Partisan Battalion. Other accomplices unknown. The body was found in the village Meoci, community Precane.

Milojica Bojovich, junior sergeant of the gendarmes, 25 years old. Community Boljanici, district Pljevlja. He was abducted and killed by the Partisan Milutin Jelovac, community Meljak, district Pljevlja. The body was found in the village Meoci, district Pljevlja.

Avram Petrovich, community Kosanica, district Pljevlja. Shot by unknown Partisans in the village Kosanica. The body was found in front of a Partisan headquarters building.

Vlado Lacmanovich, peasant, 40 years old. Community Kosanica, district Pljevlja. Partisans shot him. The body was found in the village Kosanica.

Alija Krijeshtarac, peasant, 50 years old. Community Kosanica, district Pljevlja. Partisans shot him with a rifle. The body was found in the village Lever Tara.

Gojko Ivanovich, peasant, 16 years old. Community Bobovo, district Pljevlja. He was killed by unknown Partisans.

Milan Kontich, law student, 20 years old. Community Ocevinci, district Pljevlja. Killed by unknown Partisans.

Jovica Stanich, peasant, 35 years old. Community Ocevinci, district Pljevlja.

Milorad Lukovich, peasant, 26 years old. Community Ocevinci, district Pljevlja. Partisan Aleksa Jovicevich abducted and killed him.

Bajo Cvorovich, proprietor, 35 years old. Community Ocevinci, district Pljevlja. Shot by unknown persons. The body was found on Mount Kujamusha.

Radovan Cvorovich, peasant, 45 years old. Community Ocevinci, district Pljevlja. Shot by unknown people.

Neshko Milojicich, community Prencanci, district Pljevlja. Shot by unknown persons.

Petar Vojinovich, infantry captain first class, 35 years old. Community Prencanci, district Pljevlja. Killed by unknown people.

Milosh Vojinovich, peasant. Community Prencanci, district Pljevlja. Killed by unknown Partisans. The body was found in Adrovici, district Pljevlja. His eyes had been torn out and his hands broken.

Obrad Vucinich, infantry lieutenant, 35 years old. Community Prencani, district Pljevlja. He was shot with a rifle by the Partisans: Djordjije Perunicich, Vukoman Andjelich, and Vlado Knezevich. The body was found and buried. He was a nationalist.

Ferdo Vetrih, 32 years old, stabbed by knives and tortured by unknown Partisans. He died after a few days. His body was found near the sawmill where he was killed.

Savo Damjanovich, captain first class, 40 years old. Pljevlja. He was killed by a blow from a blunt object to the head and stabbed by knives over the entire body. He had been abducted by Partisan Velimir Jakich, commandant of Sandzak Partisan Detachment. The body was discovered in Adrovici, covered in a lime kiln along with two officers and a noncommissioned officer whose names are unknown.

Stevo P. Pushelja, judge's assistant, 30 years old. Pljevlja. He was killed by the Partisans: Bogdan Kotlica, Milosh Radovich, Milan Trebjeshanin, Drago M. Cerovich, and Jovan R. Cerovich. The body was discovered in Boan, in Uskoci.

Mile Kandich, peasant, 78 years old. Pljevlja.

Alija Kondo, Pljevlja. Shot by rifle in front of his house in Pljevlja.

Dragisha Savich, master sergeant, 35 years old. Pljevlja.

Zorka Savich, housewife. Pljevlja.

Mile Tasovec, peasant, 35 years old. Pljevlja.

Luka Pejanovich, peasant, 78 years old. Pljevlja.

Zarko Pejanovich, peasant, 23 years old. Pljevlja.

Milorad Karuga, peasant, 40 years old. Community Otilovici, district Pljevlja. Killed by Partisans of the Zlatac Detachment. He was hit by a blunt object, massacred, and then finished off with fire arms. The body was found in Obord, community Matarugi, district Pljevlja.

Savo Kubar, peasant, 45 years old. Community Otilovici, district Pljevlja. First tortured, then shot by unknown people. The body was not found.

Milan Anicich, Chetnik, 33 years old. Community Otilovici, district Pljevlja.

Sredoje Joksovich, peasant, 60 years old. Community Otilovici, district Pljevlja.

Rade Trutich, peasant, 60 years old. Community Otilovici, district Pljevlja.

Panto Kezich, peasant, 40 years old. Community Otilovici, district Pljevlja.

Vukojica Perunicich. The body was found in the village Obordini.

Ilija Sharanchich, peasant, 45 years old. Community Otilovici, district Pljevlja. Killed as a courier by Partisans of the Zlatac Detachment.

He was carrying a Chetnik letter. The body was found in Kamena Gora.

Marko Pejatovich, cafe owner, 45 years old. Community Otilovici, district Pljevlja.

Ristan Grbovich, peasant, 42 years old. Community Otilovici, district Pljevlja.

Jeranija Grbovich, housewife, 85 years old. Community Otilovici, district Pljevlja.

Anica Papich, housewife, 80 years old. Community Otilovici, district Pljevlja.

Andja Kocalovich, 45 years old, from village Matarugi, community Matarugi, district Pljevlja. She was looking for plundered livestock. Partisans caught her and took her to Kosanica where she was shot by the Partisans: Olga Jovich from Shumani, Vlado Minich from Mijakovici, Gojko Tabash from Zekovica. The body was found in a pit in Kosanica.

Vojin M. Gacevich, peasant, 20 years old. Community Mataruga, district Pljevlja. Killed as Chetnik by Zecevich, commandant of a Partisan detachment. The body was found in Tihovo, community Ocevinci.

Petar Cvijovich, peasant, 54 years old. Community Gotovushka, district Pljevlja. Killed by the Partisans: Vlado Cosovich from Potpeca with others. Slaughtered by knife at his home.

Mara Lakovich, housewife, 35 years old. Community Gotovushka, district Pljevlja.

Branko Lakovich, peasant, 38 years old. Community Gotovushka, district Pljevlja.

Vojka Lakovich, 8 years old. Community Gotovushka, district Pljevlja.

Branko Lakovich, 9-month-old child. Community Gotovushka, district Pljevlja.

Dobrilo Lakovich, 3-year-old boy. Community Gotovushka, district Pljevlja.

Jelica Lakovich, 11 years old. Community Gotovushka, district Pljevlja.

Jelisaveta Lakovich, 7 years old. Community Gotovushka, district Pljevlja.

Lazar Toshich, peasant, 40 years old. Community Gotovushka, district Pljevlja.

Nikola Toshich, peasant, 27 years old. Community Gotovushka, district Pljevlja.

Veljko K. Djurovich, lieutenant, 41 years old. Community Petrushine, district Danilovgrad.

Milosh K. Djurovich, peasant, 35 years old. Community Petrushine, district Danilovgrad.

Krsto V. Djurovich, peasant, 70 years old. Community Petrushine, district Danilovgrad. All three were taken away from their house and thrown into a pit by Partisans Radosav K. Lucich, Rade M. Popovich, and

Milosh Dj. Malevich. Their bodies were found in Gostilje, three kilometers from the house.

Petar J. Milatovich, teacher, 37 years old. Community Petrushine, district Danilovgrad.

Ljubica P. Milatovich, housewife, 35 years old. Community Petrushine, district Danilovgrad. They were killed by Partisans from ambush during the night on the threshold of their home. The Partisans involved were: Milosh R. Pelevich, Sreten Pelevich, Nedjeljka Bogicevich, Savo Savovich, Marko Radonjich, Vojislav Djurovich, and Dushan Ivanovich.

Mrkoje P. Milatovich, student, 17 years old. Community Petrushine, district Danilovgrad. Killed as a nationalist.

Milosava R. Djurovich, housewife, 60 years old. Community Petrushine, district Danilovgrad.

Drago R. Djurovich, peasant, 27 years old. Community Petrushine, district Danilovgrad.

Cetna R. Djurovich, housewife, 26 years old. Community Petrushine, district Danilovgrad. Killed by Partisans Marinka M. Djurovich, Radoslava M. Djurovich, Veselina M. Djurovich, Milinka M. Bogicevich, Vlado Sekulich, Pejsa Sekulich, Ljuba Zotovich, and others.

Novica Shkerovich, teacher, 35 years old. Community Petrushine, district Danilovgrad.

Bajo Grgurovich, peasant. Community Petrushine, district Danilovgrad. He was killed fighting Partisans. He belonged to the detachment of Col. Bajo Stanishich.

Miladin Grgurovich, intellectual, 22 years old. Community Petrushine, district Danilovgrad. Disappeared.

Danica Ivanovich, student, 17 years old. Community Petrushine, district Danilovgrad.

Milorad Savovich, student, 17 years old. Community Petrushine, district Danilovgrad.

Milivoje Bojicich, peasant, 40 years old. Community Manastir, district Berane. At Mojkovac he fought the Communists. He belonged to the detachment of vojvoda Pavle Djurishich.

Vucko Bojicich, peasant, 60 years old. Community Manastir, district Berane. He was killed fighting Communists as part of Pavle Djurishich's detachment.

Djordjije Bogavac, teacher, 36 years old. Community Manastir, district Berane. Killed by a bomb thrown into his house by Partisans. His body was found in his house.

Andrija V. Vukovich, reserve lieutenant, 70 years old. Community Manastir, district Berane. Killed fighting Communists on 5-7-1942 at Mojkovac. He belonged to the detachment of vojvoda Pavle Djurishich.

Milivoje Bogovac, policeman, 33 years old. Community Manastir, district Berane. He was killed at Mojkovac by the Partisans. The body was found.

Miro M. Obradovich, peasant. Community Manastir, district Berane. He
   was killed fighting Communists at Lepenac. He belonged to the detachment of vojvoda Pavle Djurishich. The body was found.
Velimir R. Peshich, policeman. Community Manastir, district Berane.
Radonja P. Peshich, peasant. Community Manastir, district Berane. Killed
   by rifle in the village Lubnica.
Bozidar M. Vukovich, student of veterinary medicine, 20 years old. Community Manastir, district Berane. He was killed fighting Communists
   on January 29, 1942 in Ravna Rijeka.
Milonja R. Bubonja, 46 years old. Community Manastir, district Berane.
   He was killed fighting Communists. He belonged to the detachment
   of vojvoda Pavle Djurishich.
   [*Listed under the title "Abyss and Hell, People Killed by Partisans" are
   the couple Mara and Branko Lakovich with their five children from
   the community Gotovushka, district Pljevlja. Here again are their
   names and ages:*
   Mara Lakovich, housewife, 35 years old.
   Branko Lakovich, peasant, 38 years old.
   Branko Lakovich, 9-month-old child.
   Dobrilo Lakovich, 3-year-old boy.
   Jelisaveta Lakovich, 7 years old.
   Vojka Lakovich, 8 years old.
   Jelica Lakovich, 11 years old.

*It was unusual for such a family execution, including children, to be
done by the Partisans, at least in Old Montenegro. It is an undeniable fact
that in July 1941 Tito, as secretary of the Yugoslav Communist party,
ordered the provincial committees to eliminate all those, including party
members, who opposed carrying out the struggle for national liberation
and social revolution by any means possible.*

*Targeted immediately were dissenting adults, intellectuals in particular,
but not children. In that case it was probable that the order for liquidation
of the Lakovich children did not come from high in the Communist hierarchy. Then who ordered the killing? It is possible that the motive was revenge
of some kind, either personal, religious, or ethnic, carried out under the
disguise of Partisan activity.*]

People Wounded by Partisans

Pasha Dzeovich, housewife, 75 years old. Community Meljak, district
   Pljevlja.
Jovan Z. Bijedich, community Meljak, district Pljevlja. Wounded by Zivan
   Dzuver.
Josif M. Gogich, peasant, 49 years old. Community Ilino Brdo, district
   Pljevlja.

Stojan Lucich, peasant, 50 years old. Community Ilino Brdo, district Pljevlja.

Mitra Palibrk, housewife, 50 years old. Community Ocevinci, district Pljevlja. Seriously wounded by unknown persons.

Lazar Cepich, peasant, 31 years old. Community Ocevinci, district Pljevlja. Seriously wounded.

Lazar Milashinovich, peasant, 27 years old. Community Prencanci, district Pljevlja. Wounded by a bomb while working on his land.

Jaksha Maksimovich, peasant, 40 years old. Community Prencanci, district Pljevlja.

Vojin Maksimovich, peasant, 35 years old. Community Prencanci, district Pljevlja.

Maksim Maksimovich, peasant, 16 years old. community Prencanci, district Pljevlja.

Aneta Maksimovich, housewife, 23 years old. Community Prencanci, district Pljevlja.

Stanija Maksimovich, housewife, 26 years old. Community Prencanci, district Pljevlja.

Stanko Maksimovich, 4 years old. Community Prencanci, district Pljevlja. All seriously wounded by bombing while working on their land.

Dzena Dizar, housewife, 50 years old. Community Pljevlja. Wounded by Partisans.

Dura Bambur, housewife, 50 years old. Community Pljevlja.

Mevla Bambur, housewife, 18 years old. Community Pljevlja.

Bozidar O. Simovich, 13 years old. Community Pljevlja.

Vladimir Kuhal, chief of electricity plant in Pljevlja, 45 years old. Heavily wounded in both legs during Communist attack on the plant.

Lazar Nenadich, road inspector, 49 years old. Community Pljevlja. Seriously wounded fighting Communists while in the detachment of Bogoljub Irich.

Smail Bambur, innkeeper, 19 years old. Community Pljevlja. Seriously wounded.

Dzelil Bambur, worker, 26 years old. Community Pljevlja. Slightly wounded.

Suljo Mrshich, peasant, 52 years old. Community Pljevlja.

Nikola Kljaich, community Pljevlja. Seriously wounded fighting Partisans.

Marko Shljukich, Chetnik, 22 years old. Community Otolovici, district Pljevlja. Seriously wounded fighting Partisans.

Mile Shljuka, 40 years old. Community Matarugi, district Pljevlja. Wounded fighting Partisans.

Urosh Shkulja, 38 years old. Community Matarugi, district Pljevlja. Wounded fighting Partisans.

Rose Dragash, housewife, 35 years old. Community Gotovushka, district Pljevlja.

Shacir Delich, peasant, 25 years old. Community Gotovushka, district
    Pljevlja.
Milorad Velashevich, engineering student, 22 years old. Community Petru-
    shine, district Danilovgrad. Seriously wounded.
Vojin M. Grgurovich, peasant, 24 years old. Community Petrushine, district
    Danilovgrad. Slightly wounded.
Bozo Grgurovich, peasant, 39 years old. Community Petrushine, district
    Danilovgrad. Wounded fighting Partisans. He belonged to the detach-
    ment of Col. Bajo Stanishich.
Velizar B. Ivanovich, 6 years old. Community Petrushine, district Dani-
    lovgrad.
Radoje P. Pavicevich, community Petrushine, district Danilovgrad.
    Wounded, right hand severed.
Milovan T. Uskokovich, 40 years old. Community Petrushine, district Dani-
    lovgrad. Seriously wounded fighting Partisans as a nationalist.
Radovan T. Uskokovich, 25 years old. Community Petrushine, district Dan-
    ilovgrad. Seriously wounded as nationalist.
Savic Dj. Pavicevich, peasant, 20 years old. Community Petrushine, district
    Danilovgrad. Wounded fighting Communists.
Dushan M. Boshkovich, employee of tobacco station, 31 years old. Slightly
    wounded. Was in the detachment of Col. Bajo Stanishich.
Bozo S. Vujovich, policeman, 28 years old. Community Petrushine, district
    Danilovgrad.
Mirko V. Vukovich, teacher, 48 years old. Community Manastir, district
    Berane. Wounded fighting Partisans January 29, 1942, in Ravna Rijeka
    as part of the Chetnik Crnovrshaka Company, Manastir Detachment.
    Now commander of Chetnik company in Lushac.
Rako N. Bozovich, peasant, 40 years old. Community Manastir, district
    Berane. Wounded by Partisans at his home.
Milorad Mihailovich, peasant, 30 years old. Community Manastir, district
    Berane. Wounded fighting Communists. Belonged to the detachment
    of vojvoda Pavle Djurishich.
Mirko M. Vukicevich, peasant, 21 years old. Community Manastir, district
    Berane. Wounded fighting Communists. Belonged to the detachment
    of vojvoda Pavle Djurishich.
Milosav B. Jashich, peasant, 22 years old. Community Manastir, district
    Berane. Wounded fighting Partisans. Belonged to the detachment of
    vojvoda Pavle Djurishich.
Djordjije L. Tomovich, peasant, 32 years old. Community Manastir, district
    Berane. Wounded fighting Partisans. Belonged to the detachment of
    vojvoda Pavle Djurishich.
Radosav R. Shcekich, peasant, 45 years old. Community Manastir, district
    Berane. Wounded fighting Communists while in the detachment of
    vojvoda Pavle Djurishich.

Filip M. Bubonja, community Manastir, district Berane. Wounded fighting Partisans. Belonged to the detachment of vojvoda Pavle Djurishich.

Milosav Vukovich, peasant, 28 years old. Community Manastir, district Berane. Wounded fighting Partisans.

Momcilo S. Zecevich, peasant, 21 years old. Community Manastir, district Berane. Wounded fighting Partisans. Belonged to the detachment of vojvoda Pavle Djurishich.

Shemsa Beshlagich, housewife, 58 years old. Community Bukovica, district Pljevlja.

Meho Rogo, peasant, 21 years old. Community Bukovica, district Pljevlja.

Vojin S. Radojevich, peasant, 28 years old. Community Budimlje, district Berane. Seriously wounded fighting Communists. Belonged to the Chetnik detachment of vojvoda Pavle Djurishich.

Mihailo R. Dabetich, chief tax collector, 38 years old. Community Budimlje, district Berane. Seriously wounded fighting Communists on Skadarsko Jezero. Belonged to the Chetnik detachment of vojvoda Pavle Djurishich.

Milonja V. Bojovich, peasant, 52 years old. Community Budimlje, district Berane. Slightly wounded fighting Partisans.

Marijan M. Kastratovich, peasant, 48 years old. Community Budimlje, district Berane. Abducted and wounded by the Partisans Mamut Adrovich and Dzeko Odzich.

Vucich V. Djurishich, peasant, 55 years old. Community Budimlje, district Berane. Wounded fighting Communists. He belonged to the Chetnik detachment of vojvoda Pavle Djurishich.

Novica M. Shoshkich, community Polimlje, district Andrijevica. Wounded slightly in hand, nose, and forehead on April 30, 1942.

Gavro Dj. Culafich, 23 years old. Community Polimlje, district Andrijevica.

Radoslav I. Kastratovich, soldier, 22 years old. Community Shekular, district Andrijevica. Slightly wounded fighting Communists.

Aleksandar R. Dashich, lieutenant, 25 years old. Community Shekular, district Andrijevica. Slightly wounded fighting Communists.

Jusuf Bajramovich, peasant, 20 years old. Community Rasovo, district Bijelo Polje. Wounded and taken away by the Partisans: Mico Joksimovich and Radoman Tomovich from Rasovo.

Jagosh Shcepanovich, community secretary, 49 years old. Community Mojkovac, district Bijelo Polje.

Milorad Moracanin, peasant, 14 years old. Community Mojkovac, district Bijelo Polje.

Tadija P. Jelushich, 6 years old. Community Jelenak, district Danilovgrad.

Jovo Lazarevich, pensioner, 64 years old. Community Bijelo Polje, district Bijelo Polje.

Adem Martinovich, laborer, 31 years old. Community Bijelo Polje, district Bijelo Polje.

Vukadin Jocich, 20 years old. Community Zaton, district Bijelo Polje.

Grujo Mrdak, peasant, 40 years old. Community Shahovici, district Bijelo
Polje. Seriously wounded in the head by Partisans.

Milivoje Felich, peasant, 26 years old. Community Zaton, district Bijelo
Polje. Slightly wounded.

Milija Dragnich, peasant, 27 years old. Community Zaton, district Bijelo
Polje. Slightly wounded fighting Communists. He was a Chetnik in
vojvoda Pavle Djurishich's detachment.

Pero V. Radovich, peasant, 48 years old. Community Zaton, district Bijelo
Polje. Slightly wounded.

Vidak Ivanovich, peasant, 38 years old. Community Zaton, district Bijelo
Polje. Wounded while a Chetnik in the detachment of vojvoda Pavle
Djurishich.

Djoko Sh. Kalezich, peasant, 48 years old. Community Kosovi Lug, district
Danilovgrad. Wounded fighting Communists. He was in the battalion
of Jakov Jovovich, captain first class.

Milutin K. Vukovich, peasant, 22 years old. Community Komani, district
Danilovgrad. Slightly wounded fighting Communists. He belonged to
the detachment of Col. Bajo Stanishich.

Krsto Radovich, peasant, 38 years old. Community Spuz, district Danilovgrad. Taken away to shooting ground where he was wounded, but he
managed to run away. The Partisans who abducted him were: Milija
Raspovovich, Dimitrije Dragojevich, and Milan Lajovich, by order of
political commissar Vuleta Djuranovich and Zarija Stojovich, teacher,
the executioner of the main headquarters.

Milan M. Velimirovich, community Zagarac, district Danilovgrad. Slightly
wounded fighting Communists. Belonged to the Bjelopavlici Detachment.

Djoko I. Begovich, peasant, 56 years old. Community Zagarac, district
Danilovgrad. Seriously wounded fighting Communists. Belonged to
the Bjelopavlici Detachment.

Branko Dj. Begovich, peasant, 19 years old. Community Zagarac, district
Danilovgrad. Seriously wounded fighting Communists. Belonged to
the Bjelopavlici Detachment.

Nikola M. Otashevich, peasant, 19 years old. Community Zagarac, district
Danilovgrad. Slightly wounded fighting Communists. Belonged to the
Bjelopavlici Detachment.

Milutin Cupich, soldier, 20 years old. Community Zagarac, district Danilovgrad. Slightly wounded fighting Communists. Belonged to the Bjelopavlici Detachment.

Vladimir M. Begovich, peasant, 30 years old. Community Zagarac, district
Danilovgrad. Seriously wounded fighting Communists. Belonged to
the Bjelopavlici Detachment.

Mitar B. Vuletich, peasant, 24 years old. Wounded fighting Communists.

Radoje P. Vuletich, peasant, 31 years old. Community Pavkovici, district
Danilovgrad. Wounded fighting Partisans. Belonged to the detachment
of Col. Bajo Stanishich.

Milovan B. Vuletich, peasant, 35 years old. Community Pavkovici, district Danilovgrad. Wounded fighting Communists. Belonged to the detachment of Col. Bajo Stanishich.

*The corpse of Lazar
Shcepanovich*

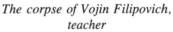

*The corpse of Vojin Filipovich,
teacher*

*Five bodies removed
from willow grove in Boan*

The corpse of Jovan Vlahovich

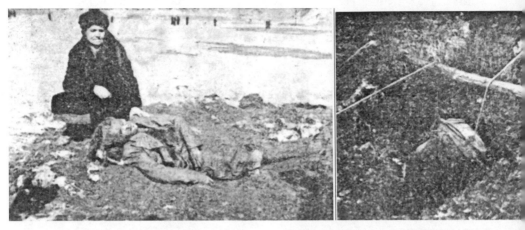

The corpse of Sofija Bojovich   *Removal of corpse from the pit 58 meters deep at Kopilje*
The body of Novo Bozovich

The corpse of Svetozar Lazarevich, former judge of court of cessation   *The team that removed bodies from the riverbed*
Komarnica President Karadzich

The corpse of Obren Aleksich,   *The corpse of Zorka Lashich*
peasant

The corpse of Saveta Tomovich   *The corpse of Dimitrije Aleksich,*
infantry lieutenant

Burnings, Plunderings, and Extortions

Community Jelenak, district Danilovgrad:

Radonja V. Bobicich, two houses damaged by cannons. Taken: 9 chickens,
1,000 kg. hay, 30 cubic meters wood, miscellaneous goods.
Approx. value: 22,150 lire

Punisha B. Jelushich, house destroyed by cannons. Taken: 75 kg. corn.
    Destroyed: 2 grapevines.
Approx. value: 50,000 lire
Mirica I. Pavicevich. Taken: Man's bicycle, wrist watch, miscellaneous
    household goods.
Approx. value: 5,500 lire
Milovan Lakich, house partially destroyed. Taken: 1 cow, 2 calves, 18
    sheep, 25 lambs, 2 goats, 4 chickens, 50 kg. corn, 100 kg. potatoes.
Approx. value: 45,000 lire
Jole M. Lakich, house partially damaged. Taken: 2 cows, 3 calves, 10 pigs,
    1 donkey, 300 kg. potatoes.
Approx. value: 40,000 lire
Novak J. Bobicich, house destroyed by cannons. Taken: 6 sheep, 2 goats,
    5 chickens, 80 kg. corn, dried meat 8 kg., bacon 6 kg., honey 10
    kg., wool 8 kg., potatoes 60 kg., hay 200 kg., wine 20 liters, brandy
    15 liters.
Approx. value: 15,160 lire
Petar J. Bobicich, house destroyed by bombing. Taken: 12 sheep, 6 goats,
    12 chickens, 150 kg. corn, 20 kg. dried meat, 15 kg. bacon, 30 kg.
    honey, butter 200 kg., 20 kg. wool, 400 liters wine, 30 liters brandy,
    40 liters mead.
Approx. value: 47,700 lire
Marica R. Djuranovich, house burned. Taken: 1 horse, 1 cow, 15 chickens,
    30 kg. cream, 30 kg. cheese, 20 kg. wool, 150 kg. potatoes, 300 kg.
    hay, 25 kg. salt, jewelry, clothes, and other household goods.
Approx. value: 100,000 lire
Vuk M. Djuranovich, house burned. Taken: 25 kg. cheese, 200 kg. pota-
    toes, miscellaneous household goods.
Approx. value: 65,000 lire
Perisha P. Djuranovich, house burned. Taken: 10 kg. cheese, 15 kg. wool,
    200 kg. potatoes, 1,250 kg. hay, miscellaneous household goods.
Approx. value: 98,000 lire
Milutin L. Djuranovich, house burned. Taken: 12 sheep, 4 chickens, 90 kg.
    wheat, 80 kg. barley, 16 kg. cheese, 35 kg. wool, 200 kg. potatoes, 15
    kg. beans, 5,500 kg. hay, miscellaneous household goods.
Approx. value: 69,000 lire
Milica K. Djuranovich, house destroyed. Taken: 6 chickens, 100 kg. pota-
    toes, 30 kg. beans, 600 kg. hay, miscellaneous household goods.
Approx. value: 30,000 iire

Community Zaton, district Bijelo Polje:

Novak N. Popovich. Taken: 15 sheep, 50 kg. cream, 100 kg. cheese, 14
    kg. wool, miscellaneous household goods.
Approx. value: 14,435

Vukojna N. Peshich. Taken: 20 sheep.
Approx. value: 24,000 lire

Community Bijelo Polje, district Bijelo Polje:

For the community, Baro A. Mekich declared. Taken: 400 kg. rice, 300 kg. sugar, a Remington typewriter.
Approx. value: 40,700 lire
Kadrija H. Kolich, house burned. Taken: 5 sheep, 100 kg. corn.
Approx. value: 20,000 lire
Shaban N. Burdzovich. Taken: 55 kg. cheese, 200 kg. walnuts, 150 kg. dried prunes. 3,050 lire in cash.
Approx. value: 12,000 lire

Community Pavino Polje, district Bijelo Polje:

Ljubo Z. Perishich. Taken: 1 sheep, 30 kg. barley, 30 kg. oats.
Approx. value: 1,575 lire
Marinko M. Grbo. Taken: 2 oxen, 60 kg. barley, 7 liters brandy.
Approx. value: 8,410 lire
Perko J. Tomashevich. Taken: 1 sheep, 100 kg. barley, 100 kg. oats.
Approx. value: 4,000 lire
Radivoje B. Tomashevich. Taken: 1 sheep, 150 kg. barley, 100 kg. oats.
Approx. value: 5,000 lire
Jeremija J. Tomashevich. Taken: 1 ox, 100 kg. barley.
Approx. value: 8,000 lire
Milisav I. Drovnjak. Taken: 1 cow, 100 kg. wheat, 65 kg. barley, 20 kg. oats.
Approx. value: 4,900 lire
Filip N. Knezevich. Taken: 1 ox, 1 horse, 100 kg. barley.
Approx. value: 6,000 lire
Milan R. Sharcevich. Taken: 3 sheep, 15 kg. barley.
Approx. value: 1,650 lire
Tomo S. Kartalovich. Taken: 1 cow, 80 kg. barley, 15 kg. oats, 10 kg. dried meat, 5 kg. cream, 7 kg. cheese, miscellaneous household goods.
Approx. value: 10,750 lire
Jagosh M. Knezevich. Taken: 3 sheep, 40 kg. barley, 20 kg. oats, 5 kg. wool.
Approx. value: 3,500 lire
Milovan R. Shestovich. Taken: 1 ox, 1 sheep, 115 kg. barley, 50 kg. wheat, 5 kg. oats.
Approx. value: 7,000 lire
Miladin S. Markovich. Taken: 1 sheep, 15 kg. barley.
Approx. value: 1,000 lire
Milka Rovcanin. Taken: 54 kg. barley.
Approx. value: 1,080 lire

Jermo M. Lekovich. Taken: 1 ox, 2 sheep, 75 kg. barley.
  Approx. value: 7,000 lire
Krsto M. Lekovich. Taken: 100 kg. barley.
  Approx. value: 2,000 lire
Milivoje A. Lekovich. Taken: 120 kg. barley, 20 kg. oats.
  Approx. value: 3,900 lire
Vukadin M. Zutich. Taken: 1 ox, 130 kg. barley, 10 kg. cream, 10 kg.
  cheese, 65 kg. potatoes
  Approx. value: 14,400 lire
Mirko Z. Perishich. Taken: 55 kg. barley. *Approx. value: 1,750 lire*
Petko M. Joksimovich. Taken: 1 sheep, 20 kg. barley, 5 kg. oats.
  Approx. value: 975 lire

Community Kosovi Lug, district Danilovgrad:

Perisha N. Brajovich. Taken: 20 chickens, 400 kg. corn, 200 kg. wheat,
  30 kg. dried meat, 200 kg. potatoes, 300 kg. cabbage, 3,500 kg. hay,
  850 kg. straw, 20 liters brandy, 50 cubic meters wood.
  Approx. value: 20,000 lire
Bogdan J. Brajovich. Taken: 20 cubic meters wood.
  Approx. value: 6,000 lire
Dobrica B. Dragovich, house burned. Taken: 600 kg. wheat, 400 kg. pota-
  toes, 4,000 kg. hay, 1,000 kg. straw, 300 liters brandy, 250 cubic
  meters wood. Destroyed 7 grapevines, 36 fruit trees.
  Approx. value: 60,000 lire
Nikola M. Dragovich. Taken: 15 cubic meters wood.
  Approx. value: 3,750 lire
Velisha F. Dragovich. Taken: 20 cubic meters wood.
  Approx. value: 5,000 lire
Zlatana R. Dragovich, house burned. Taken: 4,000 kg. hay, 300 liters
  brandy, 250 cubic meters wood.
  Approx. value: 60,000 lire

Community Komani, district Danilovgrad:

Filip S. Radulovich. Taken: 4,000 kg. hay, 400 cubic meters wood.
  Approx. value: 60,000 lire
The elementary school. Taken: 25 cubic meters wood. Miscellaneous school
  supplies. Destroyed 25 fruit trees.
  Approx. value: 30,000 lire
Jovan I. Sekulich. Taken: 1 ox, 2 sheep, 5 chickens, 8 kg. bacon, 6 kg.
  cream, 4 kg. cheese, 2,000 kg. hay, 50 liters wine, 10 liters brandy.
  Miscellaneous household goods.
  Approx. value: 10,000 lire
Djuro G. Radulovich, house burned.
  Approx. value: 100,000 lire

Janko P. Vukadinovich. Taken: 75 kg. potatoes.
Approx. value: 750 lire
Vojislav Dj. Radulovich. Taken: miscellaneous household goods.
Approx. value: 20,000 lire
Blagota S. Radonjich, 2 houses burned. Taken: 180 kg. corn, 100 kg. dried
meat, 40 kg. bacon, 50 kg. cream, 20 kg. cheese, 50 kg. honey, 20
kg. wool, 300 kg. potatoes, 20 kg. beans, 5 cubic meters wood,
furniture and miscellaneous household goods.
Approx. value: 120,000 lire
Djuro I. Radulovich. Taken: 5,000 kg. hay, 100 liters wine, 50 liters brandy,
50 cubic meters wood.
Approx. value: 10,500 lire
Cetko N. Sekulich. Taken: 1 calf, 1 pig, 1 goat, 5 beehives, 6 chickens,
100 kg. corn, 5 kg. bacon, 8 kg. cream, 100 liters wine, 50 liters
brandy.
Approx. value: 14,000 lire
Dushan N. Sekulich. Taken: 3,500 kg. hay, 4 cubic meters wood.
Approx. value: 7,800 lire
Marko J. Vukovich. Taken: 4 beehives.
Approx. value: 4,000 lire
Mashan P. Stanishich. Taken: 8 beehives, 6 chickens, 100 kg. corn, 25 kg.
dried meat, 450 kg. potatoes, 150 kg. cabbage, 3 cubic meters wood.
Approx. value: 19,050 lire
Bajo O. Vukadinovich. Taken: 100 kg. potatoes.
Approx. value: 1,000 lire
Jovan P. Stanishich. Taken: 300 kg. corn, 30 kg. dried meat, 270 kg.
potatoes, 150 kg. cabbage, 4 cubic meters wood.
Approx. value: 15,000 lire
Mitar J. Djuranovich. Taken: 250 kg. potatoes.
Approx. value: 2,500 lire
Josho I. Vukadinovich. Taken: 300 kg. potatoes.
Approx. value: 3,000 lire
Simon F. Radulovich, house and furniture burned. Taken: 80 kg. dried
meat, 30 kg. bacon, 5 kg. lard, 5 kg. cream, 15 kg. cheese.
Approx. value: 110,000 lire

Community Spuz, district Danilovgrad:

Peko P. Roganovich. Taken: 1 calf, 1 pig, 1 donkey, 5 beehives, 5 chickens,
200 kg. corn, 130 kg. wheat, 25 kg. rye, 40 kg. dried meat, 25 kg.
bacon, 10 kg. lard, 26 kg. cream, 25 kg. wool, 150 kg. potatoes, 50
kg. cabbage, 8 kg. beans, 3,000 kg. hay, 3,000 kg. straw, 5 liters
brandy, miscellaneous goods.
Approx. value: 60,000 lire
Kosto P. Milonjich, two houses burned. Taken: 1 ox, 1 pig, 50 chickens,
300 kg. corn, 300 kg. wheat, 50 kg. dried meat, 50 kg. bacon, 25 kg.

lard, 100 kg. cream, 80 kg. cheese, 100 kg. wool, 200 kg. potatoes, 50 kg. beans, 2,100 kg. hay, 450 kg. straw, 100 liters wine, 200 liters brandy, all furniture.
Approx. value: 200,000 lire

Zivko S. Miranovich, house burned. Taken: 1 pig, 2 beehives, 28 chickens, 300 kg. corn, 500 kg. potatoes, miscellaneous household goods.
Approx. value: 400,000 lire

Milovan N. Jovanovich, two-story house burned. Taken: 1 ox, 1 horse, 2 cows, 1 calf, 1 pig, 15 chickens, 5 beehives, 270 kg. corn, 150 kg. wheat, 42 kg. dried meat, 18 kg. bacon, 15 kg. lard, 20 kg. cream, 15 kg. cheese, 25 kg. honey, 10 kg. wool, 120 kg. potatoes, 8 kg. beans, 700 kg. hay, 180 kg. straw, 75 eggs. Destroyed: 30 fruit trees.
Approx. value: 57,000 lire

Ljubica S. Miranovich. Taken: All furniture. 53,000 lire in cash.
Approx. value: 100,000 lire

Milena I. Cetkovich. Taken: 20 chickens, 70 kg. corn, 30 kg. wheat, 7 kg. cheese, 15 liters brandy, 140 kg. tobacco, miscellaneous household goods.
Approx. value: 60,000 lire

Nikola M. Djurickovich, house burned. Taken: 150 kg. wheat, 75 kg. rye, 1,800 kg. hay, 1,000 kg. straw, 400 kg. apples, miscellaneous household goods.
Approx. value: 300,000 lire

Milutin B. Roganovich, two-story house burned. Taken: 3 cows, 2 pigs, 14 sheep, 34 chickens, 300 kg. corn, 300 kg. wheat, 200 kg. lard, 100 kg. cream, 120 kg. cheese, 800 kg. potatoes, 50 liters wine, 150 liters brandy, miscellaneous household goods.
Approx. value: 533,000 lire

Luka L. Kadich. Taken: 1 horse, 1 cow, 2 pigs, 12 sheep, 23 chickens, 270 kg. corn, 160 kg. wheat, 12 kg. dried meat, 8 kg. bacon, 1 kg. cream, 120 kg. potatoes, 970 kg. hay. 9,000 lire in cash, miscellaneous household goods.
Approx. value: 60,000 lire

Mirko I. Dragovich. Taken: 1,600 kg. hay, miscellaneous household goods.
Approx. value: 52,400 lire

Mirko P. Mihailovich. Taken: 1,200 kg. hay, furniture and miscellaneous household goods.
Approx. value: 3,300 lire

Community Zagarac, district Danilovgrad:

Lazar V. Otashevich. Taken: 50 liters wine, 30 liters brandy. 1 overcoat.
Approx. value: 3,000 lire

Milan M. Velimirovich. Taken: 1 pair shoes, 1 suit, 1 wrist watch.
Approx. value: 1,600 lire

Djoko I. Begovich, house burned. Taken: 50 kg. corn, 15 kg. dried meat, 7 kg. wool, 400 kg. hay, all furniture.
Approx. value: 208,000 lire

Mico V. Otashevich. Taken: 1 donkey, 30 kg. corn. 1 overcoat.
Approx. value: 45,000 lire

Tiodor M. Shcepanovich, one house burned, one house destroyed. Taken: 90 kg. corn, 20 kg. wheat, 20 kg. dried meat, 5 kg. bacon, 10 kg. cream, 8 kg. cheese, 18 kg. wool, 50 kg. potatoes, 280 kg. hay, 15 liters brandy, miscellaneous household goods.
Approx. value: 45,000 lire

Radivoje P. Shcepanovich. Taken: 45 kg. corn, 10 kg. dried meat, 10 kg. bacon, 15 kg. lard, 12 kg. cream, 6 kg. wool, miscellaneous household goods.
Approx. value: 10,000 lire

Marko M. Cupich. Taken: 1 ox, 50 kg. dried meat, 1,500 kg. potatoes, 100 kg. cabbage, 900 kg. hay, 150 liters wine, 15 liters brandy.
Approx. value: 15,000 lire

Djuro R. Markovich. Taken: 1 horse, 1 sheep, 35 liters brandy. Miscellaneous household goods.
Approx. value: 80,900 lire

Milovan I. Shepanovich, house burned. Taken: 2 chickens, 14 kg. dried meat, 3 kg. bacon, 5 kg. lard, 8 kg. cream, 180 kg. potatoes, 11 kg. beans, 12 liters brandy, 16 eggs.
Approx. value: 55,000 lire

Bozo L. Shepanovich. Taken: 1 pig, 30 kg. corn, 12 kg. dried meat, 8 kg. bacon, miscellaneous household goods.
Approx. value: 9,800 lire

Mitar I. Begovich, two houses burned. Taken: 150 kg. corn, 30 kg. wool, 100 kg. potatoes, 300 kg. cheese, 50 liters wine, 20 liters brandy, 4 cubic meters wood, miscellaneous household goods.
Approx. value: 10,000 lire

Petar R. Lazarevich, house burned. Taken: 1 pig, 3 chickens, 350 kg. corn, 45 kg. dried meat, 40 kg. bacon, 24 kg. lard, 15 kg. wool, 150 kg. potatoes, 400 kg. hay, 1,250 kg. wine, 206 liters brandy. Miscellaneous household goods.
Approx. value: 125,000 lire

Zarija M. Shepanovich, house burned. Taken: 1 chicken, 10 kg. dried meat, 5 kg. cream, 50 kg. potatoes, 5 liters brandy.
Approx. value: 117,000 lire

Various Communist Documents

(five-pointed star)
Headquarters Zeta

National Liberation Partisan Detachment No. 59
January 21, 1942
TO HEADQUARTERS OF LJESHNJANI PARTISAN BATTALION
KORNET

We confirm receipt of your letter of January 18, 1942, under No. 14 and at the same time reply as follows: Those fifth-columnist incidents are nothing but the result of your dreadful indecisiveness. If several leading fifth columnists had been liquidated, nothing of the sort would be happening.

The only remedy is to destroy fifth columnists by throwing them out of the Partisan ranks and then liquidating those quislings. Only those who are willing and determined to fight against the occupier and fifth columnists as well should be retained in the Partisan ranks. If it does not work out satisfactorily then you have to immediately mobilize all Partisan forces who are resolute and decisive. Further, call one Partisan company from Ljeshkopolje and one from Zeta. Also ask for help from one company of the Lovcen Detachment. Arrest all traitors and disarm those who help them. If anyone opposes this, shoot him on the spot. The Partisan companies should be well armed. The action should be executed at dawn. Guard the houses and keep the individual villages under siege all through the night. Be on guard against surprise from the occupier.

Consider the above to be our order.

Ljeshnjani Nahi needs to be swept clean of fifth columnists, as was done in Vasojevice. Invite the Partisan companies from Ljeshkopolje and Zeta on the basis of this order.

Keep sentries around your battalion headquarters in large numbers night and day. In case of another attack on your headquarters, open fire against the fifth columnists. For such a situation have ready about 100 trustworthy Partisans who will help you chase away that gang.

You don't have to be attached to the Gornji Ljeshnjani Battalion. On the contrary, if conditions are not adequate for a battalion formation, then you could have just one strong Partisan company. However, if you have 200 to 220 Partisans, then the conditions are right for forming one battalion.

As for the commander of the battalion: You can suggest a decisive and courageous Partisan who is best qualified for the position. In choosing him do not be guided by what clan he is from or what position he held in former Yugoslavia.

Execute actions for demolishing roads and cutting telephone wires without informing the peasants in advance.

In our opinion, Nikola and Milo Vukcevich are fifth columnists and they should be liquidated as the pillars of the fifth-column movement there.

Here in Piperi we completely routed the fifth columnists. The ring leaders were caught and will be properly punished, while the rest of them were disarmed. Some of them fled to the Italians; among them was Savo Dmitrovich. That is welcome from the political viewpoint.

DEATH TO FASCISM—FREEDOM TO THE PEOPLE!

For Political Commissar,	Commandant,
V.B.	Blazo Jovanovich
(signed)	(signed)

Headquarters Lovcen
National Liberation Partisan Detachment
February 7, 1942

TO HEADQUARTERS OF ZETA NATIONAL LIBERATION PARTISAN DETACHMENT

In the Field

Of course you know quite well what is going on in the territory of the Donjo-Ljeshnjani Battalion, which is part of our detachment.

Not long ago, fifth columnists of the Donjo Ljeshnjani Nahi frustrated the execution of an action against the occupier on their territory.

It was imperative to take appropriate measures to thwart further intentions of the fifth columnists in that region.

With your acknowledgment and with mutual cooperation with the Donjo Ljeshnjani Partisan Battalion as well, this detachment had prepared and executed actions against fifth columnists in Donja Nahija. The aim of such actions was to capture the leaders of the fifth column and to liquidate them. However, that goal was not realized because the fifth columnists were given time in advance to organize and strengthen themselves by some misled people there.

Fifth-columnist sentries met our Partisans with fire, which our Partisans returned. Two or three of the fifth columnist sentries were killed, and some of them were captured. Even though the action did not succeed in accomplishing its main task, after that event in Donjo Nahiji certain differences became apparent, as expected. In some individual villages—Kokoti, Brezine, and others—the masses tended to break away from the fifth-columnist movement and join the Partisans. As this terrain is closer to us, we took advantage of this tendency to break and isolate the fifth columnists. We invited to our headquarters and conversed with Andrija Pejovich, a federalist and honest peasant from the village of Kokoti.

We easily agreed.

After receiving our instructions he went back to talk with his friends and to prepare the ground for the arrival there of a member of our Lovcen Detachment. As that man [*Pejovich*] is obviously influential, there is the possibility of gathering around him a pack of honest men not only from the already mentioned villages but also from the Vukcevich clan, where the evil nest of the new fifth column is currently residing. Also we are getting a lot of help from Maj. Celebich from Shtitari, who joined the Partisan ranks a while ago.

The fifth columnists learned of this action. They began to make threats and will not be restrained, as can be seen from the enclosed letter. Also, we are of the opinion that you should on your side pay the utmost attention to your sector and demonstrate every help to those men with whom we are currently associated. In view of this, we'll write to the Donjo-Ljeshnjani Partisan Battalion about sending you this letter. We'll also ask Pejovich and his friends to remain unconditionally on their territory and to continue their activities. They will get every possible assistance and protection from us.

It is necessary for the headquarters of both the Zeta and Lovcen detachments to work together on the problem of Donjo Ljeshnjani Nahi and for that reason you must maintain constant contact.

DEATH TO FASCISM—FREEDOM TO THE PEOPLE!

Political Commissar,   Commandant,
in the field   (seal)   Peko
                                          (signed)

(five-pointed star) [*supposedly from Lovcen Detachment*]
Headquarters
National Liberation Partisan Detachment
            No. 159
February 14, 1942

_____

(five-pointed star)
Headquarters
National Liberation Partisan Detachment
            No. 128
February 7, 1942

TO THE HEADQUARTERS OF BRATONOSHKO BRSKUTSKI
N.L.M. BATTALION OF 18 OCTOBER

We are informing you that February 23 is the day when the Red Army was founded. This day should be celebrated by Partisans and by the entire people as well. Political commissars could give lectures about the Red Army, for which material can be found in *Struggle* (*Borba*) no. 8-9 and also from history VCP1-6. That event is important to us because today the Red Army is waging a war of liberation for the benefit not only of her own people but also for all subjugated nations. Therefore, all enslaved people especially Slavic people are watching for the Red Army to liberate them. The English and American people and even Italians and Germans were hoping for the same because they are all in jeopardy from fascism, the worst evil ever known to mankind. It is necessary to explain to the people how that strongest and most courageous army emerged and progressed to become the protector of all enslaved people.

Inform us how you carried out the exchange of Partisans in Vasojevice as it was ordered.

A certain hesitation was emerging among some Partisans, especially regarding the struggle against the treacherous Lashich gangs that were plunging the knife into the heart of our national liberation struggle. It is necessary to get rid of them because we have no reason to fight against Vasojevice, except against traitors who began the fratricidal struggle while leaning toward the occupier. Nothing could be more shameful or depressing. Besides reluctance there is a case of one traitor, Vladimir Djukich, who shamelessly joined the Partisans. He became an informer for Lashich and joined him at the end. He will not escape the people's punishment. In the meantime he should be exposed as a traitor who sold his soul to the devil. He joined the Partisan ranks at the right time to harm the national liberation movement.

All Montenegrin people were gathered around our movement except a few traitors and some misled people.

Otherwise, proceed according to our earlier orders.

DEATH TO FASCISM—FREEDOM TO THE PEOPLE!

>   Commandant,
>   Blazo Jovanovich
>   (signed)   _____

(five-star)
Headquarters Zeta
National Liberation Partisan Detachment
        Classified No. 39
February 24, 1942

TO HEADQUARTERS PIPERI N.L.M. BATTALION, SERDAR JOLE

We are sending Vidak Vukovich to your battalion headquarters so that you can proceed with him according to information already in your possession. If he deserves to be gotten rid of and liquidated do it yourself. Don't send him back to us for that reason. You surprised us when you said that you don't know what to do with him. It was well known what should be done with fifth columnists. Here we see a certain weakness and hesitation. When other battalions have to liquidate someone they do it by themselves. They don't escort him here for that purpose.

Now according to a reliable report he [Vukovich] always goes to Podgorica to see Stanko Markovich. From Rogami a small, blond, fat girl, about 14 to 15 years old, with blue coat and hood is going now instead of Bula Stamatovich—we already wrote about her. Seize her and investigate. If she should be liquidated, execute her.

In reference to Grujovich's rifle and revolver, right now we cannot send them to you for a while because they were taken by couriers on their duty. As soon as they return we will send them to you.

DEATH TO FASCISM—FREEDOM TO THE PEOPLE!

For Political Commissar,   Commandant,
V.B.   Blazo Jovanovich
                                      (signed)

(form: postcard)
Writer: Battalion headquarters   From where: From Ljeshkopolje
                                      where
To Whom: To headquarters of Zeta   which map was used
Brigade
Official No.: November 15, day hour minute

At night on the 14th of this month in Gornja Gorica an action was
executed against Milosh Milich, a spy. He was killed.

We are deeply touched to inform you that during that action the adjutant
of this battalion, Comrade Bajo Raicevich, was killed while the assistant
commander of the Gornjo Goricki Platoon, Comrade Lazo Miranovich, was
seriously wounded.

We'll try to have the funeral on November 16 at 5 o'clock in the afternoon
in Luznica.

Commandant,
Shpiro Mugosha (signed)

(on the back of postcard)
(five-pointed star)
Headquarters Zeta
National Liberation Partisan Detachment
        No. 11, November 28, 1941

According to available documents, for the Partisans the paramount goal was
Communist revolution, not national liberation. Under the motto of struggle
for the national liberation the Partisans in time realized the unpopularity of
their aims. Then they misled the masses by appealing to their patriotic
feelings. The Communists believed the execution [*of their adversaries*]
would be much easier during an occupation. From the facts it can be seen
that all real patriots, nationalists, and other honest people were proclaimed
to be fifth columnists, spies, and traitors to discredit these real and honest
leaders and more easily liquidate them.

HELL
or
Communism in Montenegro

[*picture of skull and long bone*]

Volume Number Two
An edition of *The Voice of Montenegro*
Publisher, Obod—Cetinje

Early Partisan Casualties

[*with their pictures*]

Branko Miloshevich, student of technology, killed in the Spanish civil war in 1937.
Bosko Petrovich, pilot, killed in Spanish civil war in 1937.
Vukashin M. Radunovich, Ph.D., killed in Spain.
Krsto Ljubicich, student, killed at Croatian University.

Petar (Peko) Dapcevich

He was born on June 26, 1913, in Ljubotinj. His father was Jovan Dapcevich, a deacon who after the war became banovina school superintendent and a prominent national leader; his mother was Milica, nee Jovicevich.

In 1933 he graduated from the gymnasium in Cetinje. During his school years he had financial security but did not demonstrate the success that his condition might suggest. As shown in the school records, he was slipshod in his habits, a wild and foolhardy young man.

In his early youth he already was engaged in Communist propagandizing. He continued this activity at Belgrade University, where he was a law student. (He never graduated from that institution.) He dropped his studies and slipped into Spain, where he joined the struggle of the Spanish Communists and Republicans. After the Spanish civil war he escaped across a border to France. Apparently he was in a camp there posing as a refugee.

He returned incognito to Montenegro on the eve of the events of July 13, 1941. He immediately joined the rebel leadership, taking different positions until he became commandant of all Partisan forces for Montenegro, Sandzak, and Boka.

He left behind him a bloody trail of evil that people would never forget. Carried by his restless blood, criminally disposed, cynical, and insensitive, Petar (Peko) Dapcevich not only destroyed his family, which had been known for character and virtue, but also caused many Montenegrin homes to grieve.

55

Captured Partisan Men and Women

[with their pictures]

Lazar Cokorilo from Niksic.
Stanko M. Pavicevich from Pavkovici.
Vukosava Uskokovich from Drazevina.
Several captured female Partisans [*pictured together*].
Jovanka Ulanovich from Ozrinici.
Radoica Rosandich, peasant.
Janica Kontich from Strasevina.
Capt. Djoko Mirashevich.
Cirilo Pavicevich from Jelenak, Partisan courier.
Vidna Mijanovich from Gonje Polje, belonged to Partisan strike unit.
Stanko J. Pavicevich, peasant from Pavkovici.
Radmila Popovich, student.
Nikola Burzan, mechanic from Podgorica.
Milena Kostich from Zupa, Niksic.

Commandants of Partisan Battalions, Company Commanders, and Their Assistants

[Thirty-four individuals are listed, including name, occupation, age, position, and community and district of residence.]

Political Commissars and Their Assistants

[Twenty-four individuals are listed, including name, occupation, age, position, and community and district of residence.]

Partisan Judges and Their Assistants

[Twenty-four individuals are listed, including name, occupation, age, position, and community and district of residence.]

Executioners and Their Assistants

[Seventeen individuals are listed, including name, occupation, age, position, and community and district of residence.]

Abyss and Hell

People Killed by Partisans

[Sixty-four individuals are listed, including name, occupation, age, and community and district of residence.]

People Wounded by the Partisans

[Twenty-six individuals are listed, including name, occupation, age, and community and district of residence.]

Burnings, Plunderings, and Extortions

[Forty-nine individuals are listed, including name, community and district of residence, buildings burned, items taken, and approximate value.]

Results of the Partisan Work

Various Verdicts and Crimes

<table>
<tr><td style="text-align:center">VELJO RADOVICH
Mayor of Gornjo-Zetska
Community</td><td style="text-align:center">NESHO RADOVICH
Honorary flag bearer</td></tr>
</table>

Both were killed, mutilated, and then thrown into the Moraca River on February 22, 1942. Eighty Communists bandits were involved in that deed, led by Shcepan Stijepovich and Dushan Vukovich. The executioners were Nikola Karadaglich, Vojin Ladjich, Spaso Drakich, Marko Ladjich, Velimir Cavnich, and Vlado Klikovac.

The Radovich brothers were well known as persons of integrity in their personal lives and national activity, and as such they became targets of the Communists.

After they were liquidated a Partisan document stated:

To Main Headquarters
National Liberation Partisan Detachment
for Montenegro and Boka

We received your letter no. 243 dated the 22d of this month, and we reacted appropriately. We sent orders by courier to the headquarters of Zeta, Donjo-Ljeshanski, and Ljeshkopolje and also sent Comrade Blazo Jovanovich a letter from the main headquarters.

Comrade Savo Brkovich informed us of the seizure of dishes, tools, groceries, brandy, two pigs, and other items from the fifth columnist (Mico Savovich). If you need something send us a list.

We notify you of the liquidation of the following persons: Filip Vucinich, Velika Boljevich from Donja Zeta, Veljo Radovich, former mayor of Gornja Zeta community, and his brother Nesho Radovich from Gornja Zeta, Ilija Nedovich, butcher from Podgorica, Olga Raicevich from Spuz, Milan Petkovich from Crnci, Mitar Makocevich, also from Crnci, Vuksan Djukich, and Milusha Djukich from Zavala.

We are enclosing the minutes of Mitra Makocevicha as ordered by Comrade Savo Brkovich.

DEATH TO FASCISM—FREEDOM TO THE PEOPLE!

Assistant to the Political
Commissar,
V. Bozovich
(signed)

Assistant Commandant,
Srd. Novakovich
(signed)

KOSTO LALICH
Duke and village judge of Uble, 35 years old
[picture]

He was brutally assaulted in January 1942 by nefarious Partisans in Grahovo and thrown half dead into a pit about forty meters deep.

Kosto Lalich was well known throughout Boka as a representative of the Uble peasantry. As the village judge, Kosto worked hard to improve the standard of living in his village. On his initiative a large cistern was built in Uble, solving a drinking water problem. Then he was engaged to repair the road to Uble. He had a prominent role in building the belfry of the local church. He was also a member of the local Red Cross committee. As the long-standing head of Sokol [*a patriotic organization*] he had worked for the prosperity of his village.

Kosto was an obstacle to the Partisans. Therefore, by order of the infamous Nikola Djurkovich, Kosto was taken away to Grahovo, where he was brutally tortured. He was beaten by blunt objects and held for hours in cold water before being thrown half dead into the pit.

On the way to the place of his execution, Kosto managed to grab the rifle from one of the escorting Partisans and killed one of them, a well-known, sadistic parasite, Pero Bego from Dragalj.

On Saint Vitus's Day of last year his body was found. It was solemnly moved in procession to his birthplace of Uble.

Rest in peace, duke Kosto Lalich.

KATICA JANKOVICH
Sokol head in Djenovici, Boka Kotorska
[picture]
Born in Osijek, 1913

After she graduated from the gymnasium she moved to Boka. As a nationalist and educator she participated in the activities of the local Sokol. As a true patriot she did not approve of the brutal actions of the Communists. On the contrary, she condemned them and dissuaded people from joining the Communists.

By order of the notorious Orjen headquarters she was abducted on February 13, 1942, and taken to the village Repja by local executioners. There she was brutally killed and thrown into a nearby creek.

Her body was found on July 20, 1942. The killers had stolen from her body her jewelry, overcoat, and other clothes, evidence that female Partisans had taken part in the execution.

Katica was a model in her community with her unselfish work in the national and educational fields. She was a Catholic and strongly advocated brotherly harmony between Orthodox and Roman Catholic believers. She fell as an innocent victim of the Communist ideology.

Later the authorities jailed her killers. They were youth from the neighborhood where the execution was done, acting by order of their Partisan headquarters and the notorious headquarters chief, Nikola Djurkovich.

To the Partisans any honest man who cherishes the fatherland, faith, and nationalism is a fifth columnist, traitor, and spy. To them, honest men were bloodsuckers and real traitors.

BLAZO M. CRNOJEVICH
from Gradjani
[*picture*]

Because he disagreed with what the Partisans did, an entire battalion of two hundred Partisans came to Gradjani for him and his friends. The force was led by the well-known criminals Milo Lubarda, commander of company from lower villages; Vojin I. Vojvodich, political commissar; Djuro J. Petrovich, company commander; Stanko J. Mihaljevich, the executioner; Kico Barjamovich Adzija; Mashan Djurashevich; Velisha B. Vukashevich; and others.

Eighteen Gradjani were taken away to Kunovo Prisoje. Five of them were shot, including Blazo. He was intelligent and respected in his society. He was an entrepreneur. In the army he held the rank of sergeant.

He left behind five frail children. After his liquidation the Partisans plundered his home, taking money and other objects worth about six thousand lire.

MILO M. PAVLICICH
Teacher
[*picture*]

Throughout his teaching career he stayed with his tribe the Bjelopavlici. In the last few years he taught at the monastery of Zdrebaonik.

As an exemplary Serb and faithful son of his people, loved and influential in his community, he disturbed the Partisans in their work. They came and took him away. He was thrown in some pit yet unknown.

GAVRO D. LAKICH
War invalid and landowner from Bjelopavlici

He was ambushed and killed by a salvo of over twenty rifle shots in the forest of Miljata, near his home. He fell as the first victim of the Communists on August 19, 1941. The Communists who were accused of his death and the death of many others in Martinice and surroundings were
Vuleta Djuranovich, law student, political commissar
Djuro Cagorovich, stonecutter, commandant.
The executioners and their assistants were
Vuleta Djuranovich, Djuro Cagorovich, Mihailo Zarich, Milisav Djuranovich, law student, Andrija Raspopovich, Milija Raspopovich, Milan Raspopovich, Vlado Raspopovich, and Nikola Perovich.

RISTO S. VUJACICH
Teacher and reserve captain first class
from village Podgor, Crmnica

On March 23, 1942, he was taken from his home and killed not far from his home at Smokov Vijenac.
His cousin Pavle A. Vujacich took him away from his home by giving his word of honor that Risto would not be killed, but just must appear by call of the political commissar to answer questions in an investigation.
The Partisan leaders in the same village were Blazo I. Ljutica, political commissar; Rashko Vukosavovich, jurist from Sotonici, battalion commandant; Vojo Pocek, attorney from Cetinje, company commander; and Marko Dj. Vukmanovich, peasant from the village Utrg, sergeant.
The murderers and executioners were Pavle A. Vujacich, nephew of the deceased; Branislav M. Vujacich, relative of the killed teacher; Kosto Barjamovich from Orahovo; Pavle R. Kopitovich from Brcela; and Urosh J. Markovich from Brijeg.
After Risto's death his home was plundered four times.

Various Communist Documents

Regional, District, Local Committees, and Bureaus of Cells

I

Agitation and propaganda (agit prop) are powerful tools in the hands of the Marxist-Leninist party. The party uses these tools to win over the masses and rouse them ideologically. It uses these tools to educate the masses in a particular way, by giving them the necessary consciousness and knowledge of their position in society and about society itself, by teaching the necessity for struggle, and finally, by teaching who should change society today and how. Using agitation techniques the party raises awareness among the working masses, by opening the eyes of the poor and mid-scale peasantry, by showing them who is exploiting them and how, and finally who is their friend and who their enemy. Agitation is at the first level of our work among the masses, the first step in totally taking over the masses politically. Mass propaganda is the second level in that direction. Propaganda can deepen the successes of agitation by strengthening the consciousness of the masses, increasing knowledge, raising resoluteness, and cementing everything that was accomplished by agitation. Propaganda creates bases for expanding party membership.

However, in order for the party to develop massive agitation and propaganda it is necessary to have people skilled in these areas. The first cannot be imagined without the second. They are two sides of the same coin. Massive agitation and propaganda depend on the political and ideological level of the party membership. If there is no machine capable of massive agitation the party will not be able to widen its influence and scope. Also, without such a machine it would not be able to strengthen its influence and increase the numbers of its members and of Communists in general.

During today's national liberation struggle our party is beset with problems, especially regarding agit prop. A great many people are actively engaged in armed conflict against the occupier under the direction of our party. Through that struggle our party widened its influence and acquired the trust of the masses. The aim of agit-prop work is to maximize the party's influence and trust among the masses. A further goal is to prepare the masses politically and ideologically for solving new assignments that will emerge with the development of the national liberation struggle.

II

In our party's agitation efforts today many mistakes must be corrected, many omissions must be compensated for. It is important to highlight these omissions and mistakes through critical evaluation for the sake of future efforts.

1. In some of our party organizations and forums the potential of agit-prop work in a given situation was not understood. This suggests that it may be necessary to have more access to agit prop, which in some cases had been considered secondary in relation to other facets of party work and thus was virtually ignored.

2. Previous agit-prop efforts were insufficient, unsystematic, and unorganized. There are many examples of this. *The People's Struggle* was not

published in time, cooperation was lacking, and distribution was feeble. Party newsletters, like other agit-prop materials, were not distributed outside the party membership and sympathizers. Party organizations did not distribute the material according to proper priorities. The material should primarily penetrate into villages and communities where our influence is minimal. Finally, printed agit-prop material sometimes lacked proper vocabulary and content. Many of our party organizations' leaflets treated problems stereotypically, repeated general sections, and were not concrete. The provincial committee did not pay enough attention to specific problems in the places where they were living and working.

3. The disregard of agit-prop work cannot be justified by the lack of professional party cadres during the struggle. This lack resulted from the irregular distribution of the cadres, and partly from a parochial view of certain nonparty forces, which could have been useful in areas (such as the cultural sector) where agit prop was engaged.

4. The lack of agit prop was felt strongly in the inside work of the party group. The political and theoretical education of the party cadres was neglected. The study of the history of communism was almost abandoned. Also neglected was the education of new party members who joined the struggle and through baptism by fire were qualified to become party members. It was vital to pay great attention to them, politically and theoretically, but this was not done.

5. Great omissions were made by our party organizations in agit-prop work at gatherings or meetings of Partisan units. In many of these cases the entire attempt at agit prop consisted of party proclamations and newspapers read aloud so poorly that nobody present could understand them. It was not sufficient to have the material presented by half-literate readers. The material should have been read clearly and elaborated on to ensure understanding.

6. The quality of our cultural and political shows was very poor. Most of these performances were given according to a pattern seen or learned in Belgrade or elsewhere, which was impractical for our conditions and current circumstances. Further, the performances failed in their purpose because of a misconception that the peasants lacked understanding and sophistication. In other words, the shows were written at such a low level that the performances could not elevate the cultural status of their audiences.

7. The broadcasting of radio news was very narrow, careless, and irresponsible. If news was broadcast it was usually incorrect, or carelessly transmitted. In some cases there were direct lies that were harmful to the national liberation struggle.

8. The responsible party comrades did not pay attention to or maintain the technical tools for agit-prop work. Therefore many hectographs, typewriters, radios, presses, etcetera were ruined.

III

Our agit-prop work must be systematically organized. Party members who appear in public must work out a plan with themes and present and direct it knowledgeably in view of the difficult conditions for the correct spreading of the current phase of our struggle. We suggest some themes that should be prepared in advance for party groups and mass gatherings.

1. What Partisans in Montenegro, Boka, and Sandzak were fighting for; formation of Yugoslavia; the Versailles Peace; the essence of Great Serbian politics, the plight of the subjugated Yugoslav people; the position of the CPY in regards to war; March 27 and capitulation; the character of the war and the importance of friendship with the USSR; the second imperialistic war and the position of the CPY toward the separatist question; popular politics in Yugoslavia; the nature of the second imperialistic war; the U.S.S.R. and the imperialistic war; the transformation of the imperialistic war into the national liberation struggle; the Soviet Union, 1905 and 1917; Soviet foreign policy; the internal policy and social structure of the U.S.S.R.; Stalin's constitution; the life of the peasants in the U.S.S.R.; women in the U.S.S.R.; the U.S.S.R. as a brotherhood of nations; the Red Army and its role in the national liberation struggle; the character and significance of the Partisan war at home and abroad; the solidarity of the Slavic people; and the relationship of the CPY with political parties, national liberation committees, and some government agencies.

2. The role and significance of the Communist party.
   a. The basic program and the organizational principles of the Communist party
   b. The struggle of the CPY before Yugoslavia's collapse. The role and the importance of the CPY in the national liberation struggle
   c. The CPY's future missions.

3. The lives of workers and peasants.

Explain and popularize the idea of an association of workers and peasants, while being careful about a preconceived set of problems. Pay attention to conditions in Montenegro, Boka, and Sandzak.

4. The brotherhood of the Yugoslav people necessary to explain national problems and the policy of the people's quarrel that was instigated by the occupier.

5. No return to the past.

In that theme it would be necessary to include all economic and political conditions that resulted from the bourgeois economic system that was applied in Yugoslavia before. The essential concept of the theme is that the people would be made conscious and persuaded that there cannot be a return to the past.

IV

In order to discuss all the themes in Partisan units and in front of the masses it is necessary to make prior arrangements in party groups. Without solid operations in groups we cannot realize our aim of raising the masses politically and theoretically and bringing them closer to our party. Besides these themes it is necessary to study Bolshevik Communist party groups as a bases for further agit-prop work. Without a fundamental knowledge of history there can be no talk of increasing party membership. Inner work within the party has to be more intensive and fruitful.

V

All our party organizations must pay attention to agit-prop work directed at young people. They have to insist that political and cultural performances for Montenegrin youth be on a high level. All the problems already mentioned apply also to youth performances, which should be adjusted appropriately for youths' comprehension and to specific goals of Montenegrin youth. In addition themes should be discussed at youth gatherings and performances that are directly related to youth and their struggle. Attention must be paid to the struggle, life, and work of the Comcomole, to the solidarity of youth around the world. Show by concrete examples what capitalism takes away from youth and working and peasant classes. Today Montenegrin young people are becoming more and more organized. Therefore agit-prop work with young people has to be taken seriously.

VI

In order not to make more mistakes in the future, agit prop has to be better organized. The following needs to be done:
1. In each district, local committees and bureau cells have to appoint one responsible comrade who is in harmony with the agit-prop line. In case all members are overburdened then it is permissible for each forum to designate someone from outside the forum to take care of agit-prop work under direct supervision and control of a member of the forum. Each forum has the obligation to send regular reports to the higher forum of agit-prop.
2. In each group, according to its local circumstances, a committee needs to be formed as a special agit-prop group that works in a larger sector. The group should go to all villages in their own sector. They could assist the agit-prop work of the local Partisan group by organizing lectures, conferences, performances, and mass readings of newspapers and other material with explanations. These special, elite groups have to revitalize and mobilize agit-prop work in all villages and hamlets. They have to demonstrate how effective agit prop can be. The members of the special groups do not always

have to work together. They have acted and might have to act individually as agitators and propagandists when necessary. Those special agit-prop groups would work under the direct leadership of the comrade responsible for such work or under someone else who would remain under his control. Party sympathizers could join these groups. The number of members these mobile groups should consist of depends on local circumstances and the forces available for the designated job (three to five men is optimal). The provincial committee can help these groups by sending them agit-prop instructors, but we dare not wait for the arrival of those instructors before organizing these groups. Get to work on this task.

3. Each lower forum has to inform its higher forum directly by sending regular reports about the distribution of material as well as how much material is needed. An explanation should be given of why he asks for a certain number of newspapers, proclamations, or other publications. The distribution of material is the crucial organizational problem of agit-prop work. Therefore, it requires the utmost attention.

4. All party forums have to send to the provincial committee a copy of all manuscripts and texts that were read at various meetings and performances (lectures, plays, sketches, poetry readings, etc.). The reading or performing of these texts does not depend on the approval of the provincial committee, because under today's circumstances it is impossible to organize services so fast. The provincial committee will subsequently carry out and aid regular agit-prop work. Provincial committee review of scripts ensures replacement if necessary. Effective scripts can be shared, read or shown at various places around the country.

5. Responsible members of the individual forums for agit-prop work have to organize cooperation between the people's struggle and the youth movement. Any question that arises in this area should be reported. Those reports must be correct, concise, and concrete and if possible typed. In any case they must be legible. Reports should not be sent only by the responsible comrade. His duty is to organize people from the terrain to write and not vice versa. Besides sending reports on newspapers used locally, it is necessary to send their opinion about our editions. In the first place it is the duty of all forum members to give their opinion at group gatherings from which it will routinely be transferred and acted upon.

6. All comrades responsible for agit-prop work have to insist that all the ideas of agit-prop discussed here be exposed locally. However, that does not mean that one could not take the initiative about forms of activities among the masses based on the circumstances where they work. Naturally for any initiative it is necessary to inform the responsible forums, who will inform the provincial committee. As an example of agit-prop work that cannot be realized everywhere we mention opening village libraries. Where it is possible, get to work on it.

VII

From now on the provincial committee will help much more in the agit-prop work of party organizations. Besides the regular editions of *The People's Struggle* and *Youth Movement*, larger numbers are planned. The provincial committee will prepare materials for most of the mentioned themes, either in separate pamphlets or in one of the newspapers. Very soon you will get pamphlets on why the Red Army won in 1918 to 1922, the organizational elements of the Communist party, voluminous excerpts from the history of the Boshevik Communist party, and what the Partisans of Montenegro, Boka, and Sandzak are fighting for.

An article by Comrade Tito entitled "The Role and Significance of the Communist Party in the National Liberation Struggle" will appear in the next issue of *The People's Struggle*. More articles to help you in your work on the set of themes will also be included. The provincial committee invites all party organizations to increase their work in agit-prop to compensate for the previous omissions and mistakes, but not to neglect other areas, which would be similar to the earlier mistake of neglecting agit-prop work in comparison to other sectors.

DEATH TO FASCISM—FREEDOM TO THE PEOPLE!

Communist Party of Yugoslavia
Provincial Committee for Montenegro, Boka, and Sandzak

Editor's Comment

No comment is necessary on the above document. The most uneducated man could discern the Communists under their NLM mask by their erroneous propaganda and agitation. They took advantage of an occupied people, communizing the masses and executing their revolution where they had some success.

In carrying out their intentions they first tried to liquidate all honest, popular, conscientious, and wise people. Further, they targeted intelligent people, the guardians of tradition, honesty, and dignity, and all those who did not agree with their foolish, antihumane, Godless intrigues. They covered up their brutal crimes. All conscientious and honorable men who remained faithful to their forefathers' credo and who protested these crazy actions were proclaimed by the Communists to be spies, traitors, and fifth columnists.

However, the people's soul, by both reason and instinct, could not long be deceived by false Partisan propaganda such as that spread by the Lombrozos, who committed crimes, perversions, godless acts and debauchery against men of merit. These national freaks were wandering like wild animals over mountain rocks and boulders or hiding themselves in caves and pits that were filled with innocent victims. Those bandits who were caught were prosecuted by the people, who were defending their very right to survive.

As proof of Partisan hypocrisy, witness their immorality, their deceit, how they tried to take advantage of people's patriotic feelings. All of it was channeled most conveniently to serve Partisan purposes, as the following document attests.

Headquarters
National Liberation Partisan Detachment
"Bijeli Pavle"
officially numbered
December 7, 1941
To: Partisan Battalion VPP

1. In reference to the list of items you seized and retained, we approve all of it except six rifles, which you should send to this headquarters. Those rifles include some captured at the hill of Tarash. Do this immediately, to achieve fair distribution among Partisan units of this detachment.

Note that we received from Zeta Detachment via main headquarters a number of rifles captured in Kuci that will be distributed soon.

2. Select a Partisan comrade with authority among the people and send him to Ostrog Monastery to ask for help for the national liberation army. During the conversation he should be shrewd, not irascible. Talk with them diplomatically, discoursing on a wide variety of subjects relative to saving Serbianism, Orthodoxy, etcetera. On the other hand, the comrade should find out how much food and other items the monastery has at its disposal, and a report of that information should be sent immediately to this headquarters.

3. We are sending an overcoat to the mother of the deceased Neda Jovanovicha. Deliver it right away.

(seal)   Commandant,
                                          Rad. Babich
                                          (signed)

And when things went badly they wrote as follows:

To: Comrade Blazo Jovanovich

Since yesterday the situation has grown worse and worse. It is depressing and discouraging. Last night traitors arrived in Bezjovo and a lunch was prepared for them in Uble. By direction of that old opportunist Spasoje, in the night between the 3d and 4th of March the headquarters of the Second Partisan Battalion, M.M. evacuated Orahovo with the party archives and came to Medun. We immediately sent them back to the territory of the Second Battalion.

There is nothing about the company [*a strike force designated for liquation*] we intended to form today. Here at the headquarters of the First Battalion there were ten to twenty men. This morning there are fewer of them, except Premici [*Fundina*], and there is hesitation among them, too.

We intend to defend the headquarters at all costs. However, they could go around us via Kosor and Kupusac. In many villages (Doljani, Sjenice, Kosor, Kupusac, Lijesta, Uble, Orahovo, etcetera) the five-pointed star was removed. We are surprised by such cowardice and lack of awareness. Indeed, the peasantry, the reserve of the revolution or counterrevolution, think very little about it. That is a result of insufficient political work. In any case, we'll try not to leave Kuci.

Would you agree that we should penetrate and attack the villages, taking them over and killing all prominent Chetniks? They [*Chetniks*] threaten to use several reprisal techniques against the people or the former Partisans who were not affiliated with Chetniks if anyone is killed. Or should we just kill wherever we confront them? In that case it would be very dangerous and impossible to hide party members who stayed there at certain times. In forming the strike unit we cannot gather more than ten Partisans. They will hardly dare to liquidate anyone.

General picture of the situation: massive desertion from the Partisan organization. Tomorrow everything may be changed completely.

The secretary comrade of the region is in accord with our decision.

I admit it is an unpardonable disgrace and a crime that Kuci surrendered to those traitors without firing a single shot. Despite our insistence, Comrade Zetin achieved nothing because in fact we don't have a force at all.

They were promising grain to Kuci. It is possible they'll try to buy them with it. We'll do everything possible not to be humiliated, naturally using forces that we have at our disposal now.

Comrade Zetin, whatever happens, remain steady and merciless in the struggle against those traitors.

Please send us directions as soon as possible about what to do in the present circumstances.

DEATH TO FASCISM—FREEDOM TO THE PEOPLE!

Medun,	Political Commissar,
March 4, 1942	Drag. M. Ivanovich
11 o'clock	(signed)

HELL
or
Communism in Montenegro

[*picture of skull and long bone*]

Volume Number Three
An edition of *The Voice of Montenegro*
Publisher, Obod—Cetinje

Captured Partisan Men and Women
[*with their pictures*]

Jovovich, commandant of strike battalion.
Jelena Baletich. Twelve notches were on her rifle, meaning she had committed twelve crimes. She was hung in Niksic.
Bozidar Popovich, student from Kuci, assistant commissar.
Drago Radonjich, peasant from Kosovi Lug.
Pejka Jovanovich, belonged to strike unit.
A pit eighty-five meters deep, Mackov Do near Radovce. [*picture*]
The corpse of Tomash R. Milutinovich, being removed from the pit. [*picture*]
Stana Sekulich, from Sekulici, captured at Tarash with arms.
Vidosava Petrovich, captured in Bratonozici. Her three brothers were killed as Partisans and a fourth is living illegally now.
Radovan Pavicevich, priest. Captured with arms at Timarko Polje. [*near Boan*].
Milorad Tadich, from Gornje Polje. He committed many murders.
Pekna Djurovich, organizer. During the old regime she was wounded at a Communist meeting.

Commandants of Partisan Battalions, Company Commanders, and Their Assistants

[*Twenty-two individuals are listed, including name, occupation, age, and local residence.*]

Political Commissars and Their Assistants

[*Nineteen individuals are listed, including name, occupation, age, and local residence.*]

Partisan Judges and Their Assistants

[*Eighteen individuals are listed, including name, occupation, age, and local residence.*]

Executioners and Their Assistants

[*Eleven individuals are listed, including name, occupation, age, and local residence.*]

The Abyss and Hell

People Killed by the Partisans

[*Ninety-seven individuals are listed, including name, occupation, age, local residence, and how they were killed.*]

People Wounded by the Partisans

[*Sixty-three individuals are listed, including name, occupation, age, and local residence.*]

Burnings, Plunderings, and Extortions

[*Forty individuals are listed by community and district, with their name, what was burned or taken, and the approximate value of the losses.*]

The Results of the Partisan Work

Some Communist Verdicts and Crimes

SAVO MEDENICA
Journalist

He was born in Kolashin on January 17, 1910. He attended gymnasium in Sarajevo, Sombor, and Zombolj. His permanent residence was Novi Sad, where he published a newspaper, *Export*, and later *People's Politika*. He was a correspondent for an Avala agency, and he worked for almost all of Yugoslavia's larger newspapers.

He was well known as a patriot and nationalist. He was a member of the Sokol society, National Defense, Serbian Matica (a cultural literary society) and was secretary of a temperance society.

In April of 1941 he was called for military duty. In the meantime, he moved his wife and children to the family estate in Kolashin. On December 24, 1941, the Communists picked him up from his estate in Drijenak. He was escorted under guard to Gornja Moraca. His death sentence was pronounced by the notorious Partisan leader Djuro Medenica, and the sentence was carried out by Nikola Mulevich, Lakich Simonovich, and Milinko Vujisich.

On April 18, 1942, his body, with his skull cracked open, was found and buried at the Moraca Monastery. Thus ended his martyr's life.

NOVO R. VUCICH
Teacher, reserve captain first class, and former representative
[picture]
He was born in 1893 in Shobajici, in the Danilovgrad district.

DAMJAN M. VUCICH
Long-time mayor of the community of Vrazegrmci
[picture]

In the early morning hours of March 4, 1942, there appeared in front of Novo Vucich's house the following Partisans: Miroje N. Miljevich, Vojin Sh. Vukovich, and Radivoje M. Jovanovich. They asked the teacher Novo to open the door for them because they were freezing and wanted to warm themselves. They also said they needed to talk with him, that they had something important and confidential to tell him. As soon as the teacher opened the door, seventeen Partisans entered, while two stood guard outside. They seized him and his nephew Damjan and took them away toward Bara Shumanovich.

During the night of March 5th both Vuciches were thrown alive into a pit above Slatina, in the Danilovgrad district. Still on the third day the wounded teacher, his bones broken, could be heard calling, "Water, water." But naturally no one dared to come closer to help him.

Besides those already mentioned, others who took part in that crime were Dragutin B. Grozdanich, Partisan from Podvrce, Savo P. Kadovich, assistant sergeant from Shobajici; Mileta B. Kadovich, commander of the Shabovici Company; Milat Dj. Kadovich, Milun Dj. Kadovich, Miroje R. Kadovich and Minja M. Kadovich, all Partisans from Shabovici, Mimo Sh. Jovanovich, Milisav Sh. Jovanovich, Blagoje B. Popovich, Radislav Sh. Vukovich, and Veljko B. Vukovich, all Partisans from Bara Shumanovich, Niko F. Grozdanich, Lazar Miljevich, and Milosav Miljevich, all Partisans from Podvrace; Vuksan N. Kadovich, sergeant from Shobajici, Bosko Dj. Radonjich, commissar from Mijokusovici, Bozo B. Vujadinovich, sergeant from Bara Shumanovich; Milan Z. Perovich, Partisan from Boronjine, and Radovan P. Shundich, Partisan from Shobajici.

MINJO KARADZICH
Born 1861 in Drobnjaci
[picture]

During the long reign of Prince (later King) Nicholas, Minjo was a people's representative and mayor of the community of Sharance. He was a hero of all wars, honest and a respected host. He wore many decorations for civilian as well as military merits.

For the Communists all honest and respected people were obstacles, whether an old man, old woman, or youngster, as shown in many written documents. They liquidated Minjo when he was 80 years old and sick in bed. They pronounced him a fifth columnist, spy, and traitor, this old man who had served his people his entire life, mainly as a trustee to King Nicholas and defender of the Serbs in Sandzak.

He was killed because he could not renounce his Serbian name, faith, and tradition. He refused to join the Partisans to help the corrupt Montenegrin sons who joined the international riffraff and spat on everything that had been held exalted and holy for a thousand years.

His son was killed with him, just because Minjo was his father.

LAKO (LAZAR) KARADZICH
Born in 1898
[picture]

Their house was looted and then burned by the Partisans.

The commandants and organizers for those murders were Vuk Knezevich, attorney's assistant, political commissar; Velimir Knezevich, student, political commissar; Dushan Obradovich, jurist, battalion commandant; Djoko Novosel, agronomist from Belgrade, company commander; Vojin Djerkovich, medical student, trial member; Milosh Djerkovich, agronomist, trial member.

TOMO RADOV VUKMANOVICH
From the village of Podgor, community Crmnica
[picture]

He was born in 1882 and killed in front of his house by a Partisan band on March 23, 1942, at 9 o'clock at night. As a young man he had lived for quite a while in Montreal. His nostalgia for the fatherland and love for his brothers compelled him to leave his comfortable life and properties in Montreal to spend the last days of his life among his relatives.

Even though he was not interested in politics, the Communists liquidated him because he did not approve of their criminal activities.

VASILIJE S. BOZARICH
Priest from Rogami (Piperi)

Vasilije S. Bozarich was born in 1888 the son of the priest Savo and grandson of the priest Tiodor Bozarich.

He was one of the first to be felled by the Communist terror, on November 15, 1941. Thus was destroyed a worthy, quiet, and popular man widely respected for his words and shrewd advice. He brought consolation, love, and hope for a brighter future. As Christ's true servant he was working for pacification and the salvation of his people.

Athiest carrions who called themselves Communists could not tolerate Christian work and the tremendous popularity of Father Vaso. He was an obstacle to their beastly and destructive work. Therefore they decided to eliminate him.

On November 15, 1941, Father Vaso went to Ljeshkopolje, to the village Gornja Gorica, to perform a church ritual of blessing Slava cake (Kolac). [*It was incorrectly stated in the original that the ritual was a funeral.*] The Communists knew of his departure and ambushed him. They killed him, wrapped him in canvas, and threw him into the Moraca River. On Christmas Eve his remains were found. He was buried at the church in Vukovci, naturally without any religious rites because it was forbidden by the Partisans.

JOKMA
The widow of Father Savo Bozarich
[picture]

She was killed in Rogami during an uprising that was provoked by Arso Jovanovich from Piperi, commandant of a Partisan battalion; Marko Radovich, engineer from Piperi, company commander; Milovan Djilas, student from Podgorica, political commissar for Piperi; Drago Vucinich, student from Piperi, political commissar for Piperi; Vojin Popovich, student from Piperi, assistant political commissar.

In addition to many other misdeeds, those bloodsuckers destroyed the historic village of Rogami, in which ninety-four homes were burned and fifteen people killed, among them six women.

VASO POPOVICH
Former priest in Vucji Do
[picture]

The priest Vaso Popovich was born in Baoshic (Boka Kotorska) on May 3, 1914. He was the son of Petar and Jovanka (nee Sherovich). As the son of poor parents he had difficulty continuing his education. He graduated after a year of gymnasium and seminary school in Cetinje with excellent marks. He was married and became a priest in 1939. His parish was in Vucji Do.

Early in January 1942 he was killed and thrown into a pit because he disagreed with the Communists' banditry. From the shooting ground Vaso shouted to infuriate the atheists, "You'll pay for this to God and the people." Thus as a martyr he ended his life.

Father Vaso was a faithful son of Saint Sava's church and his Serbian people joined the ranks of our clergy martyrs. He left without providing for his wife, child, and the parents who had sacrified everything they had to educate their son.

Glory and eternal memory to the young priest Vaso Popovich.

SHPIRO K. RADULOVICH
Policeman from Komani, district Danilovgrad
[picture]

He was born on April 15, 1903, in Komani. After completing his education he joined the security forces, where he spent many years. He was known as an efficient employee, good comrade, and an excellent friend. After the country's capitulation he retreated to his native region, believing he had found a haven of peace and security for himself and his family. However, on December 15, 1941, on the way to Niksic on private business, Partisans grabbed him, killed him, and threw him into some pit yet unknown.

Various Communist Documents

To: The Youth of Montenegro, Boka, and Sandzak

Young Montenegrins, both males and females, and your young Boka and Sandzak brothers, you have struggled for your future, facing attack from the rear. Horrible danger hung treacherously over each of your young heads. The traitors took up foreign rifles to leave youth without a future and the future without youth. Don't forget that because today we have to make a decision following the collapse of the Fascist invader on the main front. Will we be able to freely decide our own destiny according to our will?

For twenty years courageous young Yugoslavs have waged an ongoing, uneven struggle against Yugoslavia's imprisonment of working people and youth. In the first lines of Yugoslavia's youth army is our army of freedom, army of brotherhood, army of the future. For twenty years we have fought against national and social oppression, against tyranny and famine, darkness and imprisonment, against forces with money and protection that trade with the people's destiny and betray the people's independence. For twenty years our youth have been jailed in Yugoslav prisons, tortured in Yugoslav torture chambers, worn out and humiliated in Yugoslav military barracks, decimated on the school benches, and looted and beaten up in the fields and workshops, because the youth wanted more freedom and bread, more justice and knowledge, more rest and more books for themselves and their people. They wanted to save their homeland from betrayal and traitors, wanted the workshops not to be usury, the schools not to be banditry, the barracks not to be butchershops, torturers of souls.

Our youth defended each step of their patrimony, struggling for every ray of freedom that our forefathers sacrificed for, grabbing from the tyrants and plunderers each kernel of grain that our fathers sowed for their children. Our youth from their bloody school benches, from the prison torture rooms, from under the hooves of mounted police, shouted, "Those who plunder and torture us, they were preparing graves instead of slaves, slaves instead of fighters; instead of fields cleared of the eternal enemies of our people, they allow the Fascist invaders to run easily over our graves, they allow the fascist invaders to become slave masters." Indeed, our country, our independence was betrayed. It was betrayed by the German and Italian tyrants who turned the countryside into graveyards and the people into slaves.

For the past nine months our youth have stood in the first ranks of people struggling against disgrace and slavery into which we were thrown by the banners of Great Serbs, industrialists, higher officers, and big shots. In that struggle we have already realized great success, paid for dearly with many lives. We realized brotherhood in arms and an indivisible destiny with other

Yugoslav youth. To be faithful to our people, as well as to ourselves and to a brighter future, we fought without reserve against the Fascist invaders, the worst and most loathsome of enemies. A bastion was made up of the generation whose greatest comrade and friend was Josip Stalin. He gave hope to all subjugated people, to old and young alike, that mankind could live and that people could organize their country as they wish. Thanks to the people's struggle the enemy's treacherous heads were cut off. The masses were enlightened and prepared for tomorrow, to be capable of deciding the destiny of their country and their own future. The Great Serb bureaucracy was frightened. "When things go according to the wish of the people, it is not according to our wish," they said. Therefore they all entered into bloody service under the occupation in order to spill people's blood on the Fascist imperialistic mill. After all the sufferings and fallen victims, we endured under the Fascist occupation and persisted in the struggle against betrayal, seeking to ensure a base for tomorrow. They strive to rule again.

To Young Montenegrins, and Our Young Boka and Sandzak Brothers!

Look at the names of the traitors! We know well the murderers—Yugoslav officers who tortured and humiliated us in Yugoslav barracks, Bajo Stanishich, George Lashich, and Pavle Djurishich were the old executioners. Milutin Jelich and Mihailo Rajnvojan were old tyrants as directors of gymnasiums and the Teachers' School. They persecuted us and turned us in to the police, expelled us from school, separated us from parents and from books! Vujoshevich and Boljevich gendarme officers were old murderers. We were put on whipping posts, whipped by oxen sinews, hung by the scrotum, forcefed pepper and salt. Look at these names! All of them raised foreign rifles against us. We'll see what danger hung over each of your heads, over our struggle, over the dear fruit of our efforts, over our hopes, our future! It was not enough for them to kill Vukman Krushcich, another eight revolver shots were fired into his dead body, into his mouth!

Today it is being decided who will decide tomorrow. Today it is being decided—To be or not to be! Freedom and good fortune are the compensation for all our suffering. After the treason, we went again into slavery, into more horrible slavery from the same traitors, who together with the occupier were killing us with the occupier's cannons, machine guns, and rifles. Their deeds were more disgraceful and bloodier than those of the Italian Fascists who in their subjugated homeland forced the Italian people into services while they were hungry and frightened. Those who would not accept mercenary and fratricidal rifles could not get bread booklets. Podgorica and Niksic rabble were armed in what they called a national and "voluntary" army. They were sent under protection of Italian cannon fire, which had destroyed Montenegrin homes and monasteries in the liberated villages of Bjelopavlici, Piperi, and Niksic.

Today it is being decided who will decide tomorrow! Young Montenegrin males and females, our young Boka and Sandzak brothers, it is a question of life or death and of our future as well. Centralist and separatist officials and wealthy fifth columnists were united from occupied Cetinje! Dushan Vlahovich, former vice-governor of Zeta Banovina, threatened us and our homeland as well as our lives and honor! He let us know that officers have a word for us, those same officers who did not fulfill their duty when it was necessary to defend the freedom of our people. The Italian fifth columnist, *The Voice of Montenegro*, published the message for us: "The officers have a message. We intend to implement peace and order and to be loyal to the occupier." They proclaimed their word at the moment when our roads and rear positions were needed for the occupier's spring offensive against our Russian brothers, against us! Mercenaries and the people's enemies have a message! Up on your feet, young Montenegrin males and females, young Boka and Sandzak brothers of Montenegrin youth! Unity in the struggle against the occupier, in the struggle against traitors and mercenaries!

To Young Montenegrins and Their Young Boka and Sandzak Brothers!

Above young people's heads hangs a cruel and treacherous danger. United traitors threaten them with death sentences. They threaten with treacherous Italian bullets those who fought with pride under the national liberation Partisan banner, still bloody from the occupier and the traitors. United traitors and mercenaries sent a message to the Italian fifth columnist *The Voice of Montenegro*. They intend to liquidate all those who have bloody hands. It is a threat to our people, to our youth, because almost all of our people and youth washed out disgrace from their faces and the mud from their hands!

Prepare for fire, young Montenegrin males and females! Prepare for fire, young Boka and Sandzak brothers of Montenegrin youth, brothers by destiny and arms!

Take up the fight, young Montenegrins. Go fight, young Boka and Sandzak brothers! Ready arms, all, as united, courageous, and tireless allies of Soviet Communist youth. Our brotherly Comsomol! Take up arms! Don't let the traitors have a word! Take up arms! Don't let the workshops be torture chambers! We want to reap the fields that we have sowed. We want the barracks to be training places, the universities not to be battlefields. We want Bajo Stanishich to never again wield a whip and command and Milutin Jelich to never again wield whip and rule a gymnasium; Djordje Kosmajac to never have an opportunity, perspiring in his vest, with shirt sleeves rolled up, to enter the prison yard when the prisoners are exercising and call student Lazar Micunovich and take him to the bloody torture room number nine! Take up arms, so that we never again count the twenty strokes that cut walls and flesh!

We want to never again hear the screams from Lazar Micunovich while he was tied up and tortured. Prepare for fire, for the brotherhood and freedom of our people. Prepare yourselves for fire, for honor, pride, and equality of young females! Prepare for fire, for the brotherhood and indivisible destiny with our fellow Russian youth. All of Europe and the anti-Fascist continent are with us. In front of us is the heroic Comsomol! Forward, generation of victory, forward!

Long live the heroic youth of Montenegro, Boka, and Sandzak, their struggle and victory!

Long live the heroic youth of Yugoslavia, their brotherhood, their struggle and victory!

Long live the national liberation struggle, the brotherhood of the Yugoslav people, the right of the people to self-determination, with good fortune and freedom!

Long live the national liberation Partisan detachments!

Long live our brotherly model, Comsomol!

Long live the great friend and teacher of youth, Comrade Stalin!

Death to fascism! Extermination to traitors!

Montenegrin Youth Provincial Committee

Reading Between the Lines of the Preceding Document

Look, dear youth, how worried they were about your future, these "champions of justice and people's liberators." The people were to be liberated from everything they had. They wanted them to be rid of God, religion, morals, the roofs over their heads, and the bread in their mouths. The "liberators" liberated them from their lives, throwing them into bottomless pits, giving them the benefits of "Red paradise and social justice."

How much falsehood and deceit can be contained in just one document, you can see for yourselves. They shed an ocean of crocodile tears for the future of youth in order to seize young people with their hellish claws and use them for their treacherous aims. Those who don't recognize the sacredness of family, who kill their own parents and brothers, nevertheless call youth brothers! A strange irony! Even a blind man can readily see what they want, not to mention our progressive young people who have known them for a long time. According to a popular adage, it is known who talks the most about honesty, so they are calling the opposite real freedom fighters, traitors, spies, and fifth columnists. Under the occupation, unfortunately, the people were forced to rise up against an evil hitherto unknown.

For twenty years those wretched people boldly spoke and wrote about how they waged a struggle in Yugoslavia. Against whom and why? Against their own people and their fatherland for Judas's greed. It was indeed their unconscious admittance of their patriotism! They praised themselves for being in Yugoslav prisons for twenty years. What for, national liberators? It is unfortunate now that your heads were saved then. Otherwise fewer tears would be shed these days, and many roofs of poor people could have been saved.

The barracks where young men lived while preparing themselves for defending their fatherland for them were torture chambers for their souls and slaughterhouses of their young lives. What, people's liberators, was the food not plentiful enough for you, or because of the corporals did you not dare to bark at the stars?

They say they waged a struggle because they wanted more freedom and more bread, more justice, more knowledge, more rest, and more books for themselves and their people.

We saw, by our great misfortune the kind of liberty they were preparing for us. Last year under the yoke of social justice our peasants barely escaped famine. We don't even want to mention the knowledge, leisure time, and books. Today those "knowledgeable" people, figuratively speaking, wander like dogs among mountain boulders. They were chased by their own people because they failed to reeducate the people as they wanted. As far as leisure time was concerned, the villages knew those idlers, with unkempt heads, bent caps, and red sweaters who never worked at anything nor read any useful book, except Marxist leaflets and pamphlets. Therefore, in the people's view they were foolish as carriers of higher education, considering themselves as progressive forces. Indeed, young people, you made a great mistake. Why did you not rise up on their war cry, to protect those "advanced" people from the anger of "backward" people who could not feel the benefits of the pits? Is there any other greater social justice than the mallet over the head and then the toss into the pit? By the theory of progress, as far as the head is concerned, you can have what you need, but first those in the headquarters' harem, must be fed; later there would be relaxing. Whisper if you dare!

They were not ashamed to talk about fatherland and betrayal, those who recognize neither homeland nor nationality. Those who talk about the nationalism of the Yugoslav people even talk about nationalities of Montenegro, Boka, and Sandzak. For twenty years they undermined the foundation of their homeland, spilling over full military kettles, throwing away rifles. They tried to persuade others to do the same at the time when it was necessary to defend the homeland from those they pretend to wage war against today. They branded as traitors, murderers, and executioners those who were our outstanding leaders, such as Stanishich, Lashich, and Djurishich, who were once, as the liberators say, Yugoslav officers, who tortured and humiliated the liberators in the Yugoslav barracks. Oh, how hard life was for them in the barracks! Was it devotion to the fatherland or something else? Miserable defenders of the homeland and liberators of the people!

How can those misfits and betrayers of the people have the gall to call anyone traitor, to turn themselves toward young people and to mention the fatherland! Further, consider this whine against Jelich and Rajnvajn, that those progressives were expelled from schools, while Vujoshevich and Boljevich tortured them in the prisons. My God, why did those "reactionaries" have such spite for those "patriots?"

They really believed it would be enough to pile up phrases, slanders, and outright lies and that all youth would lose their heads and rush to save that handful of mercenary loafers from the people's anger!

The preceding document is not only characteristic of pure Communist propaganda; it also shows their obvious fear of death for their leaders. Therefore, when they could not succeed in persuading older people to go along with them, they turned toward the youth, believing that young people would be influenced by their false propaganda and join them. However, they did not have a flattering opinion about our youth. The "liberators" lost sight of the fact that the majority of our youth were not unkempt heads with bent caps and empty minds wandering aimlessly through village and town. In fact, it was a nationally conscious and responsible youth who judged with their own minds. They did not gather knowledge from leaflets and pamphlets. That youth could not be won over by a desperate "progressive" war cry. The preceding document says: "Today it is being decided who will decide tomorrow. Today it is being decided—to be or not to be." In the first place young people correctly comprehended the message of the vice-ban that the officers had the word and it was imperative to align behind them. Neither an ocean of words and phrases nor a war cry for this or that could help, because when the vigorous youth of the nation, along with their older brothers, found out how people were bleeding, they attacked and crushed the people's enemy. They were not at all touched by the muffled scream of "Comrade" Lazar Micunovich from room number nine, because they knew that comrade had helped destroy our homeland. The youth were touched by the thousands of screams from the national martyrs who were deprived of their lives in an incredibly brutal way by a handful of vermin. For that reason, God's and the people's punishment reached them.

Glory to the people's martyrs! Death to murderous traitors!

(five-pointed star)
Headquarters
National Liberation Partisan Battalion
Number: Officially dated February 24, 1942

To the Zeta National Liberation Partisan Detachment

Yesterday the courier from your headquarters, Ilija Dedovich, passed through Piperi. He talked about various matters at an outdoor party in Ozezi.

He talked about the failed situation in Matashevo: how the Chetniks took over Matashevo, how our command from Matashevo ran away to Kolashin. If the commandant of the detachment knew how the situation would develop he would not have left his position so quickly. This was not the first time couriers have spread alarming news. The couriers want to make themselves so important that they could get information before anyone else.

Please bring to your couriers' attention that they should not talk about such matters and should not talk when secrecy is required.

It should not be necessary to emphasize how important it is to keep such matters secret, when the enemy stares at anyone to learn about us and espionage is growing.

The news spread by that courier had detrimental consequences in Piperi. If the news was untrue, he should be punished severely.

We inform you that one of our company went to Bjelopavlici (Pavkovici) to suppress fifth columnists.

Please bring to the attention of Comrade Jelena Vucinich the necessity of cooperating with the women's committee. When she collects things in the capacity of detachment headquarters she should not give orders to some individuals to do this or that. It is not nice to seem as if nobody knows either who drinks or who pays. She must bring with her permission from headquarters.

Please send us the news and arms we asked for yesterday.

Also, please inform us if the news your courier was spreading yesterday is correct.

DEATH TO FASCISM! FREEDOM TO THE PEOPLE!

Commandant,
Bozo Lazarevich (signed)

(five-pointed star)
To Zeta Headquarters
of National Liberation Partisan Detachment
No. 193
February 24, 1942

Hello Blazo,
Please find out what is going on with the mobilization in Bratonozici and Brskut, as well as in Piperi.

I myself wonder how it was possible that things were allowed to fall so low. Partisans don't respond to orders to report for military service. It seems as if a great panic seized the men when they ran away from the Chetniks, as was also the case with comrades in Lijeva Rijeka. Take appropriate measures as soon as possible to send good and trustworthy men there. There were probably in each battalion from fifty to seventy trustworthy Partisans.

After you read this letter and see what was said in the accompanying letter, please tell us what was done regarding sending men.

With regards,
Milutinovich
(signed)

(five-pointed star)
Headquarters
National Liberation Partisan Battalion
''Bijeli Pavle''
Numbered officially February 15, 1942

To the Headquarters of Kosovilug Partisan Battalion

In connection with today's critical happening, liquidate the fifth columnists right away. Here you have to be very decisive and quick because any hesitation could be catastrophic and could cause revenge. If we don't kill them, they'll kill us. You were supposed to do it earlier. Why didn't you? Form a strike unit to execute the task tonight.

If you get in contact with the company from the Lovcen Detachment, send it to the headquarters of the Jelenak Battalion Bubulj.

Increase your guard against fifth columnists. Hold your units together and don't let them fall under the influence of fifth columnists and get dispersed.

If anybody appears to speak, shoot right away.
DEATH TO FASCISM! FREEDOM TO THE PEOPLE!

Political commissar,
Djuro Cagorovich (signed)   _____

(five-pointed star)
Headquarters
National Liberation Partisan Battalion
''Bijeli Pavle''

[picture]
Relatives of people whose corpses were found in front of the school in Staro Selo, Zupa.

HELL
or
Communism in Montenegro

[*picture of skull and long bone*]

Volume Number Four
An Edition of *The Voice of Montenegro*
Publisher, Obod—Cetinje

Partisan Justice

From the accompanying documents we can see they [*the Partisans*] killed people whose real names they did not even know. One phrase only sufficed—''fifth columnist, spy.'' If you interfered the least in their work or were displeasing to them you could lose your life. Using this thinking they liquidated those who had retreated to remote villages over the high mountains where they never saw any occupier soldiers.

Novak Rashovich, reserve lieutenant from Kuci, wounded in the leg April 15, 1942. On the nineteenth of the same month his head was crushed by stones. This picture shows the relatives who discovered his body.

(five-pointed star)
Headquarters N. L. Partisan Detachment
No. 91/May 27, 1942

To Zeta N. L. Partisan Battalion

We have decided to send you two automatic rifles instead of one machine gun. That will be better for you. We talked about automatic rifles that disappeared during the fighting in Piperi. We'll investigate it, though it looks as if we'll not be able to come across their trail. As soon as we get some arms we'll consider an allotment for you, though it is not necessary to repeat it in each report. Being short of arms was no excuse for saying actions were unfeasible, especially actions against fifth columnists of all colors.

For the last time we order you to take effective measures against fifth columnists. Simply give orders to certain Partisans to liquidate this and that fifth columnist. What you have failed to do up till now will be thoroughly revenged if you don't act in a Partisan manner to liquidate fifth columnists.

We already asked Velimir Terzich to return from Sandzak, but we consider it more important for you to execute actions against fifth columnists and others as feasible whether or not he comes back. You'll harden and will raise your reputation through actions, but not over this or that person.

Political commissars should hold meetings with the company, once a week to give concrete instructions so they can comprehend the meaning of today's struggle. They should clarify it for the Partisans. Without your Partisans and your actions as well, the Partisans would exist only on paper.

In your proclamation you were excessively soft toward fifth columnists. It is necessary to sharply condemn traitors and to tell people the rifle will judge them in the name of the people.

DEATH TO FASCISM—FREEDOM TO THE PEOPLE!

> Commandant,
> Blazo Jovanovich
> (signed)

———

(five-pointed star)
Headquarters N. L. Partisan Detachment
No. 89/January 27, 1942

To Headquarters of Donjo Ljeshanski N. L. Partisan Battalion

We acknowledge receipt of your letter and we reply to it.

There is no order for you not to perform actions on your terrain, but vice versa. Rather it is necessary to perform actions, especially against fifth columnists of various colors. This is the last time we will order you to destroy fifth columnists, severely and without hesitation. It angers us that you did not liquidate Nikola and Milo Vukcevich, instead disgracing yourselves. In the final reckoning, your organization was very poor. You could count on failure in advance. We hold all of you responsible, especially your political commissar.

The political commissar should hold regular meetings with company political commissars and submit a report of how many such meetings have been held since the last consultation. It is necessary to educate Partisans and to explain to them the importance of today's struggle, but you didn't do it. I asked your courier if you have ten Partisans who would perform any task given as a goal, and he replied to me that he does not know if two such could be found. That meant these Partisans are only on paper, not Partisans prepared to perform set goals. In order to elevate Partisans, actions need to be performed, because otherwise it will never become the people's army. In that regard you received goals, and now Comrade Vlado will arrive there with verbal instructions regarding what is supposed to be done.

I am surprised how many people you keep in your headquarters doing nothing. It is necessary to set before them concrete goals to execute, especially for those from Podgorica. Those earlier failures were anti-Partisan and the political commissar was responsible for them. Now he has no one beside him with the weakness of the former commandant [*Maj. Vaso Vukcevich*]. Let him roll up his sleeves.

DEATH TO FASCISM—FREEDOM TO THE PEOPLE!

> Commandant,
> Blazo Jovanovich
> (signed)

Announcement No. 2
Main Headquarters of N. L. Partisan Detachment for Montenegro and Boka

[*picture*]
Jovan Vidov Jovovich sadly watches the coffin of his son Bosko.

Sentenced to Death and Killed by the Partisans

Stevan Protich, Berane, government agent of the city of Belgrade, murderer of Vojvoda Luna and spy for the occupier.

Ivo Sutalo, Hercegovina, for spying for the benefit of the occupier in the Kolashin area.

Gavro Lakich, Bjelopavlici, old police informer, because he betrayed Vojin
   Radovich and Ljubomir Zarich to the enemy and they were subsequently shot. At the same time he gave the enemy a list of twenty-
   two community members who were subsequently interned.
Ivo Vukovich, Piperi, old police informer, counterguerrilla, because he
   persuaded the peasants to hand over their arms and threatened burning;
   he also attempted by directive of the occupier together with Ilija Milickovich, blackmailer and spy, and then with Marko Milunovich, a
   seminary school student, to organize a band to pursue Partisans.
Ilija Milickovich, counterguerrilla, because he persuaded peasants to hand
   over their arms, together with Ivo Vukovich, seminary student Marko
   Milunovich, and others. By the occupier's directives they organized
   a band to pursue Partisans.
Milutin Zarich, Bjelopavlici, former policeman and agent, because of espionage for the benefit of the occupier and activity in organizing bands
   for pursuing the Partisans. A certificate issued by the community Rovci
   was found on him from which it could be seen that he did favors for
   the occupier during the fighting around Danilovgrad and Podgorica.
Djoko Kraljevich, Ceklin, notorious spy of former anti-people's regimes,
   the right hand of one sentenced to death by Partisans, Jovan popa
   Bela Vujovich, because of espionage for the benefit of the occupier.
   Kraljevich went to Tirana to mistreat and pinpoint Montenegrins for
   shooting.
Vukosav Stankovich, pensioner, old Austro-Hungarian spy, selected by
   the occupier to serve as mayor of the community of Donja Moraca
   (Kolashin), because he persuaded peasants to hand over their arms
   and spied, for the benefit of the occupier.
Ilija Tomashevich, Crmnica, police employee, because he led occupier's
   troops, worked as a spy, and tried to organize bands to pursue Partisans.
Vaso Gvozden, former Belgrade policeman, Bosnia, because of spying
   for the benefit of the occupier. During interrogation he revealed an
   information network of seventeen spies.
Aleksa Uskokovich, district mayor of Shavnik, because he was a prominent
   agent of the occupier.
Micanovich, mayor of the community of Piva, because he spied for and
   was an agent of the occupier.
Marko Pavicevich, teacher from Grahovo, because he spied for and was an
   agent of the occupier.
Radovan Vlahovich, chief of the tax system, Kolashin, because Partisans
   found arms he received from the occupier that he tried to hide. In his
   possession were found letters to one spy, which was enough evidence
   that he had faithfully served the occupier, worked to undermine the
   people's unity, and had contact with other spies.
Shekich, Berane, because he was a dangerous spy and enemy of the people.

Vule Boljevich, Piperi, with wife and daughter, because he informed the occupier about Partisan movements while his daughter was in close relationship with occupation soldiers.

Cetko Sharanovich, Bjelopavlici, killer of two anti-Fascists by directive of the notorious chief "Belvederac," because on the occupier's order he plotted against Partisans and undermined the people's unity.

Petar Milatovich, teacher from Bjelopavlici, because he undermined the people's unity in accordance with directives, intentions, and wishes of the occupier.

Petar Sekulich, Komani, because he was a dangerous spy and the right-hand man of the bandit Musa Vukovich, who was condemned to death by the Partisans.

Nikola Jovanovich, former congressman of JRZ, from Rovci, because he undermined the people's unity and because he was secretly collaborating with the notorious spy Ljubo Minich, one of the best-known fifth columnists in Montenegro.

Marko Pavlicich, Bjelopavlici, cafe owner, because he spied for the occupier and undermined the people's unity.

Ilija Ljumovich, Piperi, because of registration in Krilashe [former Montenegrin king's guard] and recruitment of others.

Vuko Stanishich, teacher, Bratonozici, as one of the most inveterate, shrewdest, and most dangerous spies for the occupier. That bandit with cunning maneuvers frightened the people and succeeded in forcing the peasants to take arms from the occupier. Then he began to ask them to return them. Our Partisans came to his house and asked him to hand over the rifle. Then he took a bullet in his forehead, which this scoundrel had long deserved.

To be continued.

Main Headquarters of N. L. Partisan Detachment for Montenegro and Boka

[picture]
Three coffins of the Jovovich brothers. Behind them are their relatives who pulled them out from the pit.

The Justice of the National Court

Verdict re Lt. Col. Jovan Raicevich

Montenegrin National Organization
Command of the Zeta Detachment
People's Military Court
No. K.P. 125/2 1942

Record of the Main Trial

On June 25, 1942, the People's Military Court in Podgorica took up the criminal matter against Jovan P. Raicevich, who was accused by the Podgorica prosecutor of committing crimes according to Article 2, Order 14 of the Command of the People's Liberation Army for Montenegro and Hercegovina of April 1, 1942.
Those present:
President of the court
Dr. Ilija Vujovich, court captain first class

Judges
Savo Popovich, captain first class
Bajo Radovich
Mitar Mugosha
Jovan Kazich

Detachment prosecutor
Ljubomir Djukich, captain

Secretary
Vaso Perovich, attorney's assistant

Defender
Vasilija Dragutinovich, second lieutenant

Accused
Jovan P. Raicevich, lieutenant colonel

The accused is in custody.
At four o'clock the president of the court called the court to order. It was established as fact that the court had been formed according to law, under Article (Paragraph) 8, Order No. 14 and Order No. 20. The matter before the court was proclaimed; the listeners were reminded to be orderly and peaceful. They were also reminded of the consequences of disturbing the peace. The president of the court found that all invited persons were present in the courtroom.

[picture]
Jovan Raicevich, lieutenant colonel, commandant of Ljeshkopolje Partisan Battalion

After deliberation the president of the court announced the following:

Decision:

The main trial should take place.

In order to ensure the identity of the accused and the other necessary data, according to Article 15, Order No. 14 the president of the court asked the accused for any personal corrections to written questions that had been answered as follows:

1. Name and surname: Jovan Raicevich
2. Father's name: Pero
3. Name and maiden name of his mother: Mara nee Milich
4. Religion: Orthodox
5. Place of birth: Ljeshkopolje
6. Residence: Ljeshkopolje
7. Age: 56
8. Citizenship: community of Ljeshkopolje
9. Occupation: former lieutenant colonel in retirement
10. Family status: married
11. Is he literate: literate
12. Did he serve in armed forces: yes
13. What is his economic status: average
14. Was he ever convicted and what for: no
15. Is he now under investigation: yes

After the identity of the accused was established according to Article 15, Order No. 14, the president of the court summoned the witnesses and told them to pay the utmost attention to the sacred oath, which they would take when needed. The witnesses were instructed to take their seats and wait until they were called.

The president of the court established that there was no obstacle to holding the trial. The accused was reminded to follow the prosecutor's charges and the court proceedings very carefully. The prosecutor was called to read charges.

The prosecutor read charges K.P. 125/2 from June 24, 1942.

The accused was instructed according to Article 29, Order No. 14 regarding the following:

During a public hearing on the twenty-sixth of this month the accused had proposed that his defender at his trial be Dushan Vucinich, reserve captain first class. If Vucinich were not acceptable, he suggested that the court designate a defender of the officer's rank from that court.

The court accepted the proposal of the accused Jovan Raicevich that Dushan Vucinich, attorney and reserve captain first class, be informed of the accused's request.

If Cpt. Vucinich cannot undertake the defense or for any reason does not come to trial at the stated time, the trial will be held and a defender will be nominated from the officer's rank according to Article 13, Order No. 14.

Concluded and signed

Secretary,   President,
St. Pavicevich   Dr. Il. Vujovich
(signed)   (signed)

The trial was opened against the accused Jovan Raicevich, proceeding according to yesterday's conclusion of the court. Dushan Vucinich (captain first class from Podgorica) was invited by a separate letter to accept the defense of the accused. By return letter Vucinich said he could not accept the defense. Thus, according to Article 13, Order No. 14, the president of the court nominated Aleksandar Lukomski, judicatory lieutenant, to defend Jovan Raicevich at his trial.

Aleksandar Lukomski said he was willing to accept the defense of J. Raicevich.

The prosecutor read indictment K.P. 125/2 dated July twenty-fourth of this year.

After the reading of the indictment the accused Raicevich stated in his own words:

"On July 13 of last year an uprising occurred in a section of Montenegro in Drushice and Rvashe. Later the uprising spread to other parts of Montenegro. The occupation forces called up armed forces to suppress the uprising. On that occasion great numbers of our people were interned, lost their homes to burning; some were even killed. Undoubtedly the occupier did not do it intentionally, but through ignorance of the real situation.

"On November 27 of last year I decided to get out of Podgorica in order not to bring great misfortune upon my tribe. I came to cooperate with my tribesmen, not to let anybody act maliciously toward us or to persuade my tribe to attack occupation companies that were passing through the battalion's region toward Cetinje or to attack unarmed occupier's patrols as they moved more often through Ljeshkopolje. The tribe unanimously chose me to be their battalion commandant. It is true that the designation was confirmed by the main headquarters for Montenegro and Boka and the headquarters of the Zeta Detachment because I refused to accept the position of commandant of the Partisan detachment that was supposed to be formed from Podgorica, Zeta, Ljeshkopolje, and Ljeshnjani. I rejected that offer because I supposed a great number of Communists would join that battalion.

"My desire to get out of the city, besides being based on the reasons I have already mentioned, had another reason. After the Partisans attacked the occupier's columns near Bioci (as I remember on October 18 of last year), on October 20 the occupier jailed fifty to sixty prominent Podgorica citizens. Among them was my older brother Mato. My name was on that list for arrest, but I was in Cetinje. That saved me because those arrested were released after two to three days in prison because of federalist intervention. There was a rumor that all those arrested would be killed because of the Bioci incident. That was also one of the reasons that I left Podgorica, though it is less important.

"As the Partisan movement began to include crimes of anarchy, I secretly worked to destroy it. I did not execute orders from the main headquarters of the Partisan detachment for Montenegro and Boka or orders from the headquarters of the Zeta Detachment. I was told several times to order the commandant of the "Bijeli Pavle" Detachment and the commandant of the Lovcen Detachment to put at my disposal four hundred Partisans to destroy fifth columnists in Ljeshkopolje. I categorically rejected those orders and I did not execute them, feeling that there were not any fifth columnists in Ljeshkopolje. That caused my battalion to be taken away from me. However, my authority among the Ljeshkopolje tribe was not diminished, because my tribesmen openly stated they would not carry out any orders except mine. When I went to the Zeta Detachment headquarters and then to the main headquarters they told me they didn't need me anymore. Instead of giving me a decree as advisory headquarters member that the Zeta Detachment should obey my orders, the headquarters of the Ljeshkopolje Battalion was simply informed I was designated to work in that battalion, which meant that I was the least senior person in that battalion.

"Vlado Raichevich had until then been the political commissar at the headquarters of the Zeta Detachment. Now he was designated to be commandant of the Ljeshkopolje Battalion.

"Since I was relieved of my duties as battalion commandant, I came to headquarters very seldom. I didn't have to accept anyone's demand that I execute any duty. I was mainly in the field. I advised my nephew not to let Partisans from the other detachments destroy fifth columnists in Ljeshkopolje. He followed my advice, and he was quickly replaced in the position of battalion commandant. Shpiro Mugosha was chosen as his replacement.

"As battalion commandant and as an adviser without the slightest influence, during the entire period I was devoted to the well-being of my tribe and of the other tribes as well. Wherever possible I advised them to seek unity and fraternity. I spared the lives of many people who were completely innocent.

"I call upon the entire Ljeshkopolje tribe as well as the Krusko-Berska Company, on whose terrain I lived longer, to verify that these statements are correct. Regarding the roles of commandant of my battalion and political commissar, according to one detailed instruction, roles were assigned to each of them. That is, the battalion commandant was in charge of tactical matters while the political commissar and his assistant were charged with matters of a political nature, like seizing political culprits, escorting them, etc. The political commissar received a list of suspicious persons from the main headquarters via the headquarters of the Zeta Detachment. Any order had to be signed by both the commandant and the commissar, unless they were not present. In that case, orders were signed by their assistants. On matters of pure military character the political commissar did not answer to detachment headquarters but to the commandant in person, and vice versa. On matters of political content only the political commissar and his assistants were in charge. The commissar was responsible for seizing and escorting suspicious persons. In this regard I give the following testimony: Zlata Mirotich was seized and escorted from Vukovci via Grbavce by Company Commander Djoko Djurov Radinovich, Pero Simov Radinovich, and two other persons whose names she did not remember. During that ordeal her husband, Zarija Mirotich, a sergeant who was separated from her, told me: 'Yesterday the political commissar Zivko Radinovich escorted my wife Zlata to battalion headquarters. Please, if she has not yet been conveyed, try to escort her to Radovce.' I told him that was a matter for the political commissar. When I came to battalion headquarters I did not see that woman. If my signature is there, if it was not forged, it can only be that my carte blanche was used on the accompanying set. I left my carte blanche with my nephew Vlado Raicevich in case he needed to call my company for a meeting. I forbade any conferences to be held without my personally written signature. I was against the political commissar convoking conferences without my presence because he would spread Bolshevik ideas among the people. Regarding the other escorted persons, as far as my name is concerned, it could exist only as I mentioned earlier, and always, in any case, my signature did not affect their destiny nor could its absence alleviate the final results. What is true is that I was a severe enemy of all killings of complete innocents, as I proved during my entire work.

"Referring to the liquidation of Jovan Mitrov Raicevich, I was neither commandant nor participant in his death because I swear he was a right and honest man. I think in all the crimes my name was never involved as a participant, because all involved have to be confronted face to face. Also, I believe I was not accused by the family of the deceased Raicevich or anybody else because all knew I was against spilling innocent blood, which was proved by my entire work.

"I beg the court to keep in mind that for me to defy death orders meant refusing obedience to the headquarters of the Zeta Detachment and to main headquarters. I risked my life and the life of my family, which was living in the village of Vukovci. I was surrounded by well-known criminals—Marko Radovich, Vido Uskokovich, political commissar of the Ljeshanski [*Donjo Ljeshanski*] Battalion, Vlado Bozovich, assistant to the political commissar of the Zeta Detachment, and others. Also, my family was in danger from the notorious bandit Spaso Drakich, political commissar of the Zeta Battalion. As far as my other performances were concerned, get testimony from my Ljeshkopolje tribe, and the Krusko-Berska Company. Wherever I was, they would without doubt tell the truth—that I advocated accord, love, and unity among the tribe.

"As far as Communist ideology is concerned, I was always against that evil, its strongest adversary. During the Partisan movement it was forbidden in my battalion to spread it. The battalion was pure from communism, except for a minimal number who were sentenced by the law to defend their country because they had had conflicts with the police. But I held them with an iron hand and did not let them spread Bolshevik ideas.

"There were some culprits who were in the service of Marko Radovich Blazo Jovanovich, Peko Dapcevich, and others who stealthily, without my knowledge, attempted to liquidate Nikola Cirov Mugosha and Jovan Mitrov Raicevich. All my attempts against them were futile because they always rejected the accusation that they had taken part in those attempts. I swear if I succeed in finding them out I shall shoot all of them, regardless of whether it has tragic consequences not only for me and my family but also for the entire Ljeshkopolje tribe. In that case the Ljeshkopolje could find another commandant and political commissar. They could get Partisans from another detachment and Ljeshkopolje would be totally destroyed.

"I declare I have nothing to add in answer to the indictment."

In response to questioning by the court the accused replied:

"The main personnel at the headquarters of the Zeta Detachment were Blazo Jovanovich, commandant; Vlado Raicevich, political commissar for some time; Vlado Bozovich, assistant political commissar who became commissar; Djoko Mirashevich, adviser; and Srdan Novakovich, whose role I don't know because he sometimes signed as commandant and sometimes as political commissar. I don't know the roles of other people. The existing cadre numbered over thirty. I was only there one evening, and I was frightened more than ever before in my life.

"The main headquarters for Montenegro and Boka were staffed by the following people: Ivan Milutinovich, commandant; Peko Dapcevich, commandant of the Lovcen Detachment; and Lazar Djurovich, a former employee of Self-Help whose role I don't know. I was with them only once, and I stayed only half an hour. I went immediately to the headquarters of the Zeta Detachment. They had summoned me to let me know I was dismissed from the duty of battalion commandant because I was not active enough. They told Djoko Mirashevich, who was the adviser for the headquarters of the Zeta Detachment, the same about me. They took the battalion away from me because I refused to liquidate innocent people.

"The Ljeshkopolje Battalion consisted of sometime commandant and political commissar Marko Radovich, assistant political commissar Andrija Mugosha, and later my assistant was Banjo Vukcevich. Vlado Bozovich was sent by the headquarters of the Zeta Detachment on a special mission. He was at our battalion headquarters at least twenty days a month. He always insisted, well-known criminal that he was, on inviting Partisans from the Lovcen Detachment and from 'Bijeli Pavle' in order to destroy fifth columnists in Ljeshkopolje—in a word, to kill at least fifty men, to burn houses, and to take food away. I acted forcefully against it, which caused my replacement as commandant of the Ljeshkopolje Battalion.

"The most famous Communists in my battalion were Marko Radovich; Vlado Kadovich; Vlado Milich, who denied he had been actively engaged in Communist ideology since 1936; Milan Raickovich, as I heard; Zivko Radinovich; and two other Radoviches, Dragutin and Rade. Maybe there were more, but I can't recollect. They were under strict supervision of the company commander.

"I don't know who made up the Gradski bureau in Podgorica. I heard about it, but I don't know with whom that bureau was in contact.

"I testify that as long as I was battalion commandant nobody helped our movement as far as I know. During my role as battalion commandant nobody from Podgorica or anyplace else gave anything to my battalion or to the hospital in Kruse.

"Shpiro Lukin Popovich from Vukovci had no role except that he was a road worker on the Tuzi-Podgorica line. If he did something, he was not authorized, unless someone asked him to do a personal favor. Labud Vukcevich had no function in the Ljeshkopolje Battalion. I don't know if he had any link with battalion headquarters.

"On one occasion I sent a letter via Shpiro Popovich to Dr. Golubovich. I asked him to send me some medicated lice shampoo and to please lend me twenty-five hundred lire because I did not get any pension. He sent me the medicine. As for the money, he replied that his wife was not home at that time. I did not get anything else from him. I don't know if he gave anything to Popovich. I worked it with Popovich because he is my nephew.

"Referring to Tomo Krshikapa, Osman Mandich, and others I state the following:

"On December 4 of last year I went to Ljeshkopolje to find out how they felt about my designation as battalion commandant. I went to the villages Grbavci, Vukovci, and Ponari to find out whether they accepted as commandant of their battalion. My nephew Vlado Raicevich was then in Ljeshkopolje with the aim of handing over to me material for the battalion. Also, as political commissar of the Zeta Detachment Headquarters he had to reprimand all those who deserted during the attack on Pljevlja. In the meantime I went to the villages mentioned when I was informed that my wife was confined to bed with kidney illness and gallstones. Since I had to leave immediately because of my wife's illness, I took forms bearing my signature to Vlado and told him, this is for calling a meeting or issuing an order if it becomes necessary before I return. I visited villages and my family. As my wife felt better, on the fifth or seventh I went to the village of Grbavci to hold a conference. On that occasion Zivko Radinovich, political commissar of Grbavci Company, told me Vlado Raicevich had received an emergency call from Zeta Headquarters to return at once and Vlado wanted to turn over to me the material of the battalion. I went late to transport across Mishurici [*at the mouth of Sitnica into Moraca*]. I found Vlado Raicevich in Donja Gorica at the house of Bozo Milich. I asked him why he wanted me so urgently because in that bad weather I ruined my health. He told me he had to return right away to Zeta Detachment Headquarters and added, 'Instead of seizing the merchants Dervanovich and Bibezich, Tomo Krshikapa was grabbed, with two other persons, and they were escorted to detachment headquarters.' On that occasion I emphasized, 'Where was that evil Marko Radovich? This was surely his act. Why was he allowed to be an escort and mistreat a government employee?' He replied nothing would happen to Tomo. Headquarters would probably gather data about the formation of a Montenegrin state. I told him, 'If you meet him somewhere tomorrow, apologize to him, because it is a disgrace for all of us. He was your comrade from the main office, my great friend, and he only did good to everyone.'

"The next morning Vlado Raicevich departed for Radovce, while I myself went to Beri to settle the battalion headquarters there. After my return from Beri I summoned Marko Radovich after he returned from his trip. I told him it was a disgrace to him what was going on, that is, the seizure of Krshikapa and other honest people. He was faking, throwing responsibility against Vlado Raicevich. Even I could not find out who grabbed and escorted Krshikapa. I know nothing of their later fate except by courier. I was always interested and recommended to my nephew to take care of them."

As time was up, the court proceeding was interrupted, to be continued at four o'clock in the afternoon

Jov. Raicevich
(signed)

The trial continued at four o'clock.

"I told this morning everything I know about the death of Jovan M. Raicevich.

"About the death of Stana Roganovich I know nothing, except what I heard on the 'radio station' while I was imprisoned here. I think the ones who would know more about her fate are Banjo Vukcevich, my then assistant, and Vidak Miranovich. At that time I was not commandant.

"I also know nothing about the fate of Mileva Vucinich."

The court continued with the proceedings. Thus were read the minutes of the accused from March 31, 1942, given at the headquarters of the Ljeshkopolje National Battalion, which were accepted with his correction:

"I was commandant of the battalion from December 7, 1941, until about the middle of February 1942, not until March 27, as the minutes read."

The application of the accused Raicevich from April 8, 1942, was read.

The minutes were read from May 20, 1942, given to investigators at this court and also the minutes from June 24, 1942, which he acknowledged as his.

The minutes were read of the accused of May 24, 1942, given to the investigating committee, which he acknowledged as his. He added that he told in those minutes that he neither earlier nor later nor now or ever belonged to the Communist party.

A report of the community of Ljeshkopolje of May 9, 1942, was read.

The accused declared he absolutely did not know who broke into and plundered the office of the community of Ljeshkopolje, neither does he know how the community tables were moved into his office.

There was read the May 21, 1942 report of the court administrator at the main national committee, signed by the judge of the district court, Milinko Gilich, and sent to the investigatory committee in relation to the captured archives at Radovce.

After the accused Jovan P. Raicevich heard the aforementioned report, he said the content under point 1 of the report was true.

"The items under point 2 of that report I don't remember, and I believe my signature was forged or used from some form I signed carte blanche.

"As to the item under 3, I cannot attest it is true that I signed that act.

"The items under 4 could be true because I remember seeing such a report.

"The items under 5 I also cannot remember as being true.

"The item under 6 is not true. I would never send any order with such motivation, because the deceased Jovan M. Raicevich was not a fifth columnist.

"The items under 7 were true as I stated then. I did not perform any function.

"It is possible that a report such as mentioned under item 8 was sent, but I emphasize that I had to sign such reports and the responsibility for it was that of the political commissar. I never considered Nikola Mugosha a fifth columnist.

"The items under 9 I attest are true because he did it to knock off Mato Raicevich. In the main headquarters they calculated that if Mato joined us they could have influence over him to persuade me to execute killings and burnings in Ljeshkopolje."

Two or three items were read from order no. 195 of the headquarters of the Partisan Zeta Detachment from February 24, 1942. The accused stated that the order was unknown to him because he was not then battalion commandant.

On questioning by the court the accused replied: "Independently of my designation as commandant of the Ljeshkopolje Partisan Battalion by headquarters of the Zeta Detachment, I contacted all the villages in my battalion to find out their feelings about my becoming battalion commandant, proposing to them my program of work that I cited in all preceding minutes. They were all satisfied to have me as their commandant. For the truth of this I call to testify on my behalf the entire battalion.

"When I came out [*from Podgorica*] the Partisan movement was not in despair, but later it definitely was collapsing. Some Partisans were removed from front lines confronting the occupier, especially those who took part in the July uprising and went to take over Pljevlja from the occupier. The reason I came to be commandant I have already explained in detail. I would never have accepted the position of battalion commandant if the entire tribe had not wished it.

"I went to every village of my battalion's region before I took command, and I conferred with the peasants. I told them; 'I come to be commandant of the battalion with a program of preventing individual and mass killing, and preventing the burning of homes and the like.' They agreed completely with my program and the future performance.

"Besides my definition of the relationship between commandant and political commissar I would add that the political commissar had the authority to take the necessary number of men for escorting suspicious people.

"Today for the first time I heard that a 'Cika' Begovich came in my Partisan headquarters.

"During my time as battalion commandant I insisted on using my power to save what could be saved. As the commandant I had command authority, though it was curbed in great measure by the main Partisan headquarters, the headquarters of the Zeta Detachment, and the political commissar of my battalion.

"Since I became an adviser at Zeta Detachment my place was in Radovce, but I was afraid my nephew would fall under bad influences to destroy fifth columnists in Ljeshkopolje. So I intervened with the detachment commandant, Blazo Jovanovich, to return me to the Ljeshkopolje Battalion. In this I was successful.

"Earlier in my hearings and on trial I stated that the headquarters of the Zeta Detachment sent me to work in the battalion headquarters. This is not in accord with my earlier statement. I justify it. I thought it was the same.

"Since I was replaced in the capacity of battalion commandant I issued an order to let my former units know I was no longer battalion commandant and had been nominated to be adviser in Zeta Detachment. Then I went immediately to the field, where I met with the masses. They declared that, regardless of the nomination, 'We only know and want to hear orders from you. Others we don't know.'

"As battalion commandant I wore the five-pointed star symbolizing the national fight for the liberation of Montenegro.

As soon as I left Podgorica I realized the struggle and my program would not be realized as conceived. My task was national liberation. It was said that a general uprising would erupt against the enemy, and then I would have to take some role. After I came into the terrain I realized it was not a battle against the occupier but against their own people.

"Since I came out I could not return, but I remained to share my tribe's destiny, and how much I succeeded in that I leave the court to judge."

Because the accused Jovan Raicevich at today's session denied the correctness of named documents in the court administrator's report of May 21 of this year under no. 2, 3, 4, 5, 6, and 8, this session will be postponed according to Paragraph 22, Order No. 14. The next session was scheduled for Thursday July 2, 1942, at eight o'clock a.m. For that trial date the original documents that were cited in the court administrator's report of May 21, 1942 must be procured so they can be available for inspection at the trial. Then they will be returned to the court administrator, with a certified copy of each instead of the original retained in the file on the appropriate subject. Also at the time the court administrator will send data from the captured archives of Radovce about the abduction, escorting, and killing of Tomo Krshikapa, Osman Mandich, Savo Milich, and other people killed in the territory of the Ljeshkopolje Battalion.

P.P.

Concluded and signed   Jov. Raicevich
(signed)

                                         Secretary,
President,   St. Pavicevich
Dr. I. Vujovich   (signed)
(signed)

The trial was continued July 2, 1942, at eight o'clock a.m.

Those present were President Dr. Ilija Vujovich; judges Savo Popovich, Bajo Radovich, Mitar Mugosha, and Jovan Kazich; detachment prosecutor Ljubomir Djukich, defender Aleksandar Lukomski, and the accused Jovan Raicevich.

It was moved to take evidence according to the conclusion of the last session.

In answer to questions the accused replied:

"I did not order the theft of thirty-nine sheep from Krushevac, but Vlado Kadovich told me that Andrija Mugosha did order it. He [*Mugosha*] brought those sheep to our headquarters. I advised him to return the sheep as banovina property. They said they were taken on orders of the commandant of the detachment. We slaughtered eight sheep.

"The headquarters of the Zeta Detachment carried out the distribution of those sheep and sent the headquarters of the Donjo Ljeshnjani Battalion four or five pieces of meat, Zeta four pieces; for him he ordered fifteen pieces. It seems to me that some meat was sent to the provincial committee in Orahovica as well as some in exchange for grain from Zeta. How much and to whom I don't know. Andrija Perovich and Radoje Cetkovich received one sheep each. Andrija Perovich was given a sheep for producing one offspring. In return he promised to give two for that one.

"The attorney Pero Raickovich came to us voluntarily. I remember that he was to have come earlier to be assistant battalion commandant, but he did not come in time, so he was not needed later. I don't know for what purpose he stayed in our battalion. It was unknown to me how he left Podgorica. He said he only came out from Podgorica so as not to be interned.

"I don't know who invited Dr. Petar Jovanovich. I did not see him when he arrived. While Jovanovich was in Podgorica I had no contact either with him or with Dr. Jovicevich. I did not know that any medical equipment came before or after Pero Raicevich's arrival.

"I do not know whether the male nurses Ilickovich and Vukadinovich came there. I did not see them. I do not know them.

"On November 18 [*1941*] they departed for Pljevlja, while I was still in Podgorica. On their return from Pljevlja I was already in the battalion.

"I was present at the requiem for Partisans killed at Pljevlja. On that occasion were also present, Radoje Cetkovich, Blazo Jovanovich, Djoko Mirashevich, and Vlado Bozovich. I was the first to make a memorial speech in the church. Then Jovanovich, Mirashevich, and Cetkovich made speeches.

"When Nikola Pejovich was taken away to Radovce I was not in the battalion, though I was the battalion commandant. I saw him after he returned to the battalion from Radovce to appear before the political commissar who would decide his fate. I spared his life, knowing well his father and uncles.

"Mileva Vukovich was unknown to me.

"Spaso Boljevich was our courier, sometimes for companies and sometimes for Radovce. I don't remember Vasa Marinovich.

"I did not know Stana Roganovich, refugee from Pec. I assert to you that Stana Roganovich did not weep in front of me and beg me to save her life. She did not come at all that I remember. I can't say, because I don't know, whether Pero Raickovich was there on March 1, 2, or 3, but I assert for myself that on March 2 I was in Ljeshkopolje before and after noon. I remember because Nationalists came to Ljeshkopolje that day. I was in Ljeshkopolje on private business and I returned to Beri. That day when I crossed the bridge at Sitnica I saw Nationalists in Ljeshkopolje Gorica.

"I categorically swear I have no connection with Jozo Vukcevich, nor do I know if he brought anything into battalion headquarters.

"I did not know anything about the death of Dushan-Galjo Golubovich.

"About the list of spies from Podgorica, I have no knowledge of who was sentenced to death.

"I know Bozo Munov Mugosha. However, I don't know if he delivered any livestock to our headquarters.

"I know Branka Milich. I cannot say anything about her role except that she was with her ill uncle.

"I categorically assert that I neither saw Vukovich or Roganovich nor talked with them. Neither Vlado Bozovich nor Banjo Vukcevich told me anything about them.

"The highest authority in battalion headquarters for technical matters was the battalion commandant, while for political matters it was the political commissar. Each order of the battalion commandant and political commissar was signed by both.

"The cook in my battalion headquarters was Djoko Radanovich and for a short time it was Danica Carapich.

"I assert that I never saw Jelena Vukotich in the battalion headquarters. Besides, I don't know what role she played in Radovce.

"At the time of the attack in Donjo Ljeshanska Nahija I was an adviser assigned to work in battalion headquarters without any power.

"I heard about the movement of Bajo Stanishich after the road was broken through toward Niksic. I did not hear any report that the iron hand was broken and that Bajo Stanishich was squeezed and expected to be destroyed at any minute.

"I don't remember where I was in the first half of February [*1942*]—probably in Grbavci or Vukovci. I cannot say where I was in the second half of February because at that time I was continually on the move.

"I never listened to the radio news except once when I was in Baloce at the elementary school to meet with the commandant of the Donjo Ljeshanski Battalion to arrange a retreat. I had no intention of participating in any battle. I believe it happened when I was battalion commandant.

"I assert that the so-called Cika Begovich never came to me."

The court administrator's order no. 1,127 of July 1, 1942 was read and the required documents were delivered.

After the conveyance order was read, the reading and verification of the documents began.

1. Headquarters of Ljeshkopolje Partisan Battalion order no. 22 of February 2, 1942, signed by Jovan Raicevich as commandant and Marko Radovich as political commissar, registered at headquarters of Zeta Partisan Detachment as no. 119, February 5, 1942. The signature on that act was acknowledged as his.

2. Headquarters of Ljeshkopolje Partisan Battalion order no. 47 of February 21, 1942, registered at headquarters of Zeta Detachment as no. 201, February 24, 1942, which was signed by Commandant Vlado Raicevich and Political Commissar Marko Radovich.

3. Headquarters of Ljeshkopolje Partisan Battalion order no. 20 of January 23, 1942, registered at headquarters of Zeta Detachment as no. 78, January 25, 1942.

When that act was read and pointed out to the accused, the accused acknowledged his signature, but emphasized that it was a matter for the political commissar. It was ascertained that the political commissar had not signed the act, but that it was signed, "For political commissar, Bran. M. Vukcevich."

When he was asked about the first order from February 2, 1942, no 22, the accused stated it was his but that it was untrue because the headquarters of the Zeta Detachment had pressured him to liquidate of fifth columnists and destroy public objects.

4. Headquarters of Ljeshkopolje-Podgorica Battalion order of December 14, 1941, registered at headquarters of Zeta Detachment as classified no. 64, December 18, 1941. The accused stated that he had written and signed it himself. He said the content was in no way directed against people.

On court questioning about whom that act was directed against, the accused stated that it was directed against those who deserted from Pljevlja.

5. Headquarters of Ljeshkopolje Battalion order of December 23, 1941, no. official, registered at headquarters of Zeta Partisan Detachment as classified no. 72, December 23, 1941. The accused acknowledged the order and his signature. He then stated that the actions were not performed for demolishing a road and also that measures were not taken for destroying fifth columnists. "If I wanted to I could have done so while I was under pressure from the command of detachment headquarters."

6. Ljeshkopolje-Podgorica Partisan Battalion order no. official of December 14, 1941, signed by the accused Jovan Raicevich, registered at headquarters of Zeta Detachment as classified no. 72, December 23, 1941.

After that act was read the accused stated that he had written and signed it personally.

7. Headquarters of Ljeshkopolje Partisan Battalion order no. 29 of February 7, 1942, registered at headquarters of Zeta Battalion as no. 142, February 10, 1942. The accused stated: "The signature on that act I acknowledge as my own, but allow the possibility that I signed it carte blanche or that I was ill and my signature was obtained deceptively. I would never order that for Jovan M. Raicevich, knowing him as an honest man."

8. Headquarters of Zeta Detachment order no. 157 of February 14, 1942, sent to headquarters of Ljeshkopolje Battalion. The accused stated he was sure he had received that order.

9. Ljeshkopolje Partisan Battalion order no. 9 of January 16, 1942, signed by Jovan Raicevich and Marko Radovich.

The accused stated that he acknowledged the order and the signature on it. As far as Nikola Mugosha was concerned, that was a matter for the political commissar.

10. Headquarters of Ljeshkopolje Battalion order no. official, signed by Jovan Raicevich and registered at headquarters of Zeta Detachment as no. 114, December 8, 1941.

The accused stated he had signed the order. He added that it was only for the people's benefit.

11. Headquarters of Ljeshkopolje Battalion order of March 4, 1942, registered at headquarters of Zeta Detachment as no. 236, March 5, 1942. That order was signed by the commandant of Ljeshkopolje Battalion, Vlado M. Raicevich.

12. Ljeshkopolje Battalion order no. 56 of March 2, 1942, registered at headquarters of Zeta Detachment as no. 236, March 5, 1942. That order

was signed by the commandant of the battalion, Vlado Raicevich, and the political commissar, who was "in the field." Also, order no. 56 of March 2, 1942, signed by Commandant Vlado Raicevich and Political Commissar Marko Radovich. It was signed by the headquarters of Zeta Detachment "For Commandant Srdan Novakovich and Political Commissar Vlado Bozovich." For the main headquarters of Montenegro and Boka, "Milutin"—which meant Ivan Milutinovich.

13. Headquarters of Zeta Detachment order no. 236 of March 5, 1942. The order was signed, "For Commandant, Srdan Novakovich," and "For Political Commissar, Vlado Bozovich."

14. Headquarters of Zeta Detachment order no. 79 of December 10, 1941, concerning the taking of Tomo Krshikapa and others, signed by Commandant Blazo Jovanovich and Political Commissar Vlado Raicevich.

Asked to name the ten men who were the most trusted to liquidate fifth columnists in Ljeshkopolje, the accused stated that he neither appointed them nor knew them. Also, he did not know the names of four Partisans who were appointed to shoot Nikola Mugosha.

"All in all what was in the Dojbabe Monastery was unknown because it was not in the territory of my battalion."

Asked what members of the district committee of the CPY, Podgorica were present at all company conferences from January 1 to January 5, 1942, and what was said in order no. 9 of January 15, 1942, the accused stated that the existence of a committee of CPY in Podgorica was unknown to him, and that he did not know the members of that committee or what the aforementioned order said. He asserted that while he was there, nobody came out from Podgorica.

Because of the hour, the trial was adjourned until today at three o'clock.

The trial was called to order again at three o'clock on July 2, 1942.

All interested parties were present.

For the last time the accused stated that as to people mentioned today who had been killed, he had nothing more to say than what he had already said.

He asserted again that no member of the committee of the Communist party of Yugoslavia took part in the meetings and gatherings in his battalion.

The national guard order no. 197 of June 29, 1942, was read.

Excerpts from the minutes given to that court of June 29, 1942, by Djordjije Radanovich about the accused were read.

The court inspected Communist documents that were placed at the court's disposal by the military command and stated: Under general order no. 204, Jovan Perov Raicevich, lieutenant colonel retired, 56 years old, was listed as Communist; Jovan P. Raicevich, 56 years old was seconded as no. 91 on the captured Partisan list.

The prosecutor of the detachment stated that there was nothing further regarding presentation of evidence.

The defender suggests obtaining the document about the killing of Jovan M. Raicevich and about the assassination of Nikola Mugosha to establish the fact that the deceased Jovan M. Raicevich was not killed by the accused nor by his order but rather while he was being escorted to the headquarters of Zeta Detachment and because of his resistance against the escort guards. From the same documents it could be seen that his escort was not ordered by the accused but by the headquarters of Zeta Detachment. Also, by gathering documents referring to the attempt to assassinate Nikola Mugosha it would be apparent that the attempt was not by order of the accused or by his knowledge.

After secret deliberation the court pronounced the following:

Conclusion:

The suggestion of the defender was rejected as inappropriate for the following reasons: The facts cited were fully proved by public documents and could not be denied by any law; at today's trial there was read headquarters of Ljeshkopolje Partisan Battalion order no. 29 of February 29, 1942, whose complete signature was attested to by the accused, by which order was liquidated Jovan M. Raicevich on February 4, 1942. Secondly, according to battalion headquarters order no. 9 of January 16, 1942, read this morning, under the complete signature of the accused, on January 4 the assassination of the fifth columnist Nikola Mugosha was attempted by his order. In that attack only four Partisans participated, though ten of the best Partisans for liquidation were designated to the case. Those were public documents that contain in fully lawful form the total evidence such that the court according to Paragraph 22, Order no. 14 could not postpone the trial.

The accused stated: "In the documents read of the military command and captured Partisan documents I am characterized as a Communist. However, it is not true, because I never was a Communist in my life, least of all at this time. I only fought for national liberation.

"I attest that on March 27, 1942, I surrendered to the national authority. The national troops found me at the home of Luka Popovich, having been informed by my brother Mato. So the company commander came in with two soldiers who gave me asylum.

"The reason I did not surrender to the national authority from March 2 to March 27 was that I did not know exactly in which direction the national movement was developing. As soon as I learned, I joined the Nationalists.

"The reason I did not get in touch myself with the national authority was that I was for a while in Busovnik. I had a stab wound in my leg. I could not get in touch, but I told my brother to do it.

"I learned how the national movement was developing in Ljeshkopolje on March 2, though I considered it of local character. As to the broader national movement in Montenegro, I learned just on March 10.

"The reason I did not contact the national authority from March 10 to March 27 was that I wanted to persuade those ninety to a hundred comrades who belonged to the battalion of Shpiro Mugosha to surrender to the national authority. In the meantime I succeeded in persuading about seventy of them to join the national authority.''

The accused proposed to check with the Ljeshkopolje tribe about his national activities during his sojourn in the Partisan ranks, and also to find out in that regard whether there was any affidavit from seven or eight villages that saw his work when he was battalion commandant, to find out if he was a Communist or Nationalist. Asked how he learned that fact and who prepared that affidavit, the accused replied: ''I heard in the prison that there was an affidavit of the Ljeshkopolje tribe that exposed my activity at the time of my stay among the Partisans. I don't know who made that affidavit and by whom it was signed.''

After secret consultation the court made and pronounced the following:

Conclusion:

The suggestions of the accused were rejected regarding all evidence because the facts were already proven to be founded and any other proof would be irrelevant to the final decision.

After the evidence proceeding was completed, Nikola Mugosha appeared in the audience, although he had not been invited. He stated, ''I did not bring charges against anybody, and without a doubt Jovan Raicevich sentenced me. On December 11, 1941, I was in Beri with Petar Nikov Mugosha with the goal of beginning a national organization. So I did not believe I was in danger. However, at today's trial I saw and heard from the headquarters of Ljeshkopolje Partisan Battalion order no. 9 of January 16, 1942, that my liquidation had been plotted just on January 4, 1942.''

On the court question of how Mugosha could supply the court with facts when he had been sentenced to death on December 11, 1941, in Beri by Vidak Uskokovich [*political commissar of Donjo-ljesjnjani Battalion*], Mugosha stated: ''After two or more months I was told by Radoje Cetkovich; Toko and Djuro Cetkovich told me after my arrival in Beri, ten days later at my home in Donja Gorica.''

The parties having no other proposals and the court considering the interruption of Nikola Mugosha to be inappropriate, the court then considered the matter ready to be decided and invited the parties to give their final arguments. The detachment prosecutor emphasized: ''I stand by the given indictment and I suggest adding to it the other counts. I ask for punishment according to the indictment.''

In his longer statement the defender argued for bringing the indictment down from nine to four points.

''For the act of killing Jovan M. Raicevich the least responsible has been charged. In reality it was the act of the political commissar or at the worst the act was performed by order of higher command. He was not responsible for killing ordered by command of the detachment. It was clearly shown that the accused Jovan Raicevich did not have the best relationship with the detachment commandant. He was gradually degraded from battalion commandant to adviser of the detachment and from detachment adviser to battalion adviser.

"Spiritus rectus [*straight, guiding spirit*] of all misdeeds and killings was the political commissar. Also, he is not guilty of the attempt to liquidate Nikola Mugosha. He neither ordered nor knew of it; it was an act of the political commissar and the headquarters of the detachment.

"The court should take into consideration that the accused was not clever about office politics because of his age. In many cases, as shown to this court, it could be considered fraud to sign things without knowing what they were. It is necessary to take into consideration that he was retired while still a young officer because he was temperamental, cautious, and considered to be a noisemaker, not trustworthy."

The defender said he personally participated in a funeral when the accused made a farewell speech over General Vuksanovich's coffin in front of Sokol Hall and the content of that speech was patriotic.

"The government did not consider him a Communist. He remained undisturbed until November of last year, when he voluntarily left Podgorica. He went to his tribe in order to save himself, being inspired also by the highest national feelings.

"The accused did not commit any crime or slaughterings, personally or by others, but he was motivated to survive with minimal damages.

"The pronouncement of sentence could hit mercilessly, could hurt his family financially and morally, and immerse the family in a hopeless situation.

"It could be allowed that the accused was an ideological Communist, but as such he did not commit any crime.

"Regarding the disappearance of Franc Ham and Zlatija Mirotich, he could not be charged with their liquidation if such had happened, however they were only taken away for a long time. In that case the criminal responsibility does not fall on him, because he did not perform it voluntarily but by order of higher headquarters.

"I beg the court referring to Criminal Law No. 70 to accept as extenuating circumstances acknowledged good behavior. As concerns the killings of Stana Roganovich and Mileva Vukovich, the sentence should be suspended, because it was not proved and the indictment did not charge him. I beg the court to render a milder sentence. It is to his credit that the national movement in Ljeshkopolje was organized, because Ljeshkopolje was so devastated by the bombing."

The accused stated that he stands by the defense of his defender and added that he never was an ideological Communist; on the contrary, he was the bitterly sworn enemy of communism. "Also, my older brother Mato never was a Communist. Regardless of my brother's age, neither of us nor anyone else in my family was in any way inclined toward communism. In

1936 my brother Blazo was expelled from the Communist party, and since then he has always worked in the national interest. The best proof of this is he never agreed with the revolution of July 13, but rather condemned that movement."

He stated further: "I stand by my given statements and I have nothing further to say in my defense."

The court pronounced that the trial was complete and that a decision would be made immediately.

The verdict is appended to these minutes
Concluded and signed,

Secretary,   President,
V. Perovich   Dr. Il. Vujovich
(signed)   (signed)

K.P. 125/2

In the Name of the Montengrin People:

On the basis of the authority assigned by the commandant of the people's army for Montenegro and Hercegovina:

The people's military court in Podgorica was made up of the council, which consisted of President Dr. Ilija Vujovich, court captain first class, Savo Popovich, captain first class, Bajo Radovich, Mitar Mugosha, Jovan Kazich, and secretary Vaso Perovich. According to the indictment of the prosecutor of the Zeta Detachment filed with this court against Jovan P. Raicevich for criminal acts from Paragraph 2, Order no. 14, issued by the commandant of the people's army for Montenegro and Hercegovina, charges were brought and tried in the presence of the accused, who was jailed, and his defender, Aleksandar Lukomski. The composition of the main trial was set according to the proposal by the detachment prosecutor Ljubomir Djukich, who asked that judgment be passed on the accused according to the proposal presented at today's trial; the defense presented a proposal for the accused to have a milder punishment. The court declared the following:

Verdict:

Jovan Raicevich, son of Pero and Mara nee Milich, of the Orthodox religion, born and residing in Ljeshkopolje, community Ljeshkopolje, a 56-year-old retired lieutenant colonel, married, literate, a veteran of the armed forces, never convicted before nor under investigation before.

He is guilty:

Count 1. He was an active and energetic member of the Communist Partisan organization since November 27, 1941, until he was jailed on March 27, 1942. Thus he committed criminal action as defined in and punishable under Article 2, part 10, point 1, Order No. 14.

Count 2. As such he was primarily designated as commandant of the Ljeshkopolje Communist-Partisan Battalion, then as adviser of the headquarters of the Communist-Partisan Zeta Detachment. Thus he committed criminal action as defined in and punishable under Article 2, part 10, point 1, Order No. 14.

Count 3. As battalion commandant and as an advisory member of a Communist-Partisan detachment organization he made speeches and held conferences at various places on the territory of the Ljeshkopolje Battalion. Thus he committed criminal action as defined in and punishable under Article 2, part 4, point 1, Order No. 14.

Count 4. At critical moments as a professional person he was assigned according to need to work on the most difficult, most important moments and positions at the main headquarters of the Communist-Partisan Zeta Detachment as a specialist in the military view and in the political view recruited members for the Communist-Partisan ranks, where he distinguished himself. Thus he committed criminal action as defined in and punishable under Article 2, part 10, point 1, Order No. 14.

Count 5. As commandant of the Communist-Partisan Ljeshkopolje Battalion he gave orders for demolishing roads and cutting telephone and telegraph communications. Thus he committed criminal action as defined in and punishable under Article 2, part 10, point 1, Order No. 14.

Count 6. As commandant of a Communist-Partisan battalion he participated in the pilfering of thirty-nine sheep that belonged to Krushevac Hospital. Thus he committed criminal action as defined in and punishable under Article 2, part 6, Order No. 14.

Count 7. By his order was killed Jovan Mitrov Raicevich from Vranici. Thus he committed criminal action as defined in and punishable under Article 2, part 1, points 1 and 2, Order No. 14.

Count 8. By his order was organized an attempt to kill Nikola Mugosha at night between January 17 and 18 in the village Donja Gorica. Thus he committed criminal action as defined in and punishable under Article 2, part 1, points 1 and 2, Order No. 14.

Count 9. By his order were arrested Franc Ham and Zlatija Mirotich, of whom Zlatija was killed, while the fate of Ham remains unknown. Thus he committed criminal action as defined in and punishable under Article 2, part 7, in connection with part 1, points 1 and 2, Order No. 14.

Count 10. As an advisory member of the detachment assigned at headquarters of Ljeshkopolje Battalion he allowed Mileva Vukovich and Stana Roganovich to be killed. Thus he committed criminal action as defined in and punishable under Article 2, parts 1 and 2, Order No. 14 in connection with Criminal Law Paragraph 34.

Count 11. As commandant of the Communist-Partisan Ljeshkopolje Battalion he permitted to be arrested and escorted to their inevitable death: Tomo Krshikapa, Osman Mandich, and Mileva Vucinich. Thus he committed criminal action as defined in and punishable under Article 2, part 7, in connection with part 1, points 1 and 2, Order No. 14.

Therefore, on the basis of the evidence and articles 2, 24, 25, 26, 27, 28, and 29, Order No. 14 issued by the commandant of the national liberation army for Montenegro and Hercegovina:
We sentence him to death by firing squad
                                     Reasons:

The defense of the accused Jovan Raicevich was unfounded and unconvincing:
During the entire proceedings and at the trial it was found that the accused was the executor of all criminal acts as charged. Therefore by this verdict he was pronounced guilty and sentenced.

Count 1—Evidence. Count 1 of this verdict was proved by archives captured from the headquarters of the Zeta Partisan Detachment from Radovce and delivered to this court by act of the court administrator's main action committee under no. 1127 of July 1 of this year. During investigation and trial at this court the accused acknowledged that he was earlier designated by the main headquarters as commandant of the Communist-Partisan Ljeshkopolje Battalion. This was specifically shown by his minutes of May 20, 1942, from which could be seen that he indeed left Podgorica on November 27, 1941. At today's public trial he testified that he surrendered to the national authorities just on March 27, 1942

Count 2—Evidence. Count 2 was proven by the original archives of national Communist-Partisan headquarters and also by the accused's testimony in the minutes of May 20, 1942, in which he states verbatim "I had earlier been appointed commandant of a Partisan battalion that would be made up of combined forces from the Ljeshkopolje, Ljeshnjani, and Podgorica battalions. I received that decree from the commandant of the Zeta Detachment, Blazo Jovanovich. The decree was issued before I left Podgorica. After my arrival in Ljeshkopolje I learned Andrija Mugosha had been appointed as an advisory member of headquarters." That was shown by order no. 195 of the headquarters of the Zeta Partisan Battalion of February 24, 1942, and attested to by his personal acknowledgment given in his written statement of April 8, 1942, and by his assertion given in the minutes of the prosecutor of May 21, 1942, as well as in the trial minutes of this court.

Count 3—Evidence. Count 3 was proved by the original archives of the headquarters of the Ljeshkopolje Partisan Battalion thusly:
    a. Order no. 22 of February 2, 1942, point 7, where among other things was said, "It could not be said that we did not work enough at raising the political consciousness of both Partisans and the masses on our terrain. We were in constant contact with the Partisans and we told them innumerable times what Partisan duties were...."

b. By headquarters of Ljeshkopolje Partisan Battalion order no. 9 of January 16, 1942, point 3, which in part states, "On January 6 a requiem was held for Partisans fallen at Pljevlja as well as for those killed in Ljeshkopolje.... Despite bad weather a considerable number of people were present. An inspection was made by the commander of the battalion from all four Partisan companies that were under arms and a salute was given to the commandant of your detachment.... Comrade Jovan Raicevich spoke in the name of the battalion."

c. By headquarters of Ljeshkopolje Partisan Battalion order no. offical of December 17, 1941, received at the headquarters of Zeta Partisan Detachment as no. 114, December 18, 1941, in which it was said that on the evening of December 15 a conference was held to repulse fifth-columnist agitation.

d. By his battalion's very confidential order no. official of December 21, 1941, registered at headquarters of Zeta Partisan Detachment as confidential order no. 64, December 18, in which it was stated he held a conference with youth. That order was personally written and signed by the accused.

Count 4—Evidence. Count 4 was proved by the original archives of the headquarters of the Ljeshkopolje Partisan Battalion and in the court administrator's order no. 1127 of the first of this month, which at today's trial was shown to the accused, who attested his signatures were true. Besides, it was clearly proved by headquarters of Zeta Partisan Detachment order no. 236 of March 3, 1942, sent to headquarters of the Ljeshkopolje Partisan Battalion, in which, among other subjects, was the statement: "As to Comrade Jovan Raicevich, let him stay for the time being at that headquarters. We believe he would be more useful there than here."

Count 5—Evidence. Count 5 was proved by original archives of the headquarters of the Ljeshkopolje Partisan Battalion, as follows:

a. By headquarters of the Ljeshkopolje Partisan Battalion order no. 22 of February 2, 1942, by which the accused reported to the headquarters of the Zeta Partisan Detachment that between January 21 and January 22, 1942, an action was executed under Velje Brdo in which boulders were heaped up, at nine places over one kilometer of road and telephone cables were cut for a length of 500 meters. This order was signed by the accused. Also in the same order an action at Velje Brdo on the road to Niksic was described on the night between February 1 and February 2, 1942. At fourteen places the road was blocked with boulders, and several log blockades were erected. They also gathered about one and a half kilometers of telephone cable. Also an action was executed on the road to Cetinje at the place called "Lisica." Besides, as seen from order no. 79 of the main headquarters of the Zeta Detachment of December 10, 1941, the accused with his subordinate personnel incapacitated telephone lines between Podgorica and Cetinje. On December 7 [1941] the road near Velje Brdo was torn up for 300 meters, sixteen telephone poles were cut, and the wire was torn apart and taken away.

The defense of the accused that he submitted such reports to the main headquarters in order to deceive them was improper and unfounded. Those facts were asserted by public documents that were attested to by his signature in the capacity of battalion commandant.

Count 6—Evidence. Count 6 was proved by original archives of the headquarters of the Ljeshkopolje Partisan Battalion with special order no. 9 of January 16, 1942, point 7, which says: "On January 12 there were seized at the Krushevac Hospital thirty-nine banovina sheep, of which eight sterile ones were butchered." This order was signed with his personal signature. This fact was stipulated by the accused and in the minutes of the public trial in front of this court today, particularly: "We butchered eight sheep." The defense of the accused that he was not ordered to plunder thirty-nine sheep from the hospital at Krushevac was totally inappropriate, losing sight of the fact that he was battalion commandant and an adviser to main headquarters.

Count 7—Evidence. Count 7 was proved by original archives of the aforementioned headquarters and especially by order no. 29 of the headquarters of the Ljeshkopolje Partisan Battalion of February 29, 1942, by which the accused with his signature reported to the headquarters of the Zeta Partisan Detachment in the capacity of battalion commandant, saying, "On the fourth of this month about nine o'clock in the morning Partisans of our battalion by our order liquidated Jovan M. Raicevich, peasant from Vranici. The liquidation was performed in front of the house of his relatives in Luzanje." The defense of the accused that this was not his order but the order of political commissar Marko Radovich does not alleviate his responsibility. As commandant of the battalion he was the main commander and the political commissar was his executor. The other part of his defense was totally untrue. If he had acted as he portrayed at his trial, he would not have permitted Jovan M. Raicevich to be killed under any circumstances.

Count 8—Evidence. Count 8 was proved by the original archives previously mentioned of the headquarters of the Ljeshkopolje Partisan Battalion, thusly: Order no. 9 of the Ljeshkopolje Partisan Battalion of January 16, 1942, personally signed by the accused as commandant of the Ljeshkopolje Partisan Battalion, forwarded to headquarters of the Zeta Detachment, point 2 states, "On January 4 there was an attempted assassination of the fifth columnist Nikola Mugosha in Donja Gorica. Four Partisans took part. Preparations and instructions had been given to kill this scoundrel at any price.

The Partisans were indecisive and not committed, conscientious, and responsible enough for such duties. Therefore the attempt failed totally. In the ambush the four Partisans from 100 to 150 meters fired their rifles at N. Mugosha, who fell to the ground right away. The Partisans continued to shoot in his direction as they retreated. During the retreat toward Zelenika relatives of Nikola Mugosha and others opened fire on the Partisans. Ten of the most loyal Partisans were selected to liquidate the above-mentioned and other fifth columnists before Christmas Eve.'' The defense of the accused that the attempted liquidation of Nikola Mugosha was a matter for the political commissar is unfounded and does not at any rate relieve him of his criminal responsibility. The accused was commandant of the battalion, the main commander, and the political commissar was his accomplice.

Count 9—Evidence. Count 9 was proved by original archives of the aforementioned headquarters of the Ljeshkopolje Partisan Battalion thusly: By his personally written and signed report classified official no. of December 14, 1941, sent to the headquarters of the Zeta Detachment, which states: ''Herewith is conveyed Zlatija Mirotich, born in Srbija, who was seized in Grbavci at the home of her former husband, Sgt. Mirotich. She is considered to be engaged in espionage. Please verify and act according to your jurisdiction.'' That report was recorded at the headquarters of the Zeta Detachment as classified no. 72, December 23, 1941. The accused during his trial at this court completely acknowledged that report as his without any objection. Also by his order no. 20 of January 23, 1942, which was sent in his capacity of commandant of the Ljeshkopolje Partisan Battalion to the headquarters of the Zeta Partisan Detachment, ''On the twenty-third of this month on the territory of this battalion in Donja Gorica our guard caught Ham Franc from Rasovo (Bijelo Polje). It was known to us that the Italian authority marked as suspicious the I.D. issued by them to each of our honest men who were in their prison. However, the I.D. issued to Ham Franc by the Italians had nothing written on it. Thus he was suspicious to us, and as such we conveyed him to you for your further investigation.'' That act was personally signed by the accused and the signature asserted as his. The defense of the accused that this was the act of the political commissar was inappropriate because the act was not signed by the commissar but by another person altogether referring to an assistant of the battalion commandant Bran. Vukcevich ''for the political commissar,'' which in no way alleviates the guilt and criminal responsibility of the accused.

Count 10—Evidence. Count 10 was proved by the inspection of documents of this court under no. KP 15/2 on the subject of the guilt of Djordje Radanovich, who in minutes of June 29, 1942, given to this court, asserts the circumstance and says: "I categorically swear that Lt. Col. Jovan Raicevich, in the capacity of commandant and advisory member of Zeta Detachment, enjoyed complete trust as named commandant, and also the trust of his subordinates at headquarters. If he wanted he could easily have saved the lives of Milena Vukovich and Stana Roganovich, who both were seen at headquarters and with both of whom he conversed. All orders that came from headquarters were with the knowledge and approval of Lt. Col. Raicevich and were accorded maximum respect. So neither the political commissar nor his assisant, recently Vukcevich, nor anyone from headquarters could or would dare to do anything without his agreement and approval." Further, in the same minutes it was ascertained that Roganovich wept in front of Raicevich and begged him for protection, and he replied to her: "Sit down there! And nothing else!" After that those women were killed by men who were in the direct service of the accused at battalion headquarters. The defense of the accused that he did not even see those women was totally unfounded because Raicevich was precisely and clearly depicted in all events as a co-perpetrator in the killing of Stana Roganovich and as the person who was in constant and direct contact with the convicted in the capacity of cook at that time.

Count 11—Evidence. Count 11 was proved by headquarters of the Zeta Partisan Detachment order no. 79 of December 10, 1941, sent to the main headquarters for Montenegro and Boka. From this order it an be concluded that Partisans from the Ljeshkopolje Battalion on December 1, 1941, seized and shot Milka Vucinich, and on December 5, 1941, they captured a luxury car from which they seized Tomo Krshikapa and Osman Mandich. During that period the convicted was commandant of the Ljeshkopolje Battalion. The defense of the accused states that he was not present during the permitted arrest and conveyance of Tomo Krshikapa and Osman Mandich. Meanwhile, at that moment he was commandant of the bat talion, and his subordinate staff acted according to his orders and instructions. The same applies for the liquidation of Milka Vucinich, who was seized and killed by his subordinate staff. From the minutes of the hearing of the convicted of May 20, 1942, and minutes of the public trial of June 25 of this year it was determined that Vlado Raicevich, his nephew and assistant, together with Marko Radovich, political commissar, carried out those crimes according to the previous approval of the convicted. It was proved he did not take any steps to save the lives of Tomo Krshikapa and others; on the contrary, he allowed them to be conveyed under guard, mistreated, and killed, which completely coincides with order no. 195 of the main headquarters of the Zeta Partisan Detachment of February 24, 1942, which under point 11 instructed: "If you seize fifth columnists, spies, traitors, and breakers, you don't need to convey them to this headquarters, but on the spot liquidate them. Pay attention especially to the important and well-known traitors.

Learn from them what you can and then send them to this headquarters for further investigation. It is a known fact that Jovo Krshikapa occupied a prominent place in the Montenegrin committee in Cetinje. For that reason he was conveyed to Radovce and from there was told that nothing would happen to him, that headquarters just wanted to gather some data about the forming of the Montenegro state."

The defense of the accused that he was just assigned at headquarters as a secondary person cannot be accepted by the court. Such a subordinate position would not be assigned to the convicted considering his past and in regard to his profession. The accused was for a long time an officer and an educated man. Also, he is highly intelligent. It can be seen from the entire captured archives that he was trusted with the most delicate and most trustworthy assignments that were given to him with complete command of the Ljeshkopolje Battalion. On February 24, 1942 he was designated an advisory member of the Zeta Partisan Detachment, and he had full authority on the territory of the Ljeshkopolje Battalion.

That the convicted served sincerely and with devotion to the Communist terroristic actions in Montenegro is obvious because he did not want to surrender to Nationalist companies even though he saw them on March 2 of this year in Ljeshkopolje. On the contrary, he stayed with the Partisans and served them with devotion. He tried to save the Communist-Partisan situation until March 27, 1942, when he was captured by Nationalist soldiers.

By all this evidence and reasons it has been shown that the verdict is justified and based on the law, and that the convicted in reality carried out innumerable criminal acts, from which the court considered only eleven counts. For each one the death sentence was prescribed.

The crime of the convicted was proved because all acts for which judgment was passed on him were carried out by himself or by associated subordinate or superior staff totally freely and skillfully. His crime is more serious because the convicted was a highly educated person and a high officer of the Yugoslav army in pension and reserve. As such he had to foresee the consequences of his actions because he knew how many innocent victims were suppressed in the July uprising.

Under these existing orders the court cannot acknowledge any alleviating circumstances.

The court on the basis of the findings and according to free conviction, and according to articles 2, 24, and 29, Order No. 14, for the reasons already mentioned, did render that verdict and penalty.

The verdict was performed based on regulations in Order No. 14 of the commandant of the people's liberation army for Montenegro and Hercegovina from April 1, 1942.

Sentenced in Podgorica, the day of July 2, 1942.

Secretary,   President,

V. Perovich   Dr. Il. Vujovich
(signed)   (signed)

Judges:
Bajo Radovich
(signed)
Savo M. Popovich
(signed)
Mitar Mugosha
(signed)
Jovan Kazich
(signed)

Proof of Guilt

in Connection with This Verdict

(five-pointed star)
Headquarters Ljeshkopolje Partisan Battalion
No. 22/February 22, 1942

To Zeta Partisan Detachment

We deliver to you the following report:

1. During the night between January 21 and January 22, 1942, an action at Velje Brdo was carried out. At nine places boulders were heaped up on the road one kilometer in length. Telephone cables were cut along both sides of the road for a length of 500 meters. Demolition of the pavement and the "Brkovich" tunnel was not carried out because Partisans from that area did not permit it. The political commissar, Vojin Dragovich, and Sgt. Mihailo Brnovich were against it. Some Partisans protest that it is easy to order Comrade Blazo Jovanovich to perform actions here because he had moved his family out. The assistant political commissar protested such behavior of Partisans who were sabotaging the carrying out of actions on this terrain. It was not true that he [*Jovanovich*] moved out his family. The Italians burned his home and then an order was issued to move all people out from those homes. The assistant political commissar made a mistake in not taking the names of those who were talking like that. Political Commissar Dragovich said he would complain to headquarters of the "Bijeli Pavle" Detachment and to the headquarters of the Zeta Detachment not to allow actions without our prior knowledge. They sent Ljeshkopolje Partisans here for a trial run, though it was not important to perform such actions on this terrain.

2. Immediately after the requiem, conditions were at least improved on our terrain regarding fifth columnists, but for the most part, conditions remained almost the same.

3. From the seized sheep, according to your order we assigned four to the district committee, four to the headquarters of the Ljeshnjani Battalion, three to the headquarters of the Zeta Battalion, four to the N. L. committee, and one to Radoje Cetkovich. We had to give the owner of the house where headquarters was located one sheep in exchange for 300 kg. of hay to feed the sheep. One sheep was also exchanged for 200 kg. of potatoes. We could not take any sheep from Andrija Perovich without discrediting our headquarters. It is almost a month and a half since our headquarters was placed in Beri. At the beginning we were a burden to his house. He gave us room and board for fifteen days, two liters of milk a day, and did other favors for us. Our commandant was constantly there if he was not out on the terrain. However, on the terrain of Beri and Krusi we could not shelter our heads except as already mentioned. Now he began to reproach us and threatened to break off hospitality very soon. Therefore we were forced to keep one sheep for A. Perovich because he was more a materialist than a sincere helper to us. Therefore please approve that expense. If you cannot, appraise that sheep and let it fall as our burden, and then we'll send you the money for its value. We had almost no fat, so we were forced to butcher eight sterile sheep and rams. We think it was not too much considering that our headquarters has became a food station. There was not one day when fewer than fifteen to twenty people came for lunch or dinner. Comrade Bozovich was convinced in those days, that whatever happens to the main headquarters, almost all burdens fall upon us. It was a mistake to butcher some of the rams, but the political commissar did not know much about it, so it was done that way.

4. With what we have since learned, we consider it a great mistake that we let Chika Begovich go. We did not have any information that he was a spy. Some women even praised him for letting them enter the city when he was with the Italians in Pobrezje, at the entrance to Podgorica. Also, Zecani praised him for doing them many favors. He said he was going to visit his family in Kokoti where they currently live. We did not realize his true intentions.

5. Between the twenty-fourth and twenty-fifth we were preparing to carry out an action against fifth columnists in Donja Gorica. We decided to take the best Partisans from the battalion who would carry on the action without hesitation—blockade the village, arrest five or six of the worst ones or liquidate them, and disarm the rest. During a conference with the political commissar and company commanders, eighty Partisans were designated for that action. That night when they appeared at the assembly point the designated Partisans from Donji Kokoti and Grbavci were not among them. Selected Partisans from designated companies did not come to the meeting place on the designated night because the political commissar from Kokoti

Company and from Grbavci could not carry out the order from headquarters; that it. He could not select trustworthy Partisans to carry out that order. The date for the execution of that action was changed to January 25 and 26 of this year. When the Partisans arrived at the assembly point the assistant of the political commissar and the assistant to the commandant of that battalion made an inspection. They found among the Partisans some older men and some irresolute Partisans. So they decided to postpone the action until they could get more devoted and stronger Partisans to carry out the action.

In Donja Gorica there were thirty-five fifth columnists armed with rifles and two machine guns [*according to their information*]. The battalion did not have more than sixty trustworthy Partisans to carry out that action. From the morning of January 24 to the evening of January 26 the political commissar of that battalion was absent. He and the political commissar of the Ljeshnjani Battalion had been urgently summoned by the Lovcen Detachment to make a plan for carrying out an action in Ljeshnjani Nahi between January 29 and January 30 of this year. To execute that order it was necessary to select fifty of the best Partisans. Later we increased the number to sixty-eight. During the execution of that action some Partisans were not disciplined, and there was also hesitation among some of them.

[*picture*]
Coffins of the six Pavkoviches killed in Zupa Niksic

6. The political commissar regularly held meetings with the political commissars of the companies, not only once a week but several times a week.

7. From our later experiences we concluded that there was a great looseness among the Partisans from that battalion as well as lack of discipline. We cite for you several examples:

a. During the battle at Danilovgrad we issued an order to Partisan companies to be at the really so that if it became necessary they could be sent to positions from which the enemy could be attacked, a platoon from Gornja Gorica refused to obey. Thirteen Partisans from a Toloshi platoon did not reply to the call by company either.

b. On January 31 Vasiljka Mugosha, a teacher in Gornja Gorica, was arrested. She was conveyed to the Komani Bridge by two Partisans. Mugosha's fifth columnists learned of her arrest, ran in their direction and fired upon the escorts, who had to let her go. One of the escorts was the political commissar of the Gorica Company. Partisans who were on the terrain in Donja and Gornja Gorica did not respond to the call to be mobilized against fifth columnists. The Momishko-Toloshka Company did not respond to the call, if they were immediately informed of it.

c. Between January 24 and 25 of this year great hesitation was noticed when action was directed against fifth columnists.

d. During the action in Ljeshnjani Nahi there was indecisiveness and cowardice. It could not be said that we did not work enough at raising the political consciousness of both Partisans and the masses on our terrain. We were in constant contact with the Partisans and we told them innumerable times what Partisan duties were, how discipline would be carried out, and how anyone who was undisciplined would receive the hardest punishment. All of them accepted it. There was an impression that they were indeed a dependable army, but in practice it was totally different.

8. In order to improve bad conditions, we are of the opinion that it is absolutely necessary to liquidate fifth columnists on our terrain. However, because of the quality of our Partisan forces we cannot liquidate the fifth columnists by ourselves. We need half from the other battalions, as was done for the Ljeshnjani Battalion. The fifth columnists create a feeling of hesitation on our terrain as well as in Donja Gorica. We'll try to break them with conference. Comrade Vlado Bozovich has agreed to it. We'll inform you as soon as possible about our results. Last night we held a conference in Gornja Gorica that was partially successful.

9. An action at Velje Brdo was carried out at night between the first and second of this month. On the road to Niksic, boulders were heaped up at fourteen places, and several other places were blocked with logs. About one and a half kilometers of telephone cable were gathered.

Also, we ordered the Grbavci and D. Kokoti companies to perform actions on the road to Cetinje [*Lisica*]. We have not yet received a report about this action. We will send you a report later on.

Forty Partisans took part in the action at V. Brdo.

DEATH TO FASCISM—FREEDOM TO THE PEOPLE!

Political Commissar,	Commandant,
Marko Radovich	Jov. Raicevich
(signed)	(signed)

(five-pointed star)
Headquarters Ljeshkopolje Partisan Battalion
No. 29/February 7, 1942

To Headquarters of Zeta Detachment

On the fourth of this month about nine o'clock in the morning Partisans of our battalion by our order liquidated Jovan M. Raicevich, peasant from Vranici. The liquidation was performed in front of the house of his relatives in Luzanje. During the liquidation he succeeded in throwing two hand grenades and wounding one Partisan. He is now at the outpatient department in Krusi and is out of danger for his life. On the person of the deceased were found documents that proved that he was a dangerous spy and fifth columnist and a person of low character. A photograph of his wife with an Italian Fascist was also found.

On the fifth of this month the wife of the killed man was accompanied by a platoon of Italian soldiers who came to the village of Vranici to her home. She succeeded in taking her furniture from Vranici to Podgorica under Italian protection. On that occasion the village was disturbed. We received a report that Italians were moving toward the villages of Toloshi and Gorica. On account of such reports we immediately took over the position at Zelenika for defense.

We send all matters regarding your headquarters directly to you. It was not our fault that confusion arose regarding what matters should come to main headquarters. Not long ago we sent you a Continental typewriter delivered by Radoje Cetkovich. It looks as if it was delivered to main headquarters. When you get that machine, please acknowledge receipt. In addition we sent you material found at the liquidation of J. Raicevich

DEATH TO FASCISM—FREEDOM TO THE PEOPLE!

Political commissar,   Commandant,
Marko Radovich   Jov. Raicevich
(seal)   (signed)

(five-pointed star)
Headquarters Zeta N. L. Partisan Detachment
No. 142/February 10, 1942

[*picture*]
Corpse of Djoko Radonjich at Radovce

(five-pointed star)
Headquarters Ljeshkopolje-Podgorica Partisan Battalion
Classified no. official/December 14, 1941

To Headquarters of Zeta N. L. Detachment

Herewith is conveyed Zlatija Mirotich, born in Srbija, who was seized in Grbavci at the home of her former husband, Sgt. Mirotich. She is considered to be engaged in espionage. Please verify and act according to your jurisdiction.

P.S. In addition the transcript of her hearing is enclosed.

Commandant,
Jov. Raicevich (signed)

(five-pointed star)
Headquarters Zeta N. L. Partisan Detachment
Classified no. official/December 23, 1941pa

(five-pointed star)
Headquarters Ljeshkopolje-Podgorica Partisan Battalion
Very Confidential no. official/December 14, 1941
Ljeshkopolje

To the Headquarters of Zeta Partisan Detachment

The return of our Partisans from Sandzak created a very unpleasant situation among the people. It was taken advantage of by a higher circle of the Federalist party who are living in Podgorica, whose names are known to that headquarters. That treacherous action momentarily succeeded in Donja Gorica, where Mugosha's company was formed of sixty-eight to seventy men, almost their entire clan. Unfortunately a great number of Mugosha youth in whom there had been great hope have joined that company. The company commander was the old officer Risto Djokov Mugosha, with his assistant Nikola Perov Mugosha. They tried to expand their plan onto other areas of this battalion. Their action was immediately broken. They spread to Beri, though they had no success there and therefore ran away.

Last night I held a conference in Gornja Gorica with their young people as well as Partisan young people from Donja Gorica. Today I met with them again, as well as the rest of the peasants from Donja Gorica. We reached complete harmony. I'll insist on holding further conferences among our tribes. I positively believe that if we use the right tactics we'll convince people to be with us instead of against us. If the latter happens I will not feel guilty of causing it. I repeat, all depends on our tactics with the people.

To kill an unpopular person was improper because it provoked the clan, over seventy people, against us.

According to all evidence this headquarters is active with energy, and as to the purported inactivity, let's not even discuss it, as was mentioned in your order no. 91 of the twelfth of this month and year.

The person designated as the adviser at your headquarters could not be sent there because of illness. He is sick in a village. But even if he was in good health it would be more beneficial for him to remain in this area, considering the situation that has developed. In any case I propose that he remain in the rear, because he could give much more to society as the authority for Zeta than at headquarters there.

Take into consideration his seventy years of age and that he has had to endure war's hardships. I presented my argument to representatives of that headquarters. Referring to this question, please know that it urgently needs to be resolved.

Commandant,
Jov. Raicevich
(signed)

(five-pointed star)
Headquarters Zeta N. L. Partisan Detachment
Class. no. 64/December 18, 1941

To Headquarters Ljeshkopolje Partisan Battalion

We received your report of December 14 of this month. The organization of Mugosha Company on the territory of that battalion does not serve the common interest of the NLM. In that regard we order you to act most energetically, either politicially or physically, to suppress any action before it begins.

Referring to the returning Partisans from Sandzak, this headquarters does not possess a report from any battalion of the Zeta Detachment. As you stated, they created confusion and gave fifth columnists a pretext for action; because of it, such action if it appears on your territory should be completely suppressed.

We agree with your opinion that the advisory member of this headquarters, Mato Raicevich, should remain there until further notice. As to organization, do everything possible on the territory of Ljeshkopolje Battalion and Zeta.

Submit to this headquarters a detailed report about the battle in Ljeshkopolje—how many were killed, wounded, list their names and note how many were interned. Were they Partisans or volunteers?

Inform Comrade Vlado Raicevich to return immediately to this headquarters.

DEATH TO FACISM—FREEDOM TO THE PEOPLE!

For Political Commissar,   Commandant,
(seal)
V. Bozovich   Srd. Novakovich
(signed)   (signed)

(five-pointed star)
Headquarters Ljeshkopolje Partisan Battalion

No. 9/January 16, 1942

To Headquarters Zeta Partisan Detachment

This headquarters delivers to you the following reports:

1. Conferences were held with all companies in the presence of a member of the district committee of CPY Podgorica during the period January 1 to 5, 1942. Present were 466 Partisans, peasants, and peasant women [*65 women*].

2. On January 4 there was an attempted assassination of the fifth columnist Nikola Mugosha in Donja Gorica. Four Partisans took part. Preparations and instructions had been given to kill this scoundrel at any price. The Partisans were indecisive and not committed, conscientious, and responsible enough for such duties. Therefore the attempt failed totally. During the ambush the four Partisans fired their rifles at N. Mugosha from 100 to 150 meters. He fell to the ground right away. The Partisans continued to shoot in his direction as they retreated. During their retreat toward Zelenika, relatives of Nikola Mugosha and others opened fire on the Partisans. Ten of the most loyal Partisans had been selected to liquidate the above-mentioned and other fifth columnists before Christmas Eve. The reason for the failure was investigated.

3. On January 6 a requiem was held for Partisans fallen at Pljevlja as well as for those killed in Ljeshkopolje—Bajo Raicevich and Blazo Mugosha. Despite bad weather a considerable number of people were present. An inspection was made by the commander of the battalion from four Partisan companies that were under arms, and a salute was given to the commandant of your detachment. Those who spoke at the requiem were in the battalion's name, Jovan Raicevich; in the name of the main headquarters and your detachment, Comrade Blazo Jovanovich; in the name of your headquarters and Kuci, Comrade Djoko Mirashevich.

4. The celebration of Christmas Eve was observed in all companies. From Momishko-Toloshka Company, fireworks were set off on Velje Brdo, from Gorica Company on the hill of Zelenika, and from Grbavci Company on the hill above their village. Afterwards all the companies held outdoor parties, at which the significance of Badnje (Christmas) Eve was talked about. There were also prepared amusements such as sketches and recitations, etc.

5. An action was performed on the Podgorica-Cetinje road on the evening of January 10, 1942. Telephone wires were cut and four poles were knocked down. The action covered a distance of 200 meters. Grbavci Partisans were involved in that action.

6. On the eleventh of this month we ordered the commander of the Momishko-Toloshka Company to reconnoiter positions at Velje Brdo for executing an action on that road (demolishing it). When the commander of the aforementioned company came to reconnoiter the terrain, he attended a

Partisan conference at Novo Selo at which was present the political commissar from the Third Battalion of Bijeli Pavle. The aforementioned political commissar explained to the commander of the Momishko-Toloshka Company that a crew of the Third Battalion had tried to demolish that road at Velje Brdo. The enemy had noticed them and showered them with bombs from bomb throwers, wounding four Partisans. Further, the political commissar of the Third Battalion of Bijeli Pavle told our commander that he had consulted with a member of the main headquarters, who told him a professional person would be chosen to demolish the road. For that reason our headquarters abandoned that action.

7. On January 12 thirty-nine banovina sheep were seized at the Krushevac Hospital. Eight sterile ones were butchered. Several Beri peasants asked if they could barter for several sheep for breeding. We think we should satisfy some of their wishes because they do favors for us. Also, we decided to give one of the sheep to a peasant who has done many favors for us. He did not charge for thirty liters of milk that were used by headquarters. Radoje Cetkovich, adviser to Ljeshkopolje Battalion, requested that we give him one or two sheep. We told him we would ask you to make the decision on that matter.

[picture]
A group of Pavkoviches near the Zupa boulders and pits under guard of their relatives, who came with rifles at their shoulders to liberate those horrible crypts of their brothers from criminals.

8. On the twelfth of this month the enemy carried out attacks on the region of Zeta Battalion on Dajbabe, Mahala, and Goricani. As hitherto reported, arrested and conveyed to Podgorica were two monks from Dajbabe, Todor Vujoshevich, a Partisan from Kuci (who was by chance in Dajbabe), and thirty-three Partisans and peasants from Mahala and Goricani. Killed were the commandant of Zeta Battalion, Niko Marash, Partisan Vojo Bozovich, and Partisan Markovich. There were a few wounded. On that occasion the enemy plundered the Dajbabe Monastery and the villages of Mahala and Goricani.

9. A certain number of Podgorica Partisans were placed in various regions of other battalions, because the enemy appeared more frequently against those battalions' regions (especially in Zeta Battalion) and because those Partisans were poorly armed. They were forced to leave those places where they had been previously stationed. Now they are arriving to the region of our battalion and have become our burden. Please solve their relocation problem as you deem most appropriate.

10. Lately we were given information from Partisans of Grbavci and Donja Gorica, who until now had not joined the Partisan ranks. They want some kind of understanding—that is, they have laid down some conditions about command composition. Namely, those from Grbavci insisted on their choice of commander of the company or political commissar as a condition to joining the Partisan ranks. That can be seen from their enclosed letter,

which was given to our commandant. They begged him to forward it to you if we cannot solve the problem. It looks as if Donja Gorica has the same intentions since many among them were misled by Nikola Mugosha and other fifth columnists. We replied via Partisans and categorically rejected it. We don't want to accept their conditions.

We let them know that those who believe they were misled by fifth columnists could join the Partisans ranks if they say they are honest and sincere. They will place themselves at the complete discretion of the main headquarters of the Partisan detachments for Montenegro and Boka. Further, they should honestly acknowledge and expose their intrigues to the peasants and Partisans. We see through their plans and conditions. Despite our widespread conferences they often informed on our position to the occupier and to those who are helping him, steadily showing malice and crime towards the people's struggle. Those who don't participate actively in the people's liberation struggle, who don't help that struggle, and especially those who are consciously undermining the people's struggle should be considered the biggest traitors.

11. We have to deal most energetically with such freaks. Despite it all, we think you should send official word on how honest people should act in these days.

We enclose the names of Partisans who were arrested on December 16 of last year in Donja Gorica and then conveyed from Podgorica to Cetinje to the military court: Stanko Djurov Mugosha, Novica Androv Mugosha, Vaso Perov Mugosha, Mirko Stanov Mugosha, Stojan Stanov Mugosha, Mihailo Blagov Ivezich. The following Partisans and friends are still in Podgorica: Bozo Cirov Milich, Milo Filipov Milich, Vojin Petrov Sharanovich, Ciro Matov Mugosha, Savo Androv Mugosha. The rest of them were released earlier. We feel you should know this when you negotiate with the Italians for a prisoner exchange.

12. According to an agreement with the commandant of your detachment we summoned the Partisan Branislava/Banja M. Vukcevich, an active infantry lieutenant of the former Yugoslav army whom we proposed to be assistant commandant for our battallion. The named reported to our headquarters on the fourteenth of this month and he is now here.

13. This battalion has a very small number of automatic weapons and no machine guns except one out of order, which we are sending to the machine shop for repair. Future battles and actions will require use of a greater number of automatic weapons, especially machine guns. The machine gun model "breda" that Comrade Partisan Vlado Kadovich brought on his return from Pljevlja was left at your headquarters (as can be seen from the enclosed receipt). Please assign that machine gun, with ammunition, ammunition boxes, and cartridges, to this battalion as quickly as possible, and two more if possible to be ordered from the machine gun company. Comrade, the commandant of our battalion possesses only one revolver, and his assistant has none. Please, if possible, send a rifle for each of them and to each two

grenades. Besides that, for the assistant send a revolver with ammunition. Also, please get a pair of binoculars for our commandant.

DEATH TO FASCISM—FREEDOM TO THE PEOPLE!

Political commissar,   Commandant,
Marko Radovich   Jov. Raicevich
(signed)   (signed)

(five-pointed star)
Headquarters Ljeshkopolje Partisan Battalion
Class. no. official/December 23, 1941

To Headquarters Zeta Detachment

Between December 19 and 20, 1941, the action carried out at Velje Brdo had the following results: Partisans of Gorica and Momishko-Toloshka companies, together with Partisans from Novo Selo, Kosovi Lug, Zagoraca, Grba, Klikovaca, and Daljama so damaged an automobile road at two places it was impassable. Also, over a kilometer of the road was blocked by heaped boulders and rocks, with fifty cubic feet of stones or more at some places. Six telegraph poles were sawed off, and wire and cables were torn off as well.

Political Commissar Vojin Dragovich was opposed to keeping Partisans in the field with the aim of firing on the enemy if the enemy appeared. He shared the opinion of Bijeli Pavle that Partisans should not provoke the enemy on that area because of the open space. Therefore the leader for action from our territory abandoned the idea of leaving one Partisan squad to carry out the stated action. Fifty of our Partisans and forty of theirs participated in the action. Our Partisans displayed discipline, especially those who were in Sandzak.

[picture]
The corpse of Marko Vuletich from Kujava, Pavkovici

The Partisans took an oath in the presence of members of battalion head-quarters. So far the oath has been signed by forty in Gorica Company, forty in Donji Kokoti, fifty in Momishko-Toloshka, and twenty-eight in Grbavci. This does not complete the signing of the oath; later on those who did not participate when the oath was taken will sign.

Do Partisans have full rights if they signed the oath, are between 18 and 50 but do not have arms?

In Podgorica prison there are nine Partisans and twenty-two of our good peasant sympathizers. Would you take measures with the Italian authorities for exchanging prisoners?

The Partisans are: Stanko Dj. Mugosha, Vaso P. Mugosha, Stojan S. Mugosha, Ciro M. Mugosha, Filip R. Mugosha, Novica R. Mugosha, Nasto J. Mugosha, Stanko B. Mugosha, Veljko B. Mugosha, and Savo A. Mugosha. The others are: Bozo Dj. Milich, Branko K. Milich, Andro V. Mugosha, Luka J. Mugosha, Stevan K. Mugosha, Bosko S. Mugosha, Mirko S. Mugosha, Stanko S. Mugosha, Nesho A. Mugosha, Kosto N. Mugosha, Ciro P. Mugosha, Milo F. Milich, Stanko P. Mugosha, Musa M. Mugosha, Gligo K. Mugosha, Niko S. Mugosha. It was rumored that they will release all those arrested except ten from Donja Gorica.

[picture]

Corpses of Radonja Miljanov Petrovich from Kuci and Vojin Lukin Jovanovich from Bratonozici

We have great difficulty with lodging our headquarters, which hinders our work. It was impossible to lodge our headquarters on Ljeshkopolje terrain because that terrain was under occupier control. Beri does not allow us to lodge headquarters on their terrain. Currently we are in Krusi, but we are not sure if they will let us stay here much longer. The evacuation of food is partially conveyed. (1) However, we have in front of us the hard question of how to evacuate children, women, and old people with livestock and other food. (2) It is impossible to find lodging for all people from our terrain, which is controlled by the occupier, or to move to another terrain that the occupier does not control. People are in danger every day because the occupier can come on the terrain anytime he chooses to plunder cattle and other items. We don't know how to act properly to save property from the occupier. Therefore we look to you to give us more detailed instructions on how to act on this complicated question.

We think it would be most effective to suppress and destroy fifth columnists in our terrain with several companies from our terrain and others. With them we would blockade the village, destroy the most dangerous, and arrest the others. We look for help also for directives on how to act most efficiently or appropriately.

DEATH TO FASCISM—FREEDOM TO THE PEOPLE!

Political commissar, Commandant,
Marko Radovich Jov. Raicevich
 (signed)
(seal of headquarters of Ljeshkopolje N.L. Battalion with five-pointed star and three dashes under)

(five-pointed star)
Headquarters Ljeshkopolje Partisan Battalion
No. official/December 17, 1941

To Headquarters of Zeta Partisan Detachment

On the sixteenth of this month at six a.m. the enemy, with the strength of three companies armed with rifles, with machine guns, mortars, two tanks, and one armored car, took the Gorica hill by surprise. North of the village Donja Gorica was totally imperiled, while on the east, west, and south the village was surrounded by heavy forces of infantry reinforced by tanks and armored cars. That terrain offers opportunities for applying a multitude of weaponry. So we were deprived of entering into the battle theater with them. Or, better to say, the Partisans would have been deprived of a retreat if they had not set out with an energy that saved them. They retreated toward Zelenika and Beri on the right bank of the Sitnica River. We were surprised because the Italians usually go with several companies toward Kokoti every day.

I was in the village Grbavci at the moment it happened. On the evening of the thirteenth I was supposed to hold a meeting about suppressing fifth-columnist agitation that was undermining our honest struggle. Even if I had been on the spot, our comrades could not have done more except what our comrades did. For my part I commended them for their calmness in that truly ominous moment. The fifth columnists brought Italian troops. We'll find them out. Their punishment has already been pronounced.

We suffered by the enemy's entrance into our territory. Blazo Vidov Mugosha died courageously; ten others were interned in Podgorica because they were unable to retreat. Fifty to sixty people were interned from the company that had been organized on his own by Rista Dj. Mugosha, a former Montenegrin officer.

As I mentioned in the report of the fourteenth of this month and as I am again taking the opportunity to state, those who returned from Sandzak created an unpleasant situation, not only in the Donja Gorica Company but also in other parts of this battalion. The same was happening in Zeta. I think we have to operate with the real facts because the right decision can only come from the right evaluation of the situation.

It is true that in this battalion minds are shaken. We try by all available means to normalize and to calm the companies or independent platoons. The battalion is numerically weak and poorly armed, which brings great difficulties. The men ask, "What will I fight with? Give us arms and then lead us in battle," etc.

For the time being I recommend sparing the battalion from any larger action because the smallest failure could cause a desperate situation that could not ever be restored.

I am mentioning again that the person designated as adviser is ill and in bed in a village. If he recovers I propose that he remain in the rear. He could be useful for agitation, as he is very popular in these areas. In making the decision it should be taken into consideration that he is seventy years old and exhausted by the hardships of war.

(seal)   Commandant,
                                          Jov. Raicevich
                                          (signed)

(five-pointed star)
Headquarters Zeta N. L. Partisan Detachment
No. 114/December 18, 1941

Decision:
    The reply to this act was given by our classified order no. 64 of December 18 of this year. It has to be considered as final and accepted.
DEATH TO FASCISM—FREEDOM TO THE PEOPLE!

For the political commissar,   Commandant,
V. Bozovich   Sr. Novakovich
(signed)   (signed)

(five-pointed star)
Headquarters Ljeshkopolje Partisan Battalion
No. 20/January 23, 1942

To Headquarters Zeta Partisan Detachment

On the twenty-third of this month on the territory of this battalion in Donja Gorica our guard caught Ham Franc from Rasovo [*Bijelo Polje*]. It was known to us that the Italian authority marked the I.D. issued by them to each of our honest men who were in their prison as "suspicious." However, the I.D. issued to Ham Franc by the Italians had nothing written on it. Thus he was suspicious to us, and as such we conveyed him to you for your further investigation.
DEATH TO FASCISM—FREEDOM TO THE PEOPLE!

For the political commissar,   Commandant,

Bran. M. Vukcevich   Jov. Raicevich
(signed)   (signed)

(five-pointed star)
Headquarters Zeta N. L. Partisan Detachment
No. 78/January 25, 1942

For the aforementioned Ham Franc a pass was issued to go to the Partisan command in Lijeva Rijeka, where he has to appear to establish his identity. From there he'll get a new one if he is not marked suspicious.

January 26, 1942   Commandant,
                                      Blaz. Jovanovich
                                      (signed)

[*picture*]
*Mutilated body of Baca Pavlova Vuletica from the village Kujava,
Pavkovici*

(five-pointed star)
Headquarters Ljeshkopolje N. L. Partisan Battalion
No. 56—arch 2, 1942

To Headquarters Zeta N. L. Partisan Detachment
In the Field

By your order and the order of the main headquarters we could not send you the thirty-five Partisan comrades you were seeking because of a new situation in Ljeshnjani Nahi. The Donjo Ljeshnjani Battalion could not do it for the same reason.

Early yesterday morning the enemy with the strength of from two to three battalions advanced on the road toward Gornji Kokoti preceded by strong artillery fire from Podgorica, and they proceeded from there under the protection of their cannons on the left and right and with flame throwers as well as rifles and machine gun fire. The enemy occupied some positions on the territory of Donjo Ljeshnjani Battalion and already today some territory of Gornjo Ljeshnjani Battalion. We don't know which positions were occupied. It looks as if the enemy had already passed Krnicko Zdrijelo's advance guards.

The enemy took over the village of Kornet and burned a number of the houses. The battalion headquarters was evacuated in time. It looks as if the enemy will not hold the occupied positions for long because his goal was to advance toward Rijeka Crnojevia. While passing through Ljeshnjani Nahi the enemy was met with feeble fire. Surprise was possible because resistance had not been planned in advance. According to today's reports the enemy would be allowed to pass through and then be attacked at Carev Laz with stronger forces. Part of our battalion was sent into position in Ljeshnjani Nahi and the rest of the forces were deposed in positions in Zelenika, Cafa, and Beri. The response of the Partisans was poor, especially from the company of Gornja and Donja Gorica, where fifth columnists are strong and motivated. Those who were always ready for fighting are still eager today, and there are few recruits new. All our real fighting forces left Ljeshkopolje because we were afraid that the occupier could seize them and defense would be impossible.

The situation was worse, in Donjo Ljeshnjani Battalion especially among the Vukceviches, because very small numbers appeared to fight. From a reliable source we learned that Niko Milov Vukcevich was in Podgorica [*This is completely untrue*]. We are afraid that a critical situation could come about in Ljeshnjani Nahi. We'll try to use all available means to save the situation.

Comrade Jovan Raicevich, the advisory member of that headquarters, should remain in his position until your further order and until we think he is needed here in this situation.

Let us know immediately what we should do, when and where to send Partisan comrades from Podgorica who are currently in the regions of the battalions of Ljeshkopolje, Zeta, and Donjo Ljeshnjani because earlier orders were not clear. We note that those comrades are basically unarmed.

For the rest we'll submit a report later, and on your part, inform us about conditions on all fronts.

DEATH TO FASCISM—FREEDOM TO THE PEOPLE!

(round seal with five-pointed star)
Ljeshkopolje N. L. Partisan Battalion

Political commissar,   Commandant,
Marko Radovich   Vld. I. Raicevich
(signed)   (signed)

P.S. Inform main headquarters about the aforementioned.

(five-pointed star)
Headquarters Zeta N. L. Partisan Detachment
No. 236—March 5, 1942

To Main Headquarters N. L. Partisan Detachment for Montenegro and Boka

We inform you of the previous order. After acknowledging its contents, return it by our courier.

DEATH TO FASCISM—FREEDOM TO THE PEOPLE!

For political commissar,   For commandant
V. Bozovich   Srd. V. Novakovich
(signed)   (signed)

We were informed that Gornjo Ljeshnjani Battalion gave strong resistance. According to our opinion you should inform battalion headquarters that for the time being they shouldn't make trouble for occupation troops, but let them move freely on the Podgorica-Cetinje Road. Guard villages. If the occupier tries to burn a village, then defend it. Spare people and ammunition. Destroy fifth columnists more severely and effectively.

DEATH TO FASCISM—FREEDOM TO THE PEOPLE!

For Main Headquarters N. L. Partisan Detachment
for Montenegro and Boka,

Milutin (signed)

———

(five-pointed star)
Headquarters Ljeshkopolje N. L. Partisan Battalion
No. 47/February 21, 1942

To Headquarters Zeta N. L. Partisan Detachment
                                                In the Field

Comrade Vladimir Raicevich, after completing rounds and finishing his work in Donjo Ljeshnjani Partisan Battalion, appeared on duty in this headquarters. He took over the duty of battalion commandant from the previous commandant, Comrade Jovan Raicevich. A written report detailing conditions in the Donjo Ljeshnjani Partisan Battalion will be submitted soon.

We send you 34,675 lire confiscated from Stanishich, which was at that headquarters, with notification that we gave 20,000 lire on receipt to Comrade Vaso Zlaticanic for needs of that headquarters. The receipt is enclosed.

For the needs of this battalion headquarters we retain 5,000 lire because we are in short supply of necessities. For Comrade Jovanovich a wolfskin was bought from that money in the amount of 325 lire. Altogether there was 60,000 lire.

Comrade Jovan Raicevich was designated to be an advisory member at that headquarters. He will report for duty soon.

Comrade Pero Raicevich left Podgorica. Today he reported to this headquarters, where he needs to remain as an adviser; as such we recommend him.

For the time being there is nothing new. We'll go on the terrain, and submit the correct report.

We are sending you one Italian rifle no. 5533. Please repair it in our machine shop and return it as soon as possible to this headquarters. Please send a receipt for the money and the rifle.

DEATH TO FASCISM—FREEDOM TO THE PEOPLE!

Political commissar,	Commandant,
Marko Radovich	Vlad. I. Raicevich
(sgined)	(signed)

(five-pointed star)
Headquarters Ljeshkopolje N. L. Partisan Battalion

(On the reverse, the seal with a five-pointed star and on the top an inscription:)

(five-pointed star)
Headquarters Zeta N. L. Partisan Detachment
Classified no. 201/February 24, 1942

[*picture*]
The corpse of Sofija Bojovich

In the Field
March 4, 1942, 4 o'clock

To Headquarters of Zeta N. L. Partisan Detachment

The situation at this battalion the situation is critical. Fifth columnists succeeded in fortifying them selves and organizing in Gornja and Donja Gorica. M. Mugosha, Nikola Mugosha, the brothers Boljevich, and former president Markovich brought an automobile full of weapons and ammunition to distribute to their people. Maj. Dim. Boljevich was designated as assistant to the battalion commandant and M. Mugosha as his adviser. Now they are completely organized and forceful, threatening the worst reprisals. Their list is being completed, and they hold two villages entirely under their control.

They tried in the other villages too, but we were stronger than they and it was more difficult for them; however, they may succeed there as well. The occupier put everything at their disposal. Even five tanks roared through the village, and during the night the occupier burned the bridge on Sitnica/ Komani. We suppose this was to prevent us from entering the village. The fifth columnists had undoubtedly demanded it. Italians are arriving in small groups throughout Ljeshkopolje.

Our strength is too small to do anything about liquidation, especially when they succeed in organizing themselves and the occupier gives them everything they need and even helps them with his forces. With these stronger forces it is very difficult to confront the enemy in Ljeshkopolje. No success there. Our forces are still at the positions of Zelenika, Cafa, and Beri. It is very difficult to shift food back and forth, and we can barely keep them from going to their homes, which would be harmful to us.

We have guards and pistols so as not to be surprised. We have been informed that they will try to penetrate through the village Beri. We'll accept a battle there either with the occupier or with the fifth columnists. During the night we sent stronger squads to control and break up their conferences and meetings. Those traitors distributed wine, tobacco, macaroni, and other items to the people. They told them they would get more on a steady basis. They'll work for the interest of the people. All our efforts and interventions are futile because people act according to blood relationships and are politically unconscious. We try by all means to improve the situation or at least to localize it. We consider that the situation is fast becoming hopeless.

All our men whose lives were in danger escaped. They are in the field now.

From time to time they go and bring back reports about events, as well as food if there is any. We live in the houses of reactionaries of the village Cafa because our main forces are there. There is some opposition but they don't take any measures. For now the situation is as I described it. If something changes I'll inform you right away.

In Ljeshnjani Naji it is not good. The fighting was stopped and the enemy penetrated to Cetinje. What goes for … ? [*original damaged*] Inform us about the news on all fronts especially about Vasojevice because we don't have any information. I just received information that fifth columnists killed Partisan Comrade Milan Djikanovich from ambush today. We'll submit a detailed report later.

Comrade, the adviser of that headquarters, Jovan Raicevich, remains on the terrain and cooperates with us.

DEATH TO FASCISM—FREEDOM TO THE PEOPLE!

Political commissar	Battalion commandant,
on the terrain	Vlad. I. Raicevich
(signed)	(signed)

(Round seal with five-pointed star of headquarters of Ljeshkopolje Battalion)

(five-pointed star)

Headquarters Zeta N. L. Partisan Detachment
No. 246—March 5, 1942

[*picture*]
Graves of the three brothers Sharanovich

(five-pointed star)
Headquarters Zeta N. L. Partisan Detachment
No. 236—March 3, 1942

To Headquarters of Ljeshkopolje Partisan Battalion

We received your two letters: letter no. 56 of March 2 and the letter of March 4.

Don't send us the Partisans we asked for, nor Podgoricani who are currently on the territory of your headquarters. Send only their names and the names of those who are quartering in Zeta to this headquarters.

It is necessary to bind together at the battalions Komani-Zagarci, Ljeshnjani, and Zeta headquarters. If you encounter a situation like today's, rush to help one another. In that regard an order was sent to Ljeshnjani Headquarters, and we'll order Zeta.

As we could see from your letter of the fourth, fifth columnists in Ljeshkopolje are widespread, so you are on the defensive now. If you feel you don't have enough forces to do battle with the fifth columnists in Ljeshkopolje, hold such tactical positions as you can and organize nightly surprise attacks with smaller Partisan units in different directions. These units should be from thirty to forty Partisans. Organize this well, and make a safe retreat to the Sitnica Bridge (near the mill).

We are enclosing two copies verified by this headquarters of order no. 195 of main headquarters of March 2 of this year, one for you and another for the N. L. committee on your territory. Familiarize yourself with its contents and follow them completely.

The main headquarters by their letter no. 134 of March 3 of this year reminded us that while transferring things, food especially was misused, not taking into account for what purpose it was meant. That must stop. Therefore we order you to transmit the contents of the letter to the company commander and platoons as well as to those who escort material intended for headquarters, battalion, detachment, main headquarters, and the N. L. committee. When different items and food are transferred, remeasure them to gather figures that might show shortages, which the escorts should investigate to establish whether there has been abuse. Breakers should be strictly punished. If they continue to keep things for themselves, then the items will not reach those for whom they are intended. Consider this as being serious and urgent.

As to Comrade Jovan Raicevich, let him stay for the time being with that headquarters. We believe he would be more useful there than here.

The fifth columnists from Donja and Gornja Gorica will certainly visit Toloshi and possibly other villages on the territory of that battalion. Organize an ambush for them.

We send you the daily order of Comrade Stalin on the occasion of the twenty-fourth anniversary of the birth of the Red Army.

Up to now we have not received a receipt for 2500 lire. Because you sent the headquarters of the Donjo Ljeshnjani Battalion the same amount, we asked them to send us a receipt.

DEATH TO FASCISM—FREEDOM TO THE PEOPLE!

For political commissar,	For commandant,
V. N. B. (signed)	Srd. Novakovich
	(signed)

P.S. Inform the district committee that it has been given a wooden tub of jam, as has the outpatient department in Krusi. Since the district committee has no people, it is recommended you send some men for it soon because the jam will otherwise spoil. The jam has already been in the Celije Monastery for fourteen days.

For political commissar,	For commandant,
V. N. B.	Srd. Novakovich
(signed)	(signed)

[picture]
The body of Jovica Lazarevich, peasant

(five-pointed star)
Headquarters Piperi N. L. Partisan Battalion
No. classified—arch 18, 1942

To Headquarters of Zeta Detachment

We are sending Milusha Djukich, a spy, to your headquarters. She was going to Podgorica where she meets with Vidak Vukovich even though her movement was forbidden.

The situation here is bad. Mijovici are gathered at Pazarishte—Rogami and Vukovici, too. The fight against bandits is extremely hard because the occupier is very close.

We do not have time to investigate this woman. Investigate her and find out something from her. After that we are of the opinion that you should liquidate her.

Commandant,
Bozo Lazarevich
(signed)

(five-pointed star)
Headquarters Zeta N. L. Partisan Detachment
No. 79/December 10, 1941

To Main Headquarters of N. L. Detachment for Montenegro and Boka

During the night between the twenty-ninth and thirtieth of November of this year, Partisans of the Ljeshkopolje Battalion incapacitated telephone lines on the Podgorica-Cetinje road in two places. Partisans of the same battalion on December 1, 1941, seized the well-known spy Milka Vucinich. On December 5 they also seized a luxurious automobile, from which were grabbed the spies Osman Mandich and Tomo Krshikapa. On December 7 the headquarters of Ljeshkopolje Battalion carried out an action of road demolition at Velje Brdo for a length of 200 to 300 meters. Sixteen telephone poles were sawed, and wire was cut along that length and taken away. Therefore, for the last three days the occupiers hit with cannons and flame throwers from Trijebac and Gorica to Velje Brdo.

Partisans of the "Battalion of 18 October" again demolished a road in Klopot, which had been repaired by the enemy, as well as two places in Pod Krsh. They told us that since November 28 neither truck nor soldier has passed through Bratonozici in the direction from Podgorica to Kolashin. After repeated demolition of the road the Italians have not returned. This happened on December 5.

On December 7 the same Partisans seized three trucks that were going from Lijeva Rijeka toward Podgorica. In the trucks there were 5,000 kilograms of apples, six sacks of dried prunes, twenty-one tubs (wooden) of cheese and jam. That was confiscated and stored in Lutovo. The trucks and groceries were the property of Omer Kasomovich, Shaban Budzovich, and Abid Beshlich, merchants from Bijelo Polje. According to their statement it was going to Podgorica. We ordered all groceries to be transported here except a small quantity. They took the batteries and gasoline out of the trucks and then pulled them to Lutovo.

We have been informed by the Partisans that the following were sentenced to death and shot:

1. Milka Vucinich from Piperi, lived in Podgorica as a member of the Fascist organization and a spy for the occupier. During investigation she stated that she had lived in Italy for thirteen years.

2. Dimitrije Mijatov Bozovich, from Piperi, as a spy, reactionary, and fifth columnist of Yugoslav regimes and now for the occupier. He was a member of a Fascist organization.

During combat in Kuci the following were killed: Milutin Jokanovich, Partisan; Ilija S. Ivanovich, Partisan, 35 years old; Velisha P. Ivanovich, 60 years old, Partisan; Velisha Radovich; and Partisan Milun Ivanovich, member of CPY since its founding. Six Partisans were wounded, three seriously and three lightly. During the bombing an old man, Mileta Milacich, and one girl were killed. When the wife of the killed Milun Ivanovich heard of his death she told her son, "Radivoje, my only son among my seven daughters, go forward in battle with your comrades until victory over the murderers is won." The fatally wounded Milutin Jokanovich shouted to his comrades: "Forward, comrades—we have already broken them. Keep on fighting, all my three sons."

According to your order no. 41 we completely proceeded and have issued orders for actions.

Nineteen Partisans fighters from Sandzak arrived here today. They were sent by their battalion headquarters because they were sick and exhausted. Among them were two had been lightly wounded. They told us the morale of the courageous Partisans was very high. They will succeed in carrying out their assignments. They are well supplied with food because Sandzak accepts them very sympathetically. They said the mobilization of Sandzak men has begun. Many of our Partisans in Sandzak have been showing wonderful courage. The "Battalion of 18 October" had three dead and three lightly wounded, all six from Piperi. This battalion among other items seized three throwers, one heavy machine gun, twelve automatic rifles, and about thirty thousand bullets as well as ammunition for throwers.

DEATH TO FASCISM—FREEDOM TO THE PEOPLE!

Political commissar,   Commandant,
Vlad. I. Raicevich   B. Jovanovich
(signed)   (signed)

[picture]
The corpse of Milic Pavicevich, dragged by his relatives downhill on a sleigh

---

(five-pointed star)
Headquarters Zeta N. L. Partisan Detachment
No. 157/February 14, 1942

To Headquarters Ljeshkopolje N.L. Partisan Battalion

After Comrade Vlado Bozovich returned he submitted his report, and Comrade Vlado Raicevich's report. We found out many omissions had been made by that headquarters.

The comrade political commissar has not been on the terrain for one month, which is a great mistake. Indeed it is not permissible because the political commissar must be with the people most of the time. That is not the reason that "Partisans are no good" because through the actions and steady political activities Partisans become better. The comrade commandant has an incorrect relationship with the assistant of the political commissar, a bad friendship. He ignores his attitude and performance. Keep in mind the members of the headquarters are equal among themselves. They solve the problems all together. Partisans should live with the people, not run away and leave the people to fifth columnists.

Let the Partisans from Donja Gorica return to the peasants and work with them. As far as the occupier is concerned, strengthen the guard. In case of Italian attack, Partisans will evacuate as quickly as possible.

It is a mistake when conferences are held and you don't know about them. Vigilance and inspection of performance and individual movements are prerequsite to thwart their intentions in time. Don't let a hopeless situation develop. That job was for your intelligence, which is still not successful.

As you can see, the situation worsens. In addition to other factors there is your inactivity. It is not enough to hold conferences if you do not care about further developments in the village concerned. On the contrary, after conferences you should control the village and its work and give constant instructions. There is work for everybody if things are in place. It is not true that conferences were "changed," but it is necessary to have them steadily. After a conference it is necessary to inspect, perform action, make it smaller or larger, conduct outdoor parties, amusements, etc. It is necessary to mingle with the people; then the people will like them. Every member of headquarters must be known to all on the terrain.

Further, you misunderstand what was told you regarding questions that battalion headquarters should solve by itself. We wanted to raise the authority of the battalion as one of armed force and give up the habit of looking for higher authority. We cannot punish certain people, but you can according to the severity of guilt. We told the delegation the battalion would decide it. Milo Mugosha was a fifth columnist and a traitor. We did it to let them know they went astray, that a conspiracy of clan relationship is not beneficial. Partisans were right to fire at him; those who defended him committed a fifth-columnist act. Regarding forming a new company, they did not make a mistake if they have enough people. Form a personal command of the company from our trustworthy Partisans. They can give their opinion and proposals, which do not have to be adopted if they are not satisfactory. If they join the Partisans without any reserve then you can select one of them for the command even if he was not a Partisan earlier. Make the decision in the field.

In connection with all omissions we remind our comrade commandant and political commissar.

The commandant of your battalion was designated an adviser to our headquarters. We need him very much while Mato is unable to perform his duty.

Comrade Vlado Raicevich, political commissar of this headquarters, was designated commandant of that battalion. As soon as he receives duty, Comrade Jovan should come on his new job.

We remind you to pay utmost attention to the fact that Pocek came to Podgorica from Niksic to recruit people for fifth-column work. He contacted Vuko Marash among others. Vuko would agree falsely to go together with him to Zeta and to your place. Arrange with Vuko to schedule a conference and to pull out Pocek and some more from Podgorica. Then seize them or use some other way as is most appropriate.

Right away send us the money Comrade Vlado Raicevich had received from Podgorica as well as the other things he received. Send from that money 10,000 lire to Comrade Punisha Zlaticanin in Zeta for acquisition of groceries. Do it in harmony with Vlado.

DEATH TO FASCISM—FREEDOM TO THE PEOPLE!

Political commissar,   Commandant,
V. M.   (seal)   Blaz. Jovanovich
(signed)   (signed)

HELL
or
Communism in Montenegro

[*picture of skull and long bone*]

Volume Number Five
An Edition of *The Voice of Montenegro*
Publisher, Obod—Cetinje

Captured Partisan Men and Women

⌊*with their pictures*⌋
Vojislav N. Rackovich, locksmith from Podgorica.
Vidak Popovich, student from Piperi, assistant political commissar.
Blagota Mugosha, Donja Gorica.
Djordje Djuranovich, student, Jelenak.
Velisava Pavicevich, student in gymnasium seventh class, assistant battalion
    commandant.
Priest Simo Dj. Popovich from Kuci-Medun.
Djordje Vujovich, peasant, community Petrushine.
Dragutin Grozdanich, student in teachers college third class, from Podvrace,
    Shobajici.
Pavle Maksimovich, merchant from Gornja Polje, active Communist.
Milutin Radovich, Gornja Gorica.
Belo Vushurovich.
Vasilije Radovich, peasant from Kosovi Lug.
Ignjat Bijelich, five-time killer from Drobnjaci.
Raspopovich, commandant of the First Strike Partisan Battalion, wounded
    in the head and shoulder.
Aleksa Goshovich, peasant from Kuci.
Vlado J. Ivanovich, adherent of Dragisha Ivanovich.

Commandants of Partisan Battalions

Company Commanders and Their Assistants

[*Twenty-two individuals are listed, including name, age, position, commu-
    nity and district of residence, and current location.*]

[picture]
Pavkoviches carried down the corpses of Miladin S. Stanishich, infantry lieutenant,
and Stevan L. Stanishich.

Political Commissars and Their Assistants

*[Twenty-two individuals are listed, including name, occupation, age, and
community and district.]*

Partisan Judges and Their Assistants

*[Twenty-five individuals are listed, including name, occupation, age, and
community and district.]*

The Executioners and Their Assistants

[Sixteen individuals are listed, including name, occupation, age, and community and district.]

[picture]
Three disinterred corpses (two Kuca and one Bjelopavlic)

Only force, violence and unspeakable terror could unite all men and bring
them to my goal. Neither consideration nor compassion nor mercifulness,
even if they were father or mother, even if it was the wife. Who is not with
me must perish.

Lenin

Results of Partisan Work

Various Communist Verdicts and Crimes

Lazar J. Shepanovich, 32 years old
Captain first class, former adjutant of
Col. Bajo Stanishich
(picture)

Milutin J. Shepanovich
Professor, 28 years old
(picture)

The Shepanovich brothers were nationally conscious. Therefore they could not approve of criminal Partisan activities. They paid for it with their young heads. On March 16, 1942, there came to their house the Partisans Mirko Jovovich, Savo Icevich, and Krsto Raicevich. They took the Shepanoviches away for investigation to Shtitari Headquarters in Kunovo Prisoje. The brothers were killed there and thown one on top of the other in a crevice less than two meters deep, where their corpses were gnawed by foxes and dogs.

Remember these Communist criminals and their protectors for the sake of those dear national victims, whose revenge has not yet been fulfilled.

Mishko-Bozidar M. Vukovich, veterinary student
Born January 21, 1921, in the village Lushac near Berane
[picture]

As a young and nationalistic student, the late Bozidar could not adapt to the destructive, antinational work of the Communists. This was reason enough to condemn him to death. They waited for an opportunity to kill him, but instead they killed his uncle Milutin. This inflamed in Bozidar a hatred and desire for revenge. At the first stage of the formation of the Chetniks in the district of Berane he appeared and took an oath even though he was not yet subject to the draft.

He fought courageously but finally succumbed to his wounds in the presence of his commandant, vojvoda Pavle Djurishich, and his adjutant, Marko Vukovich. His father Mirko was also wounded as he fought alongside him. He stayed with his son until he died. He waited until his last spasm, arranged a farewell for him, left him, and rejoined the Chetniks. The next day the commandant picked twenty Chetniks to carry Mishko and Milisav Jovanovich to Berane for the funeral.

Mishko was a shining example of an ideal nationalist—honest and decent—who lay down his young life for the common good at the dawn of his youth. Besides his parents he was mourned by all those who had met him even once.

Rest in peace and many thanks to young Mishko-Bozidar Vukovich.

Branislav M. Cemovich
Junior sergeant from Berane, 27 years old
[picture]

The oath of the Vinici Company Monastery Chetnik Detachment was taken on January 13, 1942. The headquarters was located at the home of Milovan Seicich from the same village. At the headquarters were Maj. Bozo

Joksimovich, district commandant; Maj. Miomir M. Cemovich, commandant of the Chetnik Monastery Detachment; Savo Otovich, headquarters lieutenant adjutant; Branislav M. Cemovich, junior reserve sergeant, brother of Maj. Cemovich; and Rajko Joksimovich, junior reserve sergeant, brother of Maj. Joksimovich.

Partisans took advantage of the opportunity. About four o'clock in the morning they threw several hand grenades through the window of the house. Then they fired rifles through the doors and windows. Young Branislav guarded his brother Maj. Cemovich with his body. Branislav was hit by a bullet that went into his heart. He fell down dead. On that occasion Maj. Joksimovich was heavily wounded; Lt. Otovich, Rajko Joksimovich, and Maj. Cemovich were lightly wounded.

Branislav Cemovich fell for his Serbian people defending the people's future as well as many of his comrades who shared his views.

Branko J. Milich
Air force pilot from Bjelice, district Cetinje
[picture]

Communist banditry was antithetical to his occupation and education. So he, as well as many thousands of other Montenegrins, lost his young life because he could not renounce his national origin and traditions.

At the beginning of March 1942 he was killed in Gornje Polje near Niksic, by order of the notorious killer and thief Savo Kovacevich-Mizara.

Milija N. Jovich
Gendarme corporal from Hocevine, district Pljevlja
[picture]

He was taken from his home by Zivko Dzuver, a dropout student from the community of Bobovo, district Pljevlja. He was killed in Podborovo, community Precani, district Pljevlja.

Milivoje P. Turcinovich
Former employee of the Ministry of Foreign Affairs
[picture]

He was born in the community of Kocani, district Niksic. On October 3, 1941, there came to his house the Partisan murderers Joko Pavicevich and Janko Burich. They took him to Gornje Polje, killed him, and then threw him into a pit about 50 meters deep.

His young life ended when he was 25 years of age. He was a good nationalist, obedient son, and favorite comrade in his society because he refused to follow the Communist criminal path.

Mitar Radov Vukmanovich
Retired officer from Podgora, Crmnica

[*picture*]

He was killed in front of his house at eight o'clock on the evening of October 18, 1941, by Communists: Zarija Jovetich, Rajko Strahinja, and Savo Dj. Vukmanovich.

An honest man, he was an encumbrance to the atheist evildoers. Like thousands of other Montenegrins, he lost his life, at 56 years of age.

Novo P. Bozovich
Forest ranger from Stijena, Piperi
[*picture*]

On March 21, 1942, he was killed at Kopilje and thrown into a pit 58 meters deep. After fifteen days, Nationalists pulled his corpse from the pit and buried him at the church cemetery at Kopilje. He left behind his wife, three daughters, and one son, of whom the oldest was 13; all were unprovided for.

Jovan Mitrov Raicevich
From the village Vranici, community Ljeshkopolje
[*picture*]

He was killed on February 4, 1942, by order of the commandant of the Ljeshkopolje Battalion, his first cousin, Lt. Col. Jovan Raicevich. He was killed in the village Luzane, from where he was later moved and buried at the church cemetery in Toloshe.

He was a good Nationalist and a champion of peace and order. He paid for this with his head. It was only by chance that his family was not killed that day.

Novo N. Karadzich
Graduate seminary student from Zapala, Lijeva Rijeka
[*picture*]

Until the capitulation of Yugoslavia [*in 1941*] he lived in Metohia as a colonist. Then he came as an immigrant to Lozna, district Bijelo Polje, to his uncle, Milutin Braunovich, to find shelter for himself, his elderly father, mother, wife, and small children.

As he could not be a guest for years, he left to look for a job. First he looked in Bijelo Polje; then he went toward Mojkovac, where he was seized and brutally killed by his first cousin, Partisan Luka Zurich, and his sons.

Lazar K. Vojvodich
Former police employee
[*picture*]

On December 2, 1941, at about nine o'clock there came to the home of Bogdan Ilin Vojvodich Vojin Ivov Vojvodich, Dushan Perov Vojvodich, Milo Jovov Vojvodich (relatives of the victim), and Moashan Savov Djurashevich. Lazar had been invited to dinner by Bogdan. During dinner they told him he had to go with them to the nearest command for some investigation. They escorted him to the notorious Kunovo Prisoje, where he was interrogated and then was illusorily freed. Lazar was escorted to Ceklin by the Partisan Risto Djukanovich from Ulici. Lazar rested in the home of Andrija Pejovich, from where he tried to cover his tracks. According to the evidence he was killed somewhere in Ceklin. His corpse was found and buried in Zabrdje.

Partisans are debauched sons, led by Jewish scoundrels, Tito, Mosha, and other dissemblers. They spit on our national dignity, our past, our faith, and everything we hold sacred. Like ghouls they desecrated the family. They drank the blood of their parents, brothers, and sisters! They concocted "pejor of sins" and spilled blood that fell on their filthy heads. The people had revenge by chasing them like the wild animals they were. There could be no survival for them in Montenegro, Serbia, Hercegovina, and Bosnia. There would be for them no shelter anywhere except in the pits together with their victims.

Abyss and Hell

Persons Killed by the Partisans

[*One hundred sixty individuals are listed, including name, occupation, age, community and district, and how they were killed. Fifteen photographs illustrate the listing, with the following captions.*]

The corpse of Musa Kolakovich, with broken skull, in the grave at Radovce.

Twenty-five coffins of killed Nationalists are lined up in front of the church in Shavnik during a requiem.

The body of Veselin N. Radulovich, technician.

The well in Shavnik into which were thrown the bodies of thirteen Nationalists shot by the Communists.

*The pit in Mackov Do near Radovce, 85 meters deep,
after disinfection.*

The corpse of Veljko Jaukovich, gendarme lieutenant.

*Milena Djurovich stands over the body of her brother, Veljko Djurovich, infantry
lieutenant.*

Burial of the priest Novak Jovanovich.

*The corpse of Milosh Perutovich, second lieutenant of the people's Montenegrin
army.*

The corpse of Mljai B. Tuushunu.

Requiem for the dead at Radovce.

The corpse of Milosava Pekich, peasant from Shavnik.

Coffins of the dead, with their relatives behind.

The body of Nikola Vujovich in a ravine near Radovce.

The bridge at Lever Tara, an architectural masterpiece destroyed by the Partisans

---

Thousands of innocent victims were killed and massacred by the Partisans, thousands of homes were burned, and there were hundreds of millions in damages. Partisans place no more value on these things than a puff of cigarette smoke. The more someone is a bloodsucker, the more one is a worthy comrade.

People Wounded by the Partisans

[Seventy-nine individuals are listed, including name, occupation, age, community and district, and by whom they were wounded. Three pictures accompany the listing, with the following captions.]

The corpse of Mujo Ruzich, forest worker

Victims in coffins

207 rifles, 3 machine guns, 3 automatic rifles, and 1 thrower that Communists Partisans set on fire while leaving Piva.

Burnings, Plunderings, and Extortions

[*Sixty-four individuals are listed, including name, community and district, and the items that were taken, with approximate values.*]

[*picture*]
One of many burned houses

Various Communist Documents

To Regional, District, Local, and Bureau Cells

Through directives, publications and leaflets the provincial committee has pointed out the danger of disloyal and divided people influenced by fifth columnists. It was always pointed out that there could be no hesitation in the struggle against fifth columnists and that there must be constant vigilance against the real enemy. However, among many party members and even in some organizations it turned out that weaknesses of one kind or another prevailed. These weaknesses have caused hesitation and imprudence. Those consequences are especially apparent in the districts of Berane and Andrijevica, where fifth columnists succeeded in putting a great part of the masses under their influence. Armed by the occupier, they were led against Partisans as people who are carrying out a national liberation struggle against her party leaders who are in the forefront of the struggle.

We point out these two districts as examples of the great danger that comes from that side of the people's struggle. However, it does not mean that there is no danger in other places. Today there are signs of less severe examples. If those phenomena are not nipped in the bud they could develop into a danger of wide proportions with catastrophic consequences for the national liberation struggle of our people.

Regarding the international situation, greater class differentiation is coming, and the number of fifth columnists is increasing. Today they are recruiting from the ranks of former Yugoslav officers, higher officials, kulaks, and pensioners who are afraid for their positions. Thus they made an agreement with the occupier to incapacitate and break up the people's struggle. Today their organization and links are obvious. During the struggle the agents of the occupier succeeded by visiting places in Montenegro and Sandzak and uniting all Chetnik elements. Even today, when the German army is suffering defeat after defeat on the eastern front, the internal enemy is more and more unified and coming out more openly. Besides Vasojevici, those Chetnik fifth-columnist elements are appearing more actively in Ljeshnjani and Katuni nahijas, in Ljeshkopolje, Zeta, Piperi, and Grahovo. In the latter two places, radical measures were recently taken to thwart their treacherous intentions.

Until recently those fifth-columnist elements used perfidious methods to deceive the masses and to disunite the people's struggle. For example, "We are ready to fight against the occupier and also against the Communist party as leader." In fact, today he who is against the leadership of the national liberation struggle, our party, seeks to confuse, which is nothing but fifth-columnist work. Furthermore, they proclaimed: "It is necessary to form public courts to judge spies and fifth columnists." or "It is necessary to organize and to select command personnel." However, where our vigilance was weak and where they succeed in creating some strongholds, they enter into open struggle against Partisans and their military leadership. Today in those places they provoke fratricidal conflicts, which was their intended aim (case in point, the Vasojevici).

The duty of the party organizations is to thwart those Chetnik elements in their intentions, to frustrate their contact with the masses, to break their strongholds and any bases they have. During that work you should be careful of digression, either to the right or left, and of opportunism. Never forget the party's role as leader of the struggle that today invites all national elements to take part in the national liberation struggle. All organizations of the conspiracy against the people that are trying to break our struggle must have their impudent helpers eliminated with radical measures and without hesitation.

Therefore, because of all the mistakes made in that area, it is necessary to hit them hard. Today, at this most crucial time, mistakes could have dire consequences. Maximum vigilance must be maintained in the whole effort, both political and military, so as not to be surprised by the fifth columnists. We paid dearly with victims from the ranks of our best fighters (Vasojevici).

Party organizations must prevent all attempts to provoke fratricidal conflicts and must frustrate the enemies of the people's struggle. Without hesitation you must come forward to break up those who are against the people's unity and against today's struggle.

DEATH TO FASCISM—FREEDOM TO THE PEOPLE!

January 27, 1942   Yugoslav Communist Party
                                         Provincial Committee for
                                         Montenegro, Boka, and
                                         Sandzak

(five-pointed star)
Headquarters Zeta N. L. Partisan Detachment
No. 55/January 20, 1942

To Headquarters of Zeta Partisan Battalion

Zeta

We grieve for the losses in the Partisan ranks, especially for your battalion commandant Niko Marash, who joined the ranks of Partisan national liberation without reserve.

Herewith we express our comradely condolences to the headquarters of that battalion for their commandant and other Partisans who died courageously. Our sympathy also to the families of the killed Partisans. In the village of Ponare give a requiem for them and inform us about it. Inform the provincial committee about it also.

Those victims died because of your carelessness. You should have known that after the commandant of our detachment passed through your area the occupier would be informed by agents and fifth columnists, and you should have taken appropriate measures. The commandant warned you to take precautions.

Learn a lesson from this experience. We order you to keep a strong guard against the occupier. In the future any omissions in that regard will be the responsibility of the battalion commandant and political commissar.

Our commandant will send a letter very soon to Zecani concerning that event and the activities of the fifth columnists. On your part, explain to the people that it was the act of the fifth columnists, and harden our ranks against them. It is imperative to destroy the fifth columnists in your region. Don't feel pity and hesitation toward them. Prevent the fifth columnists from departing to Podgorica.

Recently the fifth columnists in Piperi tried to carry out a "putsch" against the national liberation movement. The ringleaders were two active officers and one district mayor—Jovica Boljevich, Savo Dmitrovich, and Milovan Beshich. They were jailed and their movement will be supressed. We mention all who joined the Partisans, not by conviction but rather by fear and by the occupier's directives, and for the occupier's benefit.

Their intrigue began when the occupier tried to break through toward Niksic and when our Partisans carried out the action. The enemy pretended they could demoralize our Partisans. They forgot one detail—our Partisans are ready to fight to the death. This event in Piperi should serve as an example to you and to others. It is necessary to recognize the occupier's methods for breaking the people's unity as well as for evading the struggle against the occupier. The worst people were involved in these antinational activities—rabble such as former Yugoslav officers and noncommissioned officers, with rare exceptions, spies, parasites, and all the reactionaries of Yugoslav regimes, and adherents of Sekula Drljevich, Novica Radovich, and Savo Vuletich. [*To the contrary, Savo Vuletich was the most honest and dignified man ever born in Serbian Sparta-Montenegro. He never collaborated or even came in contact with the occupier.*] Nothing separates them. That band was connected with the band of the traitor Maj. Lashich, who should be liquidated together with the band of the traitor Draza Mihailovich. At the same time we call your attention to the Piperi gang, which supports the spy and traitor Nikola Popovich, lieutenant colonel from Podgorica, former president of that bloody national defense and currently the mayor of that Montenegrin rabble. The designation of Draza Mihailovich to be a minister in the new Yugoslav government-in-exile was proof that the government was turning away from the national struggle. In fact, he never was for it, and Draza remains a traitorous servant of the occupier.

Be vigilant toward those who are coming from Podgorica and are now joining the Partisans.

Send couriers for a heavy machine gun that was designated to you and confirm receipt of the rifles given to you.

Send us immediately part of the 25 percent that belongs to us from the gathered food.

We inform you that our Partisans entered Kolashin and Matashevo and established authority there. We expect that in Lijeva Rijeka our authority will be established by the liquidation of the Lashich band. At Danilovgrad the enemy had heavy losses from our Partisans, but we don't have precise information yet. You will be informed later.

DEATH TO FASCISM—FREEDOM TO THE PEOPLE!

For political commissar,	(seal)	Commandant,
Srd. Novakovich		Blazo Jovanovich
(signed)		(signed)

(five-pointed star)
Headquarters N. L. Zeta Partisan Detachment
No. 120/February 7, 1942

To Comrade Electrin [*pseudonym*] (Dragisha Ivanovich)

Dear Comrade,

It will be necessary to introduce Comrade Milija Lakovich to the situation as soon as he arrives, even though we have already done so. Go into Brskut and Bratonozici and see what the circumstances are, because it looks as if they are not satisfactory. There is some hesitation among them, and it looks as if they have been infiltrated by fifth columnists, who should be cleaned from the Partisan ranks. See to it with Political Commissar Lalovich or his assistant Marovich, depending on which of them is in the field. According to a report from the headquarters of the combined N.L.M. Detachment "Radomir Mitrovich," they seized the wife of Maj. Cadjenovich as a courier for Lashich's band. They'll probably clean it up, but there are some similar incidents of hesitation.

As the Brskucani are related to the Vasojevici it is necessary to hit hard against Lashich's band, as against the traitors. It is vital to emphasize that we do not wage a struggle against the Vasojevici but against traitors. They began the fratricidal conflict by leaning on the occupier. They are responsible to history and to the people for their disgraceful acts.

In addition, the political commissar should solve all questions referring to commandants, political commissars, and their assistants, because it was not done hitherto even though the need was emphasized to them earlier. Also you must tell them to use the seal of the battalion and to keep careful books, which they don't do. See what attitude the battalion commandant has about all that. He might not be the best, as we were informed by the combined detachment. According to the same informant, Batric Markovich has been committing sabotage. That must be stopped. If necessary you should dismiss him from duty because you go there with all rights of this headquarters and also in the name of this headquarters.

See Migo Vrbica and talk with him about all of this and find out whether he knows of the circumstances, which he should. Tell him it is necessary to organize a people's committee if it has not been done yet.

Political commissars must be sure to contribute more by themselves, because their performance has not been satisfactory up to now. Let them give you our last orders to read and see if they have acted accordingly.

Instruct the political commissars how to celebrate February 23, the day of the formation of the Red Army. Explain to them the meaning of that day.

Comrade, do everything to improve any conditions there that are not satisfactory. I would go there to settle things, but I can't because all my political commissars are in the field.

The liquidation of the Lashich band goes slowly. I thought to come there to clean out what is rotten, as well as to liquidate some riffraff.

Comprehend the serious task that is imposed upon you. Let Milija assist you in your duty. Explain everything to him. Remind him to pay attention to the officers and to the assistants of commandants. He'll do it with more authority and knowledge than will Comrade Milovan, although Milovan should help him as needed. Comrade Milija is a member of the CPY. Help him with the headquarters cell.

Before you go on the trip write a long letter about everything, but go right away.

DEATH TO FASCISM—FREEDOM TO THE PEOPLE!

(seal)   Sincere comradely greetings,
                                            Zetin
                                            (signed)
                                            (Blazo Jovanovich)
                                            _____

(five-pointed star)
Headquarters Bratonoshko Brskutski N. L. Partisan Battalion
"18 October"
Brskut, February 7, 1942

To Headquarters of Zeta N. L. Partisan Detachment
                                            wherever

We inform you that I returned from the field on the fourth of this month.
The position the battalion has fallen into is very difficult. The reactionaries
had their heads up, especially in Brskut. A stronger Chetnik organization
is in preparation with Maj. Cadjenovich at the head. They tried to align
themselves with traitors from Matashevo. We succeeded in capturing material about it. In that regard the headquarters of the combined N. L. Partisan
Detachment "Rad. Mitrovich" ordered me to arrest Maj. Cadjenovich and
his close associates. For this task I was assigned the Piperi Company and
some men from the garrison at Lijeva Rijeka.
    We succeeded in arresting Maj. Cadjenovich and seven other fifth colum-
nists (traitors). Only Ivan Jankovich, former lieutenant, escaped. He is in
hiding. Patrols are looking for him. We disarmed three more, among them
Vl. Sekulovich. We will continue further.
    The situation in Brskut is improving. If we had not quickly destroyed
that contagion we could have found ourselves in a hopeless position. We
could not have carried out the order for replacing our comrades in the field
without that action. Now they report to us voluntarily.
    I have not yet been in the terrain at Bratonozici. It looks as if it is not
good at the moment, but we'll try to put things in order there. The orders
have been sent. Batric Markovich refused to execute an order to go on
position. He must be liquidated soon. I will do it if the opportunity arises.
You could do it too if you invite him to headquarters to call him to account.
    The commandant comrade is also unreliable. I think he only theorizes
about tactics. Today he did not dare to move. He agreed with all that I
recommended and demanded.
    As already explained, it is necessary to immediately designate an assistant
to the battalion commandant. Comrade Biljurich is carrying out the duty of
assistant political commissar, though he behaved poorly in Matashevo and
during this action. It was because of his mistake that Jankovich escaped.
He had not prepared a plan for the campaign against the enemy with the
squad leader.

Three days ago two of my relatives were escorted to headquarters in Matashevo. Naturally they were from militia ranks. They had connections with Lashich. I gave my opinion about them and about Cadjenovich's group—they should not be returned to my terrain anymore. Comrades, as you can see, I am determined to liquidate everyone who blocks the road of national liberation and who in the present moment would take up arms against us. If your opinion is asked, I think you would agree with what has been said.

Tomash Stanishich was designated as permanent courier at that headquarters. An order was given to him to answer a call. Enclosed is the act, with the signature of Markovich, who refused to carry out the order.

With comradely greetings,

DEATH TO FASCISM—FREEDOM TO THE PEOPLE!

Brskut, 22.00 hours	Political Commissar
February 7, 1942	Bratonoshko-Brskutski P. Bat.
(seal)	"18 October"
	Veselin Lalovich
	(signed)

(five-pointed star)
Headquarters N. L. Partisan Detachment
No. 140/February 10, 1942

To Headquarters Bratonoshko-Brskutski N. L. Partisan Battalion, "18 October"

We confirm receipt of your report and make reply as follows:

If Batric Markovich is there he must appear at detachment headquarters at once to answer for refusing obedience. Absence will be no excuse.

We totally approve of your actions against fifth columnists and traitors. In that area it is necessary to continue energetically without any hesitation. If there had not been hesitation earlier those traitors would not have been hidden, even temporarily.

Things are not any better in Bratonozici, and similar liquidations need to be carried out. Mobilize enough Partisans for that purpose.

In the name of this headquarters we sent Dragisha Ivanovich to the terrain there to help you out. Although we have informed him about the whole situation, update him about what is going on there and let him know about our orders.

Inform us immediately about the command composition of the companies, especially about political commissars and their assistants. That matter is becoming tense. We gave directives regarding who could be political commissar and assistant.

The comrade commandant should move forward harder against traitors and fifth columnists. We have information he definitely hesitates, which damages the sacred national liberation struggle.

We got angry at Biljurich for his indecisiveness against fifth columnists. We demand from him more decisiveness because the Vasojevici are example enough for us to be against those rascals, that we must be inexorable. If we don't get rid of them they will damage our struggle and kill with beastliness our best sons—real sons of the people.

DEATH TO FASCISM—FREEDOM TO THE PEOPLE!

(seal)   Commandant,
Blazo Jovanovich
(signed)

(five-pointed star)
Headquarters Zeta N. L. Partisan Detachment
No. 140/February 10, 1942

To Comrade Veselin Lalovich, Battalion Political Commissar

First, I reproach you that both you and Mirko left the terrain to the wicked Batric Markovich, who could then act undisturbed. This happened because the conditions were not laid down during the conclusions of the conference. Your return is positive. I congratulate you on your energetic steps. Just continue them. All those arrested should be shot without hesitation.

Immediately choose political commissars and assistants, our men together with Dragisha and Migo. With one order I authorized the political commissar and the assistant to designate those men. Find that order and cite it accordingly.

Arrest the five or six birds in Bratonozici and escort them to us, or to the combined detachment if it is easier for you. Disarm others as you think best. The only way to make good Partisans is through intensive political work among Partisans and among the people in the rear.

Batric should be liquidated. If he has left, let the combined detachment do it. If he is still there, tell him to come here without fail—that matter will be cleared up.

Inform us immediately whom you think should be designated as assistant to the commandant. There is no need to delay. Ask him if he is able and willing to carry out his duty without reserve. I did not want to say anything in that order before you sent me your opinion. Otherwise, Dragisha can make these changes on the terrain in the name of this headquarters and then send to us for approval.

Tell Marko we'll no longer tolerate hesitation. We reproached him in the order to prepare the commandant for harsher measures, and so it should be. Any indecisiveness toward fifth columnists warrants severe retaliation.

In all these things you should be decisive and clever, or shrewd. I hope you'll do it.

With comradely greetings,
Blazo Jovanovich-Zetin
(signed)

(five-pointed star)
Command Post N. L. Partisan Detachment
February 23, 1942
Jablan

To Headquarters of Zeta N. L. Partisan Detachment

wherever

On the twenty-second of this month during the battle that ended unsatisfactorily the positions at Matashevo were captured by Chetniks. Our detachments had retreated toward Kolashin, and a certain number of scaremongers and unthinking Partisans ran away to their homes. They spread panic in the garrison, and others left their positions. So, on the twenty-third of this month at eleven o'clock Lijeva Rijeka was abandoned. Partisans had arrived from the Bratonosko-Brskutski Battalion and the aforementioned Lijeva Rijeka Partisan Company. We retained a small Partisan band of about thirty men and took over the position at Jablan. Almost all these men were from previous assignments, which made it very hard to retain them. The mobilization of the Bratonoshko-Brskutski Battalion as First and Second Battalions Marko Miljanov was ordered. Help was urgently requested and immediate measures in that area were vital.

With the agreement of Comrade Partisan Nasto Dedich a retreat was ordered toward Vjeternik, where they would remain until further notice.

The main headquarters was also informed and asked for immediate help and needed measures. Chetnik bands were appearing even in the village Nozice, where they disarmed several of our comrades.

We urgently ask that you take necessary measures and come to our aid to solve the matter before it takes wider proportions. We are not informed about what is going on toward Kolashin because the Chetniks cut all ties by taking the positions.

DEATH TO FASCISM—FREEDOM TO THE PEOPLE!

(seal)   Post commandant,
                                Mil. Djukich
                                (signed)

(five-pointed star)
Headquarters Zeta N. L. Partisan Detachment
No. 208/February 25, 1942

———————

(five-pointed star)
Headquarters Zeta N. L. Partisan Detachment
No. 195/February 24, 1942

Order No. 3

Headquarters of Zeta N. L. Partisan Detachment to All Battalions

I

Fifth columnists, double agents, traitors, and breakers of unity who are seized should not be escorted to this headquarters. Instead, shoot them on the spot, especially those suspicious persons for whom you don't have proof for liquidation. On their way they could meet our soldiers, who could see their disposition, which could be damaging if submitted to the occupier. Important and well-known traitors could be escorted to this headquarters if some useful information could be obtained by investigation.

II

In all battalions, strike companies should be formed from Partisans in the battalion who would wage decisive battle against fifth columnists and on more dangerous places against the occupier. Those companies, composed of the best Partisans from the battalion, will carry on the battle for national liberation and will with their determination, heroism, and discipline show how it is vital to die for their people and will raise morale and militancy to the highest level. The best and bravest comrade Partisans should be designated to the command posts.

III

The Partisan ranks should be cleaned up. Those who are hesitant, insecure, and unreliable should be eliminated. Their participation in Partisan ranks could be harmful for the militant and disciplined Partisan units. They could bring confusion, panic, and indecisiveness while carrying out actions and thus cause the actions to fail. Those expelled from the Partisan units, as well as those who did not join the Partisans, need to be disarmed and their weapons given to the Partisans.

IV

Vigilance must be maintained during acceptance of Partisans because today the occupier infiltrates traitors and breakers of unity into Partisan ranks in order to disunite our Partisan army from within. They might try to eliminate our eminent fighters from today's struggle. Take into account that Partisans must be meritorious sons of our people; that is, everyone cannot be a Partisan.

V

It has been observed that Partisan comrades and other people as well carry unverified news and false accounts from the fifth columnists. That could be harmful to our national liberation struggle. An end should be put to such actions. Couriers should say nothing to anybody because they take out from headquarters various matters that are confidential. Those who spread news in the above meaning should be strictly punished. All news will be publicized through *The People's Struggle, Movement,* and official news announcements, as well as through our headquarters and national liberation committees. So all matters they need to be familiar with will be delivered to the people. There is no need to gather news from the street, which is harmful and disruptive.

VI

It has been noticed that some Partisans, their families, and others travel without marking on their passes what their purpose is. It happened that some were engaged in prohibited business. Therefore, the business the bearer is traveling on should be indicated on the travel permit. Permits without a seal are void. Therefore all battalion headquarters should issue permits; remote companies could issue blank permits that the company command will fill in and issue with the battalion seal.

VII

Regarding the high prices for some articles, they could be bought at the individual's discretion or at our markets. Most families have little or no money to buy them. Battalion headquarters and the national liberation committees should look into the possibility of determining the price of some articles, especially groceries.

VIII

For the time being the headquarters hospital is located in the Celije Monastery in Piperi. This hospital will treat Partisans from the territory of Bratonozici, Brskut, Kuci, and Piperi. Send wounded and ill Partisans there. The doctor will visit certain persons who are seriously ill in their homes.

IX

Designation as political commissar of this headquarters has been given to Comrade Dragisha Ivanovich, former political commissar of the "Marko Miljanov" Battalion. Former political commissar Comrade Vlado Raicevich was designated as commandant of the Ljeshkopolje-Podgorica Battalion. The former commandant of the latter battalion, Comrade Jovan Raicevich, former lieutenant colonel, was designated an advisory member of this headquarters. Comrade Milija Lakovich, former jurist, was designated political commissar for the "Marko Miljanov" Battalion.

X

This order should be put into effect right away. All battalions will again submit a correct list of how many Partisans they have, how many weapons, what kind of weapons, and how much ammunition.

DEATH TO FASCISM—FREEDOM TO THE PEOPLE!

Ass't. to political commissar,	Commandant,
V. Bozovich (seal)	Blazo Jovanovich
(signed)	(signed)

(five-pointed star)
Headquarters Piperi N. L. Partisan Battalion
No. official—March 2, 1942
Position

Comrade Blazo,
    We are in position to stand guard toward Pelev Brijeg. All during the night, whenever there was a changing of the guard the Chetniks opened fire

with some rifle rounds. Yesterday all the Bratonozici except a small part from Kisjelice and Zminca were at their meeting. They decided not to let any outsiders remain in the tribe. It looks as if there aren't any Partisans in Soshtica, not to mention Bolesestra. This morning the mother of Rajko Sekulich came and told us all the Brskucani had joined the Chetniks. None of the Partisans escaped except those who were with us. All the Milaciches joined the Chetniks. I asked about Dragisha Milacich, and even he had joined the Chetniks. Almost nobody from Bratonozici is with us, only those six Partisans. Even Radule Grujich, political commissar of the cheta, left two days ago. He did not come back, though he was assigned to go on patrol. Thus, from Bratonozici there is not anyone with us except those I have mentioned. The rest of them joined the Chetniks.

Tonight there were five comrades from Lijeva Rijeka at one guard post. During the night they left their sentry post, leaving a letter behind. The letter said they had to go to Lijeve Rijeka. They said they cannot endure any longer, though they remain faithful to the national Partisan army. There they will hide. This incident of their leaving their position and running away had tremendous influence on the morale of their comrades; mistrust somehow appears among them. To tell the truth, some comrades from Piperi are saying they are "plenty dissatisfied," though yesterday nothing was noticeable except a little laxness in discipline.

Blazo, how could I have known that these comrades from Lijeva Rijeka intended to throw themselves over in Stupove and wage battle through the Vasojevici as they did, until now? They went to Lutovo just now when we need to wage battle against Bratonozici. I think there is a plan to throw themselves over to Vasojevici and be helped by our fighters. Right now as I write this letter two Partisans from Lijeva Rijeka came to me and asked me to give them a pass for Kuci. Then they'll throw over for Lijeva Rijeka. They say they have to go because their families suffer from famine and one has to go to Pec as a refugee. I told them, "That is not the Partisan way. You should stay to fight with your comrades and the NLF will take care of your families in Kuci." He says he must go. He was told, "Hand over your weapon and then we'll let you go." Indeed, I'll disarm him and then let him go.

As you can see, there are hesitants among those comrades from Lijeva Rijeka, while there are also excellent comrades. However, with these kind of people and twenty comrades, Ljeshnjani could not accomplish anything in Lutovo because Lutovci would hardly decide to fight against Bratonozici, especially when they are hestitating.

It will be necessary to come for consultation with Mirko. We see how this way we lose even this small force. This is a serious matter, and you need to come before 12 o'clock because the situation is very critical. Morale among the comrades from Piperi is high—excellent behavior. Come.

DEATH TO FASCISM—FREEDOM TO THE PEOPLE!

Best regards,
Voj. Todorovich
(signed)

(five-pointed star)
Headquarters N. L. Partisan Ljeshkopolje Battalion
December 11, 1941

To Headquarters of Zeta Detachment

Dear Comrades,
In the last few days the situation has become critical. After the deserters returned from Sandzak, fifth columnists spread gossip, and they continue their treacherous activities. They had found help from the hesitants. Not too long ago they held a conference at Toloshi, where they refused to recognize Partisan authority. They will not obey them, so they'll carve their own future in the village. Our men were unable to break that conference.

Yesterday at 10:00 a.m. in Donja Gorica, fifth columnists called for a conference. The main initiator was Nikola Mugosha.

After their babbling, the fifth columnists reached a resolution choosing command personnel for their company: Risto Mugosha commander, the representative of Savo Vuletich; Nikola Mugosha assistant, well-known fifth columnist, sergeants Savo Berilaza, police officer, and Krsto Mugosha, former community secretary. Last night they began armed patrols. Before the conference started the Partisans received an order to break it up. When the Partisans saw there could be killings, they left the conference.

After some deserters returned we talked, because it was necessary to explain things to the masses. There was not much success because the fifth columnists were so organized and had begun their destructive activities with open threats. We continue to insist on breaking that band apart, but we have little hope of success.

Since we have such a situation here, we ask you to instruct us immediately what we are supposed to do. We think. Comrade Vlado Raicevich should come to a local conference here and bring detailed instructions.

Mato Raicevich came out from Podgorica and he'll depart there probably tomorrow.

We received by courier a letter of directives, which we shall follow.

DEATH TO FASCISM—FREEDOM TO THE PEOPLE!

Political commissar,   For commandant,
Marko Radovich   Andrija Mugosha

(signed)   (signed)

(five-pointed star)
Headquarters Zeta N. L. Partisan Detachment
No. 91/December 12, 1941

                               1/A

(five-pointed star)
Headquarters N. L. Partisan Radovce Detachment [*there is some*
no position   *confusion in original about the*
March 16, 1942   *sender and recipient*]

To Headquarters of Zeta N. L. Partisan *Battalion*

I confirm receipt of the envelopes and the news. I inform you that the
main headquarters wrote to me about shortages that it called criminal. It is
more than disgraceful that food was depleted and that then appeals were
made to the main headquarters asking for charity when there was a possibility of obtaining food. You don't even have meat. We spent a lot of money
for groceries, and still no food. I told Vlado that you could purchase groceries and livestock from Kuci—do it, because you still have money. Additionally, go pick up those three sheep from Kopilje and butcher them. Leave
only the one that gave birth to a lamb, because she is not for butchering.
If the lamb can survive without the mother butcher her too. Let her remain
but take the ewe in case of need. Referring to this, check the purchase
book.

Write to Vaso Zlaticanic to send purchased groceries to you as quickly
as possible to help you a little. When you receive food, be more thrifty
than you were before. Purchase in time, not late as you have done up to
now. Don't feed anybody extra except couriers. When the food is depleted
it is too late to save. I thought we at least had enough meat for a while.
Take some confiscated grain at Vucinich in Kopilje. Vojo Todorovich will
come there. I told him to do something about it, too. You are showing a
total inability to organize communal feeding. We cannot let this continue.

Liquidate all fifth columnists who are escorted to you, except in some
cases when they are obviously innocent. Don't feed those bitches and don't
wait for their interrogation. We have fondled these fifth columnists for too
long. That vermin must be radically cleared away.

DEATH TO FASCISM—FREEDOM TO THE PEOPLE!

        (seal)   Commandant,
                                         Blazo Jovanovich
                                         (signed)

                           ——————

Main Headquarters N. L. Partisan Detachment for Montenegro and Boka
No. 114/February 2, 1942

To Headquarters of Zeta N. L. Partisan Battalion

We sent you a receipt showing we received the flour sent by Mitar
Popovich, baker from Podgorica. The letter was for him. Please forward it
to him. Today we sent money and instructions to Stevan Radovanovich for
buying grain and other groceries for this headquarters. These were sent via
the headquarters of the Ljeshkopolje N.L. Partisan Battalion. If Comrade
Stevan is still there, let him wait for the money and the letter. Transfer the
grain that was bought as soon as possible.

We'll send you the shutter as soon as it is repaired.

DEATH TO FASCISM—FREEDOM TO THE PEOPLE!

(seal with   For Main Headquarters N. L.
five-pointed star)   Partisan Detachment for
                                    Montenegro and Boka,
                                    Milutin
                                    (signed)

HELL
or
Communism in Montenegro

[*picture of skull and long bone*]

Volume Number Six

An Edition of *The Voice of Montenegro*
Publisher, Obod—Cetinje, 1943

Partisan Justice

(seal)

Up to now the Partisans had worked exactly according to an agreement of Mosha Pijade and other destructive elements from 1935. We have a copy of the original agreement, of which point two says:

"The leadership of the Yugoslav Communist Party consciously acknowledges her role: the communisation of the Balkan Peninsula cannot be achieved until the spine of Serbianism and Orthodoxy is broken, because it is known that these two factors have prevented penetration of the Turks to the west and communism and Austria to the east. We agree to destroy everything that is Serbian and Orthodox, to wipe the terrain clean for the communisation of Yugoslavia and the Balkan Peninsula."

Notification No. 5

Agents and Enemies of the People Sentenced to Death and Killed by Partisan Detachments

Lazar Kalezich, chauffeur from Danilovgrad, spy for all Yugoslav regimes and the Italian occupier.

Vojo Minich, from Danilovgrad, Ljotich's bandit, Yugoslav and Italian spy.

Marko Niklich, from Niksic, king's guard and agent of the occupier. He led Italian army units during the burning of villages around Niksic.

Ruza Bulajich, from Vilusi, Italian spy, in a close relationship with an Italian captain. She had the duty of organizing an intelligence network for the Germans.

Janko Bijelich, from Boka, well-known Austrian, Yugoslav, and now Italian
    agent.
Tedesko, a member of the German intelligence service (Gestapo), assistant
    to the chief of the Gestapo for Boka.
Kosto and Justina, Russian immigrants from Igalo, Italian agents.
Mihailo Popovich, peasant from Mokre Njive (Niksic), Yugoslav and Italian
    agent. He brought Italians to the homes of Djoko Pavicevich and
    Spasoje Burich, plundered them and interned the families.
Vuksan Bulatovich, former Yugoslav policeman from Cerovice (Rovci),
    well-known thug. During the occupation he plundered Partisan ac-
    counts in Trebjesh and Sandzak and spied for the occupier.
Marija Miljevich, from Moraca, an agent of the undemocratic Yugoslav
    regimes, courier for the espionage net of Ljubo Minich, servant for
    whom she carried weapons.
Dushan Delevich, gymnasium student of the sixth grade from Berane, be-
    longed to Ljotich's band. He wore an Italian uniform. Because of him
    twenty-five men were interned.
Tomo Krshikapa, attorney's assistant from Uskoci, faithful collaborator with
    the traitor Sekula Drljevich and proposed ''commissar for building and
    agriculture'' in his [*Drljevich's*] government. He was shot as a traitor
    and fifth columnist.
Dusan Bojanich, peasant from Moraca, agent of the occupier, courier of
    the notorious people's enemy Ljubo Minich.
Milka Vucinich, from Piperi, member of a fascist organization and agent
    of the occupier.
Dimitrije M. Bozovich, peasant from Piperi, Yugoslav and Italian spy,
    well-known reactionary and fifth columnist.
Osman Mandich, vendor from Podgorica, Yugoslav and Italian agent, mem-
    ber of a ''Muslim fascist anticommunist organization'' in Podgorica.
Svetozar Cukalo, from Bukovica (Shavnik), fifth columnist, spy, organizer
    for the Italian delegation, responsible for burning villages, collaborator
    with Minja Karadzich, a spy.
Mijat Zizich, from Miloshevici (Shavnik), spy and fifth columnist.
Radivoje Janjich, from Zabljak, spy and servant of the occupier.
Djuro Miljanich, former Yugoslav policeman, well-known thug, blood-
    sucker, and fifth columnist.
Mirko Pavlovich, from Rijeka Rezevica (Pashtrovici), proprietor and spy,
    who during the July uprising sent many to death and internment.
Kristina Frnovich, from Sveti Stefan, spied on Partisans for the Italians; in
    the village where the Partisans were from she threatened the peasants
    with the occupier's revenge.
Rako Sh. Bajramovich, from Crmnica, informed on the Partisans to the
    Italians. He led the occupier to vulnerable villages and forced peasants
    to take up rifles against the Partisans.

Lazar Vojvodich, from Crmnica, chief "civil commissar" of camp in Klosi, plunderer, an oppressor of internees. He stole prisoners' food, manipulated them through food, and threatened to shoot them if they asked for their rights.

Vasilije Kovijanich, peasant from Moraca, Yugoslav and Italian informer.

Milan V. Bulatovich, president of Kolashin-Rijecinske community, well-known spy and fifth columnist, organizer of the militia (Krilashi).

Mileva Drljevich, mother of the well-known traitor Vuceta Drljevich, Italian commissar in Kolashin. She threw a bomb at the Partisans while they were searching her house.

Ljubo Boskovich, from Orja Luka, fifth columnist, opponent of the national liberation committee and the people's struggle.

Petar Lisenko, Russian immigrant, Italian informer. He was sent by the Italian command to reconnoiter the Kurilo-Zuta Greda road and Partisan strength in that sector.

(five-pointed star)
Main Headquarters N. L. Partisan Detachment for Montenegro and Boka
No. 1–ovember 24, 1941

To Headquarters of Zeta N. L. Partisan Detachment

1. We sent you Alfred Shtokinger, a spy in the Gestapo service. An investigation is in progress against him. Put him in prison and don't under any circumstances let him run away. Until he is there don't let anyone talk with him or interrogate him.

2. We send you a comrade, engineer Milorad Piper, reserve officer and specialist in heavy weapons, to organize training courses on weapon throwers. Train enough men from your detachment, and then send him back to us so we can send him to other detachments for the same purpose.

3. We send Comrade Vaso Raicevich, an attorney, for your disposition. He is from your territory. We don't need to keep him at the main headquarters.

4. Send us immediately a list of all spies who were liquidated on your territory, with annotations similar to our notifications.

5. Send us a list of all Partisans of your detachment, counting those who went to Sandzak, with information about them.

6. If you don't have enough salt, send us the necessary container and we will send you 20 kg.

7. Comrade Savo Brkovich should send an annotated list of the spies liquidated on his territory.

DEATH TO FASCISM—FREEDOM TO THE PEOPLE!

(seal)   For the Main Headquarters,
                                              N. L. Partisan Detachment for
                                              Montenegro and Boka
                                              Milutinovich (signed)

(five-pointed star)
Headquarters Zeta N. L. Partisan Detachment
Classified no. 27–November 28, 1941

We acted accordingly—save for the archives.

November 21, 1941   Commandant,
                                                    B. Jovanovich
                                                    (signed)

———

(five-pointed star)
Headquarters Zeta Partisan Detachment
Classified/December 24, 1941

To Main Headquarters for Montenegro and Boka

We inform you that these persons have been liquidated on this territory.
Their names were not previously recorded in a notification to the main
headquarters.

1. Nikola Radetich, miller from Spuz, who was a spy for the Yugoslav
reactionary and fifth-columnist regimes. He was a steady informant for the
occupier and was armed as a militiaman.

2. Djoko Miranovich, merchant from Spuz, who was a thief, tool and
agent of the Yugoslav governments and now of the occupier too.

3. Dushan Vukicevich, peasant from Sushica, who was a spy for all the
Yugoslav regimes and the occupier as well as an enemy of the people's
unity.

4. Ana Lakich, peasant woman from Martinici, who spied for the occupier
and was in a close relationship with Fascists.

5. Milutin Jocich, secretary of the Jelenak community. He was a spy
during the occupation of 1918 as well as a spy for all the Yugoslav governments and now for the occupier.

6. Savo Pavicevich, teacher from Pavkovici. He was a fifth columnist,
enemy of the national liberation struggle and slanderer of Partisans, and
otherwise a man of low morals.

7. Zarija Bozov Ivanovich, peasant from Vrbica, community of Donjo-
kuci. He was a spy for all the Yugoslav regimes and now for the occupier.

He invited the Kuci peasants to return to their homes, thus deceiving them and betraying them to the occupier. They were either killed or interned. He undermined the people's unity and thwarted them in their struggle against the occupier.

8. Vasilije Bozarich, priest from Piperi, an informer for the occupier and enemy of the people's unity in the struggle against the occupier.

9. Musa Kolakovich, coachman from Podgorica. He was a spy for all the Yugoslav regimes and now for the occupier. During interrogation he uncovered about seventy spies from Podgorica.

10. Andrija Kolakovich, coachman from Podgorica, an informer for the occupier and for all the Yugoslav regimes.

11. Amet Smakovich, grocer from Podgorica, spy for the occupier. During interrogation, like Andrija Kolakovich, he uncovered some agents from Podgorica.

12. Dusan Vukcevich, agent of the Podgorica police, spy for the occupier and a villain.

We believe there will soon be another, similar list.

DEATH TO FASCISM—FREEDOM TO THE PEOPLE!

Political commissar, in the field	Commandant, Blazo Jovanovich (signed)

———

Position
March 10, 1942
at 18.00 hours

To Comrade Blazo Jovanovich, Position

This concerns your order to arrest some men you sent here at a time of uncertainty. You wrote on March 14 of this year to the Strike Company to work and cooperate with the Piperi Battalion. At the same time you ordered some arrests without the battalion's knowledge. On the same day, on the fourteenth of this month, there was a meeting of the battalion bureau with certain members of the rear bureau of the cell, at which I was also present. We discussed the entire political and military situation in the terrain. We agreed who would be liquidated, who disarmed, and who warned. We immediately began to act according to our decisions. However, your order came to Strike Company to be executed without letting anybody know about it. None of us had any proof that some of the arrested were fifth columnists and so should be liquidated. We don't count Vujadin Cetkovich as a fifth columnist at all. He is a lazy man who could contribute much more, but with such lack of evidence we do not disarm him, much less liquidate him. He was even a platoon leader of the Crnci Company.

As for Tomash Milunovich, Seocani intervened, and I as well as the battalion bureau agreed. He is politically absolutely harmless. If he did try something destructive, he didn't accomplish it, or there is no proof of it.

The brothers of Jovica Boljevich are very quiet men, and there is no reason to arrest them, even less for their liquidation, unless we liquidate them simply because they are the brothers of Jovica Boljevich.

Regarding Niko and Ivan Vukasinovich, the battalion bureau intention was to disarm them. During their interrogation we came to the conclusion there was not even reason to disarm them. Before their interrogations (I think all of them), I was in the main headquarters, and I conversed with Comrade Milutin about what should be done with these men. We agreed, for all of them, that if there is proof that any of them acted as fifth columnists they should be liquidated, and the rest of them released to return to their homes. He told me to go and interrogate them, then to consult with the detachment headquarters about what measures should be taken. After interrogation we concluded that Vujadin Cetkovich did not deserve to be disarmed. We told him his case would be solved at once with the accord of the company command and battalion headquarters.

Niko Vukasinovich, former policeman, behaved well in Sandzak and also during the arrests of fifth columnists in Brskut. He said that he expected to be designated to the Strike Company. Ivan Vukasinovich did not act villainously. Rather, he was very lenient and not devoted enough.

In connection with the above, we decided to put their arms at the disposal of the Crnci Company command. When the command deems it appropriate, the arms can be returned. Also, we decided the arms of Tomash Milunovich should be put at the disposal of Ziva Company command, and when the command believes he deserves to get the weapons back, let it be done. When we let Tomash go home we made two Seocani guarantee his behavior. They'll watch what he does. If they notice anything they are obliged to inform us of it. Indeed, they'll take personal responsibility for him.

Blazo and Rako Cetkovich were liquidated on the spot, and Milo Cetkovich will be liquidated at detachment headquarters. All weapons the Strike Company command delivered there should be returned here without any questions, along with the ammunition. It would be inappropriate and wrong not to act accordingly, because people could think that the detachment headquarters lied to them.

I got the impression that the command of the Strike Company imagines it's their role to make everyone afraid of them.

As far as the Mijoviches are concerned, they are gathered around Pazarishte. They have with them one machine gun, and they have fun with it. Among them there is some tendency to return to their homes. We'll try by all means to separate those who did not yet go too far. If Ivan were not among them, everything would go more smoothly.

This part of the Strike Company we cannot send there, because we have to chase out the Mijovich guards from Bregovi and make life unbearable for the Pazarishte.

Comrade Milutin told me that Peko and Bajo wrote him they will send you ninety sheep. Milutin says he'll order you to keep all of them if you don't go into action right away. If you go, send about fifty of them to the Bijeli Pavle Detachment.

Write to us about your meat reserves.

DEATH TO FASCISM—FREEDOM TO THE PEOPLE!

Savo K. Brkovich
(signed)

From the above document it can be seen that at least one member of that criminal band, Savo Brkovich, sometimes had bright hours, even though on the other hand he sometimes drank human blood.

The Justice of the People's Court

[abbreviated]

Prosecutor's Office
at People's Defense Court
December 18, 1942
Podgorica

Bill of Indictment Presented to the People's Defense Court
Podgorica

On the basis of the prosecutor's office at the People's Defense Court, articles 18, 19, and 20, submits to the bureau of the People's Defense Court charges against:
1. Jovan Celebich, born in Shtitari, peasant.
2. Djuro Vujovich, born in Shtitari, peasant, 26 years old.
3. Krsto Djurovich, born in Orahe, peasant, 36 years old.
4. Ilija Vujovich, born in Shtitari, peasant, 21 years old.
5. Blagota Popovich, born in Shtitari, peasant, 26 years old.
6. Krsto Popovich, born in Shtitari, peasant, 32 years old.
7. Milutin Vukicevich, born in Releza, peasant, 24 years old.
8. Vladimir Vukicevich, born in Cepetici, student, 20 years old.
9. Vaso Vujovich, born in Shtitari, student, 23 years old.
10. Vukota Vujovich, born in Shtitari, peasant, 32 years old.

11. Jovan Popovich, born in Shtitari, teacher, 23 years old.
12. Bosko Celebich, born in Shtitari, stonemason, 63 years old.
13. Radovan Vukicevich, born in Releza, peasant, 17 years old.
14. Vidak Vukicevich, born in Releza, peasant, 38 years old.
15. Savo Vukicevich, born in Cepetici, peasant, 49 years old.
16. Mitar Vukicevich, born in Djalci, peasant, 54 years old.
17. Nikola Celebich, born in Shtitari, peasant, 30 years old.
18. Djuro Celebich, born in Shtitari, peasant, 44 years old.
19. Nikola Vujovich, born in Shtitari, peasant, 30 years old.
20. Mirko Vukicevich, born in Cepetici, law clerk, 29 years old.
21. Zlatana Vukicevich, born in Releza, hostess, 19 years old.
22. Vladimir Pejovich, born in Orahe, former junior sergeant, 22 years old.
23. Nikola Stojanovich, born in Orahe, peasant, 28 years old.
24. Vidak Stojanovich, born in Orahe, peasant, 37 years old.

They are accused on the following counts:

[*I in original very general—not translated here*]

[*picture*]
Capt. Todor Ivanovich on catafalque

II

The accused Jovan-Joko Celebich, Djuro Vujovich, Mirko Vukicevich, Milutin Vukicevich, Vladimir Vukicevich, Jovan S. Popovich, Radovan S. Vukicevich, Savo Vukicevich, Mitar Vukicevich, and Vidak Vukicevich are accused of the following:
On February 18, 1942, Josho T. Bogojevich from Staniseljici at the headquarters of the [*Gornjo*] Ljeshnjani Partisan Battalion in Releza. Josho jumped through the window of the room where he was imprisoned in an attempt to save his life. This constitutes a criminal act on the part of the accused under Article 1, Paragraph 167 concerning protection of public security and order and in connection with Article 2, Regulation 1 and 3, Paragraph 167, Point 2 of criminal law.

[*picture*]
First man descended into the pit to help pull out bodies

III

The accused Joko P. Celebich, Djuro Vujovich, Jovan-Joko S. Popovich, Nikola M. Celebich, and Vaso Vujovich in February or March of 1942 took away from the Lovcen Detachment Blazo Crnojevich, Luka Petrovich, Milo

S. Popovich, Djuro V. Popovich, and Filip J. Popovich, all from the village Gradjane (Crmnica). They were all killed by rifle fire and their belongings were taken.

IV

The accused Ilija Vujovich, Blagota S. Popovich, Jovan S. Popovich, Nikola Celebich, Djuro Vujovich, Nikola Vujovich, and Vladimir Pejovich took part in a Partisan action with other Partisans between January 29 and 30, 1942, against the Donjo-Ljeshnjani National Battalion, on the positions Brezine-Donji [*incorrect*] Gornji Kokoti-Krnjicka Komenica. Two Nationalists were killed there, Djuran Kazich and Vidak Brnovich, both from Brezine. Nikola Brnovich was arrested and taken away to the headquarters of the Lovcen Detachment in Kunovo Prisoje. Later Nikola was released.

[*picture*]
Majo Miloshevich in the ravine

V

At the end of February or the beginning of March the accused Krsto M. Djurovich, Nikola Stojanovich, and Vidak Stojanovich killed the priest Petar Vujovich from Dobrska Zupa.

VI

The accused Djuro Vujovich with other unknown Partisans brutally tortured and killed Lt. Col. Niko Jovovich.

VII

The accused Nikola Celebich and Vaso M. Vujovich sometime in March 1942, by order of the headquarters of the Lovcen Partisan Detachment in Kunovo Prisoje, took away Cpt. Lazar Shcepanovich and Prof. Milutin Shcepanovich, brothers from Zagarac. They were killed by rifle bullets and their bodies were thrown into a pit.

VIII

The accused Nikola Celebich, Djuro Celebich, and Vladimir Pejovich fought against National units until July 16, 1942, when they were captured by the Nationalists.

These defendants are bound over for trial to the People's Defense Court to answer these charges. There should be present all the defendants and these witnesses: Vaso Radunovich from Releza; Bosko R. Bogojevich from

Staniseljici; Milovan Kazich, Jovan Kazich, and Nikola Brnovich from Brezine; Ilija L. Vujovich from Mikulici, Djuro Pejovich from Orahe; and Nikola R. Vujovich, Bozo A. Vujovich, Milica Djurova Celebich, Ilija Perishich, Milivoje S. Celebich, Milica Nikolina Celebich, Vaso Celebich, Jova Boskova Celebich, and Djuro Vasov Celebich, all from the village Shtitari.

At the main trial excerpts will be read from the testimony of the witness Talaja Antonija given April 15, 1942, and a report from the clerk of the court archives shall be procured for all the defendants.

Justification:

I

By investigation it was proved that all the accused belonged to the Communist-Partisan movement.

II

On February 16, 1942 Josho T. Bogojevich from Staniselici was deprived of life at the headquarters of the Ljeshnjani Partisan Battalion in Releza. (The participants in the crime were named in count no. 2.)

III

At the beginning of 1942, by order from the headquarters of the Lovcen Partisan Detachment in Kunovo Prisoje, five men were abducted: Blazo Crnojevich, Luka Petrovich, Milo S. Popovich, Djuro V. Popovich, and Filip J. Popovich, all from the village Gradjane (Crmnica). They were brought to Partisan headquarters in Kunovo Prisoje and liquidated. (The participants in the crime were named in count no. 3.)

[picture]
Descending into the pit Markov Do near Radovce, 85 meters deep

IV

Between January 29 and 30 some of the accused took part in a punitive expedition against the Donjo-Ljeshnjani National Battalion. Nationalists Djuran Kazich and Vidak Brnovich were killed, Jovan F. Kazich was wounded. Al came from the village of Brezine. (The participants in the crime were named in count no. 4.)

V

At the end of February or the beginning of March 1942 Father Petar Vujovich from Dobrska Zupa was brought to the Lovcen Partisan Detachment in Kunovo Prisoje. He was tortured and liquidated near the village Orahe. (The participants in the crime were named in count no. 5.)

VI

At the end of February or the beginning of March 1942 Lt. Col. Niko Jovovich was escorted to Lovcen Partisan Headquarters in Kunovo Prisoje, where he was sentenced to death and executed. (The participants in the crime were named in count no. 6.)

VII

In March 1942 the brothers Lazar and Milutin Shcepanovich were seized and escorted to Lovcen Partisan Headquarters in Kunovo Prisoje. They were liquidated there and thrown into a pit. (The participants in the crime were named in count no. 7.)

VIII

The accused Nikola and Djuro Celebich remained with the Partisan units until July 16, 1942, when they were captured by the Nationalist army. Also, the accused Vladimir Pejovich fought against Vasojevici National forces at the beginning of 1942.

[picture]
The corpse of Olga Raicevich, cook at Mosha's headquarters in Radovce

Those actions and those criminally responsible for them were established by the defendants' admitted guilt in participating in the armed struggle against the Nationalists during which many Nationalists were killed.

Thus the charges are based on the law.

Prosecutor of the People's
Defense Court
Bogdan Shoshkich (signed)

Verdict Pronounced in the Name of the People:

[Biographical data about the accused not included here]

The accused were found guilty of the following:

1. The accused Djuro Vujovich joined the Partisans after the uprising of July 13, 1941. He participated in the killing of Josho Bogojevich at the headquarters of the Gornjo Ljeshnjani Battalion. He participated in the liquidations of Blazo Crnojevich, Luka Petrovich, Milo S. Popovich, Djuro V. Popovich, and Filip J. Popovich, all from the village Gradjane (Crmnica). Also, he took part in the liquidation of Lt. Col. Niko Jovovich.

2. The accused Vaso Vujovich was an active Partisan since July 13, 1941. He took part in the liquidations of five men from Gradjane (Crmnica), whose names have already been mentioned. Also, he participated in the liquidations of the brothers Shcepanovich.

3. The accused Jovan Popovich was active in the Partisan movement since July 13, 1941. He took part in the punitive expedition against Donjo-Ljeshnjani Nationalists between January 29 and 30, 1942. Also, he participated in the liquidation of Josho T. Bogojevich, as well as in the liquidations of five men from Gradjane (Crmnica).

4. The accused Nikola Celebich was an active member of Partisan units since July 13, 1941. He participated in the liquidation of five men from Gradjane (Crmnica) and of the two brothers Lazar and Milutin Shcepanovich from Zagarac.

5. The accused Jovan (Joko) Celebich was active in Partisan units since July 13, 1941. He took part in the liquidation of Josho Bogojevich from Staniselici.

6. The accused Vidak Vujovich was active in Communist-Partisan units since July 13, 1941. He took part in the liquidation of Josho Bogojevich on February 18, 1942.

7. The accused Krsto Djurovich was active in the Partisan movement since July 13, 1942. He took part in the liquidation of the priest Petar Vujovich.

8. and 9. The accused Ilija Vujovich and Blagota Popovich were active in the Partisan movement since July 13, 1941. They organized and took part in the action against the Donjo-Ljeshnjani Nationalists between January 29 and 30, 1942, when the two Nationalists Djuran Kazich and Vidak Brnovich, both from Brezine, were killed. They also attempted to kill Jovan F. Kazich from Brezine.

10. missing in original.

The corpse of Milovan Beshich, with broken arms
and eyes gouged out, in Radovce

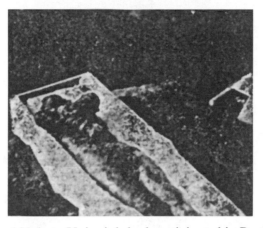

11. The accused Vukota Vujovich had participated in Partisan units since July 13, 1941. He was political commissar of the Shtitari Partisan-Communist Company. In March 1942 on the way to Vasojevici he was retained at Bioci and Rijeka Piperi, where he consulted with Blazo Jovanovich and other Communist leaders.

12. and 13. The accused Krsto Popovich and Milutin Vukicevich were active Partisans since July 13, 1941. They blindly executed all Partisan orders.

14. and 15. The accused Savo Vukicevich and Mitar Vukicevich were active Partisans since July 13, 1941. When Josho Bogojevich tried to escape, Mitar tried to catch and kill him even though Josho was unarmed at the time.

16. The accused Djuro Celebich was an active Partisan since July 13, 1941. Between January 29 and 30, 1942, he took part in the punitive expedition against Donjo-Ljeshnjani Nationalists, when two Nationalists were killed.

17. The accused Nikola Vujovich was active in the Communist-Partisan movement. Between January 29 and 30, 1942, he took part with other designated Partisans in the action against Donjo-Ljeshnjani Nationalists.

18. The accused Mirko Vukicevich belonged to the Communist-Partisan movement. He was political commissar of the Progonovici Company.

19. The accused Radovan Vukicevich was also an active member of the Partisan movement. On February 18, 1942, he helped catch Josho Bogojevich when he ran away, and collaborated in depriving Josho of his life.

[picture]
Commandant of Italian army above pit in Kopilje, 58 meters deep.

[*picture*]
The body of Gaja Pekich, an employee of the district office.

[*picture*]
The corpse of Jovica Boljevich, captain.

[*picture*]
For each recovered corpse of a Nationalist the headquarters of the National army gave a metal coffin.

On the basis of the above expositions and in connection with Paragraph 70 of Criminal Law and Article 11 as noted earlier, the People's Defense Court rules as follows:

Sentence:

The accused Djuro Jokov Vujovich, Vaso Miloshev Vujovich, Jovan Savov Popovich, Nikola Ilijin Celebich, and Jovan Petrov Celebich are sentenced to the death penalty with permanent loss of their civil rights.

The accused Krsto Markov Djurovich, Vukota Jokov Vujovich, Vidak Nikolin Vukicevich, Djuro Jokov Celebich, and Mirko Petrov Vukicevich are sentenced to twenty years imprisonment, counting from the day of their arrests, with permanent loss of their rights.

The accused Blagota Savov Popovich, Krsto Savov Popovich, Radovan Nikolin Vukicevich, Mitar Jovanov Vukicevich, and Nikola Markov Vujovich are sentenced to ten years' imprisonment, counting from the first day of their arrests, with permanent loss of rights except for the minor Radovan Vukicevich.

The accused Ilija Markov Vujovich and Milutin Nikolin Vukicevich are sentenced to five years' imprisonment, counting from the day of their arrests, with loss of rights for three years, to be counted from the first day of their arrests or parole. The accused Savo Vasov Vukicevich is sentenced to two years' imprisonment with loss of rights for one year from the first day that he begins serving the sentence. The execution of the sentence would be counted from when he was deprived of freedom.

On the basis of articles 32 and 36, by decree of the People's Defense Court, the following defendants were acquitted: Vladimir Vukicevich, Bosko Celebich, Vidak Stojanovich, and Zlatana Vukicevich. They are to be freed immediately.

Reasons:

The accused admitted their guilt during the court trial, and the witnesses attested to undeniable facts upon which the court made justified decisions.

On the basis of the expositions in accordance with Article 1, the People's Defense Court decrees judgment be passed on them as disposed.

The People's Defense Court in Podgorica

January 16, 1943

Secretary,   President of court,
Z. Babich (signed)   Dr. Il. Vujovich (signed)

Judges:
V. Vukasinovich
(signed)
J. Piletich
(signed)
I. Vuksanovich
(signed)
M. Burich
(signed)

The verdict was executed according to Article 34, by decree of the People's Defense Court

    (seal)   President of court,
                                           D. Il. Vujovich
                                           (signed)

To the Partisans every honest man who carried in his heart love of the fatherland, faith, and nation was a fifth columnist, traitor, and spy. For them only a bloodsucker and real traitor was a good man.

HELL
or
Communism in Montenegro

[*picture of skull and long bone*]

Volume Number Seven

An Edition of *The Voice of Montenegro*
Publisher, Obod—Cetinje, 1943

Partisan Fighters From the Beginning of the War July 13, 1941 and Teachers

[*Page 3: Pictures of five Communists, with their occupation and where and when they were killed.*
Pages 4 and 5: Pictures of twelve captured male and female Partisans, with their occupation and place of birth.
Page 6: Names of twenty-three Partisan battalion commandants, company commanders, and assistants. Illustrated by one photograph.
Page 7: Names of eighteen political commissars and assistants, with occupation and place of birth. Illustrated by a photograph of the positions in which five Nationalists were found in Zupa Nikshicka.
Page 8: Names of twenty-three Partisan judges and assistants, with their occupation, age, and place of residence. Names of fourteen executioners and assistants, with their occupation, age, and place of residence.]

The Results of Partisan Activities

Various Communist Verdicts and Crimes

Vasilije N. Shekarich
reserve captain first class from Pilatovci
[*picture*]

His work aroused Partisan anger. They decided to liquidate him, as they did many others. To his house came Djoko Shekarich and Aleksa Aleksich, Partisans from the Strike force from Vucji Do. They took him to their headquarters, where he was mistreated and then killed by seventeen rifle bullets.

179

Milija M. Sredojevich
peasant from the community Velika Zupa, district Mileshevo
[picture]

This poor, honest man was an obstacle to the Partisan criminal activities. He did not take part in their work. He was killed in his twenty-ninth year, leaving his parents and three small children without their breadwinner. He was a laborer with a small estate.

The bloodthirsty Partisans had not yet completed their inhuman mission. Every patriot, every Serb loyal to Njegosh's fatherland was obliged to rise up against those troublemakers and traitors to the fatherland, against the murderous, vultures, and renegades of their people, against the shameful mercenaries of Tito, Mosha, and the other self-serving rabble.

Rise up, everyone who loves his name, his people, his past, and the future. Rise up, everyone who crosses himself with the holy cross of his ancestors. Spit at all prejudices, at all the small malices of the individual, at all lies served up by some usurper leaders.

Rise up! Save yourself and your family!

Savo Gazivoda
merchant from Rijeka Crnojevica [picture]

Great misfortune befell him and many other Rijecani during the uprising. He was interned and his good estate was completely destroyed. After his return from imprisonment he started to work all over again to earn food for his four children, his wife, and himself.

The Communists did not like his industriousness, because their ideology rests on the principle, "What is worse will be better for them." For that reason and also probably for plunder, because he possessed some amount of money, the Communists seized and took from him everything they could and then killed him.

Today his widow and children live and suffer with scarcely anything in Rijeka Crnojevica.

Milusha S. Rashovich
born 1912
[picture]

A widow without property, she came to her father, Savo Djukich, in the village Zavala, Piperi to survive famine. She did not get along with the Communists. Therefore she was caught and killed, as were many others who could not get along with them and who were within their reach.

Milo R. Cetkovich
peasant, 36 years old [picture]

Blazo R. Cetkovich
artillery sergeant, 32 years old
[picture]

Their brother Milisav states:

Early in the morning of March 15, 1942, Partisans came and deprived them of their liberty, along with my mother. Not long after on that same morning near my home the Partisans killed my brother Blazo Rad. Cetkovich, and on the same spot was killed my mother Raka. They treated them like dead animals and buried them in front of the house in a garden bed.

The same day my oldest brother, Milo Rad. Cetkovich, was taken to the notorious headquarters at Radovce. On March 25, 1942, Milo was tied up, tortured, and finally killed most brutally. He was stabbed with knives and beaten black and blue. His head was so bludgeoned that every bone was broken and his skull seemed soft.

The Partisan leaders were commander of the Partisan Strike Company Milo Matich, peasant, Piperi; political commissar Radosh P. Ljumovich, employee of the district court in Danilovgrad; and assistant political commissar Blazo R. Dzankich, peasant from Piperi.

Vladimir L. Lucich
from the village Osredak, community Donja Moraca, 26 years old
[picture]

He and his 63-year-old father were taken from their home by the Partisans Strahimir A. Miloshevich, Velimir G. Mashkovich, Vladimir M. Simonovich, airman second lieutenant, Milovan M. Rakocevich, and four Partisans from the Lovcen Detachment.

On March 12, 1942, they were killed near the Moracha Monastery. Their heads were crushed almost beyond recognition.

Young Vladimir gave his life for his nation and his faith, trying to organize a national movement in his community against the notorious Communists.

Savo M. Ivanovich
from Gradjani
[picture]

In 1919 he moved with his family to Belgrade, where he completed elementary school, four years of gymnasium, and agricultural school.

For the draft call he returned to his birthplace, where momentous events were taking place.

He disagreed with the ignominious Communists. (The Partisans seized him together with some other Gradjani, known from the previous volume, and took them to the notorious Kunovo Prisoje, where he was killed.)

Miladin R. Perovich
born 1920 in the village Stubica, community Pjeshivci [picture]

He refused many times to join the Partisans. He was seized by Partisans near his home and taken away in the village Meoci Lastva Cevska. He was tortured there and killed in a beastly way on April 16, 1942.

Milivoje L. Raicevich
infantry sergeant from Rozaji
community Vrazegrmci, district Danilovgrad [picture]

After all those events, worse and worse days arrived, the most terrible episode in our history: Brother kills brother, godfather kills godfather, the father his son and vice versa. A red plague spread, and the people were expiring. It was necessary to stop that calamity and have a showdown with the Partisans. The goals were formidable. Honest people did not become discouraged; within them was born a national spirit that made them ready to die.

With his brothers and other relatives Milivoje left his hearth and under fire escaped to the salutary Robinson Island "Kujova." From there, under Bajo's flag bearer began the first national movement in Bjelopavlici.

He was a courageous and devoted patriot. On Easter Day [1942] he was killed in the village of Medjedje behind the Ostroshke Boulders.

Gorcin N. Stojovich
a contractor born in 1908 in Martinici, district Danilovgrad
[picture]

The son of poor parents, he was always busy. At the age of 15 he became a professional stonemason, and at 20 he became a contractor for government jobs. The last few years he worked in the Trepca mine as a specialist in reinforced concrete construction.

He did not agree with idlers and Partisan bloodsuckers. Therefore, they watched for a chance to deprive him of life. On September 23, 1941, their opportunity came when he went to visit his sister at Celija Monastery. The Partisans lay in ambush for him in the village Stanjevica Rupa and killed him. They also stole from him 25,000 dinars in cash.

His body has not yet been found.

Chased from Bosnia, the Partisans again knocked on our doors. They want to drink some more fraternal blood, to refill the pits with the bodies of our remaining citizens, to swallow the few remaining goats and sheep, to dishonor more women, to burn more peasants' homes! If you don't want another abyss and hell, get up, all of you!

The murderous ruffians must be finished off.

Aleksa M. Shoshkich
peasant, 50 years old, community Polimlje, district Andrijevica
[picture]

In connection with his duties as the head of the village, he was traveling on the state road Andrijevica-Murina-Cakor. At the place called Lasci, in the area of the village Lug, community Polimilje, district Andrijevica, he was ambushed by unknown Partisans and killed. His body was found at the place of his death, and he was buried the next day.

The late Aleksa was a Chetnik of Ulotska Company, Polimlje Battalion.

Krsto R. Shoshkich
peasant, 50 years old, community Polimlje, district Andrijevica
[picture]

A Chetnik, he was searching the terrain when he came across a Partisan ambush at Sharemetska Vrela (forest of the village Ulotine). He was shot with a rifle by the Partisan Ljubomir R. Shoshkich on April 30, 1942. Krsto's body was found in the forest the same day. He was carried to his village and buried.

Dushan M. Vukcevich
police employee from Podgorica
[picture]

On November 15, 1941, he went to his home in Goljemadi to spend his Slava celebration on Saint Djurdjic's Day with his family and friends. At darkness unknown Partisan criminals killed him from ambush as he was returning to his home from his visit with his relatives.

Milosh Sh. Milich
45 years old, community Ljeshkopolje, district Podgorica
[picture]

In the predawn hours of December 16, 1941, he was attacked at his house by Partisan bandits. While defending himself Milosh managed to kill with a pistol the Communists Batric (Bajo) I. Raicevich, quartermaster lieutenant, and Lazar S. Miranovich, both from Ljeshkopolje, Gornja Gorica. Two other unknown Communist assailants ran away.

The late Milosh was employed in the state border guards. He was an excellent employee and a great Nationalist.

Stana M. Roganovich
from Pjeshivci, mother of six children
refugee from Pec

On March 1, 1942, the late Stana went to Botun to get her daughter, who was a waitress there. In Ljeshko polje, Partisans intercepted her and took her away to Cafa Komani, to the headquarters of the Ljeshkopolje Battalion. She was escorted to the headquarters by Jovan M. Bulatovich from Gornja Gorica. She was tortured for three days. Then her head was crushed. After thirty-two days of searching, her husband Marko found her corpse. He carried the body to the church cemetery in the village Beri for burial.

She was sentenced to death by Marko Radovich from Podgorica. The actual executioners were Gojko and Djoko Radovich, both from Podgorica.

[picture]
Opening in the 37-meters-deep Drenovo pit in Velestovo, into which four bodies
had been thrown

[picture]
In the same pestilential pit on Dragovoljacka plate were found the three brothers
Jovovich and two more unidentified bodies. The Partisan cap pictured here was
also found there.

Abyss and Hell

People Killed by the Partisans

[One hundred forty-five individuals are listed, including name, occupation, age, and community and district of residence.]

*Pulling bodies from a well in Shavnik; coffins
of Nationalists shot in Boan by the Communists;
corpse of Maj. Petar S. Jovovich; a view of
the burial of twenty-five bodies in Shavnik; the
corpse of Radomir Jaukovich, police sergeant*]

People Wounded by the Partisans

[*Fifty-eight individuals are listed, including name, occupation, age, and
community and district of residence.*]

[*Pictures: Store of dishes and illegal material and military sectional maps buried
in the chicken coop of the house of Vukan Pavich in Ozrinici; crowd of people
watch the execution of Comm. Chupich; leg of an unidentified victim in a cast
found at the Partisan hospital in Goransko*]

Various Communist Documents

(five-pointed star)
Headquarters Zeta N. L. Partisan Detachment
No. 77/December 9, 1941

To Comrade Milutin Kazich

We acknowledge receipt of your letter. We think you should not leave
your post. When you do leave, according to your promise, you should take
more money with you for the national liberation struggle.

For the time being stay in Ljeshnjani Nahi, join the Partisans, and take
the Partisan oath. On the terrain give as much as you can for the Partisan
cause and the national struggle. Make yourself available to the headquarters
of the Ljeshnjani Partisan Battalion.

DEATH TO FASCISM—FREEDOM TO THE PEOPLE!

Political commissar,   Commandant,
V. Raicevich   B. Jovanovich
(signed)   (signed)

Situation in Vasojevice

1. The local commandant in Lijeva Rijeka is Comrade Mileta Djukich.
The Partisan flag was raised on January 19, 1942, and the same day Partisan

authorities established order. Nikola Lashich, who did not leave with La-shich's battalion, was seized in Lijeva Rijeka. He is under surveillance. George Lashich took with him about 100 Levorecani, 200 Barana, and about 100 from Moraca. The rest of them stayed at their homes and are joining the Partisans. At present, Lashich has about 400 men, but every day somebody deserts him. Lashich himself has been wounded in the cheek. Eight men from his battalion were killed.

Thirty-nine comrades from our Moraca Partisan Battalion were killed. They were treated brutally. Sixty men were captured from the same battal-ion. That happened because the Partisans did not want to fire immediately against the Lashiches because they believed it would not come to a fight between them. The Lashiches had surprised them.

Our position is north of the Djurovich factory, while Lashich's is under Kajcina Rupa-Komovi.

Our Partisans from Treshnjevik cut off the Lashiches' retreat toward Andrijevica. They hope that the liquidation of the Lashiches will come very soon.

Our strength is 200 Brskucani, 200 Kuci, about 60 Piperi, and 1,500 Rovcani and Moracani. Among the Moracani are included Poljani and Ko-lashinci.

Our store of heavy armaments is two throwers, and a sufficient number of machine guns, bombs, and rifles.

Up to now we have not noticed that Lashich has any heavy weapons. Because of the severe cold and heavy snow many of our men suffered frostbite in the legs. The communal feeding is very good. The food came from both requisitions and voluntary donations.

Morale and discipline are at a high level.

5. [*Nos. 2, 3, or 4 in original.*] Referring to your Order No. 65 of January 24, 1942, we issued the necessary order to keep an eye on those people with actions similar to those mentioned in your order. We have not noticed any similar cases up to now.

We sent two couriers according to the preceding order. Keep one of them with you. They are both good Partisans. Their names are Savo Todorovich and Nikola Markovich.

For political commissar,   Commandant of Partisan
Voj. Veljovich   Bratonoshko Brskutski Battalion,
(signed)   N. Lazovich
                                                       (signed)

(five-pointed star)
Headquarters Zeta N. L. Partisan Detachment
No. 101/February 2, 1942

(five-pointed star)

Headquarters Zeta N. L. Partisan Detachment	Note: Inform us by special order about the departure of the Partisans
No. 108/February 3, 1942	

To Headquarters of N. L. Partisan First Battalion Marko Miljanov

We order you within two days to send replacements for your Partisans who are now in Vasojevice. Send 100 Partisans even though that will leave you short. Those Partisans you send should bring with them enough food for four to five days and two pair of socks and should dress as warmly as possible. Send good Partisans from all villages because that is better than sending all from one village. The command composition of the company should be well chosen, including sergeants. As soon as they arrive they will be exchanged, and your Partisans who are here will return to you. Therefore your region will not suffer. If it becomes necessary you are authorized to strengthen your forces from the Second Battalion.

Comrade-Commandant Rashko Bozovich should go with those Partisans and be the battalion commandant. Consider this urgent. Intensify your precautions against fifth columnists and demand that all Partisans who have taken the oath wear Partisan badges. It has been noticed that some do not wear them. Such is the case with some of them in Sjenica and with some Radonjiches even though some of them wore badges earlier.

We ordered Milija Lakovich to go on duty there.

All Partisans who depart should be armed. They have to take automatic rifles and at least two machine guns and appropriate ammunition with them.

During their travel they should demonstrate complete discipline and full wartime precautions. This is necessary in case of any political influence on the local residents over whose terrain they will travel. In Lijeva Rijeka they should get in touch with the local commandant Mileta Djukich, and from there he'll send them on toward Matashevo.

DEATH TO FASCISM—FREEDOM TO THE PEOPLE!

Political commissar,	(seal)	Commandant,
V. Ristich		Blazo Jovanovich
(signed)		(signed)

(five-pointed star)
Headquarters N. L. Partisan Detachment
No. 78/December 9, 1941

To the Command of Lijeva Rijeka Partisan Company
Lijeva Rijeka

We remind you to pay the utmost attention not to be captured by the occupier with the assistance of fifth columnists around Djordje Lashich. You must be on guard day and night.

Continue to hold conferences at villages and break up the actions of Djordje Lashich and his men. Be careful of ambushes.

Continue to demolish bridges and roads on your terrain. Coordinate actions with the Partisan Battalion 18 October.

Ally yourself strongly and keep ties with headquarters of the Komski Detachment. Some men have already gone to the Komski Detachment for recovery and help.

Comrades Jagosh and Vojo should return.

DEATH TO FASCISM—FREEDOM TO THE PEOPLE!

Political commissar,	Commandant,
Vl. Raicevich	Blazo Jovanovich
(signed)	(signed)

———

(five-pointed star)
Headquarters Zeta N. L. Partisan Detachment
No. 196/February 24, 1942

To Political Commissar of Zeta Detachment, Comrade Dragisha Ivanovich

According to information from the local commandant in Lijeva Rijeka, the traitors in Vasojevice have succeeded in taking over Matashevo. It is assumed they will move in two directions, toward Kolashin and Lijeva Rijeka. They should be attacked from behind to disrupt them. For that purpose we ordered general mobilization of the Battalion 18 October and the largest number possible from the Second Battalion Marko Miljanov as well as one company from Piperi Battalion. Those Partisans have to begin their journey immediately and try to attack that band as quickly as possible.

In the name of this headquarters we designate you to command those operations in harmony with command personnel of those Partisan units. Get to work on this job right away because any delay could bring great damage to our national liberation struggle.

It is urgent!

DEATH TO FASCISM—FREEDOM TO THE PEOPLE!

For political commissar,	Commandant,
V. B.	Blazo Jovanovich

(signed)   (signed)

Local Command N. L. Partisan Detachment
No. official/February 24, 1942
   Vjeternik

To Headquarters of Zeta N. L. Partisan Detachment

Wherever it is

In connection with the report delivered to headquarters on the twenty-third of this month we add the following: the Chetnik detachments operate toward Kolashin, and only small formations are noticed toward Kolashin, Jabuka.

Regardless, on the twenty-second of this month at 10 o'clock in the evening the mobilization orders or the Bratonoshko-Brskutski Battalion were not yet executed. We can't get even ten men from the entire battalion to go toward Lijeva Rijeka to disarm some of those Chetniks who were neutral and now carry out surprise attacks on the roads and disarm our Partisans. The condition in the Bratonoshko-Brskutski Battalion is unchanged. Their opinion is to hold positions on Vjeternik and not to go any further; our opinion is to mobilize one detachment of 300 to 400 men who would rush to help their comrades who are fighting around Kolashin. That attack should be from the rear and would surely save Kolashin.

If we get the urgently needed help we'll go in that direction immediately; if we don't get any we'll go alone with our ten comrades of the Lijeva Rijeka garrison.

Please see to it urgently. That is, mobilize the units right away and send them toward Vjeternik, where we'll wait for them. If you cannot, please let us know.

Something seems to be boiling in Bolesestri. Liquidation is urgently needed. If not it could be too late, and the possible formation of new fronts there would be very damaging for us.

DEATH TO FASCISM—FREEDOM TO THE PEOPLE!

(seal)   Local commandant,
                                Mil. Djukich
                                (signed)

(five-pointed star)
Headquarters Zeta N. L. Partisan Detachment
No. 210/February 25, 1942

(five-pointed star)
Headquarters Zeta N. L. Partisan Detachment
No. 194/February 24, 1942

To Headquarters of Zeta N. L. Partisan Battalion

Send all Partisans right away from Podgorica on your territory to the headquarters of the Ljeshkopolje Battalion because we intend to organize them into a company that would operate against fifth columnists in Vasojevice. Both armed and unarmed Partisans should be considered. We expect to develop a strike company that way.

We are informed that fifth columnists and the occupier will increase their activities on your territory. Therefore, increase your vigilance and guards. Hit the fifth columnists without mercy. Don't let yourself be surprised. The situation there for fifth-columnist work is satisfactory even though you are strengthened with a number of Partisans, but they need hardness. The occupier has learned of the location of your battalion headquarters. There is no need for panic. On the contrary, you must gather strength.

Prepare replacements for your Partisans in the Montenegrin-Sandzak Detachment. You know how many of them there are. Send them via Bjelopavlici together with the Ljeshkopolje men who will also go as replacements. Recently our commandant was in Kolashin. He saw Vaso Aligrudich and Savo Bozovich there. They said that Zeta Company has showed superbly in the struggle against fifth columnists in Sandzak. In those battles was killed a Klikovac, an excellent fighter, and another from Zeta. Vaso and Savo probably will return here.

On the terrain with you is Andrija Mirocevich. As a Partisan he corresponds with his father, who is a spy in Podgorica. It looks as if he gives him some information. Verify it. If it is true, liquidate him.

We hope those automatic rifles will be sent to you soon. They were retained because of fighting in Bjelopavlice.

We inform you that the fifth-columnist movement in Bjelopavlice is generally scattered. In Vasojevice they succeeded in taking over Matashevo and Lijeva Rijeka. We'll fight fiercely against them. Despite the difficulty of the struggle we'll succeed in liquidating them.

DEATH TO FASCISM—FREEDOM TO THE PEOPLE!

For political commissar,   Commandant,
V. Bozovich   B. Jovanovich
(signed)   (signed)

Written on the paper of the People's
Assembly, Club of the People
Congressmen of the Yugoslav Radical Association

To Comrade Blazo Jovanovich

We have received your letter of March 12 of this year, and we inform
you about the situation on this side.

The fifth columnists in Gornja Moraca are camouflaged in Partisan units
and tried to carry out a putch to impose their authority in Gornja Moraca.
This happened on the eleventh of this month. They arrested the delegate of
the headquarters of the Komski Detachment, Comrade Milosh Radovich.
They replaced the people's committee and chose a new one consisting of
Col. Aleksa Bojich, an inspector of the finance ministry, Ljubisav Baoshich,
Maj. Savo Markovich, and several village peasants. The situation was terrible and serious. Therefore, it required quick intervention. Right when Peko
and I received your report we went by forced march with 105 men from
the Lovcen Detachment to purge the situation in Gornja Moraca. We seized
eighteen of the conspirators, of whom we shot ten, among them the assistant
of the Gornja Moraca N. L. Partisan Battalion.

Yesterday morning we attacked Prekobrdje. We fought all day long. The
thick fog hampered us very much, but we achieved good results. The right
column took over Sreshka Gora, Grab, and occupied Sela. Also we took
over the villages Petrova Ravan and Jabuka as well as the dominant range
of Vjeternik between Petrova Ravan and the Sjevernica River.

Our losses were one dead and one wounded. Our left column could not
take over Planinicki Vrh because of thick fog and difficult terrain. Today
we continue the attack. Possibly we will carry out a right turn to attack the
enemy from the rear. We expect to succeed; however, the fog has not lifted
today, which could postpone our success.

We'll try to send you the promised seventy sheep, though certain difficulties have arisen in that regard.

After the liquidation of Prekobrdje, Comrade Peko will move with all
available forces engaged for the liquidation in Prekobrdje via Shtavnja toward Lijeva Rijeka to make possible your pass on Vjeternik. From there
we'll act according to the established plan. This morning I went from the
front via Prekobrdje on the left sector: Crkvina-Lipovo-Trebaljevo to direct
operations with forces that are concentrated there. Today I'll send a report to
the supreme headquarters and ask again for two battalions of the proletarian
brigade, though I doubt they can send them.

This morning we received a letter from the main headquarters, and they
totally agree with our intentions and initiative for making plans to direct an
operation against the Chetnik bands.

There are all kinds of difficulties, but we'll overcome them all. As Comrade Stalin says, "The victory is ours."

DEATH TO FASCISM—FREEDOM TO THE PEOPLE!

March 14, 1942   Yours,
G. Moraca   Bajo

P.S. Please send us a long letter via Crkvina (headquarters of Kom Detachment)

———————

Headquarters Bratonoshko-Brskutski N. L. Partisan Battalion 18 October
    February 25, 1942
Vjeternik

To Headquarters of Zeta N. L. Partisan Detachment
                                              Wherever it is

In connection with the existing situation we send you the following report: According to information received from our people and from the women who pass by the Lijeva Rijeka road as well as along the Tara River, the Chetnik detachments are mostly made up of neutral people. They were not part of the main Chetnik detachments in Bare. With small reinforcement from Bare they are located in Lijeva Rijeka. Also they hold guard at Jablan with part of Batric Rakovich's Chetniks from Prekobrdje. Until dawn this morning the Chetnik detachments had not appeared near Lijeva Rijeka. According to unconfirmed reports they are on the road along Tara moving toward Lijeka Rijeka.

Regardless of several orders for general mobilization of the Bratonoshko-Brskutski Battalion to go to Lijeva Rijeka, the response was minimal. The main reason for this was that the comrades who returned from the Matashevo front brought alarming news. According to reports from Brskut the situation is a little better, though the situation could be the same there.

Some fifth columnists and traitorous elements could make the situation critical for us also. In the shortest time, armed conflict could erupt, forming a second front. As it is, there is a state of uncertainty here in Bratonozici. Please send us a stronger unit from your headquarters to our terrain, by tomorrow morning at the latest. If the unit arrives the reactionaries will be unable to take any action.

It would be helpful to send one person to this terrain from your headquarters to help us out in regard to the present situation.

Please consider it most urgent.

DEATH TO FASCISM—FREEDOM TO THE PEOPLE!

Political commissar,
Bratonoshko-Brskutski N. L.
Partisan Battalion 18 October
V. Lalovich
(signed)

(five-pointed star)
Headquarters N. L. Partisan Detachment
No. 222/February 26, 1942

———

(five-pointed star)
Headquarters N. L. Partisan Detachment
No. 297 March 22, 194[2]

To Ljeshkopolje N. L. Partisan Battalion

Field Position

According to the report from main headquarters No. 253 of March 22 of this year, the situation toward Kolashin is worsening. The Chetnik hordes succeeded in pushing back our forces from Crkvina toward Gornja and Donja Moraca. For that reason an order was issued to the Zeta N. L. Partisan Battalion to mobilize all armed Partisans and to go to the terrain of the Donjo-Ljeshnjani Battalion and together get rid of fifth columnists on that territory. Both headquarters must be in close contact with the headquarters of the Lovcen Detachment, from which they have to get orders. Therefore we order you to be alert and to send them help if needed.

Let us know about the situation on your terrain and any action you undertake against fifth columnists.

DEATH TO FASCISM—FREEDOM TO THE PEOPLE!

Assistant political commissar,   Assistant commandant,
V. B.   Srd. Novakovich
(signed)   (signed)

———

(five-pointed star)
Main Headquarters N. L. Partisan Detachment for Montenegro and Boka
No. 231 March 15, 1942

To Comrade Blazo Jovanovich, Member of Main Headquarters of N. L. Partisan Detachment for Montenegro and Boka

We received your report of the fourteenth of this month and we reply to the same.

1. We wonder why you have not been in contact with Comrades Peko and Bajo. They told us they would send couriers to be in contact with you. In case you are not yet in contact with them, send couriers to meet with them. This is vital for common operations, especially if they purge Prekobrdje.

2. We are informed by Comrades Peko and Bajo and also Comrade Budimir that our units have purged Mojkovac, Pudbishce, Polja Kolashinska, and Trebaljevo Moracko and they have arrived in Lipovo. Thanks to the lack of resourcefulness of our comrades, they did not throw the Chetniks out from Lipovo and Kolashin. Nevertheless, the Chetniks were in great panic. When the fighting began in Mojkovac they ran away, left rucksacks and dinner just to save their lives. The units from the Niksic and Lovcen detachments were engaged in purging fifth columnists in Gornja and Donja Moraca, Rovci, and Prekobrdje. They informed us they sent you seventy sheep. You did not tell us whether you got the sheep or not. If they arrived, send thirty of them. If you go into action then send forty to headquarters at Bijeli Pavle.

3. From your letter we understand what the situation is in Kuci, Bratonozici, and even in Piperi. It is too early to talk now about why fifth columnists were not purged more effectively in Piperi. I think it will be necessary to undertake a quick purge of all fifth columnists wherever they are. I don't know, but it seems to me you earlier said something else about the monk. For that reason he was sent to the flagbearer of the Piperi Battalion. Surely I did not take any part in it.

We are sending you the promised grain, some tobacco, and about three kilograms of salt. We don't have any more salt. People from your headquarters are complaining they have nothing to eat. I remember that you received money several times to buy groceries but waited until the last minute. I don't know who is responsible for this! I believe it is indeed a crime that the money is there and the food was not purchased. I hear that even the meat is gone.

DEATH TO FASCISM—FREEDOM TO THE PEOPLE!

We received three liters of brandy.

> For Main Headquarters N. L.
> Partisan Detachment for
> Montenegro and Boka
> Milutinovich

(five-pointed star)

Headquarters Zeta N. L. Partisan Detachment
No. 295 March 22, 1942

To Comrade Savo Brkovich

According to the report of main headquarters No. 253 of March 22 of this year the situation around Kolashin is deteriorating. Chetnik bands succeeded in pushing out our forces from Crkvina toward Gornja and Donja Moraca. Therefore an urgent order was sent to the Zeta N. L. Partisan Battalion to carry out an immediate mobilization of all armed Partisans and to go to the Donjo Ljeshnjani Battalion and carry out operations to purge Donjo-Ljeshnjani Nahi of fifth columnists. The headquarters of the Donjo-Ljeshnjani Battalion and of the Zeta Battalion should be closely allied with the headquarters of the Lovcen N. L. Partisan Detachment, from which they will get their orders.

We were informed that Comrade Djilas came to the main headquarters.

Please, Comrade Savo, under all circumstances send us the following from the seized items: two picks, two shovels, and two hoes, obligatory. You know yourself what we need them for [*to dig holes to bury "fifth columnists"*]. Also try to send one ax, one barrel for water, two pots—small and large, two pigs—one for us and another for main headquarters, three sieves—one for us, one for main headquarters, and a third for the technicians, one trough, one earthenware dish, some brandy, salt, and lard.

Last night at 22.00 hours (we would have done it sooner, but we needed information about Makocevich) we liquidated Cetkovich, Makocevich, Milusha Djukich, and Olga Raicevich. Please inform the headquarters of the Piperi Battalion about it, to be alert if it becomes necessary. Via the commander of Crnci Company inform Makocevich's brother of his brother's liquidation, but don't let him go to Radovce.

We send you news as well as one copy for the hospital. Try to send news to the hospital in time, not as before.

DEATH TO FASCISM—FREEDOM TO THE PEOPLE!

For political commissar,   For commandant,
V. Bozovich   Srd. Novakovich
(signed)   (signed)

(five-pointed star)
Headquarters N. L. Partisan Detachment
No. 242 March 7, 1942

To District Committee of the Communist Party

                                                    Podgorica
Dear Comrades,
   We received your letter of February 3, 1942 [*probably March 3*]. We
know well about the circumstances on the territory of our detachment. We
agree with you. Someone should come from this headquarters, but in regard
to today's situation in Kuci, Bratonozici, and Brskut as well. The main
headquarters ordered the commandant of this headquarters to go with Partisans via Bratonozici to Vasojevice because Partisans from there asked for
him. He is still in Bratonozici, while our political commissar, Comrade
Dragisha Ivanovich, is in Kuci. Comrade Perisha Vujoshevich, who recently
came from Sandzak, was also sent there by main headquarters.
   An order was issued to the battalions of Zeta, Donjo-Ljeshnjani, and
Ljeshkopolje regarding today's situation. It would be beneficial if you could
help them because otherwise the occupier and the fifth columnists will break
apart the people's struggle.
   Several good comrades as well as a certain number of party members
have come to these three battalions' territories. It would be advantageous
to contact them and assign them duties.
   We informed Kuci of the fifth columnists intentions toward them. We
also informed the headquarters of the Piperi Battalion about women from
Rogami through the commandant, for things of that nature are of some
concern. Remind him on your part, too.
   The jam assigned to you by this headquarters left here fifteen days ago.
It was taken from Bioci to the command of Crnci Company; another tub of
jam was taken for the ambulance in Krusi. We already wrote to the head-
quarters of the Ljeshkopolje Battalion to select some personnel to take the
jam there. You must insist that people are sent from headquarters as soon
as possible before the jam spoils.
   As we have been informed, Dr. Jovanovich is on the terrain of the
Ljeshnjani or Ljeshkoplje battalions. Contact him and retain him at the
ambulance in Krusi.
   Let us know if you get the items sent by our hospital.
THE RED ARMY IS WITH US—THERE IS OUR VICTORY!
DEATH TO FASCISM—FREEDOM TO THE PEOPLE!
                  (seal)   For political commissar,
                                                  V. B.
                                                  (signed)

                            ——————

February 3

   Dear Comrade,
   We are acquainted with conditions in Vasojevice. Without doubt you are
heavily engaged there. However, be alert about the terrain on this side of

Zeta. The headquarters of the Ljeshnjani and Ljeshkopolje battalions probably will let you know about the situation on their terrain. The Ljeshnjani Battalion is waging a fight. The Italians and fifth columnists in Ljeshkopolje occupied the villages near the road but the Ljeshkopolje Battalion did not take any measures. It is clear to us it would be impossible to widen the fighting on that terrain; however, they could have prevented the enemy from moving any further, and some fifth columnists have to be liquidated. The battalion headquarters does not have a complete list of those forces. We reminded headquarters, but it was futile.

Our comrades are on the terrain, but we are surprised nobody came on the terrain from detachment headquarters, though you know Zeta is in danger too. We had informed Kuci that the fifth columnists intend to attack them.

Ask the battalion in Piperi why they don't contact the women who travel from Rogami to Podgorica! Ruzica and Milena Stamatovich still maintain contact with Stanko Markovich. Don't let Vidna Vucinich go to Podgorica because she is often seen there with Raco Dervanovich.

There are mass arrests in Podgorica. Two hundred eight were arrested from Pec. Strengthen your work. We will help you.

DEATH TO FASCISM—FREEDOM TO THE PEOPLE!

O. K. (District Committee),
Podgorica

(five-pointed star)
Headquarters N. L. Partisan Detachment
No. 242 March 5, 1942

(five-pointed star)
Headquarters N. L. Partisan Detachment
No. 248 March 7, 1942

To Headquarters of Zeta N. L. Partisan Battalion

We did not receive the letters you sent this headquarters via the Partisan Milutin Radonjich because Kuci Chetniks caught him, disarmed him, and took the letters from him. Then they let him go. He came to this headquarters to tell us.

We are surprised you entrusted such a delicate duty to Radonjich. He was not the most trustworthy person for such an important job. We have good, experienced Partisans who faithfully carry out their Partisan duty—so why did you designate him for that mission? Get rid of him from your battalion headquarters as harmful; besides, he is sick with venereal disease.

We are informed that since fifteen fifth columnists came to Zeta you have lost your composure. All became incapacitated and agitated. The same thing also happened in Kuci. Our Partisans were not alert so fifth columnists succeeded in swaying our ranks. It was a pity that Partisans should come forward energetically and then that nothing would happen. For the time being don't challenge the occupier, but let him pass by freely on the roads. Watch the villages. If the occupier burns, plunders, and tortures, beat him up. Send men and ammunition. Pay the greatest attention to fifth columnists. Together with the enemy they try to break our unity and the people's struggle. Be merciless toward them and destroy them more fiercely and effectively.

We ordered the headquarters of Ljeshkopolje and Ljeshnjani to join forces with you because together you'll be more effective in waging the struggle against the occupier and fifth columnists as well.

You made a mistake in releasing Ret. Lt. Col. Niko Jovanovich, a well-known people's enemy. You did not inform us as your superior, but you asked for information about him from the headquarters of the Lovcen Detachment! In the future, ask for information about suspicious persons from the headquarters of the Ljeshkopolje Battalion.

Pay attention to your intelligence services and maintain your guard. Put passers-by under control and check their identity, so that no one can pass without your knowledge.

You cannot get the two automatic rifles you asked for now because the detachment headquarters of Bijeli Pavle needs them. The main headquarters agrees with this.

We enclose for you under 1 verified copies of Order No. 195 of main headquarters of March 2 of this year, one for you and another for the national liberation committee stationed on your territory. Familiarize yourself with its contents and follow the instructions completely.

Pay attention to our Order No. 3 recorded under No. 195 of February 24, 1942 in our records, especially items 4 and 5.

Send us a list of the Podgoricani who are on your territory.

We send you the daily order of Comrade Stalin regarding the twenty-fourth anniversary of the Red Army.

Maintain a steady guard at your headquarters, day and night. We are informed by a reliable source that fifth columnists are preparing attacks on your headquarters.

DEATH TO FASCISM—FREEDOM TO THE PEOPLE!

For political commissar,   For commandant,
V. Bozovich (signed)   Srd. Novakovich (signed)

P.S. Please inform us about the situation in Zeta as well as about liquidations.

———————

(five-pointed star)
Main Headquarters N. L. Partisan Detachment for Montenegro and Boka
No. official November 29, 1941

To Headquarters of Zeta N. L. Partisan Detachment

We forward to you a letter from Cedomir Ilickovich, laboratory helper. Reply to him and with the help of Dr. S. Bozovich make a list of all necessary hospital items, because we don't have any doctors with us now.

Why did you not reply to the Ilickovich letter about what material was received? We always complain we cannot get material; also, men who offer their services are not always used.

Send to the main headquarters via the Ljeshkopolje platoon material that will be distributed to detachments according to their needs. The Ljeshkopolje platoon, that is, the company, cannot retain any of the materials, as was done until now.

Blazo and Srdjan should dissuade the two Ljeshnjani who insist on going to Sandzak with their sons. Their departure is unnecessary. As old men and good fighters they could be much more useful in the nahija.

Order No. 5 should be given to Bozo and Budo to read. We would send it to them too, but the copy machine is not functioning. If they have an old machine that can be repaired let them send it to us.

We enclose a report from the supreme headquarters. If you get another one, return this to us.

DEATH TO FASCISM—FREEDOM TO THE PEOPLE!

(seal)　　　　　　　　　　For Main Headquarters of N. L. Partisan Detachment for Montenegro and Boka, Milutinovich (signed)

P.S. For Tuesday and Wednesday we need six packhorses with twelve sacks for transferring potatoes from Niksic Zupa. Therefore order the political commissar in Kopilje and Seoci to be with the horses and sacks at dawn in Radovce at your headquarters on December 2. We'll give one person to take care of each two horses.

Milutinovich (signed)
Send us ten pairs of peasant shoes of oxhide
(five-pointed star)
Headquarters N. L. Partisan Detachment
No. 23 November 30, 1941

(five-pointed star)
Headquarters N. L. Partisan Detachment
No. official/December 6, 1941

To Comrade Spasoje Ivanovich

Dear Comrade,
In this situation of armed struggle against the occupier and his servants it is required that you contribute more energy and resoluteness to your duty. You have to eliminate your weaknesses once and for all—that is, indecisiveness and hesitation. Comrades are saying now that you are more active than you were before, but you are not decisive enough as required by today's situation.

Make no agreement with fifth columnists. As for elements that are vacillating, tell what kind of struggle we wage and how we look at those who still hold their rifles in abeyance. Also, let them know clearly and decisively that we will not tolerate any third front, because in fact that front is for the occupier, to whom it refers. Who honestly wants to fight, let them join the Partisans. The weakness is when you say, "It is too hard to get on with this or that." It requires resoluteness and determination. There cannot be any appeasement of fifth columnists and opponents of the people's struggle.

Pay attention to the greater Kuci reaction, which is turning its view against Comrade Dragisha Ivanovich. It is necessary to take care of it so that band is totally incapacitated.

Your position is very difficult until Dragisha recovers. Therefore you have to work day and night and increase your strength tenfold.

DEATH TO FASCISM—FREEDOM TO THE PEOPLE!

For political commissar,	Commandant,
V. Bozovich	Blazo Jovanovich
(signed)	(signed)

(five-pointed star)
Headquarters N. L. Partisan Detachment
No. 48/January 16, 1942

———

To Hospital of N. L. Partisan Detachment for Montenegro and Boka
                                                                    Radovce
The Partisan woman Hilda M. Vucinich is ill. Her illness is caused by insufficient care, so day by day her health is worsening. Unforeseen complications are a cause of worry. Therefore we send her to the hospital for rest. She will be there by 13.00 hours. Prepare a bed for her.

DEATH TO FASCISM—FREEDOM TO THE PEOPLE!

For commandant,
Srd. Novakovich
(signed)

————

Headquarters Donjo-Ljeshnjani N. L. Partisan Battalion
No. 21/February 1, 1942

To Headquarters of Zeta N. L. Partisan Detachment

According to our suggestion to purge fifth columnists in Ljeshnjani Nah-ija, steps were undertaken by the Lovcen Detachment, Ljeshkopolje and Zeta battalions, and fourteen Partisans from the Bijeli Pavle Battalion. The plan was worked out at the Lovcen Detachment together with ours and the headquarters of the Ljeshkopolje Battalion.

The Battalion Carev Laz with their 110 Partisans and 10 of our Partisans had to execute an action in the village Goljemadi. Fifth- columnist sentries were met in Krinicko Zdrijelo. In the fighting two fifth columnists were killed and one was wounded. There were no casualties on our side. The Battalion Carev Laz did not arrive in time at the designated place to perform the directed task because of the clash with the sentry. Then our patrol did not come in time, which was due to the guide's error.

In Brezine fifty Cuca and Bjelica should carry out an action. A larger number was designated, but they did not show up because of the Battalion Carev Laz's skirmish. Brezine fifth columnists managed to escape from their homes. They only succeeded in catching the new candidate for community president, Brnovich, nominated by fifth columnists. It is alleged he will get a threefold supply of food if he is elected (a new trick of fifth columnists).

As for Lijeshnje and Bigor: There were designated twenty-five from Ljeshkopolje, ten from the Battalion Bijeli Pavle, and four of our guides. As soon as our Partisans approached these villages, a fifth-columnist sentry on forward position noticed them and informed other fifth columnists, who ran away from their homes. When our Partisans entered their houses they were not there. In some places Partisans found the beds empty while the bedclothes were still warm.

Podstrana: Twenty Partisans from Ljeshkopolje and two from ours were designated. The task was completely executed. The truth is, only four men were disarmed.

Kokote: There were thirty Zecani and about fifty Partisans from the Gornjo-Ljeshanski Battalion and ten Partisans from this battalion. The Partisans from the Gornjo-Ljeshnjani Battalion did not arrive in time. Our Zecani began action. During the barrage of the village they mistook each other for fifth columnists and opened fire against one another. So the task was not completed, except that one man was arrested and disarmed. The Zecani took him with them during the general confusion. That fifth columnist was only meant to be disarmed. On the way to Kokote the Gornjo-Ljeshnjani Partisans disarmed five more fifth-columnist sentries and brought them to our headquarters. After an investigation we let them go.

Steci: Seventeen Ljeshkopolje Partisans and two of our Partisans were designated. One suspicious fifth columnist was arrested. The main fifth columnist was not at home. As we learned later, he was on sentry.

Twelve rifles, four revolvers, one hand grenade, and one pair of binoculars were confiscated. We received four rifles, three revolvers, of which one was inaccurate, and one hand grenade. The hand grenade was given to Comrade V. Stajkich, while Comrade Vlado Bozovich kept the binoculars.

After the action we can state about the situation: Podstranjashi from Kokoti [*incorrect—Podstranjashi and Kokocani*] were not present at the meeting held at Barutana where preparations for an attack on our headquarters were discussed. Right now as we type this report, today's meeting is being held from two to five o'clock in the afternoon. However, we learned that they were armed and came to Barutana with rucksacks. What they intend we don't know yet. We are on the alert, although there is just a small number of resolute Partisans.

Political commissar,   (seal)   Commandant,
Vidak   V. Raickovich
                                               (signed)

(five-pointed star)
Headquarters N. L. Partisan Detachment
No. 100/February 2, 1942

(five-pointed star)
Headquarters N. L. Partisan Detachment
No. 100/February 2, 1942

To Headquarters of Ljeshnjani N. L. Partisan Battalion

There were many mistakes in the action you executed. The fundamental one is you should retain all Partisans from outside until you catch all the fifth columnists. Do not dismiss them at once. The reactionaries can now gather and mobilize themselves. If the reactionaries stayed a day or two outside of their houses they should fall apart and all honest and misled peasants would leave them. It is not a good sign that they gather freely at Barutana with their rucksacks and arms. It is necessary to remind them somehow that if they continue further with their treacherous action we'll fight until their ultimate liquidation.

Give us the names of those who have been disarmed, killed, or wounded. Don't let action be taken by fifth columnists, but by us. It is important to understand that dismissing our Partisans was not a weakness. Keep the Partisans mobilized and ready. Don't let yourself be surprised. In that regard don't trust them too much. Indeed, don't trust them at all, because some of them are fifth columnists.

Proceed to carry out actions on your terrain both separately and with other battalions.

We remind you that when an action is to be carried out you should consider all possibilities, not as this one was done.

If it is possible, forbid all suspicious persons to go to Podgorica. Make a thorough search before they go and when they return because they are connected with the treacherous committee in Podgorica.

This notification needs to be well analyzed, and you need to prepare Partisans for a fiercer and fiercer struggle against domestic traitors through conferences with Partisans and others.

DEATH TO FASCISM—FREEDOM TO THE PEOPLE!

> Commandant,
> Blazo Jovanovich
> (signed)

(five-pointed star)
Headquarters Zeta N. L. Partisan Detachment
No. 131/February 7, 1942

Comrade Migo,

It is necessary to see how things are developing among the Partisans. It looks as if some things are not going smoothly. There are phenomena not only of fluctuations but also of fifth columnists. They must be fiercely repulsed. Above all it is necessary to find out who is Partisan and who is not. In the Partisan ranks there cannot be just anyone. It is not a healthy condition not to know who is the commandant and who is the political commissar. Reach an understanding with the political commissar or his assistant, whoever is there. Tell them to do their duty resolutely, not as it was done in the past. That was not satisfactory. It was not permissible for both the political commissar and his assistant to go to Vasojevice. Only one should have gone; the other should have remained on the terrain.

As to the designation of the company's political commissar, we gave free rein to the battalion political commissar and assistant.

It looks as if Batric sabotages our work. Therefore proof needs to be gathered for his replacement. Tell Labovich and [*illegible*] about this and have them see to it and make a proposal.

The fifth columnists need to be liquidated. For that reason Comrade Dragisha Ivanovich is coming there. See to it with him.

Obtain a feeling for their work on the terrain from national liberation committees.

Give everything you have—it seems to me you could give more. You isolate yourself from the masses with feeble action and then leave the masses to someone who hesitates or to fifth columnists. Be sure to take care of everything.

DEATH TO FASCISM—FREEDOM TO THE PEOPLE!

        (seal)   With comradely greetings,
                                          Zetin (Blazo Jovanovich)

(five-pointed star)
Headquarters N. L. Partisan Detachment
No. 241—March 5, 1942

To Headquarters of Donjo-Ljeshnjani N. L. Partisan Battalion
                                              Position

We received your undated letter today, that is the fifth of this month. It was sent via courier from the Ljeshkopolje N. L. Partisan Battalion. Judging from your letter we conclude you were surprised by the occupier's attack even though you were informed about it earlier. This headquarters warned you that the occupier is preparing an attack toward Ljeshkopolje and Ljeshn-jani Nahi.

You changed the direction of the occupier toward the headquarters of the Gornjo-Ljeshnjani that is on the main Podgorica road. Don't interfere in his free movement for now; just watch the villages. If the occupier tries to burn houses then enter into battle with him. Save men and ammunition. Destroy fifth columnists more fiercely and more effectively.

Establish strong ties among yourselves—that is, with the headquarters of Ljeshkopolje, Komansko-Zagaracki, Gornjo-Ljeshanski, and Zeta as well. As we have already informed you, the last has offered help.

We expect a detailed report about the results of the fighting: about the dead and wounded and burning and in general about the situation on your battalion's territory.

We have been informed that Dr. Jovanovich left Podgorica and is now on the territory of those battalions (Zeta, Ljeshnjani, or Ljeshkopolje). Try to locate him in order to aid the wounded.

Don't send us the Partisans we asked for right now, nor the Podgoricani who are located on your terrain. Let them stay until our further order.

The Ljeshkopolje N. L. Partisan Battalion was ordered to deliver to you 2,500 Italian lire as help to headquarters for its needs. Acknowledge receipt.

We are enclosing two verified transcripts of this headquarters, one for you and the other for the national liberation committee in your region. Learn its contents and follow them completely.

We wrote a letter to Comrade Radoje Cetkovich, an advisory member of this headquarters. We reminded him not to interfere in matters of that headquarters because he is not authorized to issue and sign orders—rather, only the headquarters of that battalion.

Be watchful toward the occupier and fifth columnists. Don't let them surprise you again.

Continue with your work among the people and among Partisans through conferences, meetings, entertainments, etc.

If possible insist on finding out why the companies of Kokotsko-Lekicka and Brezinska did not respond. [*They did not take part in the fighting in March 1942.*] Investigate and after hearings strictly punish the culprits.

We agree with your opinion in the letter No. 29 of February 28 of this year regarding replacement of Comrades V. Uskokovich and V. Raickovich. This headquarters will take care of them.

Pay the utmost attention to our Order No. 3 recorded in our records as No. 195 of February 24, 1942, especially items 4 and 5.

Majo and Milo Vukcevich cannot be Partisans. Also in our Partisan units there cannot be any conditional Partisans [*"conditional" refers to more than fifty men from the Vukcevich Donjo Drazevina Company who stated they would join the Partisan ranks only if commandant Vaso Raickovich and political commissar Vidak-Vido Uskokovich were replaced in their Partisan headquarters.*] We would rather have five good Partisans than fifty or a hundred mediocre ones.

DEATH TO FASCISM—FREEDOM TO THE PEOPLE!

For political commissar,
V. B.
(signed)

For commandant,
Srd. Novakovich
(signed)

P.S. Send a list of Podgoricani on your territory. We forward to you the daily order of Comrade Stalin for the occasion of the twenty-fourth birthday of the Red Army.

HELL
or
Communism in Montenegro

[*picture of skull and long bone*]

Volume Number Eight

An Edition of *The Voice of Montenegro*
Publisher, Obod—Cetinje, 1943

Commandants of Partisan Battalions, Company Commanders, and Assistants

[*Twenty-nine individuals are listed, including name, occupation, age, and residence.*]

Political Commissars and Assistants

[*Twenty-six individuals are listed, including name, occupation, age, and residence.*]

Partisan Judges and Assistants

[*Twenty-seven individuals are listed, including name, occupation, age, and residence.*]

Executioners and Assistants

[*Twenty-two individuals are listed, including name, occupation, age, and residence.*]

Anti-Christ Perpetrators

*The Very Rev. Jagosh Simonovich, Deputy Archpriest
blasphemer and murderer from Kolashin*

Priest Blazo Markovich, well-known debaucher and murderer

———————

A decision has been reached by His Grace the Metropolitan of Montenegro-Littoral, Mr. Joanikije, as decreed in Proclamation No. 465 of April 16, 1942, to place the following under court investigation and to dismiss them from clergical services without pension rights. A ban was placed on their clergical services because canon law deems punishable their active participation in the Communist movement. That includes denying belief in God, which is central to Christ's representative and which denial is an abomination to the faithful and brings shame to the profession of the clergy. Those named below are now engaged in underground activities:

Jagosh Simonovich, former deputy archpriest in Kolashin.

Blazo Markovich, former prosecutor of the diocesan court in Cetinje.

Vidak Drakich, former parish priest of Brskut, district Podgorica.

Djordjije Kalezich, former parish priest of Slatina-Gostilje, in Danilovgrad.

By the same decree was punished Rufine Zizich, former superintendent of the Bijele Monastery, district Shavnik, who was then with the Partisans.

[picture]
The body of Maj. Petar S. Jovovich being pulled out from a pit into a tent.

Our Church Martyrs Killed by the Communists

Archimandrite Nikodim Janjushevich, head of the Zupa Monastery near Niksic
[picture and biography]

Father Petar Vujovich, parish priest of Meterizi-Drushici from Zupa Dobrska
[picture and biography]

Father Pavic Kekovich, parish priest of Pavkovici
[picture and biography]

Father Risto S. Jaramaz, parish priest of Kosijere
[picture and biography]

Father Vasilije Bozarich, parish priest of Rogami-Djurkovici, from Rogami
[*picture and biography*]

Father Rade Popovich, retired parish priest from Velika, district Andrijevica
[*picture and biography*]

Archpriest Varnava Bucan, head of the Podlastve Monastery
[*biography*]

Father Bogdan Cerovich, parish priest from Zabljak
[*picture and biography*]

Brother Teofan Beatovich, friar of Kosijerevo Monastery
[*biography*]

Father Vaso Popovich, parish priest of Vucido from Baoshici (Boka Kotorska)
[*biography*]

Brother Gavrilo Dabich, friar of Zupa Monastery near Niksic
[*biography*]

Father Novo Delich, parish priest from Planinopivska, district Shavnik
[*biography*]

[*picture*]
The corpse of Father Novo Delich

Laymen Killed by the Communists

Mico Ivov Kopitovich
[*biography and picture*]

Novo Medenica
head of the district court in Kolashin

*Blagota L. Vukcevich, reserve captain from village Popratnica, community
Ljeshnjani Nahi,
district Podgorica*
[*picture and biography*]

Niko (Nikola) St. Djurkovich from Kosijeri, district Cetinje
[*picture and biography*]

Milovan Jacheglav, teacher and reserve lieutenant
[*picture and biography*]

[*picture*]
In a ravine during excavation of corpses

Abyss and Hell

People Killed by the Partisans

[*One hundred twenty individuals are listed, including name, occupation, age, and community and district of residence.*]

[*Pictures:*] The body of Jovic Lazarevich in his coffin; the body of Milan Cvorovich, contractor from Shavnik; four bodies covered with sand in Zupa: (1) Stojan M. Lakovich and (2) Petar S. Rashkovich, both from Kuci; (3) Bozo Jovanovich and (4) Mileta Pavicevich from Pavkovici-Bjelopavlici; the body of Lt. Col. Savo Vujoshevich; families of those killed stand by in Radovce; the body of Radosav Pekich, second lieutenant; the body of Gledo Aleksich, peasant; the body of Mijat S. Jankovich, gendarme sergeant; the body of Mitar Karadzich, president of Drobnjak community, after being taken out of the Komarnica River; the body of Vaso Milashinovich, teacher; the body of Radosav Bogicevich, head of the village Bogicevici; excavation of bodies from limekiln in Shavnik; the body of Arso Minich.

Thousands of families are overwhelmed by grief, thousands of burned homes gape like ghosts, thousands of corpses of the most prominent citizens are still in pits today, the action of our monstrous "liberators."

People Wounded by the Partisans

[*Seventy individuals are listed, including name, occupation, age, and community and district of residence.*]

[*Pictures: The body of Nedeljko Jaukovich, peasant; moving six bodies from Pavkovici; one of the many burned houses; the road demolished above Kujava*]

Various Communist Documents

Headquarters Montenegrin Detachment

To Main Headquarters for Montenegro and Boka

Our attack on Pljevlja failed. We had losses of about 400 dead and wounded. The reasons for the failure:
— The units were not familiar enough with the terrain, and the officers were unfit for that kind of fighting. In that regard the guides from the

Pljevlja Company failed. The men involved did not have strict military discipline; they partly succumbed to panic and were afraid of the bombing, etc. The Italians succeeded in routing the entire Zeta Battalion, while others retreated at the first sign of fire and demoralized the rest.

— A good portion of the lead cadres fell, which demoralized the people, and in the meanwhile they could not find strong hands to lead the units.

— Part of the population [*Turks and Ustashe*] made our street fighting more difficult.

— The enemy was completely informed about our action even though we marched through Sandzak at night.

— Our excessive optimism about the enemy's actions hurt us. Our fighters had believed they would take over Pljevlja after the first attack. However, the enemy gave strong resistance, while our side began to hesitate.

— Regardless of the enemy's strength (3,000), we could have taken over Pljevlja if our units and commandants had taken the task seriously. Only three battalions carried out their assignments: Cetinje, Bjelopavlici, and Piperi. These three battalions protected the lines of communication between Prijepolje and Pljevlja, got good booty, and took seventy prisoners while having only three casualties, respectively. The Niksic Battalion was partially successful. All the other battalions failed, though there were scattered heroic acts. There was partial penetration into the city, whose buildings were defended all during the day. During the night they pulled out. All the last-ditch efforts to penetrate had failed. At dawn people began retreating and came out, as they did in the aftermath of the penetration at Velje Brdo.

One more lesson: An army is created through its actions, not in any other way. There was very weak organization in the battalions Komski, Pivski, Niksic, and Shavnik.

Otherwise we would have penetrated to the center of the city. The director of the gymnasium and the priory were killed at the center of the city. Two important fortresses were taken; it needed but two more, but our commanders could not cope with it. We suffered losses during the retreat that we had not conceived of earlier. The long, arduous marches had tired our troops. Because of the need for secrecy on Sandzak territory we could not rest. The communal feeding was inadequate because of the need for secrecy. The mistakes of the leaders were that they didn't send two or three waves of soldiers, so if one hesitated the next would hold up the first and carry the first to action. The attack did not come from all directions at once; therefore, the Italians concentrated their fire on one group after another.

Conclusion: We overrated the quality of our soldiers. Any leader who trusted his troops should choose to attack after reconnaissance. The fortresses taken by the Cetinjani and Bjelopavlici were not more vulnerable than those that were not taken by other troops. The situation after the unsuccessful attack is that: All volunteers left their units. There were repeated cases of this with Velje Brdo, Lijeva Rijeka, etc. Most of the best leaders were killed at the heads of their units. The rest of the leadership is not suitable for their present positions. Democratic election is not good.

During the march we recognized many deficiencies of our people and also the difficulty of the attack. However, we were optimistic, believing in our total success in this action, and we could not give up the attack.

There are new goals before us now. The situation in Serbia is worsening. The Germans took over all the cities, and they reached Uvca. The supreme headquarters is located in the village Drenovo. Therefore with the people remaining (1,600 Partisans) we blockaded all cities in Sandzak, Pljevlja, Prijepolje from this side, the bridge between Rudo and Priboj, and Bijelo Polje, and we try to demolish communications. You should take all measures to destroy connections and to hit the enemy on the roads. This is important especially on the roads Podgorica-Kolashin and Berane-Bijelo Polje. We'll do everything we can to carry out our task. The morale of the people is improving. In Serbia we'll throw over 1,000 Partisans by demand of the supreme headquarters, with which we established ties. In Serbia the situation will improve. From now on we'll inform you regularly. We'll inform you in detail about the battles at Pljevlja.

Political commissar,   Commandant,
Bajo Sekulich   Arso Jovanovich
(signed)   (signed)

(five-pointed star)
Headquarters Zeta N. L. Partisan Detachment
Very confidential No. 48/December 9, 1941

To Headquarters of Podgorica Battalion Position

Dear Comrades,

The Montenegro-Sandzak Headquarters for operation in Sandzak has informed us your headquarters is located in Toci and that we should contact you for coordination. At the same time, headquarters asked for one doctor and lotion for mange. We sent you the lotion, doctor, and a courier. However, since Chetnik bands are located in Toci, we don't know anything about the destiny of those comrades. That is a terrible omission on the part of the operations headquarters in Sandzak and on your part as well. In the letter I sent by the doctor I said you were to send us couriers twice weekly. Furthermore, the operations headquarters in Sandzak should send us one delegate for the formation of a special command. Both orders have to be carried out immediately.

Regarding the political circumstances, there is a move to destroy the people's movement by the bourgeois and reactionary Great Serbian clique rising in class defense. Referring to the military circumstances, there is a move more and more toward the collapse of fascism from outside and stronger Chetnik bands from within. It is therefore necessary (1) to hold conferences with Partisans and in the villages as well to explain the movements of forces and the regrouping of forces under these new conditions and (2) to purge Partisan companies and increase them numerically, penetrating the core of their social layers.

You had the task of carrying out actions in the district of Podgorica. However, you did nothing, nothing at all, except liquidate a couple of spies. Therefore I'm ordering:

1. That you contact us.

2. That you immediately begin purging Chetnik bands in the villages Toci, Bjelobaba, Babine, etc. in the zone of Kamena Gora to the Lim River and north to Izbicana and Djurova. Carry out nightly actions thusly: After you receive advance information, seize the village, disarm all armed bandits and their leaders, and liquidate the main criminals on the spot. Confiscate the property (cattle, dry meat, food supplies, clothes, and other) only of those you liquidate. Don't give any consideration or hesitation toward the enemy. Bivouacking so that you do not execute the actions is equal to treason. In the same way, chase the Muslim bands, and destroy their leaders. In a word, the terrain on the line from Gracanica on the south to Djurova on the north has to be purged of Chetnik bands, which want to pull out Italians or to attack on Nova Varosh in cooperation with Nedich's bands from Serbia. We have to seize Prijepolje if the Italians surrender to the Chetniks' Lim bands. You should be prepared for that task in advance.

3. Forward this letter to the operations headquarters in Sandzak

S.F.S.H.

January 14, 1942

The delegate from supreme headquarters,

Djido [*Milovan Djilas*]

(five-pointed star)
Headquarters Piperi N. L. Partisan Battalion
Classified No. 24/January 17, 1942

To Zeta N. L. Partisan Detachment

This morning at 7 o'clock the anti-Partisan organizers Jovica Boljevich, Pavle Beshich, and Milovan Beshich were arrested and disarmed. They are being escorted to headquarters by the commander of Stijena Company along with twenty Partisan comrades of that company. They resisted arrest, especially Jovica Boljevich, but later he was disarmed too.

During the search and disarming two rifles, two hand grenades, twelve sticks of dynamite, and several meters of detonating wire were taken.

The companies had received orders to be prepared to prevent any movement of people without permits on company territory.

Savo Mitrovich will get a summons to appear tomorrow at this headquarters for a hearing, and we'll escort him to your headquarters for further investigation.

DEATH TO FASCISM—FREEDOM TO THE PEOPLE!

Political commissar,
V. Todorovich (signed)

(five-pointed star)
Headquarters Zeta N. L. Partisan Detachment
Classified No. 11/January 17, 1942

(five-pointed star)
Headquarters II Kuci N. L. Partisan Battalion Marko Miljanov
Classified No. 24/February 23, 1942
Kuci

Report Delivered to Headquarters of Zeta N. L. Partisan Detachment Piperi

On February 18 at 5 o'clock our brave Partisans at Ubli liquidated Milovan M. Rashovich, Vaso M. Rashovich, and their sister Mirosava, called "Corna." Milovan was a well-known criminal, bandit, thief, and notorious fifth columnist—a terror to all in Momce. He was active in breaking up the people's struggle. The people feel relieved that he was liquidated.

Vaso had collaborated with Mihailo. He says, "We'll get each other." Mirosava had served as a courier between Milovan and fifth columnists in Podgorica. She had threatened to kill ten Partisans with a pick-ax if Milovan were killed. Now it is excellent in Momce, because we had put it in order earlier. Our alertness toward fifth columnists is not lessened, even though their right strike wing was destroyed on this territory.

On February 22 a meeting of Kuci was held at Ubli. The meeting was magnificent and well attended. There was order and discipline. Comrade Dragisha Ivanovich, delegate of that headquarters, explained the political situation without and within. The masses were enthusiastic about his speech.

The alliance with Albania momentarily is slowed down because Ljucovich hasn't come since February 5, though he promised he would be back earlier. We don't know why! The Kuci have informed us that there is no longer any danger from Albania.

The national liberation committee let us know they'll not take care of our headquarter's communal feeding. Now we are in a great crisis regarding our food. Please assign something for us. Referring to the communal feeding they told us the main headquarters of the N. L. Provincial Detachment for Montenegro and Boka would take care of it. Please take the necessary steps immediately. There are seven people at this headquarters.

The situation is good in the battalion. On February 19 we sent our replacement to Matashevo.

DEATH TO FASCISM—FREEDOM TO THE PEOPLE!

For political commissar,   (seal)   Commandant,
Rade Prelevich   Arso L. Perich
                                          (signed)

(five-pointed star)
Headquarters N. L. Partisan Detachment
No. 200/February 24, 1942

———

To Comrade Zetin [*Blazo Jovanovich*],

We are surprised by the beastly fear that possesses some Partisans and an even greater number of party members.

I gave directions to the First Battalion and I formed a strike group. However, people are afraid to leave their homes despite the strict directives I have assigned. Last night a group of ten men demolished the road below Fundina, which Chetniks were repairing.

All men are mobilized. Some former Partisans searched the terrain with astonishing zeal. Some began to tire, but orders are strict. The courier Drakulovich was seized and escorted to Orahovo. Savo Petrov let him go because he is one of his friends.

The Partisans have not yet liquidated any fifth columnists. The criminal Caricich, who had received 60,000 lire for Marko Biljurich, is in Kuci. Vlado Dukich, Nikola Mirkov Vujoshevich, and Dragoje Spahich passed through Kuci on the way to Podgorica. Not even one Partisan tried to liquidate any of them. Comrade Zetin! This cowardice of party members has to be strictly punished. For instance, Spasoje could not be found. He is secluded somewhere in some hole, and he does not have any ties with Orahovo.

Some party members from Podgorica told us that five days ago there arrived fifty to sixty Kuci traitors with Italian rifles, heavy soldiers' boots, and the Montenegrin flag. Some of them returned to Podgorica.

At night I meet with party members and Partisans, but their fighting spirit can be criticized.

Rely on many operations in Vasojevice.

Previously an order was given that about 150 men come to Orahovo with food for four days. The order was carried out. Most of them thought they were being assigned to Vasojevice; however, it was a "flying company" for searching the Kuci terrain.

As you can see, the situation in Kuci is bad. We retain those Partisans illegally, because around all "suspicious" houses there lie in ambush ten to twenty men, who inquire where the person is from that house, etc.

We'll do everything we can, but the people with whom we are working are not energetic at all.

Perisha is on Medun. His task is to explain the real situation on Medun. We delivered forty to fifty copies of the proclamation for distribution throughout Kuci.

I wrote several letters. It would be great if you have time to write those letters.

DEATH TO FASCISM—FREEDOM TO THE PEOPLE!

March 17, 1942   R. Electrin
                                       [*Dragisha Ivanovich*]
                                       (signed)

———

Dear Blazo,

We passed through all of Bratonozici as we fought the Chetniks on each and every hill. The attack was initiated at 7:30. Positions were taken toward Lijeva Rijeka, where there remains a guard of about thirty Partisans. With other Partisans we took Vjeternik and crossed Bolesestra, Orahovo. Last night at 6:30 we arrived at Prelev Brijeg, where we stayed overnight in the school. This morning we sent a squad of twenty-five comrades to take positions above Prelev Brijeg, toward Lutovo.

We need help in holding all the positions in Bratonozici because rifle fire is all around us.

We used a lot of ammunition and we'll need to get more. We had two heavily wounded who immediately succumbed to their wounds, Perisha Lalovich and a Partisan from Boka. One was lightly wounded. On their side there were two dead as far as we know. There are probably more, as well as wounded.

It is necessary to come here right away to see what we should do.

Give an order to bring flour and other foodstuffs. We don't have meat, either.

We wait for you.

DEATH TO FASCISM—FREEDOM TO THE PEOPLE!

Position, March 21, 1942, 7:30

Regards,
Vojo Todorovich
(signed)

(back of letter)

Comrade Blazo Jovanovich

Urgent   Position

COMMENTARY ON *HELL OR COMMUNISM IN MONTENEGRO*

It was not unusual for Montenegrins to state their birth year in terms of history (leaders and natural events) and the day in terms of the church calendar. Though often lacking a formal education, these simple, dignified people had a clear sense of self-definition that was in harmony with their fatherland and the Serbian Orthodox Church. Thus, Aleksa Popovich, a Montenegrin representative at the parliament convened by King Nicholas I, was quoted as saying, "I was born in Smail-aga's year, during the Assumption fast." Lakich Vojvodich said, "I was born in the year when the winter was hard with heavy snow." Mihailo Mishin, "The story was I was born in the year when many people died from epidemics. Then five people were buried in a single grave." One might say, "I was born on Saint Sava's Day in the year that the rivers rose over their banks." In such genealogy there is a connection with their traditions and heroes and a comradely sense of having been strengthened by surviving natural disasters.

But what will be the birth statements of those Montenegrins born in the nine months from the end of 1941 to the middle of 1942? With church after church left empty by the murder of their priests, there were no baptisms or baptismal certificates. The birth events recalled bespeak a tragedy of incredible proportions, a hellishness far beyond natural disasters. What a birthright! "I was born in the winter of the pits, when men were buried alive." "I was born in the time of torture." "I was born in the time when brothers killed brothers and sons killed their fathers."

Alas, such genealogy is not hyperbole. It evokes stories such as that of the octogenarian Petar Kovacevich from Grahovo, killed by his own sons early in 1942. Such sons were publicly lauded by Tito in a speech in January 1942, praised as those "whose hands do not tremble even as they kill their own father." When Pavle Kovacevich followed orders to liquidate his own father, he was rewarded as an example to others, by being promoted to the position of political commissar in the Partisan operations headquarters in Hercegovina.

The enormity of the tragedy behind such events is documented in *Hell or Communism in Montenegro*. Its eight volumes show in words and pictures one of the blackest episodes of Serbian history in Montenegro. Relentlessly the lists add up: the goods stolen, the houses burned, the men—and some-times women—wounded and killed. As the statistics show, not even old age was protection against slaughter. The descriptions of the photographs leave indelible images of horror: old men in their coffins, dozens of bodies pulled out of mass graves, mutilated corpses with sunken skulls and gaping eye sockets.

Equally appalling are the testimony and documents that establish the guilt of those charged with the heinous crimes of this period. No one takes any responsibility. "I was just the commandant. The political commissar would have been in charge of such things, and I wasn't in control of him." And the political commissar would say, "I only carried out my orders." And orders there definitely were. Letters from one commandant to another re-printed in the volumes of *Hell* bear complaints about lack of ruthlessness and resolve. And order after meticulously logged order exhorts the Partisan commanders to find men who won't be cowardly and who will carry out liquidations urgently, without fail.

The orders never used the words *kill* or *murder*, or even *shoot*. The directives were always to *liquidate*. It's a cold word, *liquidation*. It sounds so unfeeling and bureaucratic. But that word could set in place an ambush outside a man's home, could pull the triggers on four machine guns aimed at one target, could bring a bludgeon crashing down on a priest's head, could callously kick a still-warm body onto the top of another one in the depths of a pit. Interspersed in the same official communications that insist on liquidations there is interminable bickering about how to divide thirty-nine stolen sheep, whining about meat purchases, and detailed instructions for sending a convoy to escort a tub of jam before it spoils. It is as if more feeling is engendered by animals and foodstuffs than by the human victims of this fratricidal conflict.

To this day the volumes of *Hell* have not been made available to Montene-grins searching for details of the events that happened fifty years ago. The original volumes that have been translated here were literally smuggled out of Yugoslavia at peril to the participants, and they traveled a very circuitous route to the author. But the knowledge of what happened exists in Yugosla-via, in stories and in birth accounts and in the national consciousness. What needs to be known on a broader scale is who was responsible for the hell.

The "god" in the Partisan supreme headquarters was Josip Broz Tito. He and his close associates Milovan Djilas, Mosha Pijade, Ivan Milutino-vich, and others orchestrated the tragedy.

Petar Kovacevich, whose son killed him and then was rewarded for it, was one of sixty-six Chetniks killed by order of Partisan headquarters in Grahovo as "fifth columnists" simply because they had refused to carry out the ubiquitous orders to liquidate innocent countrymen. Among the leaders issuing orders in Grahovo, in addition to Montenegrin Partisans, were Croatian Ustashe from Zagreb; Ernest Fisher, who is currently living in Zagreb; and the jurist Marija Kos from Shibenik, now living a comfortable life in Belgrade.

Another example of injustice with a tragic epilogue involved the Serbian clan Karadzich from the district Shavnik. From that clan over forty-one people were killed by Tito's pitmen. One of them was Branko Karadzich, former captain in the king's army. In the summer of 1941, when the uprising against the occupier broke out in Montenegro, Branko took an active part. He was wounded in December 1941 in Pljevlja. Despite his own injuries, Branko helped pull some of his wounded comrades from the center of the city so they would not be captured by the occupier. In one of the pogroms carried out in Montenegro as ordered from above, Branko was arrested and tortured. The inquisitors broke his hands and legs and cut off one of his fingers to take the ring from it. While he was still alive they pulled out his teeth and gouged out his eyes. Then his head was crushed with a mallet.

How could such atrocities be instigated? Various Communist documents have shown that Tito, the secretary of the Communist party, gave orders for the barbaric executions in Montenegro. It is difficult for the rational mind to fathom the criminal devastation wrought by these orders in Montenegro in just nine months.

On January 14, 1942, Milovan Djilas as a delegate of the supreme head-quarters ordered the leadership of the Podgorica Battalion to liquidate fifth columnists and to confiscate their properties. In March 1942 Mosha Pijade, responding to earlier instructions from his supreme commander, sent Tito a letter in which he reported that the "Niksic Proletariat" had killed 150 "vagabonds" and burned the village of Ozrinici. "Only with vehemence can we destroy the despised fifth columnists," Pijade concluded. On March 5, 1942, Comintern sent a letter to the central committee of the Communist Party of Yugoslavia (CCCPY) calling for intervention against the "left deviates" of the CPY; in April of that year the CCCPY convened a meeting in Foca at which the primary topic of discussion was the source and eradication of such "left deviation." The deviates who terrorized innocent people were denounced by their own party, and Dr. Branko Petranovich called them a "Red terror."

Who were the victims of this terror? Many, like Petar Kovacevich and his compatriots, were patriots who wanted to get on with resistance and sabotage against the occupier and who refused to carry out orders for mass murder of their neighbors and clansmen. Local leaders who would not join the Partisans were immediately targeted, as was anyone who openly criticized Partisan methods. In particular, Orthodox priests were doomed by the atheistic Communist leadership, which abhorred their resolute faith and feared the influence they had among their congregations. The followers of Njegosh and Marko Miljanov were put on hit lists. People of good stock were struck down. Ancient clans that had fought and survived the Turks were decimated. In summary, anyone who was honest and humane and self-respecting was in danger. With their demise the very culture and traditions of

a people were in jeopardy. The Communists acted on the belief that everything must be destroyed to create something new. Djilas observed, "Those
who wage war and revolution must be prepared to kill people, compatriots
and even their friends and relatives."

Ironically, the brutal killings that were intended to put an end to opposition to Partisan plans probably had the opposite effect. In Montenegro it
was widely believed that the Chetnik movement would not have been so
strong if the Partisans had not waged their bloody ideological vendetta.
Their brutality forced even would-be noncombatants to take a stand against
them.

The Communists were not content to eradicate their opponents physically;
they also tried to blacken their reputations. Thus the knee-jerk epithet of
"fifth columnist" was bandied about so casually that opportunists within
Partisan ranks, the dregs of society, could use it as an excuse for murder
and mayhem. Although the decent Montenegrins who were their targets
never collaborated with the occupier, they were branded as traitors by their
killers. The diabolical tendency of the Communists to twist facts and skewer
reputations even extended to perjuring the background of the Montenegrin
people and creating fictional ethnicities and supposed schisms, as will be
explored in the next chapter.

The editors of *Hell or Communism in Montenegro* did their best to illumi-
nate the horrors inflicted in a nine-month period on the innocent citizenry
of that region and to document the orders that caused them. But these
volumes are still not public, and people caught up in the cauldron of the
fratricidal conflict must have puzzled deeply over how their ordered, peaceful world could have gone so incredibly wrong. An anecdote illustrates the
anguish:

When Spasoje Tadich was in hiding he was surrounded by a group of
Partisans sent to eliminate him. Spasoje succeeded in killing two and
wounding several of them. His nephew Tadija, a student, was accused of
warning his uncle of the raid. He was arrested and sentenced to death.
When Spasoje was in hiding, Tadija met him at the home of Spasoje's
sister. Their dialogue might have gone like this:

Spasoje: "My nephew, I would be delighted with you if you were not
with such unscrupulous guys like Veljko Milushin [*Micanovich*]."

Tadija: "Veljko compared to some others is shining gold, especially
compared to those in the highest positions."

Spasoje, with surprise: "How can you think like that?!"

Tadija, in a lower voice: "It's true! I think, Uncle, you might have
judged Veljko wrong. In any revolution mistakes are made!"

Spasoje: "I am afraid the Partisans could go too far with liquidations."

Tadija with surprise: "I don't think so!"

Spasoje with sadness: "Just look at the 'Dogs Cemetery' near Kolashin!
Some victims were mutilated and some were thrown alive into the pits or
into the wells!"

Tadija: "It sounds to me as if the Chetniks have been spreading false propaganda against the Partisans and their struggle."

Spasoje: "Remember that nobody can bring those innocent people who were murdered back to life again!"

Tadija: "True! However, we'll bring better lives to all the people."

Spasoje: "It depends on whether anyone survives this cataclysm."

Tadija, anxiously: "There is no doubt! There will surely be some survivors!"

Spasoje: "God only knows how many Serbs will survive this paranoid period."

Tragically, many of them did not!

We end with the words of Dr. Radoje Vukcevich: "Terror is the method of communism, and fear is its weapon. Self-interest is their truth, and hatred is their faith. Chains are their freedom, and coercion is their justice."

PART II

Chapter Two

QUO VADIS MONTENEGRIN LATINASHI?[1]

Montenegro is small geographically; however, through the centuries it has been important politically and ideologically. Conflicting forces and warmongers have attempted both to draw on its strengths and to deny them. An awakening of an ancient, mythical, individual, and collective psyche as well as forces of division, schism, and immense evil have marked its trail of glory and distress through history.

The Montenegrin Ethos

Montenegro is a unique area populated by Serbs, fierce Dinaric mountain people who are a bit different from the Serbs of the flatter agricultural land[2] but who fully share—indeed, have cherished and preserved—their proud Serbian origin.

The tiny, independent principality that was later called the kingdom of Montenegro was centered around the town of Cetinje until World War I broke out. Cetinje was surrounded by bare limestone mountains that were perfectly suited for resistance against the Turks, as well as against Venice and Austria for over five centuries. The people of Montenegro are remarkable, as full of contrast as is the country in which they proudly live.

The inhabitants of those tough, inaccessible mountains were known as uncompromising fighters for liberty and human dignity. Lord Tennyson said of them, "And never, since the beginning of the world, was there a prouder tribe breathing than thine. . . . These are men who, when asked to pay tribute, offer stones. These are men who dress cowards in women's clothes and whose wives, when need requires, boldly grab hold of the gun."[3] Yes, such was Montenegro, until tragedy was fomented by unscrupulous revolutionaries in 1941.

The term *ethos* in regard to Serb-Montenegrins refers to more than the ethnicity of a people physically related to each other. Ethos embraces the characteristics of a people—the traditions, beliefs, and values that link them with their past and guide them in the present. Though harsh coercion and calculated manipulation can temporarily undermine the outward expression of an ethos, as has been the case in Montenegro in the twentieth century, its latent power cannot be forever denied. The Serb-Montenegrin ethos is a rich blend of poetry, faith, military and spiritual heroism, and an abiding sense of human decency and dignity. Philosophers and historians worldwide have lauded the spirit of these proud mountain people.

There are nine cycles of collected Serbian folksongs that express the sufferings as well as the heroism of the Serbian people during and after the tragic events of Kosovo (the defeat by the Turks in 1389). Goethe, the German philosopher, learned Serbian in order to understand the depth of meaning of the Serbian folksongs, which have expressed the aspirations of the Serbian people throughout centuries. They are a real Serbian treasury. In art, the themes of the folksongs are depicted in medieval frescos of monasteries and churches. Accompanied by the strumming of simple instruments like the *gusle*, the folksongs were handed down from one generation to another. Some Serbian renegades of Montenegro try to denigrate the simple beauty of the music by calling it "guslarenje." But with those songs, known and otherwise unknown heroes were kept in the mind of many generations. How should someone be judged who belittles his own glorious past and tradition?

According to Dr. Branislav Djurdjev, the Serbian nobility concluded their conversation at a supper at Kosovo by saying that if the Serbs were defeated at Kosovo they would not recuperate soon. Therefore, the nobility came to the conclusion that whoever survived should remove to some natural fortresses and remain there until they could regain control of their own territory. They judged that the most suitable territory to defend would be the area of the Zeta Serbs, later known as Montenegro, a state that had sometimes been taken but never subjugated.

Thus, after the Kosovo tragedy many Serbian clans began to move from the Kosovo area. Among those clans were the Vukcevich and the Vojinovich, later called Vujovich, who left their beloved land of Vucitrn ten miles south of Kosovska Mitrovica. The Vujovich clan inhabited the western shore of Lake Skutari (Skadarsko jezero), which they called Ljubotinj. The Vukcevich clan retreated via Ljesh (Albania) and in the midfifteenth century with some other Ljeshnjani clans (from whence came their name) moved to Zeta, which was ruled by Stevan Charnojevich.

The Petrovich dynasty called themselves Serbs, and they ruled Montenegro for over 200 years despite very harsh circumstances. Danilo the First, who was the founder of the Petrovich dynasty, took as his title "Danilo, Bishop of Cetinje, Njegosh, ruler of Serbian land."

In 1754, Metropolitan (Archbishop) Vasilije said all Serbs look at Montenegro as the country from where sunshine begins, as the lighthouse that illuminates them in the darkness that covered the Serbian land. In 1757 the Metropolitans Sava and Vasilije together with other Montenegrin chieftains wrote to the prince of Venice "from our glorious Serbian empire."

On February 26, 1766, Metropolitan Sava Petrovich appealed to his counterpart in Moscow, Metropolitan Platon, to intervene with Empress Catherine the Great to have her representative at Porta "persuade the Greeks not to intervene in the Serbian nation."

In 1788 and 1789 gubernator Ivan Radonjich wrote two letters to Empress Catherine, including in the first letter the words "Now, all we Montenegrin Serbs." The other letter refers to "all Serbs from Montenegro and Hercegovina."

In 1796 at the eve of battle in Kruse, Saint Peter the First wrote, "Our unquenchable Serbian heart beats and our Serbian blood is boiling."

In 1833 Petar II Petrovich-Njegosh sent a letter to Vuk Karadzich, proclaiming proudly:

> My name is Veroljub [one devoted to the faith]
> Surname is Rodoljub [patriot].
> Montenegro my native country,
> Stone around on all sides.
> In Serbian I write and speak.
> I loudly say to everyone:
> My nationality is Serbian;
> My mind and soul are Slavic.
>
> (Ime mi je Veroljub,
> Prezime mi Rodoljub.
> Crnu goru, rodnu grudu
> Kamen pashe odasvud.
> Srpski pisem i zborim,
> Svakom gromko govorim:
> Narodnost mi Srbinska,
> Um i dusa Slavjanska.

In the presence of Njegosh, the Bishop of Uzica Nikiphor added the following to Njegosh's poem:

> He who climbs to the top of Lovcen,
> Let him live there.
> And with Njegosh fly closer to the sky,
> And to the sunshine that we all need.
>
> (Ko se pope na vrh Lovcena,
> Nek prebiva ondjena.
> S Njegoshem se tune blize neba,
> I sunce koje nam svima treba.)

In August 1833, Njegosh departed for Russia, where he was consecrated an Orthodox bishop.

The year after Njegosh's death in 1851, Nikanor Ivanovich was chosen Metropolitan of Montenegro. He left for Russia in 1860. The metropolitan could not get along with the ambitious young Montenegrin prince Nicholas. The prince then designated Mitrophan Ban, who was a vehement adherent of Serbian unification in 1918, as metropolitan.

The epoch of King Nicholas represents the last shelter of the current Separatists. Some of them followed their master, Josip Broz from Kumrovac, and accepted acts of King Nicholas that were anti-judicial and anti-canon. However, the Separatists remain silent in regard to King Nicholas's literary work, especially his poetry and the speeches made before Montenegrins went to war. One Separatist, Vidoje Zarkovich, calls King Nicholas an "exaggerated Serb." The Separatists have been trying to hide behind the king's popularity.

Here are a few lines of the king's patriotic hymn:

> There, to that place, behind those hills,
> They say Milosh's tomb rests!
> There my soul will find peace,
> When Serbs will never be slaves again!

> (Onamo, 'namo, za brda ona,
> Miloshev kazu, prebiva grob!
> Onamo pokoj dobicu dushi,
> Kad Srbin vishe ne bude rob!)

In 1852 Prince Danilo wrote to Omer-pashe, "Don't forget, Omer, just a handful of Montenegrin Serbs hold the entire Turkish might at bay!"

In 1855 the code of Prince Danilo says in paragraph 92, "In this country there is no nationality except Serbian, and no faith except Eastern Orthodox."

According to Savo Brkovich, who claims himself a hundred percent Montenegrin, the Nemanjich and Petrovich dynasties "borrowed" the Serbian origin to enhance their personal ambitions and prestige, but the facts clearly show otherwise.

Here are some verses from the talented contemporary Serbian poet Milan Petrovich:

> So told us Mosha Pijade,
> That Bishop Rade is not Serb . . .
> Don't Mosho and also Saro
> Touch that old Serbian hearth,
> Because the Sultan touched it once.
> Since then Smirnu never saw again.

(Tako nam rece Mosa Pijade
Da Srbin nije vladika Rade . . .
Nemoj Moso, i nemoj Saro
Dirati to srpsko ognjiste staro.
Jer Sultan jednom u njega dirnu
Pa nikad vise ne vide Smirnu.)

Duke (Vojvoda) Marko Miljanov appealed through an Austrian delegate to the Austrian tzar to let all Serbian land be united in promising that if he did so they would hold the tzar in high esteem instead of maligning him.

In 1914 King Nicholas the First proposed to King Petar the First the formation of a military, diplomatic, and financial union between Montenegro and Serbia—"So as to leave to our sons one unified soul and a strong Serbdom."

Many European authors praised Montenegro as a Spartan state. Gerhard Gezemann, the German Slavist, in his book *The Humaneness and Heroism of Old Montenegrins*, wrote: "The Montenegrin by his legendary belief is not only the best fighter in the world but also the best Serb, a better Serb than any other Serb. He is the typical Serbian Dinaric soul."

The de-Serbianization of Montenegro would be the same as de-Germanizing the Prussians. Is there today any Serb who would turn his back to Kosovo and to Milosh's tomb?

To turn away from the Serbian ethos of Montenegrins is to distance oneself from the humaneness that characterizes the Serbian soul. Humaneness is the synthesis of all human virtues. Says Marko Miljanov: "If there is a man who drives another man away, open the door to the real man, but close it to the one who is driving away the other man."

Throughout the centuries Montenegrin-Serbian Sparta was the guardian of Serbian identity and the beacon of liberty. With Lovcen, the Serbian Olympus, it has been the spiritual center for all Serbs. Montenegro stood as a symbol of patriotism, courage, morality, dignity, pride, and sacrifice whenever those virtues were in jeopardy. For over five centuries Montenegro kept the torch of liberty burning. After the Serbian Good Friday at Kosovo Field, Kosovo remains as special for Serbs as Jerusalem is to Jews, as Rome is to Catholics, and as Mecca is to Muslims.

Montenegrins have been proud to be Serbs. Circumstances led them from war cry (poklich) to war cry, from one shot to another. Montenegro was a war camp where heroism was considered as a supreme virtue, a quality that left a strong stamp on Montenegrin society.

William Gladstone said that Montenegro is a "miracle in history."

Serbian men in Montenegro earned respect through history, an esteem that some of their detractors have disregarded. Separatist "historians," for example, talk about the imaginary theories of the origin of the Montenegrin people but intentionally avoid mentioning such things as the Croats' behavior during the thirty years war in the nineteenth century. On a wall of the Munich Cathedral of the Croats' ally Bavaria was written the famous sentence: "God save me from the plague (kuga), war (hunger), and Croats." The French cardinal Tisserant mentioned Croats, reporting that in his region (Lorraine) they had burned several towns and had a reputation as evil men. How did the Croatian quisling army behave on the Soviet front during World War II?

Attempted Breaking Apart of the Serbian Ethos

During and after World War II a very small number of Montenegrin forces, called "Montenegrin Ustashe" by their adversaries, performed a disgraceful job. For a long time, influenced by Vatican clerics and Muslim (dzihad) forces, they tried to dig a grave for the Serbian people. However, history, tradition, culture, and truth were against them, because man cannot live his entire life with lies and injustice. The great lie was that Montenegrins are a separate and non-Serbian entity; the greatest injustice is that Montenegrin youth of today have been coerced into that lie, which in denying them their roots robs them of their chance to blossom in the future as proud citizens of a noble birthright.

The first concept of a separate Montenegrin nation was presented by racist Italian anthropologists. Then it was embraced by the Comintern and—last and most importantly—by Titoists, whose CPY endeavored to turn that idea into reality.

An international meeting of the Communist party was held in Moscow on March 30, 1925. The party then embraced a program to break up Yugoslavia (which was considered an artifact of the Treaty of Versailles) and to create Balkan Soviet republics, one of which would be Montenegro. Thus, the Montenegrin nation was created by Communist decree. The chicks were hatched under Lenin and Stalin's carts.

Why did the international community of the Communist party want to break up the Yugoslav entity? In the Comintern were members from countries defeated in the first world war, like Bulgaria (her representative in Comintern was Dimitrov), Germany, Austria, Hungary, Croatia, and Italy (which believed it should have Dalmatia[4]).

The "Independent" State of Montenegro

On July 12, 1941, in Cetinje, Sekula Drljevich and his cohorts proclaimed the Independent Montenegrin State under Italian protection. The following day the Montenegrin people in protest of such humiliation began an armed uprising against the occupier for their national liberation.

Montenegrin statehood has existed since Zeta under the Balshich, Crno-jevich, and Petrovich dynasties that ruled Montenegro. Meanwhile, in Montenegro nobody paid attention to Montenegrin nationality until Titoism came in power. Why not? The Montenegrin entity was acknowledged by Tito's AVNOY decree in Jajce in November 1943. Titoistic history began with the "new era"—that is, from 1941, when the Communists began the revolution in Yugoslavia. A separate, non-Serbian Montenegrin ethos was not determined by historical facts or the will of the Montenegrin people. With Tito's dictatorial decision Montenegrin pride and dignity were raped. No honest, rational person will recognize this new Montenegrin ethnos. Some tried to confuse uninformed people into identifying statehood with national origin.

It is a paradox of Titoist duality that Serbian enemies, Croats in particular, have used Montenegrin nationality in two ways, depending on whether the wind blows in their favor or not. For example, when statistics of individual nationalities in the Yugoslav armed forces were gathered, Montenegrins were counted as Serbs so Croats and Slovenes could complain of superfluous Serb representation. In other cases they were regarded as members of a separate Montenegrin ethos. Such irony!

Montenegrin Titoists versus the Serbian Orthodox Church in Montenegro

The Serbian Orthodox church played a dominant and decisive role in national and political life throughout Serbian history, especially in the period of Serbian slavery under the Turkish empire. The church is central to the concept of Serbdom as the bones and flesh together make up the human body. Therefore, the Serbian church was extolled by her friends and steadily attacked and fanatically hated by her enemies. Indeed, her enemies undertook the total destruction of the Serbian Orthodox church in Montenegro.

People with different cultures have diverse views, and religion has an important role in their lives. Culture is understood by civilized people as the thoughts that bind certain people in a given time. Ideology, on the other hand, is a doctrine that more often separates people. Religion is a pattern of beliefs and conduct that involves a code of ethics. What is tolerant in religion belongs to culture; what is not belongs to ideology.

Real faith is based on love, while hatred is a complex of weakness that springs from hell. Blasphemy has disastrous consequences on the moral behavior of man. The simple man is directed toward God, submitting his account only to God. When belief in God is destroyed in such a man, he directs himself toward his self-interests. Says Leo Tolstoy, if man does not believe in God he becomes God himself. Then he can do whatever he wants to.

When the Titoists won over the people in 1945 in Ljeshkopolje, now a suburb of Podgorica, they tried by all means to destroy humaneness in people. Thus they dressed a horse in priest's garments and paraded it through the village. As if aware of the humiliation, the horse walked with bowed head. It showed more dignity than its masters did![5] This example demonstrates in a small way how Titoists tried—and often succeeded—to shake the people's faith in God, by eliminating the caretakers and teachers of the faith, the priests, whose wanton murders are documented in *Hell or Communism in Montenegro*. Titoists have to ask themselves who they are and what they are! Unfortunately, today's generations know little or nothing about their past.

Professor Milorad Ekmecich in a study juxtaposed the term *Orthodoxy* with the title Apostate and Schism, to destroy the concept and importance of Orthodoxy in favor of the Catholic church.

Some who called themselves one hundred percent Montenegrins betrayed their Serbian origins, as Judas Iscariot betrayed Jesus for money. Where did the money come from? Some publications assert it continues to come from the highest and largest religious institutions!

During the "Blasphemous Period," violence was done not only to the beliefs to which Montenegrins had been loyal but also to the very persons who had worked to spread those beliefs. From 1941 to 1946, Montenegrin Communists, the "avant garde of the working class," killed about 120 priests, monks, deacons, and seminarians. A brutal culmination came when the metropolitan of Montenegro's Littoral diocese, Joanikije Lipovac, and Dr. Luka Vukmanovich were killed by mallet blows at the foot of Bukulja, Arangelovac in 1946. During this period was heard the popular Communist slogan: "I don't believe in heaven, but in Marx and Engels" (Ne vjerujem u nebesa, vec u Marksa i Engelsa).

Indirect and Direct Vatican Involvement in Balkan Matters

Attacks on the Serbian Orthodox Church in Montenegro were paralleled by arbitrary elimination in Croatia by calling it the Croatian Catholic church. In the Independent State of Croatia (ISC) there was no longer room for the Serbian church organization. Poglavnik (Pavelich), a new "pope" for the persecuted church in Croatia, defined her status by special law, decreeing how the Croatian Orthodox church, a thinly disguised Catholic church, should be organized.[6] Pavelich said in a speech at the Croatian parliament: The Croatian Orthodoxy will be left alone. Meanwhile, the Serbian Orthodox church cannot exist in Croatia. Why not? Because all Orthodox churches throughout the world are national churches. The Serbian Orthodox church is a part of the Serbian state. The Serbian Orthodox church is hierarchical. In Serbia, her state representatives appoint the patriarch, or at least take part in his appointment. The patriarch is in charge of the entire clergy in his church jurisdiction. Such rules could be applied in Serbia, perhaps in the former unfortunate Yugoslavia, but they cannot and will not be in the

Croatian state. If a church organization is not international but particular, then it can only be Croatian, under control of the Croatian state.[7]

Does this show equal treatment? The Croatian Catholic church must be under the direct jurisdiction of the Vatican, while the Serbian Orthodox church in Croatia could not be under the jurisdiction of her mother church in Belgrade!

Further, world reaction against the genocide committed by the Croatian Ustashe in the ISC moved Pavelich to camouflage his crimes by creating the so-called Croatian Orthodox church. The French cardinal Tisserant stated: "Pavelich had decided by one stroke of the pen to create the Croatian Orthodox church so he could in the same way renounce it."

The "theocratic" position that rationalized the essentially forced conversion of Orthodox congregations to Catholic ones was the contention that Serbs in Croatia were but renegade Catholics who needed—and desired—to be returned to the papal fold. The political reality was that the Vatican had long involved itself in Balkan affairs, and this was no exception.

In fact, the Vatican was well known for its anti-Yugoslav policy. In 1925 the Holy See had agreed to negotiate a concord with the Yugoslav government. Both delegations met in Rome. However, the Catholic bishops had requested the pope not to sign the concord until conditions of the church—political matters—were accepted. De facto, it meant returning to the position of 1918 regarding the former Catholic Austro-Hungarian Empire. The Holy See accepted the bishops' recommendations. Then the Yugoslav minister of education, Stjepan Radich, a Croat and chief of the strongest Catholic party in Croatia, came out energetically against the hostile attitude of the Vatican and the higher clergy. He condemned the pretensions of the clergy and demanded from them complete respect for Yugoslav sovereignty.

Unfortunately, during and after the Second World War, the Croatian politicians did not follow Radich's example, and they dared not appeal to the Croatian clergy to devote themselves to the well-being of all people living in Croatia regardless of their creed, ethnicity, and differences in ideology and political leanings.

Between 1925 and 1992 the Vatican reversed its position by recognizing the independence and sovereignty of Croatia and Slovenia ahead of the European Community (EC) representatives. Did the Vatican act in good faith, in both cases if not with Christian love then with understanding and fairness to others in the full Christian meaning of the word?

Dr. Krunislav Draganovich was known as a notorious clerofascist during World War II. He was accused as a war criminal for misdeeds toward Orthodox people in Croatia. In 1937 his doctoral dissertation centered on Orthodox people living in the Croatian linguistic domain. Research into the facts, of course, shows no basis whatsoever for his claims. According to him, the Orthodox Serbs once were Roman Catholics. Then Orthodoxy began to spread into Croatia. Under unbearable pressures many Catholics succumbed and under duress abandoned their Catholic faith. Some were converted to Islam by Turks, while others pressured by Greeks turned to Orthodoxy. This view of the Orthodox people in Croatia as renegades of the Catholic church[8] dovetailed with the Catholic desire for expansion and domination. The views and desires of the Vatican and Draganovich are discussed here just to show how different forces played a part in the orchestration of malevolent events.

One enigma: Did Churchill have a secret plan with the Vatican for the restoration of the Sub-Danube Catholic Federation? In the nineteenth century was formed in the Danube Basin a chauvinistic Pan-Croatian movement under the patronage of the Vatican. This movement was trying to extend Croatian influence, and thus expand Catholicism. They tried to be friendly with the Montenegrins, whom they called "Red Croats," translated by Shtedimlija as "Southern Croats." Bosnia and Hercegovina were called "Turkish Croatia"; Dalmatia, "White Croatia"; Korushka and Shtajerska, "Karantinska Croatia"; Slovenia, "Alp Croatia"; and other Serbs, "Orthodox Croats." Is it not appropriate to call such nomenclature a phantasm of invention?

The Formulators of the Ethos Fraud

Who were the men who promulgated the fantastic ideas that found expression in such brutal reality? Two were particularly involved in the creation of the Croatian "Orthodox" church and the Independent State of Montenegro. They represent the sad ability of men to delude themselves about their past until they so believe their own lies they are utterly corrupted and doomed by them. These two Separatists are Savic Markovich Shtedimlija and Sekula Drljevich. Correctly or incorrectly, their adversaries called them Montenegrin Ustashe. The reader can judge from the material that follows whether they were renegades of the Serbian nation.[9]

Savich Markovich Shtedimlija was a distinctive Ustashe ideologist. As a young man he declared himself by national orientation a Serb and by religion Orthodox. In the first phase of his writing, in his work *The Elements of Montenegrin Nationalism*, he treated Montenegrins as Serbs. Yet he took part in the abortive declaration of the Independent State of Montenegro (ISM). In 1941 he wrote two articles in which he stated that Drljevich and his adherents were ready with Italian help to form an independent state of Montenegro. The declaration of Montenegrin students living in Zagreb on April 11, 1941, was written by him in accord with Drljevich's opinion. And he happily participated in organizing the Croatian Orthodox church. Under the auspices of the Croatian Ustashe authority, he was the writer and editor for various publications. He edited the *Orthodox Calendar* for 1944.[10]

Radovan Zogovich says that Shtedimlija died twice. His first "death" was in the summer of 1930, when his demise was announced in the newspaper *Vreme* on August 6. He personally spread the news, to find out what the public thought about him.

His second death began with his collaboration with Mile Budak. When he moved to Zagreb he changed completely. There he came in contact with Croatian historiographers, who influenced him to change his nationality from Serbian to Croatian! Rather than agreeing that Montenegrins are autohton, who came from Dukljanian Slavs and from the old Balkan people found there, Shtedimlija asserted that after Nemanja took over Zeta (later called Montenegro), Croatians disappeared under the influence and the pressure of the authorities of the Orthodox church, swallowed up into the Serbian national consciousness with the Montenegrin ancestors. (In the Middle Ages there was neither religious identification nor national determination.)

Shtedimlija wrote a pamphlet called "Red (southern) Croatia," which he attempted to distinguish from "White" (western) Croatia. He tried to prove that today's Montenegro is Red Croatia, which would mean that the descendants of Montenegrins were Croats. He continues his version of history by saying that Red Croatia was weakened by internal conflicts so she came to the edge of destruction. Then she formed an alliance with the Serbian Rashka and remained there by restoring the name of the kingdom. She remained faithful to the Roman Catholic church until the disintegration of Dushan's Serbian empire in the late fourteenth century. Under the foreign domination of Serbs, Albanians, and Greeks, the Croatian name and national conscience began to fade away. At least, that's what Shtedimlija claimed! Thus the Montenegrin Separatists of Shtedimlija's and Drljevich's persuasion were apologists who pretended that the Montenegrins' genetic origin came from Goths and Red Croats.

Marko Kavaja labeled Shtedimlija a degenerate faker. When Rade Drainac met him in Zagreb, Shtedimlija slipped a Jesuit's black mantle over his head. Indeed, he acted like a megalomaniac. Tanasije Mladenovich believes Shtedimlija became a camouflaged Fascist and that he directly espoused Franciscan clerocatholicism for personal advantages.

Shtedimlija was certainly capable of taking advantage of a situation. Through a committee formed with Pavelich's accord under the auspices of the Italians, Shtedimlija acquired wealth from the hapless Jews by providing them with documentation of Montenegrin nationality in order to be protected from execution by the Croatian Ustashe. They paid dearly to obtain these papers, which spared many of their lives.

Shtedimlija was a Montenegrin Separatist and Gestapo agent before the war. In Zagreb he was a close friend of the Montenegrin Separatist Sekula Drljevich. He wrote editorials for *The Croatian State*, Ante Pavelich's official newspaper, and he also sent intelligence reports to Hans Helm, chief of the Croatian Gestapo.

Before liberation, Shtedimlija fled from Zagreb. In Vienna he was arrested by the Soviet intelligence service. In 1956, he appeared again in Zagreb, allegedly as a former Informbureau adherent. He started to write again under a pseudonym. Soon after, under his own name, he became one of the leaders of the mass movement! He even published a series of stories about the secret archives of the secret police, the UDBA.

Shtedimlija's third—and final—death came in 1970, after the kind of long illness that makes people say "Thank God!" for the final release. In his obituary he was characterized as a "meritorious writer." The bills for his burial were paid by writers of the Croatian Association.[11]

Sekula Drljevich

During World War I, Sekula Drljevich was interned in Boldagason, Hungary by the Austrian-Hungarian occupier. There he was a vehement adversary of his king, Nicholas I of Montenegro. By 1918 Drljevich was in favor of the unification of Montenegro with Serbia. He was ready to steadily change his shirts. Later he became a Serbian renegade just out of spite.

During his political career in Belgrade, true to his unstable character, he left Belgrade and joined the Croatian opposition in Zagreb, just to tweak the nose of the Serbian authority. During World War II, Drljevich seriously thought that if he could arrest some adherents of Serbian unification he would be able to rule Montenegro without major problems. Paradoxically, he would have had to arrest himself first, because he had been a strong adherent of Serbian unification in 1918.

In 1941 Biroli, the governor of Montenegro, expelled Drljevich from Montenegro to San Remo, Italy because the overwhelming majority of Montenegrins rejected his separatist and antagonistic policy toward the Serbian ethos. From there Drljevich clandestinely managed to reach Zagreb hospital, where he hid himself under an alias. It was there that he wrote the articles in the *Gracanica* in which he urged the Ustashe to totally exterminate the Serbian people.

The Germans were even more against Drljevich than the Italians. Hermann Neubacher, the minister of the Reich for the southeast, wrote a report that called Drljevich a thief. First he was paid by the Italians and then abandoned; then the Croats took care of him. Says Dr. Dragoljub Jovanovich in his book *Oh men! Oh men!* about Drljevich, one who does not know him could never believe a Montenegrin could hate Serbia to such an extent that he even hates Yugoslavia because Serbia is located in her.

The Yugoslav Commission for War Crimes later concluded that the articles published by Drljevich (whom it called a usurper who was calling himself the president of the Montenegrin government) had caused the Ustashe and their regime to persecute, plunder, and kill our people, especially Serbs, not only in the city of Zemun but in the entire district.

Concerning Dr. Drljevich, the People's Commission stated he had played the role of a Yugoslav Goebbels. In any regard he was a monster to his people and a freak of humanity. During the war he boldly tried to persuade Germans, Italians, and Ustashe that Montenegrins are not Serbs. Rather, they are descendants of Illyrians who are closest to Albanians, with the same distinctive characteristics.

Drljevich was a close friend of Ante Pavelich, who had a villa in his neighborhood. Drljevich visited Pavelich often with his friend Vancha Mihajlov, leader of the pro-Bulgarian terrorist organization VMRO.

Ante Pavelich

Dr. Ante Pavelich, the Croatian Fuhrer, found a close bond with Dr. Sekula Drljevich in their mutual attitudes toward the Serbian people. Pavelich flattered Drljevich that Croatians only have Montenegrins as real brothers! Drljevich proudly replied that the Montenegrin people shared the same views with the Croatian people. He believed few people in Montenegro were misled by Belgrade propaganda. He believed evil needed to be exterminated from the flock on both sides.

Pavelich told Drljevich the Serbs were the greatest enemy of both Montenegro and Croatia. They were an evil force in the Balkans and throughout Europe as well. (This statement of Pavelich's about the Serbs is identical with Tudjman's after he appeared on the policial scene in Croatia.) Pavelich also claimed that Montenegrins are not Serbs but descendants of old Illyrians. His fantasy extended even further, claiming that somehow there even existed some kinship with the Germans!

The Actions and Effects of Extreme Separatism

Did Montenegrin Separatists correctly read the minds of the Montenegrin people? What motivated Drljevich and others to proclaim an independent Montenegrin state under an occupier? Was it to serve their people or to serve their own ambitions and interests? How could those mercenaries serve the most extreme form of fascism, the Croatian Ustashe under the leadereship of Ante Pavelich? How could anyone justify such betrayal of their own people, call them what you wish, either just Montenegrins or Serb Montenegrins? Was it in accord with the heroic struggle of Montenegro through the centuries of fighting for "holy cross and golden liberty?" How could anyone accept Shtedimlija's accumulation of wealth drawn from others' distress and misfortune? Was it in accord with the humaneness of Marko Miljanov and the tradition and pride of the Montenegrin people? Were Drljevich and Shtedimlija really patriots and honest representatives of their people? If they were not, then what were they? After World War II there spread from somewhere in Montenegro the words "Great Lamentation through Montenegro for Savic and Sekula" (Velja tuga Crnom Gorom za Savicem i Sekulom).

Similarities of Separatist Actions in the ISC and Montenegro

Drljevich and Shtedimlija, two sworn enemies of the Serbian people, directed their loyalties toward the Croatian Ustashe, the most extreme variance of fascism, on whom they depended financially and morally. The small group of Montenegrin Separatists in the USC was unique and active in intelligence services concerning their imagined Serbian enemies both inside and outside Croatia.

Meanwhile, in Montenegro, Separatists (or by a broader concept Zelenashi) did not agree. Why not? The majority of them were against any provocative action toward Montenegrin Serbs, who were for the Montenegrin unification with Serbia in 1918. The leaders of those moderate Montenegrin Federalists were Savo Vuletich, former minister of justice in the government of King Nicholas I; Tomash Grujovich; Jevrem Shaulich; Milo Bakocevich; and others. Unfortunately, on Ljeshnjani territory the leadership of the Zelenashi of Drljevich's persuasion abandoned Vuletich as their leader during World War II.

So, on August 29, 1941, Jovan Belov Vujovich, "gayettlia," (named for the adherents of King Nicholas I who left for Gayeta, Italy) brought Italians from Cetinje to the nahija. The Italian occupier then arrested over eighty Ljeshnjani who were well-known Serbs.[12]

Pejovich, a Manipulator of Drljevich's Persuasion

Another arrest was conducted by the pliant Italians in 1942. The person who manipulated the occupier into serving Separatist aims was Andrija Pejovich.

Since January 29/30, 1942, the date of a punitive expedition against the Donjo Ljeshnjani Battalion directed by Jovanovich but initiated by Headquarters of Lovcen Determen, the battalion had been on the alert every night to guard against surprise Partisan attacks. The primary targets for liquidation in that expedition were prominent persons from the Vukcevich clan.

In the middle of February, Andrija Pejovich with two armed escorts from the Bojanich clan came to the home of Pero Tomasheva in Lijeshnje while Maj. Vaso Vukcevich and the very popular Nikola Vukcevich were visiting. Pejovich was looking for both of them.[13] A few nights before, the Partisans had tried—and failed—to assassinate Nikola. Pejovich also was unsuccessful in his attempt at Pero's house. (A letter sent from the Lovcen Partisan Detachment to the headquarters of the Zeta Detachment illuminates Pejovich's standing with the Partisans and also shows perplexing calculations and intentions. This letter is quoted extensively in endnote 14 of this chapter.)

On February 20, 1942 Andrija went to Podgorica and submitted a list of "Communists" from the sector of Donjo Ljeshnjani to the Italian command.

On that list were the same names that had been targeted for liquidation by Jovanovich's punitive expedition of January 29/30. This shows that Savo Celebich and his son, Milovan from the Lovcen Detachment, had secretly conspired with Pejovich to liquidate their poliqical adversaries either by Partisans or by the Italians or by both, whichever would succeed first.

How was it possible that Pejovich was trusted by the Italian occupier and by the Lovcen Partisan Detachment at the same time, when the Partisans were supposed to be such archenemies of fascism? He was an Italian informer. Through Maj. Celebich and Milovan (a party member), Andrija became also a trusted man at the Lovcen Partisan Headquarters, which was located in their village, Shtitari. What was he trusted to do? Celebich was a political leader of the Ljeshnjani Separatists. Both he and Pejovich were ready to use all means to get rid of Ljeshnjanis who favored the Serbian entity.

On March 1, 1942, the Italian occupier attacked the territory of the Donjo Ljeshnjani Battalion. Once again Pejovich and his marionettes did not succeed in liquidating the people who were named on the list submitted by him to the Italians earlier in Podgorica. Why not? Thanks to an Italian interpreter of Slovenian descent who was a former Yugoslav officer. He was an honest man. He saved the lives of most of the targeted people because he found they had been labeled "Communists" out of malice.

Was there any retaliation later against Pejovich's gendarme company by the Ljeshnjani Chetnik Battalion? Not at all. No Ljeshnjani Separatist ever lost one hair from his head because of the Ljeshnjani Chetniks.

As far as the Ljeshnjani Separatists were concerned: In May of 1943 Maj. Vaso Vukcevich asked Capt. Ilija Brnovich, a Separatist, to take over the unified battalion command. He refused to accept on the excuse of poor health!

On September 8, 1943, Italy capitulated. All patriots celebrated that day. On September 10, Maj. Vaso Vukcevich was arrested by a German detachment led by the same Andrija Pejovich and incarcerated for two months.

On December 1, 1943, Partisan brigades and three rear Partisan battalions encircled and then attacked the Ljeshnjani Battalion. At the same time, the Partisans attacked the Germans for the first time on the territory of Montenegro. The Partisans hoped the Germans would retaliate against the Ljeshnjani inhabitants because the attack was executed on their territory.

Pejovich and his gendarme company joined the Partisans on the eve of the attack, though they were fed and paid by the Germans for services to the German Reich. During the five-day fighting, the Ljeshnjani Battalion had about 50 dead and wounded, while the Partisans, most of them untrained men, lost over 340 dead. Some Vukceviches were killed by the Germans, too.

What happened with the Ljeshnjani Separatists who allied with everybody in attempting to liquidate their adversaries on their territory? Again, nothing!

Because the Ljeshnjani Chetniks primarily and honestly stood to defend their people, not kill their opponents.

In 1944 the Ljeshnjani Brigade under the command of Capt. Ilija Markovich attempted to negotiate with both the Partisans and Ljeshnjani separatists, but failed. The intention was to attack the Germans together under separate commands. The Partisan representative, Lt. Col. Milutin Dapcevich, demanded that the brigade either come under Partisan command or attack the Germans alone and then the Partisans would help them out. Experience had taught the lesson that in such cases the Partisans always attacked the Chetniks from the rear to destroy them completely. So both Partisan offers were unacceptable to the Ljeshnjani Brigade. Indeed, both ideological groups, the Partisans and the Ljeshnjani Separatists, though different, shared a desire for the annihilation of their political adversaries, the Chetniks. Neither group negotiated in good faith.

Deceit and Betrayal

Lies and deceit were the tools of those who were using all possible means to bring to murderous reality the hatred in their hearts. They tried to get rid of honest men who would not embrace treacherous acts against their own people, who would not condone throwing them into pits and wells or spying against them to the occupier. Pejovich and his ilk were "Separatists" even contrary from the ideals of their own ancestry. Honesty and dignity were not only always more important than any political affiliation for true Montenegrins; they were also prized above one's own life, which is still a characteristic of Montenegrin Serbs.

Effects of Titoism

What role did Titoism play in the period of the reign of the "convicts" (Communists who had been arrested during the monarchy)? In Montenegro in particular, Titoism was an antireligious ideology that had been promoted for over fifty years with disastrous, catastrophic consequences. Tito's perfidious ideologists have been pressing to confuse and destroy the concept of Serbian ethos by using the most unscrupulous methods. There was a period of contagious disease that greatly afflicted the young generations who were without national consciousness and whose religious feelings had died out.

Those who yesterday were atheists, hard-core Communists and antireligious persecutors, overnight became fanatical defenders of the Montenegrin entity. Only yesterday they were the eyes and ears against their community, against their friends. Such irony!

As far as former Titoist leaders were concerned, one should note that they did not move a finger to bring the remains of Nicholas I from San

Remo to his capital of Cetinje—because the king was an "exaggerated" Serb! Meanwhile, thoses former Montenegrin Titoists flew by helicopter for weekends in their villas where they cooked their lamb in milk, while many Montenegrin children didn't have any milk to go with their meager bread! That is Titoist equality and justice, is it not?

As secretary of the CPY Tito took all strings of power in his hands. He ruled the country as a dictator, using the most deceptive methods. He and his cohorts invented the false slogan: "Brotherhood and Unity" to hide the Croatian Ustashe genocide committed in World War II.

After fifty years of Titoism the cynicism of that slogan was apparent. Croatia was the only part of Europe where neofascism was not destroyed right after the end of the war. Thanks for this go primarily to Tito and his Croatian Communists, who cooperated with neofascist Ustashism, covertly and overtly, within and without Yugoslavia.

In eastern Hercegovina thirty-eight pits were filled with innocent Serbian men, women, and children. After the war those pits were covered up with cement, hidden to foster "brotherhood and unity."

During the revolution of 1941-1945 people were thrown into pits, ravines, forests, wells, and rivers. Partisans committed or condoned a degree of barbaric genocide against their own people that had been unknown in the history of mankind. Just one example: A dog that was loyal to its master was shot. It had followed its master who was taken away from his home by the Communists and executed. The Communists skinned the dog, crucified the hide on a cross, and put it above the burial mound of its master. That place was marked by the Communists as the "Dog's Cemetary."

Furthermore, in April 1945 genocide was committed by the Drljevich group, together with Ustashe in Stara Gradishka. Titoists were also responsible for the intentional retention in Croatia of about ten thousand Chetniks who were not able to reach Italy and join the Allied forces out of Communist reach. So they met their death by Titoist executioners in Slovenia. These deaths were just a small fraction of "the tragedy within tragedy."

Dr. Mladen Ivekovich, a Croat, states that the pen is not capable of telling the horror and terror of the atmosphere of Jasenovac, the Ustashe-run concentration camp in Croatia. It surpasses human imagining. Imagine hell, the Inquisition, a terror more dreadful than any that ever before existed anywhere, run by bloodthirsty animals whose most hidden and disgusting instincts had erupted onto the surface in a way never before seen in human beings—and still you have not said enough! In this Yugoslav Dachau, human skulls and arm and hand bones were used in the macabre manufacture of lamps that sold for 100 to 300 marks.

Could any person of pride and dignity associate himself with such villains who belonged to the neo-Fascist Ustashe or with the cover-up of their crimes by Titoists? The Ustashe's genocide against Serbs, Gypsies, and Jews could never be forgotten nor forgiven by a civilized society. Do young Montenegrins want in any way, either directly or indirectly, to be associated with villains who have been mortal enemies of humanity and human dignity?

"Tito after Tito"

Even today twisted human minds, nationalistic and religious intolerance, still exist in the Marxist utopia, hardening the anti-Serbian ethos. Serbs and Serbia are tarnished by epithets like "Great Serbs," "reactionaries," "Chauvinistic," "hegemonistic"—expressions borrowed from the former Austro-Hungarian Empire since 1903. That is one among many paradoxes!

The apologists of Titoism should be seen through the mirror of reality. They are only concerned for their own advantages, neglecting the common people. Serbian Communists of Tito's persuasion who even now favor "Tito after Tito" became the renegades of the Serbian nation. They abandoned their own Serbian identity while embracing internationalism or Yugoslavism as their identity. However, they remain titular representatives of the Serbian people, and they hold their positions and all privileges while riding on the back of the Serbian people. During Titoism it was the law that the Montenegrin ethos must be recognized as such because Comintern says so, the Vatican wants it, and AVNOY with Tito as the master of deceit and his puppets declared it.

Did the Titoists really succeed in creating robots from men? Tito's megalomaniac, eccentric views could not vaporize overnight. On such fictitious premises many of his robots built their careers, which brought them tremendous advantages—political as well as financial gain. Why not? As Tito himself says, they fought to enjoy the fruits of their struggle! Division on the premises of ethnic and religious affiliation flatly means sowing discord among the people.

During Titoism all bridges of decency and respect among the people collapsed. It was not unusual for children to become informers on their own parents! The youth were encouraged to refuse to obey elderly people unless they were Communists. In fact, Titoism created an almost incomprehensible psychological chaos and moral decadence. Intellectuals without real academic roots came to the surface. They received the highest educational degrees. However, they had to be ready to change their opinions overnight in order to serve anyone in power. The results of their teachings and the actions of other Titoists in high positions have been hatred, envy, slander, lies, and all kinds of intrigues. The corrupters tried to inject poison into a healthy organism, into uninformed young people, to cause brother to quarrel with brother. The enemies of the Serbian people do not have what the Serbians have: a proud ethos, a glorious history. Serbians fought against them as foreign vassals. They liberated them and then they were accepted as equal brothers even though yesterday they had been enemies. The Titoists were willing to destroy the social and economic life. They were arrogant toward work and to progressive, instructive ideas. Traditional spiritual leaders were either killed or pushed aside.

Mixing Politics with Religion

Lately the interference with religion has increasingly taken the form of politically motivated interruptions of actual church services, as exemplified by the following incident in Bar.

A stranger from Zagreb sat with the Bar congregation and interrupted Father Femich during his church sermon by asking who Prince Vladimir was. "A Serbian," replied Father Femich. At that moment a "Croatian" writer from Piperi stood up and said, "Don't lie, Father! Prince Vladimir was Dukljanian, not Serbian!" (Prince Vladimir was killed in 1016. However, his cross was preserved and has been kept to this day in the Bar congregation.) At the same time, a mob was shouting primitive slogans around the church.

Common sense demands answers to some questions if we pretend to be a civilized society. Did the stranger from Zagreb look for information in the right place? Or did he want the incident to be shown on TV the next day in Zagreb? Are churches public libraries, and are worship services proper sources for finding out historical facts? Did the stranger from Zagreb ever look for historical data from the Croatian archbishop Kuharich or from any other clergy? Was his question of a religious or political nature? What motivated the Croatian writer to bring his guest from Zagreb to the Bar congregation? Had the "Croatian" writer been baptized? If he were a real Christian in his heart and mind, would he have acted as he did? Was this ugliness a residue of Titoism? In a democratic and civilized society nobody looks for political answers in religious institutions. Edmund Burke, British statesman, says, "For evil to win, it is necessary that good men do nothing."

At Cetinje Monastery a requiem mass was held to commemorate Patriarch Arsenije Charnojevich and his faithful followers who lived 300 years ago. They had to leave their beloved land to escape from Turkish genocide. During the requiem the metropolitan was interrupted by shameless lawbreakers who had no reverence for the sacred ceremony. A similar interruption occurred when the metropolitan baptized refugees from Albania, where religious institutions were closed down and clergy of all denominations were being persecuted.

On July 12, 1991, at Cetinje Monastery a most dramatic and unfortunate event happened during the traditional religious celebration of Saint Peter I, who had been called a saint by his people before his death. During the commemoration, nonbelievers shouted out rude slogans, especially against the metropolitan of Montenegro-Littoral-Skenderejski.

Outside, another confrontation centered around two flags. One flag based on an ancient Orthodox flag with symbols taken from the Bysantia represented the believers. That flag had been flying over the Cetinje Monastery since it was built by the Crnojevich dynasty in 1483. Since then the monastery had become the Serbian spiritual and cultural center, the Serbian Mecca after the Kosovo defeat. The other flag also depicted the royal Montenegrin crown with the two-headed eagle. In the long history of the Montenegrin people, the two flags had never been displayed opposite each other. However, a group of atheists insisted on forcibly replacing the first flag on the monastery building with the second flag that expressed their wishes. That group was led by a leader of the Montenegrin Liberal Alliance. In an interview the leader himself stated he was an atheist. His group included other atheists from SUBNOR (a Titoist veterans group[15]) and members of the new Alliance of Communists of Yugoslavia (ACY). The agitators were joined by people of other faiths and ethos, also. Thus so-called liberal leaders from SUBNOR and ACY marched together arm in arm in front of the Cetinje Monastery against believers. How could they call themselves liberals when they used the same methods the Titoists did against their adversaries?

During the long years of Turkish oppression the ancient Serbian books were held sacred, and monasteries were protected by special behest of the sultan. How about today? Deeds speak louder than words. Do the protagonists of Mediterranean culture apply it in practice as loudly as they talk about it in public?

Despite such assaults, the Metropolitan of the Cetinje Monastery remains calm and faithful to the Petrovich throne, his Saint Sava church, and his Serbian people. He admires the descendants of Obilich and glorifies the Petroviches while he disdains the followers of Drljevich-Shtedimlija as neo-Fascist Ustashe servants.

The People and Reasons Behind an Autocephalous Atheist Montenegrin Church

The Russian thinker Nikolay Berdjayev says the danger of the Communist philosophy is its opposition to human intellect and to spiritual life.

During and after World War II, Tito dictatorially took over the helm of the Yugoslav Communist hierarchy. He continued to follow Comintern policy of breaking the Serbian entity into fragments; from the Serb ethos were created two more nationalities, Macedonian and Montenegrin. Also, after the war Tito continued to control the Serbian Orthodox church. First he initiated the separation of the Macedonian church from the Serbian Orthodox church. Tito's marionette Krsto Crvenkovski played the role of executioner in that instance, applying tyrannical anti-canonical methods. In the whole world, no one recognized the Macedonian Orthodox church as independent except the Roman Catholic pope!

However, Montenegrin Communists rendered their churches and monasteries incapable of performing any religious rites. At the same time, in the Montenegrin diocese, Communists liquidated most of the clergy most barbarously. Why? To totally suppress any spiritual life among the people.

And how did their ideological comrades in Croatia and Slovenia who predominantly belonged to the Catholic faith behave? In fact, they did nothing, even while Croatian Communists destroyed an additional fifty Orthodox churches that had remained after Ustashe pogroms destroyed over five hundred Serbian churches and monasteries.

At that particular time in Montenegro, Tito and his cohorts did not need to form an independent atheistic Montenegrin church. The Orthodox clergy in Montenegro had almost perished at the hands of Communist sadists. Meanwhile, when Metropolitan Amphilohije Radovich took over the metropolis of Montenegro Littoral, spiritual life began to revitalize. The anti-Serbian followers in Montenegro did not like this. Those "religious atheists," as they call themselves, wanted to have an autocephalous atheist Montenegrin church! How could they have a church in the first place, when most of them had never been baptized and when they didn't believe in God, except for some Muslims and Catholics who joined with the Montenegrins merely for political advantage? They want to break the unity of the Serbian Orthodox church from the Belgrade patriarchate. Furthermore, those "religious atheists" know nothing about Christianity, neither in theory nor in practice. Those atheists with their destructive intent did more harm to the Orthodox faith in Montenegro during fifty years of rule than the Turks did in over five centuries!

The Communist rulers have been promoting hatred and moral stumbling. Montenegrin atheists have been fabricating the lie that once the Montenegrin church was autocephalous! There is no truth or historical basis for their statements. The protagonists of the autocephalous church should realize the following:

1. Before 1766 the Montenegrin metropolis was part of the Pec patriarchate.

2. In 1766 the occupying Ottoman Empire broke apart the unity of the Serbian Orthodox church.

3. The Pec patriarchate was then subordinated to the Carigrad/Istanbul patriarchate.

4. The Montenegrin metropolitan was never under either Greek or Turkish authority.

5. In 1767 the Montenegrin in metropolitan Sava sought Russian intervention for help in reestablishing the authority of the Pec patriarchate.

6. In 1779 the governor of Montenegro, Radonjich, sent his envoy to the Austrian czar in Vienna to propose an agreement. It was stressed that the Montenegrin metropolis depended on the Pec patriarchate in Serbia.

7. In the seventeenth century, Patriarch Arsenije Charnojevich (Crnojevich from Cetinje) made Karlovac the greatest spiritual center of Saint Sava's Orthodox faith.

8. In July 1804, Montenegrin chiefs gathered in Cetinje to reply to the Russian Holy Synod:

After the Serbian empire fell in 1389, our ancestors retreated into the Montenegrin mountains before the strong enemy of Christianity, depending on no one except the authority of the metropolitans who taught them to defend Orthodoxy and liberty. We never heard that the Russian Holy Synod had any authority over the Serbian people. Montenegrins were not Russian citizens. They were only under moral Russian patronage because they were affiliated with the same faith. So, Serbian tribes were loyal to the Russian throne.

Father Vasilije Tarasjev, a Russian, states that the Montenegrin diocese was never autocephalous.

One "Croatian" writer from Piperi (district of Podgorica) recommends the unification of Croatia, Montenegro, and Albania into one Catholic state! Zagreb with its Catholic church expects something from the Montenegrin Latinashi in return for giving them full support financially and morally!

In short, Communists and their followers deal with two sensitive problems: the ethnicity of the Montenegrin people and whether their church should be autocephalous or remain as part of the Serbian Orthodox patriarchate in Belgrade.

The newspaper *Free Thought*, published in Niksic, on April 10, 1938, mentioned the contents of a leaflet claiming that Montenegrins by origin are not Serbs, but were subordinated under Serbian hegemony! The newspaper refused to continue discussion with people of such mentality. "If they prefer to call themselves Gypsies that would be their right," the paper says. However, today all Montenegrins, from the ordinary man to the highest intellectual, know that Montenegro is inhabited by the purest race of Serbian people. It was attested to be so by the late patriarch German, though later his statement was denounced by the almighty Communists. Indeed, to negate one's own national origin is rare in the world of ethics!*

Dilemma for Montenegrin Youth: Betrayal versus Heroism

A moral problem rose when Tito took over the helm of the Yugoslav ship. Titoism seeks to destroy the human soul, especially in the young people.

Vuk Brankovich has been a symbol of treason to the Serbian people since the Kosovo tragedy. His opposite there was Milosh Obilich, the symbol of Serbian heroism who personally killed the Turkish sultan Murat. Every Serb from Montenegro and elsewhere has the right to align himself with either Vuk or Milosh. The moral standards and education obtained at home and from educational and social institutions along with other factors would determine what values a person embraces.

Today's youth, especially in Montenegro, is faced with a dilemma—either to choose an earthly (materialistic) or a heavenly (spiritual) kingdom. Montenegrin King Nicholas I said a hero will hold the reins of the horse of Marko Miljanova, the epitome of humaneness. Titoism exemplifies a sordid, earthly kingdom in which Tito is considered as the Messiah, that is the God from Kumrovac! Titoism tried, and unfortunately succeeded in many ways especially in traditionally Serbian areas, to destroy man's soul, his humaneness, dignity, and pride by creating robots who would readily execute any unfounded order and commit any atrocity. To Tito's revolutionaries one could apply the expression of Madame Roland on her way to the guillotine: "Oh, Liberty, Liberty! What crimes are committed in your name!"

Montenegrin youth should not let themselves be manipulated by scoundrels, as they may have been on Christmas Eve recently when they lit bonfires in front of the former palace of the King Nicholas the First. Were the youth motivated to evoke sympathy and respect for the former king, or were they led to stir up hatred and intolerance toward the Serbian Orthodox church and those people who were for Serbian unity? The young people have the right to celebrate the holiday wherever they choose if they are peacefully gathered and they are tolerant toward others. A democratic society requires respect for the law and order of society. In a democratic, civilized society different political views are discussed or dealt with in an atmosphere of mutual respect, and dignity and tolerance prevail. Unfortunately, this is not always happening in Montenegro.

When someone reads *Hell or Communism in Montenegro* he will discover a twentieth-century history that contrasts starkly with events in the more distant Montenegrin past. The volumes of *Hell* testify to the villainous genocide committed by Communists in Montenegro, where the Titoist criminal performed acts that were identical to Croatian Ustashe bestialities on their territory, with the pope's blessing. Current events have confirmed Ustashe misdeeds, which have been supported by "the most democratic Croatian republic in the world." Have Titoists been following the Ustashe line for the biological and psychological destruction of the Serbian nation?

In Montenegro, Titoists tortured and brutally killed clergy of the Serbian Orthodox Church, as did the Ustashe in the ISC. In essence both ideologies, regardless of their polarized goals, had in common one aim: to destroy Orthodoxy and Serbs as a unique entity. So, Catholic friars were flagbearers of the Ustashe ideology, while Communists in Montenegro performed atrocities that had never before been done by any Serbian enemy, Turks or Nazis or any others! Under such circumstances a pathological hatred was created that still exists in the residue of Titoism, as in the personality of the SUBNOR prseident and the Liberal Alliance leader whose actions were criticized even by his relatives.[16]

Vucji Do Flag Used for Chauvinistic Purposes

The flag from Vucji Do is a national symbol. It symbolizes the heroic struggle of Montenegrins and their national successes against the Turks, who were the oppressors of the Serbian people for centuries. At the battle of Vucji Do in 1876 the fierce hand-to-hand combat lasted five full hours. The Montenegrin army threw out from the battlefield 110,000 Turkish soldiers, of whom 51,692 were dead, 41,255 wounded, and 11,333 captured. Also captured were 58,200 rifles, 136 artillery pieces, and 168 flags. On the Montenegrin side there were 2,972 dead and 6,513 wounded. None were captured.

In 1907 in London at a Balkan exhibition the flag from Vucji Do with 404 bullet holes was displayed.

On April 5, 1991, some Montenegrin Separatists—or, as they call themselves, liberals—flew to Zagreb to celebrate with Croatian Separatists fifty years of the ISC formation under the auspices of Nazi Germany and Fascist Italy. The shahovnica, the Croatian flag used by the Ustashe during the war, was exhibited, and beneath it, the flag from Vucji Do. The juxtaposition was jarring, a sickening blow to the Montenegrin consciousness.

Though both the Vucji Do flag and the shahovnica symbolize blood, their meanings are diametrically opposed to each other. On one hand, the shahovnica symbolizes mass genocide of their own people during World War II. There were over a million victims—Serbs, Jews, Gypsies, Yugoslav-oriented Croats, and Muslims. The Montenegrin flag symbolizes the honor and dignity of her people, while the shahovnica symbolizes the machiavellianism of the Vatican with the Croatian Catholic church that played a tragic and anti-Christian role in the genocide. To put the shahovnica publicly above the bullet-riddled banner of Vucji Do claims the lives and honor of those thousands of innocent victims all over again, and brings tears to the eyes of honest descendants of the heroic Vucji Do veterans.

Challenges of the Future

Today's youth has a tremendous challenge to rise to the challenge of reconciliation and brotherly love. There is a need to accumulate as much knowledge as possible, quality knowledge that advocates man's virtues. Libraries, not the street, are a primary source of such knowledge. Reading material should be selected that reflects the highest levels of Montenegrin morality and ethical standards. Titoism insinuated into youth poisonous germs that could destroy them. The people would be immune to such Satanism if they were highly educated from sources that teach about the people's unity and democratic principles. They should keep the value of man uppermost, extolling him, not destroying him. In civilized society, God is respected, as well as those who worship Him. From the basics of the Judeo-Christian faith, the Ten Commandments, young people could get inspiration to revitalize their spirit and body. Leave those who still possess and use weapons of hatred and intolerance and who have no respect for others. One day they'll spit on themselves and sink in their own sauce, where they would deserve their eternal rest right there.

Finally, it is necessary to stress reconciliation as the Orthodox church is recommending. Such reconciliation does not mean, however, that justice will be denied. The statute of limitations for some crimes never runs out. Therefore, everyone who took part in the civil war in Yugoslavia should come one day under scrutiny of the law. The Ljeshnjani Brigade would be eager for that day to come. The Titoists' genocide in Montenegro and elsewhere and the Ustashe genocide during World War II will not be forgotten.

It is time to turn away from over a half century of oppression, of "might makes right," and lack of pride and dignity. It is necessary to return to Njegosh and Marko Miljanov and to the reality and gracefulness of all knights of proud Montenegro.

Vices like hatred, envy, slander, and lies should be replaced with the love, tolerance, respect, and humaneness of Marko Miljanov, and the Spartanism of Njegosh, who was admired and respected throughout the civilized world. Njegosh was the moral pillar of his Serbian people for the last two centuries. His *Mountain Wreath* is a masterpiece of Serbian literature, and, like Kosovo Cult, is integral to the Serbian national identity.

The Montenegrin ethos cannot be separated from its proud Serbian origins. Those who have attempted to do so used the false identity to foster divisiveness and undermine faith. Their machinations have hurt all of Yugoslavia. It is fervently to be hoped that a new generation of leaders will find a true identity that reconciles rather than divides, heals rather than kills, honors truth, not lies. Only then can today's generations reclaim their heritage and look to the future with pride and with the expectancy of peace.

NOTES

1. A convention was held in Split in 925 and 928 to discuss the differences between Latinashi priests and Glagoljashi priests. The latter were against conversion to Catholicism, against using the Latin language in the church, and against abolishing the Glagoljica alphabet. The Glagoljica was preserved in Istra until the Fascists took over in the Independent State of Croatia (ISC).

2. Michael Lees, *The Rape of Serbia* (San Diego, New York, London: Harcourt Brace Jovanovich, 1990), p. 72.

3. *Fodor's Yugoslavia* (New York: David McKay, 1969), p. 225.

4. By the London Agreement of 1915 the Allies agreed to give Dalmatia to Italy after the war was over if Italy joined the Allies against Austro-Hungary and Germany. At the Versailles Conference the Allies changed their minds, due to the tremendous popularity of Nikola Pashich, president of the Serbian government. Pashich was the only dignitary at Versailles who was personally given a warm welcome by Woodrow Wilson, president of the United States.

5. However, that horse did not commit suicide, as according to Communist myth the mount of Lola Ribar did when it realized the loss of its master!

6. S. M. Shtedimlija, *Orthodoxy in Croatia*, p . 138.

7. Ibid., p. 139.

8. Sima Simich, cited in Vladimir Dedijer, *The Vatican and Jasenovac* (Belgrade: Rad, 1987), p. 483.

9. The information about Drljevich and Shtedimlija was mainly gathered from the book *The Conspiracy Against the Serbs* by Dr. Rastislav Petrovich.

10. Publisher: Milan Shuffleja, Zagreb, pp. 45–60; *Collection, Our Homeland* (Zagreb: Main Ustashe Stan [GUS], 1943), pp. 289-334.

11. Dragan Kljakich, *Dossier on Hebrang* (Belgrade: Publishing Printing Institute, 1983), pp. 115–116.

12. Jovan Vujovich inquired if "King" Veljo Gosheljin Vukcevich was still alive. (After the unification Veljo had played the role of king in a short sketch.) No, they told him. But, one added, one of his sons was living in Cetinje. Jovan asked for his name. "Ah, Djoko Vukcevich! If one of us two ever has to be arrested, I'll go first." Those present were surprised, and someone asked Jovan why. Vujovich explained that when he returned from Italy, as King Nicholas' adherent he was detained in jail in Rijeka Crnojevica. Djoko was then a government employee. "He came to talk with me in jail," continued Vujovich. He told me it would be worthless to resist the current establishment. He wanted me to be free, and said he would send me home if I gave him my word of honor I would not join the guerillas again. I gave him my pledge. Djoko succeeded in persuading his superiors to let me go home. Later I received a pension, and I continue to live in peace together with my loved ones. I'll always appreciate what Djoko Vukcevich did for me," concluded Jovan.

13. Andrija asked his two escorts to tell their eyewitness stories during their recent trip to Katuni Nahi. One of them said they saw people with the king's cockade who were enthusiastically shouting, "Long live King Peter." Maj. Vaso's face showed a broad, happy smile, but Nikola greeted the shouts with reserve and suspicion. Pejovich was obviously trying to deceive them in order to achieve their liquidation more easily, because the Partisans were mortal enemies of the monarchy.

14. In the first volume of *Hell or Communism in Montenegro* there was an important letter, dated February 7, 1942, referring to the situation in the Donjo Ljeshnjani Partisan Battalion. The letter was sent from the headquarters of the Lovcen N. L. Partisan Detachment to the headquarters of the Zeta N. L. Partisan Detachment and is signed by the Lovcen commandment, Peko Dapcevich. Part of that letter is translated as follows: ". . . Of course you know quite well the facts of what is going on in the territory of the Donjo-Ljeshnjani Battalion, which is part of our detachment. [How could all or part of a battalion be under command at the same time of *two* Partisan detachments, Zeta and Lovcen?!]

"It is imperative to take appropriate measures to thwart further intentions of the fifth columnists in that region. With your acknowledgment and with mutual cooperation of the Donjo-Ljeshnjani Partisan Battalion [which was exclusively under the jurisdiction of the Zeta Detachment] as well, this detachment prepared and executed actions against fifth columnists in Donja Nahija. The aim of such actions was to capture the leaders of the fifth columnists and to liquidate them. . . .

"In some individual villages—Kokoti, Brezine, and others—the masses tended to break away from the fifth-columnist movement and join the Partisans. As this terrain is closer to us, we took the initiative of taking advantage of it in order to break and isolate the fifth columnists. We invited to our headquarters and conversed with Andrija Pejovich, a Federalist and honest peasant from the village of Kokoti. . . . As that man [Pejovich] is obviously influential, there is a possibility of gathering around him a group of honest men not only from the already mentioned villages but also from the Vukcevich clan, where the evil nest of the new fifth columnists is currently residing. [The "honest men" referred to the Lazarevich branch of the clan except the families of Pera and Mila Markova Vukcevich, whch was part of Pejovich's gendarme company.]

"Also, we are getting a lot of help from Maj. Celebich from Shtitari, who joined the Partisan ranks a while ago. . . ."

"We'll also write to Pejovich and to his friends to remain unconditionally on their territory and to continue their activities. They will get from us every possible assistance and protection. . . ."

During that period, as a matter of fact, Bajo Sekulich, political commissar of the Lovcen Detachment, was designated to lead Partisan units against Nationalist (Chetnik) insurgents in Moracha and Vasojevice.

15. The SUBNOR prseident refused to accept as new members those who had been fighting against the Ustashe. Would he have accepted them if they had fought against Serbia even without reason? It seems the SUBNOR president is still a faithful Titoist! Do the majority of SUBNOR members share his view in that matter? Was it true that some SUBNOR members became members by only two signatures of "witnesses" and were not required to be active fighters on the battlefield? Once Tito himself stated that if he had had as many fighters during World War II as he had veterans after the war he could have conquered all of Europe!

16. The SUBNOR president had attended the peace meeting held in Podgorica at which they disapproved of Montenegrin involvement in the unfortunate Yugoslav internal revolution. It was not only unfortunate but shameful, a tragedy caused by those Titoists that resulted in the deaths of many young people! In fact, neo-Fascist Croatian Ustashe with their mercenaries of the international Black Croatian Brigade appeared at Prevlaka with a force of 20,000 men. Why did they come—to threaten or attack Serbian Boka! Those Montenegrins who refused to defend their soil were called "heroes"! What kind of morality is this? Titoists' morality, is not it? Traitors became heroes, and vice versa! That was a typical example of Titoism—"Tito after Tito"—which was the main culprit of the later Yugoslav tragedy because the Croatian neo-Fascist Ustashe had been nurtured and preserved by Tito himself since 1941!

Chapter Three

TITO: HERO OR VILLAIN?

During World War II and the revolution there appeared on the Yugoslav scene two adversaries: General Draza Mihailovich and Josip Broz Tito. Mihailovich was a native of Ivanica, Serbia. Tito was born in Kumrovac, Croatia.

For centuries the Yugoslav people, and the Serbs in particular, had nurtured seeds of resistance against any foreign occupier. They felt humiliated by the rapid collapse of their state under the German onslaught.

Mihailovich repudiated the capitulation. When confusion reigned, he emerged dramatically on the scene as a professional soldier ready to save the honor of Serbian men at arms. He was the first guerrilla leader in occupied Europe.

In 1942 *Time Magazine* proclaimed Mihailovich Man of the Year. He was extolled as a rare patriot who was fighting under unbearable hardship for the liberation of his country. Twenty thousand square miles of Yugoslav land had been liberated, creating an "island of democracy."

Draza was a man of strong character, possessed of integrity and ability, traits seldom appreciated in the world of politics. David Martin affirms that the Mihailovich movement was one of resistance, not a collaborationist effort, as a few Comintern agents proclaimed it in May-June 1942 at the PanSlavic Congress held in Moscow.

Dr. Veselin Djuretich says the Mihailovich movement was an anti-occupier and anti-quisling entity. Dr. Branko Petranovich also states that Mihailovich's Chetniks were organized on an anti-Fascist platform.

Josip Broz Tito was already experienced in international revolution. He was a perfidious, unscrupulous Comintern type of commander who worked together with his subordinates to divide his country.

Filip Radulovich in his book *Loves of Josip Broz* characterized him exactly as he was: a man with elegant manners toward companions of the opposite sex, a man willing to lie and cheat. Countless times he disappeared from his girlfriends when the girls discovered they had conceived and were making wedding plans! During his love affair with Liza Shpurer in Vienna, Broz purloined material for his suit from the company he worked for as a salesman. So there were early signs of his inborn criminal traits.

To add to his biography: On July 2, 1990 Ante Ciliga, a Croatian Communist, was interviewed by Politika Express in Rome about Tito. Ciliga states that Tito completed school as an Austrian noncommissioned officer. In 1914 and 1915 he fought against Serbia on the Podrinski front. From there he was transferred to the Russian front. Once he managed to capture eleven Russian soldiers as they slept and took them across the front line into an Austrian prison camp. Later Broz himself was captured by the Russians. During his Russian captivity Broz had an opportunity to join the Serbian army in Corfu (Greece), but he refused to fight with other southern Slavs and the Western Allies against the Austro-Hungarian Empire.

Reports reached Vienna about the heroic behavior of a 23-year-old sergeant major, Josip Broz. His supreme military commander, Kaiser Franz Joseph, awarded him a medal, but it could not be delivered because of his captivity. In 1918 the Allies defeated the Austro-Hungarian Empire, so Broz probably lost his bright future with the Austrian military! When Broz visited Vienna in 1964 the Austrian chancellor Joseph Klaus had the high military decoration awarded by the Habsburg ruler in 1915 delivered to him. Did any Yugoslav news agency report Tito had received the decoration? If not, why did Tito hide it?

Tito's Activities in Moscow

During Broz's captivity in Moscow he embraced the Marxist ideology after the October Revolution in 1917. He returned to Yugoslavia in 1919.

In 1935 he was known in Moscow as Friedrich Walter, an alias he retained until the end of World War II. His biographer, Vladimir Dedijer, mentioned that Josip Broz used more than seventy aliases during his career as an international underground revolutionary.

Moma Markovich, a Comintern intelligence officer, told a story that he had learned from the Soviet intelligence officers Gen. Jakov Anastasijevich and NKVD Lt. Col. Aljosha Tuljenin. The activities of Yugoslav revolutionaries were emphasized in the Comintern. Tuljenin knew extremely well the fundamental causes and the effects, the rises and falls of the Yugoslav revolutionaries in Moscow. He talked about the lives of men whose liquidations were sponsored by "three to four men who later lived in Yugoslavia." There was a belief that Tito played an important role in the Kremlin underground.

Thanks to Tito's influence in Moscow, the entire Orthodox wing was executed: Sima Markovich, Milan Gorkich, Ratko Miletich, Kosta Novakovich, Filip Filipovich, and others.

Sima Markovich (1888-1939) was a university professor. He was one of the first organizers of the CPY. He was jailed in 1935 and later killed.

In Moscow it was believed that after the liquidation of Sima Markovich, Josip Kopinich recommended Tito to Dimitrov to replace Markovich as secretary of the CPY. Dimitrov took the advice. After World War II Tito wanted to return the favor to Kopinich by sending him to Washington as the Yugoslav ambassador, but Kardelj refused.

Milan Gorkich (1904-1937), a brilliant intellectual and resolute revolutionary, was also liquidated. Gorkich was in close relationship with Rodoljub Colakovich, Labud Kusovac, Mustafa Golubich, Kristina Kusovac, and Sima Markovich. On the other side of the aisle were their rivals: Josip Broz, Edward Kardelj, Lavro Kuhar, Ivan Srebrnjakov, Veljko Vlahovich, and Josip Kopinich.

Ratko Miletich, a carpenter and professional revolutionary, had been a veteran of the CPY since 1919. He was accused, mysteriously jailed, and sentenced. He was in bitter conflict with Josip Broz and Mosha Pijade.

Kosta Novakovich (1886-1938) was a journalist and publicist. He was in steady conflict with Tito's and Kardelj's group. In the 1938 purge he was jailed, sentenced, and shot.

Filip Filipovich (1878-1938) was the organizer of the CPY. He was liquidated in 1938.

Behind these liquidations was Josip Broz, alias Fridrih Georgijevich. Broz's synthesis of a German name and Russian surname was not unintentional. He worked for both intelligence services, German and Russian, and even for a third one, the British intelligence, which he hid like a snake does legs.

Because of the purges Tito's life was in danger in Moscow, although he was protected by those representatives whose countries were against the Allies during World War I, such as George Dimitrov, William Pick, and Andrey Andrejeyev.

After Moscow's Purges Tito Continues Against His Rivals

During the Spanish civil war, Tito continued liquidating possible rivals. In that war Tito was a master of commando intelligence work. He helped Stalin's executioners, like Stevo Krajacich helped the Ustashe liquidate the left wing of Croatian Communists in Kerestinac during World War II. Tito was an unsurpassed master of conspiracy, a characteristic of his Austro-Hungarian mentality. In 1940 Tito was secretly transferred by the German intelligence to Yugoslavia.

By Tito's orders victims were shot most treacherously on various Yugoslav shooting grounds—then they were proclaimed "people's heroes"!

Among those killed were Cirko Pavlovich, Vukman Krushcich, Mijat Laki-cevich, Rade Koncar, Ivo Lola Ribar, Ivan Milutinovich, August Cesarac, Vladimir Rolovich, and only Tito knew how many more!

Tito was an aggressive professional revolutionary. He was flexible in adjusting to new situations while maintaining iron-handed discipline. Com-intern instructions, an international Communist spy ring, and a propaganda network were the keys to his later successes. He was indeed a talented international agent.

In 1940 he was writing for the *Comintern Journal*, applauding the take-over of Poland and echoing the Stalinist line that "English and French imperialists" were responsible for the conflict. As Nora Beloff notes, for Yugoslav Communists this era of party history remains something of an embarrassment.

Consequences of Yugoslav Collapse in April 1941

After Yugoslavia's capitulation, Nazi Germany and Fascist Italy caused her disintegration. Tito did not defend his country against either the foreign invaders or internal quislings.

Croatian Ustashe formed their Independent State of Croatia (ISC), thanks to German and Italian bayonets and tanks. The racist Ustashe declared a war of extermination against Serbs, Jews, and Gypsies on their territory. Thus began a real "tragedy within tragedy." Looking closely at the complex events, Dedijer reported that on April 17, 1941, Bakarich and Hebrang and possibly Pavle Popa as representatives of the CCCCP signed a secret agreement with Lorkovich and Budak (Ustashe representatives) forming an independent Communist party of Croatia (CPC). Their idea was Croatia was to be an independent state in which the CCP would be recognized as a key factor in parliament. The agreement contained the acceptance of the dismemberment of Yugoslavia, the establishment of the independent state, and the disintegration of the CPY.

Dr. Ante Pavelich, head of the new quisling Croatian state, was willing to accept such a proposition. How was it possible that there was cooperation between the CCP and the extreme neo-Fascist Ustashe ideology? It was not the first time. In 1932, during Artukovich's Velebit uprising, *Proletarian (Proleter)*, the official Communist newspaper, supported the Artukovich mutiny.

Did Tito as the secretary of the Communist party central committee of Yugoslavia (CCCCPY) know about it? What was his reaction, if any? Was a Croatian party member reprimanded for it? Was Tito, even then a prudent politician, able to handle it properly in regards to the influential Serbs in the CCCPY?[1] According to Dedijer, Tito shrewdly camouflaged himself in the sickle and hammer in the article "Why Are We Still a Part of the Communist Party of Yugoslavia?" in the official magazine of the Communist party. He mildly remarked about inappropriate contacts of Croatian Communists with the Ustashe and allegedly opposed the dismemberment of Yugoslavia and the forming of an independent CPC.

What was Tito doing during that period? He just promenaded through the streets of Zagreb. Along the way he was informing the Comintern in order to facilitate a quick Yugoslav collapse, blaming it on Serbian reactionaries and her hegemonistic policy. Why did he not inform Comintern about the Croatian treachery and Ustashe pogroms that were in progress! Says historian C. L. Sulzberger, "Yugoslavia was riddled with fifth-column movements among its Croatian, Albanian, and German Volksdeutsch minorities."

During the first half of 1941, uprisings flared up in the Serbian provinces of Bosnia, Hercegovina, and in the ISC. Ninety-nine percent of the insurgents were Serbs. On July 13, 1941, an uprising broke out in Montenegro against the Italian occupier, and it was extended in Serbia against the Nazis, first by Mihailovich and then together with Tito's Communists, until they split among themselves.

Tito moved from Zagreb to Belgrade to encourage such uprisings among Serbs on their territories because they would invite reprisals from the occupier. The Germans responded by killing 100 Serbs for every dead German or 50 Serbs for every wounded German. So, all over the Yugoslav territory the Serbs were in danger of annihilation, either at the hands of their internal enemies or by foreign occupiers. Tito knew well that Croatians were pro-Nazi while Serbs were pro-Western. On September 18, 1941, Tito joined the Partisans in Serbia.

Dr. Ivan Avakumovich asked a series of pointed questions of Tito's biographer, Dedijer:[2]

1. Who is the person who appears in the archives of the Third Reich as the "Croat who does not work for money" in occupied Belgrade in the late spring and summer of 1941?

2. What part did that person play in the attack by the Gestapo and the German military intelligence (Abwehr) against the secret center of Soviet intelligence in Belgrade in 1941, when the Germans arrested Mustafu Golubich?

3. Did the arrest of Golubich, a Yugoslav revolutionary and prominent Soviet intelligence agent [who incidently had a poor opinion of both Hitler's "New Order" and of the CPCCY], aggravate or alleviate Soviet consideration of Tito's activities and the German occupier?

4. What part did the "Croat who does not work for money" play in the successful undertaking of the Gestapo against Belgrade's Communist organization in the summer of 1941?

5. Which "Croat who does not work for money" was transferred to another terrain after completing his Belgrade assignment?

6. Did this useful Croat in the fall of 1941 leave Belgrade alone, or did he have an escort to facilitate his departure?

7. Tito left Belgrade in mid-September 1941 and traveled by train to the free territory of western Serbia, accompanied by the assistant commandant of the Nazi SS "Prince Eugene" Division. Was it a regular practice for general secretaries of Communist parties to travel with escorts of SS officers at a time when Hitler was intensifying his all-out attack against the Soviet Union?

8. If it was not a regular practice, why was an exception made for Tito?

9. According to Nazi documents, the Germans informed Tito before they attacked Drvar in 1944 that he would be attacked by parachutes. Was it standard German policy during World War II to inform the "enemy" ahead of time of how he would be attacked?[3]

10. Did the Germans try to undermine or shore up the defense of the supreme headquarters of the National Liberation Army and Marshal Tito?

The Plight of Serbs on the Croatian Front During World War II

On the territory of the ISC, events were happening that rational minds could not understand, much less accept, unless the person was a Croat of Avari origin, whose history leans toward genocide. The genocide, a racist, ideological, religious, political, and chauvinistic effort, was instigated by Dr. Ante Starcevich and Josip Frank, who tried to satanize Serbs in Croatia. Frank organized a Franciscan Croatian movement from which was built an Ustashe nest on Starcevich-Franciscan ideas. The Croatian writer Eugen Kumichick called Starcevich "Pater Patri"—the Father of the Homeland."[4] Starcevich's conservative, racist, national-chauvinistic ideology was later epitomized by Hitler and embraced by Pavelich. Today in western Europe the extreme right are neo-Nazis, of whom the Ustashe are the most extreme apologists of the ideology against which the democratic world fought during the second world war.

Serbs in Croatia came between the hammer and the anvil. First they were hit by the Ustashe, then by both the Ustashe and Croatian Communists. The genocide escalated. On May 6, 1941, there was a massive killing of Serbs by the Ustashe in Kordun.

Rade Koncar, a member of the CCCPC, personally appealed to Tito to protect Serbs in Croatia. Tito replied the party was not strong enough to protect them. What Tito meant was the party was strong enough when he ordered attacks against Germans in Serbia and against Italians in Montenegro and elsewhere, but it was not strong enough against the Ustashe!

Soon after, Koncar, a Serb, was betrayed by a chauvinistic Croatian group of Srebrnjak's persuasion. (Hebrang was among the first involved in the conspiracy against him.) On May 22, 1942, Koncar was shot by Italians in Shibenik. Bakarich tried to explain the betrayal to Dedijer. Koncar was shot, says Bakarich, for a new pair of Italian boots. (Allegedly, a Partisan had shot an Italian officer for his new boots and the Italians retaliated!)

Croatia was interwoven by espionage nets of all colors. Ivan Srebrnjak's intelligence net leaned to the right and was connected with the Italian-Vatican branch. His network was also tied in with the Kopinich center. Srebrnjak's men probably wanted to eliminate Koncar first to frustrate the liberation of left-wing Croatian Communists and continue on later at Kerenstinac.

Where did Ivan-Stevo Krajecich stand? Srebrnjak's center insisted on taking over at any price the leadership of the uprising in Croatia and not letting Serbs lead alone. Further, the ties with the Ustashe must be maintained, said Srebrnjak, who was in close contact with Hebrang. Srebrnjak was first arrested and then killed, while Hebrang was sent to the notorious Jasenovac camp, where he made a secret deal with the Ustashe authority. Josip Kopinich had planted three agents inside the Ustashe apparatus. One of them, Tibor Vaska, informed Kopinich of Hebrang's collaboration with the Ustashe. Kopinich immediately informed the Comintern and Tito's headquarters of Hebrang's betrayal. Tito denied that he ever received any information from Kopinich about Hebrang!

In February 1942 in Kordun, Veco Holjevac, a Croat, had ordered Canica Opacich to have all Chetnik insignias (traditional Serbian symbols) replaced by a five-pointed star. Serbs were the only ones to wear those insignia because there were no Croats in the Partisan ranks at that period except a few at the top of the Partisan command. The Serbs refused to obey the order. Holjevac chose Canica as a Serb to be prosecutor. Thus, Cpt. Lalich with eighty other Serbs were sentenced to death for refusing to replace their traditional insignia.

On February 18, 1942, Tito gave the green light to Milovan Djilas, a Montenegrin extremist, to purge Partisan battalions from Serbia. Djilas disqualified 200 Partisans as unfit for the execution of Partisan higher duties.

From February through April 1942 the Communists and Ustashe combined to carry out attacks against Dagnich's Chetniks. The collaboration of Partisans and Ustashe was noted on several German reports. On March 20, 1942, Gen. Brader, a German commandant in Serbia, submitted a report that "between Croatian Communists, Ustashe, and Montenegrin proletarian brigades there exists an agreement not to fight each other."

The main intelligence net between Ustashe and Partisan coordination and collaboration was directed from Zagreb.[5]

Ustashe-Partisan symbiosis utilized all means against Serbs in Croatia to make them either slaves or put them in their graves. If a Serb in the Partisan ranks wanted to be promoted he had to kill Serbs, while a Croat would get a promotion if he saved the life of a fellow Croat.[6]

Partisan Serbs were mobilized and sent against enemies who were informed in advance. Thus, on November 4, 1942, Bihac finally fell after heavy fighting against the Ustashe; on November 26, 1942, Krajina Partisans (Serbs) attacked the Germans in Bosanski Novi during daylight. The Germans repulsed the attack. The Partisans had heavy casualties because the Germans were informed in advance. Before the Partisans attacked the Ustashe at Udbine Jakob Blazevich informed them. So the Ustashe made an orderly retreat, taking with them everything they wanted! On Catholic Christmas, Ustashe were attacked at Lovinje. The order stated not to fire at the Ustashe if they were running away but to try to capture them alive. By contrast, an order was given to attack Chetniks at Gracac, saying shoot anyone who moves!

There was a concerted campaign to villify Serbs in general and their guerrilla units in particular. Andrija Hebrang, secretary of the CPC, wrote that people must be persuaded that the Chetniks were their greatest enemy. Such bandits cut off the noses and ears of all captured Partisans and then pulled out their eyes and slit their throats with knives. [*This was a bald lie by the secretary of the CPC!*][7] Hebrang called Mihailovich a "German mercenary," while all German documents show that Mihailovich never had any contact with the German occupier during the entire war! However, Hebrang himself was a German, Soviet, and Ustashe agent. There is as much evidence for this as any historian would want.

On July 2, 1943, Tito sent directions to all Domobrans and to the other Croatian formations to join the NLM freely, in return for which they would be guaranteed every security. They would get their former rank in the armed forces as well as promotions, as long as they fought together with NLM units to destroy Chetniks. Joco Jeremich asked Canica Opacich what that directive meant. Did it mean they should accept Ustashe into the Partisan ranks?

The annihilation of Serbs proceeded on two fronts, spiritual and military. One encyclopedia[8] states that in Croatia the indigenous fascist regime set about a policy of "racial purification" that went beyond even Nazi practices. *Encyclopedia Americana* describes the Ustashe regime as a force organized to annihilate or convert Serbian Orthodox into the Catholic faith. On August 30, 1943, Tito ordered the First Bosnia Strike Corps of the NLMY to destroy as many Chetniks as possible!

At the end of 1943, Jakob Blazevich, a Croatian attorney from Gospich and an influential party member, gave an order: If you cannot catch Ustashe alive, don't fire at them. They are good men—they have just been misled.

Tito's Policy: Total Extermination of Chetniks

Typically, Tito did not order fighting against the occupier but against his main adversary in the civil conflict, Draza Mihailovich. However, the

Germans considered the Chetniks and the Partisans as two insurgent movements regardless of their polarized ideologies, believing that they represented two sides of the same coin.

On January 12, 1942, Tito, as head of the NLM headquarters, issued a statement saying: Chetnik forces in Lijeva Rijeka and Lim have had close ties with Draza Mihailovich. The Supreme Headquarters considers that any vacillation or indecisiveness regarding the speedy liquidation of Chetnik forces in Andrijevica [*Lashich's area*] and Berane [*Djurishich's area*] may later be revenged.

Also in January 1942 Tito praised sons whose hands did not tremble in settling accounts with their own fathers if they were Chetniks! Why did Tito never recommend, symmetrically, the same treatment for Ustashe fathers as he did for Chetnik ones? Was it true that Chetniks were aligned with the Western Allies, that they were assigned to missions with them? How could Titoists in talking about crimes always balance Ustashe and Chetniks?! During the civil conflict, Titoists shrewdly evaded the correct conclusion, that the Partisans were just waging a civil war.

In February 1942 Tito ordered the First and Second Proletarian Brigades to eradicate the Chetniks from eastern Bosnia. On February 28, 1942, Tito through his supreme headquarters of the CPY directed an order for the total liquidation of the Chetnik forces: That should be your primary goal.... Resort to force in carrying out reprisals against Chetniks. Burn all the houses of Chetnik leaders and their gang leaders. All properties shall be confiscated. Any fighting against the Italians should be avoided until you liquidate the Chetniks.

At a meeting in Foca in March 1942 Tito declared war against the Serbian peasantry, even though the peasants were the backbone for both resistances. He stated: If the peasants [*meaning Serbians*] go over to the invader we'll also burn their homes! Was Tito using persuasion or scare tactics to turn peasants away from Mihailovich? With whom was the Croatian peasantry aligned during the civil war and during the entire second world war?

In November 1942 the supreme headquarters of the NLM sent instructions to local headquarters in Montenegro and Boka to shoot all who help Chetniks or sympathize with them.

On March 23, 1943, Tito confirmed that the Montenegrin Chetniks were "the greatest threat" in that area. He sent a letter to the Partisan commander in Bosnia, saying, On your way [*toward Zaborak and Coajnice*] don't fight the Germans. Your most important task at this moment is to annihilate the Chetniks of Draza Mihailovich and to destroy their command apparatus, which represents the greatest threat to the progress of the NLM.

Over and over again Tito slandered Mihailovich and his adherents. The Comintern rebuked the Partisans for "acquiring Communist character" so openly. It is difficult to agree that London and the Yugoslav government-in-exile were siding with the invaders. There must be some great misunderstanding here. It is not opportune to emphasize that the struggle is mainly against the Chetniks. World opinion must first and foremost be mobilized against the invaders—mentioning or remarking about the Chetniks is secondary! But despite Comintern's cautions, Tito was undeterred in his priorities, and the Allies were seemingly unaware of his true motives.

Judging by Tito's orders, one must come to the conclusion that Tito's main objective during the Yugoslav war drama was to get rid of Chetniks by using all available means, no matter how unscrupulous, while he put the occupiers and their auxiliary quisling groups on the back burner. Throughout the entire war the Chetniks were Tito's nightmare.

Tito's Treatment of Croatian, Fascist Ustashe

Tito, a shrewd politician, invented the slogan "Brotherhood and Unity!" What for? Regardless, the Croatian Ustashe were categorized as war criminals by the world tribunal in Nurenburg.[9]

After the war the process of de-Nazification in Croatia was never carried out.

The policy of Starcevich, Kvaternik, Pavelich, Hebrang, and Bakarich was confirmed by Tito and by Tudjman, who wanted to chase Serbs not only from Croatian territory but also from Croatian history. Recent events in Croatia and Yugoslavia are the consequences of Tito's achievements and those of the Croatian Communist party. The federal Yugoslav administration marked Yugoslavia for disintegration, and the brutalities condoned by that adminstration during and after the war ensured that the disintegration would be explosively violent.

On May 7, 1944, Tito wired to the main headquarters in Croatia that "the main fighting is for destroying Draza's army." And on September 12, 1944, Tito ordered the headquarters of the First Proletarian Strike Corps to "destroy Draza and his staff." Tito also sent additional orders to the main headquarters in Croatia, summoning to the Partisan ranks the Homeguard and those who had been "forced" to join the Ustashe. The order was as follows: Headquarters invites the Homeguards and the forced Ustashe to come to our side within ten days from this order. For those units that were unable for any reason to join the NOV [*National Liberation Army*] before September 15, their joining would be acceptable under the same conditions as before the 15th.

In Broz's Yugoslavia double social security (pension) was given to the Nazi collaborators, Ustashe and Domobrans, who joined the Yugoslav people's army in the fall of 1944.

Under Pavelich, ties existed between the main Partisan headquarters of Croatia in the hills and the main Ustashe headquarters in Zagreb. What message did Pavelich send directly to Tito regarding the protection of the

Croatian national forces just before he fled from Zagreb or disappeared through a "Ratline"? (There was an organized channel with the Vatican center to bring Nazis of all colors to freedom, like Pavelich, Artukovich, and many others.[10] In fact, both sides, Partisans and Croatian Ustashe, were ready to exchange roles whenever possible. A network of informers throughout Croatia connected leading Croatian Ustashe and Partisan commandants.)[11]

Tito's General Djurich found out that on the terrain in Bosnia the Ustashe sold a Serbian woman to an old Muslim. Her child was killed and her husband sent to Germany to work. When the Partisans arrived on that territory the woman told her appalling story to Djurich and begged him to free her from the slavery. The Ustashe had retained three other Serbian girls for themselves. Was Tito silent toward slavery, adultery, and rape? If not, why then did he not order the investigation and trial of all those who were lawbreakers and against Christian and ethical principles? Would Tito betray himself?

Partisan morals degraded the family, rejected God, and deprived people of their personal property, religion, and freedom. Moral chaos was being created. It is indeed a delicate and slow process to get out of a situation that has had protection from military police and the judicial system for half a century.

Dushan Vilich stated that a hundred years ago Ustashism began a conspiracy using terrorism, assassinations, and other acts of tyranny. Tito purposefully hid it. Titoists always looked for symmetry—that is, claiming that Ustashe and Chetniks are the same. Nothing could be further from the truth. The conspiracy was a continuation of the ploy that Croatian immigrants and the clergy had accomplished to perfection.

According to Milenko Doder, the school of terrorism in Kumrovac was formerly a party school. Mirko Bareshich, the killer of Vladimir Rolovich, the Yugoslav ambassador in Stockholm and a Tudjman protegee, became a professor for training terrorists there.

Jelena Popovich said Tito killed her brother, Vladimir Rolovich. After his assassination Tito immediately decorated him with a medal proclaiming him as a people's hero. How ironic! Tito was trying to cover his crimes by decorating his victims. Rolovich was targeted for liquidation by the Croatian Ustashe and the Croatian UDBA. He gathered secret documents of conspiracy between the Croatian Ustashe (Branko Jelich, Branko Salaj) and the Croatian Communist leadership (Bakarich, Savka Dabcevich-Kucar, Miko Tripalo).

Rolovich was killed to suppress the truth about what really was going on in the Croatian political theater. The Montenegrin leadership was informed of that conspiracy, which was represented by Veljko Milatovich, Veselin Djuranovich, and Vidoje Zarkovich ("Police hits—Vidoje laughs"; Policija bije—Vidoje se smije).

In 1971 Stana Dolanc formed a commission on Brioni to investigate Rolovich's case, which was covered up by Dolanc's conclusion that there was no conspiracy between the Croatian Ustashe and the Croatian UDBA. Tito ordered the formation of the commission to deceive those who demanded a complete investigation of the case.

Dr. Branko Petranovich, one of today's best-known historians, says that Ustashe criminal pathology surpasses even the Nazis'. It was probably for this reason that President Roosevelt recommended that Croatians as immature people should be put under guardianship of the United Nations after the end of the war.[12]

On September 15, 1944, Tito sent a telegram to Hebrang saying that he was very surprised that ZAVNOH had made a decision to require catechism as a mandatory subject in Croatia. None of the democratic countries require Catholic education in their public schools. Obviously, he was afraid of negative reactions from his central committee members, where Serbs were still in the majority. Tito still needed Serbs because the war was not yet over and power was still up for grabs.

On September 19, 1944, Tito sent a telegram to the main Croatian headquarters saying: Zagreb does not dare attack without our approval. It will always be necessary to have ready forces that could be used in a favorable situation. The city should be attacked only when we are sure it will remain under our control. The German forces are still strong in our area. During their retreat through our northern and western parts, they could hold out longer.[13] Tito did not fear German strength on the Srem front enough to avoid sending the youth of Serbia, though untrained, badly armed, poorly fed and clad, to be slaughtered in mass there. Did Tito with his cohorts commit genocide when he intentionally sent youth to be massacred? Djilas states that Serbia had not yet spilled enough blood!

On December 26, 1944, Tito sent a personal communique not to bomb main cities with no strategic importance: I forbid bombing in the immediate vicinity of Zagreb!

On April 6, 1941, Belgrade was bombed by Nazi warplanes, and over 20,000 civilians were killed. Despite this, Tito ordered the Allied air force to bomb Belgrade and other Serbian cities on Orthodox Easter, 1944.

On January 15, 1945, Tito sent a telegram to Velebit: Inform the delegates that our desire is not only to spare the Croatian people, but also to spare their villages and cities, especially Zagreb, from destruction. It is important that the Croatian army help itself, to slow the immediate use against the Germans.

Michael Lees says that Tito, like Hitler before him, hated and feared Serbs and he drew the boundaries of the postwar republics so as to make Serbia as small as possible.

Meanwhile, Tito insisted on beating Serbs with Serbs. Among the Serbs he looked to for Brankoviches-poltroons were Stamboliches, Markoviches, Ljubicich, Minich, and others, while he succeeded in eliminating Obiliches (heroic fighters). In order to succeed in his endeavor, to humiliate and destroy the Serbian people, Tito found men who were willing to dig their own grave and negate their own existence. There were Serbian janissaries (Serbian boys indoctrinated by the Turks who became more fanatical Muslims than their occupiers) who were putting themselves in danger to make lucrative careers. Serbian Communists was their name; they called themselves internationalists. They have been competing among themselves as to who would hurt their own people more, by renouncing their history, tradition, and religion. In fact, Serbian Communists lost their vision, morals, and the instincts for their ethnic survival amid Tito's negativism and his lust for personal gain and state extravagence.

Why Tito Insisted on Peace with Nazi Germany in World War II

Willy Frischauer Lohr's orders to his subordinates referred to Serbs as sworn enemies who deserve to die from famine. Don't be misled by their false sentimentality, he said. Take away their last piece of bread, and their last apple, too. This attitude paved the way for Tito's negotiations with the German authorities in Yugoslavia, because Tito could be useful on their side.

In March 1943 negotiations took place between the general of the German Fifth Division and representatives of Tito's supreme staff, "Milosh Markovich" (Milovan Djilas), "Vladimir Petrovich" (Vlatko Velebit), and Koca Popovich (the only one who used his real name). Their names were recorded in the secret diplomatic archives of Siegfried Kasche, the German minister in Zagreb and a strong supporter of Pavelich, and also by Glaise von Horstenau, Hitler's personal military envoy to Zagreb.

The pretext was that the Partisan delegation wanted to discuss an exchange of prisoners. In fact, Tito wanted recognition of the Partisans as the regular army and a complete ceasefire during the negotiations. They emphasized that the Chetniks with their support from the British were the Germans' main enemy. The Partisans themselves, they said, would be willing to fight the British if they tried to land on Yugoslav soil. The Partisan delegates asked that this request for nonhostility be kept secret.

The Comintern was outraged to learn Tito had negotiated with the Germans. Djilas asked Tito about the Russian reaction. He was not overly concerned. "They think first about their people and their enemy," Tito said.

The German Col. Pfapfenroth mentioned a fourth point that the Partisans included in their memorandum: "They didn't want to fight against the Croatian state, nor in any case against the Germans, but exclusively against Chetniks. They are armed and ready to resist any enemies that we point out to them, including the British."

In contrast to Tito's treasonous negotiations, according to German documents, Mihailovich never tried to collaborate with the Nazis.

Any impartial historian could easily judge from Tito's actions whether he was a hero or a villain. When his negotiations with the Germans stated that the Chetniks were the Germans' main enemy, they entirely contradicted their false propaganda that Chetniks were collaborators and Mihailovich was a "German mercenary." When were the Partisans right?

Furthermore, Tito's negotiators stated also that they were ready to resist any enemies that the Germans pointed out to them, including the British! The British already had their missions in Partisan headquarters and had supplied the Partisans with arms, medicine, and food. Regardless of this British help, the Partisans were ready to fight even them if the Germans asked them to. What more could Tito's Partisans do except to dress dead Chetniks in Nazi uniforms?[14]

Jasenovac—Why Didn't Titoists Liberate the Place of Torture

Aggression is characteristic of man. The imagination raises man above the animal kingdom and at the same time in a certain sense lowers him beneath that kingdom, too. Animals predominantly make their kills to defend themselves or to satisfy vital biological necessities. Man can kill without definite need. Man has an inborn tendency to aggression, destruction, and cruelty. During World War II victims were tortured in beastly ways before they were slaughtered. For instance, some victims in the ISC had their eyes gouged out before they were killed. In Jasenovac and other places of execution the victims were shamefully mistreated.

From 600,000 to 700,000 Serbs, Jews and Gypsies—all innocent people—were liquidated at Jasenovac for one main reason: They belonged to a different ethos or religion. The terror in Jasenovac lasted 1,335 days. Ivan Supek, a professor from Zagreb, wrote: "The Jasenovac camp was the greatest torture chamber in the ISC. About 50,000 hostages were killed, most left-wing Croats, then Serbs, Gypsies and Jews." Supek added that all other numbers were "a fantastic overexaggeration, as much as tenfold." German documents state otherwise as an impartial occupier.

Referring to the number of victims, one of the survivors of the camp puts it in this perspective: If all the skeletons from Jasenovac were returned by freight wagons to avenge their horrible deaths, in front of us would pass 15,000 wagons with forty skeletons in each of them. By his estimates, 600,000 perished at Jasenovac.

In the Yugoslav Dachau, hostages were killed in the most brutal ways, as in unique "gladiator fights." The captors picked two people, if possible brothers. The two were instructed to hit each other with wooden sticks until one fell down.

Says Pauline Weiss, an English Jewess who was interned first in Jasenovac and then at Stara Gradiska, every night prisoners were slaughtered and strangled. Jasenovac was filled with corpses. Captives were tortured.

The most brutal punishment at Jasenovac was the "bivouac on the wire." There was a space of some ten cubic meters. The height of the cage was less than one meter. A prisoner could not stand straight up nor could he lie down, because there was water up to knee height.

Jasenovac victims were hit by wooden mallets or metal bars. Then their throats were cut by daggers and they were thrown half dead into a hot furnace to perish without a trace. German occupation forces compared Jasenovac with Dante's inferno.

There were attempts at sabotage to stop the Jasenovac horrors. The headquarters of the Fifth Krajishka Brigade sent a letter to the headquarters of the NLM saying volunteers were ready to attack Jasenovac, Bukvica, and Stara Gradiska. From Tito's supreme headquarters a notice was sent that no measure was to be taken against the Ustashe at Jasenovac!

On April 22, 1945, about 600 half-dead prisoners, with only sticks as weapons, jumped on armed sentries from the inside camp. In their heroic struggle seventy-five captives succeeded in escaping, thus saving themselves from certain death.

The Ustashe horrors at Jasenovac were racial and religious genocide on a scale previously unparalleled in history. But a "conspiracy of silence" exists, an institutionalized strategy of denial so the crimes are not included in history books or known to decent people. There are many who know the truth. But they keep silent about it or minimize its importance.

The minimizing of the victims in the Jasenovac camp was strategically organized by the Croatian state, their Catholic church, and the Croatian Communist party and imposed through propaganda. Bertrand Russell came to the conclusion that the Vatican is responsible for concealing the truth of what really happened in Yugoslavia during the second world war. (This topic will be discussed further in Chapter 6.)

Tito, supreme commander of the NLM, and his marionettes would be the most competent to answer the following questions:

1. How was it possible that in the Jasenovac camp top functionaries of the Croatian Communist party such as Andrija Hebrang, secretary of the CCCPC, had special treatment while Serbs, on the other hand—peasants, old men, women, and children—as well as Jews, Gypsies, and Croats of Yugoslav orientation—were tortured, then liquidated, mostly by the gas chamber?

2. How could Tito explain what happened in April 1945 at Lijevce Polje? Was it coincidence or not that two Partisan Krajishke brigades, the Sixth and Eleventh from Kozara, attacked Montenegrin-Hercegovina Chetniks from the rear when they were making attacks against the Ustashe there? Who ordered the Partisan brigades to help the Ustashe?

3. Why was the horrifying Jasenovac shooting ground not liberated before May 1945? On the contrary, Tito forbade volunteer Serbian commanders to attack and liberate the thousands of innocent hostages from the Ustashe. Did Tito's conscience ever trouble him about it, if he even had one?

4. Why did Tito never visit that camp, the largest underground Serbian city?

5. Why were those pits and ravines, those terrifying Serbian crypts, covered in concrete for decades until Serbian relatives and friends of the murdered victims opened up those so-called museums as symbols of the incredible inhumanity of man to man?

6. How could Tito allow notorious neo-Fascists and war criminals like fra Dr. Krunislav Draganovich to return and to live freely without shame, recriminations, or punishment? Such Brozomania brought Yugoslavia from one catastrophic civil war into another one fifty years later.

In the Western democratic world, how could Tito be judged a hero of the Yugoslav people when he committed directly or indirectly thousands and thousands of the most heinous crimes? What could anyone say about such a system as Titoism that did not let close relatives and friends sing a requiem for the eternal peace of the victims in Jasenovac or those who were thrown alive into the pits and ravines or the others killed by the Ustashe?

A Serb in the Croatian republic could only survive by denying his ethos—his spiritual, cultural, and political being. In 1986, Radovan Trivundzich states, someone decided to have the inhabitants of Jasenovac, both Serbs and Croats, abandon the tainted ground and resettle elsewhere. Someone decided to demolish everything, to plant trees and forget what had happened there. Hebrang sent a message to the people of Jasenovac that economic misery was forcing them to resettle. All in all, Jasenovac and its inhabitants have been sorely and continuously punished.

The greatness of men and of nations is measured, in large part, by the dignity with which they dominate. To the dead, especially to innocent victims, we owe at least a dignified burial or a marked place to sing a requiem for eternal peace in their graves. Also, toward the dead we have at the least a moral obligation to tell the truth. Where does Titoism stand on these measures of morality?

Dr. Nikola Nikolich, a Croat and a doctor at the Jasenovac camp, submitted a project with the title "Jasenovac—Mausoleum" with the intention that the concentration camp remains should serve as a memorial with educational and instructive facilities as an "eternal reminder" so such evil would never be repeated. Nikolich's humanistic proposal was ignored by the Croatian authority.

Consequences of AVNOY Decisions in 1943

The decisions of the Anti-Fascist Council of National Liberation of Yugoslavia (AVNOY) were nothing but farce, illusion, and deceit. During Tito's

Communist revolution (1941-1945) the most important decisions were made at AVNOY sessions, with irrevocable consequences. The second AVNOY in Jajce, as it was known afterwards, did not succeed. A police state was created according to the Bolshevik model. After Broz became dominant on the political scene, the Serbian people were subjugated, physically and culturally destroyed, spiritually decimated, forced into disunification, despised by the world and smeared. Today the Serbian is at the most dangerous crossroads in his entire history.

By Tito's decree new "nations" were formed: Macedonian, Montenegrin on account of the Serbian ethos, and later in 1961 a Muslim nation, according to religious affiliation. Tito formed a Muslim nation to have a new role in the new Serbophobia. The concept of nationalism was emphasized with the obvious aim of giving more rights to the minorities, such as Albanians in the Kosovo province. What irony! By the Constitution, the Serbian provinces Kosovo and Vojvodina had more rights than citizens of the Serbian republic itself! Kosovo and Vojvodina could make or repeal laws without agreement from Serbia, while Serbia could not do so herself.

In addition, Tito had promised Kosovo to the Albanians if Albania liberalized her government (i.e., renounced Stalinism as he did). How could Tito dare to give anybody property that does not belong to them! Could Tito realize that Kosovo for Serbs is a sacred place, a symbol of holiness, which he was generously willing to give away?

How did Tito accomplish the weakening of Serbia? He kept all the republics and autonomies in a state of constant dissension and rivalry. The Titoist system was corruptive, inefficient, morally disgraceful, and economically catstrophic. The system neither functioned properly nor was able to make good decisions, thus securing Tito's position as a giant among his henchmen.

There was injustice and discrimination with the Serbian minority in the Croatian republic. Mosha Pijade was for Serbian autonomy in Croatia, while Djilas, Rankovich, and Kardelj were against it since they desired to please Tito. He cleverly explained that those boundaries among republics were just for administrative purposes, not state borders. As it is today, drawing administrative borders is only a pretext to establish state borders. Those boundaries were not based on ethnic identity so they could not be valid.

Furthermore, representatives of the national Communist party of Croatia and Slovenia were at the AVNOY convention, while Serbs did not have their own national party. Also, by the Constitution of 1974 the republics have advantages over the structure of federal authority. The aim of that constitution was to drive Serbs into a corner from which they could not escape. Tito had it in mind after he became secretary of the CPY, but he moved with extreme caution.

The constitution was also intended to prevent Serbia from being united on the basis of ethnic factors. Tito forced Kardelj (whom he feared as a rival for his presidency) to write a separate article asking Tito to remain head of the Yugoslav state for the rest of his life. Tito held two blades of the cutting tool: One was Rankovich, who disagreed with Tito to get rid of Kardelj, and the other was Kardelj himself, who had to secure Tito's presidency for life!

According to the new Constitution, Serbia ceased to be a state in 1974. Instead two autonomous provinces with all attributes of states were formed. These then became guardians of their original state. Thanks for this go to some Serbs who were Tito's poltroons and were ready to execute any order of Tito's for the sake of retaining or gaining benefits and positions. A unique base of solidarity was broken down.

Through the Constitution of 1974 Tito with Kardelj and Bakarich secured so to speak six nearly independent republics. In other words, the republics could separate themselves from Yugoslavia whenever they decided to.[15] By that constitution the federal republics with the two provinces became constitutional elements of the federation. Such a constitution sanctioned the division of Yugoslavia and as things look now broke her apart forever.

Breaking up Yugoslavia was harder than predicted by the creators of the AVNOY concepts. Serbia alone lost 27 percent of her population for the liberation and unification of south Slavs. Furthermore, for Yugoslavia to survive the attacks of the Comintern and Vatican, Serbia had to sacrifice her democracy and constitutional parliamentary system that she had before the south Slavs were unified into one state.

Tito's codes of the Constitution of 1974 for self-management make a mockery of the judicial system of democratic societies. In 1974 when Serbs in Croatia asked for more human rights, Vladimir Bakarich stated that they would punch them (Serbs) in the teeth if they asked for their national rights, and Croatians have other nationals besides Serbs. Bakarich further recommended force, consistent with his long-standing advocacy of spiritual and physical genocide.

It was the same Bakarich who during the war had promised the most to Serbs. He states, referring to Serbs, "the surrounding areas [*dominantly Serbian*] in the new Croatia would be gold plated." Thus were the majority of Croatian leaders ready to deceive and lie to naive Serbs.

Alive and well today is not the boogyman of Marx or Engels of communism but the ogre of nationalism reinforced by Tito's decision to allow each republic to handle her own territorial defense if she chose to. Thanks to Tito's pretorian guard, the Yugoslav army enjoyed the status of social parasitism. Ivan Zvonimir-Chichak, a Croat, called the officers of the military academy the Forest Academy! Each republic could have its own army, but Serbia had to trust its safety to the federal troops. Territorial defense was a wild army directed by hatred, envy, and greed, often filled with persons with dark pasts.

All of Europe, whether former friends or foes, should bear in mind that before Yugoslavia ever existed, only two legitimate states, Serbia and Montenegro, were recognized by the Berlin Congress of 1878. What about

Croatia and Slovenia? Croatia lost her independence in 1102, while the Slovenes had lost it thousands of years ago. Since then both became part of the Austro-Hungarian Empire. Return back to Zvonimir-Chichak, who stated not long ago that Belgrade never was the Croatian capital, but Vienna. They have the right to choose freely with whom they like to live, then to stop committing genocide. So far, no Croats have apologized for the crimes of the Ustashe during World War II.

To achieve peace between Serbs and Croats, the following goals need to be met:

1. Right for self-determination to be respected.

2. Titoist/AVNOY administrative borders must be flexible and drawn according to the ethnic majority among federal republics and autonomies.

3. Some kind of mechanism needs to be invented to protect the human rights of each individual including those with the status of national minorities.

Titoists Committed Genocide in May 1945

Erich Fromm says no war among countries calls out such hatred and cruelty as does a civil war, when the quarreling parties know each other.

The Communist movement with its international Comintern agents used the "big lie" technique of repeating lies over and over again until one day they are accepted as truth. In fact, the truth was hermetically sealed. The Communists used force rather than persuasion, to pay back in kind.

In May 1945 Milan Basta, political commissar of the Fifty-First Vojvodina Division, stated that about 100,000 Ustashe and Domobran soldiers and a few thousand Montenegrin Hercegovina Chetniks had reached the Austrian border. Fikreta Jelich-Butich believes no more than 170,000 people were involved in the repatriation by the British in 1945.

Dr. Franjo Tudjman, Tito's general and political commissar and later a protagonist of neo-fascist Ustashe ideology in his book *Seamless Historical Truth*, believes the Croatian Ustashe did not create a Bleiburg myth about hundreds of thousands of Croats slaughtered "by Chetniks and Serbo-Communists." Tudjman has lost touch with rationality and common sense. How could the Chetniks kill Ustashe when the Chetniks were also slaughtered by Titoists? Tudjman will say whatever pleases the neo-Fascist Ustashe, who have been his main financial support. What did Tudjman himself do when he was political commissar in Tito's army?

Gen. Kosta Nadj, commandant of the Third Partisan Army, in his book *Comrade Tito, the War Is Over* states that Tito ordered on May 11, 1945: Proceed to Korushka by destroying the enemy.

British views about the Ustashe treatment at the Austrian border are represented by Brig. T. P. Scott, then commandant of the Thirty-Eighth Irish Brigade. He gave captured Croatians three alternatives: to surrender to the Communists; to retain their current position, where they would be attacked by the Yugoslav army; or to try to penetrate through the British lines, where they would be attacked by both sides, the British and the Yugoslav Partisan army.

Ralph Stevenson, British ambassador in Belgrade, recommended that those defeated forces be used as "auxiliary units" extradicted to the Yugoslav army or they could be disarmed and lodged in a displaced persons camp.

On May 5, 1945, Macmillan sent a telegram to Ambassador Stevenson in Belgrade.[16] He instructed Stevenson to inform Tito that the British would not make any negotiations with the ISC representatives, though the Ustashe government unsuccessfully tried to contact Field Marshal Alexander.

Macmillan and Alexander believed the highest orders of the American and British authorities could not be applied to the Ustashe regime, but only to Chetniks, Slovenes, Domobrans, and Balists.

The British Foreign Office (BFO) on May 26, 1945, telegraphed their units: Croatian troops are in a different position than the other units from Yugoslav territory. We are encouraging Croatian troops in southern Austria to hand over to Tito's forces because such an act could please them.

On May 10-20, 1945, into just one pit called Ponor were thrown 20,000 unarmed youth loyal to Mihailovich. The pit is 200 to 300 meters deep and is located in Miljevina, between Foca and Kalinovik.[17]

On May 27, 1945, in Ljubljana, Tito said: As far as those traitors are concerned, the hand of justice, the hand of revenge of our people, will recheck them. Only a small number succeeded in running away to protection outside our country.[18] In 1945 Stalin told Polish Communist leaders that Tito was a smart man—now he has no problems with his enemies because he already solved them.

On May 29, 1945, the position of the BFO in relation to Ustashe was that Croatian units de facto were regular forces of the quisling government that had operated under German leadership. Therefore, they should deport Croatian units from southern Austria to Tito's forces.

Bora Karapandzich in his book *Kochevye* states that in the Kochevye Forest alone 12,000 Slovenian Homeguardsmen, 3,000 Serbian volunteers, 2,000 Croatian Homeguardsmen, and 1,000 Montenegrin Chetniks were shot and thrown into pits. Says Milovan Djilas, according to its structure and party hierarchy, something like that could not happen without permission from the top. Before it happened, an atmosphere of revenge and the use of force had been created. In Tito's Yugoslavia executions were common, depending on various factors for their intensity and extent.

Tito was at the top of his autocratic government and was responsible for the crimes executed by his faithful Partisans. Their war prisoners were shot on the Pohorje slopes, Kocevje, and Teharje near Celje, and for all these crimes Tito almost was rewarded by a Nobel Peace prize!

In 1946 after the Bleiburg deportation of Yugoslav subjects, the BFO was engaged again in the matter of prisoners. According to documentation, all Ustashe in an Italian POW camp should be extradicted together to the Yugoslav authority. According to Churchill's conservative government in 1945 and, a year later, to Attlee's Labor party government, all Croatian military prisoners, without exception, should be considered not only as spies but also as a group of criminals who don't deserve any treatment according to the principles of international and war justice.[19]

The American State Department in April 1948 secretly investigated the matter under the title: No. 61—Policy of the United States Toward the Ustashe.

Pavelich as the official head of the Croatian government declared war against Britain and France and later the United States. What then could his Ustashe expect—when they loyally and faithfully served Nazi Germany, could they expect the Allied governments to treat them as if they had been their allies? However, it was unfair and inhumane to send them back to Yugoslavia, where all met brutal executions. The criminals were the Ustashe themselves; most of those so severely punished were innocent people. The Allies should have kept them and screened them instead of sending them back in a hurry.

The Chetniks who retreated to Italy were not returned to the Allies. Most of them came to the United States, where they continued successful lives.[20]

Titoists Victors over Their Own People

In Serbia, in particular, the victorious Partisans could eliminate anyone without investigation or trial. Was it a perfidious, planned campaign for Serbian destruction? In Belgrade, Serbs were hunted like dogs for over six months after Tito won over the Yugoslav people, while in Zagreb such pursuit lasted for only three days. Some sources say that in Serbia alone Titoists killed over 150,000 in the period from the second half of 1944 and the beginning of 1945. Serbia was again crucified after the war was over.

There was a terrifying confession by a Partisan executioner who committed crimes at the end of the war. He says: Yes, I killed people. I was under such stressful circumstances. I was young then, in fact, crazy without really knowing what I was doing. Now in my dreams those crimes have been frequently appearing before me. The entire world trembles at the idea of what I did. Let truth uncover the secrets about those who forced me to kill. I dream more frequently about unknown people who are staring me as if asking me what kind of mania made me kill them. I don't ask either them or myself who they are! Do you want to blame me for depriving them of their lives? It was sometimes unbearable for me. During the nights those dreams awaken me from sleep and I race toward the window like a madman. Therefore, for the last two years I sleep alone, in the isolated part of my home. On my window there are steel shutters that I lock each evening. During those terrible nightmares I want to be alone. I let myself suffer alone, because I only have to amend for my mistakes. During that infamous period when hotheads were trying to establish a new order, a better human society in the new environs, they said it was necessary to be rid of all reactionary scum and the bourgeoisie decay that was deposited before and during the war that was not in accord with the spirit of progressive people.... Indeed, the time is long overdue to separate the truth from the lie, to separate chaff from the wheat. No doubt there have always been black sheep in any flock. Then a man's weaknesses came to the surface, against which were struggling the human virtues like personal honor, dignity, and human decency....

At the conclusion of his confession he advises others: Don't commit a crime unless you want to be wretched the rest of your life. It would be easier to lose your head—that pain would last just a few seconds—than having your soul, your conscience suffer forever. I say it from my own horrible experience. My life is death, yet it would be much better to rest in the grave than to live and confront the nightmare every time I decide to go to sleep. You want to rest but you can't! Oh God! Who forced me to have such an unbearable life! Will society ever stop committing crimes in the name of higher ideals of liberty and social justice? Stay away from the cursed Satan who is dressed in human clothes, the lion in the lamb's hide, if you want to have tranquility and a modest life....

People tried to relieve their minds and their sufferings from Tito's hypocrisy through anecdotes, songs, and the like. One of the songs is recorded here:

> From the Ovcar and Kablar
> Shepherd was saying:
> King Peter of the white face,
> When would you come to Uzica?
> And to see your Serbs,
> How they are hanging on gallows:
> Son next to father, brother next to brother,
> With ropes around their necks.
>
> (Sa Ovcara i Kablara,
> Chobanica progovara:
> Kralju Pero, bela lica
> Kad cesh doci do Uzica?
> Pa da vidish Srbe Tvoje
> Na veshala kako stoje,
> Sin do oca, brat do brata
> Sa konopom oko vrata.)

Nikolay Tolstoy in his book *Minister and Massacres* said that after Tito took control in Yugoslavia about 350,000 of his political adversaries were killed. Michael Lees in his book *Rape of Serbia* says he understands that about 250,000 were liquidated on a narrowed perimeter. In 1974 Willy Brandt, chancellor of West Germany, submitted to Tito a list of 130,000 Volksdeutscher Germans whom Partisans killed at the end of the war.

Should Yugoslavia Be Broken Up?

In 1956 Kardelj told Dobrica Cosich: Historically, Yugoslavia is a temporary formation. She is a phenomenon, the result of an imperialistic epoch and the constellation of international relations in that epoch. With the development of a world process of integration and a new association based on a civilized and spiritual affinity, it is unavoidable that Yugoslavia will decompose as a nation.

In March 1962 Tito called a secret three-day conference of the party leadership from the federation and the republics. Tito opened by asking: Can we preserve or should we break up Yugoslavia?

According to Kardelj's opinion, which was shared by Bakarich, Kucan, and Racan, one day Yugoslavia will be reorganized as a historical necessity. Kardelj continues: Slovenia will join with Austria and Italy, while Serbs naturally will join Bulgaria as Orthodox nations, historically predetermined to live closer to each other.

Yugoslavia was an illusion, an artificial creation that was held together like a marriage. Indeed, Kardelj's notion sounds like the idea of the restoration of the Habsburg dynasty in the Catholic "sub-Danube federation." Churchill himself was a protagonist of such an idea, though it was not realized during his lifetime. Intellectuals of the prospective new federation were known as the Alps-Adriatic community. This organization was wrapped in secrecy in order not to give anyone suspicion of the restoration of the Habsburg Empire and the increase of Vatican influence toward dominance of the east. In that conference, Slovenian and Croatian leaders unveiled their intentions for a new map of Yugoslavia. They completely ignored the Serbs. However, in 1918 both Slovenians and Croats had cried loudly that Serbs, Croats, and Slovenes were one nation with three tribes. Until then, various enemies had thwarted their natural unification. But what was going on in 1962?

Tito said there were many problems, not only economic crises, but political ones. Then he asked: Could the country hold together, or was it to be broken up?

Alexander Rankovich reacted with surprise. He like the majority of Serbs present thought they were gathered not to destroy the country but to find the best solution for its reorganization and proper functioning to save Yugoslavia from its deep political crises and economic collapse. Some republics were going too far in their particularism. As Goshnjak says, the republics had been changing Yugoslavia's orientation since the end of the 1950s and the beginning of the 1960s. Djuro Pucar could not believe that such chauvinism and particularism could prevail, every big city like a forest in which can be hidden every wolf.

The architects of a policy of disintegration were, besides Tito, Kardelj, Bakarich, Kavcich, and Stevan Doronjski. There was no doubt that the dictator Tito had to know in advance the intentions of the Croatian and Slovenian leaders for Yugoslav disintegration without the presence of any Serb. Kardelj as a Slovenian was chosen at that meeting to speak up because Serbs considered Slovenes less anti-Yugoslav than Croats. Besides, between Serbs and Croats there was an abyss caused by the genocide committed by the Croatian Ustashe.

After defeating the Yugoslav army in Slovenia in June 1991, Gen. Veljko Kadijevich, secretary of defense, attributed the current events to the happenings in 1962!

In the middle of 1962 Tito declared himself for the decentralization of Yugoslavia. He attacked centralism and dogmatism in interpreting party politics. Tito could not blame anyone but himself for the concept of centralism because he held all the strings of power in his hands. Additionally, in 1945 he had favored unity and centralism of the Yugoslav state because it was then in the best interest of Croatia to hide the crimes committed by the Ustashe. Later Tito was willing to reverse his own policy.

He also suffered from a "Serbian complex." He did not mention this complex openly, but only in allusions referring to "Belgrade charshija" (people) and "different kitchens." He was always afraid of Serbian superiority in the ruling party and in the country as well. They knew they could not keep Serbia in a subordinate position forever, taking from her but giving nothing in return. Those complicities and various manipulations were hard, even impossible, for many Yugoslav experts to understand.

The roots of the latest Yugoslav crises lie primarily in the inheritance of Tito's autocratic Communist system. He founded a special type of political system primarily to protect and secure his personal authority. He had gradually and quietly worked to slacken political and economic cohesion among the Yugoslav republics. He succeeded sooner than expected.

Croatian Masspok—"Croatian Spring": Tendency for a Sovereign and Independent Croatian State

Masspok was Ustashe ideology reaching out. The Croatian *masspok* (mass movement) was preparing a putsch for the New Year of 1971. The leaders of Ustashe immigrants in the United States concluded that Croatian Communists finally understood it was imperative for Croatians to put Croatian money in their pockets and Croatian rifles over Croatian shoulders. Masspok was favored by the powerful headquarters of Matica Hrvatska and Zagreb and was supported by functionaries from the CCCPC: Tripalo, Dabcevich, Pirker, Gen. Shible, and Rector Supek and by Kapitol (the highest body of the Catholic church in Croatia).

Bakarich stated: Croatians will not and cannot be either a dowry for anybody or a province beseiged from the sea. If Croatian nationalism were not correctly understood and blocked, it would expand uncontrollably.

Interpreted rightly, "Croatian Spring" means Croatian chauvinists wanted much more than the Serbs in Croatia had demanded in 1950. The Serbs were ready to fight to the last man, but they hesitated to begin until they could win.

Mass movements planned before the putsch included the following:

1. About 200 men from Hercegovina, young members of Matica Hrvatska, had received orders to dress in military uniforms and were provided with falsified documents. Around Christmas several hundred prvoboraca (those who fought from the beginning of the war) were to be picked up in Zagreb and then in the nearby forest or Zagrebacka Gora to be liquidated. It was a prelude to the putsch, which then would be taken over by the authority of Matica Hrvatska.

2. Actions by postmen: On New Year's Day 300 postmen would ring bells at the doors of some functionaries targeted for liquidation in Zagreb. The moment they opened their doors with "Happy New Year" on their lips, they would be shot in the forehead or in the chest.

There were rumors that those actions were under the direct supervision of Dragutin Haramija, then president of the executive council of the Croatian parliament (sabor).

Masspok was prevented by intervention of the Yugoslav army. The Yugoslav general staff was worried about the mass movement. They decided to visit Tito at Brioni and ask him what was going on. Tito replied: Comrades, you don't know what the mouse thinks until it comes out of its hole!

Savka Dabcevich-Kucar was frustrated and surprised by Tito's cowardly manner. She looked him right in the eye and told him whatever the masspok planners did he was informed. He knew all of their moves and he completely approved of it. He promised them help if they succeeded; if they failed he would help them even more.

Savka was frustrated and called Tito a coward because he changed his mind and had to approve the military blockade of the borders and Zagreb as well in order to arrest the organizers of the reprising.

The following people fell as victims of Masspok: Miko Tripalo, Savka Dabcevich-Kucar, Pero Pirker, Ivan Shible, and others.

By preventing the putsch the death of Yugoslavia was postponed. Croatian Separatist forces were pushed back for a while, but they were not destroyed.

Tito was between the anvil and the hammer. As an expert of manipulation and treachery he proclaimed the weeds were cut off, which did not mean to cut off the heads. Forced by the military, Tito succeeded in stopping both masspok and the entering of the Red Army into Yugoslavia. (In April 1971 Brezhnev had contacted Tito and asked him if he needed help in retaining Yugoslav unity.)

Yugoslav separatists planned to divide Yugoslavia thusly:

1. United republics of western Yugoslavia—Croatia, Slovenia, Bosnia, and Hercegovina.

2. Southern Yugoslavia—Serbia, Montenegro, and Macedonia, while Kosovo should be either a sovereign state or join Albania.

In February 1989 nationalistic tendencies resurfaced in Zagreb. On February 28, 1989, messages were sent by Franjo Tudjman and from Cancar Dom, Jubljana that sounded like masspok. In March 1989 texts appeared in Belgrade newspapers with many harsh and provocative sentences that conveyed the message "Croatia is in peril."

Hrvoje Hitrec, a Croatian writer, called for the unity of all Croatians to defend the sovereignty of Croatia. Tudjman states: In Croatia tragic consequences have been felt since masspok was crushed. Silence was imposed on Croatia, but Croatian thought had not faded away.

It was necessary to realize that the majority of the Croatian people were stamped as nationalistic, separatist by sharing Ustashe's views for over three decades!

Was the prognosis correct?

Catholic attorney Ivo Polar wrote in German about the Yugoslav problem. He said Yugoslavia became the "embryo for the expansion of Serbian nationalism." Serbianism and Orthodoxy cannot exist without expansion and conquering, "like fish without water." The only alternative to stop it was to form a great Croatian state from Kotor along the Drina River to Zemun.

On the Yugoslav political scene there were two opposing trends of Tito-ism. Both drew Communist concepts from the same source. One was inspired by the sovereignty of the republics, by the second congress of AV-NOY, and later by the Constitution of 1974 that shook the federation. The other rested on ties between the Yugoslav army and the ideology as a basic lever of authority.

Croatia and Slovenia find strong supporters if not initiators for expansion of Austro-Hungary and the Vatican toward Drang nach Osten (prodor na istok).

Tito's Poltroons and Intelligence Agents

Alexander Rankovich and His Fall

A French adage says: Things should be abandoned before they abandon you.

For Rankovich, Tito was an idol to whom he was loyal like a dog. He was without the Comintern education Kardelj, Veselinov, Vlahovich, and others had. Rankovich had negated himself as a most subordinate person, which left in him some degree of human honesty and relative modesty. Before the Brioni plenum he was vice-president of Tito's government.

A plenum at which Rankovich was dismissed was held at Brioni in 1966. At that session Rankovich's executor was Edward Kardelj; Ivan-Stevo Krajacich was a direct player against him. The anticentralist policy began at this plenum.

Secret preparations for the Brioni plenum began in the spring of 1966. Members of the Central Committee Plenum (CCP) were informed and consulted. Tito and army authorities were behind the CCP.

On June 16 a meeting of the executive committee was held. Tito made a speech for the legalization of Krsto Crvenkovski's committee for the investigation of Alexander Rankovich. Men from Croatia, Slovenia, and the army were activated, while those from Belgrade and Serbia were eyed with suspicion.

What were Rankovich and Stefanovich accused of at the Brioni plenum?

Their accusers brought up evidence of "crimes" at Kosmet (Kosovo and Metohia) executed by the UDBA. Behind the UDBA stood Rankovich, executing the nationalistic and chauvinistic tendencies common to his group. Those "crimes" were acknowledged by the Kosovo and Serbian leadership and had already been condemned at the sixth plenum of the central committee.

In fact, Rankovich or Stefanovich routinely informed four men—Tito, Kardelj, Djilas, and Rankovich—of all activities of the security service (UDBA).

In 1964 the UDBA was praised by Bakarich for showing persistence and courage. Kardelj also stated that it was great fortune for society that there was such an organization working in the struggle for the victory of socialism. Tito also stated he had followed the UDBA's work for the entire period.

On the first day of the plenum Rankovich was totally isolated. After two Rankovich appearances and despite a heart attack, the Brioni plotters did not lose their determination to be rid of him.

Selim Numich, assistant federal secretary of security forces, denied all accusations of wiretapping. He defended Rankovich as the head of Yugoslav security forces.

The Communist Party of Slovenia was the greatest stimulus for Albanian irredentists and for other nationalists and chauvinistic elements in Croatia and Slovenia. Scapegoats were found: Vojin Lukich, Numich, Zivotije Srba Savich, and technical personnel in the federal UDBA who were arrested, interrogated, and finally given "amnesty." During Rankovich's fall only the federal UDBA, the UDBA of the Serbian republic, and the Belgrade UDBA were combed.

The plenum could not bring Rankovich to trial because there was no evidence against him. Therefore, the plenum wanted to "forgive" all the accused in a behind-the-scenes scenario. Tito once told Rankovich that "either Kardelj or me" would stay in government, but Rankovich succeeded in calming him down for the sake of world reaction.

There were several reasons for Rankovich's downfall. Rankovich was an instrumental obstacle to destroying the central function of the Yugoslav state. Disintegration of Yugoslavia was inevitable, as Kardelj insisted and Tito supported. So, Rankovich as the head of federal security had to fall first. Kardelj consistently sacrificed Yugoslavia to bolster his Slovenian sovereign state (dezela).

Tito acted as the judge during Rankovich's and Milosh Zanko's executions, as well as the leader of the CPY with his "first strike" of secret police and the Yugoslav army. In March of 1967 a Declaration of Croatian Literary language, separated from Serbian, was issued.

In 1970 Dr. Milosh Zanko, the greatest Yugoslav-oriented Croat of the time, was castigated as Rankovich had been in 1966. Both were accused of unitarism, trying to break Yugoslav unity (they both acted oppositely) as a political and economic entity. The executor of Zanko was Bakarich, who told a "joke" that if one scratches to blood under the skin of every Serb there will appear Saint Sava.

The most inveterate adversary of the new Croatian concept of independence and sovereignty was Zanko, who was defeated. He was finished off so he would never raise his head again. "In advance he dared to show and to frustrate our great plans.... He is dead, while our idea is continuing," said Dr. Savka Dabcevich.

At the end, Tito first used Rankovich to get rid of Kardelj, then did the opposite. Kardelj was chosen so that "Vlasi could not recall" the Tito-Krajacich circle of conspiracy. Tito was a friend to somebody while he needed him. As a professional KGB executor he was a villain in the full meaning of the word.

Slobodan Penezich "Krcun"—Titoist and Member of Tito's Guard

Penezich was a high school teacher from Uzice, Serbia. He was a brutal, bloodthirsty person and was often compared with the Soviet chief of police, Beria. Penezich "Krcun" tortured his innocent victims, bragging that he would choke them with his own hands and suck their blood, so they would breathe their last under his hands to tell the dead who Slobodan Penezich was! Krcun, Rankovich, and Dedijer tortured Zivojin Pavlovich, who was the first Yugoslav to say no to Stalin. He wrote a book *Balance of Soviet Termidor*. Witnesses stated that Pavlovich was kicked repeatedly by Petar Stambolich and Vladimir Dedijer. Finally, Tito sentenced him to death. Communists like Tito were merciless toward their fellow Communists!

In 1963 Tito, Marko (Alexander Rankovich), and Krcun went to Brioni. During that trip Krcun under the influence of alcohol scolded Tito:

1. Tito was welcomed by Serbs when he arrived on the free territory from Belgrade.
2. Serbs brought him to liberated Uzucu in November 1941.
3. Serbs guarded him there.
4. Serbs including Krcun continued to guard him.
5. Throughout the entire war Tito was guarded by Serbs. They continued until Tito forgot them!

Krcun continued that there was no intention of mentioning either Sreten Zujovich-Crni, Blagoje Neshkovich or Ljube Djurich, who were under suspicion. How did it happen that only Serb commandants were suspect, such as Pavle Jakshich, Miloje Milojevich, Radivoje Jovanovich-Bradonja, Sredoje Uroshevich, and others?

Tito lost his patience, jumped from his seat, and yelled to Krcun that he was drunk and didn't know what he was talking about.

Krcun replied, "I know, I know.... Only I don't know when the two of us will be next" (meaning Rankovich and himself).

Tito shut the door while Krcun had another drink.

None of the Serbian generals could advance in their careers if they refused to become Tito's vassals, as did Gen. Ljubicich. If any showed the slightest disagreement with Tito, he was forced to retire early.

Krcun was one of the first Serbian Communists, with exceptional instincts and intuition, to point out the existence of nationalism and economic egoism. He was the strongest and most difficult obstacle for Kardelj and Tito in realizing the formation of the sovereign national states that began with ANVOY. Krcun was then considered a "dangerous Serb." He was under steady surveillance, and Broz targeted him for elimination.

He was a melancholy person, a revolutionary and rebel. He was unhappy with Tito's politics toward Serbs, Serbian cadres, and Serbia. Krcun once said (again under the influence of alcohol): "We did not fight for unkempt Marx but for Serbia." He felt Tito's sword over Serbia, which distressed him very much.[21]

Was an "accident" plotted against Krcun?

Gen. Djurich was Tito's trustee and former chief of Tito's cabinet until 1952, when he was jailed at the Sixth Congress of the CPY-ACY held from November 2-7, 1952. In 1965 Djurich went with his wife to Uzicu to visit their relatives.

In November 1964, near Lazarevac, Krcun's automobile swerved off the road, hitting a big tree. He was killed instantly, along with his comrade Svetolik Lazarevich, who was political commissar of the Third Battalion, Second Proletarian Brigade.

The conspiracy against Krcun was planned by Tito, Kardelj, Krajacich, Bakarich, and the Mishkovich brothers, Milan and Ivan.[22]

Tito had always complained that others deceived him. However, he always made all important decisions personally, while the others obediently executed his decisions, as did Rankovich, Djurich, and the like.

In 1952 Gen. Ljubo Djurich, chief of Tito's cabinet, was eliminated, and Tito ordered him taken away from the podium where he was presiding over the Sixth Congress of the CPY. Djurich accused Petar Stambolich of adultery with his wife. The party chose Djurich's second and third wives. During an anti-Tito period by Comintern adherents, Tito invited Djurich and told him flatly, "Djurich, party or family!" The brother of Djurich's wife was arrested as a Cominformist. Djurich chose the party. He divorced his wife, leaving two children (and a third child from the first marriage). When he decided to get married a third time he asked the party to find a wife acceptable to the party. After a thorough UDBA investigation they selected a female with "good" moral qualifications fit for party members. So Djurich married her. Soon after, he found that she was continuing to have a close relationship with Petar Stambolich, who was Tito's poltroon and as such was an influential party member. Stambolich had a "harem." Regardless, Tito protected Stambolich and threw Djurich in jail. That was the morality and justice of Josip Broz Tito!

Kardelj, Tito's Associate from Moscow

In 1944 during the war, Kardelj wrote to Tito that Serbian processes on liberated territory in Croatia in many ways were the result of an incorrect policy toward Serbs. Kardelj defended Serbs as great contributors to the Partisan victory, though lately he changed his position toward them.

Soviet intelligence did not get along well with Kardelj. Jovanka Broz also was against Kardelj, probably because she did not get along with Kardelj's wife, Pepsa.

In fact, Rankovich strongly defended Kardelj while Tito was trying to get rid of him. Why was Tito afraid of Kardelj? The cause was cursed power: either to get it or to retain the current position.

The ink on the Constitution of 1964 was not yet dry when Kardelj began to prepare another one. In February 1974 a new constitution was written that thrust a spear into Yugoslavia. As the story goes, instead of making Yugoslavia a prosperous and happy country taking advantage of its natural richness and beauty Tito did just the opposite: Yugoslavia was wrapped in mourning and thrown into a dark tunnel! Kardelj's new constitution was not a demonstration of statesmanship but a denunciation of law and justice. That constitution was called by judicial experts "a judicial and constitutional monster." The Yugoslav republics had supported Kardelj in his efforts to write a new constitution!

In 1974 with the new constitution Kardelj purposefully gave more autonomy to the republics. So each republic could form its own army for so-called territorial defense. This instigated in the first place separatist tendencies in

Croatia and Slovenia led incognito by Tito, Kardelj, Bakarich, Kucan, and Racan.

However, the Serbian republic was an unequal partner in the federation, with even less authority than her two provinces, Kosovo and Vojvodina. For instance, she could not make any law without confirmation by both Kosovo and Vojvodina, while those two entities could make laws without consent of the Serbian republic. Tito's motto was "A weaker Serbia, a stronger Yugoslavia."

Tito's motto mirrored the Tito-Subashich formula from 1944. In April 1981, when the Yugoslav presidency was convened to discuss the mutiny at Kosovo, Lazar Kolishevski thought Yugoslavia would collapse if she did not abandon the Tito-Subashich concept. He said, Yugoslavia can only survive and be strong if Serbia is strong! Those words of Kolishevski caused the end of his political career in ACY and in the Yugoslav government. Indeed, his statement was an outspoken expression of Yugoslav political reality. Croatian and Slovenian separatists decided if they could not take Serbia as a vassal republic, they would have to break the Yugoslav entity. Later events resulted from that uncompromising trend.

Tito and his cohorts insisted on a weaker Serbia, politically, militarily, and economically. The military industry was moved out of Serbia. Heavy industries were relocated from Serbia to Bosnia and Slovenia. Somebody was always afraid of Serbia. Austro-Hungary and the Vatican and their followers have been going along with their masters.

In 1974 the new constitution of the ACY (Alliance of Yugoslav Communists) characterized Serbs and Serbia as a main danger for Yugoslav "democracy" and for "equal treatment of all nationalities and nations." The wishes of national people were fulfilled even though they were former Nazi allies, except for Slovenia. Only the Serbian people were deprived of their statehood and their equal rights.

Earlier, in 1971, the ACY saw the danger of Serbian liberalism in the agricultural reforms. Serbia was insisting on being included in the European Common Market. Therefore, Nikezich with his entire agricultural apparatus—specialists and directors—was removed. So Serbian agriculture was destroyed and her ties with Europe were cut off.

Tito and his marionettes used all possible perfidious means to destroy the Serbian people, both politically and ecoonomically. Those are the irrefutable facts.

According to Dr. Branko Petranovich, a renowned and respected historian, Kardelj's idea for reorganizing society remains a permanent testament to the nonsense that had dangerous consequences for the state concept, the democratic system, the classic experience of the civilized world, the pragmatic strip of the most different empiric and theoretical genesis (from Christian socialism via bourgeois thinkers to deforming self-management from the past).

Tito's Yugoslavia could survive if with the same concept and structure Serbia agreed to remain in a subordinate position. It was mere illusion to expect people with a developed statehood consciousness to reconcile with their fate and current role. Mutiny was unavoidable. It was prepared secretly during Tito's reign by his heirs. In 1987 came a party revolution. A people's insurrection began as a national revival and grew to include equal partnership.

Kardelj with his ambitious plans and new constitution brought to the people in Yugoslavia (even to his Slovenian dezela time would tell) chaos, despair, and, above all, the worst animosity that had ever existed.

Stevo-Ivan Krajacich, Tito's Right-hand Man

Stevo Krajacich was the most influential person around Tito. He recruited Jovanka Broz as his agent in order to know what was going on around Tito. He gave "gifts" to Tito ("black pears"), wiretappers, to dispatch and receive, that he installed in Tito's office. So Tito could hear any conversation around him, while the others' offices could not.

Krajacich supported Hebrang's view of nationalism, and he had an explicitly chauvinistic attitude toward Serbs. He was painted with all colors. He had direct ties between Tito and the supreme headquarters of Ante Pavelich; he was the highest authority to arrange contacts between these two "warring" parties. He played a direct role in negotiations between Tito and the Ustashe. Documents about Ustashe barbarism that were not destroyed by the Ustashe were destroyed by Krajacich. He lived in Zagreb most of the time during the war. He dressed in an Ustashe uniform. He traveled to Hungary in the guise of a "swine merchant." He contacted a former Austro-Hungarian colonel designated to defend Zagreb. They agreed during Pavelich's celebration of the New Year in 1943 to hit Banske Dvore, where a reception would be held. Krajacich was told he could destroy everything within artillery's reach. The hit would be about a hundred meters; however, Tito ordered the hit cancelled because the civilian population might suffer.

There was a rumor that Krajacich as a great Serbophobe went to Belgrade via Zemun to organize the liquidation of some German officers so the Germans would retaliate against the Serbs, probably by the ratio of 100 Serbs for each German killed or 50 for each one wounded, as the Germans did during Kragujevac and other reprisals. Via Broz, Krajacich and Bakarich intended to strengthen their positions in the CPY, with the possible aim of weakening or temporarily eliminating Hebrang's influence. This trio—Tito, Krajacich, and Bakarich—were perfidious and ready to destroy anything that stood in the way of accomplishing their goal.

Quarrel Between Krajacich and Krcun

As an intelligence officer Krajacich travelled wherever duty required. He was involved in the intelligence of the Ustashe, Germans, and the Soviet military. From Croatian Partisan headquarters he was dispatched to the supreme Partisan headquarters in Bosnia. Tito assigned him to the Second Partisan Brigade (Srbijanaca) to find out how the brigade was organized. He could later transmit his experience to Croatian units.

During Krajacich's stay with the brigade from Serbia he complained to Krcun (Slobodon Penezich) that Srbijanci had plundered a village. One woman pointed a finger at a fighter who had taken a pair of woolen socks. Stevo advised Krcun that as the party leader he should not tolerate but strike hard at plunderers. Stevo then added: Srbijanci plundered before and now they do the same against us. You, Krcun, don't you see it?

Krcun in the excitement jumped to his feet, shouting at Stevo. If they plundered it was a Serbian village, not your Ustashe one.

Stevo got up and went toward the door while Krcun swore at Stevo and anyone who had sent him, shouting, If you were worthwhile they would not have sent you here from the Croatian headquarters!

In 1944 in Kordun there were liquidations of "hesitant" Serbs. Krajacich was then OZNA chief in Croatia. He played a dominant role in Serb liquidations there.

Stevo Krajacich played a decisive role in eliminating all of Tito's adversaries or unneeded collaborators, including Rankovich. Even Tito's barber was replaced by a Krajacich appointee. Stevo played the darkest role in the history of the CPY. He and Bakarich wanted to take control over the Serb uprising in Croatia. Soviet intelligence through Kopinich also wanted to keep the uprising in Croatia under their own control. Krajacich ordered Tibor Vaska to liquidate Srebrnjak (February 23, 1942) and Hebrang (February 24, 1942). Through the Ustashe Vaska liquidated Srebrnjak. His intelligence center was completely interwoven with the existing ISC authority and leaned also toward the Vatican. During Hebrang's arrest, Pavelich visited him in jail! Then Hebrang was transferred to the notorious Jasenovac camp, where he secretly agreed to collaborate with the Ustashe under one condition—all documentation about it must be destroyed. Tibor Vaska was Kopinich's agent planted among the Ustashe. He informed Kopinich of Hebrang's behavior in Jasenovac. So Kopinich informed the Comintern and Tito, who denied ever getting such information!

After the war, Hebrang and Francisca, Srebrnjak's wife, were arrested. In 1948 both committed "suicide" in prison under mysterious circumstances. The chief of the prison then was Stevo Krajacich, and his assistant was Josip Manolich, who was currently in Tudjman's government.

After those purges Krajacich became the absolute boss inside the CPC. He gradually expanded his influence via "Walter" to other national Communists in the Balkans.

On July 3, 1966, Krajacich was present during the unveiling of a monument in Jasenovac. When the commemorative speeches concluded, Krajacich approached the delegation of the Veterans Federation from Serbia, saying, "We killed too few Serbs here" (malo smo vas ovde pobili.)

Josip Kopinich, Comintern Representative

Josip Kopinich can be considered an encyclopedia of collected documents of the various intelligence services. He was a four-fold experienced agent. He was proud of his activities on behalf of the Soviet Union. In the Spanish civil war he distinguished himself with rare intelligence, resoluteness, and courage. He informed the Soviets of what the Germans and British were doing, told the British what they were interested in knowing about the Soviets and Germans, and told the Germans about the Soviets and the British.

Josip Broz was thus informed before any of those major countries. He was informed by Kopinich, his old comrade and friend from the Moscow underground.

Kopinich was the Comintern representative for six countries: Austria, Czechoslovakia, Greece, Italy, Switzerland, and Yugoslavia. In 1948, through Kopinich, Tito was told of Stalin's letter about getting rid of Tito.

During World War II Kopinich had three Communist party members planted in the Ustashe and Gestapo intelligence services. Through those three agents he received information and word on the status of imprisoned comrades. Kopinich told Krajacich to let Tito know about Hebrang. At the end of the war Kopinich saved Vaska's life. He was secretly transferred to Belgrade under a false identity.

The other two Kopinich agents, Zivko Fuchich and Zdenko Zezeljich, did not fare so well. Fuchich's liquidation was ordered by the military authority; Zezeljich was suffocated one night by a cyclone bomb in his bedroom in Zemun.

Kopinich is still alive. After his death we hope he will allow documents of his activities to be published.

Tito and the Yugoslav Plight

Did Tito fight for the liberation or the subjugation of his people? Broz was known to the world as an invulnerable ruler-dictator. Such an expensive statesman, history does not remember.

For years, Croatian and Slovenian leadership insisted that historically they did not belong to the Yugoslav state. In 1917 at Corfu, Dr. Ante Trumbich, representing Yugoslav people from the Austro-Hungarian Empire, signed a joint proclamation with the Serbian government for the unification of the south Slav people after the end of the war. As later events showed, that act did not symbolize joy and a sincere desire for their unification, but mere necessity. Trumbich states after the war that he didn't want to see Croatian under rubble with the Austro-Hungarian Empire. Croatians throughout history have been devoted Catholics, and they believed in Catholicism being the advance guard in the Balkans. They also remained faithful to the former Austro-Hungarian Empire, hoping for her ressurection one day. With such fanaticism toward the Vatican and loyalty to Austro-Hungary in their hearts and minds they could never accept Yugoslavia as their real country. There was antagonism toward Serbia as an Orthodox nation that was in a position to dictate peace conditions in the Balkans in 1918. Croatia and Slovenia have jointly complained about the Yugoslav structure, though both received the maximum from Yugoslavia with the minimum possible given in return.

The Serbs were too naive; the formation of Yugoslavia cost them dearly in lives and goods. In 1918 Croatians and Slovenes united with Serbs to evade war reparations as defeated nations and interboundary demarcations. However, in 1991 both were in different bargaining positions and ready for Yugoslav disintegration, especially since the Serbian republic had equal status with other Yugoslav republics, thanks to Tito with his cynical and perfidious temper who did everything in such an unscrupulous manner to break Yugoslavia's unique statehood! Serbs have to accept the reality that they were deceived and plundered under Tito's dictatorship. If the republics don't want to live together nobody has the moral and ethical right to hold them together against their will and desire.

In 1945 after the war, Croatians were silent regarding Yugoslav disintegration in order to hush up the Ustashe genocide. During Tito's rule anyone who mentioned Jasenovac was mercilessly persecuted. Serbs, Jews, and Gypsies could never forget such bestialities, especially when Croats, except for Dr. Grizigono, did not condemn the genocide, much less apologize for such crimes, as did the Germans to the Jews and the Japanese to the Chinese. The Croatian Catholic church headed by Archbishop Dr. Kuharich, whose clergy (part of it) took a direct part in the genocide, is trying to minimize the number of victims annihilated in the period of World War II. Such an un-Christian position of the Croatian Catholic church and the Vatican infuriated Serbs and well-informed people worldwide. There was no longer a Tito to suppress the justified reactions against such inhuman behavior!

Titoism lulled people into feeling strength and security; this gave them the illusion of Yugoslav prestige in the world and the eternity of their regime. Therefore they use the slogan "Tito after Tito." Politicians use this phrase to set forth their idol as a rare, extinct animal to prolong their imperial lives and to retain for themselves what the people earned by their sweat. They further keep the people immorally and shamelessly in the darkness of one way of thinking (jednoumlja). Circumstances were changing, so Titoists found themselves in a new situation looking for new political support. Primarily, they insist on preserving their acquired privileges and covering up the innumerable usurpations and thefts of state and community properties.

Tito did not have any predecessor or successor, but he was unique in amassing luxuries. He spent enormous amounts of money for kumstvo (by the tradition to be godfather for the ninth male child), as well as mountain palaces, villas, Vanga Island, vineyards, orchards, a zoo, horses for riding, books, goods, hunting grounds, and the Brioni complex, with about twenty-eight buildings. The complex was supervised by Stevo Krajacich. There were employed 1,150 people, from maids to members of security. Krajacich and the Croatian UDBA presented Tito with a vineyard with a small villa, a villa in Split, and an old palace near Kranj (Slovenia). All these objects except the villa in Opatia were maintained from the federal budget.

Tito's poltroons mystified him as if he were the delegate of God on earth.

Alexander Rankovich made the greatest mistakes when he eagerly executed all Tito's orders without question or hesitation! Those poltroons played a decisive role in forming Tito's cult of personality with conceit and a tendency to autocracy. The pleiad of flatterers and poltroons included Rankovich, Kardelj, Bakarich, Stambolich, Krajacich, and Todorovich. Some of Tito's associates and advisors hold fundamental positions while expressing their independent opinions, like Sreten Zujovich-Crni, Boris Kidrich, Blagoje Neshkovich, Lazar Kolishevski, Ivan Goshnjak, Svetozar Vukmanovich-Tempo, and Djuro Pucar. In the third group of Tito's associates were those who noticed deficiencies in Tito's character and performance and showed it indirectly, like Krleza, Koca Popovich, and Mosha Pijade.

During his lifetime Tito even brought Yugoslavia to disappear by sanctions, changing personnel in his autocratic regime, the encirclement of Serbia, and her demotion to a lower level than were her autonomous provinces!

Tito reserved two alternatives for Yugoslavia:

1. To retain a Yugoslavia in which Serbia would have inferior status, and be outvoted, deprived of any independent position or declaration.

2. To disintegrate Yugoslavia.

The roots of the Yugoslav crisis were caused by Tito himself and his autocratic, corruptive, unethical, antisocial, and anti-Christian brand of communism, primarily in the Serbian regions and republics. Tito split not only the Serbian ethos but also the Serbian Orthodox church into three parts:

1. The Serbian free church in the United States and Canada

2. Serbian church under an obedient German patriarch

3. Macedonian church, which is still de jure Serbian church because the civil authority doesn't make final decisions in Christian church matters.

To divide people on the premises of ethnic or religious affiliation flatly means sowing discord among the people.[24] Just as Tito interfered in Serbian church matters, in 1991 Pope John himself aligned one side of the Yugoslav conflict. Judging by Christian ethics this is not permissible because the Pope cannot interfere in the internal affairs of a sovereign country. As the head of the Catholic church he is betraying his apostolic mission for peace on earth among all people!

Yugoslavia is a country of the Mediterranean, Balkan, Panonian, and Alps. It is a continent in itself.

At the same time, Yugoslavia is a country with some horrible historical experiences that were catastrophic for the Serbian nation! The Serbs were acting inside the boundaries of their national interests. Nothing can heal the wounds as can political and economic processes: free exchange of thought, national freedom, human rights, and political diversities. At the end, Tito's "brotherhood and unity" were but camouflage to hide the beastly crimes committed. The cause and effects of Yugoslavia's disintegration are almost beyond comprehension by rational human minds and conventional wisdom. The hatred, both racial or religious, that caused the genocide can never be erased from the minds of the "residues of butchered people," though they were willing to forgive, though never to forget. How could the innocent victims be forgotten? The guilty consciences of those who either committed or hid crimes should make them come to their senses and in accord with Judeo-Christian ethics and morality make them want to prevent evil in the future.

The people should speak up for the honor of the innocent victims, for respect and for justice. Primarily, the mighty leaders with guilty consciences should also come under the blade of justice, regardless of whether they were representatives of civil or spiritual institutions. Yugoslav integration could have some positive aspects if racial and religious hatred were replaced by tolerance and mutual understanding. Tito did not accomplish it, not because he could not but because he would not. That was because of his character.

Recapitulation

Here are some questions for the posthumous Tito. Only God knows how many more could be asked.

1. In 1940 did the German intelligence service give Tito and his associates a lift over the Yugoslav border?

2. In 1940 why did Tito call Britain and France "imperialistic" countries?

3. In April 1941 did Tito as secretary of the CPY take part in the defense of his country against Italian fascism and German nazism?

4. After the Yugoslav capitulation, did Tito still remain in and promenade with Germans through the streets of Zagreb?

5. Was a secret agreement signed on April 17, 1941, between the CPC and Ustashe representatives without Tito's knowledge? What was his reaction?

6. Was Tito objective when he sent a report to Comintern blaming the Serbs for Yugoslavia's quick capitulation without mentioning himself as secretary of the CPY and many Croatian military formations?

7. What did Tito tell Rade Koncar, a member of the CCCPC, when he asked Tito to protect the Serbs in Croatia against Ustashe genocide?

8. Why did Tito move on Serbian territory to fight against the occupiers and leave Croatia without demanding that Croatia take part in the uprising too?

9. In 1941 when the CCCPC refused to organize an armed uprising against the Nazi Germany occupiers, what kind of measures was Tito taking? In July 1941 in Belgrade Tito instructed Djilas to shoot anyone including members of the provincial committee who showed hesitancy and undiscipline.

10. Did Tito officially condemn the Ustashe genocide against Jews, Serbs and Gypsies?

11. Why did Tito never send a report to Comintern about the Ustashe genocide?

12. Did Tito have strong control of the Croatian Communist leadership as he did of Serbian?

13. Why did Tito discriminate by praising a son who kills his own father if he is a Chetnik when he did not reciprically mention the Ustashe?

14. Did Tito order the total annihilation of Mihailovich Chetniks, their sympathizers, and even Chetnik families as in Montenegro?

15. Did Tito invite Domobrans and conscript Ustashe to join the NLM with all equal rights and benefits in the armed services with Partisans to fight together against Chetniks?

16. In September 1944 did Tito invite Ustashe to join the NLM with promises of double social security/pension?

17. Did Tito ever offer something similar to Serbian Chetniks or to any other ideological or political affiliation?

18. Why did Tito forbid an artillery attack on Banske Dvore where Pavelich's Ustashe headquarters were preparing to celebrate New Year's in 1943?

19. Why did Tito forbid the bombing of Croatian cities but not Serbian cities by the Allied air force?

20. Why did Tito forbid Yugoslav pilots under British command to bomb German headquarters at Brioni on May 1, 1945?

21. On November 29, 1943, an AVNOY conference was held at Jajce. By what right did Tito split the Serbian ethos by adding two more nations: Macedonia and Montenegro, and in 1961 the Muslim nation? Was Tito's Yugoslavia a paradox when a nation was formed by religious affiliation? At an AVNOY session, Croatia and Slovenia had full representation, while Serbia did not, though Serbs then made up over 40 percent of the Yugoslav population. What were the AVNOY repercussions for Yugoslavia's existence as a unique state?

22. Why did Tito form two autonomous provinces as part of Serbia while Istria, a new territory, was attached to the Croatian republic? Dalmatia also never was under direct Croatian rule until 1939, when Serbian premier Cvetkovich agreed with Prince Paul to win Croatians over to the Serbian side to fight together against nazism. Did they succeed?

23. By what rule of thumb did Tito make so-called administrative boundaries, one between the Serbian and Croatian republics? Did those borders cause civil war in Yugoslavia in 1991?

24. For six months after World War II Partisans in Belgrade could prosecute anyone without interrogation or truth, while such activities lasted only three days in Zagreb. Was this intentional?

25. How did Tito interpret his slogan of "Brotherhood and Unity" when the Serbian nation aligned with the Allies and was broken into three parts ethnically and her church as well? In 1941 the Croatian quisling president Dr. Ante Pavelich declared war against Britain and France and later against the United States. At the end of the war Croatia was not only rewarded with new territory, but her genocide was hidden.

26. Did Tito visit the Pope and other Catholic prelates while he split the Serbian Orthodox church in three parts?

27. In 1962 what did Tito mean by the query could they preserve Yugoslav unity or must she be disintegrated?

28. Why was Krcun-Penezich killed in 1964 and Rankovich released in 1966 from any governmental duty although he was faithful as a dog to Tito?

29. Why was Milosh Zanko, a Croat, dismissed from his job because he was against Ustashe neofascism?

30. Was Tito for or against Croatian masspok, the "Croatian Spring"? Why did Savka Dabcevich-Kucar call Tito a coward?

31. In the new Constitution of 1974 was it Tito's action behind the scenes together with Croatian and Slovenian leaders that was the main catalyst for disintegration?

32. Why did Tito give so many privileges to the army that it became parasitic, obsolete, and unable to perform her military duty?

33. The Constitution of 1974 approved the formation of territorial defenses for each republic if they wanted. Was this for Yugoslavia's further unity or an obvious step toward her disintegration?

34. Why did Tito earn legendary status by being called "the supreme protector of anti-Serbs?"

35. Will Tito and Croatian leadership (past and present) and the Croatian Catholic church ever admit and apologize for genocide committed against Serbs, Jews, and Gypsies?

36. How could Tito play real politics with the Serbian sacred place of Kosovo as if it were his dowry? He had promised Kosovo to Albania if she subordinated herself to his megalomaniac intentions! Did he know that Kosovo is the cradle of Serbian culture and tradition?

37. When Tito was surrounded by Croats he told Meshtrovich, "Serbs are megalomaniacs." During the war and revolution who guarded and protected Tito—Croats or Serbs? Were Serbs megalomaniacs at that time? If they were not megalomaniacs, were most of them naive or corrupted?

38. Who was the most responsible for causing bloody civil war in Yugoslavia in 1991?

These questions deserve to be answered by those of Tito's cohorts who still prefer to continue the status quo of "Tito after Tito."

Following the notes to this chapter the reader will find some illuminating material from original sources. Appendix A contains the personal recollections of three people captured by the Nazi occupier. Appendix B contains stories of those who ran away from the shooting ground. Appendix C lists those of the Ljeshnjani Brigade who lost their lives in fighting against the occupiers and the Communists. Appendix D tells some stories of those who stayed as guerrillas and were eventually liquidated. Appendix E consists of translations of original OZNA documents about those who survived the 1945 calamity and emigrated to the United States or Britain and whose relatives in Yugoslavia are still under surveillance on their account.

Notes

1. Against the Yugoslav entity there were two influential forces: the Vatican and the Comintern. In early 1930, Croatian Fascists collaborated with the CPY in order to destroy Yugoslavia. Was Tito the strategist behind it? However, Tito kept Serbian Communists under his control.

2. Ivan Avakumovich, "New Stories," *Chicago Herald*, pp. 81-82.

3. Tito was also informed of a German attack on Sutjeska in March 1943. Hans Ott, a German engineer and Gestapo agent, warned Tito of the impending attack on his headquarters at Sutjeska, saying, "If Tito is there, he should be made aware of the attack; he could perish because the attack will be fierce, and an encirclement is being prepared."

4. In Croatia for many decades the work of Ante Starcevich was wrongly identified with the French bourgeois revolution! In the second half of the nineteenth century, Starcevich introduced his racist theory, which later served as a steppingstone for the Nazi Ustashe movement. In fact, Starcevich, a Budapest doctor, passionately hated Serbs. The motto of his Right party was "Croatia only for Croatians." He preached, "Vlasi and Gypsies are synonyms for Serbs." He studied with devotion the origin and characteristics of Serbs in Croatia. His book *Slavs* depicted Serbs as a lower race. Starcevich further stated that neither Croatia nor Europe could have peace until the wedge was removed from the Croatian body. Serbs had to be pushed out over the Drina River where they came from. Is there any difference in statements between Starcevich in the 1800s and Tudjman in 1991?

5. Nikola Plecash, former commandant of a Partisan battalion and later commandant of a Chetnik brigade, had captured the entire supply units of the Sixth Partisan Division during a Partisan attack against the Chetniks: 50 butchered pigs, 10 barrels of lard, 5 barrels of oil, 1,000 kg of sugar, and nearly 3,000 pieces of bread. Those supplies came from Zagreb, as proved by their Zagreb labels!

6. Oh Serbs! Oh Serbs! For all, we are wrong
   Because we are Serbs and we are still alive.
   (Oh, Srbi, Srbi za sve smo krivi;
   i shto smo Srbi, i shto smo zivi.)

7. On August 13, 1941, Hebrang described the ISC as the expression of the "ancient dream of the Croatian people." He forgot that since 1102 the Croats had never fought for their freedom or independence. Someone else did it for them. So, during both world wars the Serbs were victorious with their allies, while the Croats fought together with Austro-Hungary or with Nazi Germany! One might wonder whether Croats will recognize the truth!

8. Macropedia, vol. 29, 1991, p. 1111.

9. *Foreign Service Journal*, October 1991, pp. 20-21, and *Encyclopedia of the Holocaust*, in which records of the Nuremberg trials list Ustashe crimes during the world war. Second, the Croatian Nazi government carried out pogroms against Serbs and Jews that amounted to genocide, which shocked even the Germans.

10. During Spellman's visit in Rome he met with Pavelich's representative, though the ISC had declared war against the United States at the end of 1941 under the Nazi Pavelich!

Alexander Cockburn says current scenes in Slovenia, Croatia, and Serbia evoke bitter memories from World War II, when "the fanaticism of Catholic Croats raised catacombs of Serbian bodies on the altars of their religious frenzies"—which makes Rome happy while Serbs can hardly control their vengeful furies.

11. Not so long ago it was learned how Luburich, a notorious Ustashe, came to Slovenia from Austria in 1945. After the Ustashe tragedy in Bleiburg, Luburich arrived in Slovenia with a Partisan passport. The CCCP of Slovenia had interrogated and then punished some Montenegrin commandants who protested such a relationship between the Ustashe and Slovenian Partisans.

From Slovenia, Luburich crossed to Croatia to continue resistance against Tito's Partisans. However, he soon realized it was impossible at that time to resist the Communists. Luburich then used a secure channel to cross over the Hungarian border. Later he proceeded via Austria and Switzerland to Spain. He married a Spanish girl. They had four children. Under the conspiratorial name "Gen. Drinjanin" Luburich informed his adherents that Spain and the United States were ready to give them aid to overthrow the Communist government in Yugoslavia. To get the aid there were some requirements: to be anti-Communist, aggressive, and democratically oriented. Luburich appealed to all Croats, regardless of their past political affiliations and ideology, to join under his command and fight together for an independent and free Croatia.

On April 25, 1969, Luburich was assassinated by the professional killer Ilija Stanich (probably a conspiratorial name). Says Bogdan Radica, Tito and the Croatian Communists made a mistake in not retaining the Croatian Ustashe state in 1945 then transforming her into a Communist state. In 1950 Dr. Branko Jelich, an influential Ustashe, broke off relations with Pavelich because of their rivalry. Jelich later contacted Bakarich, Gen. Hojevac, mayor of Zagreb, to lead the Croatian Communist movement out of their impasse. Jelich scolded Bakarich, when he was political commissar, about what happened then in Bleiburg. Bakarich allegedly liquidated Hebrang to become boss of the Croatians. Ivo Rojnica wanted to know what happened in Bleiburg in order to get world sympathy toward Croatia.

Bozo Lazarevich, an old Montenegrin Communist, could not understand how Tito could choose Franja Pirc commandant of the Partisan air force when Pirc was chief of staff of the ISC. In 1946 Tito's government appointed Pirc ambassador to Argentina. Afterwards he joined the Ustashe movement there. Tito was the only one who could understand and explain that tragi-comedy on the Yugoslav political scene. Only he knew why he picked Pirc, Marko Mesich, and others to be his close associates!

12. Nikola Tesla, a Serb and well-known scientist, asked his nephew Sava Kosanovich to intervene directly with President Roosevelt and tell him Serbs and Croats could live together in peace and prosperity. Return your spirit, Tesla, to your native Lika and find out if you were right!

13. Churchill promised Tito two squadrons, each with twenty Spitfires and twenty Hurricane planes, to be assigned to the NLM. The squadrons had Yugoslav pilots and technical personnel. Other facilities were supplied by the British.

In August 1944 the Spitfires went into action, while in February 1945 they were moved to the island of Vis. In April 1945 they were moved again, this time to the Skabrinja airport near Zadar. German ships sailing to Rijeka and Trieste were attacked.

An order came around May 1945 for the squadron of Spitfires to attack the German main headquarters at Brioni. One of the Yugoslav pilots designated for that mission was Ljubomir N. Vukcevich, a lieutenant and later colonel of the Yugoslav air force. The planes with their pilots were ready to execute their mission. However, at the last minute the Brioni bombing was cancelled! Why? Did Tito even at that time intend Brioni for his personal resort?

14. During Djilas's imprisonment, Loncarevich, a Mihailovich adherent, told Djilas that when Partisans killed Chetniks, they disguised them in German uniforms to show the Allied missions how many "Germans" the Partisans had killed! Tito was a brilliant master at deceiving his enemy, in this case British and American members of their missions!

15. Serbs in Krajina never denied rights to Croatians for their self-determination. However, by the same token, there was a justifiable and logical demand to get the same rights for themselves.

16. No. 133, R8237/6/92; FO 371/8814.

17. Witnesses of the crimes committed at Ponor Pit were Milenko Mirkov Vukovich and Miladin Kabara.

18. Croatian leaders, including Ivan Zvonimir-Chicak, president of the CPP, were extremely illogical in equating Ustashe with Chetniks. For once the Croats should accept the truth that the Ustashe were and remain criminals, with pathological states of mind, while the Chetniks, deficient in organization, were pro-Western and were attached to the Allied military missions. Titoists and international agents used a propaganda machine to distort the facts by slandering the Mihailovich movement, including left and right extremists, contrary to German documents from the war and many Allied sources.

19. In an article Dr. Marko Grcich concludes that the British government and the British army considered the Ustashe regime criminals who don't deserve civilized treatment according to international and war law.

20. Milan Basta and Ivan Kovacich, representatives of the Yugoslav army (JA), negotiated with the British officials for the surrender of those who had retreated. Professor Crljen from Split and Gen. Herencich, both Croats, negotiated with both the British and JA representatives. An ultimatum came down: Total surrender! At the Meza River and Gornji Dolic the Ustashe fought against the Partisans. Eyewitnesses said Partisans who were captured by the Ustashe had their throats slit. A lieutenant Franc Strl, 18 years old at the time, wrote in his book *Veliki finale na Korushkem* that the Partisan Shtefan Vertica from Ptuj saw the Ustashe barbeque one captured Partisan on a spit.

When the Montenegrin-Hercegovina Chetniks reached the Austrian border, their representatives sent a letter via a young girl to the British occupation forces in Bleiburg. The girl was afraid and embarrassed when the letter was delivered to JA by mistake. The letter stated that the Yugoslav army of the fatherland, from the areas of Montenegro, Boka, Sandzak, and Hercegovina, appeals to the Allied government to give them shelter and political asylum until they return. During their struggle against the occupier another struggle had been forced upon them by the Communists. They hope in the near future to continue the struggle together against Communist bands.

21. Krcun sensed how much Tito disliked Serbs in the northwestern parts of Yugoslavia: Croatia and Slovenia. Serbia was exploited for precious stones, food, mineral richness, and electrical energy. As conceived by Broz-Kardelj-Bakarich, Serbia was to be a primary source of raw materials.

22. In Uzice, Djurich visited Krcun's mother. During their conversation the mother turned to Djurich's wife Hajra and said, "Please, Hajra, guard our Ljubo who is our gold. They'll kill him as they did my son Sloba!" Then she kissed Hajra, repeating, "They'll... they'll... He is the next!" Ljubo Djurich had to console her, assuring her that they probably would not, since they hadn't gotten rid of him when he had been arrested.

Krcun's sister, who was also present, confirmed that the steering wheel had been tampered with so that when a sharp turn in the road came, a tragedy was inevitable!

23. Tito was buried in Dedinje like a pharoah. His grave, "the house of flowers," is guarded as if it were a shrine. The cost of maintaining his memorial is very high. One hundred forty-six people are employed there. No wonder Yugoslavia has all kinds of economic problems, because they are most concerned with how to spend rather than how to earn money.

24. During a visit Tito made to New York, Serbian demonstrations were held in front of Tito's hotel, led by the Serbian Orthodox bishop for the United States and Canada, His Grace Bishop Dionisije Milojevich. When Tito saw the bishop, he immediately ordered him dismissed without delay when they returned to Yugoslavia. The Yugoslav secret police (UDBA) pressured the Holy Synod of the Serbian Orthodox church to defrock Bishop Dionisije. After three consecutive days in session the Holy Synod under duress finally agreed in order to save anything possible from total destruction of the Serbian church by despotic Titoism. That event brought tragic consequences of a split among the faithful in the United States and Canada. Later Patriarch German in the magazine *Communists and Me* confessed that under unbearable personal pressure by Tito the church synod had to defrock Bishop Dionisije!

That's the real personality of Josip Broz Tito—his direct involvement in making decisions not only in Serbian political life but also in their church matters! Did Tito give equal treatment to other Yugoslav religious denominations?

The split in the Serbian Orthodox church in 1963 was healed in 1991 by the true servant of God and Christianity, Serbian Patriarch Pavle.

Appendix A-1

Twenty Months in German Captivity as a Mihailovich Chetnik
by Ignjat Aleksich

Before World War II, I served in the Yugoslav gendarmes in Macedonia, then in Serbia. After the Yugoslav capitulation, in April 1941, I returned back to my native place Bogdashici near Bileca.

Right after the capitulation we were confronted by Croatian SS Ustashe who made death threats because they promoted racist ideology, as did their masters in Nazi Germany.

The rest of us fought together against our internal and external enemies until Tito's Communist headquarters ordered the liquidation of prominent people, like Mihailovich's delegate Maj. Bosko Todorovich. In a word, it was the beginning of a fratricidal and political civil war.

In Hercegovina near the Montenegro border we were reorganized into one national battalion, in which I had various positions until I was captured by the German "Prince Eugen" Division on May 14, 1943, at a Plana defensive position.

Our group of captured Chetniks was transported by the Germans to Zenica. Another, larger Chetnik unit from Hercegovina that had operated around Kalinovik was captured by the Germans and they were also dispatched to Zenica. Around the barbed-wire camp were many German and Ustashe sentries. Conditions were extremely miserable, including little or no food. The Machiavellian news was spread that whoever declared himself captured without arms by the Germans would be sent to Germany to work. As for those who were captured with arms, their destiny remained uncertain and critical. In fact, all those who said they were captured unarmed were transported to Zemun, and they disappeared without a trace. Zemun then was under Ustashe control. However, those who stated they were captured under arms were protected by the Geneva Convention and declared prisoners of war.

We were loaded into cattle boxcars. Along the way, in Rashka or Vucitrn, we were joined by a contingent of Montenegrin Chetniks of Pavle Djurishich. Our destination was Salonica, Greece.

299

The living conditions in that prison camp in Salonica were below any standards of hygiene. It was an old camp left by the Turks in 1912. The Germans named the camp Stalag 185.

Later on the living conditions were slightly improved by the help of the International Red Cross. Hunger and misery still existed, causing many illnesses. Typhus was the most dangerous. It took away eighty young lives whose bodies were never returned to their birth places for a traditional burial.

In November 1944 we were liberated by British forces. The camp conditions were better. Later on we were transferred to a displaced persons camp in Italy. We emigrated to any country that opened its doors to us. Indeed, our destiny was confronting harsh reality!

Appendix A–2

Being Captured by Nazis Was Later My Salvation
by Vuceta Rutovich

On May 14, 1943, I was captured by Germans after two years of fighting in the free Serbian mountains, first against the Italian occupier and then against the Partisans. Our Chetnik commandant, Pavle Djurishich, was also apprehended with over 2,000 of his Chetniks. The Germans brought one group of captured Chetniks to Zaton. On the first day, a Muslim guard was deployed around the captured Chetniks. They showed their belligerence toward Chetniks. The Germans noticed it right away and replaced them with German guards. By this prompt action some Chetnik lives were spared.

After three days, about 600 Chetniks were transported by German military trucks to Pec, then by cattle cars via Kosovska Mitrovica, Kraljevo, Belgrade to Sajmishte, Zemun. Croatian Ustashe under a commander named Baneta were ready to attack us with bars. A previous group was beaten till they became unconscious, then were thrown into the Sava River one by one. The Germans frustrated their beastial intentions. Soon we were transported in box cars to the camp Krems near Vienna. From there we were moved to Buchenwald, Camp 4B, near Holland's border. There were many prisoners there of different nationalities. Besides Serbs, there were Frenchmen, Poles, Russians, and others. Inside the camp the nationalities were separated by barbed wire like that which surrounded the camp.

We were completely exhausted by our long trip with minimum food, sleeping mostly on the ground or locked in the box cars. The prisoners in Buchenwald gave us some food from parcels received from the American Red Cross.

Our officers were separated from us here and taken away to an officer prison camp. Noncommissioned officers and soldiers were taken to Duesseldorf to clean up debris from the American bombing.

It was June 1943. During the debris clean-up, first we were supervised by Hungarians, then by Germans, who treated us much better.

Living conditions began to improve. We were dressed in French uniforms and shoes received from the Red Cross. After a month we began to get parcels from the Red Cross.

The Germans moved us from one place to another, to Belgium and Holland. Finally we were located in the forest Grile between Torgau and Leipzig, where we were liberated by the American and British allies.

From my group in the German prison camp there are currently living in Chicago: Mihailo Dulovich, Marko Radojicich, Djordje Vujoshevich, Vuka Devich, Petar Bojovich, Milorad Ralevich, the Durkovich brothers, Radovan Cimbaljevich, Rajko Rosich, Nikodin Djurashkovich, and many others.

Also, Chetniks captured in May 1943 and transported by the Germans to Greece were liberated by the British army in November 1944. They were: Velimir Boricich, Ljubo Shukovich, Marko Lalich, Ignjat Aleksich, Branko Savovich, and others.

After World War II many Serbs were not fortunate enough to live in freedom together with their families in their native country.

Meanwhile, they are grateful to our allies, especially to the Americans, for giving us an opportunity to enjoy freedom and democracy with them.

Appendix A–3

From the Mountains to a Nazi Prison Camp by Vukosav Kljajich

At the time when Nazi Germany attacked Yugoslavia I was employed in Niksic as a superintendent of the government food supply.

On July 13, 1941, in the district of Berane there was an uprising against the Italian occupier as well as an uprising that was spreading through all of

Montenegro. After our heavy fighting, especially with carabinieri, Berane was liberated.

Captain Pavle Djurishich distinguished himself with rare courage. He and Rudolf Perhinenk had negotiated the Italian commandant for their surrender.

Right after the uprising, the judge Ilija Lutovac tried to raise a Communist flag with a hammer and sickle. The majority reacted against it.

At a meeting at Milovan Sajcich's home in the village of Vinicka, Communists threw a bomb through a window, killing Branislav M. Cemovich. His brother, Maj. Momir, was heavily wounded.

Not long after that we split into two belligerent groups: anti-Communists, or Chetniks, and Communist, or Partisans. The first group was led by Gen. Draza Mihailovich; the other group was led by the international villain Josip Broz Tito.

After that, uneven fighting continued against the occupier and the Partisans. On May 14, 1943, German divisions with Croatian Ustashe, Bulgarian, and Albanian divisions encircled the headquarters of Mihailovich and Djurishich outside of Kolashin. Draza succeeded in penetrating the German lines, while Djurishich was captured with his chief of staff, Cpt. Rajo Popovich, and Cpt. Mitar Bukumira. They were flown by German airplane to Berlin. Then they were transferred to the Strij prison camp at the foot of Karpati. With Djurishich were captured over 2,000 Chetniks. Our group contained 500 officers, noncommissioned officers, and soldiers. We were escorted under heavy German guard through Matashevo via Cakor and Pec, and then to Sajmishte in Zemun. We had the status of war prisoners and were saved from Ustashe torture. The lodging and food were extremely bad. We were transported in box cars to Krems near Vienna, where we were registered. Then we arrived in Buchenwald. My new name was No. 85141 XVII B—that remained until we were liberated. They sent us to the Ruhr region to clean up debris from Allied bombing. On June 22, 1943, twenty-seven officers, among them Milorad T. Joksimovich and Miomir Cemovich, were sent to Osnabrueck. In that camp were 5,000 Serb officers; Croatian and Bulgarian officers were released earlier by the Germans as their allies.

On December 6, 1944, the camp was bombed by the British and 114 Serbian officers were killed. The camp was officially registered Oflag VIC. Our worst enemy in that camp was hunger.

On March 30, 1945, the Germans separated us into three columns and marched us in the direction of Osnabrueck-Sulingen, while 400 older and sick officers stayed behind. On April 6, 1945, I arrived with my column at Kuchdorf near Sulingen, where we were liberated by the Second Montgomery army. After one month we were transferred by military trucks to Osnabrueck.

Most of our group refused to return to Communist Yugoslavia, because we had to choose between freedom or slavery. We chose freedom, regardless of uncertainty and sacrificing our country and our families. In the countries where each of us emigrated our life's destiny was uncertain and we had to start from the beginning.

Appendix B-1

Proud to Be in the Escort of Vojvoda Pavle Djurishich
by Veljo Radunovich

While I was growing up I was educated by epic folk songs about Kosovo, Milosh Obilich, and many other Serbian heroes who fought with pride and dignity to defend Orthodoxy and the Serbian nation. Strong traditions, close clan and tribe relationships, and respect for each other were the best compass for my orientation and for deciding which kingdom, heavenly or earthly, I would choose.

Throughout history Montenegrin Serbs always fought for ''the holy Cross and golden liberty'' and for their total independence.

In July 1941 Montenegrin Serbs were happy to take an active role in fighting the occupier in order to contribute to the Allied cause for a quicker victory.

In the fall of the same year Tito as secretary of the CPY ordered an attack against occupiers just in the Serbian regions.

The Communists in Montenegro did not hide their yearning for power, and they were ready to destroy anything that was a barrier on their road to total victory. There were detachments organized to fight only the occupier. However, Communists, who later were called Partisans, began a civil war even though the Comintern ordered them to fight only against the occupier, not to wage social revolution at that particular time. In the notorious Kunovo Prisoje in the vicinity of my birth place was the headquarters of the Lovcen Detachment where liquidations began of the best-known Montenegrin sons, like medical general Milo Ilickovich, Lt. Col. Niko Jovovich, the Shcepanovich brothers, and others. Therefore, people began to disassociate themselves from the Communists who murdered innocent citizens.

All my Radunovich clan, so to speak, were organized into a National company to fight against Partisan terrorism. As a youth I took part in fighting Partisans when they attacked us on December 1, 1943, in May 1944 at Chevo, and in November of the same year when Cetinje was encircled by Tito's Partisans. Tito's orders said it would be the greatest disappointment for him if the Montenegrin National forces were not totally destroyed.

In 1944 I joined the escort of vojvoda Pavle Djurishich, who succeeded in escaping from German captivity.

In September 1944 Djurishich negotiated with the Albanian prince Mark Djoni for a common defense against Communists and the eventual retreat via Albania to Greece to meet our British ally there. On the Cijevna River Pavle was ambushed and wounded by terrorists. He recovered, even though a bullet had gone through his lungs.

Who was vojvoda Pavle Djurishich? He was an unparalleled brave person and a man of great endurance. In an attack he was the first and in a tactical guerrilla warfare retreat he was the last. The National youth was crazy about him. Every fighter considered it the greatest honor for himself if he could be accepted in Pavle's escort, regardless of risking his life more often throughout battles. No doubt, there was iron discipline. I stayed in Pavle's escort until I was wounded in February 1945. During our retreat over Bosnia, Croatia, and Slovenia toward Austria, where finally the British ally returned us back to Yugoslav Communists, our destiny was sealed; at the same time we buried our national ideals for which Serbian generations had eagerly died.

On that trip my father and two of my brothers, not to mention many of my uncles and cousins, perished. I hope younger generations will learn to be more realistic (not materialistic) than we were.

Appendix B–2

There Is No Death Until Judgment Day Comes
by Todor Stanjevich

Let me state very briefly my origin. In the fourteenth century, during the period of Tsar Dushan, lived the vojvoda Nikola Stanjevich. As a monk he built a memorial church to Saint Stevan in Konca. The monk was buried in the Hilandar Monastery. My ancestors were raised in the Kosovo cult, epics, and the Christian epics. I was born in 1921 in the village Kazanci, district Gacko, Hercegovina. I was in military school in Bileca when Yugoslavia was attacked in April 1941. First we had to defend our lives against SS Croatian Ustashe. On June 5, 1941, the Ustashe threw 300 Serbs into Koritska jama (pit). The next day we chose for our leader Father Radojica Perishich, the most clever and popular person in that region. In September 1942 he was promoted to the highest respected rank, to vojvoda.

On June 26, 1941, we attacked the Italian occupier on Kobilja Glava and captured three trucks with Italian soldiers. Further, we fought against the occupiers at Krstac, Goransko, Foca, Vishegrad, Goradzde, Trebinje, Popovo Polje, and many other places. In a word, we fought against the occupiers, first the Italians and then the Germans. We were forced also to fight against internal enemies: Ustashe and later Tito's Communists.

After we liberated Hercegovina from the Communist yoke we Chetniks went to Dalmatia, then to Lika, Gracac. We fought on the Serbian New Year of 1943 and I was wounded. I had various duties in the Chetnik Strike units. Since I was wounded three times, Cpt. Milo Lazarevich recommended me for the Obilic's medal with two white eagles and swords, as well as for the Karageorge's star with swords. During the entire war we waged a struggle against our bitter enemy, the Croatian Ustashe, in various regions: Faslagica Kula, Borac, Midjenovichi, Ravno, Gacko, Avtovac, Nevesinje, Kifino Selo, Kallinovik, Foca, Konjic, Siroki Brijeg, Livno, Duvno, and God only knows how many more.

In April 1945 after our defeat at Lijevce Polje I retreated through Croatia with great difficulties. Finally we reached the British ally in Austria. Unfortunately, the British sent us back to Yugoslavia, into the jaws of Tito's Partisans.

In Radovljice, the Partisans tied me and Prof. Acim Grgur with wire and took us to the shooting ground. I managed to untie myself and with two other Chetniks to escape certain death. We reached Austria again. That time the British forces did not turn us back because they had learned what Tito did with captured Chetniks and others regardless of whether they were prisoners of war.

Later on I crossed to Italy and remained in Camp Jesi where there were some Chetnik survivors from Hercegovina. To my surprise I saw Laza Bodanjac, who was with the Partisans at the shooting ground. He was an agent of the Yugoslav intelligence service. He gathered data about Yugoslav emigrants in the camp. Later he moved to Rome, working as secretary to vojvoda Jevdjevich. One day he returned to Yugoslavia, after secretly collecting all necessary data from Jevdjevich's archives.

At Camp Jesi I remember another agent from Serbia, a young man named Todorovich. In order to camouflage himself he had actual pictures of Mihailovich and Djurishich that he gave free of charge to some Chetniks there! Todorovich succeeded in gathering all documents of Serbian students in the camp who desired to continue their education. He turned those documents in to Tito's Yugoslav embassy in Rome instead of to the Serbian national committee there. American Serbs had asked for their documents to give financial help to those students who wanted to continue their education abroad. Finally my dream was realized when I emigrated to the United States.

Appendix B–3

Tragic Epilogue of One Chetnik's Family by Branko Pejovich

Let me first introduce myself. I am Branko Nikolin Pejovich, born in 1924 in Orahe in the region of Cetinje. Besides my parents, Nikola and Jova, I had three brothers and four sisters. My father, a veteran officer of the Serbian army in World War I, all his four sons, and one of our not yet married sisters were all Chetniks.

My village, Orasi, is located close to Mt. Stavor and the infamous Kunovo Prisoje. During the tyrannical Communist regime of nine months (the end of 1941 through the first half of 1942) the Montenegrin elite was decimated. They were tortured and sadistically killed. My family was intact despite the fighting with various enemies until the retreat of our Chetniks through Bosnia in 1945.

During our Bosnian Golgotha we were confronted not only by fighting Ustashe and Partisans but also by typhus, hunger, and severe cold.

In early 1945 my brother Svetozar was killed in Bosnia.

We had to defy all those calamities, hoping dawn would come soon. When we arrived at Lijevce Polje we met fierce fighting with Ustashe, Croatian SS Nazi who were superbly armed, fed, and clad. Our commandants, Pavle Djurishich, Zarija Ostoich, Petar Bacevich, and Milorad Popovich, with their escorts personally took part by attacking Ustashe tanks with hand grenades. The Hercegovina Chetnik Division had penetrated through Ustashe lines in order to attack them from the rear. Meanwhile, two Partisan Krajishka brigades, if I remember correctly the Sixth and Eleventh, attacked the Hercegovina Division from the rear, helped by the Ustashe. The collaboration between the Ustashe and Partisans was well known. Stevo Krajacich was a bridge between Tito and Ante Pavelich!

At Lijevce Polje we lost the battle, but nevertheless most of us succeeded in crossing Croatia and Slovenia to reach the Austrian border. To our surprise, the British army returned us to Tito's criminals.

From Maribor prison camp on the way to the shooting ground, my brother Dimitrije and I with Krsto Radusinovich and Rajko B. Vukcevich succeeded in untieing ourselves and running away. On our second trip to Austria my brother and I reached Austria again, saving our lives, while Krsto Radusinovich was killed and Rajko Vukcevich was captured by Partisans.

The fate of our father is unknown. My sister Ljeposava and my youngest brother Petar were returned to Cetinje. All Chetnik returnees—old men, women, and children—were humiliated and treated by the Partisans in a beastly manner! Petar, 12 years old, was captured by the Bulgarian army. First he was sent to Novi Sad, then to Cetinje. The Communists put him on trial. Pejoviches from Orahe sentenced and executed him!

This tragic epilogue of my family is not a singular one—it reflects the destiny of many Serbian families who took the road of Golgotha with honesty and dignity.

Titoists could not totally eradicate the Serbian nation, despite their Geobbels-like cynicism and primitivism and terrorism unknown in the annals of the civilized world.

Appendix B–4

Escaping from the Shooting Ground by Rajko Vukcevich

During World War II and the revolution it was, indeed, a miracle that I survived inevitable death three times. It first happened at the end of 1942 in Bosnia when only by God's will was I saved from Communist capture; the second time was in October 1943 at Ostrog Monastery when Blazo Jovanovich shot all but me; and the third time was in Slovenia in May 1945. Here is my story from the prison camp in Maribor to the shooting ground and my escape from certain death.

From the Maribor camp the Partisans took us to an adjacent building and took away clothes. I was completely naked. Then they began to strike us with rifle butts, sticks, and whatever they could get their hands on. Our hands were individually tied with wire; then with the same wire we were tied together three by three. On one side of me was Dimitrije Pejovich from Orasi, while on the other side was Krsto Radusinovich from Buronje. Nine groups were thrown onto a covered truck. Between the cab and the bed of the truck was a window with a machine gun installed. At the rear door there were three young Slovenes with rifles. They did not like to talk with us. In that group were all Ljeshnjanis, three sons of Pera Markova: Milutin, Mirko, and Bosko.

In front of me was Dimitrije's brother Branko. Says he, "Rajko, you're stepping on my foot. Bend yourself a little." I did and felt untied. My hands were free. It was dark in the truckbed. On the curves the truck was knocked to the side because it was climbing up toward Saint Arap. For several days our brothers had been brought there and killed and thrown into ditches. We succeeded in untieing Krsto and Dimitrije and attacked the sentries. I hit one in the middle. I pressed his legs against the rear door with one hand. With the other hand I opened the door, and the guard fell off the truckbed. The four of us who were untied got out. The truck stopped. We ran away into the nearby forest. We heard steady machine gun bursts. They fired at us but the forest was our safe cover. I was naked and barefoot, while Krsto and Dimitrije had underpants, I believe. The three of us proceeded through the forest. The pursuit stopped.

At dusk we noticed a vacant house. We found some clothes, a kettle with warm beans, and a little flour. We ran farther. The next morning a young lady who was cutting the grass in her meadow told us that at night the houses are empty because the Partisans come, pick up men and then shoot them. This had happened to her brother the previous night. She made corn meal with warm milk for us.

We were moving slowly. On the fifteenth day we entered a home. Within half an hour armed Partisans appeared at the house. Krsto and Dimitrije ran away. I could not because I had a wound on my leg. Dimitrije met his brother Branko during his escape but I have not heard anything about Krsto since then!

The Partisans took me to the local commandant. A student from Belgrade investigated me. I told him the alias name Zivojin Janovac from Senta, Vojvodina. Allegedly I came from prison camp. All captured Montenegrins were shot. The Partisans took me from one place to another until I arrived by plane at Podgorica prison. In jail a 78-year-old man begged them in vain to let us go free.

After two years they brought me to trial. The judge was Popovich from Zeta; one juror was from Parce, and another juror, Lamar (a sheet metal man), was from Podgorica. The public prosecutor was Novak Vujoshevich. His substitute was Milovan Vukovich from Piperi.

At the trial Novak Vujoshevich let me go free. Lamar from Podgorica shouted, "You see, you see, even now he did not say 'Long live Tito.'" Not then, or ever...

Appendix C

The following lists of Ljeshnjanis who were casualties of World War II were obtained from various sources, whose identity must still be kept secret. However, their efforts and sacrifices for the sake of truth and justice should be greatly appreciated by all, especially the younger generations, who finally have an opportunity to learn exactly what happened during those tragic and bloody days in Ljeshnjani Nahi.

The Ljeshnjani Nahi as a microcosm could exemplify for the world what Tito's megalomaniacal atrocities accomplished, through blood and tears, against their own people. Why? Because people were against any "ism"—either fascism or communism—applied not by logic but by brutal barbarism. In such endeavors Tito was backed by the West, consciously or unconsciously, in making the Yugoslav realm a Communist dictatorship. The mistakes made then by the West, used cleverly by Tito, have been paid for dearly by the polarized religious and ethnic contenders in the current tragic Yugoslav war.

Ljeshnjanis Killed by the Italian Occupier

Kazich Pantelija and his brother
Pejovich (Ilija) Milo
Radusinovich (Nikole) Krsto
Vukcevich (Blaga) Lazar
Vukcevich (Mitra) Lazo

Vukcevich (Mitra) Luka
Vukcevich (Rista) Milutin
Vukcevich (Sava) Stevan
Vukcevich (Ilije) Vaso

Ljeshnjanis Killed by the German Occupier

Markovich (Ilije) Nikola
Radunovich (Djura) Milo, colonel
Radusinovich (Nikole) Radomir
Vukcevich (Stojana) Gligorije
Vukcevich (Ivana) Joko

Vukcevich (Ilije) Luka
Vukcevich (Marka) Milo
Vukcevich (Sava) Radoje
Vukcevich (Malishina) Savo
Vukcevich (Anta) Spasoje

Vukceviches Killed by Albanians (in Kosovo and Metohia)

Vukcevich (Blaga) Ivan

Vukcevich (Milosha) Savo

Vukceviches Killed by Hungarians (Vojvodina)

Vukcevich (Nikole) Milo[1]

Vukceviches Killed by Croatian Ustashe

Vukcevich (Sava) Aleksa

Ljeshnjanis Killed or Shot by the Occupiers as Tito's Partisans

(list incomplete)

The above listed Partisans, in our view, had joined the Partisan ranks voluntarily during the war. However, can those who were mobilized by Partisan forces, either military or secret police, whether they were killed under the insignia of the five-pointed star or not really be judged Partisan volunteers? Let future impartial historians sort out those who really should be judged by facts gathered from still-living eyewitnesses or even from those who took part in the immoral, bestial liquidations!

At first the Yugoslav Communist Party's practice was to shoot their innocent victims and throw their bodies, sometimes half alive, into pits, crevices, wells, or shallow mass graves. Then the Partisans changed their tactics and turned to killing their apparent political adversaries by shooting them in the back during actual fighting. In fact, it was a different means used to accomplish the same ends!

Burzanovich (Petra) Veselin   Burzanovich (Mica) Milovan
Burzanovich (Petra) Dushan   Burzanovich (Jovana) Petar
Burzanovich (Toma) Dushan   Burzanovich (Peja) Petar
Burzanovich (Ilije) Djoko   Burzanovich (Spasoje) Radoje
Burzanovich (Spasoje) Konstadin   Globarevich (Sava) Dushan
Kazich (Andrije) Savo (died in Partisan ranks from typhus in 1943)
Kazich (Toma) Milutin   Vukcevich (Labuda) Veselin
Popovich (Ilije) Milo   Vukcevich (Rista) Vasilije
Raickovich (Stevana) Vaso   Vukcevich (Alekse) Drago
Uskokovich ( ) Vido   Vukcevich (Lazara) Blazo
Vukcevich (Boska) Labud-Anto
Vukcevich (Mila) Simo (committed suicide rather than follow orders to kill his
    brothers Lazar and Risto)

Ljeshnjanis Who Left Montenegro in Front of Communist Terrorism in 1944

(Names are recorded by village [selo], not by any military formation.)

Selo Lijesnje—23:

Vukcevich (Sima) Vaso   Vukcevich (Mila) Nikola
Vukcevich (Sima) Jovan   Vukcevich (Petra) Mihailo
Vukcevich (Marka) Pero   Vukcevich (Gligorija) Milan
Vukcevich (Pera) Milutin   Vukcevich (Krsta) Perisa
Vukcevich (Pera) Mirko   Vukcevich (Kosta) Raso
Vukcevich (Pera) Bosko   Vukcevich (Janka) Jovan
Vukcevich (Pera) Blagota   Vukcevich (Janka) Slobodan
Vukcevich (Djura) Spasoje   Vukcevich (Vela) Vaso
Vukcevich (Stevena) Dusan   Vukcevich (Bogdana) Rajko
Vukcevich (Krsta) Milutin   Vukcevich (Bogdana) Zorka
Vukcevich (Andrije) Vladimir   Vukcevich (Joka) Djordjije

Vukcevich (Vladimira) Radovan

Selo Podstrana—9:

Vukcevich (Todora) Ilija
Vukcevich (Nikole) Jovan
Vukcevich (Nikole) Spasoje
Vukcevich (Sava) Milovan
Vukcevich (Musa) Petar

Vukcevich (Joka) Vasilije
Vukcevich (Laza) Savo
Vukcevich (Laza) Marko
Vukcevich (Laza) Ilija

Selo Steke—13:

Vukcevich (Sima) Lazar
Vukcevich (Sima) Risto
Vukcevich (Filipa) Mihailo
Vukcevich (Mihaila) Danilo
Vukcevich (Mihaila) Milutin
Vukcevich (Mihaila) Vaso
Vukcevich (Sava) Marko

Vukcevich (Marka) Radovan
Vukcevich (Marka) Luka
Vukcevich (Sima) Mitar
Vukcevich (Sima) Djuro
Vukcevich (Mata) Petar
Vukcevich (Mata) Risto

Selo Bigor—8:

Vukcevich (Sava) Petar
Vukcevich (Sava) Vojin
Vukcevich (Mitra) Marko
Vukcevich (Mitra) Andrija

Vukcevich (Joka) Djuro
Vukcevich (Radoja) Bosko
Vukcevich (Vasa) Luka
Vukcevich (Nikole) Ilija

Selo Goljemadi—11:

Vukcevich (Ilije) Milo
Vukcevich (Ilije) Marko[2]
Vukcevich (Joleze) Branko
Vukcevich (Sava) Aleksa
Vukcevich (Radoja) Savo
Vukcevich (Sava) Bosko

Vukcevich (Sava) Zarija
Vukcevich (Marka) Bosko
Vukcevich (Mila) Nikola
Vukcevich (Blagote) Milorad
Vukcevich (Mila) Schcpan

Selo Farmaci—2:

Vukcevich (Marka) Pero

Radunovich (Nika) Velisa

Selo Popratnica i Kornet—5:

Vukcevich (Luke) Lazar
Vukcevich (Lazara) Milan
Vukcevich (Lazara) Bogich

Vukcevich (Blagote) Rade
Uskokovich (Petra) Milovan

Selo Botun—9: (Doseljenici iz Ljesanske nahije)

Vukcevich (Ilije) Drago
Vukcevich (Peka) Djoko

Djurisich (Sima) Vojin
Djurisich (Blagoja) Vaso

Vukcevich (Nikole) Rako   Djurisich (Joka) Vukota
Stojanovich (Radoja) Dusan

Selo Lekichi—6:

Vukcevich (Pera) Vaso
Vukcevich (Pera) Djuro
Lakovich (Jovana) Petar-Penjo
Lakovich (Petka) Vido
Lakovich (Petka) pop Andrija
Lakovich ( ) Ilija

Selo Staniseljichi—10:

Bogojevich (Sava) Dusan   Popovich (Mitra) Radomir
Bogojevich (Nikole) Bosko   Popovich (Spasoja) Marko
Bogojevich (Boska) Blagota   Popovich (Matana) Djuro
Popovich (Matana) Pero   Knezevich (Filipa) Spasoje
Popovich (Matana) Bego   Davidovich (Sava) Vaso

Selo Orahe—24:

Pejovich (Sava) Ljubo   Pejovich (Nikole) Svetozar
Pejovich (Sava) Vladimir   Pejovich (Nikole) Dimitrije
Pejovich (Andrije) Spasoje   Pejovich (Nikole) Branko
Pejovich (Jovana) Mirko   Pejovich (Nikole) Petar
Pejovich (Sava) Blazo   Pejovich (Nikole) Ljeposava
Pejovich (Perise) Jovan   Pejovich (Andrije) Becir
Pejovich (Toma) Marko   Stojanovich (Krsta) Milovan
Pejovich (Toma) Dusan   Stojanovich (Krsta) Vidak
Pejovich (Novaka) Lazo   Stojanovich (Boza) Vukadin
Pejovich (Laza) Radovan   Stojanovich (Ilije) Vidak
Pejovich (Laza) Milovan   Stojanovich (Raka) Nikola
Pejovich (Blagote) Nikola   Stojanovich (Andrije) Marko

Selo Krusi—2:

Bojanovich (Nikole) Novak   Bojanovich (Vasa) Mirko

Selo Beri—8:

Cetkovich (Nikole) Blazo   Cetkovich (Jovana) Savo
Cetkovich (Nikole) Mito   Rackovich (Sava) Petko
Cetkovich (Sava) Jovan   Rackovich (Petka) Veselin
Cetkovich (Sava) Pero   Raicevich (Vida) Jovan

Selo Progonovichi—38:

Radunovich (Blagota) Mitar   Radunovich (Zivka) Zarija

Radunovich (Blagota) Luka
Radunovich (Rista) Novica
Radunovich (Vasa) Zivko
Radunovich (Vasa) Pajo
Radunovich (Joka) Milos
Radunovich (Joka) Bogich
Radunovich (Pera) Konstadin
Radunovich (Nikole) Petko
Radunovich (Bogdana) Milos
Radunovich (Rista) Dusan
Radunovich (Ivana) Krsto
Radunovich (Alekse) Panto
Radunovich (Rista) Vukasin
Radunovich (Rista) Dusan
Radunovich (Joka) Vuko
Radunovich (Vasa) Petar
Radunovich (Vasa) Stevo

Radunovich (Pera) Savo
Radunovich (Pera) Bozo
Radunovich (Vasa) Savo
Radunovich (Kica) Simo
Radunovich (Stanise) Milovan
Radunovich (Ilije) Stanisa
Radunovich (Ilije) Radoje
Radunovich (Mitra) Stanko
Radunovich (Boza) Branko
Radunovich (Petra) Mirko
Radunovich (Stevana) Radun
Radonjich (Nikole) Pavle
Radonjich (Ivana) Krsto
Radonjich (Nikole) Vukola
Radonjich (Petra) Mirko
Radonjich (Nikole) Zivko
Roganovich ( ) pop Krsto
Roganovich ( ) Savo

Selo Releza—4:

Radunovich (Blagota) Ljubo
Radunovich (Krcuna) Dusan

Radunovich (Krcuna) Marko
Radunovich (Mrguda) Lazo

Selo Buronji—13:

Radusinovich (Pera) Krsto
Radusinovich (Pera) Mihailo
Radusinovich (Pera) Vidak
Radusinovich (Iva) Dusan
Radusinovich (Iva) Vlado
Radusinovich (Iva) Marko-Vracen
Radusinovich (Steva) Dusan

Radusinovich (Vasa) Rako
Radusinovich (Tomana) Bozo
Radusinovich (Vasa) Petar
Markovich (Marka) Ilija
Markovich (Rista) Milutin
Radusinvoch (Rista) Djuro

Selo Gornja Drazevina—3:

Globarevich (Luke) Marko
Globarevich (Ilije) Bozina

Globarevich (Mice) Nikola

Selo Brezine—9:

Bojanich (Filipa) Jovan
Bojanich (Filipa) Mihailo
Bojanich (Nikole) Dusan
Bojanich (Mihaila) Ilija
Brnovich (Filipa) Marko

Brnovich (Nikole) Dusan
Brnovich (Nikole) Petar
Kazich (Jovana) Peko
Kovacevich (Sava) Marko

Additional Names—15:

Bojanich ( ) Ilija
Celebich ( ) Filip
Celebich (Petra), two brothers
Kovacevich brothers from Botun
Markovich (Nikole) Dragutin
Radunovich (Milosha) Blazo
Radunovich (Ilije) Dushan

Radusinovich (Stevana) Milovan
Radusinovich (Vasa) Petar
Radusinovich (Vasa) Radovan
Vukcevich (Rista) Ilija
Vukcevich (Cetka) Migo
Vukcevich (Cetka) Zivko

Additional Names of Ljeshnjani Victims of Tito's Partisan Barbarism

Selo Buronji—29:

Radusinovich (Ilije) Pero
Radusinovich (Pera) Krsto
Radusinovich (Vasa) Djuro
Radusinovich (Rista) Djuro
Radusinovich (Iva) Dushan
Radusinovich (Iva) Vlado
Radusinovich (Stevana) Dushan
Radusinovich (Rista) Branko
Radusinovich (Tomana) Bozo
Radusinovich (Andrije) Konstadin
Radusinovich (Stevana) Milovan
Markovich (Marka) Ilija
Markovich (Nikole) Dragutin
Markovich (Peka) Ilija
Markovich (Andrije) Marko

Markovich (Djura) Blagota
Markovich (Stevana) Nikola
Markovich (Stevana) Spasoje
Markovich (Stevana) pop Krsto
Markovich (Stevana) Blagota
Markovich (Rista) Milutin
Cetkovich (Boska) Spasoje
Cetkovich (Spasoja) Ljubo
Nenadovich (Scepana) Maso
Nenadovich (Ilije) Branko
Radusinovich (Vasa) Petar
Radusinovich (Nikole) Milutin[3]
Radusinovich (Marka) Mitar
Radusinovich (Vasa) Rista

Selo Drazevina—4:

Globarevich (Luke) Marko
Globarevich (Ilije) Bozina

Globarevich (Mica) Nikola
Globarevich (Mica) Novka

Selo Krusi—12:

Bojanovich (Nikole) Novak
Bojanovich (Vasa) Mirko
Bojanovich (Baca) Mirko
Bojanovich ( ) Vaso
Bojanovich (Milosa) Baco
Bojanovich (Baca) Stane

Bojanovich (Iva) Nikola
Bojanovich (Spasoje)
Bojanovich (Baca)'s son
Cetkovich (Mila) Cetko
Cetkovich (Mila) Pero
Rackovich ( ) Vido

Progonovici—41:

Radunovich (Nika) Andrija

Radunovich (Jakova) Bogic

Radunovich (Ivana) Aleksa
Radunovich (Rista) Vukale
Radunovich (Vasa) Lazar
Radunovich (Gigoja) Risto
Radunovich (Mrguda) Vaso
Radunovich (Blagote) Milorad
Radunovich (Zivka) Zarije
Radunovich (Vasa) Petar
Radunovich (Vasa) Stevan
Radunovich (Kica) Simo
Radunovich (Petra) Bozo
Radunovich (Petra) Savo
Radunovich (Ilije) Padoje
Radunovich (Jakova) Vuko
Radunovich (Vidaka) Risto
Radunovich (Rista) Dushan
Radunovich (Rista) Vukasin
Radunovich (Alekse) Panto
Radunovich (Bogdana) Milos
Radunovich (Rista) Dushan

Radunovich (Nikole) Petko
Radunovich (Stevana) Jovan
Radunovich (Vasa) Zivko
Radunovich (Rista) Novica
Radunovich (Blagote) Mitar
Radunovich (Blagote) Luka
Radunovich (Boza) Branko
Radunovich (Mitra) pop Stanko
Radunovich (Krcuna) Dushan
Radunovich (Krcuna) Marko
Radunovich (Milosa) Maso
Radunovich (Pera) Konstadin
Radunovich (Stanise) Milovan
Radonjich (Nikole) Pajo
Radonjich (Nikole) Vukale
Radonjich (Nikole) Zivko
Radonjich (Ivana) Krsto
Roganovich (Vasa) Savo
Roganovich (Vasa) Mirko

Parci—5:

Durisich (Krsta) Dragutin
Durisich (Milovana) Bogic
Durisich (Dushana) Novak

Raickovich (Marka) Mitar
Raickovich (Mitra) Ilija

Orasi—21:

Pejovich (Nikole) Svetozar
Pejovich (Nikole) Petar
Pejovich (Sava) Ljubo
Pejovich (Sava) Vladimir
Pejovich (Andrije) Spasoje
Pejovich (Jovana) Marko
Pejovich (Sava) Blazo
Pejovich (Toma) Marko
Pejovich (Novaka) Lazar
Pejovich (Lazara) Radovan
Pejovich (Blagota) Nikola

Pejovich (Andrije) Becir
Pejovich (Mica) Gojko
Stojanovich (Krsta) Milovan
Stojanovich (Krsta) Vidak
Stojanovich (Boza) Vukadin
Stojanovich (Ilije) Vidak
Stojanovich (Raka) Nikola
Stojanovich (Andrije) Marko
Durovich (Jovana) Vaso
Durovich (Sima) Vojin

Staniseljici—13:

Bogojevich (Tomasa) Joso
Bogojevich (Nikole) Dushan
Bogojevich (Boska) Nikola
Bogojevich (Boska) Blagota

Davidovich (Filipa) Spasoje
Pejovich (Mitra) Duro
Popovich (Matana) Pero
Popovich (Matana) Bego

Bogojevich (Nikole) Bosko
Bogojevich (Toma) Jovan
Davidovich (Sava) Vaso

Popovich (Spasoja) Marko
Popovich (Matana) Duro

Beri—13:

Cetkovich (Nikole) Blazo
Cetkovich (Sava) Jovan
Cetkovich (Sava) Pero
Cetkovich (Jovana) Savo
Cetkovich (Peja) Radoje
Cetkovich (Jovana) Masan
Cetkovich (Spasoja) Marko

Raickovich (Vida) Jovan
Rackovich (Sava) Luka
Rackovich (Sava) Petko
Rackovich (Marka) Andrija
Perovich (Dura) Petko
Perovich (Petka) Ilija

Selo Lijesnje—20:

Vukcevich (Sima) Drago
Vukcevich (Janka) Vidak
Vukcevich (Perise) Mitar
Vukcevich (Gligorije) Milan
Vukcevich (Krsta) Perisa
Vukcevich (Djura) Savo
Vukcevich (Joka) Risto
Vukcevich (Janka) Jovan
Vukcevich (Andrije) Vladimir
Vukcevich (Mila) Nikola

Vukcevich (Petra) Mihailo
Vukcevich (Sima) Jovan
Vukcevich (Sima) Vaso
Vukcevich (Pera) Milutin
Vukcevich (Pera) Mirko
Vukcevich (Pera) Bosko
Vukcevich (Djura) Spasoje
Vukcevich (Stevana) Dushan
Vukcevich (Pera) T. Radovan
Vukcevich (Kosta) Raso

Podstrana—7:

Vukcevich (Jova) Banjo
Vukcevich (Todora) Ilija
Vukcevich (Sava) Milovan
Vukcevich (Djuke) Marko

Vukcevich (Joka) Vasilije
Vukcevich (Laza) Savo
Vukcevich (Laza) Marko

Selo Steci i Farmaci—16:

Vukcevich (Sima) Lazar
Vukcevich (Sima) Risto
Vukcevich (Filipa) Mihailo
Vukcevich (Mihaila) Danilo
Vukcevich (Mihaila) Milutin
Vukcevich (Sava) Marko
Vukcevich (Marka) Rako
Vukcevich (Marka) Luka

Vukcevich (Sima) Mitar
Vukcevich (Sima) Djuro
Vukcevich (Mata) Risto
Vukcevich (Mata) Pero
Vukcevich (Mata) S. Pero
Radunovich (Nika) Velisa
Petkovich (Jovana) Djoko
Petkovich (Jovana) Ivan

Kokoti—4:

Pejovich (Zeka) Savo
Pejovich (Jovana) Andrija

Pejovich (Vida) Ilinka
Pejovich (Nika) Mishko

Bigor—10:

Vukcevich (Milosa) Joko
Vukcevich (Sava) Petar
Vukcevich (Sava) Vojin
Vukcevich (Mitra) Marko
Vukcevich (Mitra) Andrija

Vukcevich (Radoja) Bosko
Vukcevich (Lazara) Jovan
Vukcevich (Joka) Djuro
Vukcevich (Vasa) Luka
Vukcevich (Nikole) Kosto

Selo Kornet—2:

Uskokovich (Nikole) Milovan

Vukcevich (Marka) Dushan

Selo Bridje—2:

Brnovich (Mitra) Bosko

Vukcevich (Nikole) Marko

Selo Goljemadi—13:

Vukcevich (Mila) Dushan
Vukcevich (Joka) Lazar
Vukcevich (Vucine) Ivo
Vukcevich (Marka) Bosko
Vukcevich (Marka) Andja
Vukcevich (Marka) Dushan
Vukcevich (Sava) Aleksa

Vukcevich (Joleze) Branko
Vukcevich (Mila) Nikola
Vukcevich (Stevana) Marko
Vukcevich (Blagote) Peko
Vukcevich (Joka) Andrija
Vukcevich (Mila) Stevan

Selo Popratnica—5:

Vukcevich (Luke) Blagota
Vukcevich (Luke) Lazar
Vukcevich (Lazara) Milan

Vukcevich (Blagote) Drago
Vukcevich (Rista) Ilija

Selo Lekici—4:

Lakovich (Jovana) Petar
Novakovich (Mila) Vasilije

Vukcevich (Pera) Djuro
Vukcevich (Pera) Vaso

Selo Brezine—10:

Kazich (Vukala) Djuran
Brnovich (Marka) Vidak
Bojanich (Nikole) Stojan
Bojanich (Nikole) Dushan
Bojanich (Ilija)

Brnovich (Nikole) Petar
Brnovich (Nikole) Dushan
Brnovich (Filipa) Marko
Brnovich (Dragise) ''Musa''
Kovacevich (Sava) Marko

Notes

1. Professor Milo Vukcevich was shot in Alibunar along with seventy students. They were in civilian clothes. They had volunteered for the military and were awaiting recruitment

2. In Slovenia in May 1945 the life of Blagota Perov Vukcevich, from the village of Lijeshnje, was spared by Yugoslav Partisans because he was a minor. He was conscripted into the Partisan army instead of being shot by them.

Meanwhile, Blagota's three older brothers, Milutin, Mirko, and Bosko, were shot barbarically along with other Chetniks in Pohorje, Slovenia, by Tito's Partisans. His father Pero was returned home, where he was sentenced to fifteen years in prison. The only crime he had committed was being against the fratricidal conflicts caused and led by Tito's Communists.

Since then, forty-six years have passed, and Blagota was apparently free to write an article about his experiences. He titled it "Communist Culprits and the Sufferings of Ljeshnjani Chetniks in Slovenia." It was published in the weekly magazine *Mirror* in 1991.

He states that he himself was present when the Communists gave their word of honor that everyone's life would be spared. They would be sent to their birth places or to the places where they lived during the year. The old men, women, and children would be immediately transported by train to their destination, while the others would march to Maribor, from where they would be transported to Belgrade. In Belgrade, according to the Partisans, there was an Allied commission of American, British, and Soviet representatives who would formally take charge of them.

What happened? In Maribor their hands were tied behind their backs with telephone wires, and they were packed into trucks accompanied by guards. They were taken to shooting grounds and liquidated.

In his article Blagota included the names of nine Ljeshnjani Chetniks who miraculously escaped death because they did not trust the Partisans. They ran away from their groups into the nearby forest of Karavanke. British troops in Austria were confused but did not return them to Yugoslavia. The persons were: Marko, Milo, Savo, Vaso, Bosko (the author of this book), and Zarija Vukcevich; Mihailo-Mrgud and Jovan Bojanich; and the priest Krsto Roganovich. Later all the Vukceviches and Father Roganovich emigrated to the United States. The Bojanich brothers emigrated to Great Britain.

We greatly appreciate Blagota's tragic story about the cursed destiny of the Ljeshnjani Chetniks. There is an old saying, it only happened what was written down.

3. In 1945 Milutin Radusinovich was killed by his relative, Savo Filipa Radusinovich. At the court trial held in Podgorica, Savo stated that he personally killed Milutin because he was a Chetnik. The court dismissed the case; Savo was acquitted. Justice, was it not? An apt adage says, "Plato is dear to me, but the truth is dearer."

Appendix D

Pursuit of Chetnik Guerrillas after World War II

(The following information has not yet been publicly announced by the Yugoslav secret police.)

According to Tito's orders, the Yugoslav secret police (UDBA) mercilessly persecuted all their political adversaries, within and without.

Here are two cases where the UDBA even liquidated two party members who were against the torture, plundering, and killing of innocent people.

Uros N. Vukcevich, law student and party member, was mysteriously liquidated by UDBA agents in February 1944. To cover up their deed, the agents spread the word Uros had been assassinated by Chetniks!

According to one version: the Communist party of the Podgorica community held a meeting in Piperi at the beginning of 1944. At that meeting was present the accused, Uros Vukcevich, secretary of the Communist party for Ljeshnjani nahi.

Dragutin Radovich acutely criticized Uros for his hesitant, conciliatory position toward the party's class enemies, because he did not join the Partisans in the class struggle but only to fight against the occupier. Uros energetically repulsed all accusations as baseless. The party members decided to dismiss him from party membership. He was replaced by Luka M. Vukcevich, formerly Uros's assistant.

On his return to Ljeshnjani nahi Uros called a meeting of the membership. At that meeting he delivered the written decision to his replacement, Luka M. Vukcevich. During the meeting the debate was bitter, because Uros was regarded as a highly intelligent, fair, and democratically minded person who was against any usurpation, persecution, or mistreatment. Uros quieted them down. He told them the party decision must be obeyed and respected. Allegedly there was danger from the Chetniks' penetration in the upper Ljeshnjani nahi, so some party members including the new party secretary Luka Vukcevich with Vaso Lukin Vukcevich were designated for the lower nahi (under Chetniks' control), while Nivak Perov, Ilija Mihailov Vukcevich, and Uros Vukcevich were designated to go to the upper nahi (then under Partisan control) terrain. Luka and Vaso hid themselves in a stable near their homes. During the funeral of Marine lieutenant Risto Vukcevich, who was killed in action at Cevo in May 1944, the honor guard fired rifle salutes over Risto's coffin. Luka and Vaso were then hiding in a cave in Oblun, near the village Bridze. They thought they were surrounded by Chetniks.

Uros also came into conflict with Andrija Pejovich, an influential and unscrupulous party member at Lovcen Partisan Headquarters. Pejovich, from Rijeka nahi, cynically accused Uros of acting like a Judas when Uros spared the lives of two Chetnik youngsters who were designated by Pejovich to the "Thirteenth Brigade" (which meant to be liquidated). Uros had emphasized that the Partisan struggle must be waged nobly, sparing not destroying lives whenever possible. However, Uros paid for this dearly with his own life! Later Pejovich was transferred to Dapcevich's corps in Kolashin as the chief of OZNA.

Now here are some questions: Who informed Dragutin Radovich of what was going on in Ljeshnjani nahi terrain? Was the meeting held in Piperi just camouflage for those Ljeshnjani Partisans who were insisting on Uros's elimination from the party and then his actual liquidation? In fact, how could any Partisan with common sense know the real circumstances in Ljeshnjani nahi if he were not directly involved in everyday business there? Was a conspiracy made in advance for Uros's liquidation when some members were designated for the lower nahi and some for the upper? The doubt obviously exists that local party members recommended Uros's liquidation and that they probably took part in the execution, too.

Jakov-Jagosh M. Vukcevich, an attorney, was an old party member and a classmate of Blazo Jovanovich. Though devoted to Marxist-Leninist doctrine, he was against fratricidal conflict, like Andelich, Marushich, and many others. From him I learned about secret orders from Partisan headquarters. From 1942 to 1944 he continued this dual role. In 1944 he joined the Partisan military, but he was liquidated before the war was over, unable to save the lives of any Chetniks. Because of his efforts, nobody had been killed by troikas on his territory. No one from Jakov's inner circle was surprised that he was assassinated in Croatia in April 1945, just before the war ended. The Partisans blamed the Ustashe for the assassination; the truth is that one more member of the Communist party had been killed by his own political brethren.

Vukcevich was a Marxist who strongly believed in that ideology as the best one for the well-being of the future of humanity. However, Tito and his marionettes were international conspirators who misled people, imposed autocracy, and encouraged corruption, and as a consequence brought the people to the edge of economic collapse.

Stojan Nikolin Bojanich was a very brave and honest man. At the end of 1944 Stojan could not join his brother and other Chetniks on the retreat to Bosnia because of his poor health. First he was hidden in Grbavce; then he moved to Grubane. One day while he was hiding, a Partisan conference was held in Barutana. Stojan came out of his cave and climbed up on a high rock from where he could see the people moving at Barutana.

Unfortunately, at that moment he was seen by Lubica Lazara Djukanova Bojanich. She immediately informed secret agents at Kokoti. UDBA agents encircled him. He resisted but could not penetrate through the UDBA circle. He was killed on the spot.

The National movement lost tremendously when Stojan was killed.

Liquidation of Markovich's Troikas by OZNA Agents

Nikola Stevanov, teacher, Spasoje Stevanov Markovich, and Blagota Djurov Markovich were hidden near their homes after the war. At the end of January 1945 OZNA agents (or, as they were called for camouflage, the "People's Defense") received information that those men were hiding in

Busovnik. OZNA encircled Busovnik. Spasoje Stevanov managed to escape, though he was wounded. Nikola was hidden among the rocks. Someone said, "You see they escaped." Blagota Djurov was ambushed and he surrendered. An OZNA agent from Crmnica shot Blagota on the spot in February 1945. A few days earlier near Drushice, Chetnik guerrillas had killed the brother of that Crmnicanin. So he got his revenge.

Nikola and Spasoje remained in hiding. OZNA was looking for them, turning heaven and earth to catch them. OZNA found out from an informer where they were hidden. They encircled them. Spasoje resisted. He wounded one OZNA agent. He was captured and immediately killed. Nikola was shot on the spot. That happened in April 1945.

The only sin of those patriotic and honest men was that they were not criminals, neither Communists nor Communist sympathizers.

Large Group of Chetnik Guerrillas Attacked at Tvrdosh

Ljubo Cetkovich and Branko Nenadovich from Buronje remained in the guerillas after the war was over. They joined Barjamovica's Chetnik group of about thirty men, mainly from Cpt. Jovan Nikolich's Katuni nahi group. They found shelter in a very secure cave that OZNA was unable to locate.

The commander of this group was Rade Markov Djurovich from Orasi. The guerrillas were very active, targeting UDBA agents and prominent Communist leaders. Their domain of operation was on the Podgorica-Cetinje road at two points, Koshcele and Kosica. They had succeeded in liquidating, among others, Vlahovich and Rolovich from Crmnica.

One night they went to Gornja Drazevina, where they took some groceries necessary for their survival. If they caught Skoj members or party activists they beat them up to scare them, but they did not kill them. Therefore, people were more careful about what they did in order to evade reprisals from the guerillas. The UDBA used every available means to catch them, but without any success.

The UDBA finally tried via a Djurovich to make contact with the commander of that group, Rade Djurovich. He agreed to betray his group if the UDBA guaranteed him safety after the action was executed. They did.

One morning at dawn the UDBA massed around the cave's main entrance for an attack. Ljubo Cetkovich was on guard with his machine gun. He opened fire and made it possible for Branko Nenadovich, Rade Durovich, and Jovo Turcinovich to escape through another cave exit. Ljubo was first wounded and then killed and was buried in the meadow near the cave the same day. The rest of them were liquidated on the spot, except for Rade Drashkovich and the brothers Djuranovich, who stayed in the cave during the fighting. It is possible Drashkovich had already contacted the UDBA to help them discover and liquidate that group. Drashkovich was freed and was employed in the steel plant in Niksic. The Djuranovich brothers were given amnesty. They went to their home in Bandice, where they remain on their farm.

Jovo Turcinovich went to Komane and continued to live in hiding. In June 1947 Jovo was surrounded in his shelter by UDBA. A shepherd had informed the UDBA of his whereabouts. First the UDBA invited him to surrender voluntarily. He refused. He opened fire on the agents. At that moment a UDBA sniper cut off his life. He was buried in a nearby hole the same day, and his remains are still there. The UDBA was led by Ljubo Radojev Uskokovich. They sang a song: "This song is new to us, there is no more Turcinovich Jova" (Ova pjesma nam je nova, Turcinovich nema Jova).

Branko Nenadovich and Rade Djurovich ran away to Curilac in Bjelopavlice, where they lived illegally in a stable. One day they were noticed by a 10-year-old-boy. Since their lives were in danger if the UDBA learned where they were hiding, they decided to risk going to Greece via the mountains. It was a long and hideous trip. On the way to Greece near Kosovska Mitrovica they were confronted by the UDBA. Both were killed. It happened in August 1947.

All those Chetniks from Buronje Company (Nikola, Spasoje and Blagota Markovich, Ljubo Cetkovich, and Branko Nenadovich) who had remained in the guerrillas were patriotic, brave, and honest men of endurance who knew no fear. It was understandable that they could not join the retreat together with other Chetniks who made their way via the mountains in the harsh winter over Bosnia to meet the Allies in the west. Common sense told them that direction was unrealistic; instead they decided to retreat toward Greece, where the trip would be shorter and easier. Unfortunately, adventurism prevailed. On that retreat across Bosnia very few survived!

Heroism of Krsto Popovich

Krsto Popovich was well known among the Montenegrin people. He was an honest and dignified man from the Katuni nahi. In 1920 Krsto visited Belgium. On his passport his nationality was listed as Serb. Through his entire life Popovich remained a strong adherent of Petrovich dynasty. He exercised political acumen with pride and dignity, which is a characteristic of men from the Katuni nahi.

During the revolution Krsto refused to wash his hands in the brothers' blood! That was the main reason Montenegrins turned against the Partisans. The Communists, including his own son Nikola, were fanatical internationalists who were ready to do anything to achieve victory for the international proletariat.

In order to save the Montenegrin people from total extermination, Popovich, like many Nationalist leaders in other regions, was forced to reach temporary accommodations with the Italian occupier. Some have accused Popovich of collaborating with the occupier, but they forget that Tito with his entire leadership of the CPC collaborated with various enemies of the Allies. Was it true that Stevo Krajachich served as liaison officer between Tito and Ante Pavelich, the head of the quisling Croatian government?

Krsto's friends and foes confirmed he was neither a murderer nor a criminal! Further, judging by political sense and personal character, Krsto's actions could never be compared to performances of Drljevich, Shtedimlija, and the like. He was a man of dignity and integrity without malice toward his political adversaries. Besides, by his heroic death he would become a legend.

The rest of the Popovich family was affiliated with the Partisans. After the war Krsto remained in hiding. His close friend Savo Celebich, Tito's general, unsuccessfully tried to persuade Blazo Jovanovich, the secretary of the CPM, to give amnesty to Popovich.

The UDBA knew well of Krsto's bravery and incomparable experience as a guerrilla soldier. Thus the UDBA had only one weapon with which to catch him—deceit. Hiding with Krsto was Bigovich. Krsto's daughter brought them food. So the UBDA contacted Krsto's daughter and promised her if Bigovich betrayed her father, the UDBA would let Bigovich be free so he could marry Krsto's daughter if she chose. The UDBA told Bigovich to deactivate Krsto's weapons: rifle, hand grenade, and pistol. Bigovich deactivated all except for the pistol.

Bigovich then arranged to meet Krsto in a ruined building without a roof. The UDBA's aim was to catch Krsto alive. (By the way, Rako Mugosha boasted that he himself would catch Krsto alive and then he would "ride" him. Indeed, that was an utterly sarcastic and crude statement like only Titoists would utter.) Hiding inside the building were Veljko Milatovich, assistant to the interior secretary of Montenegro, UDBA colonel Mihailo-Sharo Brajovich, and Lt. Rako Mugosha.

Krsto approached the building from the opposite side. He saw the UDBA agents inside the building. He threw a hand grenade at them, but the grenade had been deactivated by Bigovich. Mugosha then jumped up and ran out of the building to catch Krsto alive. Krsto killed Mugosha instantly with his pistol. Krsto tried to run away, but Milatovich killed Krsto with a blast from his machine gun.

To hide the crime that Milatovich killed him the UDBA spread the word that when Krsto shot at Mugosha, Mugosha returned fire. So both were dead. Krsto became a national hero among the people in Montenegro. When Mugosha's coffin was brought to Ljeskopolje for the funeral, his mother lamented, "Don't you know that Krsto was not a rabbit from the forest, but a Montenegrin knight?" (Krsto nije zec iz gore, nego vitez Crne Gore).

Nothing short of it! Krsto fell heroically on March 13, 1947. Today Milatovich lives in Herceg Novi, while Sharo Brajovich lives in Spuz. Milatovich
and Rako Mugosha became people's heroes. A bust was erected in Mugosha's honor near the cooperative hall on the Cetinje road. Montenegrins
were insulted. Indeed, all honest people would pay tribute to the heroic
death of Krsto Popovich.

Dushan Vukovich

During the war Dushan Vukovich was commandant of Krsto Popovich's
military units. After the war he went into hiding, like Popovich. He hid at
the home of Nikola Savov Brnovich in Crni Brijeg (Ljeshnjani nahi). With
Vukovich was the nephew of Father Radoje Durishich. Before the war
young Djurishich had been a policeman.

The UDBA was informed of where they could find them. So the UDBA
encircled them. Vukovich was killed, while Djurishich managed to escape.
However, after a few months Djurishich was killed too. That happened in
1947.

Gen. Ljubomir Novakovich

Gen. Ljubomir Novakovich was born at Novo Selo, Bjelopavlici. He was
with Krsto Popovich in the Montenegrin military academy. After 1918 he
continued his career as a military man, while Krsto Popovich retired.

After World War II Novakovich joined the Mihailovich headquarters, but
he could not reconcile himself to being subordinate to Mihailovich as a
lower-ranking officer. Therefore, he left Mihailovich and returned to his
native Montenegro. He insisted on waging a struggle against the occupier.
Later he moved to Katuni nahi together with his son, who was a captain in
the Yugoslav army.

Gen. Novakovich had maintained contact with Dushan Vukovich, but
not directly with Krsto Popovich.

In 1943 after the Italian capitulation, Gen. Novakovich was liquidated
by the Partisans. The crime was executed under the leadership of Krsto
Popivoda, a well-known Communist.

Over and over again, as Gen. Novakovich's case makes crystal clear,
the Communists were allegedly fighting for national liberation, while instead
they fought for sheer power.

Misuse of Word of Honor by Communists

Vaso Mrgudov Radunovich with his relative Milorad Radunovich retreated with the Chetniks toward Bosnia in December 1944. During the trip

they changed their minds and decided to return secretly to their native place Releza, Ljeshnjani nahi. On the way home for a few days they stayed with his wife's family for a little rest.

When they came back, Vaso and Milorad immediately made a very well-camouflaged shelter inside Vaso's house.

Right after the war Communist policy strictly forbade party members to maintain any friendly relationship with Nationalist females. Afterwards, the Communists reversed their policy and ordered party members to form close relationships with females from anti-Communist families in order to obtain information from them about the locations of those guerrillas who were still in hiding.

So, a young lady saw Vaso in his house and turned him in to a UDBA agent who was probably her close friend. The UDBA blocked Vaso's home, but they could not find anything suspicious inside the house. The UDBA again used deceit, leaving an agent to hide himself in the house to listen to the family's conversations.

Soon after, Vaso and Milorad came out from their shelter. The UDBA agent informed his superiors. First they invited them to surrender. As the story goes, Luka Simonov.Vukcevich gave them his word of honor that if they voluntarily surrendered, their lives would be safe. They did. What happened then? Luka broke his promise and shot both of them.

The following day Luka was rewarded for the crime he committed by being accepted into the party ranks. Once in the ranks one could earn promotions for getting bloody hands.

Stevan (Bajo) Milov Vukcevich

Stevan was a quiet and hard-working man. Part of his farm was located on a hill about a mile from his house. He never had enough time to worry much about local politics. Therefore, he told his relative Petar Ristov if anything important came up to let him know. He was always ready to be with his relatives, to share with them whatever comes, for good or for bad. He never did harm to anyone. Because of his age he was physically not able to take the long and uncertain trip with the other Chetniks in 1944.

After the Communists took over but before they had achieved complete control they imposed iron discipline, including a curfew hour. One evening as Stevan was returning from his farm he was ambushed and killed by UDBA agents. He was an innocent victim, like so many others!

Radovan (Raco) Perov Vukcevich

Radovan was a farmer, a very energetic man. After the war it was a big surprise for all who knew him that he went into hiding. For some time he was hidden at the home of his kum (godfather), Marko Milov Vukcevich. Secret agents and informers were practically everywhere. So Radovan had to move somewhere else. He came closer to his home, where his family and relatives could supply him with food.

One day the UDBA was informed where he was located. They encircled him and in a surprise attack he was killed. One more anti-Communist victim!

Vojin S. Djurovich, Teacher and Reserve Officer

At the teachers school in Cetinje, Vojin was an outstanding student. After World War II he joined the guerrillas fighting against Communist usurpation. They executed actions against individual Communists who unscrupulously terrorized the citizens.

According to Branko Pejovich, who is currently living in Canada, Vojin joined a guerrilla group in which there were, among others, Ljubo Cetkovich and Branko Nenadovich, both from the village of Buronje.

They were hiding in Tvrdosh. One of Barjamovica's guerrillas had surrendered to the UDBA. He told them where other guerillas were hiding. UDBA agents encircled them. Vojin was captured.

He was brutally treated. They tied him up with rope and tied the other end of the rope to a horse's saddle. In this horrible way, with the horse dragging him behind, they reached Vojin's house in the village Orahe. The UDBA men took Vojin to a nearby threshing floor, where he was shot. One agent went to Vojin's parents' home to tell them what had happened. The parents came to see their son's corpse, which was beyond recognition. The agent told the parents that was their son. The mother first wailed and then fainted. After that tragic scene the UDBA let Vojin's parents take his body for burial. His father asked one of his relatives to help him take the corpse to the church cemetery. They carried him on a blanket and buried him in the cemetery.

After all this, the UDBA agents went to the home of the prominent Chetnik Nikola Blagotin Pejovich, who had left his home with four sons and daughter to join the Chetniks in December 1944. Since then Nikola's house was used as Partisan headquarters, while his wife Jove was driven away to stay in one of her sheds.

Vojin Djurovich was an outstanding intellectual and an uncompromising fighter against Communism despotism. This modest obituary is dedicated to his memory.

Evaluation of Some Original Documents of the Secret Police on the Terrain of Ljeshnjani Nahi

Here we intend to raise the lid a little on the large reservoir of secret UDBA documents. The archives of the UDBA (Yugoslav secret police) are still classified top-secret state documents. However, the day is coming when all the crimes and wrong-doings of that infamous bureau will be open to the public. Here is just a small contribution.

OZNA, later the UDBA, listed the names of some men who miraculously escaped execution by Tito's Communists in May 1945. Mihailo (Mileta) P. Radusinovich, Vidak P. Radusinovich, Djuro Kovacevich, Mihailo F. Bojanich, Jovan (Josho) F. Bojanich, Vaso Veljov Vukcevich, Savo Popovich, and Petar St. Kovacevich.

Mihailo Radusinovich's father, Pero, was jailed, tortured, and summarily killed in prison by the UDBA. Mihailo was an active officer of the Yugoslav military establishment. His older brother Krsto, also an officer, had retreated with Djurishich's Chetniks across Bosnia. They reached Slovenia in May 1945. Krsto and thousands of other Chetniks were captured by the Partisans. They were undressed, their hands were tied behind their backs with wire, and they were taken by military trucks to the shooting ground for execution. Krsto was miraculously untied, as were the brothers Dimitrija and Branko Pejovich, Rajko Vukcevich, and Djuro Kovacevich. Along the road they escaped into the unfamiliar Slovenian forest. After a long and horrendous journey the brothers Pejovich and Djuro reached the British occupiers in Austria. Rajko was recaptured by the Partisans but he cleverly passed himself off as a war prisoner, so they sent him under guard to Montenegro, where he was jailed, tried, and finally released. The most unfortunate of the escapees was Krsto. He was killed by a Partisan ambush troika in the Slovenian forest. He left behind his young wife Ljubica and an eight-month-old son, Chedomir. Another of Mihailo's brothers, Vidak (Vido), also escaped capture.

Djuro Kovacevich was a policeman of the former royal Yugoslavia. He escaped certain death on the Solvenian mountain Pohorje and later succeeded in emigrating to America.

Mihailo F. Bojanich was in the Yugoslav air force. Inspired by democratic principles, he and his brother Jovan joined the liberation army of Gen. Draza Mihailovich, the first guerrilla leader in occupied Europe. In May 1945 the brothers both escaped Partisan capture in Slovenia. Later they emigrated to Britain.

Vaso Veljov Vukcevich was purported by OZNA/UDBA to be an opponent of the NLM and was thus marked for liquidation as a "people's enemy." On the contrary, Vaso was a staunch opponent of any dictatorial regime, either from the right or from the left, that abused the principles of liberty and human dignity. Vaso, the brothers Bojanich, and six others succeeded in breaking through a Partisan encirclement.

[Blagota Vukcevich, "About Communist Crimes and the Sufferings of Chetniks in Slovenia," part 3, *People's Mirror* (Podgorica), no. 7, 1991, p. 8.]

Savo Popovich was accused by the unscrupulous, half-literate UDBA of being involved in Partisan persecution during the Italian occupation of Montenegro and was regarded as an ideaological "enemy of the people." Indeed, the UDBA was ready to liquidate anyone who opposed the Communist crimes committed against innocent people.

In May 1943 Petar Kovacevich and Milan and Branko Djurishich were rounded up by the Italian occupier and interned in southern Italy. That same year, after the Italian capitulation, they were liberated by the Allies. They enlisted in the royal Yugoslav navy under British command to continue the war against the Nazis. Petar distinguished himself as a courageous, devoted officer. After the war, all three former prisoners refused to return to the hell of Tito's Yugoslavia. Regardless of what Petar had done for his country and for the Allied victory, he was also stamped as the people's enemy. That was Tito's justice!

Professor Branko Djurishich suggested that a monument of appreciation be erected in memory of those who were slaughtered by Tito's Communists in May 1945 in Slovenia. They deserve it as the best of Ljeshnjanis, whose only sin was they believed in God.[1]

What is the meaning behind Djurishich's idea for a monument? During the revolution the Communist driving force, controlled by the secret police, was like a hurricane destroying everything in order to achieve the ultimate goal—power. Innocent opponents, like the patriot Petar Kovacevich, were branded "traitors," "collaborators," "quislings," and "people's enemies." Beneath this hurricane force the human spirit was destroyed, physically and morally, in the most barbaric and uncivilized way.

Notes

1. Jovan Stamatovich, "Never Again Brother Against Brother," *Victory/Pobjeda*, December 6, 1992, p. 13.

Chapter Four

TITOISTS TURN THEIR BRUTALITIES ON THEIR OWN COLLEAGUES

It is not the purpose here to analyze the causes and effects of the ideological split between Cominformists, Stalin, and the Soviet Union on one side and Titoists and the CPY on the other. We merely intend to show how the rapacities of the revolution continued with different groups as victims at the war's end and after.

After the Yugoslav Communists, Serbians in particular, rid themselves of their political adversaries, they could not stand not having imagined or real enemies to think about. So they had to invent them. During their stay in power Titoists lost their vision, their morals, and their wisdom, the compass that differentiates good from bad, democracy from autocracy, civilized behavior from primitivism. The anti-Cominform movement culminated in nearly a decade of disregard for human decency and continued the entries in the criminal record of Titoism.

Virulent Anti-Bolshevism: More Deceit and Sham Democracy

The Cominform resolution IB that caused a split between Stalin and Tito signalled the beginning of an anti-Bolshevic trend. The Serbian people then mistakenly expected the Western Allies to replace Stalinism with democracy in Yugoslavia.

Tito identified himself as a "democrat" in Europe and to the world as well. But the Fascist rabble, former Nazi allies, were part of his government apparatus, especially in Macedonia, Kosovo, and Metohia, in Bosnia and Croatia (the center for future nationalism).

It could have been different. In 1948 the doors were wide open to the anti-Bolshevik elements to rehabilitate themselves and to prove they truly were democrats. During World War II and afterwards the same Fascist elements had identified Serbs as "Serbo-Communists." Instead, the postwar, post-Stalinist coalition combined the delusions of Goebbels and the dictatorship of Mussolini with the Austro-Hungarian marshal and Jerusalem mufti el Husein who during World War II had formed Muslim and Albanian SS divisions in Yugoslavia.

Cominform Resolution of June 1948

In June 1948 the Cominform, or Informbureau, issued a resolution sponsored by Stalin and Molotov in order to retain a monolithic Communist empire. It meant keeping the "gang of four" (Djilas, Kardelj, Rankovich, and Tito) under their direct control. The entire world was then asking if Tito was being educated by Stalin!

The Informbureau held a congress in Bucharest. The Yugoslav Communist party (YCP) boycotted the congress because Josip Kopinich informed Tito his life could be in jeopardy. (At that particular time Kopinich was in Turkey, sent by Alexander Rankovich to the Yugoslav embassy there.)

There were Titoists who declared themselves for the IB resolution, that is, in favor of Yugoslavia remaining in the socialist camp to promote world proletarianism. Their dilemma as they saw it was to choose either bourgeois nationalism or proletarian internationalism. Those who chose to support the resolution were arrested, beaten, spat on, and called traitors, Stalinists, toadies, bandits, NKVD agents, and everything else their former colleagues could think of. Those Cominformists were represented to the people as their greatest enemies, without giving them a chance to defend their views publicly.

Swift Retaliation Against Those Who Did Not Support Tito

Tito and his cohorts lost no time in arresting those who did not share their view of a Communist dictatorship run Tito-style. If you were not for him, you were against him—even if you had proven yourself a trusted colleague. Hundreds of men and women suspected of disloyalty were swiftly arrested and interned without proper trials in brutal political prison camps, of which the worst was the notorious island torture chamber, Goli Otok.

Who was arrested, and for what?

— Those who asked why Titoists did not go to the congress at Bucharest

— Those who asked why peasant cooperatives were formed so quickly and forcibly

— Anyone caught listening to Radio Moscow or retelling news from Radio Moscow

— Anyone mentioning the name of the Soviet Union or Stalin

In a democratic society none of these reasons would be enough to have someone arrested. But in Yugoslavia anything was possible.

The Role of UDBA and KOS in 1948 and Afterwards

The Yugoslav UDBA and KOS (counterintelligence service in the armed forces) had the task of settling accounts with Informbureau adherents. After the split in 1948 the UDBA imprisoned thousands of supporters of Stalin and the Soviet Union. Those jailed were mainly from Serbian provinces: 12,500 from Montenegro, and from Bosnia, Hercegovina, and Serbia 50,000 to 60,000. The YCP had taught their party members to be loyal to international solidarity and to their idol Stalin. They could not change their ideological views overnight to renounce the Soviet Union and Stalin's brutality.

At the end of 1948 the Fifth Congress of the YCP was held, at which Stalin was personally praised by Tito! Was this another example of Tito's Machiavellian double standards? He praised Stalin while others were condemning him and then arrested those who did the same. It is believed that 50 percent of jailed Cominformists were innocent of the charges against them.

UDBA state security agents held the reins in their hands. At that period, by Tito's authorization, the UDBA was the supreme executor, ignoring party and state authority. Therefore, UDBA agents began to misuse their officials positions: Women were raped, jewelry was stolen, young women were blackmailed in order to free their husbands. They demanded that wives of jailed men renounce their husbands, that children renounce their parents, brothers, sisters! Such coerced acts caused much damage in marriage relationships and undermined family ties, friendship, respect, dignity, sincerity, honesty, decisiveness, and morality. Liars, thieves, and especially spies were gaining ground. In fact, all traditional values in Montenegro were turned upside down. There was too much spying on one another with reciprocal accusations.

Why did UDBA people behave this way? They could do whatever they wanted to without fearing any legal consequences. The majority of UDBA personnel had no more than an elementary education and little knowledge of proper, civilized behavior. They were free to act on their most primitive impulses because Tito allowed them to be the law or above it.

In fact, the UDBA executors of Tito's political strategies used the most inhumane and bestial methods. In essence, psychological terrorism was carried out against convicts to "reeducate them": to "persuade them" to renounce Stalin and the Soviet Union, then to praise Tito, the party, and the Yugoslav party!

Tito's subordinates in security matters were authorized to use two approaches toward convicts: persuasion to get them to renounce their "wrongdoing" or application of the stick or lash to their backs. Tito was the supreme commander of life and death. He set the tone and issued directives for everything. When Blazo Jovanovich complained to Tito about excessive arrests, Tito replied, "With dry wood burns green lumber, too. It is better to have several innocent people in jail than have one culprit remain free." How far individual UDBA agents went in applying the match to Cominformist timber was up to them. According to UDBA general Jovo Kapicich-Kapa, it would be absurd to involve Tito, Kardelj, and even Rankovich, who was the best informed in such matters.

Under the existing circumstances, says Kapicich, the suffering was caused by unbridled elements and primitivism, by the prisoners themselves as well as by certain security workers. However, on May 13, 1949, during a celebration of security forces (a gathering of about 200 UDBA and KOS officers), Tito told them, "Comrades UDBA-shi, destroy all of them."

Bozo Ljumovich was an old Montenegrin Communist. He states that it wasn't necessary to be a Marxist. Any impartial and honest person had to come to the conclusion that UDBA mistreatments under Tito's encouragement demonstrated a pattern of monstrous, sadistic, and immoral behavior previously unknown in the annals of the civilized world.

Here we will discuss two UDBA representatives, of the highest and the lowest education, who were the best known for their brutalities to prisoners: Jovo Kapicich and Blazo Stankov Jankovich.

Jovo Kapicich-Kapa

Jovo Kapicich was Tito's general of the Yugoslav police and his people's hero. He was Rankovich's assistant at the Yugoslav ministry of the interior. Kapicich was the most responsible functionary in the state security police.

According to Kapicich's statement, it was imperative to isolate dangerous people in case of Soviet Union attacks on Yugoslavia. Therefore those adversaries of Tito (Cominformists) were gathered into various camps like Goli Otok, Gradishka, Bileca, Sveti Grgur, Zagreb, Ugljen, and Zadar.

In 1945, says Kapicich, Montenegrins filled top positions in the Yugoslav state army, SUP and SIP, and even in the navy. However, Montenegrins changed their nationality, being either Montenegrins or Serbs every few years. These top officers, by his rationalization, had to be interned to ensure state security.

In 1949 Kapicich made a speech at Goli Otok, warning the prisoners that whoever refuses "to revise his position" would leave his bones on the island. So the bloody revisions of position continued in the various camps.

The first victim in Goli Otok was professor Dr. Blazo Raicevich, who was brutally tortured and succumbed to his injuries. Among others was Col. Savo Vukcevich, chief editor of the People's army newspaper.[1] He died in Goli Otok's "prison of prisons," R-101, called Petrova rupa (pit).

Nikola Zivanovich states that Jovo Kapicich sent word clearly and loudly to all prisoners of Goli Otok that nobody could leave without a replacement, "because under is terra, up is high, and around is sea." There was no escape except "reeducation," and even recantations did not always result in freedom.

Kapicich did not admit publicly that camp police (UDBA and militia) forced prisoners to be against each other. (That was done to instill bone-deep fear in each prisoner.) Jovo Kapicich says that on Goli Otok/"Marko's (Rankovich) Hawaii" prisoners made the most trouble for each other. He doesn't even remember that any investigator or other official mistreated any prisoner there! In fact, Goli Otok was a Mediterranean gulag unique in contemporary history.

Bozo Stankov Jankovich

Another UDBA "hero" was Bozo Stankov Jankovich, a Montenegrin Goebbels, the turnkey of Bogdanov Kraj and Kotor prisons.

Bozo Stankov Jankovich was born in 1901 in Rijecka nahija. After the summer of 1944 he took part in the NLM. He had only an elementary school education. Regardless of this, he was later promoted to be the head of the Podgorica prison. He is currently living as a pensioner near Cacak, Serbia. As he states, he has been living with a nightmare from his past "cursed life."

Here are some opinions by prisoners about Jankovich's behavior as an "almighty God."

One prisoner states: Bozo Jankovich was a beast, a monster of a man, a terrible human being.

From time to time Jankovich pursued a hobby in the prisons of Bogdanov Kraj and Kotor, personally commanding, "With military equipment [dish and spoon] into the corridor right away!" Each prisoner then took his dish and spoon, moving quickly to evade beating by Bozo's bundle of keys that he always carried and lining up in the corridor. Then the command came: "Let's hear metal music!" What did that mean?

The first prisoner had to hit his metal dish with the spoon while others in the line followed; each had to hit the head of the prisoner with his dish in front of him, while the spoon in the dish created some kind of sound. So on it went to the last prisoner in line. Bozo was obviously enthusiastic. Then he commanded: "Arms in the racks!" That meant every prisoner had to bend his head close to the concrete floor, pointing to it with the index finger of the right hand. Then with the left hand holding the right ear, he had to turn around in circles until he fell down. If any prisoner fell too soon he was hit by Bozo's keys because Bozo's criterion was bad performance of the "Game."

Bosa Danilovich-Abramovich narrates: "In Kotor prison there was one Bozo Jankovich! Until then I had never met such a monster. He was able to deliver seven to eight hundred lunches of soup in a half hour. You could hear him going from one cell to another with the soup kettle. He sometimes spilled hot soup over a prisoner's hand. Also, if someone did not hold onto the dish tightly before Bozo scooped the soup he could be hit on his head with the ladle. Bozo also played with an electric wire with prisoners who were unfamiliar with current. He would tell an unsuspecting prisoner to touch the wire with a finger, and the prisoner was unexpectedly shocked. And Bozo would smile broadly and happily. Prisoners leaving their cells had to cover their backs with towels as best they could to try to protect themselves from Bozo's clubbing.

Olga Perishich says when she was transferred by truck from Bogdanov Kraj (Cetinje) to Kotor prison, the prisoners were tied together five by five with wire soaked in tar. In Kotor prison they met the turnkey, Bozo Jankovich. Each prisoner was hit at least once by the warden's bundle of keys. Petar, the husband of Bojana Boshkovich, steadily repeated in his cell: "What are you filthy men doing to those innocent people? Why don't you take their lives in a human way?" Petar later became insane as a consequence of unbearable tortures. Prisoners were sometimes forced to clean blood from cells like in a slaughterhouse!

A sword of Damocles steadily hung over a prisoner's head. A Muslim girl was imprisoned as a Cominformist. She complained about Jankovich's behavior in the Kotor prison. For her it was most repulsive when Bozo called his hodza (Turkish priest), who assaulted her in a way that won't be described here. Once Bozo tied her hands and let current flow until she fell down. They took her half dead back to her cell.

Draginja Vushovich from Niksic says that prisoners were under steady physical and psychological torture. Bozo Jankovich was the sole ruler there (Bog i batina). He was a monster, a hyena in human shape. He was anything but a human being. It was hardest for the prisoners when some men were beaten during the night. The other side of the prison echoed with their cries, and sometimes over the groans could be heard someone shouting, "Kill me! Can't you shoot? Why don't you kill me at once?"

Jankovich in an interview tried to excuse himself for his crimes by blaming the prisoners! Yet he admitted that since then he has not fallen into a quiet sleep. But that apparent twinge of conscience was the only punishment he ever received for his cruel deeds—mild repercussions indeed for such a monster!

Besides Bozo Jankovich there were tortures and beatings from other UDBA officers, like Veljko Rashkovich. A blow from Rashkovich was worse than nine electric shocks, says one prisoner. Rashkovich used a special whip for hitting prisoners: three ox sinews tied together and at the top formed into a ball. Many prisoners were instantly killed by a hard blow from that instrument of torture.

Looking at Some UDBA Agents from the Opposite Side of the Coin

Not all UDBA agents were of vicious character and behavior. On the other side of the coin were some who did not lose their human characteristics even if their own lives could be in jeopardy. There were not many among them who acted like human beings. However, in the judgment of past prisoners, two UDBA agents deserve to be mentioned: V. Popovich and Drago Mijovich.

V. Popovich was a UDBA major from Doljani, near Podgorica, who took part in the NLM in 1941. He was employed in the Yugoslav counterintelligence. After the Tito-Stalin split in the Communist hierarchy, Popovich was designated director of a women's convict camp in Ramski Rit, along the Danube River. There were 306 women detained in that camp. They worked hard from dawn to dusk, under harsh conditions.

Popovich was against the mistreatment of prisoners. Trials against Cominformists were not held because they were treated as "bands" and "traitors." Despite this, Popovich released thirty-three female convicts on February 20, 1950. Then he was under fire from his UDBA superiors, and he had to run away to Romania to escape arrest.

Popovich believed if a person is honest with high principles, moral satisfaction must come, regardless of difficulties and even possible persecution. A clear conscience was very important because new generations would judge with a perspective of impartiality and justice.

Drago Mijovich was another UDBA officer who was praised by some prisoners. In the period from 1953 to 1955 Mijovich served first as assistant director of the Bileca prison. Djoko Mirashevich, a hero from both world wars, was thankful to Mijovich for helping him survive Bileca camp. Later Mijovich became director of the notorious Goli Otak. During his camp reign Stalin was already dead.

Cominformists were "hawthorne sticks" for the Communist general movement, especially for the CPY.

Incomprehensible Crimes of Prison Camps

Some Victims Turn into Tyrants

During the incredible terror against Cominformists, humaneness died in human beings, as revolution participants were mistreated physically and psychologically. Those crimes were hidden from the people and from generations to come. Nobody could believe that Communists regardless of their different opinions would build camps for one another! The camps were built for Cominform prisoners under the pretext of "social benefits."

The stories that came from the prison camps were worse than those that came from the gulags—of cruelty, brutality, and unimaginable torture chambers. In the context of the strange relationship between victim and tyrant, there were stories of victims being transformed into tyrants and enduring the impossible. It is beyond comprehension how friends could suffer to such a degree at the hands of friends, or one man from another of like mind, one convict from another with the same misfortune, brother denying brother by breaking all moral codes and principles. How could anyone excuse the heartlessness of some convicts, revisionists? The men were under such unbearable repression that they simply were not men of dignity any longer. However, some convicts, despite various tortures and humiliations, succeeded in preserving their dignity and pride.

Methods of Torture and Humiliation

Prison within a Prison

On Goli Otok was a "prison within a prison" called Petrova rupa (pit), named for Petar Komnenich, who was president of the Montenegrin People's Assembly before he was arrested. He refused to revise his political views. In other words, the UDBA could not "re-educate" him so that he would renounce himself regarding Tito and the CPY. In Petrova rupa were held the top intellectuals and prisoners of strong character who refused to change their views in regard to the Soviet Union and Stalin on one side and Tito on the other.

Prison "Manners"

When prisoners passed a militia man or when an investigator stopped, they bowed their heads and took off their caps.

"Dry Diving" or "Spanish Swimming"

The victim was placed down on his back. Several UDBA agents held him in that position by sitting on his legs, stomach, and chest. The victim's mouth was stuffed with rags so he could not breathe. Then water was poured through a nozzle inserted in his nose. The victim's head was turned so the chin angled up. In a few minutes the victim fell unconscious. Such a method was used in Cetinje and Kotor prisons.

Hanging by the Legs

The prisoner's legs were tied with rope and his hands were tied behind his back. The body was then hung upside down from a beam. A pot filled with human excrement and urine was set beneath the prisoner, whose head was dipped into it at intervals.

The Landing of Prisoners on Goli Otok and Their Passing Between Ranks of Prisoners

The scene was reminiscent of the ceremonies of some African tribes. Before Rankovich visited Goli Otok a bloody reception was prepared for new prisoners, which began by their passing through "tigers and lions," through a formation of two rows leading from the disembarking ship to the upper part of the compound. As soon as the first prisoner jumped on the ground he was mercilessly beaten from both sides of the gauntlet amid a wild uproar of cursing, spitting, and whistling. If anyone lined up in the row did not hit the new prisoner hard, the news came quickly to the room's guardian. Such a prisoner was assigned to be mistreated among the newcomers and then "rewarded" by sticking his head into a barrel of dirty salt water.

The Corner of Shame

"Boycotted" prisoners were those who refused to revise their political views. They had to carry work tools back and forth. In front of the building they ground rock against rock just to keep them steadily occupied. After the other prisoners went to rest, the boycotted ones stood with their heads bowed near the edge of a pot filled with human excrement mixed with urine. Their hands were behind their backs. The boycotted prisoners were sometimes ordered to wade naked in the sea water in the winter.

Evening Classes

Every evening political classes were held for the "re-education" of prisoners.

Another Type of Reeducation

A wire chain was put around the neck of a boycotted man. The leader (revisionist) held the end of the wire, pulling the "dog" along, walking on hands and knees. They walked in a closed area. Then followed different kinds of tortures.

The Treatment of Milija Lakovich, Colonel and President of Draza Mihailovich's Trial

Lakovich was brutally treated on Goli Otok. His pursuers put a heavy rock on his back and tied it down with a wire over his shoulders. His head was turned so that he was constantly looking into the sun. One of his legs had been broken earlier. When he could not run any longer he was exposed to extreme mistreatments. His ears were ripped off by heavy blows and pulling.

Other Conditions

The food in the prison camps was miserable by any standard of quality and quantity. Hygiene was beneath any human standards.

Goli Otok

The Yugoslav Goli Otok was a symbol of gulag archipelago. Goli Otok was called by Tito's adversaries "the island of shame," "the wall of humiliation," "Marko's Hawaii." To be on that island was to be in hell.

Origins of Island Inferno

What were the origins of this hellish place? During World War I the Austro-Hungarian Empire had brought Russian prisoners to Goli Otok. They lived under the open sky and they dug marble for Austria. Most of those prisoners left their bones there. During World War II the Italians mined marble there to export to Venice.

Ivan-Stevo Krajacich, a general of the Yugoslav UDBA and a favorite of Tito, told Augustincich about the isolated island near Rijeka. It was ideal for a Cominform camp as far as security, being seven kilometers from the nearest coast.

In short, Goli Otok was organized on the initiative of Krajacich, the interior minister of Croatia, and his assistant Drakulovich.

The Aim of Goli Otok

The aim of Goli Otok was to destroy the dignity and pride in man, to humiliate him to the lowest degree so he would never feel like a man again. Goli Otok is a harsh place by nature, but under Tito's UDBA, what happened there was even harsher. It was a horrible torture place, a special blacksmith shop for testing men's character. What was done on Goli Otok the normal human mind could not adequately picture. A Frenchman says that the more he thinks about men, the more he likes animals. The prisoners on Goli Otok, or to call them what they were, Yugoslav slaves, did not look like human beings after such tortures. Scabs formed over the entire body: Face, nose, forehead, ears, shoulders, back, and the entire upper torso were torn and scarred by innumerable blows. Various primitive measures were used against the prisoners in order to force them to return to Tito and the party. On Goli Otok, in particular, the most horrible thing was not the constant beatings, nor hunger, thirst, and dirt, nor the tormented work or sleeplessness, but the atmosphere of horror. A rational man must ask himself, are there among the creatures of the earth any greater beast than man himself, especially when man has unlimited power over other men!

The Goli Otok mill ground men with its millstone in order to create from a former politically and ethically aware person a political nobody, or simple rabble. It was also a mechanism to scare leading cadres who were free, not prisoners. In some ways the gulag organizers succeeded in their satanic goals.

Who Directed the Terror on Goli Otok

In that horrible period the executors of the terror were the camp's interrogators, their assistants from the UDBA, and the leader and assistants from KOS, then their collaborators and various groups of disguised, uniformed civilians.

Comparison of Titoists' Goli Otok with Occupier and Chetnik Prison Camps

In 1942 Dushan Dozich was captured by Chetniks and detained in the Chetnik camp in Kolashin. Dozich considered Chetniks his class enemies. However, he states that the Chetniks did not do what the Titoists did against Cominformists, who were their fellow soldiers and war comrades. In the Chetniks' jail after the verdict was pronounced no one bothered him any more. All had its limits; the Chetnik prison was like a vacation compared with his Goli Otok treatment.

Did Tempo, Popovich, and Djilas Know about Goli Otok?

During the persecutions of Cominformists, Tempo was chief of the political department of the general staff of the Yugoslav army. He states that he had never heard about Goli Otok before it was destroyed.

Koca Popovich, of the general staff of the Yugoslav army, said the same thing—he never heard of that camp for the accommodation of those "incorrigible bandits."

Those two men were in top positions in the Yugoslav army. How could they not know when many of their subordinate officers were arrested by the KOS? Such statements by Tempo and Popovich and similar ones by Djilas were nothing but stories for children. That is typical of Titoist morals and ethics!

Conclusion

It would be a great mistake to believe that Tito and his cohorts began their criminal activities with the prosecution of the Cominformists in 1948. That was just a continuation of their "professional" work performance.

Who was behind the scene when eight secretaries of the YCP were liquidated in Moscow? Was Tito himself?

Radovan Lukovich, secretary of the PCCPS (Provincial Committee of the Communist Party of Serbia) when Petko Miletich was dismissed as secretary of the YCP, says about Tito: "He is an opportunist and a very suspicious person."

It is needless to state what role Tito played during the Spanish and Yugoslav revolutions and afterwards!

But it is imperative for people to know what draconian policies and torture methods were employed by the top Yugoslav leadership. It is bitterly ironic that most of their postwar victims were their fellow soldiers and war comrades, who had survived the war struggle only to fall before the vicious onslaught of political repression waged by their former ideological brothers.

Notes

1. Savo M. Vukcevich was my classmate at the Podgorica gymnasium. As a young Communist he was expelled from the school there. As a private student he graduated high school at Cetinje gymnasium. At his final examination Marko Z. Rakocevich was his professor for the Serbo-Croatian language. When Savo submitted his written theme, Prof. Rakocevich was surprised by the exceptional intelligence and rare talent the writing demonstrated. The professor showed the other students Savo's paper as an example of outstanding thinking.

Many talented men like Savo were swallowed by the very beginning of the revolution in 1941. Goli Otok exemplifies the prison grinding mills. Dr. Cedomir Ilickovich was together with Savo in the torture chamber R-101 at the moment when he died. The camp doctor did not even dare to check Savo's pulse before he was pronounced dead. Another witness, Vlado Dapcevich, was also with Savo before he died. His last words were: "Oh, my children! Oh, my wife! Now what will happen to you!"

Chapter Five

THE DESECRATION OF LOVCEN CHAPEL

What Shakespeare is to the British, Njegosh is to Serbians. Great men of culture sometimes suffer the most from those who consider themselves energetic defenders of that culture.

Njegosh once said, "When Nature creates the man of genius and then lights a torch above his head, she tells him, 'Go, be unfortunate.'"

During their celebration of slava (the family patron saint ritual) Serbs in Bosnia sing the following song:

> At Lovcen Njegosh is sleeping,
> The wisest Serbian poet.

> (Na Lovcenu Njegosh spava,
> Najmudrija srpska glava.)

Njegosh's Life

Petar Petrovich-Njegosh was born November 1, 1813, in Njegushi, located on the lower slopes of Mount Lovcen. There he spent his childhood and his early youth as a shepherd. When he was baptized he received the name Rade. As a shepherd, Rade Petrovich spent the most joyous days of his life. There like young King David he watched his father's sheep as they grazed. The rifle was his first entertainment and the gusle his first teacher. Serbian glory was his first love, and the sky and the stars his first puzzle, says Ljubomir Nekadovich, a Serbian writer. His teacher was Sima Milutinovich. Like Plato, Milutinovich taught his students while walking in the green meadows or sitting in the shade of a big tree. Frequently he would give his students ten-minute discourses about Greek gods, the sowing of potatoes, or philosophy. "Spartans and Montenegrins are never taken alive," Milutinovich told them. He showed Rade the path that leads across Parnos to the pantheon of eternal glory. He was the most talented man in memory from without or within the tribe, who brought us the artistic inheritance of the world.

In 1830, after the death of his uncle Bishop Petar I, Rade succeeded him. He was chosen by the Montenegrin chieftains to become Prince and Bishop of Montenegro, Petar II Petrovich-Njegosh.

Njegosh accumulated his knowledge and enlarged his experience from Russian literature, which is rich in all fields, as well as from Italian and French. He had a fantastic memory that enabled him to study all the humanistic disciplines and to undertake serious study of the poetry of Pushkin, Mickievich, Homer, and Dante. Throughout his life Njegosh gravitated toward the sophisticated European model of civilization.

Vuk Karadzich states, "Njegosh is a very talented man, a great patriot and well educated."

Njegosh's Literary Accomplishments

The greatest treasures in Serbian culture are its folk poetry, the frescoes in the monasteries from the medieval period, and Njegosh's literary work.

His literary work with its great artistic qualities is as important and valuable today as ever before. In his deep thoughts and strong expressions are preserved the moral and spiritual strength of his time. He had neither great predecessors nor, as yet, successors. As a poet and philosopher he stands alone, straight as a monument. The genius of his talent is as yet unequaled, though he died when he was only 38 years of age.

Njegosh's Curse

Njegosh chose the mountain Lovcen to build a chapel in memory of his uncle, Bishop Petar I. Lovcen is the highest peak of Montenegro, from which you can see most of the Serbian land. Njegosh's chapel was dedicated to Bishop Petar I and with Mount Lovcen became the beacon of freedom, humanity, and the dignity of all people. Mount Lovcen is the Serbian Olympus, the Serbian spiritual center.

Njegosh in his last will and testament stated: "I want to be buried in the chapel on Lovcen Mountain. That is my last wish to be fulfilled by you. If you don't promise me what I ask you to do then I shall have to leave a curse upon you. In such a case my last hours of life would be extremely sad, which would afflict your soul, also."

His wish was fulfilled.

Lovcen with Njegosh is the highest Serbian mountain. Without him it would be just a little higher than the other Njegushi hills.

Why Was There Animosity Toward Njegosh?

The decadent Austrian culture had nothing to compare to Njegosh as a poet of liberty who was also identified with his people.

One Serbian foe was the Austrian tzar Franz Joseph I.

During World War I, Austrian artillery hit Njegosh's Lovcen Chapel. On August 12, 1916, Austrian occupation forces in Montegro, like dogs, dug up Njegosh's remains from Lovcen Chapel and took them to Cetinje Monastery. This was done secretly. The Austrian occupier was afraid that the Montenegrin people would mutiny against such a disgraceful act. This was a humiliating act of desecration of the Njegosh monument.

Why did the Austrian authority remove the Njegosh relics from Mount Lovcen? They knew well Bishop Rade's greatness and glory among the Serbian people. They knew the Serbian Olympus with Njegosh's relics would become a holy place for pilgrimages. Furthermore, the Austrian aggressor was trying to make Lovcen lose its luminescence in order to prepare the climate for future annexation of that region and eventually the entire region of Montenegro. Then Austria planned to erect on Mount Lovcen a monument to Franz Joseph. Therefore, during World War I the Austrian occupier was preparing public opinion through various newspapers (Montenegrin and occupation) for the erection of such a monument.

On January 12, 1916, the Vienna newspaper *Neue Freie Presse* announced the following news: Lovcen was a sign of defiance like an enormous banner driven into the rock of the Montenegrin kingdom that provoked their monarchy just like some legation of the great Russian empire, whenever a signal was given to them from Petrograd. Now that banner is toppled and Austrian fighters are converging from all directions to exterminate that haiduk's nest.

On October 19, 1916, an official newspaper in Cetinje reported that a large monument would very soon be erected on Lovcen as a symbol of conquering Gibraltar Andria.

The editor of a Belgrade newspaper, K. Herman, emphasized that the consequences of Russia's defeat and her retreat from Galicia, the fall of all Russian fortresses that were built by billions of French money, and the complete destruction of the Petrovich dynasty did not exhilarate the Austrians as much as the fall of Lovcen. On Lovcen, the haiduk's nest, stands a huge Montenegrin banner stuck into the rocks that provokes the Austrian monarchy like a consulate of the great Russian empire.

The *Obzor* (Horizon) newspaper of Zagreb stated that half a year had passed since the Austrian army waged battle against Lovcen. The monument to the tzar would be seen from the sea. Therefore, every Austro-Hungarian flag had to salute it.

The Vienna position toward Lovcen was to undermine the spiritual influence of Njegosh upon Serbian Sparta. Austro-Hungary lost the war, and she did not realize her imperialistic intentions of humiliating Lovcen and the tiny state of Montenegro. Njegosh, like Saint Sava, was a thorn in the eyes of Serbian foes that gave them neither peace nor tranquility.

In 1925 Njegosh's relics were returned. The renovation of the chapel was a complex and expensive job. King Alexander paid the cost from his personal fund. Some 100-percent Montenegrins as they called themselves interpreted the king's generosity as a plan to subjugate Montenegro to Serbia! Actually, the Montenegrin people were exhausted from the war. They were poor in the material sense, though they were always spiritually rich.

Hegel's View of Cemeteries

The German philosopher Hegel says that if ancient people did not have a steady residence they together gathered in cemeteries. According to Hegel, tombs and monuments unite people. They represent holy places for defenders to protect at any cost.

From such a perspective should be evaluated the barbaric act of Sinan pasha of burning the relics of Saint Sava as well as the despotic tendencies of Tzar Franz Joseph.

And what about the razing of Lovcen Chapel by Tito, the god from Kumrovac, with the help of Montenegrin Titoists?

Who Destroyed Njegosh's Chapel, and Why?

No Yugoslav artist went through so many humiliations after death as Njegosh did. He was the greatest poet of the south Slavs, and his destiny was identified with Montenegro and his people.

One does not need great intelligence but only basic honesty to realize the scurrilous perfidy of the policy acted out by Serbians' enemies including Josip Broz Tito.

Tito's marionettes in the Cetinje community and the state of Montenegro agreed to replace Njegosh's chapel by a mausoleum designed by Meshtrovich.

Marxist ideology was systematically destroying God in the soul of human beings. As soon as God's decency is forgotten, man becomes like a wolf toward his fellow men. However, in the cases of Saint Sava and Njegosh, the actions against them reflected religious fanaticism and imperialistic chauvinism of the Muslim faith and Austro-Hungarian imperialistic Catholicism.

Tyranny had destroyed the dignity of man. Just in the diocese of Montenegro-Littoral-Skenderijski ruffians barbously tortured and butchered the clergy so relentlessly that fewer than twenty out of two hundred survived by the end of the war! The practice of observing religious customs was forbidden, such as performing rites like slava, baptism, weddings, and burials in the church. The spiritual meaning of candles was neglected.

Keeping people mindful of the need to respect each other, to treat and to esteem every human being as a supreme creation, was systematically neglected.

The generation that performed the shameful act of the desecration of Lovcen Chapel must apologize for the primitivism they committed and restore the chapel. Do they know that they humiliated proud Lovcen, stepped on the legacy of Bishop Rade, and desecrated a holy temple once erected by the most famous people ever born in the invincible Lovcen-Serbian Olympus, the Serbian spiritual center?

Needless to say, those acts against religion and the chapel were more or less ordered and executed by the same ruffians who during the revolution filled pits, ravines, and wells with the most honest and dignified people. They razed to the ground the graves of their ideological adversaries. Those hotheads wore brass decorations covered with tin. They believe their "merits" belong to history! For them, all the past was darkness, degradation, and desperation.

Besides the destruction of Lovcen Chapel, Montenegro experienced other lawlessness during and after the war. The monument in Rudo Polje near Niksic that had been erected in memory of seventy-two people shot by the Austro-Hungarian occupier during World War I was destroyed.

An enigma: Who ordered such vandalism against the occupier's victims? Was it a former Austrian sergeant who was decorated by his tzar Franz Joseph for capturing a Russian patrol in World War I? He had remained loyal and faithful to the former Austro-Hungarian Empire. Could it be anyone else but the villain from Kumrovac?

Should the Chapel Be Replaced by a Mausoleum?

The journal *Art* no. 278, Belgrade 1971 listed some fifty names of Montenegrin and Serbian government officials who at that time favored the Meshtrovich project. However, they cynically hid the fundamental reason why in 1916 the occupier's newspapers in Cetinje and Belgrade supported action to erect a monument to the Austrian tzar Franz Joseph in order to get rid of the Lovcen "commemoration of Orthodoxy" and to mark the day of liberation of Lovcen by "our [Austrian] invincible army." Then Lovcen would become a different guardian of Montenegrin history.

How will history judge despots like Sinan pasha, who burned Saint Sava's relics, Franz Joseph, and Tito and his henchmen for their desecration of Njegosh's chapel?

Whoever violates the will of the poet, an anathema upon him!

Broz irrevocably declared war against the holy Mount Lovcen.

Montenegrin leaders decided to erect a Meshtrovich mausoleum for Njegosh, unconcerned about the similarity to German/pharoah tombs/pyramids.

The Montenegrin tyrants did not realize that mausoleums are for autocrats, despots, dictators, and tyrants not for poets and bishops. This was a perfidious act against Njogosh's tomb and against the history as well as the culture and dignity of the Serbian people. It was against Mount Lovcen itself.

If hills and men ever disappear, the twin collossi, Lovcen and Bishop Rade, will forever remain in Montenegro.

Brozovici cut the peak of Mount Lovcen down about four meters and then on it they installed the Meshtrovich mausoleum, which represents a shameful epoch.

There came into power those who needed neither light nor cross. Njegosh's chapel was replaced by a dark mausoleum without one cross. At one time Cetinje was the eternal spiritual capitol of Montenegro, the residence of great Montenegrin bishops, capitol of a small but glorified Serbia country. Kosovo is the foundation of the temple on Mount Lovcen. In the period of the Montenegrin hotheads, when malice had the advantage over reason and honor, Cetinje was humiliated and ideologically condemned.

Government Decision to Install Mausoleum

In 1959 in the *Encyclopedia of Zagreb* it was written that a mausoleum to Njegosh would be erected on Lovcen. The monument would be a sculpture of Ivan Meshtrovich, instead of a chapel. This is unique when an encyclopedia announces future events!

According to international convention, destroying a monument of culture, especially a church, is a barbaric act. The destruction of Lovcen Chapel became part of the anti-Serb politics of Josip Broz. His word was the law for the Montenegrin party forum and the community organizations of Cetinje.

In 1966 the Commission for the Organization of a Mausoleum at Cetinje recommended to the Montenegrin secretary for education and culture *not* to build a mausoleum on Mount Lovcen.

Despite the recommendation, on February 28, 1969, Bill No. 02107 of the community of Cetinje got approval for the demolition of Lovcen Chapel, because the demolition of a chapel is not sacrilege (svetogrdje).

Josip Broz and his Brozovici were guided by hatred and ideological and imperialistic tendencies as faithful adherents of Tzar Franz Joseph. They barbarically attacked the culture, tradition, and above all the pride and dignity of Montenegrin Serbs.

The Yugoslav supreme political body and the parliament of Montenegro had decided well in advance to approve the erection of a mausoleum. In April 1952 the Montenegrin government instructed Vladimir Popovich, the Yugoslav ambassador to the United States, to contact Ivan Meshtrovich about a mausoleum. Meshtrovich was a staunch anti-Communist who during the war had wholeheartedly embraced the Ustashe ideology. He enthusiastically agreed to do the job even without an honorarium, except "a piece of cheese or a shoulder of ram." On May 21, 1952, Blazo Jovanovich, president of the Montenegrin government, sent a letter to Meshtrovich expressing satisfaction if he could make a splendid mausoleum expressing Njegosh's "justice, liberty, and dignity of man and the people." To be fair, it is necessary to emphasize that Meshtrovich did not ask the state authority to let him make a mausoleum on the top of Lovcen. To the contrary, the Montenegrin government approached under the presidency of Blazo Jovanovich.

The enemies of the Serbian people were united in their insistence that the chapel had to be replaced with a mausoleum. It is attested that the poor maintenance of the mausoleum shows that ruffians were more concerned about removing the chapel that had been restored by King Alexander than with erecting its graceless, soulless replacement.

Savic Markovich-Shtedimlija was once again appearing on the Ustashe-Communist scene:

On April 26, 1970, Savic Markovich wrote in Zagreb's *Herald* (Vjesnik), that the campaign against the Meshtrovich mausoleum on Lovcen had let up, while abroad it was intensified by the Chetnik-Ljoticevska immigrant press. The campaign spread to some foreign newspapers who were misled by Chetnik propaganda.

On May 14, 1970, Bishop Vasilija of Zica wrote that an unqualified reporter had been writing from time to time in Zagreb newspapers. He should be silent! He was Savic Markovich-Shtedimlija.

Against the Meshtrovich Mausoleum

It was a paradox of the times that the Communist Yugoslav authority let Meshtrovich, a Croatian Catholic who during World War II wrote odes glorifying the Fascist Pavelich, desecrate Lovcen Chapel! About two hundred names renowned in Serbian culture joined by three Croatians (Krleza, Cvito Fiskovich, and M. Glanurich) condemned the destruction of the chapel. The nation felt depressed at the lack of respect for its shrines. People who do not know anything greater than themselves do not deserve to exist. To escape such damnation we must return our shrines to their original places. Those who destroyed the chapel had forgotten that Serbs never forget their holy objects, not as an expression of fanaticism but as the highest homage to those personalities and places that had earned it by their own merits. The Serbs renovated what was once destroyed regardless of price, moral and material. It will be the same with the chapel. The sooner the better.

Among those who opposed the destruction of the chapel were the Metropolitan of Montenegro-Littoral-Skenderiski; the Serbian patriarchate; the Montenegrin secretary for education and culture, then Lazar Trifkovich; the well-known historian of arts, France Stele; Slovenian academician Dr. Luc Menash; and Miroslav Krleza. Many voices against the mausoleum were heard, especially those of literary men, artists, and journalists. In a word, men of culture were against such primitivism!

On March 18, 1969, high school students demonstrated against the demolition of Lovcen Chapel in Cetinje.

Dr. Ljubomir Durkovich-Jakshich stated, "The destruction of the chapel on Lovcen is a way of extinguishing the Serbian candle," because Njegosh's supreme loyalty was to the holy cross and to Obilich's people.

Pavle Ilich, the academician, could not comprehend how the man who was the epitome of hatred against the Serbian people could erect a mausoleum monument to the greatest Serbian poet. On Serbian Olympus Lovcen, Njegosh's chapel was erected by God's hand as a monument to liberty and her defenders. The demolition of the chapel was a crime that could never be healed or forgotten.

Voices against the mausoleum were not only heard in Yugoslavia but throughout the entire civilized world. These persons of principle and sensitivity had a broad knowledge in harmony with world events, contrary to those narrow-minded people whose hatred and chauvinism controlled their minds and hearts as well.

Willard Ben Quan, an American philosopher from Harvard University, asked, "Is it possible that Montenegrins, who were so proud and hold to their tradition, will let the oath of their greatest Yugoslav poet be broken?" Other people who spoke out were Andre Malraux, the French minister of culture in Gen. DeGaulle's government; Marcel Gabriel, a great Christian thinker; Zana Kresia, who unsuccessfully begged the Yugoslav government to spare Lovcen Chapel; P. Emanuel, a poet and member of the French Academy and president of an international writers club who directly contacted Broz Tito and his Brozovici without avail; Andre Mandeva, a great French thinker and writer; Skender Kulenovich, a Muslim who called the Meshtrovich mausoleum the "pack saddle of Lovcen"; Petar Lubarda; Mihailo Lalich; Dr. Niko Martinovich; and many others were aghast at the demolition of the chapel and the desecration of what it represented.

Njegosh's defenders, the defenders of Serbian Orthodoxy and Kosovo determination, knew that Njegosh was neither a pharoah nor a Lenin who needed a mausoleum. Njegosh was Saint Sava's bishop, the head of poor Montenegro, the spiritual leader of Serbianism crucified on the cross, the poet of tragic Kosovo determination. His cries remain a voice crying in the wilderness. The final decision to destroy Njegosh's chapel was made by crude, arrogant Communist atheists, Tito's flatterers, who were ruling by brutal force and destroying the roof of the Serbian Fatherland.

The Meshtrovich mausoleum is architecture without spirit. It remains a symbol of a time when national, historical, and religious sacredness were not respected, especially in the Serbian land. Brutal men found their expression in it, as a negative marker of their absurdity and primitivism.

That monster mausoleum is a nightmare, a nightmare of lack of culture and of tyranny, a nightmare of Asiatic torture, a nightmare lived out during a period that is irredeemable.

The majority of Croatian and Montenegrin intellectuals were scum who maliciously tried to execute spiritual blasphemy with the mausoleum on Lovcen and in so doing disgrace unprotected Montenegro, which had stood for centuries as a paradigm of Kosovo epics and Christian ethics.

That national desecration was maliciously planned and performed as part of the long-lived, ongoing, Machiavellian intent to destroy Serbs, physically and spiritually as well.

The Mausoleum Ceremony

On July 28, 1974, a mausoleum ceremony was held. Veljko Milatovich, then president of the Montenegrin Republic, said, "We had an obligation to interpret his [Njegosh's] work, both poetic and constitutional. We want to get rid of romantic deadwood and folklore naivete, from Orthodox and civil mythomania and scenery as well...." (By the way, after the war Milatovich personally killed Krsto Popovich, the Montenegrin guerrilla leader.) Indeed, what interpretative "geniuses" could dare offer advice to the Petrovich bishops and King Nicholas I about Serbianism and other human qualities!

At that ceremony, during a recitation from *The Montenegrin Wreath*, verses were omitted that referred to Serbianism, Kosovo, or Milosh Obilich. The desecration of *Mountain Wreath* was a policy of the Montenegrin leadership who were writing to de-Serbianize the Montenegrin people. Is there any other example in the world of people willingly renouncing their origin, their nationality, except Montenegrins of Drljevich's and Savic Markovich's persuasion?

Conclusion

Was there any justification for the removal of Njegosh's chapel? In a civilized world it could only be justified if criteria are reversed and virtues are replaced by vices!

The final judgment will nullify the tragic error made by a disgraceful and soulless generation. They were so narrow-minded they could not accept the opinion of knowledgeable people. The time will come when they will be buried alive, in the moral sense, for committing such a crime.

Lovcen was shaped by eternity and by Njegosh himself. Together they were part of the Serbian people's spiritual, cultural, historical, and geographic existence. The Lovcen tragedy was mourned by all civilized society.

The eventual resurrection of the chapel on Lovcen would clearly mean not only victory for the Serbian people but also a victory for justice to all democratic, freedom-loving people who respect Judeo-Christian ethics, morality, and higher cultural values. In a word, those with great minds and even greater humanitarian hearts. Most of the money for the mausoleum came from the West. Now let others contribute to restore the chapel. Some people promised their share when they were asked to contribute to the mausoleum.

Posthumous Martyrdom
by Matija Beckovich

Lovcen is a temple; on its cupola is the chapel. At the time of its destruction the chapel was one of the most beautiful Orthodox temples ever built. This crime could be compared with the destroying of Christ Church in Moscow. In Moscow the church was replaced with a fountain, while the chapel on Lovcen was replaced by a motel called a mausoleum. Men drowned in the fountain. People perished beside the mausoleum.

According to the bishop's wishes he was buried on the top of Lovcen to defend his church and faith in death as he had in life. That is when his martyrdom began. If the chapel belonged to any other denomination it would not have been destroyed. It was destroyed only because it belonged to the Serbian Orthodox church.

In our time, Njegosh is the only bishop who was not buried either by candle or by clergy. So he can share his destiny with his counterparts of today!

Indeed, Njegosh was not buried; rather he was enslaved in a prison that was built for him. That hostage is held under lock and key and defended with guns. The question of the renovation of the chapel is at the same time a question of the renovation of Lovcen, if people still exist who would exist with Njegosh.

Chapter Six

From Vatican to Tudjman

Under the concept of "Vatican" we consider those cabals of Nazis and Fascist priests and diplomats who took the non-Christian role of forceful extermination or conversion of other races or religious afiliations. It also encompasses those villains engaged in "Ratline" activities.

If the Vatican wants to exert moral authority it must at least be unequivocal and truly neutral as shown by its deeds; peace on earth and good will to all humanity regardless of race, creed, and ideological beliefs.

> The evil is not only those who commit it
> But also those who
> Could thwart it but do not.
> —Tukidid

> (Zlo nije samo djelo ko ga cini,
> Vec i onih koji
> Mogu da gu sprijece, ali tu ne cine.)

During World War II the complexities of Yugoslav events and personalities could be seen in three aspects of the war: religious, opposition to the occupier for national liberation, and ideological factors.

Before the split in the Christian church in 1054 the harassment between non-Christians and Christians had existed as early as the fourth century A.D. In 1054 a schism occurred in the Christian church. In the eleventh century Cardinal Humburt branded the faithful of the Orthodox church as heretics. In 1332 Brikard, a Catholic monk, recommended that two schismatic states, Serbia and Greece, be destroyed. Thus the Orthodox Satanization began. Ever since then, the Catholic church has had strong aspirations for earthly rule, especially in the Balkan vacuum. Also, satanization of Serbs in Croatia meant the creation of a totally false description of an entire ethos, in which they were represented by myths of monsters and dream fables.

During the Spanish inquisition in 1478 125,000 lost their lives, within a period of eighteen years: 10,222 persons were burned at the stake; 114,401 perished from hunger and torture in their prisons; 18,000 died in Holland; 100,000 in France. Those inquisitions were led by Dominicans and Franciscans with unlimited power given them by the popes.

351

In 1483 the inquisitor Jacob de Marci came to Slavonia "to persecute schismatic Serbs." Thus began another salvo of religious-political conflict between the Catholic church (which believed only she is in charge of the salvation of souls for all Christians) and the Orthodox church.

During Bartholomew's Night in 1573 in Paris the pope's warriors slaughtered several thousand Huguenots (French Protestants), their religious adversaries.

Three inquisitions in the world's history did not swallow as many victims, though their record is frightening enough, as the "Croatian Ustashe in the twentieth century in its persecution of unarmed Serbian people on the territory of Hitler and Mussolini's formation of the Independent State of Croatia!"

In 1985 the Catholic News Agency observed that the victims under the Ustashe authority in Croatia between 1941 and 1945 (as martyrs of the Orthodox faith) should not only be celebrated and honored by Serbs in the future, but also by the Greek church as well. The genocide that occurred in Croatia was a new inquisition of the twentieth century!

Historical Importance of Serbs in Croatia, Slavonia, and Dalmatia

Serbs began migrating to northern Croatia right after the Slavs moved in. Their settlements continued in the twelfth ceuntry when Queen Jelena, daughter of Urosh of Zupan (head of the tribal state) Rashka, married the king of Hungary.

In 1454 in Varazdin a codex of Apostles to bless and bestow Christ's love on Princess Katakuzin, countess of Celje, daughter of the despot (title of Serbian ruler after the Battle of Kosovo) Djurdja, autocrat of Serbia was preserved in the Cyrillic alphabet.

In 1469-1482 the Hungarian-Croatian king, Matija Korvin, gave the despot Vuk Grugurovich (famous hero from folksongs as the ardent dragon) several cities around Kostajnica, Bela Stena of Pakrac, and nearly all of Posavina from Stara Gradishka to Sisak, with a hundred villages. He did this to defend Croatia and Slavonia from the Turks.

In 1493 at Krbavsko Polje the Turks defeated the Croats. More than ten thousand soldiers were killed. At the end of the fifteenth century there was a bishopric in Zagreb with forty-six parishes, while in 1501 there had been only sixteen.

Before the Turks invaded there were 280 Serb settlements in the Zadar region. After the Turkish invasion only 85 survived.

Lika Sandzakat was organized in 1527. In 1540 old Croatia fell under the Turks.

From the fifteenth to the eighteenth century it was the Serbs who with spiritual power defended, cultivated, and later liberated Croatian territory from the Turkish agressor.

In 1576 the Austrian archduke Karlo (Karlovac was named after him) stated that the majority of dukes in Krajina near Shtajerska were not Roman Catholics but Uskoks (invaders of Turkish territory) who were of the Orthodox religion.

In 1598 the main commander of Krajina, General Baron Herberstajn, stated that Serbs are the most decisive Krajishnici. They did not move to Croatia out of any fear. They are sincere and faithful Christians. Their honor does not let them suffer under Turkish tyranny.

Serbs are exceptionally courageous, skillful, and worthy soldiers. They did not move to Croatia empty-handed. They brought with them livestock and other wealth. They are very popular, well behaved, well dressed, and armed.

On September 7, 1599, Archduke Ferdinand submitted information to Tzar Rudolph that Serbs had moved to Croatia under the condition that they would remain independent from Croatian masters there. Those masters are trying to subordinate Serbs under their authority. In return for privileges given them by the Austrian authority the Serbs had obligated themselves to defend Krajina from the Turks at any time.

In 1670 the Coratian ban Peter Zrinski and his brother-in-law Krsto Frankopan were jailed and beheaded by the Austrian tzar. They had refused to revoke the historical rights given Serbs earlier. Also, Bishop Gavrilo Mijakich was jailed and died, walled into a living tomb.

Serbian representatives (vojvode) were always ready to defend the guaranteed rights given their people by both the Austrian authority or the Zagreb bishopric against rulings by local judges or from forcible proselytism. For centuries, actions have been led by Catholic clergy to convert Serbs. They succeeded to a great extent in Dalmatia, Lika, Kordun, Banija, and all of Zumberak. In 1755 there was a "severinski" rebellion led by the Serb Petar Ljubojevich from Veliki Grdjenac near Bjelovar, caused by forcible uniatism as well as the revocation of old rights to Serbian frontiersmen.

In 1788 a Serbian school was organized for Orthodox children in Bjelovar. The first teacher was Jovan Rajacich. During that century most of the Orthodox churches were built, to preserve, in addition to religion, the national identity of Serbs. Seminary schools were organized in Metak, Zaluznica, Plashko, and Karlovac. Also, eighty Serbian schools were formed by Lukijan Mushicki, bishop of the Gornjo-Karlovci diocese.

On May 31, 1791, the Illyrian palace in Vienna informed Serbian Gornjo-Karlovac, Bishop Genadija Dimovich that the Austrian tzar in considering the interests of his own country was willing to extend benefits to Serb immigrants. The tzar and king of the hereditary land was willing to broaden the old rights and benefits already given to the Serbian people.

According to medieval principle, the religion should be in accord with (cuius regio, illus religio) whomever the land (country) belongs to.

Croatian Patriots Recognized Serbs' Merits in Croatian History

In the mid-nineteenth century in Croatia there was a strong Illyrian movement for the unity of South Slavs among the intelligentsia. They were guided by cultural, socioeconomic, and linguistic ties, as in Germany and Italy under Bismarck and Mazzini. Serbia was not so enthusiastic for a Yugoslav entity from the pragmatic position of monarchy interests.

In 1848 the new Croatian ban Josip Jelacich invited "all Croatian and Serbian people" in the tripartite kingdom of Dalmatia, Croatia, and Slavonia to work together on an equal basis for the benefit of their fatherland, which was imperiled by the enemy (Turks). Among the first to respond was the new Serbian patriarch Rajacich, who came to the Sabor (Parliament) in Zagreb on June 2, 1848.

The Orthodox patriarch had administered the oath of office to the new Croatian ban Jelacich, which then seemed a real triumph of brotherly accord between Croats and Serbs.

On June 6, 1848, at the same Sabor, Ivan Kukuljevich-Sakcinski recounted Serbs' merits for Croatia in the most important period. The Serbian people had preserved the Croatian pure nationality when the Croatians moaned under aristocracy, Latinism, and Germanism.

At the same Sabor, the Croatian Ljudevit Gaj said the future of brotherhood of Serbs and Croats would be ensured. He dared to say, "Gentlemen, these Serbian people have great merits for Croats. Think about it—Serbs alone defend Kordun with their muscles."

The Croatian poet Ivan Mazuranich sent a letter from the same Sabor to Austrian archduke Johan in which Mazuranich emphasized that the Croatian Parliament sets the same demands "for our Serbian brothers" because we are the same people and so strongly merged that nobody in the world could disassociate us. . . .

At the conclusion of Parliament, Article VII was passed, stating that the Croatian Sabor, on the basis of freedom and complete equality, accepts all the wishes of the Serbian people as their own representatives acknowledged.

On June 17, 1861, a Croatian Sabor was held at which the Serbian patriarch Rajacich appealed to the Sabor to stop pressuring the Orthodox people to be converted. The Sabor promised the patriarch that Croats could live with Serbs in brotherly harmony.

On April 29, 1867, the Sabor of the tripartite kingdom passed a motion of Ivan Voncina that "Serbian people who are living there have the same rights as Croatian people."

Unfortunately, regardless of Sabor promises, a third group with a Jesuit tendency tried to create a split between Serbs and Croats, or at least to proselytyze Serbs.

Serbs in Croatia not only contributed a great deal to the military and political establishments, but also in the promotion and preservation of their spiritual culture in Croatia.

Ljudevit Gaj emphasized that Croats should be thankful to God that the Croats together with the Serbs had a written, Illyrian language now. The Illyrian language was preserved among Serbs from their altar to their shepherd. In order to understand the Croatian Sabors, their spirit toward Serbs, at least two factors need to be considered.

At a time of direct danger from Turks, Serbs received from Vienna some privileges, such as easing the religious pressure for conversion, in return for defending the country against the Turkish aggressor. But in times of tranquility and peace, those privileges were in jeopardy!

Furthermore, in the nineteenth century, as shown, Croatian patriots at their Sabors had expressed a great appreciation to Serbs for what they had contributed to Croats at a time when even the Croatian national identity was in question. De facto, those Croats were protagonists and sincere ideologists for the unification of Southern Slavs, which was realized in 1918.

Why some Croats later completely reversed their positions, currently causing catastrophic consequences, will be discussed later.

Serbs in Slavonia

During the reign of King Dragutin Nemanjich, who married the Hungarian princess Katarina in 1282, Serbs settled in Slavonia and Vojvodina. Dragutin was given Srem, Belgrade, Macva, and Semberija. Therefore, he gave up the crown of Rashka by giving her to his brother Milutin. So Dragutin became the king of Srem (1282-1316). Those settlements continued during the reign of prince/despot Stevan Lazarevich (1389-1427), Djuradj Brankovich, and their successors (1427-1459).

In Slavonia the so-called Vienna Wars resulted in settlements of Serbs over the Sava River and the Danube.

After the Kosovo tragedy a great number of Serbs moved to Slavonia, where they built over 150 Orthodox churches and 3 monasteries: Pakrac, Orahovica, and Saint Ana.

Slavonia fell under Turkish rule in 1453.

In June of 1690 in Belgrade, when the Austrian forces were defeated by the Turks, Patriarch Arsenije held an assembly where they decided to retreat in front of the Turkish penetration. In that same year, Patriarch Arsenije III Charnojevich retreated with his faithful from Kosovo to the north to escape Turkish/Tatarian-Shiptarsko-Albanian genocide. At that particular period, people suffered under the Ottoman yoke on all sides: fear and misfortune were widespread; mothers were separated from their children, sons from their fathers; young women were taken away as slaves; older people were hacked and strangled. People sought death rather than live under such conditions.

On August 19, 1691, just a year after Patriarch Arsenije had to leave Kosovo, 10,000 Serbian men at arms in the Austrian army under Jovan Manastirlija and 3,600 cavalry participated in a battle near Slankamen. Serbs were the first to penetrate through the Turkish ranks; they captured thrity-four flags. In that battle the Turkish vizir Mustafa pasha Cuprilija, eighteen pashas, and about 20,000 Turks were killed.

The next day the Austrian tzar gave new privileges to Patriarch Arsenije, giving him authority over the people in the same measure he had had under the Turks. The Catholic church traditionally was against giving such privileges to Serbs. However, Austria was in great danger from the Turks, and her War Council gave the patriarch the right to canonically visit his congregations.

A little earlier, in 1684-1688 in Dalmatia, the legendary hero Stojan Jankovich, Uskok liberated some cities in northern Dalmatia to Cetina, Skadrin, Drnish, Sinj, and Knin in 1691.

In 1704 in Slavonia, Patriarch Arsenije redeemed the bishop's palace and church, and replaced the uniat bishop Petronije Ljubibratich by Bishop Sophronie Podgoricanin, who succeeded to a certain degree in holding up the Uniati of Serbs in Slavonia. Patriarch Arsenije was most remembered in Slavonia. He held up further expansion of uniatization by Rome—that is, he stopped the further conversion of Serbs to Catholicism.

In the eighteenth century during the Austrian rule, Serbs in Pakrac had a seminary that was later transformed to a teachers' school. There was a printing press that not only had Cyrillic and Latin letters but also Greek and Hebrew. Various books were published there as well as the magazine *Good Shepherd*. Many other cultural and educational institutions were there also.

What do the Serbs in Slavonia have today, spiritually and culturally? Almost nothing! During World War II almost every Serbian home suffered from the Ustashe madness (bezumlje). During World War II in Croatia, 456 Orthodox churches were destroyed; then in the period until 1957 an additional 57 churches were demolished.[1]

Recently monuments were discovered in the village Sheovici near Pakrac, the strongest medieval fortress in Slavonia, with a printing press that was moved to Zagreb! Many monuments in Slavonia have chiseled Cyrillic inscriptions that date from the end of the fourteenth century.

The Slavonian Orthodox diocese possesses fine objects of cultural, historical, and artistic values; a library with old manuscripts and the first published books, including the *Incunabula*, the very first stage, printed before 1500; a treasury with precious icons; and other priceless holy objects.

In the eighteenth century the Croatian poet Antun-Matija Reljkovich wrote the following verse:

Your old people read the books,
In Serbian read and in Serbian wrote.
(Tvoji stari knjige shtili (chitali),
Srpski shtili i srpski pisali.)

Today in Slavonia all Serbs' cultural contributions from the Austrian and Austro-Hungarian period have disappeared, destroyed. The Cyrillic alphabet was not allowed to be used, either in the Serbian schools or in the official Croatian press! Before that, there was preserved an act of Tzar Franz Joseph written in the Cyrillic alphabet with his own Cyrillic signature! Could anyone believe that the Austrian tzar was more tolerant toward Serbs than the Croatian authority with Tudjman today?

Now the Serbian Orthodox institutions in Slavonia are penniless. Most of the church properties were confiscated. Therefore they are in ruins, and the church remains a voice crying in the wilderness, till the present time.

What Can Serbs Expect in Slavonia Now?

Serbs are still waiting for the real truth of the dreadful camps in Jasenovac, Glina, Jadovno, and others to be consolidated and revealed, hearing from all sides in order to guarantee that such evil will never be repeated. Additionally, there is a Christian moral duty, as well as a humanitarian and historical obligation, toward these innocent victims who have not yet been buried with Christian rites.

To summarize in brief what would be the minimum Serb expectations from a new Croatian authority:

1. Serbs to be recognized as a sovereign people
2. Recognition of their ethnic and civil rights and the freedoms enjoyed by any minority in the civilized world
3. To develop their culture in their own language and letters
4. To organize schools and cultural institutions and to develop information networks
5. Most imperative, the solution of the fundamental Serb-Croatian relationship
6. To have mutual democratic behavior, tolerance, and civilized endeavor observed in the mutual state of Croatia
7. To reject Machiavellianism so as to embrace real Christian tolerance, reciprocal respect, pride, and human dignity.

Serbs in Dalmatia

In 1869 Krivoshije as an official part of Boka revolted against the Austrian authority in serving in their military formations. The inhabitants of Bay of Kotor did not serve in the military, either under Venice or during French rule. The Serbian representatives Stepan Mitrov Ljubisha and deputy Rodich barely succeeded in reconciling Krivoshije.

In mixed Dalmatia, collusion was proved by Mihe Pavlinovich, a Catholic (at one time a strong protagonist for Croatian and Serbian unity), in his newspaper *Il Nazionale*. The newspaper also praised the occupation of Bosnia to please the Austrian authority. In 1879 Serbs formed their People party and began to publish a Serbian newspaper in 1880 under the editorship of Sava Bjelanovich.

Serbs demanded their natural rights regardless of national origin and religious affiliation, because a Serb was a Serb before he embraced Christianity. But the Croatian party stated there were no Serbs in Dalmatia and that Serbian thought had no place there. The Serbian party was pure invention by the Orthodox clergy, they said. Again and again Orthodoxy was blamed for everything that did not favor Catholic expansionism.

In 1879 Serbs, together with Zadar's autonomous region, won an election for the Austrian king's council when the autonomashi promised to defend Serbian interests, their name, the Serbian language, and the Cyrillic alphabet.

The Serbian party won a community election in 1890 in Dubrovnik because the Serbian party's members were mostly Serb Catholics.

Zagreb's *Obzor* says that the Serbian and Croatian parties were not divided by religious lines, at least in Dalmatia.

If that trend of mutual religious tolerance and respect had continued, the "tragedy within a tragedy" in Yugoslavia since 1941 and after would not have happened.

Uniatism and Proselytism of Serbs under Austrian and Vatican Domain

In the sixteenth and seventeenth centuries, as a first step, the Catholic church made endeavors to convince the Orthodox faithful to accept the pope alone as the spiritual and religious head of the Christian church. Those just converted uniats could temporarily continue their Orthodox religious rites until Serb-uniats were proclaimed Catholics by Catholic clergy without their prior consent. After that they were forbidden to come in contact with any Orthodox clergy. Serbs by changing their religion automatically became not only Catholics but Croats as well.

Serb emigrants who escaped from Turkish territory to the Austrian jurisdiction in order to preserve their identity, their ethos, and religion paradoxically went through the process of forced conversion from Orthodoxy to
Catholicism. The process of proselytism was executed very shrewdly, with
utmost skill by the pope's missionaries.

Conversion to Catholicism under Direct Vatican Supervision

Marko Jacov in his book *Conversion to Catholicism* published secret
documents of religious propaganda. The book contains several hundred
original documents hitherto unknown. Also, the book contains some letters
from the Bar and Kotor bishoprics. Once or twice a month they informed
a congregation in the Vatican about Catholic successes in Montenegrin
Littoral during the sixteenth and seventeenth centuries. Those missionaries
of Kotor, Bar, and other bishoprics were authorized by the pope to work
on the conversion of Orthodox people to the Catholic faith on that particular
territory. In those letters it was mentioned precisely with whom they conversed and what they replied in order to accept a Uniat. For centuries in
Yugoslavia the Vatican has been waging war against orthodoxy. According
to Dr. Novica Vojinovich's research, there have been killers working in
God's name for the conversion or the annihilation of Orthodox faithful for
almost a thousand years.[2]

Commission of Saint Congregation

Even today each Catholic bishopric in Yugoslavia has a department called
the Commission of Saint Congregation for religious propaganda. At each
bishopric the chief of this congregation is usually the most educated and
popular friar. Those friars are the most trusted of the pope's faithful, sometimes more than bishops.

That is their "agitprop," as the Communists would call it. The aim of
the Saint Congregation is to destroy Orthodoxy regardless of the material
cost, not even sparing blood if it becomes necessary. Tens of thousands of
missionaries are working in Yugoslavia today.

The expansion of Croatianism on account of Serbianism as well as Catholicism on account of Orthodoxy and the formation of a Great Croatian state
in the framework of Austro-Hungary was and is the fundamental task of
Catholic clericalism in Croatia. Help has been received from the Vatican
and Vienna.

When people lose their constitutional rights, as Serbs have in Croatia
today by being given minority status, they can be neither satisfied nor

prosperous. Despite the tremendous contributions of Serbs in Croatia against fascism and nazism, what did they get in return? Bakarich's promises that Serbs would be rewarded for their merits after the war have remained empty. Instead, Serbian regions in Croatia are the poorest since the end of World War II.

When the poet Alphonse Lamartine (1790-1869) saw several hundred skulls in Cele-Kula, he cried out and at the same time admired the Serbian people. What would Lamartine say, if he were alive today, about the Ustashe genocide committed in the Yugoslav Dachau, Jasenovac, the largest Serbian underground city?

Vatican Mission in the Balkan Countries

The Vatican in its millenium-old tradition was anti-Orthodox, just as the Franciscans were anti-Serbs, which caused the spread of racist genocide in the state of Croatia.

Even in the nineteenth century a Pan-Croatian chauvinist movement based on Catholicism in an unyielding position and struggle against the Orthodox church was organized.

The conversion of Serbs throughout history has had a tremendous effect on their denationalization and religious affiliation for the final assimilation. From a sociological point of view forceful denationalization of any ethos is considered nothing less than a reactionary act of duress.

In the period between 1918 and 1990 the Latin motto "sempeer idem" (uvijek isti) could be applied to Croatian Franciscan politicians. Franciscans were trying to wear out the Serbs, like water on rocks, drop by drop, year after year until they were destroyed and finally indistinguishable from the dirt.

In Montenegro every Jesuit and Franciscan is a missionary, but they don't publicly express themselves. The fundamental task for each bishopric is missionary work. The sword of Damocles is still hanging over the heads of Orthodox people.

In its expansionistic policy the Roman Catholic church is also based on the principles "Extra Romanum ecclesiam non est sallus" (Outside the Roman Catholic church there is no salvation) and "Greaca fides, nulla fides" (Greek faith is not faith—Grcka vjera nije vjera).

Traditional Vatican policy takes an uncompromising position toward Orthodoxy. The negation of Serbian nationality on the "Croatian linguistic territory" and their Orthodox affiliation was the first step toward proselytism.

The Vatican policy in South Slav countries, Serbia and Montenegro in particular, was characteristic because the Vatican did not sit with folded hands in the Balkans.[3]

Accusations and Persecutions of Serbs in Croatia

Anyone looking back into history to record all the persecution of Serbs in Croatia for their national identity and religion would have a long and tedious task. Therefore, just some of the events from the second half of the nineteenth century and continuing into the twentieth will be discussed here.

In 1878, Serbs were arrested as "great traitors" in Pakrac, Bjelovar, Karlovac, Daruvar, and Osijek. The Serbian Orthodox schools were closed down.

At that time voices on the Croatian side were saying that Italians, Germans, and Hungarians (Ag. Tagblatt) were closer to Croatians than Serbs were! In Croatian opinion, Serbian identity and religion were very dangerous to the entire monarchy.

Serbs were forced to defend themselves. They organized their own political party, the Serbian party, and they began to publish a newspaper, *Srbobran*.

In 1895 during the opening of a new theater in Zagreb, large demonstrations were held against the Serbs because they flew a Serbian flag on their church building.

On October 14-15, 1895, Dr. Jovan Pachu wrote, There was a wild attack by Croats against the Serbian flag and the Serbian church. It lasted for two days. The Orthodox clergy was publicly attacked by calling them Vallach (Vlasi) pigs! The police were indifferent toward the demonstrations. Some European countries condemned the demonstrations as a national shame of the first rank. The demonstrations in 1895 were justified by Josip Frank, contrary to Stjepan Radich. Frank thought it was a meritorious action for Croatians because there was not room for Serbs on that territory.

On June 26, 1899, Pachu continues: A Croatian mob together with Croatian clergymen threw eggs and rocks at men and women alike. The mob shouted against "Vallach's priests" and "Vallach breed." The reason for the demonstration? Serbs had dared to arrange a Serbian celebration in Zagreb. Young Stjepan Radich condemned the demonstrations, and at a trial against Serbs he called the demonstrations "swine" performances.

In 1900 a Catholic congress was held in Zagreb. The archbishop of Sarajevo, Dr. J. Shadler, read a report that openly encouraged Catholic Croats to physically exterminate Serbs. He said that this world, including us, dear to our Croatia, exists only for Christ's own. "We have to do anything as Christ's right men. Christ himself razed and destroyed many cities, people, and kingdoms because he did not find his real right men." Shadler publicly invited genocide, particularly against Orthodox Serbs who live in the "Croatian homeland."

The head of the clero-fascist coalition was the new bishop of Zagreb, Ante Bauer. That coalition executed many bestial crimes against Serbs during World War I.

In 1902, demonstrations lasted for three days. The Croats' actions against Serbs were wild. Their shops, houses, and schools were attacked, destroyed, burned, and plundered. Serbian employees in Croatian shops were laid off.

In 1909 in Zagreb, trials against Adam Pribicevich and fifty-two other Serbs were held against Serbs as "great traitors." Falsified documents were used against the accused, and witnesses like Djordje Mastich were bribed. The verdicts against Serbs in Croatia became a European scandal. Under European pressure the verdicts were suspended.[4]

After their early settlements, the Serbs in Croatia had continued their own spiritual life. The uniats caused their national conscience to be lost. The Orthodox church preserved her status among Serbian people, although Serb Orthodox schools were mostly forbidden and children were educated in Croatian schools. (Now and then the Serbian church was freed from the Catholic pressure—this depended greatly on whether Serbs were waging war with the Austrian army against the Turkish aggressor.)

In 1912, according to Croatian statistics, there were twenty-one Serbian newspapers in Croatia. They were all banned during Titoists' rule. The influence of Serbian literature and education was spread through the entire Serbian land, including Croatia.

Adam Pribicevich was one of the most popular Serbs in Croatia. His brother Svetozar was a politician and publicist along with Bogdan Medakovich and Dushan Popovich. Nikola Tesla, born in Lika, Croatia, the son of a Serbian priest, became a world-renowned scientist. He immigrated to the United States, where he developed and applied his scientific talent.

Holy See and Concordat

Pope Pius XII was a cunning politician. More than anyone else from outside Germany, he helped Hitler come into power. He allied himself with the Catholics of Italy, Germany, and Spanish fascists. Later the pope was a central figure in leading the cold war against communism. He also played a paramount role in transferring the Catholic church into a global political institution.

Pope Pius XII should not have been involved with the Black Orchestra or Technica (tendency for revival of postwar intermarium). If he were involved then the Vatican obstructed justice, did it not? Should the pope with his clergy from the Saint Congregation of Cardinals of the Eastern Institute act in a Christian way, to save rather than to destroy the lives of innocent persons like Serbs, Jews, and Gypsies who were outlawed in Croatia for the entire four years of Ustashe bestiality? Did anyone hear the pope publicly raise his voice against such inhumane acts against Jews? Did he try to find a way of smuggling them out instead of smuggling out Nazi criminals? Was it obstruction of justice when all means were used to save Nazis?

In the Balkans the Vatican's age-old policy was to convert Orthodox people there to the Catholic faith. If this was not true, why had religious war in Yugoslavia flared up in such proportion that the human race could not recall anything similar happening before?

Serbian politicians were short-sighted and unable to cope with Yugoslav reality. Yugoslav King Alexander's premiers, Jevtich and Stojadinovich, had prepared a draft of a concordat for approval by the Yugoslav National Assembly. The relationship between the Yugoslav state and the other churches was regulated by law, except with the Roman Catholic church, which had to be regulated by a concordat. The proposed concordat favored the Roman Catholic church over Serbian Orthodoxy, which caused great worries among Serbs.[5]

In July 1935 a concordat was signed between the Holy See and Yugoslavia. It was signed for the Vatican by Cardinal Pacelli, state secretary of the Holy See, who on March 2, 1939, became Pope Pius XII (1939-1958). According to Article I of the concordat, Yugoslavia was announced as terra mission (missionary country), where the Catholic mission would be freely promoted. This was the first time the Vatican had gained unlimited rights in a European or non-European country for missionary activities.

The concordat was not approved because of the strong reaction against it by the Serbian church and Serbs as a whole.[6]

Referring to the failure to sign the concordat, on December 15, 1937, the Holy Father Pope Pius XII stated: "I'm deeply convinced that the day will come when many souls will regret that the great gift of goodness was not accepted. It was offered to their country by the representatives of Jesus Christ. This was not done solely for the ecclesiastical and religious unity of the nation but also for its social and political accord, though we resolutely reject politics as our aim or our aspiration."

The prophecy of the Holy Father was realized—after only three and a half years, knives were sharpened by the Ustashe to use against Serbs. In 1939 Prince Paul visited Archbishop Stepinac a few times, begging him for help in reaching an agreement between Serbs and Croats. No Serb, neither diplomat nor politician, scientist nor clergyman, noticed that Stepinac hated Serbs. In 1941, during a Belgrade demonstration against the Nazi Pact of March 25-27, Archbishop Stepinac recorded in his diary: "Serbs and Croats are two worlds. They will never unite until only one is still alive." Those words were written by the head of the Croatian Catholic church!

Consequences for Serbs of Ante Starcevich's Racist Theory

In the former Austro-Hungarian territory, Croatian, Slavonian, and Dalmatian Serbs were only wanted in time of war, as canon fodder in the struggle against enemies; in peacetime Serbs were unwanted under the pretext that they disturbed the others. In 1918 when Yugoslavia was founded, Serbs, then popular and strong, were desirable and respected because Croat and Slovene national interests dictated the use of demagoguery.

Throughout their thorny history, Serbs only wanted to live on their own land, not to be against others or against themselves. But Serbs in Croatia, Slavonia, and Dalmatia in order to preserve their cross and their identity became a sword in the hands of others.

Croatian racism appeared more than half a century before the appearance of German racism. Dr. Ante Starcevich prompted genocidal tendencies against the "satanic, monstrous Serbs." To be exact, in the ISC the annihilation of the Serbs was not only motivated by religious-biological bigotry but also by racial genocide. Croatian chauvinists tried to represent Serbs as a lower race, an "impure breed" with criminal dispositions (cud).

In the second half of the nineteenth century, Dr. Ante Starcevich introduced his racist theory, characterizing Slavo Serbs as "the slave breed, beasts more filthy than anyone else." According to him, there are three levels of human development: animal stage, common sense, and intellect. Slavo Serbs had not yet reached the lowest level.

Starcevich went to a further extreme when he said the history of the entire middle ages had belonged to the Croatians! Serbian mythical heroes Obilich and Marko Kraljevich were Croats, not Serbs! Starcevich's motto was "Croatia to Croatians," the same as Tudjman's pressures today. He could not accomplish anything against the stronger Croatian aggressor, Austro-Hungary. Therefore he turned against a less powerful target, Serbs, whom he accused of being "responsible for somebody else's guilt" (scapegoating). Thus began the satanization of Serbs, which was the embryo of later genocide.

Starcevich was called the "father of the Homeland" by Croats, but he was not the father for Serbs on Croatian territory. He was the wickedest spirit that could ever be imagined. Hitler could sooner be called the father of the Jewish nation than Starcevich could be called the father of the Serbian people. It would be ironic to hang the epithet only upon him when the Starcevich Rights party was followed by the lawyer Josip Frank (1844-1911) and down the line to Pavelich and Tudjman. They hated Serbs pathologically. A nightmare of Serbophobia was spread. Genocide has been alive ever since, though it was closed up as in a bottle, waiting to burst out.

In those horrible years, in 1914 and especially 1941-1945, the entire arsenal of profanity and tirades against Serbs was resurrected in a wild and tragic simplicity that resulted in the breaking of skulls and gouging out of eyes. Not only were Serbs attacked but also "Poscrbice" (Yugoslav-oriented Croats). The written slogan was "Death to all Serbian traitors and their Poscrbice."

Racism is present in Croatia today as the Croatian president, Dr. Tudjman, Tito's general, states with satisfaction that his wife is "neither Jewish nor Serbian."

Zidland Polar states that the Croats had bad luck with Europeans and historians. To the contrary, the great Serbophiles were Chech Shapharic, Franjo Mikloshich, Medo Pucich from Dubrovnik, and the historian Constantin Jurichek. Among the Serbophiles was also Constantin Porfirogenit, Byzantine tzar (905-959), who wrote about the migration of South Slavs, Serbs, and Croats in the Balkans. Porfirogenit's sources were the oldest ones interpreting settlements of South Slavs.

In the middle of the nineteenth century, Austria wanted to move toward the east (the Balkans) with an imperialistic goal that was embraced by the pope and the Vatican for spreading Catholicism.

Vienna-Vatican interest in the Balkans was embraced by Starcevich, who hoped to form a "Great Croatia" that would include Bosnia and Hercegovina.

The idea of the genocide of the Serbian people was begun by Starcevich and the Catholic clergy. For Starcevich, Serbs were nothing but Orthodox Croats!

Croatian Sovereignty of Thirty Days

Miroslav Krleza, a Croat, states that in a period of eight hundred years, Croatia had only thirty days of real sovereignty, which is the entire Croatian balance. His book *A Few Words about Petit Bourgeois History* explains it. The period of thirty days occurred from October 29, 1918, when the Croats broke an agreement with Hungary, until December 1, 1918, when Croatia united with Serbia.[7]

Adil Zulfikarpashich, a Muslim, asks if Yugoslavia could exist as one federal entity. Says he, referring to the complicated Yugoslav drama, we are so intertwined that no power could demarcate our borders and satisfy both sides, on the left and on the right. Consequently, either destiny or history assigned for us would probably have had tragic results. Therefore, we cannot separate from each other without great difficulty.

How do some representatives in the Croatian ruling party behave today? Prof. Ivo Jelich resigned as a representative in Tudjman's parliament. Vladimir Sheks sent word: "Mr. Jelich, you got into parliament through the party and also through the party you could get out." Jelich replied, "Such a statement you may wrap around your hat!" Jelich further continued: "God creates men equal, including Serbs and Jews, regardless of their religion and ethnic background."

Jelich continued his article, in the newspaper *Borba*, saying his grandfather had lost his life in World War I, which had seriously affected his father. In World War II he lost his father and his uncle, which affected himself. Therefore, he sent word to all people he was not interested in who stands better with a rifle on their shoulders because he thinks nobody with common sense needs it.

In 1918, Should South Slavs Be Unified in One State?

According to the London Pact in 1915 a major portion of the Adriatic coast was assigned to Italy. Meanwhile, the Serbian government persuaded its allies to nullify the London Agreement and add the entire Adriatic coast to a new South Slav state. The Croats certainly forgot it. Under a favorable climate an agreement was reached in 1917 on the island of Corfu between Pashich, the head of the Serbian government, and the "Yugoslav Committee" from the Austro-Hungarian Empire.

In 1918 on the eve of the South Slavs' unification, politicians from the western regions (Croatia and Slovenia) said that "in Yugoslavia lives one people composed of three tribes. They speak one language, so a man at the foot of Triglav Mountain and Zagorje could easily understand a peasant from Shumadija (Serbia) and those who live at the foot of Mount Lovcen." However, later those politicians became bitter adversaries of their own deeds.

Dr. Ante Trumbich, a Croatian politician, said, "Serbia had proved ready to sacrifice her own independence in order to form one South Slav common state of old Serbs, Croats, and Slovenes. And, doing so, she attained the absolute right to be called the Yugoslav Piedmont."

In 1926 when Trumbich was asked why he had signed the Corfu declaration, his answer was simple: He wanted to save Croatia from being buried under Austro-Hungarian rubble after the war was over. Was it really an illusion, as events later proved, that there was "one people with three tribes"?

The Croatian sculptor Meshtrovich stated: It is not important who is Serb or who is Croat; though he is a Croat, it is the same! In 1941 the same Meshtrovich became a strong supporter of Dr. Ante Pavelich, who led racial and religious exterminations against Serbs, Jews, and Gypsies. Could this be called a chameleon-like metamorphosis?

On the other side of the spectrum, the influential members of the Croatian Catholic church, except for a very few including Bishop Strosmajer, have been faithful followers and executors of Austro-Hungarian policy before and after World War I regardless that she was defeated in that war. The political campaign was taken from the Austro-Hungarian arsenal, like "Great Serbian bourgeoisie," "Great Serbian imperialism," "Great Serbian hegemony," "Belgrade capitol," "Great Serbian unitarism," and the like.

It is necessary to state that in 1903 a conspiracy against Serbia was organized in the Austro-Hungarian Empire after the assassination of Alexander Obrenovich. Serbia had become disturbing to the Viennese palace because Serbia was an independent, well-organized democratic state. From the Vienna centers, slanders were spread against Serbia through Europe by the Austro-Hungarian press. In fact, in 1941 that conspiracy against Serbia was transformed into a conspiracy against Serbs as racial and religious adversaries!

During World War I the Allies offered Serbia Vojvodina, Bosnia and Hercegovina, Montenegro, and part of today's Croatia—that is, two-thirds of today's Yugoslav territory as a reward for her great contributions to the victorious end of the war: Serbia lost 28 percent of her population in that war. According to official data submitted by Serbia at the peace conference in Paris in 1919, Serbia lost 1,247,435 people, of whom 402,435 were military and 845,000 were civilians.

During those four years, Croatian and Slovenian conscripts and some volunteers fought in the Austro-Hungarian army. When Croatian and Slovenian politicians realized the Allies would win the war, they rushed to realign themselves on the winning side. They began intensively lobbying the Serbian government and Allied capitols for the formation of a unique South Slav state on the ruins of the Austro-Hungarian Empire.

On December 1, 1918, representatives of Croats and Slovenes came to Belgrade to press for immediate unification with Serbia to defend their national interests. They wanted to preserve their territorial and linguistic integrity before the victorious Allies convened in Versailles to sign the peace treaty. Therefore, on December 1, 1918, the representative of the Croatian Peasant party (CPP), Dr. Ante Pavelich, in front of the regent Alexander read a proclamation that Croatia was ready to unify with the Serbian kingdom under the mace of the Karadjordjevich dynasty. In fact, Serbia and Montenegro entered Yugoslavia as sovereign and independent states as well as winners in the war. The other parts of the new state came from the territory of the defeated Austro-Hungarian monarchy or the Ottoman empire.

Croatia benefitted the most from the unification, while Serbia lost her democracy and parliamentary system. Among the benefits to Croatia were:

1. Croatia overnight changed her political status from defeated to victorious.

2. By that act she no longer had to pay war reparations that would have been due from the Austro-Hungarian Empire, on the losing side.

3. The border was not drawn between Serbia and Croatia as had been recommended by the French president Clemanceau to the Serbian president Nikola Peshich. This was an inexcusable act for which Serbs would pay dearly later. In other words, if the borders had been drawn correctly at that time, the catastrophic war and revolution inside Yugoslavia in 1991-1993 might well have been avoided.

As soon as the unification of Yugoslavia was realized, a great historical and political misunderstanding arose. Croats wanted to organize Yugoslavia as a federation, while Stojan Protich, a Serbian politician, pretended to organize the historical entities with wide autonomies. If regent Alexander, pragmatically speaking, really wanted the South Slav unification and was able to read correctly the Croatian political mind, he should first have abdicated his throne and then organized the state on a federation base. The Croats would only be satisfied to form their own independent state, as they did in 1941 under the auspices of Nazi Germany and Fascist Italy. It was obvious that the Croats had accepted Yugoslavia as a necessary lesser evil to evade border demarcations with Serbs. It was a wise move for them, was it not?

As soon as the Yugoslav unification was accomplished, Croatians pressed for solving their national problem. Their separatist tendencies and ambitions brought the new state to a political crisis. Nine administrative banovinas were introduced, which was an obvious concession that was the precedent for a serious concession when a Croatian banovina was formed in 1939 (corpus separatum).

All Yugoslav nationalities, except Serbs, formed political parties along ethnic lines. In order to preserve the Yugoslav entity Serbs were forced to go step by step to solve the national problem imposed by Croatia. The Yugoslav state was called by her enemies "the prison of the people," and her formation was an artificial creation of the Versailles agreement. Indeed, if Yugoslavia was a prison for some, it was a veritable graveyard for Serbs from 1941 up to the current time. According to Prof. Dr. Smilja Avramov, of the victims of World War II in Yugoslavia, 95 percent were Serbs.[8]

Yugoslav "Tragedy Within a Tragedy"

Sadly for all concerned, it is time to confront the darkest history that ever existed in Croatia and her Catholic church. By this is meant the genocide against Serbs, Jews, and Gypsies, which according to the number of victims and the cruelty of their tortures and executions can be called "the most monstrous events in current history."[9] In April of 1941 the so-called Independent State of Croatia (ISC) by Nazi and Fascist bayonets and cannons was formed. The head of that puppet government was Dr. Ante Pavelich.

In 1927 Pavelich said Croats could not coexist with the Orthodox, who were "rough, savage, and ruthless Serbs." Croatians possess "a richness of western culture, Latin and German culture, Italian humanistic culture, and German romanticism!"

On November 11, 1940, before Yugoslavia was attacked by the Nazis, Croatian intellectuals from Zagreb sent a letter to Adolf Hitler. They asked him for the creation of a new "Croatian state" in Hitler's "New Europe." If he agreed, they assured him with enclosed documentation that it would not be a state of unpopular Slavs but a state of real Goths. (Both Hitler and Rozenburg had a negative opinion of Slavs. Therefore, to please the Germans, the theory was born among the Croats that they were not Slavs but Goths. This theory was repeated during the mass movement [maspok] in

1971.) The signers of the letter concluded by referring to a close relationship between Croatian and German people based on blood kinship and similar culture and history. Was this pure treason committed by Zagreb Croatian intellectuals in regard to their Yugoslav country?

Tito and his cohorts bore the guilt and responsibility for later Croats becoming vampires of neofascism in Croatia!

According to Hermann Neubacher, Hitler said that Serbs were not Communist-oriented. Serbs are people who possess great statesmanship ability. Therefore, I have serious reason not to encourage those people in their ambitions, concluded Hitler.

Also, Ribbentrop says that Germany had waged war in the Balkans to destroy, once and forever, the Serbian center of resistance. Therefore, we don't have any interest in inflaming again the great Serbian spirit.

The most bitter terror and slaughter of Serbs occurred in 1941 and 1942. From June 24-28, 1941, on Saint Vitus Day (Vidovdan), over 100,000 Serbs in Bosnia, Hercegovina, Dalmatia, Lika, Croatia, and Srem were slaughtered. For four days in Bihac over 9,000 people were slaughtered when the Ustashe paid a Gypsy-Muslim rabble for an hour of murder 50 dinars, one kilogram of mutton, and one liter of brandy!

In Banja Luka the Ustashe committed horrible atrocities, among others killing five Orthodox priests and brutally torturing Bishop Platon by nailing horseshoes to his feet. The Roman Catholic bishop Garich did not lift a finger to protect his brother in Christ! For four years of Ustashe pogroms no Croatian Catholic clergy or civilian authority, except Dr. Prvoslav Grizogono, publicly condemned such bestiality, similar to the cannibalism committed by men at the lowest levels of civilization.

The well-known Croatian Communist Ante Ciliga says, "We Croats have long accused Serbs as Balkan peoples and murderers, while we Croats showed ourselves uncomparably worse and more bloodthirsty than they ever were."

Dr. Andrija Artukovich, minister of the interior under Pavelich, known as the Duce and Croatian Fuhrer who later became minister of justice, said on July 13, 1943, that the creation of the ISC was "the expression of an ancient dream of the Croatian people." In February 1990 Dr. Tudjman, currently president of the Croatian government, expressed an opinion similar to Artukovich's. At his trial in Zagreb in April 1986 Artukovich stated: "The moral principles and laws that I followed were identical with the principles of the Catholic church. There is no difference between the latter and my principles." Andrija Artukovich was known as the "butcher of the Balkans." He committed the greatest number of war crimes in the period from April 17, 1941, to October 10, 1942, and from April 29, 1943, to October 9, 1943.[10]

Massacre in Glina Serbian Orthodox Church

The reader will find in Appendix B at the end of this chapter the full statement of a rare survivor of a terrible massacre at the Glina Serbian Orthodox Church, an event typical of the crimes committed under Artukovich and Pavelich.

The world's history does not record a more horrifying sight in a religious context than that executed by the Ustashe against the Serbian civilian population in the Serbian Orthodox church in Glina in 1941.[11] At one time 1,200 innocent people in that church were slaughtered. Alija Konjhodzich, Muslim journalist, stated, "All together there were slaughtered in just that one church about three thousand Serbs."

The first massacre in Glina Church, when 300 innocent Serbs were executed, took place between May 12-13, 1941. The main crime was at the beginning of August 1941, on Saint Elie's Day. In the church Serbs were "proselytzed" by Ustashe daggers. The Ustashe had invited Serbs to come in Vrgin Most under a pretext for conversion. Twenty-two hundred Serbs arrived there. The Ustashe surrounded them and drove them away to Sokol Hall (an athletic hall). About 400 Serbs succeeded in running away.

Before the major genocide in the Orthodox church in Glina, on June 2, 1941, in Nova Gradishka, the minister of justice, Dr. Milovan Zanich, stated: This state is only for Croats, not for anyone else. There are no ways nor means we Croats will not use to make our country truly ours, and cleanse her from all Orthodox Serbs. All those who came into our country 300 years ago must disappear. We don't hide our intention. It is the policy of our state, and during its promotion we shall do nothing else but follow the principles of the Ustashe.

Zanich was right. To mention just the following: The Italian occupier at Dubrovnik took pictures of an Ustasha wearing two "necklaces," one a string of gouged-out eyes, the other a string of tongues of murdered Serbs. Croatian priests, often friars, took an oath to fight with dagger and gun for the "triumph of Christ and Croatia."

On July 6, 1941, Dr. Mirko Puk, a native of Glina and Pavelich's minister, said, "There is only one God and one people who rule, and they are the Croats."

In that same month Stavko Kvaternik said, "All Serbs are Communists, from the patriarch to the last peasant."

Cardinal Gutich from Banja Luka vowed he would be an iron broomstick and he most definitely would not allow anyone to come pleading to him for his enemies. Dr. Fra. Srecko Perich, a Franciscan from the Livno monastery, called upon his brother Croats to go forth and slaughter all Serbs. First they should kill his sister who was married to a Serb and then deal with all other Serbs in the same way. When they finished that job they were to come to him in his church, where he would hear their confession and give them communion and then all their sins would be forgiven. Friar Filipovich, a Jesuit from the Petricevac monastery near Banja Luka, said, "You just kill, and I will absolve your sins."

The Roman Catholic church was embroiled in all these antireligious movements of the state authorities and even of individuals, so that instead of demonstrating Christian love, tolerance, and compassion towards the unprotected and helpless victims it sent its Ustashe clergymen to murder unnamed Serbs and their children with knives and bombs and proclaimed from its pulpits: "Kill them and the church will absolve your sins."

On November 12, 1941, Muslims from Banja Luka sent a memorandum to the Croatian Ustashe government, stating that Serbs in the ISC were being subjugated without "precedent in the history of any people."

On March 1, 1942, Slovenian Catholic priests sent a letter to Belgrade, to Slovenian archbishop Dr. Josip Ujcich. The letter stated that in the Slovenian Catholic church they did not kill bishops or clergymen, neither were their bodies thrown into rivers. In their land they did not burn and destroy churches, nor did they kill the faithful during holy mass. They did not slaughter the population of whole villages overnight as cattle were slaughtered. They did not kill the fathers of families in the doorways of their homes before the very eyes of their wives and children, and they did not bury people alive. (All those references were to deeds of the Croatian Ustashe and the Croatian people and clergy.)

Was Jasenovac Indeed the Yugoslav Dachau?

Jasenovac was a Nazi-Fascist concentration camp in Yugoslavia, the third largest in occupied Europe.

It is reasonable to state here again the words of Dr. Mladen Ivekovich, a Croat and an inmate of Jasenovac: "There is not a pen capable of describing the horror and terror of the atmosphere at Jasenovac. It surpasses any human fantasy. Imagine Hell, the Inquisition, a terror more dreadful than any that ever before existed anywhere, run by bloodthirsty wild animals whose most hidden and disgusting instincts had come to the surface in a way never before seen in human beings—and still you have not said enough."[12]

The ISC was unique in occupied Europe as it destroyed a great number of Serbian cultural-historical monuments and various documents.

The aim of the Ustashe regime was not only to destroy Serbs in all domains of human creativity but also to completely exterminate the Serbian ethos in Croatia as well as to erase the Serbs' history and their past.

In Jasenovac, the Yugoslav Dachau, the Ustashe brought icons and frescoes of Serbian medieval times from the neighboring Orthodox churches.

From those sacred objects the Ustashe made a fire to warm up the camp. In the winter of 1941-1942, while Ustashe were killing Serbs, they turned their bloody axes also on holy objects, as if to destroy the events they represented: Palm Sunday, Resurrection of Christ, Transfiguration, Descent of Holy Spirit, etc.

The icons and other church relics were from the temples: Novska, Okucani, Paklenici, Hrvatska Dubica, Bogicevac, Nova Gradishka, Gredjani, Gradina, and Ralic. Their holy treasures were burned in the furnace of the camp commandant, Sotona/Devil Miroslav Majstorovich-Filipovich, who was previously a chaplain of the monastery Petricevac near Banja Luka.

Nearly fifty years have passed since those crimes were committed. Neither the Croatian Catholic church nor Croatian political leaders have admitted guilt for what was done in the name of one nation and "their historical aspirations." Crimes were committed by one of the most monstrous products, called Fascist Endehazija, ever developed.

What about Jasenovac, the "largest Serbian underground city," which for decades has been shrouded in a well-thought-out plan of silence despite the tragic experiences of an unprecedented genocide? Both the Catholic church in Croatia and Croatian secular leaders have chosen silence, and they act as if their consciences are clean while others are condemned.

The silence about the committed crimes is sometimes harder to take than the crimes themselves. Those crimes have created a bloody abyss between two nations with different religious affiliations and divergent political views. Silence can neither calm the restless conscience of innocent Croats nor comfort the relatives of the one million resting in cemeteries.

Says Esref Bradnjevich, who was an inmate of Jasenovac, in about three months over a hundred thousand people were killed there. Jasenovac became a hell in which people died like flies.

To mention just one of the thousands of reports from the occupiers during World War II:

On March 16, 1944, German SS general Ernest Fick sent a letter to SS Reichfuehrer Heinrich Himmler in Berlin, stating that the Ustashe in the ISC had taken approximately 600,000 to 700,000 "politically undesirable" people into concentration camps and slaughtered them "in the Balkan way. They are fighting against Chetniks and Partisans. They consider themselves as SS."[13]

Vladimir Dedijer, Tito's biographer, states that Hebrang, Stevo Krajacich, and some other leading Croatian Communists forbade the preservation of buildings, including the torture chambers of the monstrous Jasenovac, contrary to what was done in other civilized countries like postwar Germany and Poland. That decision was made, without the slightest doubt, with the full knowledge of the Yugoslav dictator Josip Broz Tito.

Christian Miller, a Swiss journalist, stated that just in Jasenovac 750,000 Serbs were slaughtered in the most barbaric way, among them tens of thousands of children. Also, 240,000 Orthodox faithful were converted under threat of death (umorstva). These monstrous acts were done not only in front of his eyes, but with the active support of the Croatian archbishop Aloiz Stepinac, a close associate of the chief of state Pavelich and with the full knowledge of the Roman Curia.

In his two-volume book *The Fall of the Yugoslav Kingdom* Gen. Velimir Terzich, at one time Tito's chief of staff, says that in Jasenovac camp alone over one million Serbs were killed, which nobody has then denied. The thousands of documents, eye-witness reports, and writings of prominent Croatian authors and over fifty world authorities testify to the Croatian Ustashe genocide. (See, for example, the dramatic story of a young boy who was a prisoner in Jasenovac, found in Appendix A at the end of the chapter.) To refute these facts we'll mention here just two Croats who stubbornly cling to their own interpretation of the "facts."

Ivan Supek, a Zagreb professor, claimed that according to his statistics, about 50,000 hostages were killed in Jasenovac camp, most of them left-wing Croats, then Serbs, Gypsies, and Jews. All other statistics were a "ten-fold exaggeration" with the purpose of forcing reparations and war compensation.

In February 1981, Cardinal Kuharich gave a sermon during the commemoration of the twenty-first anniversary of the death of Archbishop Stepinac. According to *Le Monde* of Paris, the cardinal stated that "some say Catholic priests were commanders of that human slaughterhouse, which is a shameless lie!" The purpose of such irresponsible accusations was to make Cardinal Stepinac seem responsible for the 40,000 from the camp in Jasenovac.

Dr. Nikola Nikolich, a Croat, was an eyewitness of crimes committed in the concentration camp of Jasenovac. He was interned in that camp, where he practiced his profession as best he could under the circumstances. He wrote the book *Jasenovac Camp*, published in Zagreb in 1948. He recorded one story heard from an Ustasha murderer about some Vukashin from Klepci, near Chapljine. The entire Vukashin family was slaughtered. First Vukashin was cutting wood; then he was sent to Jasenovac. An Ustasha ordered him to shout, "Long live Paglavnik!" Vukashin refused to do so. The Ustasha cut off one of his ears and ordered him a second time to say "Long live Paglavnik." Vukashin refused a second time and the Ustashe cut off his other ear. After a third refusal, the Ustasha cut off his nose. The fourth time the Ustasha told him if he did not say it he would cut out his heart. How did Vukashin react? He said calmly, "Continue to do your job, young man." Did Archbishop Kuharich and his subordinate Catholic clergy ever hear or read that horrible story?

In 1961 in Bosanska Dubica a three-member committee of the War Veterans Organization was given the task of carrying out anthropological and archeological studies of the concentration camp in Jasenovac. The report of the committee referring to Gradina states that they could not find a brochure allegedly written by the ex-inmate of the Jasenovac camp, Dr.

Nikola Nikolich. He was then living in Zagreb. The committee wanted to read his book and use it as a basis for their study. But the book was not available.

At the end of 1945 in Zagreb, Djordje Milisha published the book *A Place of Torture—The Inferno of Jasenovac*. The book was exhibited in a shop window and then was quickly withdrawn. Why? Milisha was accused of "jeopardizing the national interests" and doing "moral damage" and even of "instigating crime." Milisha's book strongly criticized the Catholic clergy for direct responsibility for the Ustashe's crimes.[14]

What was the fate of Dr. Victor Novak's book, *Magnum Crimen*? In December 1948 the *National Daily–arodni List* in Zagreb reported that Novak's book had been burned at a Catholic stake!

Bakarich favored oblivion for the genocide of Jasenovac, stating that he would support forgiveness. Yet the harm caused by those criminals is unforgettable![15]

Did the Vatican Bless Serb Genocide?

According to Vatican documents, it is irrefutable that cardinals Tisserant and Maljonea gave directives to Croatian bishoprics:

1. The first document contains directives of Cardinal Tisserant, head of the Congregation for the Eastern Church, of July 17, 1941, to Archbishop Stepinac. In that official document, the Congregation for the Eastern Church proclaimed Serbs in the ISC as "renegades of the Catholic church." That view was in accord with that of the priest Dr. Drajanovich, because all such directives were directly or indirectly coming from the Vatican.

2. A second document of January 25, 1942 states that the secretary of the Holy See had replied to a protest note from the legation of the Yugoslav kingdom to the Holy See No. 1/2 from January 24 in regard to the forceful coercion of Serbs in Pavelich's ISC. In his reply, the secretary of the Holy See showed how deeply he was interested in defending Ustashe crimes. That document had considered all Serbs outside of Serbia on "Croatian linguistic territory" as "Croatian dissidents." It is important to mention that those "Croatian dissidents" allegedly returned en masse to the faith of their fathers!

3. A third document of February 21, 1942 contains the directives of Cardinal Maljonea, secretary of the Holy See, to Croatian bishops to accelerate the process of Serb conversion. Also it was mentioned that the word "Orthodox" should be replaced by the words "renegade and schismatic."

There is no doubt that during the period of troubled waters for Serbs during the Yugoslav occupation the Vatican had promoted forceful Serb conversion. The Ustashe were induced for Serb conversion. The old pope's thesis of proselytism was restored on the border zone between Eastern and Western churches. In a word, the conversion of Orthodox people has been a main goal of the Catholic mission on the Catholic linguistic territory. Neither the Vatican nor the Catholic church ever claimed any responsibility for the atrocities committed in the ISC. They kept silent, which practically meant approval. Serb conversions had been fully applied during World War II. As was shown previously, those attempts succeeded in many areas where Serbs were living.

It is worth mentioning that at the end of World War I, Bishop Antun Mahnich had the idea of unifying all Serbs, Croats, and Slovenes in a Catholic state under the mace of the Habsburg dynasty. He thought the field was ripe on the east for a Catholic harvest.

During World War II, Monsignor Janko Shimrak was president of the committee for proselytism. He instigated the Ustashe to Serb conversion by emphasizing that their work was legitimate and in harmony with the Holy See's will and the Saint Congregation of Cardinals of the Eastern church. Shimrak said it had taken "a thousand years" for Jesus' wish for "schisms" to be destroyed—that is, Orthodoxy, which Archbishop Stepinac called "the greatest evil in Europe." For his "accomplishments" Shimrak was decorated by Ante Pavelich.

According to Slovenian scientist Dr. Niko Zupanich and Serbian historian Dr. Aleksa Ivich, the settlers of Zumberk were once Orthodox Serbs. In the second half of the seventeenth century they were forced to accept the Uniat. By changing their religion, Serbs were also denationalized.

In 1751 and 1752 it was forbidden for Orthodox clergy to interfere in the internal affairs of their congregations, and Orthodox bishops were not allowed to make canonical visits to their flocks. Serbs in Zumberk in particular were forced to accept the Uniat. Vienna uncompromisingly (as long as there was no immediate danger from the Turks) executed Roman policies. The identical aim of the Austrian palace and the Holy See—to proselytize Orthodox Serbs into Roman Catholicism—was vigorously executed, especially during the rule of Maria Thera (1717-1780), queen of Hungary and Bohemia.

Did Ante Pavelich Become a Protégé of Vatican and British Intelligence?

The power of Ante Pavelich during World War II in the ISC was comparable to that of the German fuhrer, although he was brought into power by Italian Fascists and German Nazis, who exercised the real authority in satellite Croatia.

In 1929 Pavelich went into exile for the first time. During this time he built up a clandestine network of Ustashe terrorists (called "a crowd of barbarians and cannibals").

In April 1941 Pavelich was received by Pope Pius XII (called "the German pope"). The British Foreign Office was outraged that the pope would receive such a notorious criminal. The pope was stamped as "the greatest moral coward of our age."

Brigadier Maclean, head of the British mission with Tito, said the ISC government was a dictatorship on Fascist or Nazi lines, with Pavelich in the role of Paglavnik or fuhrer and the Ustashe as his Praetorian guards. In addition to the Ustashe, who formed units of their own corresponding to Hitler's SS, the new Croatian state boasted its own army and air force, both under German occupational control.

Pavelich's accession to power was followed by a reign of terror unprecedented even in the Balkans. He had many old scores to settle. There were widespread massacres and atrocities—of Serbs, first of all, especially in Bosnia, where there was a large Serb population; then, to please his Nazi masters, Jews; and, finally, when he could catch them, Communists and Communist sympathizers.

Racial and political persecution was accompanied by equally ferocious religious persecution. The Ustashe were fervent Roman Catholics. Now that they were at last in a position to do so, they set about liquidating the Greek Orthodox church in their domain. Orthodox villages were sacked and pillaged and their inhabitants—old and young, men, women, and children alike—were massacred. Orthodox clergy were tortured and killed; Orthodox churches were desecrated and destroyed, or burned down with their screaming congregations inside (an Ustashe specialty, this). The Bosnian Moslems, equally fanatical and organized in special units by Pavelich and the Germans and helped by the Mufti of Jerusalem, joined in with gusto and a refined cruelty all of their own, delighting in the opportunity to massacre Christians of all denominations. (At last, the Croats were getting their own back after twenty years of Serbian domination.)[16]

Just one example of Ustashe barbarism: The Italian writer Curzio Malaparte interviewed Pavelich in Zagreb. "While he talked," Malaparte wrote, "I kept looking at a wicker basket at the right of the Paglovnik's desk. 'Oysters from Dalmatia?' I inquired. Ante Pavelich raised the lid of the basket and showed me the contents that looked like a mess of sticky, gelatinous oysters. He said with a tired, kindly smile, 'A gift from my loyal Ustashe. Forty pounds of human eyes.' "[17]

In 1942 Pavelich boasted that great deeds were being done by Croats and Germans together. "We can proudly say we succeeded in our attempt to break the Serb nation, which after the British is the most thick-headed, the most stubborn, and the most stupid!"[18]

What happened to Pavelich after he fled Yugoslavia in 1945? In May 1945 Pavelich left Croatia with 500 Catholic priests and entered Austria, where he hid under the name "Father Gomez" in Saint Gilgen's Catholic monastery near Salzburg in the British zone. When the Yugoslav Communist intelligence found out where Pavelich was, the Yugoslav authority asked the British authority in Austria for Pavelich's extradition, telling them exactly where Pavelich was lodging. The British refused to acknowledge anything about Pavelich at that time. However, the U.S. army's counterintelligence corps said their British ally had been lying all along. They knew exactly where Pavelich was!

The Roman Catholic clergy, most of them of Croatian extraction, protected Pavelich. In 1948 he succeeded in emigrating to Argentina through the "Ratline" channel. He took with him three things: a Papal blessing; looted gold and other precious objects from Serbs, Jews, and Gypsies; and an Ustashe programme.

Ater a failed assassination attempt against him, Pavelich moved to Spain, where he lived in a Franciscan monastery. On December 26, 1954, he died in a German hospital in Madrid, after receiving Holy Communion with the personal blessing of Pope Pius XII.

Ustashe crimes then were well known, especially to the Vatican. But Pavelich was a faithful Catholic and a strong proponent of the Vatican and two popes, Pius XI and Pius XII, whose politics were based on theological traditionalism, "Roma eterna," and the infallibility of Catholocism as the only right religion.

Ideologically, the Vatican was definitely against communism. However, if Orthodoxy was in question, Rome supported communism as a means to destroy the Orthodox countries of the East. Under such a pretext ties were maintained between the Vatican and Josip Broz Tito.[19]

The British intelligence not only sheltered Pavelich; they smuggled from the Ustashe at least two trucks of gold. They helped the Ustashe make a mass escape from Rimini and other camps. The British intelligence was also involved in the Ratline operation, smuggling Nazi criminals to escape justice for the crimes they had committed. That was contrary to the statement made July 30, 1943, by President Roosevelt that no neutral or Allied country would dare give asylum to war criminals of Axis powers and their satellites. The territories of neutral countries should not become refuges for war criminals. Sweden was the first country to react favorably to Roosevelt's statement. She would not allow any such persons to enter! After the war was over, did even the United States respect President Roosevelt's statement?

In 1948, Britain secretly demanded an end to further investigation against Nazi war criminals, when they found cover in Intermarium, Prometheus, and NTS. The British government contacted the Vatican to help her resettle "grey" Nazis, and asked America to help them sabotage the screening process of the Nazis.

In fact, behind the Nazis was the Vatican; behind the Vatican were the British; and possibly behind the British were the Communists as well.

The *London Times* stated that the United States has classified documents referring to Nazi criminals in order to protect all governments involved from certain embarrassment. Right after the war, France and Britain revived former Nazi organizations, and the intelligence agencies of France, Britain, Australia, Canada, Austria, West Germany, Italy, and the Vatican recruited former Nazi criminals. They recruited and funded them, and they helped about 30,000 of them immigrate! Most of the central governments of these countries were unaware of such intelligence activities.

Why the intelligence agencies of these countries acted as they did will be known when the embargo is lifted on those documents that are still classified.

The Criminal Role of Fra. Dr. Krunislav S. Draganovich

In 1932, on the recommendation of Sarajevo bishop Sharich, Fra. Krunislav Draganovich went to Rome as a cadet of St. Jeronime in the Eastern Institute. After three years of study he earned a doctoral degree.

Draganovich became a Croatian chauvinistic star and as such he was the best known among the cadre at Eastern Institute in Rome. He was put in charge of Catholic-Orthodox relations in southern Slavic countries. His dissertation was "Massive Conversion of Catholics to Orthodoxy."[20] Material for his dissertation was found in the archives of the propaganda commission. Draganovich's dissertation centered on Orthodox people living in the Croatian linguistic domain. According to his interpretation, once Orthodox Serbs were Roman Catholics. Under unbearable pressures, many Catholics succumbed and abandoned their Catholic faith under duress. Some were either converted to Islam or Orthodoxy. However, the French cardinal Tisserant flatly denied that claim.

Before the war, Draganovich had been a professor of Catholic theology in Zagreb. He was enthusiastic about the formation of the ISC, even though it was under the control of Nazi Germany and Fascist Italy. He leaned toward the Ustashe apparatus "as a citizen according to the laws of the Lord."

Fra. Krunislav S. Draganovich was Archbishop Stepinac's liaison with the Vatican. He was also a member of the committee for the conversion of Serbs and a chaplain at Jasenovac. Witnesses confirmed that Draganovich took part in the bloody Kozara offensive against Serbs. In the Kozara region Draganovich forced requisitions during German and Ustashe offensives. Kurt Waldheim, current president of Austria, took part as a Nazi officer in that offensive and was rewarded by Pavelich.[21] As vice-president of the Ustashe committee for colonization Draganovich played a key role in the annihilation of the Serbian population in Kozara. Draganovich took various roles in the clero-Ustashe hierarchy. In order to promote relations between the Vatican and the ISC he issued a special edition, *Croatia Sacre*. That book was praised by Italian cardinal Frumasoni, which meant that clero-Ustashe propaganda received authoritative acknowledgment and praise.

During a bishops' conference from November 17-20, 1941, in Zagreb, Serb status in the ISC and their conversion were discussed. Dragonovich as an expert joined the "working commitee referring to the conversion of Greek Orthodox to the Catholic faith," which amounted to denationalizing Serbs and assimilating them as Croats.

On his return to Rome in 1943 Draganovich became a representative of the Ustashe Red Cross. His prestige was promoted by Stepinac, who was very influential among Vatican officials. He also maintained close contact with Axis diplomats at the Vatican. With the help of Pope Pius XII he established contact with senior officials of the Vatican Secretariat of State and Italian intelligence. Western intelligence knew Draganovich as "the golden priest" because he controlled much of the stolen Ustashe treasury. British colonel Johnson took two truckloads of gold to finance Krizari forces, while another portion was given to Draganovich to finance a terrorist network.[22] Draganovich was well treated by Western diplomats, by Americans in particular. His sophisticated network was expanded through Italy, Austria, and Germany. One British officer remembered Draganovich as being like "all Croats, very conspiratorial."

Following the rules set down by Vatican policy, Croatian missionaries were induced to form a pure Catholic country whose territory was already marked in the pope's Eastern Institute "on Croatian linguistic territory."

After the war Draganovich lived at the Vatican. Later he was chief of the National Catholic Voluntary organization at the Vatican, whose purpose was to aid immigration of persons who lacked passports.

Draganovich helped notorious Ustashe like Andrija Artukovich (Ustashe interior minister), emmigrate to the United States. He also helped Ante Pavelich, who impersonated a Franciscan priest, emmigrate to South America.

Draganovich's Ratline (so called because that was the CIA code name for the operation) was professional, so many war criminals found haven in Canada, Britain, and Australia. The personnel that ran the Ratline smuggling network were almost all Croatian Catholic priests.

The Croatian Ustashe stood as the avant garde of the Vatican toward Orthodoxy in the Balkans. They were ready to fight against Serbs who were allegedly tools of Russia for the conquest of the Balkans. The Vatican was delighted to hear it.

Dragonovich turned the Croatian Institute of Saint Girolamo into a sanctuary for Nazi criminals. Acting as a "charitable" organization, Saint Girolamo was a main conduit key for Nazi smuggling. Several religious orders, including Franciscans and Jesuits, supplied forged documents. Giovanni Montini, later Pope Paul VI, secretly supervised Draganovich's Ratline, and he lobbied Western authorities for the release of war criminals.

U.S. army intelligence staged a burglary at Draganovich's office and learned Pavelich had been living there before he immigrated to Argentina.

During the cold war Draganovich was a liaison officer to the intelligence services of Italy, Britain, and the United States.

One British officer says Draganovich was working closely with Italian intelligence by smuggling arms to Yugoslavia under cover of the Italian Red Cross. That was a political and military operation using money from drug smugglers and black marketeers to help Krizari volunteers cross the Yugoslav border. The volunteers were trained near Udine at an American training camp. Then Americans transported them armed to Austria, from where they intruded into Yugoslavia.[23]

During the Krizari operations, Yugoslav secret police obtained radio codes used by Krizari and all details of Krizari operations. In 1948 in Zagreb a "trial show" of captured Krizari was held. Those operations were carried out by Ustashe adherents, the Austrian government, and the Catholic church, with the purpose of forming a "sub-Danube" federation of all Catholic states in southeastern Europe.

Ratline Directed by Draganovich and Other Catholic Priests

Draganovich skillfully used San Girolamo for building a professional Nazi-smuggling system. He and other Croatian fanatics succeeded in making San Girolamo the main center of the Ratline.

According to one state department official, there were nearly two dozen covert Vatican relief and welfare organizations engaged in handling illegal emigration. Thus, the Holy See was engaged in illicitly obtaining Red Cross papers "under an alias or false nationality." Later, Americans learned the Vatican was willing to smuggle Fascists of every stripe, first Germans and then other non-German Nazi collaborators.

The summer residence of Pope Pius XII became a shelter for notorious Nazi criminals like Pavelich and Ference Vajta, a Hungarian Nazi. After the war Vajta served in the French and Vatican intelligence. Finally he told the Americans all the secrets he knew.

The Vatican recruited ex-Nazis to fight communism, while Communist agents had penetrated the Vatican-sponsored command structure from top to bottom. The Catholic church was waging a life and death struggle with communism. Therefore, the Catholic church used all means to justify its aims, like International Red Cross identity cards, Italian identity papers, false birth certificates, and even visas for their country of destination. In 1947, according to the American ambassador in Belgrade, the Vatican and Argentina made arrangements to settle Yugoslav quislings who had committed crimes during World War II. Later, unfortunately, the Vatican was helped by British and American intelligence in unjustified acts that were contrary to the principles and ideals of democratic and civilized societies.

In 1947, U.S. intelligence discovered the British-Vatican Nazi network and took it over under the code name "Operation Ratline." Then many of those Nazi criminals succeeded in penetrating Allied intelligence services.

On the other side, Soviet intelligence succeeded in effectively penetrating the Vatican's Nazi programs through the British spy Kim Philby. In fact, the Vatican played a symbiotic role, one knowingly trying to save the lives of Nazis, the other unknowingly supplying Soviet intelligence, primarily Stalin, with valuable data.

Among many collaborators, in addition to Father Draganovich, was Bishop Hudal, who was called a Nazi-Fascist bishop. He primarily sheltered German and Austrian Nazis. He was instrumental in helping those Nazi criminals escape from the Allied prison camps, as Draganovich had helped Croatian racist criminals escape.

Did those two highly educated persons in the Catholic hierarchy commit crimes all by themselves? Instead of those criminals being brought to trial, their work was secretly blessed. What could anyone say about Christian morality when the clergy in the Ratline used illegal means under the cover of charitable organizations? Should clergymen undermine the prestige of their church? Did the pope ever try to protect innocent victims in Croatia or wherever? Where were Christian ethics when on one side all means were used to protect notorious criminals from justice while on the other side silence was kept to protect or avoid acknowledging crimes committed against innocent people by those of different racial and religious affiliations?

Lt. Col. Father Cecelj played an important role in Draganovich's Ratline. A "sworn Ustasha," he remained loyal to Pavelich and his Ustashe movement. Cecelj was supplied by documents from the Red Cross and the Americans so he could travel freely through the American zone.

Draganovich, Cecelj, and other Croatian priests played a Jesuit role either as humanitarians or as opponents of the Pavelich regime! How could Draganovich be against Pavelich when he personally helped Pavelich emigrate to Argentina? It is hard to comprehend how some American politicians and intelligence agents could be so naive as to believe anything or to play politics by turning a blind eye to such matters!

During President Nixon's administration the Australian government asked the State Department for advice about how to handle the problem of Fascist Ustashe residents. The State Department secretly told the Australian government not to take any repressive measures against Ustashe fugitives because they needed them as useful ethnic voters "in several federal, state and municipal elections"! The Jewish community in the United States was warned about Nazi criminals in America. Therefore, to cover up that scandal, Nazi criminals were transferred to the Pentagon as "consultants" on "special operations."

In 1968, Ronald Reagan, then governor of California, proclaimed April 10 Independence Day of the Croatian state. In fact, the quisling Pavelich state had been proclaimed an independent state on April 10, 1941, although it was formed under the auspices of Nazi Germany and Fascist Italy. Soon after, Pavelich declared war against England and France, and later against the United States after she was attacked by Japan. Nixon's administration reminded U.S. politicians not to take part in a Croatian April 10 celebration; however, presidential candidate Bush's campaign published a calendar on which April 10 was marked as a Croatian holiday. It was impossible that Bush, one-time head of the CIA, did not know anything about Croatian terrorists.

It is imperative to mention a few more Ustashe priests:

The Croatian priest Dr. Dragutin Kamber was a notorious Ustasha with a Nazi orientation. He took direct part in liquidations of Serbs in the Doboj region. He ordered Jews to wear yellow armbands, while Serbs had to wear white ones for public discrimination.

Father Dominic Mandich was the official Vatican representative at San Girolamo. Gatherings of a political nature, not religious rites, were held at the San Girolamo monastery. By Mandich's order, false identity papers were printed, and the Franciscan press was put at the Ustashe's disposal. He also played an important role in Draganovich's Ratline. He was in close cooperation with the Italian police.

After the war Monsignor Karlo Petranovich, a priest of Ogulin, was designated to operate a sophisticated Ratline at Genoa. Many criminals left Italy via Genoa. Petranovich emigrated to Niagara Falls, Canada. He "saw nothing" regarding the massacres in Croatia!

By the way, it is worthwhile noting that both Washington and London had arranged with the Holy See to assist many Nazi collaborators to emigrate via Draganovich's Ratline.

During the war British captain Evelyn Waugh was a liaison officer at Tito's headquarters. He investigated Father Bujanovich's activities in Gospic. Bujanovich was responsible for the massacre of Orthodox peasants in the Gospic area. He first fled Croatia, then joined the Krizari as an officer under the command of Kavran and Sushich. He arranged Pavelich's trip to Argentina through the Ratline network, joining the Paglavnik on that trip. Bujanovich finally settled in Australia.

Bishop Gregory Rozman was a political leader of the Slovenian Krizari. He first collaborated with the Italian occupier, who got arms from him. After the Italian capitulation he collaborated with the Germans. At the end of the war Rozman went to Austria. The Vatican intervened by sending Father Draganovich to bring him to Rome. Rozman "escaped" from Klagenfurt in the British zone to the American zone of Salzburg and went to Switzerland. In Berne he took care of Ustashe monies deposited in a Swiss bank. He finally emigrated to the United States and settled in Cleveland, Ohio.

Father Draganovich's Last Mission in Yugoslavia

In 1967, Father Draganovich returned to Yugoslavia, despite his having been declared a war criminal by Tito's government during World War II.

Western intelligence was surprised by Draganovich's decision to go back to Sarajevo. After Draganovich's arrival in Sarajevo he was formally investigated but not mistreated. Thanks to Father Draganovich's Ratline, about 30,000 criminals found havens in South America, the United States, Canada, Britain, and Australia.

Some private sources who were present at a banquet for Draganovich sponsored by the UDBA apparatus before he left for Yugoslavia stated that Draganovich had been hired by the Yugoslav UDBA. If that is true, it means the Yugoslav UDBA or at least the Croatian UDBA was indirectly involved in helping Ustashe criminals escape justice.

According to Alija Konjhodzich, a Muslim, Draganovich came back to Bosnia to dig a deeper abyss between Serbs and Muslims there. Inoslav Beshkar, a correspondent for Zagreb's *Vjesnik*, wrote on March 16, 1986, that some offenders from the Catholic hierarchy, like Father Dr. Krunislav S. Draganovich, "had repented and admitted their guilt." However, Beshkar did not mention either the time or the place of any "trial" held for Draganovich.

Zivko Cerovich, in *Struggle (Borba)* of March 27, 1986, gave the opinion that Beshkar was trying to hush up history and crimes, pushing the idea of forgetting everything for the sake of a deceitful peace.

Draganovich died in 1982.

Vatican Political Perplexities

There are twenty vaults of Vatican secrets hidden from the public in the state of Maryland in the United States. The Vatican Ratline passed from history to secrecy the sad story of the Vatican intelligence service. Those hidden scandals covered three important matters: religion, espionage, and politics. For American intelligence, involvement in such matters was disgraceful. There were contradictions in American politics. The U.S. intelligence—to be more precise, the Jewish community—was hunting Nazis while the State Department was readmitting them with British, French, and Vatican help!

Furthermore, did the Vatican benefit financially from the Pavelich gold bullion war booty that was taken from Serbian, Jewish, and Gypsy victims? Did the Vatican violate deplomatic rules when criminals were driven in vehicles with diplomatic plates? Thus they were protected from arrest. Could the Ratline have operated successfully without the Vatican's coordination and diplomatic intervention?

High Vatican officials had obtained documents for Bishop Hudel, Father Draganovich, Bishop Buchor, and others from the Western Allies in order to freely operate the Ratline under cover of performing charitable duties.

Two clergymen testified as witnesses to Vatican involvement: Monsignor Milan Simcich and Father Cecelj. Both maintained close relations with

Draganovich. They were certain that the top hierarchy of the Vatican knew about Draganovich's activities and approved them. In a word, the Vatican was strongly and undeniably behind the Fascist Draganovich's activities!

Also, through the Mafia of southern Italy the Vatican succeeded in transferring to the Vatican silver from the altar of Saint Januarius the Germans intended to melt down to pay for the occupation of southern Italy.

As the Vatican has its own private state, it is immune from any outside intervention. The Vatican promotes its geopolitical interests regardless of the price in victims and their property as an intermarium, which means fermenting insurrections regardless of losses during either an active or a cold war. The authors of the book *Unholy Trinity* state that the "Vatican was guilty of crimes against humanity." Thus, Pope Pius XII "chose diplomacy over truth, temporal power over his moral duty."

Statistics of Ethnicity in Croatia

The crimes in Croatia are a Serbian tragedy, but even more tragic to the Croatian people; however, the plight of the Serbian people in their suffering is dignified and historic. Under such circumstances it is better, from a humanitarian and Christian point of view, to be a victim than to be the executioner. By the judgment of history only God is sinless.

The guilt of spilling of innocent blood cannot be washed out by any means, except by repentance, by asking sincerely for forgiveness. If the Croats hid their crimes from the world, as they did from themselves, one day they would appear again, as they did in 1991.

The Orthodox people have one virtue: They never proclaimed evil as good, never justified their own crimes. Even though a crime can be hidden from the people, it cannot be hidden from God. The Orthodox church throughout her historic endeavors never renounced the fundamental principles of the Gospel. So, for instance, Jasenovac victims could be hidden from the people and manipulated by Archbishop Kuharich and Tito's general Tudjman, but they could not be hidden from God and eventually from those who believe in Him, and in truth and justice as well.

Mr. Manhattan asked Eleanor Roosevelt why those Catholic crimes were not as well known to the world as German Nazi crimes. Mrs. Roosevelt replied that Nazi Germany does not exist any more. We still have the Catholic church with us. She is more powerful than ever. With her own press and the world press at her bidding, anything published about the atrocities would not be believed.... Despite its horror, the genocide in Croatia did not get publicity because the Vatican hid it.

Mr. Manhattan told Mrs. Roosevelt that he was writing a book. She replied, "Your book might convince a few. But what about the hundreds of millions already brainwashed by Catholic propaganda?"[24]

According to Joseph Shapharik,[25] there were then 801,000 Croats and 5,294,000 Serbs. So the Serbs who survived genocide in Croatia are not trees without roots.

In 1921 a census by religious affiliation was taken in Yugoslavia. There were 5,602,207 Orthodox, or 46.6 percent; 4,735,154 Roman Catholics, or 39.4 percent; and 14 percent of other affiliations.

At the end of 1940, according to German intelligence, in the ISC there were 3,069,000 (or 50.78%) Croats; 1,847,000 (or 30.56%) Serbs; 717,000 (11.86%) Muslims; and 410,000 (6.80%) others.

In 1941 at the beginning of World War II, according to Ustashe statistics, there were 3,200,000 Croats; 1,848,400 Serbs; and 800,000 Muslims.

In 1943 the Croat Sergio Krizman in Washington presented a map with the legend: The slaughter of innocent Serbian population was recorded "from April 1941 to August 1942. In that period the total number of slaughtered Serbs was 744,000 (78,000 killed by Germans, 20,000 by Italians, 30,000 by Hungarians, 60,000 by Albanians, 6,000 by Bulgarians, while Pavelich's Ustashe killed 600,000)."

According to Avro Manhattan, the population in Croatia was composed of a total 6,700,000: 3,300,000 Croatians; 2,000,000 Serbs; 700,000 Muslims; and 45,000 Jews. According to all statistics in 1941 there were living 1,847,000 Serbs in Croatia. Currently some 500,000 to 600,000 Serbs live in Croatia.

Could Archbishop Kuharich and President Tudjman give an explanation for the Serbs' diminishing numbers in their "most democratic country," Croatia? There is an imperative and moral need for dignified and responsible people to work with facts instead of propaganda. Could we ask Archbishop Kuharich, head of the Croatian Catholic church, and Tito's former general who is now president where they stand in this regard?

Serbs were persecuted in the ISC for the following reasons:

1. The ISC had the broadest boundaries that Croatia had ever imagined.

2. Because of Serbs' Catholization then Croatization they were vulnerable.

3. Serbian property was pillaged and plundered.

4. Croats had demonstrated a deep-seated and unbridled hatred and envy toward everything that was Serbian, an unfortunate Croatian characteristic. They showed primitivism, poor upbringing, and moral laxity.

In the middle of 1942, Dr. Fedor Lukach, director of the Mostar hospital, stated that there were killed "no less than 700,000 Serbs and 300,000 of them had to escape to Serbia."

In May of 1942 the Croatian diplomat Nikola Pavelich disembarked in Rio de Janeiro. Said Pavelich, when the civilized world finds out, there would be revulsion and indignation, and nobody knows what would happen with us Croats. Just one detail was mentioned: In the streets of Croatian cities Serbs' eyes, thirty to forty in a bunch, were offered for sale in order to spite them![26]

Book Excerpts from Corroborators and Eyewitnesses of Ustashe Genocide

German Authors

Hermann Neubacher, *Sanderauftrag Suedosten, 1940-1945, Benicht lines fliegenden Diplomate* (Goettingen, 1956): Ante Pavelich remains the architect of one of the bloodiest religious wars, when some three-quarters of a million were slaughtered.

Walter Hagen, *Die geheime Front, Organization, Personen und Aktionen des deutshen Geheimdienstes* (Zurich, 1950): There was deep hatred against Jews and Serbs, of whom it was officially declared that "everyone is free to kill them."

Gert Fricke, *Kroatien 1941-1944*: Eugen Kvaternik waged terror against Orthodox Serbs with the approval of the central government in Zagreb. "There were hundreds of thousands of victims."

Karl Hulicka, *Das Ende auf dem Balkan 1944-45*: The Croatian Ustashe are Catholics who slaughtered by Balkan methods 600,000 to 700,000 persons of different religious affiliation and political beliefs.

Walter Goerlitz, *Der Zweite Wellbrief 1939-1945* (Stuttgart, 1952): The Catholic Ustashe waged a war for Serbs' extermination that caused a civil war in that young country.

Karlheinz Deschner, *Mit Gott und then Faschisten* (Stuttgart, 1962): Serbs became slaughterhouse victims though they were of the highest cultural level in the Balkans. They were not Catholics, which was mostly the reason for their persecution as Orthodox. Of two million Serbs, almost 600,000 were killed. Deschner found new proof that the Ustashe killed more Serbs than he had earlier reported.

Italian Authors

Giuseppe Angelina, *Fuochi di bivacco in Croazia, Regionale in Roma* (Rome, 1946): Thousands of Serbs were tortured and massacred. After executing crimes the murderers organized banquets, as did the son of the Gospich director when he celebrated "his one thousandth victim."

Italian daily *Il Tempo*, Rome, September 9, 1953: On May 21, 1941, the Franciscan priest Fra. Shimic came to Knin. He told an Italian general, the commandant of the "Sesari Division," that they intend "to kill all Serbs in the shortest possible time. This is our program." Franciscans had received orders from Rome saying, "There should be no interference in local politics. And so they started." Orders from whom? Who could say the Vatican was not involved?

Salvatore Loi, *Yugoslavia 1941* (Torino, 1953): Salvatore, an eyewitness of massacres in Lika in 1941, wrote, "Under the skies of the Balkans there is no people that is more proud, more noble, more loyal or heroic than the Serbian people, with a soul fortified by centuries' long tortures."

Enzo Gataldi, *La Yugoslavia alle porte. Tra cronaca e documenta una storia che nessuno racconta* (1968): Between 1941 and 1942 Croats killed Serbs, "of whom 356,000 were Orthodox persons, and several thousands of Jews."

Il Tempo of September 10, 1953: When somebody reads what happened in China, they could consider it to be an exaggeration. However, what has been happening in Croatia was here in Europe, "two steps away from the civilized world." In Veljun, in the district of Slunj, Serbian priest Branko Dobrosavljevich and his son were tortured, as beyond human comprehension. Then both were massacred in the most barbaric way.

One lady from Gospic came to the Ustashe inquiring what had happened to her 16-year-old son. She took with her her 12-year-old daughter. When she refused to pass the girl to the Ustashe, one of them brought a bundle containing the eyes of her son. She instantly fainted. "This is what Croats were doing to Serbs. It is understandable that we cannot continue with these bloodcurdling stories; they would fill volumes and volumes."

Alfiro Russo, *Revoluziane in Yugoslavia* (Rome, 1944): "Even the most extraordinary massacres in the darkest era of history would not soil its name [Croatia]. 'Kill, kill,' scream the Ustashe against the Serbs. And they cut their heads off and threw their bodies into the Sava River, which flows slowly and gravely in the direction of Belgrade."

" 'Go back to your motherland, go back to your motherland.' "

Neither Fascists nor Nazis could be compared to the Ustashe in their use of torture and methods of killing.

Carlo Falconi, *Il silenzio di Pio XII* (Milan, 1965): On the basis of documents from Zagreb and Warsaw still unpublished, Falconi wrote, "This sadism was nothing more than an accentuation of the methods applied during 'normal' mass executions. The sadism was performed with savage energy. Victims were dismembered into four pieces and then often hung, for fun, in butcher shops labeled 'human meat'. The sadism was also accompanied by burning down houses from Vlasenice and Kladanj and churches full of victims. But one should not forget the impaled children and the games the Ustashe played torturing their victims during nocturnal orgies."

Corrado Zoli, in the Italian newspaper *Risto del Carlina,* September 18, 1941: "Events are developing and acquiring the most dangerous forms of a religious war. Catholic priests and monks were leading and instigating gangs of murderers and are probably still doing so. There is more than adequate proof of that. The ISC is full of hatred killing innocents who share the same language, blood and country of origin. They kill. Then they bury people alive or throw dead bodies into rivers, into the sea and pits."

Roberto Buttaglia, *La Seconda Guerra Mondiale,* 1962: The kingdom of Croatia was established by Nazi-Fascist invaders in which Pavelich the executioner under the auspices of Hitler and Mussolini "is trying to completely annihilate the Serbs."

Curzio Malaparte, *Kaputt*, Roma-Milan, 1948: The *Chicago Sun* said about his book, "This terrible *Kaputt* comes to us from Italy, greeted by the prominent Italian critics as the most lasting post-war literary event." The book discusses fascism not only in Germany and Italy but in Croatia as well. It is in this book that Malaparte recounted the incident, described previously, of Pavelich's basket of eyes.

Alija Konjhodzich Proudly Defends Serbian Nation

[*Brotherhood*, Toronto, Canada, September 1969]

In Buenos Aires in 1961 the Croatian sculptor Ivan Meshtrovich, formerly a close friend of the late Yugoslav king Alexander, published a book, *Memories of Political Men and Events*, in which, as Alija Konjhodzich states, he poured out his bitterness and slanders against the Serbian people and their representatives.

It was obvious that Meshtrovich always switched his political views to agree with those with power and prestige. During World War I and after it in old Yugoslavia he was the "best friend of Serbs." However, after the Yugoslav capitulation in 1941, he pledged allegiance to the racist ideology of the Croats Starcevich and Pavelich.

Serbs who had emigrated to the United States and Canada reacted negatively to Meshtrovich's book, while inside Yugoslavia, Serbian historians, publicists, and Marxist-oriented politicians remained silent.

Konjhodzich continues: In the diaspora all honest Muslims and Orthodox people of good will have been getting along well, though Ustashe emigrants have been using all available means to divide them on a religious basis according to the Latin motto "Divide and conquer."

Alija Konjhodzich was one of the most prominent Muslim intellectuals abroad. He was the editor of the magazine *Bratstvo (Brotherhood)* in Toronto, Canada. He gathered the best possible minds of both denominations for his magazine. In the September 1969 issue, Alija wrote that there is nothing new about Satan-directed attacks against Serbs both by Ustashe and Croatian Communists, who both measure Serbs as identically as a pair of boots.

In 1918 the creators of the Yugoslav state imagined statehood as a unique entity along classical lines, based on a parliamentary monarchy with equal rights for all citizens. Croatia benefited the most from that unity; however, Serbia, which before the war was an independent state, lost her real democracy and parliamentary system after the unification. Nationalistic and separatist tendencies were appearing that gradually dominated Yugoslav statehood and real democracy.

Belgrade politicians were completely unaware of Zagreb's political perplexities, the domination of the Vatican not only in religious but also in political matters, and the desire to resurrect the former Austria-Hungary.

In his masterpiece *Magnum Crimen* Dr. Victor Novak pointed out that King Alexander and his government were totally naive and shortsighted when they did not let some Croatian Catholic clergy organize their own autonomous Catholic church that would be independent from the Vatican. Why did those clerics want to break with the Vatican? Because they felt strong Slavic ties, as did Dr. Novak, one of the most prominent Yugoslav intellectuals.

As long as the Croatian Catholic church stays under Vatican domination they cannot act in good spirit as a real component of the Slavic family. The Vatican steadily promotes Latinization, contrary to Slavic unity. In the Balkans, Catholic missionaries have pursued the same goal of Orthodox subjugation since the Christian church split in 1054.

Furthermore, Serbian politicians like Stojadinovich, Jevtich, and Cvetkovich were ready at a nod from Croatian politicians, either Radich or Macek, to sacrifice Serbian national interests in order to preserve a politically paralyzed Yugoslav state and to stay in power themselves.

The rational mind could not understand that small Serbia was able to defeat the Ottoman Empire in the war of 1912 and also the Austro-Hungarian Empire during World War I; when the Yugoslav state was established, Serbian politicians lost touch with political reality by trying to rescue the Yugoslav sinking ship.

Konjhodzich continues: Ethics and human pride and dignity demand the Croatian people apologize to the world for Ustashe-committed genocide against Serbs, Jews, and Gypsies. De facto, the Croatian people are guilty because none of them apologized, except Dr. Prvoslav Grizogono, who was shocked by what he heard about the atrocities that had been committed. A greater tragedy was that Grizogono's letter to Archbishop Stepinac remained a voice crying in the wilderness. Therefore, Starcevich's theory of racism and discrimination succeeded in sowing primordial hatred toward Serbs.

Konjhodzich further says that Croats lack principles of logic, rationality, and, at the least, ethics, because they never possessed them. As proof, there was intense hatred toward Serbs even by the head of the CPP and the former vice-president of the Yugoslav government-in-exile in London, Dr. Juraj Krnjevich, who never could rid himself of his pathological hatred toward Serbs.

People with integrity and rational minds accept that for a thousand years Croatians were trying to carve out an independent state. Let them have it, under the condition not to be racist and against other religious denominations. That means, Croats should neither be against Serbs, Jews, or Gypsies nor be militaristic, racist, or Fascist. During World War II Hitler gave an opportunity to Croatians to allow their uncontrollable passions full sway. They fanatically endeavored to create a pure ethnic state with limitations on minorities. Mussolini accomplished the restoration of Great Albania in Kosovo. Tito and his marionettes continued in the same spirit.

After World War II Tito issued an order forbidding Serbs from Serbia and Montenegro to return to their homes in Kosovo and Metohia, while the doors were opened wide for Albanians from Albania to replace Serbs in those regions. Dushan Mugosha, Tito's representative, turned back all the Serbian refugees!

All Croatian publications in and out of Croatia, like the archbishop's organ of Zagreb, *Glas Concila (Voice of Council)* and the Croatian literary newspaper *Vjesnik (Herald)*, recently went so far as to advocate denying Serbs their nationality on Croatian territory, "Croats of Orthodox religion." Croats are again forming camps for those Serbs who survived! Is there any conscience and justice in this world? Now "unslaughtered Serbs," who lost countless lives, properties, and holy objects, could not sit idly by.

Konjhodzich also says Croatian publications all use the same dishonest language, reminiscent of Goebbels propaganda methods, to spread constant hatred toward the Serbian people. Croatians also play an immoral role by reducing the number of Serb victims killed from 800,000 to 60,000 including Yugoslav-oriented Croats and Muslims. A Croatian literary newspaper tried to revive Starcevich and Pavelich ideology. The author of that article, "War's Victims," was one Bruno Bushich. Then, in *Glas Concila* again a friar claimed that more Croats than any other nationality were killed during the last war.

Konjhodzich also reminds his Islamic compatriots that such ostensible Croatian love toward Muslims exemplified by calling them "Croatian flowers" was ordinary lies and hypocrisy. Croats never denied either their guilt of Serbophobia nor their intensive Catholicism, Konjhodzich concludes.

Tudjman Remains a Faithful Follower of Titoism

Indeed, Franjo Tudjman remains a faithful follower of the Titoist hierarchy, by hiding and nurturing neo-fascism in Croatia even after the war ended. The Ustashe's admiration for Tito is best illustrated in their song dedicated to him: "Comrade Tito, I kiss you on the forehead, let yourself be dressed in Ustashe uniform" (Druze Tito, ljubim te u chelo, daj obuci Ustashko odelo). A proper investigation of Ustashe atrocities was not allowed in Yugoslavia, although, as has been already described, they were condemned by the Nuremburg tribunal. The Communists refused to acknowledge what they called an "anti-Fascist struggle"—which in fact was a religious massacre on an unparalleled scale. In that regard, as in many others, Croatia was a unique exception in Europe, as Croats caused new tragedy and continued the civil war in Yugoslavia.

Just to mention one case: After the war, if anyone dared to mention the notorious Jasenovac camp, regardless of how many members of his family were slaughtered or burned in the camp furnaces, he would be mercilessly persecuted. Such suppression of facts and psychological repression were certainly unbearable, especially for those families directly affected by Jasenovac's Dachau.

Franjo Tudjman held various positions in Tito's hierarchy. Someone explained the derivation of the word Tudjman thusly: Tito's ucenik (student), Djilas's miljenik (favorite), and Antin's (Pavelich's) naslednik (heir). In 1945 Tudjman was a political commissar of a Partisan division of the Tenth Corps stationed on Zagreb territory under the command of Ivan Shabl.

Did Tudjman forget his war comrades? Not at all! At one time Bojkovec was chief of OZNA in the Karlovac region, and Manojlich was chief of OZNA in Croatia. In Tudjman's government, Bojkovec is currently minister of police and Manojlich is vice-president. Tudjman continues Hebrang's policy, surrounding himself with cohorts of a real democratic background, as he possesses himself!

The program of the Croatian Democratic Association (CDZ) clearly states that nationally oriented Croatian Communists could play "the key role in Croatian liberation." For that very reason the motto was for national reconciliation between Croatian Ustashe and Croatian Communists. Whoever watched the Alliance of Croatian Communists closely would come to the conclusion that Croatian Communists had created Tudjman and the Croatian Democratic Association (HDZ). Both Josip Vrhovec's and Racan's policies were a continuation of Hebrang-Bakarich intentions. On the eve of Yugoslavia's official capitulation on April 17, 1941, Hebrang and Bakarich made an agreement with Ustashe representatives to cooperate and form and recognize the independent Communist Party of Croatia—all under Tito's awareness and approval.

The first coalition of Ustashe emigrants in the United States was organized under a Washington watchdog.[27]

As we understand Tudjman's book, his interpretation of crime and genocide was judged by the position of might, not right. In any judicial and democratic society, crime remains crime, regardless of whoever performed in the chain of authority. Tudjman states that the crimes were the consequences of war acts in which everybody took part. He claimed the actions performed by the NLM were not criminal. He meant crimes could not be committed by Tito's Communists, including himself. On the contrary, according to his interpretation, the Allied (British) repatriation of members of the Endehazia (ISC) army to the Yugoslav authority in May 1945 was a crime.

According to Tudjman, genocide is a natural phenomenon, in harmony with society and with a mythologically divine nature! Genocide is not only permissible; it is also recommended, even commanded by the word of the diety, whenever it is useful. That means it is permissible to ensure the survival or the restoration of the kingdom of the chosen nation, or preserve and spread the one true faith.

Tudjman offers examples related to the Jews. Quoting the Bible, he asserts that the act of retribution has been legal since ancient times. The law of the stronger was the one that was consecrated; thus all dispassion in destroying an enemy is justified.

Tudjman's Obvious Anti-Semitism and Ustashe Sympathies

Tudjman wrote about the participation of Jews in the liquidation of Gypsies in Jasenovac. According to him, they jealously guarded their monopoly of top-level administration. In the camp, Jews took the initiative in preparing and provoking not only individual atrocities but also the mass slaughter of non-Jews, Communists, Partisans, and Serbs.[28]

In Croatia the new neo-Fascist Ustashe, like the shadow of the malicious "U" (a symbol of Pavelich's ISC/Endehoazia), was restored as "the historical aspiration of the Croatian people." In Pavelich's state the Ustashe tried to solve the perceived Serbian and Jewish problem through a process of genocide, which disgusted even the Nazis in its barbarism.

In 1989 during his campaign, Tudjman did not conceal his anti-Semetism and sympathy for the Ustashe. During his party congress he declared the Nazi Independent Croatian state "was the crowning accomplishment of the thousand-year efforts of the Croatian people."

Tudjman has been celebrated among the Ustashe for over fifteen years. Indeed the Ustashe proclaimed him "the greatest Croatian historian." The new Croatian president embraced many political theses from Ustashe emigrants represented by Nikola Shtedul, a fanatic follower of Marx Luburich. Now Tudjman must execute extreme Ustashe plans. De facto, Tudjman was drawn into the war against the Yugoslav army and the Yugoslav state as a federal entity.

Why has Tudjman been so extreme toward Serbs and Jews? Judging pragmatically from events, without applying any moral scruples or ethics, Tudjman obviously tries to minimize the number of Ustashe crimes to please Ustashe abroad and at home in return for financial contributions and votes. Is everything permissible in politics? Tudjman is continuing racist genocide as was both suggested and attempted by Starcevich, Frank, and Pavelich. He wants to be Pavelich's successor not only in the territorial sense of the Croatian state but also in carrying out his particular ideas.[29]

His tactics remind us of Stalin's politics, that the Soviet Union only pretended to be democratic. It is necessary to see Tudjman's pretensions for Croatia in such a light.[30]

Tudjman's policy is like that of Josip Frank, who believed a Great Croatia could only be created on the ruins of Serbia. Since that Croats are loyal to an able leader, all Croats are invited to join in a decisive and holy war against "Serbo-Communists," "military Bolsheviks," "hegemonistic-Bolshevik Belgrade," Serbian-Communist generals, and Chetnik bands of "idiotic revolutionaries." The Serbian demon is threatening all of Europe, even the entire world! He also pours out his anger on Belgrade, calling the city Stalinist, military Communistic, imperialistic, and anything else he can think of!

Serbia has been unfortunate beyond belief. The largest Yugoslav republic turned out to be a scapegoat for all the evils happening in Yugoslavia. An anti-Serbian coalition was successful. There was a conspiracy to salvage Titoism through Yugoslavia's national problems. The Yugoslav crises are the current consequences of a planned Titoist campaign of Serbian degradation and national numbness that affected the Serbian entity and its culture.

In Tudjman's parliament, anti-Serbianism and anti-Belgrade feelings were blended in one large pot to flare up not only against Belgrade but also against Knin and its surroundings. As Croatian leader, Tudjman gave Belgrade a last chance to redeem itself with Europe and the former Allies, the British and American governments, as well as Austrian and German media that respond urgently to the motto "Bolshevik danger!" Allegedly Tudjman spoke as a politician from a great democratic country; however, he was silent regarding brutal terror against Serbs on Croatian territory.

The Serbs in Croatia and Bosnia and Hercegovina have to defend themselves so that genocide against them is not repeated. They only resist the injustice, tyranny, and terror that have come to life again like a vampire. The Serbian Democratic party is a witness to the brutal terror carried out by the HDZ authority. Serbs in Croatia don't need Croatian guardianship, as President Roosevelt suggested for Croats when he heard about the horrible persecutions they had carried out in World War II.

What the Croatian trio of Mesich, Markovich, and Loncar had done had been done before them by Tito himself to accomplish the disintegration of Yugoslavia and the annihilation of Serbs as a national entity.

Since Tudjman took the helm of the Croatian republic, Serbs in Croatia have become vulnerable in their jobs, their safety, and even their very lives.

Persecution of Serbs under Tudjman in Croatia, 1990-1991

Tudjman's ruling party, the Croatian Democratic Union (CDU), has been mercilessly persecuting Serbs in Croatia, trying to erase the Serbian national identity, name, language, alphabet, and religion.

Tudjman's followers are preparing a mass extermination of Serbs like that Ante Pavelich attempted from 1941-1945. Needless to say, Serbs are feeling insecure. Their basic human and civil rights are threatened or completely destroyed.

How does Tudjman intend to accomplish this genocide? In December 1990 a new Croatian constitution was adopted, under which Serbs lost the status of a nation; they became a national minority despite the fact that Yugoslavia was a country of Serbs, Croats, and Slovenes with international recognition.

Croats by simple decree intend the Croatization of the Serbian language by depriving Serbs of their Cyrillic alphabet and replacing it with the Latin alphabet. Croats also banned all Serbian publications in the Croatian republic and Serbian television and radio programs. In a word, Croats are treating Serbs in their republic as if they don't exist at all. On the other hand, the Albanians, Italians, Slovenes, Hungarians, and others have their own programs on Croatian radio and television even though they are much smaller minorities. Furthermore, Serbs don't even have their own cultural center.

For these stated reasons and others, Serbs are forced by circumstances to form their autonomy (cultural, political, and territorial).

Tudjman's party took as its official symbol the Ustashe-Fascist flag![31] De facto, Tudjman had officially rehabilitated Ustashe-Fascist criminals. In May 1991, signs were posted against Serbs like those that were seen during Pavelich's Ustashe reign. Pavelich never hid it, but Tudjman "makes legs" under the cover "Croatia is the most democratic country."

The Croatian establishment is currently fundamentally undemocratic, with a pathological hatred toward Serbs. Why couldn't the Serbs have their own ethnic and religious affiliation? If Serbs were Catholic, would they be persecuted, not to mention subject to genocide? Serbs in Croatia are again suffering like Jews did in Hitler's Nazi Germany.

Perhaps Tudjman's government's biggest mistake was never admitting the full scale of the killing. They deny it like some deny the Holocaust ever took place. If Tudjman came out and recognized it as one of the greatest tragedies of this country, then Serbs would forgive even if they could not forget, hoping such evil would never happen again. The catharsis that took place in postwar Germany never happened in Croatia. On the other hand, anti-semetism is on the rise!

Serbian property is constantly destroyed. In Zadar, for instance, 148 residences and business buildings owned by Serbs were demolished and looted; in Zarma near Dubrovnik, 11 Serbian houses were destroyed; 50 sales outlets of the Belgrade Borba (Stuggle) were demolished, etc.[32]

Extortion of Loyalty

In Zagreb, Zadar, Shibenik, Split, and other places where Serbs were a minority, the Croatian authority introduced signing statements of loyalty to the current Croatian authority. Serbs who failed to sign the "letter of support" could lose their jobs and end up on the street with their families.

Under the new constitution Serbs became second-class citizens. Therefore they had to accept the founding of the Croatian independent state. As mentioned earlier, in 1941 the first ISC was formed under Axis auspices. The other ISC was reborn in 1991 with the support of the Western Allies. (Germany and Austria, staunch Serbian enemies in both world wars, were the first to recognize the new state.) If Serbs in any way resisted the new Croatian establishment they were pronounced "terrorists of a militant minority, encouraged by support from Serbia." Serbs who signed the letters of support were issued certificates that were proof of their loyalty to the existing republic. On May 6, 1991, Adria Enterprises in Zadar dismissed all employees who failed to sign their loyalty oaths, like Srboljub Oluich, Ljubica Vukcevich, Dushanka Budimir, Dushanka Knezevich, and many others.

Murder, Beating, and Mistreatment of Serbs in the Republic of Croatia

The policy of Serb persecution continued in the "new democratic" state of Croatia.

On May 1, 1991, Stevan Inich of the village Vrshadin, member of the SDP, was murdered because he was carrying a Serbian flag in his village. On May 2, 1991, Croatian police killed Vaso Pecar, 21, from Polac, near Knin. Croatian police beat up Dushan Vitas, an 80-year-old invalid with highest decorations for participation in the liberation of his country. Serb Zoran Panich from Gospic, Milivoje Vishich from the village Smokvic near Zadar, and Milenko Popovich also from Smokvic were beaten and suffered heavy injuries; on April 1, 1991, Dushan Drakulich and Zeljko Prica from Titova Korenica were beaten up; on May 21, 1991, Branko Krunich from Osijek was beaten. Many Serbs were taken to Osijek and beaten up, mistreated, and humiliated in the local Croatian police station. These and similar, even worse events occurred under Tudjman's rule. No wonder, since many of Tudjman's subordinates, like himself, were former political commissars under Tito in the Yugoslav Communist army, where they persecuted and killed hundreds of thousands of innocent citizens. In Serbia alone from November 1944 to the new Communist occupation of Serbia and in May 1945 in Slovenia hundreds of thousands of all Yugoslav nationalities, primarily Serbs in Serbia, were slaughtered.

Croatian governments continued pogroms against Serbs under Croatian fuhrer Ante Pavelich, Croatian villain Josip Broz Tito, and president of the "new democratic state," Tito's general Franjo Tudjman. Why? Because Serbs remain Serbs regardless of threats of physical annihilation. What kind of "new democracy" exists in Croatia? Does the civilized and democratic world want to know or not?

Judging from the great horrible experiences, Serbs in the Croatian and Bosnian republics have nothing to lose in their national struggle for survival.

The EC and America were silent while the tigers swallowed unprotected Serbs there. They already could see it would not go as smoothly as they had predicted or wanted, despite subjective Western media.

In June 1991 in Croatia two concentration camps were set up, one near Gospic and another near the Slavonian village of Tenja. Arrests of Serbs have been made, besides in Gospic, in Karlovac, Virovitica, Zadar, Shibenik, Biograd na moru (on the sea), Drnish, Zagreb, Slavonski Brad, and Osijek.

These cases are but a fraction of the frightening record in the twelve months between May 1990 and May 1991.These fundamental violations of human and civil rights that deny Serb national identity in Croatia could have serious consequences for all of Europe.

Tudjman's behavior is a classic example of the absurdity of today's world confusion and misinterpretation of facts, of twisting truth without applying moral or ethical principles. Tudjman is following the line of his Machiavellian predecessors in accusing Serbia of being the most dangerous place for peace not only in Europe but in the world as well. He sounds the alarm against Serbs and Serbia instead of against himself, he who does a perfidious disservice to the world community, justice, and real peace!

The Voice from the Catholic Church

During and after World War II, the Croatian Catholic church and the Vatican never acknowledged the racial and religious genocide committed by the notorious Ustashe in their ISC.

According to Vladimir Dedijer, Tito's biographer, a collection of documents was published in the Federal Republic of Germany in the book *The Vatican and Jasenovac*. Among others were documents with captions like the following:

1. Vatican as the incitor of forcible conversion and genocidal actions in the Balkans.

2. Roman Catholic church in Croatia assisted Nazi-Fascist party of Ustashe before the war and its foundation on Yugoslav territory, thus the first such secret cell was formed on Kapitol in Zegred.

3. In May 1941, Pope Pius XII gave an audience to Pavelich.

4. The Roman Catholic church gave full support to Pavelich's new regime in the ISC.

5. Many Roman Catholic priests together with the Ustashe took part in the genocidal slaughter of Serbs, Jews, and other nationals to create a pure Croatian state.

6. Representatives of the Roman Catholic church took an active role in organizing the Jasenovac camp. In the spring of 1942 the chief of the camp was a Roman Catholic friar, Majstorovich-Filipovich, who personally took part in killing Serbs in western Bosnia.

7. During the anti-Serb German-Ustashe offensive, in the spring of 1942, Kurt Waldheim served under the command of the German general Shtal. Waldheim was later decorated by the Croatian fuhrer Ante Pavelich for his active participation in the Kozara offensive. Pope Ivan Paul invited Waldheim to the Vatican during his tenure as Austrian president. That fact also helps explain the "bloody role of the Vatican in the last war," as Dedijer concluded his statement.

8. At the beginning of 1943, Pope Pius XII gave an audience to 120 Ustashe gendarmes and policemen, among them many guards and criminals from Jasenovac camp. A Vatican official agency published photos of the visit of those criminals to the pope, who gave them a special blessing.

Vatican and Archbishop Kuharich Activities

On August 20, 1991, in Hungary, Pope John Paul met with a group of Croatian faithful led by Archbishop Kuharich and assured them he would ask the international community to help Croats in those harsh days of their history. One day in the near future, the pope continued, he would visit them.

The Vatican acts like a state and a multinational center. Vatican propaganda presents Serbia and Serbian people as "terrorists that should be exterminated."

On August 4, 1991, Spanish reporters were shocked when Cardinal Kuharich said in his Zagreb cathedral that he yearns and cries for vengeance against Serbian terrorists. Archbishop Kuharich forgets that in 1941 there were about two million Serbs living in Croatia, and the "remnants of the slaughtered people" would not let the Croats butcher them like sheep. Could anyone be called a terrorist for defending his family from physical extermination? Who is provoking revolt in Croatia, Serbs or Tudjman's new constitution of December 1990?

Pope John Paul asked the entire Catholic world to get up on their feet and pray with him for peace in Croatia and in the other Yugoslav republics. Archbishop Kuharich sent a telegram to the pope, expressing his worry about the great strain of the situation. The pope obviously intended to create sympathy for Tudjman and an anti-Serb attitude by using the scarecrow of communism to enlist the Catholic world behind him.

For centuries Vatican aspirations toward the east have been hampered by Serb resoluteness.

The pope expressed sadness and worry for the destiny of the Croatian people and other Yugoslav people as well. He also expressed solidarity with the Croatian people.

The world expects the Vatican to speak with understanding, tolerance, and reality. We completely agree with Richard West when he stated in the

Sunday Telegraph of London that the pope is the only man who could stop the bloodshed in Yugoslavia. West further said that executions of Serbs during World War II were carried out by a great many of the Roman Catholic hierarchy.

West also recorded that when he was in Mostar in the autumn of 1991, an elderly Muslim told him the worst thing that had happened was the Catholic church never apologized for the crimes the Ustashe committed. The Serbs and their Orthodox church were not given a chance to put the case of genocide before a world crime tribunal or the United Nations. Silence was ordered to hush up the crimes.

Traditional Role of the Serbian Orthodox Church

The Serbian Orthodox church as an autocephalous entity has preserved among the Serbian people spiritual values and national identity during long centuries of slavery under the Ottoman Empire. During those darkest periods of suffering, Islamization, and annihilation, Serbs were between two grinding wheels, that is, between the hammer and the anvil, or more clearly between the repressive Turks and the aggressive Austro-Hungarian Empire and the Vatican. On their apocolyptic voyages many Orthodox faithful were forced to swallow bitter pills. If they were to survive they had to change their faith and ethos—to be Islamized, converted, proselytzed, or made part of a Uniat. Unethical and uncivilized processes were destroying Serbian national and cultural traditions. However, they were being forced to live according to the motto "Who has the might has the right."

In the long history of suffering and unbearable humiliations of the Serbian nation, the Serbian church, like the Star of Bethlehem, led them in the spiritual survival of their Orthodoxy. She was not only the guardian of national and religious life but also the source of ideas of statehood, especially in a time when the Serbian people were without national and even religious leaders.

Meanwhile, the Pec patriarchate played a multilateral role and had to deal with the Catholic church, which in essence was always missionary, aggressive, and expansionistic and devoted to fomenting religious intolerance between Croats and Serbs. The new tactics of physical destruction and spiritual subjugation of the Serbian Orthodox church had come with Tito and his Brozovici (cohorts) after they took over the Yugoslav helm in 1945.

Again, the Serbian church found herself alone, without any real backing from within or without. Tito secretly contacted the Vatican and the Croatian Catholic church during the war and the Catholic clergy in Bosnia whenever favorable circumstances allowed. Also, Tito maintained close relations and cooperation with Arab Muslim countries, giving them every possible moral as well as material support. These policies resulted in more freedom to Yugoslav Muslims (especially since 1971) to promote their national and religious aspirations. There was nothing left for the Serbian Orthodox church except to moan under the oppression of Tito's rule. That is not an unfounded fabrication, but an undeniable, documented fact. In her book *Genocide in Yugoslavia* Prof. Smilja Abramov attested that the Vatican cooperated with some Communist parties (like Tito's) to subjugate or destroy the Orthodox faith whenever possible. Therefore, it was imperative for the Serbian Orthodox church and her people to find an exit, if any existed, from the despair caused by a half century of Communist tyranny and the current apostasy of the entire world.

The Serbian ruling Socialist party differs in the substance of its principles and behavior from the other European Socialist countries no less than does the South Arabian monarchy differ from the British one, in reference to the Orthodox religion. The current tendency for full religious freedom and free activities is a nightmare for some ruling authorities in the Serbian land, in Montenegro in particular. The civilian authorities view with envy the church's popularity among their people. For them the Orthodox church is a monster that threatens their government of usurpation and corruption. They are still using undemocratic methods to subjugate people's national and religious feelings. Could any country be considered judicial and democratic, even with a Mediterranean culture, as some call themselves, that treats the highest clergy so dismally? There are many examples of such primitive, undemocratic behavior. To mention just a few:

Church services were interrupted with the most vulgar language and even with threats of physical force. The security organs of the Montenegrin republic used brutal force and even jailed some junior high school students from Bijelo Polje whose only sin was they had been in the monastery of Ostrog. Not long ago the Montenegrin government allowed the formation of a new Ministry of Religious Affairs. Dr. Slobodan Tomovich was appointed head of that department. Such an act might be considered hypocritical and meant only to camouflage its real intentions and behavior toward the Serbian Orthodox church, intervening in her jurisdiction.

The Serbian Orthodox church always taught and led Serbian generations in true Christian ethics, justice, and morality that honor human pride and dignity. She always opposed personal ambitions that seek power and enjoyment within the context of sacred authority.

According to the constitution of each Yugoslav republic the church is separate from the state. The church has a moral obligation to promote real democracy among the people with respect to the human rights of all individuals regardless of creed, color, or ethnicity. No political party should manipulate the church for its own political gains. Such interference would be against canon law as well as contrary to legislative separation of church and state.

The history of the Serbian Orthodox church proves that unspeakable repressions, humiliations, and barbarisms have never succeeded in subjugating the voice of the Serbian church in advocating what is right and just.

During the Bosnian calamity that started in 1991 the Orthodox church has helped people of all three warring parties in that republic. In Serbia there are over 700,000 refugees, of whom more than 150,000 are Croats and Muslims. In Montenegro alone almost 75,000 of the refugees are Muslims. They all get equal treatment, despite what the media says. That has been the credo of the Serbian Orthodox church in the past and it will be in the future as long as she exists.

Notes

1. The Orthodox church has had priority over the Catholic church since the sixth century because the Catholic west survived by grace of help from the Orthodox center in Carigrad Constantinople/Istanbul. From the eleventh to thirteenth century the Crusades began to recover the Holy Land from the Muslims. Carigrad, the cradle of Christianity and civilization, was destroyed.

2. On July 31, 1914, just three days after Austro-Hungary's declaration of war on Serbia, the archbishop of Zagreb, Ante Bauer, told Croatian troops in the Austro-Hungarian army the following:

Croatian soldiers! The Fatherland calls you to battle! Be courageous because Croatians never ignore the voice of their king of the Habsburg dynasty. During critical times your grandfathers were always faithful to the throne. Be ready to sacrifice your life for the king. The Fatherland is threatened by the enemy [Serbs] to tear her apart....

God and eternal justice call you to be avengers of the crime that happened in Sarajevo. It threatens to grab away support from our king and intends to seize hope for a great future. Let victory be given to you and your weaponry as well.

In his circular to the Catholic clergy Archbishop Bauer said peace is impossible with an enemy who plots against the monarchy by inflaming citizens' dissatisfaction.

Bishop Jeglich stated that Serbs are not only the enemy of the monarchy, but of Jesus as well.

Bishop Mishich, like Archbishop Bauer, reminded Croatian soldiers they should not regret dying for the Saint Apostolic throne, for the well-being of their Fatherland. There was a holy duty to become a martyr, so God would give a heavenly reward....

Stjepan Radich sent a telegram to the Habsburg dynasty under the motto "God lives to protect the king and our people."

In 1831 in Bosnia there was a strong Catholic movement to break away from the pope and to recognize either "the head of the church of the patriarch of Constantinople or the bishop of Montenegro."

After Yugoslav unity the Catholic church and Assembly of Serbs, Croats, and Slovenes did a great injustice to their priests, who had deep national aspirations to be independent from the Vatican. The priests were excommunicated by Archbishop Bauer. Those priests were in favor of the sovereignty of a national Croatian church. The other church always drives water to a strange watermill, not to the national (Croatian) one.

The rejection of the Croatian clergy's request for their own national church was strongly criticized by Dr. Victor Novak, a Croat and university professor, in his book *Magnum Crimen*

3. Dr. Ante Starcevich was the ideological father of the Ustashe organization. A nineteenth-century protagonist of unity for southern Slavs, Bishop Jurej Strossmayer, said, "My

soul is embittered. You cannot imagine how much I mourn the behavior of the friars (fratere). It is a pity that our clergy, who should 'serve the people as the only way to serve God,' serve instead the Roman Curia."

Stjepan Radich was a Croat whose motto was "Believe in God, but not in a priest." He believed that clericalism "is so dangerous that the Croatian people will never really unite with the Serbs, unless they are completely rid of Rome."

Another Croat, Dr. Victor Novak, professor of Zagreb and later Belgrade University and a prominent scholar, wrote about Croats as devoted Catholics who were subject to the influence of the Vatican. A small percentage of Croats "identified themselves as Slavs, letting go of traditional ties and reorienting themselves toward Pan-Slavism. Even that small percentage was decimated by Ustashe pogroms during the war!"

4. In 1991-1992, where were the consciences and ethics of the European Community countries and the United States, who pretend they are acting in the name of civilized society concerning the treatment of Serbs in Croatia?

As expressed recently by Edgar Morin, cultural and political sociologist, the Yugoslav disintegration is the introduction of the new schism between east and west, as it was between Rome and Byzantium, between Christianity and the Ottoman world, which would inevitably bring new iron curtains!

The Catholic Croatian-Germanized world will continue with the west, while the Serbs will be exiled from "exemplary" Europe! Says Sir Alfred Sherman, the bloodshed will continue as long as Germany dominates EC foreign policy.

The historical pattern of the Drang nach Osten, Germany's anti-Serb movement, was an interlude of supporting Croatian Catholic nationalism.

With the satanization of Serbs in the ethnically mixed republics, Croatia and Bosnia-Hercegovina, Serbs have nothing to lose if they continue to fight to the end of their lives!

Professor Salvatorloy wrote in his book *Yugoslavia 1941* that no people under the Balkan sky are more noble, prouder, more loyal, or more courageous than the Serbs, for whom through centuries the soul was tougher.

German historian and poet Johan Kristof Fridrih wrote about the Croats: In the seventeenth century in Magdenburg Park there was a cemetery with a monument. At the bottom of the monument was the inscription "God save us from the plague, famine, and Croats."

General Tilija led Croatian soldiers who committed genocide against local people.

5. On January 6, 1929, King Alexander proclaimed his authoritarian role, which caused grave consequences for the Yugoslav state and her prestige abroad. The Serbian Orthodox church did not agree with the king's policy. Time had proved that the king and his politicians were short-sighted. Their greatest mistake was the formation of Yugoslavia in 1918 based on three nationalities—Serbs, Croats, and Slovenes. The Croats, as was shown later by their behavior, could only be satisfied if they had their own independent state. Serbs could not understand nor much less accept Yugoslavia's disintegration!

King Alexander tried hard to please the Croats, the Catholic church, and the Vatican with the concordat, hoping for their sincere cooperation for their common interests. Nobody could accomplish anything constructive if hated dominated over logic.

6. The Vatican had tremendous experience signing condorats with various nations.

Thus in 1886 a concordat was signed with Montenegro and was ratified by the Serbian Parliament in July 1914. A concordat was signed with Mussolini in 1929 based purely on a moral base; one with Hitler in 1933; and one with Austria in 1934.

Referring to the Montenegrin and Serbian concordats, there was not one word about mission activities; rather, "the religion of the Roman Catholic Apostolic" church could be executed freely and publicly in Montenegro as well as in Serbia.

It is worth noting what the Roman Catholic author Tomislav Vukovich said in an article titled "Who Prevented the Concordat in the Kingdom of Yugoslavia?" (*The Voice of the Council*, no. 26, July 26, 1986). He says that in the kingdom of SCS the government because of her various interests had insisted on regulating the judicial relationship between herself and the Catholic church as she did with other faiths—Orthodox, Jewish, Muslim, and the old Catholic Croatian church. In that context, the concordat would mean equal treatment of the Catholic church with other faiths (Mihailo Simich, *Dossier* [Belgrade: Politika-Svet, March 6, 1991], p. 10). Therefore, according to the Vidovdan constitution, all religions in Yugoslavia were treated equally in relation to the state. However, that relationship was regulated by law, except for the Roman Catholic church, whose relationship could only be regulated by concordat.

Furthermore, in 1922, Roman Catholic bishops drafted a concordat that was later submitted to the Yugoslav government. King Alexander was strongly in favor of the concordat in order to draw the Catholic church closer to him and his government; however, the king was dead wrong when he officially abolished the Serbian name, and replaced it with a Yugoslav one to please the Croats, because the idea of Yugoslavia was first born among the Croats.

The Serbian Orthodox church was opposed to the draft of the concordat because she was put in an unequal position.

The Serbian people were behind their church authority, knowing exactly what role their church played in the preservation of the Serbian nationality during long centuries of slavery.

Was it coincidence the Serbian Orthodox patriarch died the same day the Yugoslav Parliament voted on the concordat? Though the concordat passed in the Parliament, Stojadinovich's government was forced to shelve it. The patriarch's two brothers, Urosh and Alex, also died, during a visit to their ailing brother, Patriarch Varnava, in the Belgrade patriarchate. People became suspicious that perhaps the three brothers had been poisoned!

7. *Literary Republic*, No. 3, Zagreb, 1926.

8. Avramov Smilja, *Genocide in Yugoslavia* (Belgrade: Politika, 1992).

9. *Ibid*.

10. In 1941 in the ISC, Artukovich issued a decree that all Serbs and Jews living in Zagreb must leave within 12 hours. If any citizen sheltered them he would immediately be executed on the spot. In 1945, Artukovich fled from his country, living for the most part in Switzerland, Austria, and Ireland. In 1948 he entered the United States as a priest under the name of Alois Anich. In 1951 the Yugoslav government asked for his extradition. The entire Catholic apparatus in the United States worked to refute the accusations against him. After thirty years of legal battles he was finally extradicted to Zagreb in 1986.

11. Glina Church was built in 1826 and destroyed by the Ustashe in 1941. In 1969 the Croatian Communist authority razed the church walls to the foundation and erected a Commemoration Hall for cultural and recreational community activities. The Communist local authority rejected an application of the Serbian Orthodox church to rebuild the church on old church grounds that had been used as a shooting ground. Finally, Croatian Communists gave permission to build a new church approximately 150 meters from where the old church was. The unfortunate Serbs saw what they built during the day was knocked down by monsters at night.

The song "Pretty Our Homeland" written by Antun Mihanovich, a Croat, was performed for the first time, in 1846, in the old Orthodox church. It was set to music by a Serb from Glina, Joseph Runjanin. The song was sung by the Serbian Orthodox choir from Glina. Imagine such harmony and respect between Serbs and Croats during the Austro-Hungarian rule!

12. Antun Miletich, *Concentration Camp Jasenovac, 1941-1945* (Belgrade: People's Books, 1986), p. 7

13. Archive VII; cited in Miletich, *ibid.*, pp. 720-721

14. The book *Mission in Croatia 1941-1946* was written by Guiseppe Masucci, secretary of the Apostolic representation, envoy of Pope Pius XII to the Croatian Episcopate. In his diary on February 2, 1946, Masucci wrote that he had sent a protest to the Croatian prime minister Bakarich, Nazor, and Monsignor Ritting against the book *Jasenovac* written by Djordje Milisha. In that book it was stated that Prof. Dabinovich had submitted a memorandum against the Ustashe, to the Apostolic Nunzio Marcone after Marcone reported him to the police. Masucci complained that was shameless slander! The complaints went on....

Masucci was trying to extricate the Holy See from any hint of wrongdoing concerning the Ustashe regime.

15. It is imperative to mention here some of the barbaric Ustashe methods used against their victims in Jasenovac and other Croatian concentration camps.

Jasenovac victims were hit by wooden mallets or metal bars. Then their throats were cut with daggers and they were thrown half dead into a hot furnace to perish without a trace. Also, hands and legs were tied so the victims formed a ball, and they were rolled on boards with nails. Their soles were burned, flesh was cut from their ribs, and then salt was poured into the wounds. After inmates were stunned by a mallet, their stomachs were ripped out and a heavy item was tied around the neck to weight the victims down so they wouldn't float to the surface of the Sava River. To prolong sufferings, besides various tortures, victims were put in "bivouac" in wire cages or separate cells to die without food and water; girls were raped before execution, and the like.

One Ustasha would throw a child into the air to be "caught" by another on his dagger. They would rip open the stomach of a pregnant woman and pull out the unborn baby and then tear open the stomach of an unpregnant woman and thrust in the fetus.

The pattern of cruelty was similar wherever there were Serbs to be victimized. Old men, women, and children were all tortured terribly before they were murdered. Victims were impaled; they were burned on the chest or burned alive on a stake or in their homes or churches. Boiling water was poured on them. Eyes were gouged out while the victims were still alive, and noses, ears, et cetera were cut off. The genitals of Orthodox clergy were cut off and stuffed into their mouths. Men were tied to the backs of trucks that then drove off at high speed. They were impaled to the floor with large nails hammered through their heads. They were thrown into pits and wells and abysses. Children were thrown into the fire, or their heads were crushed against a wall or their spines broken against rocks. Thousands and thousands of Serbian bodies floated in the rivers Sava, Drava, Dunav, and their tributaries. Some corpses bore a sign: "Direct to Belgrade to King Peter." A boat was found on the Sava River heaped with children's heads and the head of one woman (the mother of some of the children?), and a sign: "Meat for Jovanova pijaca (market), Belgrade." Roasted heads were found in Bosnia, and Serbs were forced to drink out of dishes filled with the blood of their brothers. Mothers were raped in front of their daughters, and vice versa. Many girls were taken away for Ustashe harems. There were rapes on the altars of Orthodox churches.

For all these unspeakable horrors there are witnesses and documents attesting to the dreadful details. (Smilja Avramov, *Genocide in Yugoslavia* [Belgrade: NIP Politika, 1992], p. 42.)

16. Fitzroy Maclean, *Eastern Approaches* (London: Lowe and Brydone, 1944), p. 487.

17. Curzio Malaparte, *Kaput* (Rome: Milano, 1948), p. 130.

18. Edmond Paris, *Genocide in Satellite Croatia, 1941-1945* (Chicago: American Institute for Balkan Affairs, 1961), p. 63.

19. Smilja Avramov, *Genocide, op. cit.*, p. 274.

20. Reviews of Draganovich's book *Massive Conversion of Catholics to Orthodoxy*:

Yugoslavia was a conventional heterogeneous country. Therefore, ultra clero-Fascists got the green light for destroying the Yugoslav state. By such conspiracy was realized the ISC as a "resurrected state" whose "sovereignty represents the crown of King Zvonimir," who was a vassal of Pope Grgur VII.

Reviews of Draganovich's book deeply touched the root of Croatian falsification of historical facts. Stanoje Stanojevich, a professor at Belgrade University, reviewed Draganovich's book, but he did not completely grasp its meaning and intention. Stanojevich's main remarks about the book were about the lack of "tolerance and respect toward those who have different opinions."

Meanwhile, two Ustashe, Juraj Jurjevich and Mladen Lorkovich, also reviewed Draganovich's book in an extremely positive light.

Jurjevich says the Balkan Catholic church "always had a defensive character." During Turkish rule, the Catholic church was persecuted while the Orthodox church was expanding under normal circumstances. In fact, however, the Catholic church with its missionary zeal was solving religious problems with fire and sword.

Victor Igo stated on the floor of the French parliament that Europe was helping Turkey destroy the Serbian land.

Popes in Rome and Avignon (a city in southern France) organized Catholic wars on the Balkan peninsula.

Another reviewer, Mladen Lorkovich, a distinguished Ustasha, says Draganovich's dissertation should be worked out reflecting the effect of apostasy.

Referring to Bosnia and Hercegovina, their descendants today are both Catholics and Muslims who have a common Croatian name.

In essence, the historical reality of Bosnia and Hercegovina requires such a review, wrote a Catholic newspaper, which obviously needed a historical falsification of Bosnia. It is impossible to debate with those who don't respect historical facts and truth, as a majority of Croatians were regarding Serbs in mixed areas. Says Josip Butovac, historiography knows that some Orthodox people were converted to the Catholic religion. It was wrongly represented what was done by duress, that is, religious persecutions.

Those reviewers greatly appreciated Draganovich's book, because it gave them a key for understanding, as they say, that in Montenegro, Bosnia, and Hercegovina there once was a Catholic majority! They were massively converted to the Orthodox faith and so almost lost the character of Catholic countries! This is absolutely untrue!

The conversion of Serbs on Croatian territory was put on the agenda as an actual problem and was discussed in "Massive Conversion of Catholics to Orthodox on the Croatian Linguistic Territory during Turkish Rule" published in the magazine *Croatian Review*.

21. As a most loyal and devoted Catholic country the postwar Austrian government supported the Vatican plans.

Waldheim denied his participation in the Kozara massacre. When Vladimir Dedijer demanded that Waldheim's dossier be submitted so the Russell committee could investigate his case, Croatians flatly denied having any information about him. Why then, did Pavelich decorate Waldheim for successful Kozara operations?

Did the Croatian Communist government deny the wrongdoings—the criminalities of their predecessors, the Ustashe government of Ante Pavelich—when the entire free world knew they had occurred?

22. Croatian Krizari (crusaders) in the British zone in Austria had received military equipment, including weapons from the British. Ustashe pamphlets signed by Pavelich were dropped in Croatia by British planes. In a word, the Ustashe had strong support from both Britain and the Vatican, where the command center was located.

23. Former Ustashe minister Lovro Sushich controlled stolen money (over a billion in war booty) from Serbian churches, monasteries, and from innocent Serbs, Jews, and even Gypsies. Sushich held 400 kilos of gold and a considerable amount of foreign currency.

In mid-1945 Draganovich secretly went to Austria to secure the stolen treasure of the Ustashe while it was hidden there. On his return to Rome, Draganovich took forty kilos of gold bars with him. Later the Ustashe treasury was controlled by a committee of three persons: Draganovich, Ustashe Stjepan Hefer, and Gen. Vilko Pechnikar, Pavelich's son-in-law. U.S. intelligence officers discovered the whereabouts of the Ustashe treasure that Pavelich had transferred to Switzerland in early 1944. There were 2,400 kilos of gold and other valuables in Berne that were intended for exchange on the black market for U.S. dollars and Austrian schillings by the Ustashe. Draganovich had lobbied the British ambassador at the Vatican by submitting to him a memo from Ustashe ministers in Zagreb. The memo was then sent to London via the Vatican, urging the formation of a Pan-Danubian confederation, in early 1944.

24. Avro Manhattan, *The Vatican/ Holocaust* (Springfield, Mo.: Ozark Books, 1988).

25. Joseph Shaparic, a famous Slovak and prominent scholar, was well educated and idealistic. He stood for Slavic mutual respect. He was the founder of Slavic studies.

In Croatia, Shaparic's followers were Croatian journalist Imbro Tkalac, Franc Kurelec, Marko Bogovich, and others. At that time, according to Shaparic, there were no Croats living in Slavonia, Dalmatia, and Istra. Croats then were living around today's Tito Zagorje and its surroundings.

26. Yugoslav Archive 103-27-180, Representative in Rio de Janeiro to Ivan Subashich, May 15, 1942.

27. Milo Boshkovich, *Victory*, Feb. 3, 1991, p. 6.

28. Regarding how many Jews were killed, Tudjman says the number of six million Jews exterminated is based to a great extent on emotionally biased testimony. It also comes, he claims, from one-sided, exaggerated data in the postwar reckonings of war crimes for squaring accounts with the defeated perpetrators of war crimes.

29. In 1990, Franjo Tudjman identified himself with the ISC during his political campaign. After the war, if Croatia chose to remain as the ISC, similar to Pavelich's model, the Soviet Union and the Serbs would have the right to demand war reparations from Croatia. "Kalashnjikov" was the Soviet weapon for defending the Slavic people. That was Tudjman's creation. Tudjman's Croatia is currently flattering Western Europeans, playing cards with Austria and Germany against Russia, Serbia, and Orthodoxy. Today's Yugoslav people, like all nationalities with common sense, should pray for the long lives of all their honest people and for the disappearance of sinful leadership, the sooner the better.

30. Tudjman has been using similar methods against Serbs as Pavelich did. State and civilian terror against Serbs has been "legalized."

A comparison of Hebrang and Tudjman expressions:

On July 13, 1941, Andrija Hebrang said the ISC is an expression of an ancient dream of the Croatian people. In February 1990, Franjo Tudjman stated that the independence of Croatia was the expression of the centuries-old aspirations of the Croatian people. Both Hebrang and Tudjman had a legitimate right to struggle for and to obtain freedom and independence for their Croatian state. However, nobody should put his head in the sand or escape by covering the face with mud without answering the fundamental question: How and under what circumstances was that independence acquired? Was it an armed or political struggle (or both) for their national liberation, or was it obtained under the auspices of their Nazi and Fascist occupiers?

31. From "Public Appearances of Neofascist Symbols in Croatia," Zagreb's *Vjesnik*, June 24, 1991: Public appearances of Ante Pavelich's posters and Ustashe symbols do not present a praiseworthy picture of Croatia, especially since she is pretending to be the most democratic republic in Yugoslavia. The defenders of such doings in Belgrade may say, Chetnik symbols and posters of Draza Mihailovich are being sold. It does not mean one's own sins can be excused by what others do. The world's democratic governments are condemning most energetically the appearances of neo-fascism and neo-Nazi works. Why? Because the whole world knows how much evil was done under those symbols, which are not only beginning to appear but are also prevailing in Zagreb.

After the Croatian republic declared itself an independent state, free of the federal government in Yugoslavia, the inhumanity and hatred of Croats toward Serbs continued. The Holocaust during World War II was the pinnacle, but the force seems as powerful as ever. Serbs again are fearful of a repetition of 1941, and they are endeavoring to hold a peaceful referendum.

The word "pure" in racist and religious terms is being used again, as it was used by the Nazis, Fascists, and Croat Ustashe. The current officials in Croatia have given every indication that they intend to "purify" those who work and live within the Croatian boundaries. How? By allowing only persons who are third or fourth generations of "pure" Croatian to work in the police force and by dismissing all persons who are employed within the government if they are linked in any way to Serbians, such as having Serbian in-laws or a spouse, for instance.

32. Monuments to the victims of fascism were destroyed in Split on January. The monument to Jozo Lozovina-Mosor, a well-known anti-Fascist, was blown up; thirty or so monuments in Dalmatia, reminders of the anti-Fascist struggle, have been demolished over the last twelve months. A sign was placed at the entrance to the Borovo Rubber and Footwear works in May 1991 saying "No entry for Serbs!" In some restaurants in Zagreb, in the Dubrava district in particular, signs saying, "No Serbs or dogs," were posted. Also, Serbian cemeteries were razed and their homes and libraries were burned, especially after a film was shown depicting preparations for the continuation of Serb liquidation in Croatia.

On October 30, 1990, on the door of the Serbian Democratic Party (SDP) in Zagreb were carved with a knife the words "Srbe o vibe" (Hang Serbs on the willows); in 1990, on the Orthodox Christmas Eve, someone wrote, "Serbs, you are condemned to death" and "We want Serbian blood," "We will cut your throats." In May 1991 in Zagreb the SDP premises were drenched with gasoline and ignited.

Also, the Serbian Orthodox church in Croatia was brutally attacked. Bishop Simeon Zlokovich in Karlovac and Father Dragan Glumac were injured by the Croatian police; Father Hrizoston Jovich from Skradin was attacked and mistreated. On March 3, 1991, the Serbian Orthodox Church in Pakich was stormed by Croatian policemen. They took down the icons of Serbian saints and they left a terrible mess, as the Ustashe had when they slaughtered Serbs in Glina Church in 1941.

Appendix A

From Kozara Mountain to the Hell of Jawenovac
by Ilija Bradarich

Could any rational mind understand when neighbors and friends of yesterday become bestial enemies of today? In the name of Christ and the Croatian "thousand years of culture" those culprits used the most sadistic methods—they gouged out a victim's eyes and cut off the ears and nose before plunging their knife into the victim's heart or throat to end the agony. For four full years during World War II these acts were performed by the Croatian Ustashe, at the instigation of a large number of Croatian Catholic clergy.

Such deeds were done against whom? Those crimes were committed against innocent Orthodox Serbs, Jews and Gypsies! Why? Simply because they had a different ethos and religious affiliation. Under such threats and fear, Serbs were forced to move from the plains areas in Croatia to regions in Bosnia in the hope of salvation.

I was born in the village Slabinje, Dubica region. When World War II broke out I was not yet a teenager.

In the spring of 1942 the Serbian exodus from naturally unprotected areas like Bosanski Novi, Bosan, Kostajnica, Dubica, Gradiska, and Prijedor reached Kozara Mountain.

In the summer of the same year, Croatian Ustashe together with their Nazi protectors launched an offensive against innocent Serbs who had taken refuge there. Kozara Mountain was encircled and then hit by heavy artillery and by airplanes that attacked refugee shelters in the Kozara area. As I learned later, one who took part in that German offensive was the Austrian officer Kurt Waldheim, later Austrian president, who was decorated by the Croatian fuhrer Ante Pavelich. Also, Father Krunislav S. Draganovich took part in that offensive, not with a rifle in his hands but as the person in charge of forced food requisitions for the Ustashe units.

Partisan units encircled together with the people of Kozara, like always, succeeded in penetrating through German and Ustashe lines, leaving the Serbian refugees at the mercy of the Croatian Ustashe.

Unfortunately, I was there. I personally saw heaps of dead Serbian people in one small Kozara village.

All Serbian survivors were taken to Bosnian Dubica. Along the way, older people and women with children became exhausted and were unable to continue. The Ustashe simply plunged bayonets or knives into them or shot them on the spot. Oh, that tragic scene, I will never forget it!

During that arduous trip Croatian peasants barked at us like furious dogs, cursing King Petar, Churchill, Roosevelt, and Stalin as our allies. They had been educated by the Croatian clergy to hate not only Serbs but also those who were allied with Serbs.

In Bosnian Dubica I saw one Muslim lady crying when she saw us in such miserable physical condition and psychological deprivation!

On the trip the idea came into my mind to run away. But where? I had lost my orientation.

After a short stop in Dubica we continued our march toward the notorious Jasenovac camp. Along the way, the stronger men were beaten up by the merciless and sadistic Ustashe.

When we neared the camp we saw a high metal gate and barbed wires all around the camp. Also, around the camp there were thrown various utensils and clothes.

When we entered the camp I noticed Jovo Binkovich, who had been there since 1941. Right away he came up to us and asked if we knew anything about his family. Jovo had not yet been liquidated because the Ustashe needed him to operate the brick kiln in the camp. He had had a kiln himself in his native village. Jovo told us that in that camp 600,000 to 700,000 innocent people had been killed. People were burned alive in brick kilns. In Gradina they were killed with mallets and axes; in Zvonara, victims were slaughtered by daggers; women were raped, tortured, and killed in front of their children. In Kula of Stara Gradishka, children were poisoned with cyanide gas or run through with bayonets in front of their mothers. The terror in Jasenovac lasted 1,335 days.

That did not happen in the Stone Age, but in the first half of the twentieth century! What kind of civilization is it when law breakers tried to hide those crimes with silence?

Jovo also told us we were lucky because until recently all people gathered in the camp were killed or burned in the camp's furnaces. The Germans took away the stronger and healthier prisoners to work in Germany as forced labor.

In the camp the men were separated from their wives and children, to make their lives even more anguished and unbearable.

I was in Jasenovac for a few months. Each day there was an eternity. Many inmates became ill from exhaustion caused by lack of food and clean drinking water and by the filth. People died like flies. In the morning a peasant cart, filthy and blood-soaked, was driven in carrying some spoiled food like corn bread and some kind of soup made from only God knew what! On its return the cart was piled with corpses that had died the night before.

There was a swamp inside the camp. Its water was filthy. Despite that, people used to drink the water because they preferred to get sick and die rather than just die of thirst.

One afternoon some Catholic nuns came with large hats on their heads and with crosses around their necks. The inquired if there were any sick children. Oh yes! Many mothers brought their feeble children for help. The nuns gave them some kind of medicine. Only they and God knew what kind of medicine it was! During the next night many babies died; if the older children survived they had diarrhea.

There were no bathrooms inside the camp. All physiological necessities were performed under the open sky.

Every day the stronger men were picked up to perform forced labor. Whoever could not go was liquidated on the spot. No mercy! Who could expect it from wild animales?

When my neighbor Dushan Dragovich passed by his wife he asked her about their baby. Then he threw her a piece of his own bread hoping the baby would survive. People sometimes have hope even when there isn't any.

One day I approached the swamp to take some dirty water to drink. I heard a voice near me asking, "Listen, young Bradarich, I want to ask you about my family. Are they still alive or not?" It was Jovo Simich. I could not recognize him. His hair was cut to the skin, and he had no moustache or eyebrows. He had returned from the United States just before the war started. Jovo stayed in a barracks with very sick people.

My relative Zdravko Kolor was there. He died there before he was even twenty!

One day I saw a few Croats from Crkveni Bok. They were looking for their friends, Croats and Serbs, to let them get out from the camp because they needed help. I don't know if they succeeded in their humanitarian mission. Few Croats were like them!

One afternoon the Ustashe came and asked us who wanted to work or go to another camp because this one was overcrowded. Most of my relatives volunteered for work, and I joined them. We expected they would send us to another camp or simply shoot us. Anyway, we had nothing to lose. The girl Dragica Gacich helped me pass the Ustasha guard and to continue the trip with that group.

We walked under guard from Jasenovac camp to Novska. In the suburb of Novska was a brick plant. It had been productive but the plant was idle then. We were assigned lodging around the plant.

The Ustashe often mistreated camp inmates by beating them up, especially when they were lined up for a meal.

One day the camp administration expected some commission to visit. They ordered us to take off all our clothes to be boiled and disinfected against lice and various epidemics. The same day the Ustashe took away some men under the pretext of sending them to the Zemun camp. They were killed after they had been taken away.

Fortunately, my mother had succeeded in running away from the Ustashe escort on her journey to the camp at Stara Gradishka. She was told I was still alive in the camp of Novska. Therefore, she bought a new set of clothes for me. She arrived in camp together with her son-in-law, who was a Croat. They managed to pass the suit to me. The Ustashe then thought I was a young Croat. So I left the camp without any problem. That was the happiest day of my life.

At the end of my sad story I would like to apologize to my readers if they could not grasp what I was trying to say. It is always extremely hard to express something adequately when logic, honesty, and love are replaced by irrationality, dishonesty, and hatred.

Appendix B

Massacre in the Glina Church

Ljuban Jednak, peasant from Selishte, Bosnia, was the only survivor of the massacre of 1,200 people in Glina. He told his own tragic story.

''Here is what happened.'' Ljuban began his narration without excitement, in a quiet voice. On August 29, 1941, Ljuban was at home in Selishte. The people in and around the village were fearful because rumors had already spread that the Ustashe were killing all Serbs above 16 years of age. Therefore, all men were on guard! On August 29 the Ustashe suddenly surrounded his village. Women began wailing and crying. The Ustashe picked up all males from the houses. Ljuban succeeded in penetrating through the Ustashe ranks and escaped capture. At Balinac he rested for a while, until an old lady ran into the house shouting, "Run away, the Ustashe are coming!"

Ljuban again succeeded in escaping. He ran to the village Gredjane. The Ustashe were already looking for him. They had already taken away all men over 16 years old. Only the females and boys and old men remained. Fear and horror took over the village.

Nobody knew what had happened to those who had been taken away. The mothers and wives of the captured men lamented and cursed the Ustashe.

Ljuban left his hiding place to look for safer shelter. He pulled himself up onto the road at just the wrong time. An Ustasha caught him and threw him into a truck. In the truck were more arrested Serbs. They were all fearful, asking each other what the Ustashe intended to do with them. "Oh, how stupid I was," says Ljuban, "to let one Ustasha arrest me. I should have jumped on him and then run away."

The Ustashe brought them to Topusko. During the trip they cursed their prisoners' Serbian mothers and made fun of them by telling them, while winking at each other, how they would prepare a welcoming reception for them. The fearful captives doubted it. The Ustashe asked if they wanted to lodge on the church floor or at the community hall. They received different replies. They asked Ljuban, too. He told them it did not matter because he felt it was a senseless choice.

Ljuban was taken to the community hall. It was impossible to run away from there. They were surrounded by the bandit Ustashe. They were armed to the teeth and growled at the captives like furious dogs. The men trembled and sweated, and one youngster was crying. Ljuban recognized two Ustashe, Franjo Butorac and Stevo Mulac. Ljuban could not believe those men would kill them. They had known each other for a long time and they had never quarreled.

At about 3 p.m. a truck began to hum in front of the community hall. Ljuban looked through a window and saw a truck full of Serbs from Staro Selo, Katinovac, and Perne. When the truck stopped, Ustasha Tusich shouted to check those arrested to see if they had weapons. One by one they took them off the truck. They beat them with rifle butts over the back and head. The innocent victims screamed for help, saying, "Don't do it, brothers! Spare our lives, for Christ's sake!" The Ustashe swore at them and continued to hit them with rifle butts, feet, fists, and everything that could be used.

One old man was hit by a Ustasha over his back as if he were a tree stump. From the unfortunate man were heard only quiet sighs. The man fell once but got up again. The Ustasha hit him against the door and blood dripped over his white shirt. There were chaotic moments. Vulgar curses, blows, and laughter of the Ustashe were mixed with the yelling and screaming of innocent victims.

"Mother, you Serbian! You'll bleed today!" roared the wild Ustashe.

"Sir, what could I be blamed for? Don't do it, for God's sake. Have mercy on us!" various voices cried out.

After beating the captives heavily, the bandits took money from them. Some men voluntarily gave money in order to stop further beating. The Ustashe then quarreled among themselves about who should get the plundered goods.

Ljuban saw Djuro Vukinovac, and he begged him to spare his life. Djuro replied, "Ljuban, I would help you, but you can see yourself I do not dare."

He turned away.

The men from the truck were driven back to it by rifle butts and barrels. Those wretched persons climbed up quietly into the truck.

When the truck left, Djuro ran toward Ljuban, who had earlier begged him to spare his life. Before Ljuban could say anything else, Djuro hit him over the head with his fist. Ljuban was very surprised. He could not understand how a man could change himself in a moment to become a beast. From where had come such hatred? Who nourished that hatred from the cradle to the grave? And for what? How could any real Christian become such an uncontrollable beast?

Ljuban then continued his horrible story.

They came to Topusko by train. They were sorted like sardines and they could not breathe, especially the older men. There was not enough air, no water, no food. Through a small window in the boxcar Ljuban noticed Stanko Zuzich, from Gradjane, who was on guard.

"Please, Stanko, open the door a little. Don't let us be choked," begged Ljuban.

"Get out, swine!" Stanko replied.

"Stanko, for God's sake, pass me a drop of water!"

"Get out!" Stanko shouted.

The next morning they heard the Ustashe saying they would go to forced labor. The arrestees reasoned that if the Ustashe stopped beating and killing them, forced labor would not be the worst thing, and it would not last forever. There was probably some justice for them in the world, after all.

With such hope the train brought them to Glina. They met more Ustashe there, who looked at the captives with blood-red eyes. One Ustasha, the cutthroat Nikica Vidakovich, barked, "You came, mother you Walach (vlashku). Bring them to pray to the Serbian God! It will be good for their souls. Run for the keys to lock them all into the church!"

They took the captives into the church. The Ustashe locked the church door and put sentries around the church. In the church the men had plenty of room to stretch their exhausted bodies and they could breathe. They were alone. They could talk quietly. Some of them shook their heads, saying the Ustashe intended to kill them here. The majority of them still believed the Ustashe finally would not deceive them but would send them to forced labor. Men still hoped. As the old adage says, "People born with hope, live and die with it." They were very thirsty and hungry, lying on the church floor exhausted. All were so quiet that even the buzzing of a fly was noticeable.

Not long after, the lock of the church door clicked. Rajo Kreshtalica and Milich came in yelling. "Get up!" They took the men's names. They needed the list, they said, to assign them to labor in Lika.

Around noon the Ustashe second lieutenant entered the church and asked if anyone was converted. Two answered the call, and the Ustasha took them with him. Some offered the consolation that those two had not gone to forced labor.

After noon the Ustashe came in again. "Who is Pero Miljevich?" one asked. "Come closer, 'dove.' What do you know about the Chetniks? Tell us all you know about them!"

Pero replied fearfully, "I know there is a list of Chetniks in the recorder's office."

"Are you a Chetnik?"

"No."

"You are not?! God be cursed!... You are Chetnik! Aren't you, Wallach whore. In 1935 who fired at Malinca, ha! Your Serbian mother...."

The Ustasha rushed toward Pero. He carried a thick rope from the belfry. The Ustasha told Pero to lie down on the floor. He beat him so hard and long until Pero's body became totally black. At first Pero screamed, but then only his moaning was heard.

The Ustashe left again.

At dusk they came back. One Ustasha asked whoever had any money to bring it forward to buy food. Six thousand dinars were collected. The captives were hungry and they all gladly accepted the Ustasha's offer. A while later a motor was heard buzzing outside the church.

Now armed Ustashe entered the church.

"Light the candles!" Some big candles would not light. "It is a great sign," whispered an older man with trembling lips.

The lighted candles gave enough light inside the church. The bandits walked around the captives and glared at their victims. The hearts of the men beat faster.

"Do you believe in our paglavnik" (Ante Pavelich) screamed one Ustasha.

"Yes," a few frightened voices called out.

"Shout then, 'Long live Paglavnik.'"

Some did.

"Louder, mother your Serbian, louder."

Suddenly a carbine was fired over the captives' heads.

"Lie down!" shouted one murderer. Then, "Get up!" "Lie down!" "Up!" "Down!"...

One murderer roared like a tiger toward another, "Why are you playing?" (by cursing their God). Then he turned toward the captives. "Take off all your clothes and shoes!"

Hurriedly the men dropped their coats and trousers onto the church floor. Men had to sit down to take their shoes off. Nobody asked why.

In that darkest time that could be imagined, while the men took off their apparel, they heard the Ustashe breaking the church altar apart and throwing icons all around. Some holy objects were thrown at the captives.

They forced the men to lie down. They were only in their underwear. In a frenzy the Ustashe began to stomp on them and beat them with rifle butts and barrels. The church filled with the sounds of lamenting, weeping, and screaming for help. Help from whom?

"Where is Pero Miljevich?" an Ustasha asked again.

Pero replied in a feeble voice. He already was severely beaten, and he begged the Ustashe to stop. They interrogated him again about the Chetniks.

During that horrible scene a knife in the hand of one Ustasha shone in the candlelight. Their breath stopped. The Ustasha slowly approached Pero and thrust the knife into Pero's neck. Pero fell without a word. Blood gushed from his neck. The only sound was the man's labored breathing. It was obvious the Ustasha was professional in his bloody trade.

Now the Ustasha asked again if anyone knew anything about the Chetniks. Stojan Bojich pretended to know, hoping it would help him be released. "Say something, then we'll let you go home," a bandit encouraged him.

"I'll tell everything, just let me be free," said Stojan. Stojan began talking. He had not even ended his story when he was slaughtered.

Then the general slaughter began. "Kill, kill! (Kolji, kolji!) screamed one Ustasha. The scene was indescribable. It was worse than Dante's inferno.

One Ustasha noticed that a victim who had been hit was wiggling. He ordered him to get up and put his head on a table. The Ustasha simply grabbed the victim by his hair and pressed his head hard against the table. Then he put the sharp point of his knife against his neck and ordered him to sing. Blood gushed from the man's neck, while from his throat could be heard wheezing. Another Ustasha cracked his head open with a rifle butt.

Three captives hid in the altar. Later they climbed to the belfry. They remained there for two days and nights, until a Ustasha sniper, Stevo Mulac, cut them down.

Ljuban lay in a puddle of blood among the victims. He awaited his fate. The Ustashe were congratulating themselves and each other on their great deeds.

Meanwhile, a teenager raised his head. An Ustasha saw him and hit him with a rifle butt. Then the Ustashe methodically went among all their victims, hitting them with rifle butts and then with knives. When they knew their victims were all dead they began pulling corpses out of the church and throwing them into a truck.

Ljuban was pulled by one leg over the stone floor. He pretended to be dead. He was thrown into a truck that was already full of bodies. In the truck he lay on his back, as the Ustashe continued to throw even more corpses in. In one horrific moment a body landed on Ljuban, its cut throat bleeding into Ljuban's mouth.

The truck began to move ahead. Ljuban heard a command to drive closer to the pit. The Ustashe threw the bodies from the truck into a pit. They also stacked bodies like logs in the pit in order to fit in as many as possible. Other trucks continued to come with live men. Above the pit they were hit on the heads by hatchets and hammers and then they were thrown into the pit. The Ustashe brought one young woman. Ljuban thinks she was a schoolteacher. The wild animals raped her first and then threw her into the pit. Some victims were moving in the pit. The Ustashe opened fire with carbines and pistols. Ljuban was wounded in the leg.

Late at night the job was done. The Ustashe left the pit. Ljuban was preparing to get out of the pit and run away. He noticed an apparition among the corpses crawling toward him, asking in a whisper if he were alive. They both pulled themselves out of the pit. Then they went their own ways.

Ljuban came to Majske Poljane, to the home of his uncle Pavle Loncar, where he stayed for six months. Ljuban was the only survivor from that group. The comrade who came out of the pit with him was later caught by the Ustashe and killed.

Chapter Seven

Serbs Demonized by Their Old Allies and Their Traditional Enemies

The recent coalition against Serbs is inevitable: the old Allies (the United States, France, and Britain) who formed the Yugoslav state in 1919 and the old traditional enemies (Germany, the former Austro-Hungarian Empire, and the Vatican) who were defeated, militarily and politically, by the end of World War I.

All Serbian friends and foes should know at least the fact that through their thorny history the Serbian people have never been the aggressor; rather they have been stoically defending their independence, sovereignty, and above all liberty. They did it in the past; they will continue to do so in the future to the last Serbian man, against all kinds of subjugation, either ideological or religious.

There is no race which has shown a more heroic desire for freedom than the Serbs, or achieved it with less aid from others or at more sacrifice to itself.

—Temperley, British historian

Serdjo Krizman, a Croat, published a map in 1943 in Washington, with the legend that in fifteen months 749,000 Serbs were killed in Yugoslavia by the occupiers: Germans, Italians, Hungarians, Albanians, Bulgarians; the Croatian Ustashe alone killed over 600,000.

To be historically accurate, according to Italian and other sources, including witnesses who are still living, Italian occupation forces on the territory of the Independent State of Croatia (ISC) saved over 200,000 Serbian lives from the Ustashe genocide, even though paradoxically both Italians and Croats are Roman Catholics. Croatian Nazi policy, from Ante Starcevich who exhorted "Serbs to the willows" (Serbe o vrbe) to Tito's general Tudjman, espoused the total annihilation of Serbs, as Nazi Germany called for the annihilation of the Jews during World War II. And there is yet another paradox: The German Catholic church protested against Jewish genocide in Germany, while the Croatian Catholic church did not lift a finger to save the lives of innocent victims, and silence is still being kept

415

to the present time! Says Edmond Paris in his book *Genocide in Satellite Croatia 1941-1945*: The greatest genocide did not happen in Nazi Germany but in Ustashe Croatia.

By whom was this genocide hidden from the world's attention? Undoubtedly Tito and his cohorts would have reminded all around them that anyone who dared to mention the crimes would be mercilessly persecuted. Therefore, Tito should be credited, along with his police apparatus, for the survival of fascism in Croatia after the end of World War II. It meant that the Ustashe who committed the crimes were never brought to justice.

At the third meeting of ZAVNOH (Provincial Anti-Fascist Council of National Liberation of Croatia), among the first laws passed were those forbidding provocation of national racial and religious hatred or sowing discord. What did those lawmakers do in 1941 to prevent genocide in the ISC?

Dr. Milan Bulajich is the author of the books *Ustashe Crimes of Genocide* (vol. 1 & 2, 1988; vol. 3 & 4, 1989) and *The Mission of the Vatican in the ISC* (vol. 1 & 2, 1992). He appeals to his generation to look for the truth through the facts to reach a right and just conclusion. Those facts should be gathered by scientific historical analysis, free of personal emotions and prejudice, regardless of who is involved—the Ustashe Ante Pavelich or Bulajich's commandant in World War II, Tito, or His Eminence Pope Pius XII.

Serbs Always in Jeopardy

In a diplomatic conversation the secretary of state of His Eminence Meri del Val revealed that the pope and the Roman curia saw a destructive disease in Serbia that would little by little damage the monarchy and in time would entirely corrode her. The Austro-Hungarian Empire was the superlative Catholic state, the strongest rampart in Christ's church. Destroying that bulwark would mean destroying the strongest fulcrum in the church's struggle against Orthodoxy. For those very reasons, for her self-existence, she must rid her organism of the evil biting into her body. So, the Catholic church should do whatever was necessary to achieve that goal.[1] Pope Pius X said he regretted that Austria-Hungary had failed to punish her dangerous neighbors (Serbia).[2]

The Vatican considers the Serbs a barrier to expanding the Catholic faith to the east. In that regard, Tito faithfully continued the policy of the Vatican and Austria-Hungary as a loyal Catholic and a former Austrian soldier during World War I, when he was captured by the Russians on their battlefield. During World War II and the Yugoslav revolution, when the Partisans were stationed in western Bosnia, in Ustashe territory, Tito slipped over once a week to pay a visit to the nearest Catholic church authority there.[3]

Did Tito Visit the Pope, and Why?

On August 6, 1944, Tito flew to Caserta, Italy to converse with Gen. Wilson and Gen. Alexander about military matters. He also talked with Winston Churchill, who was the instrumental architect of installing Tito on the Yugoslav throne. They talked about the political structure of postwar Europe. Tito shrewdly deceived Churchill by telling him he did not intend to impose communism in Yugoslavia. That would be contrary to the intention of the other European countries!

On August 9, 1944, Tito secretly visited the Vatican and Basilica of Saint Peter. The visit with the Pope was carefully planned to go unnoticed by the world media and not to disturb his main military protectors, the Serbs. On the same day, Tito sent letters to Marko (Alexander Rankovich) and to Bevc (Edward Kardelj), without mentioning his visit to the Holy See.

On August 11, 1944, the Italian ambassador at the Holy See informed his ministry of foreign affairs that the newspapers had reported the Yugoslav officer's visit to the Church of Saint Peter. On the 9th the Vatican also announced that Marshal Tito and his guard had visited the Basilica of Saint Peter, obviously incognito. Nothing more. On August 12 the Italian embassy at the Holy See offered more information:

On August 9, 1944, five military automobiles accompanied by a camionette holding British policemen armed with machine guns stopped at the stairs of the Basilica. About twenty Yugoslav officers came out. Some of them were in military uniforms, and they surrounded one of them who was most authoritative. Later he was recognized as Marshal Tito.

The group, about seven or eight policemen, all with machine guns kept ready to fire, went upstairs to the Basilica. Before the group entered the church, on the priest's demand everyone except Tito had to lay down their weapons. Some newspaper photographers followed them, but it was forbidden to take any photographs.

Early in the afternoon, Marshal Tito and his guard left the Basilica.[4]

Italian political and military authorities investigated why Tito and his representatives had visited the Vatican. His representatives had to explain why some Catholic priests had been killed by Tito's liberation army! Tito's representatives tried to convince the Vatican that despite this, Tito held the Catholic church in high esteem and desired to maintain a cordial relationship with her.

In conclusion, the Italian ambassador states, Tito representatives' visits to the Vatican were not the first.[5] On that secret mission to the Vatican in August 1944 Tito was accompanied by Brig. Fitzroy Maclean, the head of the British mission at Tito's headquarters; Maj. Gen. Ivan Rukavina; Lt. Col. Jefto Shashich; the translator Olga Ninchich-Humo; and Tito's personal escort, Capt. Nikola Prlja. On August 10, Radio Vatican briefly mentioned Tito's visit to Rome.[6]

The assertion of Miladin Milatovich, Tito's ambassador to Rome, that Tito did not contact the Holy See was unfounded, says Bulajich.

What about Edward Kocbek, a Slovenian who submitted a memorandum to the Holy See? Tito gave instructions in advance, and the advice was passed on to Kocbek by his compatriot Edward Kardelj. Kocbek was chosen as a former Catholic seminarian whom the Vatican could trust. The National Committee for Yugoslav Liberation had approved the memorandum. It expressed the desire for reconciliation and the sincere cooperation of Tito's Communist party with the Vatican for the mutual benefit of Yugoslav Catholics and the Vatican. The Vatican was pleased with those contacts, even though the new Yugoslav representatives were Communists. Old Vatican tactics and diplomacy dictate never closing the door completely to anyone if they might be beneficial to the Vatican's goals.

How and why did Milatovich come in contact with Krunislav Draganovich, a notorious Ustasha and war criminal? It raises many questions. Draganovich was sent to Italy by Archbishop Stepinac. Through the Vatican he was to try to save Ustashe lives after the war. Did Milatovich as a member of the Yugoslav military mission know who Draganovich was and about his activities to break Yugoslav unity, for which Milatovich was allegedly fighting?

In 1971 Tito visited Pope John Paul II at the Vatican. They were scheduled to discuss a project for the formation of a Sub-Danube federation in which Croatia would have the role of "Catholic perivoj" (poetic—"park"). Prof. Vladeta Koshutich, a member of the board of the Association of Serbian Writers, reports on the content of Tito's conversation with the pope. The secret of the conversation came to the public through confidential Catholic sources in Italy. As documented, Tito secretly paid visits to either Pope Pius XII or to Pope John Paul II, in his capacity as secretary of the Yugoslav Communist Party (YCP) or as Yugoslav president. Tito continually tried to please the Vatican, while he was extremely cautious not to arouse suspicion among non-Catholics in Yugoslavia.

Was it permissible for Tito, who was at the top of the Yugoslav party hierarchy, to publicly or secretly visit any pope? Was such behavior insubordinate to international Communist policy and discipline?

Bulajich complained that the Vatican failed to allow its archives from that period to be opened. Historians like Bulajich have the right to ask what has been hidden about those secret meetings behind the back of the Yugoslav people!

Right after the war Tito visited Zagreb. He had expressed his desire to meet with Catholic authorities to consolidate the relationship between the new Yugoslav government and the Croatian Catholic church. At a meeting on June 2, 1945, Bishop Salis-Seewis greeted Tito and told him the Catholic church could work quietly and without any interference to lead souls on the path of truth and God's justice for the benefit of the entire country. Tito replied in a moderate and friendly tone, emphasizing his desire to work together on a proposal to guarantee the position of the Catholic church in Croatia. Tito emphasized the Catholic church needed to be closer to the people than it was, meaning it should be more loyal to the Yugoslav community than to the Croatian state.[7] Tito treated the Serbian Orthodox church in quite a different way, as has already been discussed in previous chapters.

During World War II, Tito was praised and supported as a champion of democracy, liberty, and human rights by the Western Allies, especially by the Western liberal press, the BBC, British prime minister Churchill, and some British SOE agents who worked for the Comintern. Those influential forces brought Tito to the helm of the Yugoslav ship; he was not elevated by the Yugoslav people, especially the Serbs who under Mihailovich had broken with him in 1941 because Tito had begun an internal revolution against multiple occupiers in the Serbian lands.

After the war the Western Allies continued to support Tito, economically, militarily, and politically, to stay in power against the will of the majority of Yugoslav people. As the former British foreign secretary Lord David Owen said, he ruled his country with an iron fist. Some Westerners still condemn Serbian leadership as Communist though they themselves brought and kept Tito and his associates in their lucrative and corruptive positions.

Croatian and Slovenian leaders have been more flexible than the Serbian leadership. They have been trying to protect their Separatist national interests regardless of Yugoslavia's national interests.

The U.S. ambassador in Belgrade, Zimmermann, noted there was more freedom in Serbia than in Croatia and Slovenia.

Jelena Lovric, a Croatian journalist, says the gloomy outlook for the free media in Croatia is not yet at an end. His article referred to the Split newspaper *Free Dalmatia*, which finally fell under Tudjman's supervision, though Tudjman claims Croatia is the most democratic country in the world.[8]

Stepinac's Role in the Independent State of Croatia[9]

The ISC was the main culprit in provoking Yugoslav disunity through unforgettable ethnic hatred, intolerance, and genocide. It was successful because it was supported by the Croatian Catholic church and the Vatican.

The Croatian Catholic church has been instrumental in helping and nourishing the ISC, while the Vatican provided moral protection. Therefore, to understand correctly what is happening today and why, it is imperative to know what happened yesterday.

During the reign of the quisling Ante Pavelich, Alojzija (Vjekoslav) Stepinac had the title of President of the Bishops' Conference and was the military vicar of the Ustashe forces, appointed by Pope Pius XII at the beginning of 1942. The Croatian army (Ustashe and Domobrans) committed horrible crimes against Serbs, Jews, and Gypsies. Stepinac as head of the Croatian Catholic church wholeheartedly assisted the Croatian Nazi Pavelich in his ISC. He was a perfidious and sworn enemy of the Yugoslav state. Croats did not fight for the formation of Yugoslavia nor defend her in 1941. The majority of Croatian civilian and ecclesiastical authorities tried to bury her as quickly as possible.

In the Vatican strategy, Croatia was regarded as the "bulwark of Christianity" against Slavic Orthodoxy as first demonstrated by Serbian Orthodox "schismatics."

Stepinac deeply believed:

1. The dogma of the Catholic church—her authority is derived directly from God; therefore, the Catholic church is the only church, true, universal, and unerring.

2. Freemasons and Jews are a great evil in Yugoslavia.

3. Communism represents a punishment from God. If Russia were a Catholic country, Communists could never have succeeded in coming to power.

In Stepinac's view (shared by the Vatican), a "schismatic" Orthodox church rules Yugoslavia. In Yugoslavia the Catholic church and the Orthodox Serbs have nothing in common. Orthodoxy represents a dangerous obstacle for the fulfillment of Catholic dogma. Such a Yugoslavia should be destroyed by the secession of Croatia and Slovenia as independent Catholic states.

Under a religious veil Archbishop Stepinac involved the Croatian Catholic church in political matters. In July 1934 he told Robert Schumann, a member of the French parliament, in five years more blood was spilled in Croatia by Serbian gendarmes than by Austria in a hundred years! It is already the eleventh hour! France could only count on Yugoslavia if Yugoslavia could solve her internal problems.

Stepinac also asked for help from Hungary, through consuls Revicsky and Horthy, and from the Italian fascist government. In his contacts, Stepinac recommended the Serbs return to the faith of their ancestors, that is, bow to the Holy Father. We could then get our breath in this part of Europe, where Byzantium played a horrible role in history. The Catholic church is the one true church of God.

Dr. Victor Novak, a Croat, says that Stepinac not only destroyed lives; he also destroyed the souls and the conscience of man. His name should remain among the darkest and the most disgraced in the history of world civilization. He could not defend himself with his hypocritical, Jesuit lies that the conversions were in the interest of the converted because their lives were spared. The horrible memory of a quarter million Orthodox converted to Catholicism is the harshest indictment of not only Stepinac but also all those in the Vatican who protected him. He as well as Marcone and the entire episcopate should be put on canonical trial for the violation of canon law no. 1351.[10]

Addone Talpo, the author of the book *Dalmatia—Chronicle for History* (*Dalmatia—Una Cronica per la Storia*), asked Stepinac why he had not resisted Pavelich. The Ustashe plan forcefully converted hundreds of thousands of Serbs to the Catholic faith in a period of several months. The Catholic church aided in that conversion. During that unChristian process, Bishop Stepinac's only intervention to the Ustashe Pavelich was to say that Orthodox Serbs should not pay a tax for their conversion.[11]

In 1943 Stepinac said that for Croatia, Chetniks are a greater danger than Partisans.

On July 13, 1944, the pope sent a letter to Churchill via Churchill's son Randolph, saying there was a dangerous situation in Yugoslavia. The pope, of course, had in mind the interests of the Catholic church. In 1944 Stepinac submitted letters via the Vatican's ambasadors to the U.S. and British governments referring to Allied bombing of Croatian territory, especially the open city of Zagreb. What would Stepinac say about Belgrade, which was bombed by the Germans on April 6, 1941 despite being an open city and suffered over 20,000 casualties? In 1944 on Orthodox Easter, during the hour of church services, the bombing of Belgrade was repeated, not by Germans but by Allied air forces in the Balkans!

Stepinac asserts: It is no exaggeration to say that no nation was hit so hard during the war as unfortunate Croatia. Croats were devoted to Western principles and ideas more than any other people in that part of Europe. Stepinac tried to explain the loyalty of the Croatian people by saying their political structure was similar to that of western Europe. How could he say something like this when Croatia was incorporated into the Austro-Hungarian Empire during World War I and then fought against the Allies? In World War II, Pavelich, the head of the Ustashe regime whom Stepinac was trying to save, declared war against Britain, France, and the United States!

Stepinac was more concerned about political and ideological matters than about religious ones. On July 9, 1944, he said that for centuries the Croatian people had been gravitating toward freedom, and so today they were defending their sovereignty with an unmeasured number of victims.[12]

Responding to that statement, Radio London noted on July 20, 1944, that the Ustashe were the only ones to say that their regime defends their freedom and sovereignty. They themselves were neither free nor independent. Archbishop Stepinac added his name to those on the list defending Germans and Ustashe, which means he is an enemy of the Allies.[13]

On August 8, 1944, Stepinac sent a letter to Pavelich saying that Croatia does not have to die—she must live. Also, on August 9, 1944, he sent a letter to the Nazi commander of Zagreb, Adolf Sabljak, saying Croatia has to live, not die.[14] He was tireless in contacting various dignitaries on both sides of the political spectrum to save Ustashe lives and the ISC.

Stepinac sent Dr. Krunislav Draganovich to the Vatican, supplying him with "facts" to defend the Croatian cause:

1. Croatia belongs with the West, in spirit and culture, while the Serbs have gravitated toward the East (Byzantium).

2. Throughout their history Serbs and Croats never had the same political interests.

3. 99 percent of the Croatian people favor the ISC.

4. The souls of Croats were anti-dictatorship, while the Ustashe were Germanophiles.

5. More Croats than Serbs were killed. The Chetniks of Draza Mihailovich used excesses against Croats, especially in Bosnia, Hercegovina, and Sandzak. (In May 1943 Stepinac submitted some documents, among which was a copy of the Chetniks' proclamation to the state secretary of the Vatican to fight to the last drop of blood against the Germans, Ustashe, and Italians.[15])

6. Serbs and Slovenes collaborated more closely with the Germans, while Croats are against the Germans, even in governmental circles. (After the Italian capitulation in September 1943 the Croats realized the Germans would be defeated. They then began to reorient themselves toward the victorious West, not by conviction but rather for political opportunism.)

7. Croatia should enter into a European Danube federation.

Stepinac simply ignored the Ustashe genocide committed against Serbs, Jews, and Gypsies.

The Croats demanded freedom and independence and respect for their religious and cultural tradition from the Western leaders.

On September 20, 1945, the Croatian Bishops Conference adopted a proposal of Archbishop Stepinac embracing his pastoral letter. The essence was the rejection of the formation of a new Yugoslav state. In fact the bishops supported the continuation of the ISC created by Hitler and Mussolini. The Catholic bishops also defended against claims of crimes committed against humanity by Ustashe Catholic priests (Shiroki Brijeg-Hercegovina). The Catholic clergy were trying to make martyrs of criminals. Where had Christian ethics and truth vanished?

Dr. Zarko Vimprolsher, who presided at Stepinac's trial, accused the bishop of being responsible for many deaths, persecutions, mistreatments, and forcible conversions. In his public appearances, Stepinac spoke on behalf of the Ustashe and the occupiers.

Was the Vatican Directly or Indirectly Involved in Croatian Ustashe Genocide?

Pope Leon X (1519) honored the Croatian people as "Fortissimum Antemurale Christianitatis" (najchvrshci bedem krishcanstvra). In November 1939 Pope Pius XII saluted some Croatian pilgrims and exhorted them to be as strong in their faith as Velebit (a mountain in Lika), steady as a rock that defies the waves and storms.[16]

The main goal of the Croatian Holy Year (July 1940 to July 1941) was, as Archbishop Stepinac articulated it, to "return the Orthodox to the faith of their ancestors," to the Catholic faith, with a program of conversion.[17] The committee responsible for organizing Serb conversion to Catholicism was formed in accordance with the Holy See.[18]

Academician Vladimir Dedijer, Tito's biographer, and another member of Russell's tribunal, Christopher Farley, sent a letter to Pope John Paul II. That letter stated that recently, at the trial of Andrija Artukovich, former interior minister of Pavelich's quisling government in Croatia, close ties were revealed between the Pavelich government and the Croatian Catholic church regarding genocide against Serbs, Jews, and Gypsies by Croatian Ustashe in the ISC. At that trial Artukovich himself stated that as interior minister and a faithful son of the Catholic church, he first asked for the opinion of the high dignitaries of the Catholic church in Croatia before doing anything. According to Dedijer, the available documents confirmed Artukovich's statement.

The former vice-president of the Yugoslav government-in-exile, Juraj Krnjevich, sent a letter to the Los Angeles judge stating that Artukovich was innocent of the crimes of which he was accused by the Yugoslav Communist government. On June 10, 1942, Monsignor Augustin Juretich had informed Krnjevich that Jasenovac was a place of execution. Such horrors as the Ustashe were committing there had never been heard of before, not even under Soviet political rule or the Gestapo. The tortures were beyond the wildest imagination. Jasenovac was the center of Ustashe work, where thousands were sadistically executed, said Juretich.

On January 15, 1959, a federal judge in Los Angeles, Theodore Hocke, dismissed the case of Artukovich's extradition to Yugoslavia as a war criminal. The Croatian Catholic *Herald* praised the victory of Artukovich as a victory for the Croatian cause.

In 1983 the truth came out about Artukovich in the book *Quiet Neighbors: Protecting Nazi War Criminals in America* by special assistant to the U.S. Justice Department Allen A. Ryan. Artukovich had had full support and protection from the Catholic church.

Pavelich's connections with the Vatican were such that his extradition would have had serious consequences for the Roman Catholic church.[19] Bertrand Russell was disappointed at the Vatican's coverup of crimes committed in Croatia.

Dr. Ivo Mashtruko, an ambassador for the Federal Republic of Yugoslavia, stated, "There is only one truth—the pope's truth, the truth of the Catholic church."[20] The French bishop at the Vatican told Bulajich that the roads to truth are very difficult.

Statement of Janko Shimrak, Bishopric Administrator

The administrator of the Krizevac bishopric, Janko Shimrak, said that for centuries there has been theoretical talk about conversion. Every great work has its adversaries. Our work is legal according to the decision of the Holy See and also according to the decision of the eastern branch of the Congregation of Cardinals as well as of the circular of July 30, 1941, of the government of the ISC, which intends to convert Greek-Easterners to the Catholic faith.[21]

Pope Pius XII Was Well Informed about the Conversions[22]

Pope Pius XII was well informed by the Catholic press about mistakes made in handling the mass conversion of Orthodox Serbs in the ISC. The pope knew what had happened at the beginning of December 1941 when the Ustashe committed genocide against Orthodox Serbs in Ljubinje, and when Serbs were thrown, some still alive, into the pit of Shumarnica near Chapljina (August 6, 1941). The horrors continued in Duvno Polje, Klepci, and Goranci.

According to documents of the Holy See, what was most important was the creation of a pure Catholic church (Civitas Dei—God's government) and moving historical Christian boundaries. This could only be accomplished by destroying Orthodox "schismatics."

There is not the slightest doubt that Stepinac coordinated his policy with the accord of the Holy Father. During his visits to the Vatican, Stepinac told the Vatican secretary that the Croatian government had not committed as many crimes as the Serbs claimed. On the contrary, she did many good things for the benefit of the Catholic church!

Apostolic Representative Marcone's Role in the ISC

Ramilo Marcone, the pope's representative in Zagreb, agreed to establish diplomatic relations with the ISC. Thus, the Holy See had to break diplomatic relations with the recognized royal Yugoslav government, then in exile in London.

On August 5, 1941, Marcone paid a visit to the Ustashe poglavnik Pavelich, the head of the Croatian state. Pavelich was delighted by the visit and grateful to the Holy See. Stepinac recorded the event in his diary. Stepinac notes further that the Holy See had recognized the ISC "de facto"; "de jure" recognition was withheld because of the foreseen negative Allied reaction.[23]

Marcone stated regretfully that the schismatic hierarchy in Belgrade had not only rejected but also excommunicated the metropolitan newly appointed by the Croatian government to head the Croatian Orthodox church! Pavelich formed a new "Croatian Orthodox church" by decree in order to calm the world reaction to the genocide against Serbs, Jews, and Gypsies in the ISC.

Marcone as apostolic representative defended the fascist Croatian government, saying the current Croatian government never engaged in religious persecutions against schismatics. On the contrary, for over a year, schismatics had been favored by the Croatian civil authority. Thus, the ministry of religious affairs has one schismatic priest as an employee. In the ISC, 222 Serbian bishops and priests were killed and 334 other priests were either expelled or fled from Croatia. Furthermore, the Croatian authority was seriously considering the problem of recruiting new schismatic clergy. Some young men had already been sent into Bulgaria for their education to the priesthood. (Bulgaria was an ally of Nazi Germany.) Marcone also emphasized that he appealed to Pavelich for a slow and careful approach to schismatic conversion and to refrain from destroying Orthodox churches.

Archbishop Ivan Sharich, a War Criminal

The archbishop of Sarajevo, Dr. Ivan Sharich, a sworn Ustasha, stated in the presence of apostolic delegate Marcone and Archbishop Stepinac, today comes the moment for Catholics to settle accounts with Serbs. A Catholic rebellion is the only way to fulfill justice, truth, and honesty.[24]

Many Croatian Catholic clergy were strongly associated with the racist Ustashe ideology. Bulajich has submitted a still incomplete list of 694 Croatian clergy who belonged to or were assistants of the Ustashe terrorist organization or who collaborated with the occupiers.

Spellman Visits Pope Pius XII

During World War II the archbishop of New York, Dr. Spellman, was called "the flying bishop." At the request of President Roosevelt he went to the Vatican. During his stay in Rome he visited the pope four times. Spellman, a chaplain for American Catholics in the armed forces, said his visit to Rome was strictly religious. However, rumors spread that during his stay in Italy he had two real objectives: to clarify how the West should handle the danger of postwar Soviet communism that might spread through Europe and how to stop the hostilities among the Western countries.

During his stay at the Vatican the Ustashe plenipotentiary Lobkowics told him the Ustashe state stood as "the Antemurale Christianitatis." He said the River Drina should be the border between East and West and insisted the restoration of Yugoslavia could have deterimental consequences for the Croatian people and for the Catholic church as well.

During their conversation, Lobkowics presented two books to Spellman: *Ustashe Principles* and the "Gray book." Spellman asked if he should give the books to Roosevelt, and Lobkowics said no, because we had declared war against the United States.

Most of the thoughts of Starcevich were exposed in *Ustashe Principles*. The book openly proclaimed Serbophobism and anti-Semitic genocide. The bond between the Catholic church and Ustashe principles, proclaimed the Ustashe line, is the principles of "God and Croats." The gray book contained "documentation" for world consumption, purporting to show that any genocide in the ISC had been executed against Catholics, not against Orthodox Serbs!

What Did Lorkovich Plan for Serbs Who Survived in the ISC?

Lorkovich had connections with a Reich representative who assured him that they understood Croatia's "problem," meaning the Serbs. After the final victory, said Lorkovich, the Nazis and Croats would resettle surviving Serbs to Siberia.[25]

Slovenian Priests Against Ustashe Genocide

Is it Christian to force someone by the sword to change his or her religion? That is the spiritual equivalent of murder.

The Slovenian Catholic priests and other refugees from Slovenia were accepted as Nazi victims in brotherly Serbia even though Serbia herself had suffered terribly under Nazi occupation.

The Slovenian priests asked their bishops for help. Bishop Ujcich forwarded their petition to the Holy See asking for the following:

1. The Holy See should condemn the bloody persecution of the Serbian Orthodox faithful in the ISC.

2. As long as the tyrannical regime lasts in Croatia, the Holy See should forbid the conversion of Orthodox to Catholicism.

3. The Holy See should advise Croatian bishops to defend Orthodox Serbs regardless of the consequences, even at the risk of their lives.

Meanwhile, the Croatian episcopate and the secular authority did the opposite. They worked together for conversion. Just one example: Dr. Mirko Puk, the minister of justice and religion in the ISC, wholeheartedly supported the conversion of the Greek Orthodox to the Catholic faith under the pretext that conversion was a legal action for returning to the faith of their ancestors.

The Serbs could not understand why the Holy See did not raise a voice against such crimes committed by her faithful, the Croatian Ustashe, especially since the Vatican had protested against persecutions in the Soviet Union.

A Voice Raised Too Late

In June 1989, fifty years after the crimes were committed, Serbian Orthodox bishops sent a letter to the Croatian Catholic Bishops Conference, saying the Christian conscience is astonished that the Croatian Catholic hierarchy with its archbishop Alojzije Stepinac, in a time of pressure and fear of annihilation, applied the principle of conversion.[26]

According to an official report of the Archbishops Synod of the Serbian Orthodox church, 240,000 Orthodox Serbs were converted during the existence of the ISC. Says Avro Manhattan in an official document of May 8, 1944, Archbishop Stepinac sent a report to the Holy See informing the Vatican that up till then "244,000 Orthodox Serbs were converted to God's church."[27]

Why had the Serbian Orthodox church been silent for so long concerning the conversions and genocide of Serbs? The atrocities were hidden behind the veil of the Communist motto "Brotherhood and unity," which was invented to hide the crimes committed against humanity by the extreme right wingers, the Croatian neo-Nazi Ustashe! Anyone who dared to mention any of those crimes, including the existence of Jasenovac, the Yugoslav Dachau, was mercilessly punished by courts that blindly executed Tito's orders.

Repetition of Yugoslav "Tragedy within Tragedy"

To understand better what is happening today and why, it is necessary to look briefly at the events of the past.

In the thirteenth and fourteenth centuries, Serbia was one of the most advanced and prosperous countries. The Serbian tzar Dushan (1331-1355) created a code of laws under which even servants could publicly seek justice against noblemen. Those codes are still studied at some European universities. Jevrosima, the mother of the popular hero Marko Kraljevich, taught her son, "It is better to lose one's head than to commit a sin" (to perform an unjust act).

In 1377, at the tomb of Saint Sava, Tvrtko Kotromanich was crowned as "king of the Serbs and Bosnia and of the coastland." Tvrtko sent some of his forces under the command of the vojvoda (general) Vlatko Vukovich to help his friend the Serbian prince Lazar at Kosovo Field. He was defeated by the Ottoman Empire in 1389, over a hundred years before Columbus discovered America. From that time on the Serbs continued to fight against the Turks' penetration into the heart of Europe.

In 1914 the Austro-Hungarian Empire attacked Serbia. Tito was then within the empire's ranks. In that uneven battle Serbia lost over half of her soldiers. In 1914 the vojvoda Zivojin Mishich counterattacked the Austro-Hungarian army, capturing 190,000 of her soldiers. And the Serbs regained control, for one week, of the territory they had lost in a three-month retreat. Such was the spirit and the morale of the Serbian soldiers. But Austro-Hungary, helped by Germany and Bulgaria, took the counteroffensive and the outnumbered Serbs again had to retreat.

In 1915 Russian tzar Nicholas II sent telegrams to France and Britain saying if they didn't evacuate the exhausted survivors of the Serbian army to safety he would sign an armistice with Austria-Hungary. So the rest of the Serbian army was evacuated to the Greek island of Corfu. In April 1915 the Allies, France and Britain, signed the London Agreement with Italy, pledging that if Italy joined the Allied side she would get Dalmatia when the war was over. The Serbian government appealed through its Russian ally not to make any concession to Italy without consulting the Serbian government. The Kingdom of Serbs, Croats, and Slovenes was formed in 1918, uniting these people for the first time in their history. The regent Alexander and his Serbian government generously united with the Croats and Slovenes without any preconditions and on an equal basis. Alexander accepted over 20,000 noncommissioned officers and other officers from the Austro-Hungarian army into the Yugoslav army, promoting them one or two ranks. The regent hoped the country would gradually progress toward a real democracy as had existed in Serbia before World War I. He strongly (and naively) believed that Yugoslavia would become a "melting pot" like the United States.

The Allies asked Serbia to unite with Montenegro, Macedonia, Bosnia, and part of Dalmatia if the rest of Dalmatia was given to Italy. Serbia refused. Since that time Italy has been an unfriendly neighbor to Yugoslavia. At the Versailles Peace Conference in 1919, American president Wilson met with the Serbian president Nikola Pashich as a symbol of respect and appreciation for what tiny Serbia had contributed toward the Allied victory. Serbia was particularly rewarded for all the favors she did for Croatia, which enjoyed the benefits of unification, when the Croatian Ustashe Pavelich organized the assassination of King Alexander and the French foreign minister Bartu in Marseilles on October 9, 1934!

Unfortunately, the darkest forces in Yugoslavia by hatred, intolerance, and envy erupted like a volcano in 1941, spewing unprecedented genocidal violence. In 1968 the Austrian historian Friedrich Heer noted that what happened in the ISC was "the singular murder of the twentieth century," following the racist ideology of Ante Starcevich. Croatian generations born after the end of World War II wear T-shirts adorned with Starcevich's picture. Representatives of the Western media fail to comprehend what such symbolism portends.[28]

Does Tudjman Faithfully Follow Starcevich and Pavelich?

According to Gen. Alexander Vasiljevich, chief of the Yugoslav army counterintelligence service, in October 1990 Croatia secretly imported weapons (18,000 "Kalashnjikov") from Hungary under the code name "Shtit." The Croatian defense minister, Tito's general Martin Shpegelj, and Interior Minister Josip Boljkovec, also a Tito general, were responsible.

That action was not officially condemned by the Yugoslav government because the Yugoslav defense secretary, Gen. Veljko Kadijevich, was indecisive. The Croatians were feverishly preparing to form their pure "civitas dei" (God's government) state.

Tudjman's victory in attaining leadership was a victory of the most extreme form of Croatian radicalism combined with chauvinism and clericalism. Croatian archbishop Franjo Kuharich blessed a baby's cradle to symbolize the rebirth of the ISC at a rally in Jelacich Square in Zagreb. In December 1990 the Croatians adopted a new constitution. Its first sentence read: "Croatia is the state of the Croatian people." This clearly means that the constitution sanctions apartheid regarding Serbs within Croatian boundaries. It was recognized by fifty nations of the world. Tudjman's constitution deprives Serbs of any rights and protections under the law. Tudjman is anti-Serbian not only in rhetoric; he applies it in practice. Despite camouflaging himself as a democrat, he is in fact a close follower of the racist philosophy of Ante Starcevich and Ante Pavelich. Nora Beloff, a well-known writer and observer of the Balkan scene, compares Tudjman's constitution with Stalin's in 1935, even though Tudjman poses as a strong anti-Communist.

Lord Carrington, a former chairman of the EC peace initiative, described Tito's former general Tudjman as an evil man, under whose leadership chauvinism is promoted and intensified. Tudjman calls his a new Croatian nation. In fact it is actually a continuation of the former Nazi Ustashe state currently supported by Kohl's Germany as the ISC was in Hitler's era. Many Serbs have lost their jobs in Croatia because of what they are. Serbian schools, their publications, and even their Cyrillic alphabet have been banned. In short, not only physical but cultural genocide is being promoted. In 1980 the Croatian Communist government cynically banned all political and cultural associations of Serbs as "harmful" for Serbs as well as Croats. After the Croatian proclamation of independence and sovereignty on July 25, 1991, foreign and domestic journalists were harassed by Croatian extremists if they dared to criticize the Croatian government and politics. In 1991 in Croatia some journalists were killed because they failed to submit their reports to the Croatian government before publication.

Fear of the secret police still exists in Croatia. Judges remain under the control of the ruling party, as do the press and television stations. How can Tudjman truly call the new Republic of Croatia "part of the West, part of Europe," when it is ruled by one party like a neo-Nazi Ustashe state? Democracy is treated there like a golden apple: Look but don't touch, much less grab or eat. There is neither civil nor intellectual freedom, says Croatian journalist Jelena Lovric.

In his book *Wasteland of Historical Reality* Tudjman interprets genocide as a natural phenomenon that is not only permissible but recommended for the survival or restoration of a chosen nation!

Russian historian Dr. Jelena Yuryevna Guskova did not say without reason that "Fascism was born in Croatia before war broke out, and it was the fascist behavior of the government of President Franjo Tudjman.'' She is preparing to publish a book called *Yugoslavia in Flames*. Croatia realized that she can only become independent through war. Thus the ethnic cleansing of Serbs in areas where they have lived for centuries began in Croatia.

Evgeni Ambratsumov, the president of the Russian foreign policy committee, was interviewed in Zagreb by Globus. He said that international recognition of some Yugoslav republics had ignited war inside the former Yugoslavia. The recognition was based on mistaken premises and the irresponsible judgment that the restoration of a Bosnia and Hercegovina republic would prevent war.

Also, Croatia, with its mixed ethnic and religious population, should have first reached agreement among all its people before recognition was given. For reasons that might include preventing such an agreement, Croatia was recognized in a hurry by Germany, the Vatican, and Iran.

What Do Serbs in Croatia, Bosnia, and Hercegovina Fear?

President Tudjman welcomed back from abroad all Ustashe, including Ante Pavelich's family, even though they had committed genocide during the war and had escaped from the country without being brought to justice.

In 1990 the Ustashe in Croatia adopted their old checkered symbol as the Croatian national flag (shahovnica). It was reminiscent of the Ustashe genocide during World War II, and is as repulsive to Serbs as the swastika is to Jews. Some Croatian fighters wore armbands with a skull and crossbones and the letter *U*, which for Serbs is also reminiscent of the Nazi Ustashe SS. Any soldier including Ustashe who had committed a crime was unworthy to wear the Cross, says the Serbian Metropolitan Jovan of Zagreb and Ljubljana. Serbs feared the rebirth of neo-Nazism, as happened in Croatia.

Tudjman wants to have a "purified" Croatian state. Does purification mean the same as ethnic cleansing? Why do Croatian Nazis want to exterminate Serbs on their territory? Because Serbs remain Serbs, with their distinctive Orthodox religion. They are proud of their ethnicity and the principles they live for. We do believe that if the Serbs were Catholics there would not be any persecution against those living under Croatian jurisdiction.

The Serbs of Krajina as well as those in Bosnia and Hercegovina must defend their human rights to survive. They have learned from horrible experiences in the past. The international public was deceived by the one-sided information coming from the media. Serbs in Croatia were wrongly stamped as "terrorists," "aggressors," and the like. The Serbs were called criminals, but in reality they were victims rather than oppressors.

After a referendum, the Serbs proclaimed their Republic of Serbian Krajina with administrative borders of secessionist Croatia. Did the Serbs have the right to self-determination as did the Croats, Slovenes, and Muslims?

Herb Brin, editor of *Heritage*, said on March 26, 1993, that the Serbs were fighting like Israelis who refuse to be hurled into the sea. The German-led EC was calling secessionist Slovenia, Croatia, and Bosnia-Hercegovina the epitome of "democratic aspiration toward self-determination." However, Serbs were called "hegemonists" and "unitarians" even though they were asking for independence for sheer survival, while the other republics were already, so to speak, independent "states within a state," according to Tito's constitution of 1974.

The Serbian tragedy is repeating itself.

Tito did recognize two autonomous provinces, Kosovo and Vojvodina, at the expense of the Serbian republic, but not autonomous Krajina.[29]

Germany's Role in the Break-up of Yugoslavia

What is happening in Yugoslavia in 1991-93 is the continuation of World War II.

Germany, the Vatican, and Iran were among the first to recognize the independence of Slovenia, Croatia, and Bosnia-Hercegovina. For Germany, the Balkans are an opportunity for territorial or influential expansion (Drang nach Asten), while for the Vatican the area is marked for spiritual expansion. Croatia, Slovenia, and Bosnian Muslims were always German allies. For that reason, as well as a desire to perpetuate her national interests, Germany rewarded them as independent governments.

Germany was happy to get an opportunity to expand her influence eastward to the Balkans. With her dominant economy, she also succeeded diplomatically in imposing upon the EC her desire to create small client states in the Balkans. Mitterand, the president of France, was weak and indecisive in objecting to it, while Britain had insufficient weight in the European diplomatic theater.

Kohl calculated rightly that the Americans would follow the European lead (Europe is first the responsibility of Europeans), so he proceeded further and recognized independence of Bosnia and Hercegovina. In his efforts he was backed by the German foreign minister Geshner, who had worked diplomatically behind the scene for years.

This was a decisive factor in Yugoslavia's disintegration. The aggressive Catholic church, with the help of Marxist atheists like Tito and Croatian Communists in particular, had kept the lid on the boiling pot and waited until the appropriate time to escalate the war.

From Kohl's Germany came the second premature recognition of Croatia (the first was from Hitler), with the aim of achieving its ends of controlling transportation lines to the east (Balkans—for the oil supply) and also to central port facilities in the Adriatic Sea. These two issues would bring power and influence to the German republic. Also, Germany plans to build a highway from Hamburg to Saint Petersburg to give Germany domination in the Balkan countries as well as in the former Soviet republics. Is it true that recently Germany rewarded all living former Latvian SS (from Hitler's era) with retroactive pensions? Germany also has it in mind to link Budapest with Trieste and Rijeka via Zagreb. Thus, German economic might would have access to the Mediterranean.

Germany, de facto, forced the EC under the pretext of European political and economic unity to act hurriedly for Yugoslav disintegration along the line of Tito's internal demarcations. Beloff says the British and French governments tried unsuccessfully to persuade Germany and the Vatican not to rush to recognize the former Yugoslav republics. Germany primarily hoped for a quick end to the war "to teach the Serbs a lesson," as the Austro-Hungarian Empire had tried to do with its ultimatum in 1914. The time also has come for the Serbs to be punished for restraining German expansion toward the east. Both Germany and the Vatican have been manipulating the mass media, representing Serbs as barbarian residues of Bolshevism that might threaten not only democratic Europe but also the entire world, as Tudjman often says. During World War II in Yugoslavia more crimes were committed, but the world remained uninformed because some influential powers hid them!

Vladan Desnica observes that evil done and not repented becomes the source of new evils. That is exactly what is now happening in Yugoslavia.

A knowledgeable and professional politician, George Kenon is a former U.S. ambassador to Yugoslavia. In an interview he said that all three sides were committing crimes in Bosnia and Hercegovina. After this tragic war is over, impartial historians will judge "truth through the facts" to give the world as accurately as they can the dimensions and nature of the crimes that have been committed by all involved in these conflicts.

If crimes are only being committed by Serbs, why are there more refugees in Serbia (700,000) and Montenegro (75,000) than there are Croatian and Muslim refugees combined? In the *Calgary Sun*, columnist Eric Margolio claims there were two to three million Muslim refugees! In the 1981 census, the population of Bosnia and Hercegovina was 39 percent Muslim, 32 percent Serb, 18 percent Croatian, and 8 percent Yugoslav (most of them Serbs). The total Muslim population in Bosnia is 1.9 million. Was Margolio's claim exaggerated? This inflated number of Muslim refugees is reminiscent of similar claims made by Partisans during World War II.[30]

"We die when we have to or when we don't want to"—Dobrica Cosic

The Serbs of the republics of Croatia and Bosnia-Hercegovina were unfortunately right to fear the resumption of genocide, as events showed. In September 1990, Serbs were driven out of coastal cities like Zadar. Three hundred Serbian businesses and 163 houses burned.

Simon Wiesenthal told Reuters, "The first refugees in the Yugoslav conflict were the 40,000 Serbs who fled Croatia after a constitutional amendment defined them as a minority." In the meantime, Tudjman's government fired Serbs en masse from their jobs. At the same time only Serbian land-owners were to be taxed in Croatia.

During Tudjman's "new democracy" in Croatia over 200 Serbian Ortho-dox churches were destroyed.

Under Tudjman the Croats were psychologically and materially prepared to execute any order against Serbs. They were supplied with modern military weapons by Germany and Austria. From Poland alone were smuggled about fifty tons of weapons. They also received radioactive materials through secret channels thanks to a German woman, Rita Draxler, and a Croatian, Marijan Sokolovich. They also smuggled in uranium and plutonium. Nu-clear material was transferred from Siberia via Bulgaria to Iraq and then driven by truck to Baghdad.[31]

The top administrative leadership of Yugoslavia was mainly in Croatian hands. The president of Yugoslvia was the Croat Stipe Mesich, who prom-ised he would be the last Yugoslav president before conflict erupted; the Yugoslav prime minister was the Croat Ante Markovich; the secretary of foreign affairs was again a Croat, Loncar; etc.

So everyone was ready at a given signal to do their designated jobs quickly and effectively. Many Serbs could not believe it, let alone understand the core of it.

Premature recognition of the republics of Croatia and Bosnia-Hercegovina forced the Serbs to fight rather than be slaughtered by the same criminals who killed their parents and relatives during World War II. Those mighty representatives of a "New World order" provoked a tragedy by a stroke of the pen for which they bear the moral responsibility. None of them wanted to remember Churchill's words when during World War II he called Yugoslavia "a tragedy within a tragedy." Who carried out that tragedy—the Serbs, or the Croats with the help of Bosnian-Hercegovinian Muslims and German SS troops? It is easiest to blame the Serbs, because they don't have the backing of economically strong Germany, the powerful Vatican, and the weak and ambitious Jelshin who is only interested in maintaining his power and privileges like his predecessor Communists. Also, Serbs do not have petro-dollars like the Bosnian Muslims and therefore cannot hire the most powerful public relations firms in Washington to defend them. As Alexander of Macedonia stated, "There is no donkey packed with gold that could not jump over any wall."

The EC and the United States should know that Bosnia was recognized first by Tito in order to break Serbian unity, that is, to prevent Serbs from forming a "great Serbia." Those who most loudly denounce the Serbs could form a greater united Germany and Croatia, thus expanding borders that were never within her domain before.

In Bosnia, as in Croatia, Serbs were the first victims of ethnic cleansing. They were driven out of Bosanski Brod and, later, Mostar. There was no reaction from the West to these first cleansings; they were not even reported by the media. If the West had acted to stop them, the entire later carnage done by extremists from all sides could have been prevented.

It is an open secret that the Gulf Cooperation Council poured $100,000,000 into Bosnia in just six months. The Islamic countries, notably Iran, were sending weapons and mujahideen via Croatia to fight against Serbs. Their fighting spirit and courage were very low, especially in the rural areas. However, the mujahideen fought more resolutely in the cities to defend themselves. The entire Muslim leadership is dedicated to the Bosnian cause, as if they have no problems of their own. Do they have no less moral obligation to help starving Somalians and unfortunates in other Muslim countries than to intervene in Bosnia?

The powerful media spread misinformation about land grabbing by Serbs in Croatia and Bosnia-Hercegovina. Here is the truth: Serbs have been living in Croatia since the fifteenth century. They lived as the majority in one-third of Croatian territory. In 1941 there were 1,855,000 Serbs in Croatia, one-third of the entire Croatian population. Before the last war started in 1991 there were 600,000 Serbs in Croatia. Where had the rest disappeared? The same is true in Bosnia-Hercegovina. Before this war broke out, the Serbs held 63.4 percent of the Bosnian territory.

In 1389, as mentioned earlier, Serbs from Bosnia came to Kosovo to help Prince Lazar of Serbia repulse Ottoman aggression. The media and politicians should know at least that Bosnian Serbs have been living there for well over five centuries! Why would Serbs leave the territory where their ancestors had lived for so long? The Vance-Owen map would designate to the Serbs about 42 percent of that territory. This would force them to leave about 21 percent of their ancestral property. Who would leave their property willingly, or submit under mandate because of someone's whim or the stroke of a pen?

The international media and decision makers were brainwashed by a coalition of Croats and Muslims who misrepresented and distorted the facts by sophisticated "big lie" techniques developed to hide their genocidal activities. Thus, pictures of dead, wounded, or raped Serbs victimized by Croats or Muslims were labeled as Croat or Muslim victims. On April 19, 1993, the *New York Times* published a picture of 90 Muslim victims of Croats in a mass grave. The next day, on April 30, 1993, the *Oakland Tribune* printed the same picture with the caption "Bosnian Muslims bury 90 victims of Serbian 'ethnic cleansing' in a mass grave." For too many reporters, propaganda that comes from the "vile, neo-Communist authorities" of Belgrade is rejected, while whatever comes from Zagreb is considered authentic and justified!

Here are just a few examples of Croatian vandalism and barbarism. After gathering various materials from all three warring parties in Bosnia, future knowledgeable, impartial historians will inform the world who did what and why.

Gospic was one of the most tragic cities for the Serbs in Croatia. Milica Smiljanich, a witness to the sad events there, tells what happened to Serbs in that city. She states that Tudjman's regime in Croatia differs from the previous Ustashe regime in one respect: committing crimes against the truth by covering up crimes against people. In Gospic, where the chief of police was the notorious Zeljko Bolfa, the crime wave lasted from August 28 to the first half of November. People like herself hid in the cellars to try to save themselves. Croatian extremists arrived on October 16, 1991. They all wore masks. Among them she recognized by his voice Martin Mataija. He was an extremist who before the war was employed as a gravedigger until he was caught taking jewelry from corpses. The masked Ustashe abducted Milica's husband.

An honest Croat (who shall remain anonymous) gave Milica written permission to travel to Zagreb. By secret channels she fled from Zagreb to Belgrade, where she found her children, who had been evacuated earlier. In Belgrade she wanted to publicize the crimes committed against Serbs in Gospic.

The Fourth Lika Reconnaissance Brigade discovered twenty-four bodies near Perushici, above the village Lipova Glavica. Milica's husband, Stanko Smiljanich, was among them. The head of Mico Vranesh, was found at the Rijeka cemetery, and his body was found near Senj. This was reported in Zagreb's evening paper.

Bruce Connac (Konak), the first secretary of the U.S. embassy in Belgrade, went to Zagreb to give the names of massacred victims to Tudjman. Milica had also told the Catholic bishop in Belgrade about the massacres in Gospic, appealing to him to inform the world of this death storm.

Milica also remembered well Tihomir Oreskovich, an emigrant who had returned from Australia, currently commander of the ZNG in Gospic, and Jadranka Markovich, who helped him compile a list of Serbs who were to be liquidated; Bashich worked with these two.

In 1991 President Tudjman bulldozed buildings in the Jasenovac death camp that had been preserved as a memorial to the 750,000 Serbs, Jews, Gypsies, and some Yugoslav-oriented Croats and Muslims who were slaughtered there. For some people like Tudjman, nothing is dear or sacred.

The Committee for Human Rights was informed via their representative Catherine at the American embassy in Belgrade. *New York Times* reporters Stephen Engelberg and Sudetich wrote about that case.

The Helsinki Watch recorded instances when Croatian armed forces broke the rules of war, as in Gospic, Marino Selo near Pakrac in May and September 1991. Captured Serbs were tortured and mistreated while detained. In addition, arbitrary arrests and disappearances, destruction of civilian properties, and robberies were among the violations noted.[32]

Other hellish stories came from Gacka Dolina-Hercegovina. In the first half of 1991 the Ustashoidna Croatian authority did everything it could to make the lives of Serbians miserable, by applying constant psychological pressure. The Croatian MUP (police) invaded villages to demonstrate their power, frightening and mistreating Serb villagers.

The fate of more than 1,500 Serbs in Otocac is unknown. Serbs who could not run away from their homes were slaughtered or burned alive in their houses. It is known that the most fanatic Croats from Otocac, Senj, and Brinjci participated in these destructive, criminal attacks. Following old practices, the Croatian media informed the public that Chetniks burned everything during their retreats! People might wonder why anyone would want to abandon his home voluntarily to be burned and then go to an uncertain hell! The Ustashe plundered everything before burning the houses.

In Drenov Klanac the Serbs' homes were burned by their close neighbors, the Croats. On December 12, 1991, Ustashe attacked Podrum, Dabar, and other neighboring villages. One elderly man was slaughtered, and a woman over 80 years old perished in the fire of her home. On January 7, 1992, on Orthodox Christmas, Croatian armed guardists entered the Orthodox church in the center of Zagreb. They expelled all the faithful by threatening to kill them. Tudjman knew about it.[33]

Tragedy repeated itself in Prebilovci. On August 4, 1941, the town was surrounded by over 3,000 Ustashe composed of Croatian Catholic and Hercegovina Muslim neighbors. As always, the Ustashe committed crimes whenever they could catch Serbs. They threw infants up in the air or hit their heads against walls, and raped young girls in front of their mothers. Many innocent victims were killed. People captured in Prebilovci were taken by railcars to Golubinka pit and thrown into it. Forty-five victims managed to come out at night and tell the world the horrible story of a holocaust hitherto unknown. What crimes had the Serbs committed for which they were so barbarously punished? Only the crime of belonging to Serbian Orthodoxy.

Dr. Victor Novak asked who taught those Ustashe criminals to fanatically hate Serbs.

Franciscan Ilija Tomash, a sworn Ustashe and priest in Klepce, forced Serbs from surrounding villages to convert to Catholicism. Then he gave them Holy Communion. After the mass he sent them to the local school, where the Ustashe were waiting for them. They were all slaughtered. Tomash explains that by conversion the Catholic church did not have in mind saving either their property or their lives, only their souls![34]

In August 1991, exactly fifty years after their death, remains of the Serbs were dug up from the Golubinka pit. They were finally buried with Christian rites, personally performed by the head of the Serbian Orthodox church, Patriarch Paul II, assisted by other clergy. The remains were buried in 126 boxes in the crypt in Prebilovci.

In 1992, when the Bosnia-Hercegovina civil war erupted, Croatian Ustashe came back and took over that region. They blew up the crypt, sending over 3,500 human remains flying into the air. This was the horrible destiny of those victims whose remains would never know peace in this unethical world.

Following is a statement by Ivan Zvonimir Cicak, president of the Croatian Peasant Party. Cicak was a renowned Croatian intellectual who was interviewed by the Belgian daily *Le Son* on April 9, 1993. He stated that Serbs were being exposed to systemic ethnic cleansings in Croatia. More than 100,000 Serbs' houses were destroyed by explosives. No one was arrested or punished for the crimes. Cicak says those actions were taken to scare Serbs into leaving Croatia. "This is pure ethnic cleansing," he declared.

It might be worthwhile to conclude with what the Italians thought about their Croatian allies from World War II. In August 1941, Italian general Pirzio Biroli, then governor of occupied Montenegro, sent a report to the Italian supreme headquarters about the military-political situation in Montenegro. He said that in his opinion Serbs are one of the best Balkan people, despite their temperamental character. Croats are mean and vile, two-faced, real hypocrites, and cowards. In contrast, Serbs are warriors with the spirit of knights. If one put aside their political mistake of opposing the Axis powers, the Italian occupation governor continues, it would be more suitable for us to support Serbs and Montenegrins than Croats and Albanians. After Russia falls, it would not be a wrong policy to try to bring Serbs into the Roman sphere.

Biroli continues, the Montenegrins have been badly hurt by the Ustashe's barbaric treatment of the Serbs before the Italian military authority. Considering what the Serbs are exposed to there, they cannot comprehend why Italy does not intervene to stop this unnecessary slaughter.[35]

Three Questions for a Cardinal

Veljko Guberina, attorney at law, wrote a letter to the head of the Croatian Catholic church, which was published in *Politika*, March 8, 1991. In July 1941 Guberina, then a teenager, was forced to leave Croatia to escape Ustashe genocide. After the war he completed his education in Serbia and Ljubljana (Slovenia), where he graduated from law school. He never was a member of the Communist party. In his profession he was dedicated to defending justice and the rights of every individual according to the law and his conscience. He was a staunch opponent of the death penalty, and he became a member of Amnesty International in London.

In his remarks directed to Franjo Kuharich, head of the Catholic church in Croatia, he calls on the cardinal to "speak up and call all believers to religious tolerance." He points out that Serbs never acted toward the Croatians like the Croatians acted toward them, such as screaming "Hang the Croatians" or forcing their alphabet on them. He sarcastically asks whether Kuharich ever visited the death camps, or said masses for the souls of slaughtered Serbians. Guberina asks Kuharich as "the only one who has powerful influence upon the development of the present and the future situation in Croatia" to answer three questions: (1) Is there any Catholic church whose members were rounded up and slaughtered during the war? (2) Is there any place where Orthodox priests carried out a program of forced conversion to their faith? (3) How many Catholic churches were destroyed or plundered of their valuables during the war? Kuharich would not be able to answer these questions.

The Role of Pope John Paul II in Yugoslav Political Matters

Pope John Paul II (Vojtila) was the first to recognize the independence of Slovenia and Croatia, on January 13, 1992. Regarding Yugoslav matters, the pope worked in two ways: through diplomatic channels and through personal papal intervention.

The Italian newspaper *Corriere de La Serra* (Rome, May 30, 1993), analyzing the geo-political views of *Limes* magazine, states that the Yugoslav tragedy was caused by extreme nationalism that "had been smoldering for half a century." However, the decisive blows for Yugoslav disintegration came from outside. Both the German influence on the EC and the Vatican were factors. In November 1991 the Holy See had already divided "Tito's Federation" into dioceses that best fit the newly recognized republics, Slovenia, Croatia, and Bosnia-Hercegovina, two days before the EC recognized them.

The pope put his authority and influence behind the German foreign minister Geshner, who had been instrumental in breaking up Yugoslav unity. Was it normal diplomatic routine to move so quickly? The creators of Yugoslavia in 1918 would not be surprised by such acts by the Vatican and Germany, because Yugoslavia had been formed partly on the ashes of the former Austro-Hungarian Empire.

In 1919, U.S. president Wilson was a main Yugoslav supporter along with France and Britain as allies with Serbia. In 1991, when the Yugoslav disintegration began, the United States was unaware of the magnitude and complexity of her ethnic and religious divisions. Tito had forbidden anyone in Yugoslavia to mention, much less to write about, the crimes of the Nazi Croatian Ustashe. However, it was permissible and encouraged to demonize the Chetniks of Mihailovich, the first guerrilla leader in occupied Europe, who contributed to the Allied victory. President Truman decorated him with the Legion of Merit for having "contributed materially to the Allied cause, and for having been instrumental in obtaining a final Allied victory."

When the Bosnian conflict in particular started, the pope pleaded four times for military intervention. Was it the Vatican tradition to advocate military intervention in any conflict? If not, then why was Pope Vojtila the first to ask for it?

Since July 1992 the head of the Catholic church has persistently pleaded for peace to the EC, NATO, and the UN Security Council. At the same time he continues to ask for military intervention to hit military installations! He wanted to disarm the Serbian hand (meaning the republic of Serbia) that kills. The pope conveniently forgot there was not one single soldier from Serbia in the Bosnian conflict. However, there were then and are now from 40,000 to 60,000 Croatian soldiers on Bosnia-Hercegovina territory. Does the pope also apply the adage "Might makes right?"

Furthermore, the Vatican says the Bosnian conflict is ideological in substance, which means democracy versus bolshevism, a conflict between Western democracy and Serbian totalitarianism! The pope had access to the best information from the former ambassador in Belgrade, Mr. Zimmerman, so he should have asked, where is there more democracy—in Croatia or in Serbia?

In our view, the Bosnian conflict is based more on religious overtones than on racial and ideological implications. Bosnian Muslims are getting weapons from Arab fundamentalists.

Some political analysts noticed correctly that the pope appealed for intervention in Bosnia on the eve of important sessions of the highest EC, from KEBS to the Security Council. But against whom? No doubt, against Serbian Orthodoxy, through economic and military means.

The Vatican secretary of state, Angelo Sodano, says military intervention in Bosnia is necessary because it is a legitimate struggle against aggression. Isn't it the Christian duty of any real prelate to carry in one hand the cross and in the other an olive branch, instead of steel and fire?

The Vatican insists Serbs are the evil forces in the Balkans. What does the pope think about Catholic Croats—are they lambs or wolves in sheep's clothing? The Serbs are demonized through Vatican media such as *Observatore Romano* and Radio Vatican. Information programs on three Italian channels (Roi uno duo and tre) lead off with headlines like "Hundreds of thousands of murdered Muslims," "Tens of thousands of Muslim women raped by Serbs...."

Beloff states that the claim that Bosnian Serbs rape Muslim women as a deliberate policy of intimidation has been challenged. "The material came partly from the Izetbegovich government and partly from the Roman Catholic charity Caritas."[36] Dr. Ijubica Tokolj, professor of gynecology at Belgrade University, reported there were only 119 proved pregnancies of Muslim, Serb, and Croat women held by all three combatants. This was confirmed by Helsinki Watch and the International Red Cross.[37] No war exists without crimes, but war cannot justify the means, and usually no side in war is blameless.

Responding to the pope's plan to visit the epicenter, the "Balkan Lenjigrad," to step on Sarajevo soil, academic Milorad Ekmechich, a university professor, called it "the Vaticanization of the Bosnian crisis." In his article "Yugoslavs Need the Pope" Richard West said Rome has a role to play in bringing about reconciliation between Croats and Serbs—that is, peace, not the sword!

In March 1993, Amphilohije Radovich, metropolitan of Montenegro-Littoral, Zeta-Highlands, and Skenderijski, and Bishop Irinej Bulovich of Backa visited Pope John Paul II. (The Serbian Orthodox patriarchate had not had any direct contact with a pope since the days of Saint Sava, over 700 years before.) The crux of their discussion was the question of the appropriate timing of the Vatican recognition of the former Yugoslav republics Slovenia, Croatia, and Bosnia-Hercegovina. Why should the Vatican recognize them first rather than last as was the tradition? What were the repercussions of early recognition of Bosnia-Hercegovina when the genocide caused by sharp religious and racial differences was ignored? Radovich was pleased to hear the pope say, "We are men—we make mistakes!"—thus calling into question the dogma of papal infallibility.

Both Christian churches agreed to play greater roles in stopping the fratricidal war in Bosnia and Hercegovina. The metropolitan believes if both churches in the name of truth and justice kneel before the martyrs of Jasenovac and Jadovno as did Willy Brandt in Auschwitz, the temperature of hatred, intolerance, and disrespect would drop in the beleaguered, unfortunate country once called Yugoslavia.[38]

Manipulations and Misrepresentations of Serbs by the Media

In politics today, "the pen is indeed mightier than the sword—and the television camera mightier than the missile." How can the public understand what is going on in Bosnia when many journalists, radio and television commentators do not really grasp it at all?

Daniel Salvatore Schiffer, an Italian philosopher and humanist, states that the world was trying to put the Serbs into a ghetto. Schiffer, a close friend of Elie Wiesel, says European policy is leading to a disastrous end. Croatian and Muslim leadership have the backing of Germany and the United States. Germany is using the secessionist republics as a steppingstone for her expansion in her Drang nach Osten (drive to the east). The West was wrong to recognize Bosnia and Hercegovina without considering Serbian rights to self-determination. The trap for Serbs was prepared by fascists and nationalists as well.[39]

The Serbs in Bosnia today have been demonized, which is in effect a threatening form of moral genocide, a threat the Serbs know all too well. Who is responsible? The mass media with disinformation and a dose of racial hatred are representing the Serbs as barbarians and the only culprits in the atrocities of the conflict. This representation is untrue and unprofessional. It is inappropriate to sow lies and condemn one side in this complex and delicate conflict. The media simply ignore or does not even know that the Serbs are a freedom-loving people with a rich tradition of Hellenic-Christian culture. According to Schiffer, there is an international plot against the Serbs, one that is orchestrated to some extent by some parties within the strife-torn region to promote their own interests and their megalomaniacal aspirations.

The Countess Visconti, a friend of Schiffer, wrote about the Croats after visiting them at Zagreb.[40] Even before that ugly war began, she states, the Croats were shrewd people who hired powerful Washington public relations firms like Pear. The Croatian international image was carefully crafted. Another public relations firm, Sachi and Sachi from Paris, used an organization of world doctors. In their name were printed thousands of huge posters showing pictures of Miloshevich and Hitler. The Croatian and Muslim sides also hired the public relations firm Finn and Hill and Knowlton, which staged the bombing of Dubrovnik in 1991. Was Dubrovnik damaged, or was it a set-up unverified by the EC, the United States, or media watchdogs? Thus, according to Visconti, Croatian propaganda penetrated the world community without any investigation. If the media impartially reported the truth, events in the Bosnian conflict would have developed differently.

Dubrovnik was not destroyed by the bombing in 1991. John Peter Moher, a professor of linguistics at Illinois University, visited Dubrovnik as a tourist on March 25, 1992. He states that there was no shooting at that time except between Croatians themselves—police who wanted to surrender to the Yugoslav national army and Dobroslav Paraga units, Nazi-oriented Croats. The synagogue was not damaged, but some structures in the Old City were damaged. A collection of rare books and priceless icons in the Serbian Orthodox church had gone up in flames. Moher stopped at the Cafe Minseta, where about thirty young men were singing an Ustashe song: "We Croats drink no wine, but the blood of Serbs from Knin."

So Croatia was successful in creating an image of dirty, primitive Serbian soldiers and fanatical Bolshevic Serbian politicians.

Was the report correct, based on files of the Justice Department under the Foreign Agents Registration Act, that three former Yugoslav regions, Croatia, Bosnia, and Kosovo, had hired the Ruder-Finn public relations firm? They spent almost $250,000 in the period between June and December 1992. The Ruder-Finn firm set up over thirty interviews with U.S. news organizations. Also, it arranged meetings between Bosnian officials and then vice-presidential candidate Al Gore, the acting secretary of state Lawrence Eagleburger, and other influential U.S. officials. Democratic majority leader George Mitchell was contacted, as well as the Republican minority leader Bob Dole, who is known as a staunch supporter of Albanians in Kosovo.

The Serbs need a new diplomatic approach and a new credibility to face this dangerous challenge head on. At the end of the twentieth century, wars can primarily be won through the media and shrewd diplomacy.

Countess Visconti suggests that the Serbs should emphasize to the world their rich culture, especially of their middle century Byzantine-style churches and monasteries, frescos, and folk epics that inspired Goethe to learn Serbian so he could read the poetry in the original.

Are Schiffer and Visconti right? These two prominent and outspoken, highly respected Italian intellectuals have the intuition and capability to penetrate deeply into the labyrinth of unscrupulous world politics. The following examples serve to prove their theories including the twisting of the facts by Muslims.

— The first conflict between Muslims and Serbs was provoked by Muslims, when they killed the father of the bridegroom at a Serbian wedding in Sarajevo.

— On August 22, 1992, the London weekly *Independent* confirmed that a Muslim "bread queue massacre" in Sarajevo was executed by Muslims' mortar in order to blame Serbs for it. At least twenty-eight innocent people were killed. In reaction, the United Nations imposed sanctions against Serbia and Montenegro.

— At least two French soldiers who were part of the UN peacekeeping force in Bosnia and Hercegovina were killed, and ABC correspondent David Kaplan was murdered.

— An Italian air force GE-222 plane supplying Bosnia was downed by Croats, not by Serbs as originally claimed.

— An attack at a Muslim funeral was directed and executed by Muslim snipers.

— Many stories were publicized about alleged rapes of Muslim women by Bosnian Serbs when in many cases non-Muslim women were dressed as Muslims in order to blame Serbs.

According to Gen. Lewis Mackenzie, commandant of the UN peacekeeping forces in Bosnia, the Bosnian Muslim leadership was using all means to provoke international involvement in Bosnia because they wanted someone else to pull their chestnuts out of the fire.

By manipulating the international media, the war in Yugoslavia is being won by Croatian Ustashe and Bosnian Muslims against the Serbs, while all three parties have committed crimes. Germany does not hesitate to use her influence to distort the truth in the media and prevent a workable, permanent peace solution.

The Vance-Owen peace plan for Bosnia is impractical, as recent events have proved. Even the old allies against the Serbs, the Croats and Muslims, recently fought each other, though the American media are shy about reporting it. The only right solution in Bosnia would be a bitter pill to be swallowed by all three sides. As Dr. Karazich states, it is impossible for dogs and cats to live together in one cage.

If the EC and the United States had stood firmly against pressure from Germany and the Vatican to recognize those republics so quickly, the bloodshed could have been avoided.

"War Within War"—Why Do Croats and Muslims Fight Between Themselves in Bosnia?

Serbs, Croats, and Bosnian Muslims are ethnically indistinguishable. All are of the same Slavic stock. The ethnicity of Croats and Muslims depends on which side the wind blows from, with the least political resistance. To please Muslim countries, Tito's proteges, the Muslims, have identified their nationality by religious affiliation, which is unique in world annals.

In the Bosnian conflict, Croatian forces helped the Muslims get involved against Bosnian Serbs, and for thirteen months allied with them against the Serbs. Then the Croatian forces withdrew and left the Muslims to fight the Serbs alone.

Until October 29, 1992, the Bosnian town of Prozor was held by Slavic Muslims. Croatian major Mijo Jozic led Croats in attacking Muslims in Prozor, and the Muslims suffered six dead and sixty-eight wounded. The Muslim government in Bosnia estimated at least 300 Muslim casualties.

On April 20, 1993, John F. Burns of the *New York Times* brought news of a break-up of the old alliance between Croats and Muslims, who hitherto were officially together against the Serbs. Casualties were in the hundreds, and the crimes committed were "often associated with Serbian forces." The fighting had gone on for five or six days straight when UN peacekeeping forces intervened to stop the fighting between them. There was more rivalry between these two groups, but American media in particular failed to publicize it. They probably do not like to change the old routine of demonizing the Serbs in the ugly Bosnian conflict.

Some Americans, among them A. M. Rosenthal, believe the only solution for the Bosnian conflict is a political one. The United States should not repeat the tragedy of the U.S. Marines in Lebanon during the Reagan administration or a prolonged war like Britain has in Ulster, which has gone on for twenty-four years with no sign of ending soon.

On May 6, 1993, the Paris daily *Le Monde* published an article by Yves Heller under the above "War Within War" title. In Bosnia, British UN officials confirmed that in Croat-held Vitez everything was razed or burned down, including minarets! The Croats there were doing "ethnic cleansing," while Muslims from Jablanica expelled Croats from their homes. In Konjic, Muslims were encircled by Croats, and a fierce battle was raging.

One UN officer says both parties had committed crimes. Bosnian Serbian massacre victims were exhumed from a mass grave. The victims had been killed by Muslims on July 21, 1992 in Ratkovici. That stands as proof that all three sides in the war bear guilt in Bosnia. After that tragic event, the Muslims ran into their enclave Srebrnica, which was later encircled by the Serbs to stop further massacres in the nearby Serbian villages. To this and similar events the powerful Western media, including Washington public relations firms, turned deaf ears and concentrated only on Serbian ethnic aggressors who were allegedly battering the peaceful "innocent" Muslims.

Recently, fighting also broke out between the alleged allies—Croats and Muslims—against Serbs. Regardless of media misrepresentation of facts in that conflict, there were many armed confrontations between Croats and Muslims.

The U.S. Congress is still hesitant to approve troops against Bosnian Serbs. According to Rep. Lee Hamilton, the members of Congress are frustrated. They want more information about goals, objectives, and costs, since America is currently in a poor economic position, before the U.S. becomes involved in the Bosnian war. However, the morality of the Bosnian war, as some politicians emphasize, would take a back seat in the "rational world" of politics. Every war carries criminal consequences. Democrat Sam Nunn, chairman of the Senate Armed Services Committee, referring to the division of opinion among government, Congress, the military, and the public, asks what would be the most appropriate action to take to bring the Bosnian war to an end. He stresses that there would have to be a clear exit point. The U.S. people ought to know, in case of involvement, how they are going to get out.

Anthony Lewis, a *New York Times* correspondent, judges the dangers of involvement more lightly because he believes the Serbs are cowards! If Lewis is right, why did the Bosnian Serbs reject the Vance-Owen plan by 96 percent in their referendum? Contrary to Lewis, Hamilton pointed out that the Serbs are a brave and proud people who fought in the past against Germany and the Austro-Hungarian and Ottoman empires. They are not likely to be scared by air strikes.

Recently, six American journalists debated the Bosnian crisis on public television. One of them, the editor of *Progressive* magazine from Wisconsin, suggested that Washington and New York journalists take machine guns themselves and go fight in Bosnia. Otherwise, they should stop promoting irresponsible professional ethics.

The world must soon realize that in order to survive under current circumstances, the Serbs have no alternative but to fight and die to the last one. This is realistic but very tragic.

Meanwhile, the former U.S. secretary of state Henry A. Kissinger, a knowledgeable and pragmatic, experienced politician, states that Bosnia never has been a sovereign state, nor has she ever had a cultural identity. After the fifteenth century she was divided between the Ottoman and Austro-Hungarian empires. She was liberated by the Serbian army and unified into the Yugoslav state in 1918. At the Berlin Congress in 1878, Serbia and Montenegro were the only Yugoslav states that were recognized as sovereign. Kissinger believes that the only way to deal with the ethnic and religious hatred is for the groups to be divided into three parts by their ethnicities. How could they all live together in Bosnia when Croats and Serbs could not co-exist in the former Yugoslavia?

For the United States there is no national or strategic interest, regardless of what some claim, in being involved in the Bosnian war. The war between Armenians and Azerbaijan was very frustrating, although the world community including Arab Muslim states remains silent. Are matters any better in the Sudan now?

A group of Stanford scholars including some from the Hoover Institution sent an open letter to President Clinton about the Bosnian quagmire. They clearly stated the causes and conducts in the conflict and said it would not be in the best interest of the United States nor in the interest of the affected people for the United States to take a side or to be involved in that civil war.

The time for living together is over. They might be able to live in Bosnia side by side, but never again together.

How do the warring parties in Bosnia judge the Vance-Owen plan? According to the Muslims, the plan is bad because it would give the Croats the green light to conquer more territory whenever they decide to. The plan was resented by Serbs because it gave them too little and conceded too much to the Muslims. In fact, Croats want a confederate Bosnian state, while Muslims prefer a unitary state based on majority rule. Croats already are establishing their "state within a state," labeling it the sovereign state of Herceg-Bosnia.

What does the Vance-Owen plan offer to the three ethnic groups in Bosnia? Banja Luka was the only one of Bosnia's ten industrial centers allocated to Serbs. Three of the five Serbian Orthodox dioceses, six of eight monasteries and about half of the churches would not be included in the Serbian provinces. Muslims would receive about 18.1 billion, Croats about 7.2 billion, and Serbs about 6.1 billion in assets. Translated into income per capita, that means $9,500 for Muslims; $8,100 for Croats; and $5,000 for Serbs. Muslims would receive 45 percent of the electrical power, Croats 31 percent, and Serbs 24 percent. Furthermore, about 46 percent, or 629,000, of the Serbian populace would live outside their provinces, and 29 percent of Croats would be similarly "misplaced." Serbs would have to give up 17 to 20 percent of the territories that have belonged to them for centuries.

The world community considered it permissible to break up Yugoslavia, but not Bosnia! The provinces of the former Yugoslavia had the right to self-determination, but not to the division of Bosnia along ethnic lines.

In conclusion, Serbs have neither an oil lobby nor Catholic political power behind them. On the eve of Yugoslavia's break-up, the pope appealed to the world Catholic community to influence their respective national governments for the secession of the Yugoslav republics. The world can already see the tragic consequences.

An example of media distortion of the tragedy comes from coverage of fighting around Mostar. Before Mostar was attacked it was predominantly inhabited by Muslims, though the surrounding villages were populated by ardently nationalist Croats. According to UN military observers from a Spanish battalion near Mostar, some Muslim headquarters and other buildings were set on fire by Croats at dawn on Saturday, May 8, 1993. According to a *Washington Post* article of May 9, 1993, the Bosnian Croatian militia attacked Muslims at Mostar. About 60,000 Croatian troops from Dalmatia and Croatia are located in Bosnia-Hercegovina, though the media said nothing about their presence. Croatian paramilitary troops forced Muslims from their homes and herded women and children into a soccer stadium, as Croats claimed, for their own protection. Men were segregated and taken to another location. UN officials believe that Croats were applying "ethnic cleansing" by the forcible removal of civilians. If that had been done by Serbs, the media would have cried out, but powerful public relations firms in Washington keep such actions by either Croats or Muslims hermetically sealed from public knowledge. On May 11, 1993, the Madrid daily *El Pais* reported that Croats were carrying out ethnic cleansing in Bosnia-Hercegovina, seizing more territory and establishing concentration camps, without any reaction from the international community.

The current U.S. secretary of state, Warren Christopher, characterizes the Bosnian war as "the war of all against all," with atrocities on all sides. He says Muslims as well as Croats have been trying to seize territory. The Croats were attacking Muslims in order to grab more territory west and south of Sarajevo. The Vance-Owen peace plan, unfortunately, intensified the fighting between the warring groups. After further Croatian attacks against Muslims, their president, Alija Izetbegovich, appealed to Croatian president Franjo Tudjman to stop the fighting. Reports also came that Croatian troops were moving by train toward the Bosnian town of Konjice, held by Muslims. Izetbegovich then was forced to say that, if that was true, he would "accuse Croatia of being an aggressor in our country."

Where Do the Jewish People Stand Regarding the Bosnian War?

Most Jewish intellectuals comprehend the essence of the Yugoslav complexities because world injustice to the Serbs today reminds them of their own treatment. They have the prudence and courage to speak the truth and to defend what is just.

Bosnian Jew Shlomit Lussic, a member of the Association of Yugoslav Immigrants in Israel, reminded pro-Serbian Jews that Bosnian refugees were accepted in Israel. They were allegedly rescued from concentration camps run by the Serbs. That was just one side of the story, because all three sides involved in the Bosnian tragedy committed crimes.

Israel's acceptance of eighty-three Muslim refugees from Bosnia stirred up debate among Jews from various Yugoslav republics. The Chinese press mentioned that the U.S. and Israeli governments have been pleasing Bosnian Muslims. What for? Rabbi Zvi Azariya says that, unlike Bosnian Muslims and Croatians, Serbs protected Jews during World War II. Azariya reminded the Israeli government that Croatian and Bosnian governments cooperated with the Nazi occupier and that the current conflict has unfairly maligned the reputation of the Serbian people. Azariya served in the Serbian army in World War II, while the Croatian-Bosnian government was helping the Germans round up both Jews and Serbs on their territory, persecuting them most bestially. Most of them were transported to the Jasenovac camp, where all perished.

The Croatian Ustashe behaved like the SS Nazi. During 1943, El Husein, a Jerusalem mufti, arrived in Berlin via Istanbul to meet with some of Hitler's dignataries. Heinrich Himmler, chief of the Gestapo, sent him to Sarajevo to organize another Muslim SS division, the notorious Handzar division.

Says Jewish historian Jenny Leibi, there were conflicting reports about the number of Jews killed in Yugoslavia during World War II. No doubt, he asserts, local Bosnian and Croatian authorities "collaborated with the Nazis against both the Jews and the Serbs." He states further that Bosnian president Izetbegovich is "an active member in various international" Islamic conferences and has taken a clear anti-Jewish, anti-Israeli stand.[41] Also, it is worth mentioning that in his "Islamic Declaration" Izetbegovich was preaching the Koran from Morocco to Indonesia. He also served six years in prison for anti-Serb terrorist activities. There cannot be peace or co-existence between the Islamic and non-Islamic faith and institutions. The Islamic movement believes it must and can take power as soon as it is morally and numerically strong enough, not only to destroy the non-Islamic powers, but to build up a greater Islamic one.[42]

"Holocaust History Misappropriated"

Dr. Philip Cohen, a dermatologist and immunologist, used the above title as a springboard to wage a Goebells-type propaganda war against the Serbs, replete with unprecedented misrepresentation of the facts. Such representation was without verification of so-called facts and without any moral scruples. It is nothing less than a cheap shot on the reader's intelligence and judgment. There is a moral imperative to expose some of Cohen's misrepresentations.

Cohen portrayed Serbs as anti-Semites who created propaganda about the holocaust that had occurred in Croatia and Bosnia during World War II. They proclaimed a war against "Judaism as the source of world evil and advocated the humiliation and violent subjugation of Jews that had begun during Ottoman rule in the Balkans." He said Serbs don't talk about their own holocaust committed against other people, including Jews in Serbia.

The truth is as follows: In 1804, Jews heroically fought alongside Serbs in Karageorge's uprising against the Turks. In addition to bearing arms, they supplied the rebels materially and morally. During the Balkan wars and World War I, there were about six thousand Jews in Serbia, of whom six hundred fought in the Serbian army. One hundred fifty Jews were killed.

At the end of 1917, Milenko Vesnich, a Serbian royalist representative, sent a letter to Capt. David Albali, a military doctor who was then representing Serbia in the United States. In the letter Vesnich expressed the direct support of the Serbian people for the formation of an independent Jewish state. Says Vesnich, we must support the aspirations and sufferings of the Jewish people. Our countrymen of your faith fought courageously for their Serbian homeland as did our best Serbian sons.[43]

In Belgrade, the persecution of Jews was carried out by the Gestapo. General Nedich personally told the Germans the Serbian government refused to take part in the genocide.[44] The Jews, contrary to Cohen's statement, were treated differently in the ISC.

Worth mentioning here is an exchange of letters between Vuk Drashkovich[45] and Joseph Gottfried[46] that emphasize and celebrate that Serbs and Jews considered themselves "blood brothers," related by history and common suffering and a common desire for justice and freedom. Cohen asserts that Serbian citizens and the police received cash bounties for Jews captured and delivered to the German occupier. Says Enrico Josif, the representative of the Jewish community in Serbia, a horrid spiritual crime was the fact that what happened to the Serbs during World War II was concealed from the entire world. In fact, after the war the horrid crimes of genocide continued.

Cohen continues: The Serbian Orthodox church turned over Jews to the Nazis, with whom many Serbian priests collaborated. Cohen should address this claim to the Catholic clergy in Croatia instead of the Serbians. In fact, the heads of the Serbian Orthodox church, Patriarch Gavrilo Dozich and Bishop Nikolay Velimirovich, were first interned inside Serbia right after Yugoslavia capitulted in 1941.

The Germans transferred them to the German prison camp Dachau, where they remained until the German capitulation in May 1945. According to Cohen, Bishop Nikolay was taken to Dachau only for the sake of German propaganda! Could any rational person believe Cohen's assertion that the Nazis brought only one Serb to Germany, the detained Serbian bishop? This seems like the epitome of propaganda.

Also, Cohen accused Metropolitan Josif of Skoplje of being anti-Semitic. Josif took the patriarch's position when Gavrilo was detained by the German occupier. Slovenes expelled from Slovenia to Serbia submitted their wishe to convert to the Orthodox faith to the Serbian metropolitan Josif. Josif as a true and faithful son and servant of the Christian church told them, "My children, this is not the time to do it. Now go and save your heads; after the war we'll talk about everything, including conversion, according to your wishes."

Meanwhile, Slovenian priests then living in Serbia said the final goal of the current Zagreb policy is destroying Serbian people in the ISC. It is an immoral goal to force anyone, including Serbs, to be converted to Catholicism.[47]

Letter from Professor Thomas to *Midstream*

Raju Thomas, professor of political science at Marquette University, replied to Philip Cohen's letter in *Midstream*,[48] a Jewish monthly review. Thomas is neither a Serb nor a Jew, but an Eastern Orthodox Christian from Kerala, South India. He could not understand Cohen's hatred toward Serbs and especially against the Serbian Orthodox church. Cohen seemed to be following Napoleon's adage: "Slander! Slander! Something must stick!" If Croatian propaganda could convince anyone that there was no Holocaust against Serbs, then the Holocaust against the Jews did not happen either. In the *Jerusalem Post* (December 21, 1991), Israeli journalist Teddy Preuss says, "Goebbels lives in Zagreb!"

Thomas tells how all Serbs—men, women, and children—were subjected to psychological and cultural genocide that decimated their culture, religion, and self-esteem. The Western media, American in particular, are leading a one-sided smear campaign.

According to Cohen, Jews and Croats are getting along wonderfully, while Jews continue to suffer from Serb anti-Semitism not only recently but also under the Ottoman Empire!

Thanks to Dr. Ante Starcevich, the nineteenth-century father of racism in Croatia, the Croatian roots of hatred and zeal against Serbs, especially their church, have sunk immeasurably deep.

The history of the Holocaust was being revised and falsified. According to Cohen, Serbs suffered less than others during World War II. The Serbian Orthodox church and the Chetniks were anti-Semitic, while the Croatians, the Vatican, and Germans (minus the Nazis) were not anti-Semitic!

Thomas states correctly that while the Croatian Ustashe committed massacres, only a few of them were ever brought to justice. Serbs feared the union of the Ustashe with the Communists, whose cooperation was known before World War II began. Thus, the Yugoslav Communist Party (YCP) greeted the Ustashe movement of the Lika and Dalmatia peasantry with enthusiasm. The YCP expressed the desire to join the Ustashe side against the judicial state of Yugoslavia. The party declared that the duty of all Communist organizations was to help organize and lead that movement.[49]

John Hamilton (Sterling Hayden) had boundless admiration for the Partisan movement. He was attached to the Partisan Tenth Corps as an Allied officer in Croatia. On September 28, 1944, Hamilton reported that "the Partisan movement is not the expression of the people's will. Whenever the enemy wanted to take over territory, the Partisans took to the hills.... The Germans, as well as local Fascists [Ustashe] plundered farms, raped women, burned a few houses, and moved on. Then the Partisans returned, and the cycle was ready to commence anew.''[50]

Colonel McDowell, a Balkan expert, was an Allied OSS officer attached to the headquarters of General Mihailovich. He wrote: ''All the evidence, including collected earlier by British and American liaison officers, cries out against the hypocrisy and dishonesty of the Partisan efforts to destroy the Nationalist Movement [Mihailovich] by labelling it collaborationist or quisling…. Compelling evidence accepted by the British suggested that Partisans and Ustashe units were cooperating in joint attacks on the Chetniks. Ustashe criminals who had taken part in the massacres of great numbers of Serbs in 1941 had joined the Partisans to escape punishment for their deeds.''[51]

Another American source is a report of the American consul in Istanbul. On February 23, 1943, the American consulate general in Istanbul, Turkey, sent an intelligence report about the ''bloody terror'' against Serbs in Glina, Vrginmost, Vojnic, Dvor at Una, Kostajnica, Petrinje in the district of Kordun, Slunj, Ogulin, Vrbovska, Karlovac, Susak, Lika, Grachac, Bosanska Krajina, Bjelovar, Slavonska Pozega, Hercegovina, central Bosnia, and Srem. He also reported the deportation of Serbs and Slovenes.

This report of the consul Burton Y. Berry contains a chapter about a camp in Danica, near Koprivica, Jadovno, where 30,000 victims perished; and about the Jasenovac camp in particular, where the most brutal tortures and killings took place. The report gave the exact camp locations and names and the names of the camp commanders, Max Luburich and Ljubo Milosh.

Using machine guns, rifles, pistols, knives, axes, and hammers the Ustashe have been killing Serbs in groups and individually night and day, the report said. To save ammunition the Ustashe brought groups of Serbs in front of a burning brick oven. One by one the victims were first hit with a hammer, then thrown alive into the oven. Others were drowned in the Sava River, which flowed with their corpses.

The bloodiest villain was Milosh, who personally killed at least 3,000 Serbs. He used his knife to cut victims' throats; then he would lick the bloody knife, smiling and shouting how sweet Serbian blood was.

At the Jasenovac camp most prisoners were liquidated soon after entering. Thus, a group from Pakrac arrived there on Catholic Christmas. Almost all of them were immediately killed. The Ustasha Matkovich asked Milosh to give him one Serb as a Christmas present. Matkovich picked Joco Divljak, a restaurant owner from Lishika. He and two other Ustashe grabbed him. The unfortunate victim was put on the ground. Matkovich took off his clothing. Then he began to hack at the victim's flesh with a knife. After half an hour, while Joco was still alive, Matkovich pulled out his heart. All the prisoners who were present had to calmly observe that horrible scene, and even had to smile while the unfortunate Divljak suffered indescribable pain. If anyone tried to turn his head aside or showed any disgust, he was killed instantly.

The American consul also described how "undisciplined" victims were confined in the space of ten square meters, fenced with barbed wire, where they stayed all night in freezing water and then were let out to work all day. Dr. Otto Gavrancich, "Sokol" (Yugoslav patriotic organization) from Zagreb endured nine days of the cage and labor and died completely exhausted. In such barbaric ways many Serbian officers who were captured in Croatia ended their lives.

That report also mentioned how the international commission was duped during their visit to the Jasenovac camp on February 6, 1942. The Vatican had not yet lifted the ban on reports submitted by two clergymen of the Holy See about their impressions of Jasenovac. The apostolic secretary Giusappe Masucci and the secretary of Archbishop Stepinac of Zagreb served on that international commission. Dr. Stjepan Lackovich also visited the Jasenovac camp, together with an executor of Ustashe crimes, Eugene-Dido Kvaternik. When the international commission visited Jasenovac, the camp was camouflaged like Potemkin's villages. That same day the Holy See received the son of the Ustashe leader Kvaternik, whose mother was killed by the Ustashe because she was a Jew. This is one of many examples of pathological hatred leading to inexplicable activities, such as the killing of one's own mother! Was it an expression of racist loyalty to Nazism or an incurable criminal pathology embraced by Croatian Ustashe who were wholeheartedly (except for a very small percent) supported by the Croatian Catholic church?

Here, Mr. Cohen, we have some more facts, free of your unfortunate fabrication. In the same report of February 23, 1943, the American consul general Berry wrote a chapter titled "Bloody Rivers of Catholic Clergy in Croatia." He said Catholic clergy in Croatia, Hercegovina, and Dalmatia were spreading intense propaganda in favor of the Ustashe movement. They had done so even during the existence of the former Yugoslavia. For years they held so-called Eucharistic Congresses under the name of religious convocations, but they were really nothing but extreme political demonstrations.

After the fall of Yugoslavia, the Catholic clergy worked more closely with the Ustashe in the massacres of Serbs. Those clergy executed the crimes methodically and systemically. Here are just a few well-known Croatian Catholic clergy, criminals dressed in friars' clothing: Sarajevo's bishop, Dr. Ivan Sharich; Livno—Dr. Srecko Perich; Ogulin—Ivan Mikan; Brcko—fra. Anto Tepeluk; Knin—Vjekoslav Shimic; Nashice—Sidonije Sholc; Slavonski Brod—Gruncovich and Dragutin Marjanovich; Glina—German Castimir; etc.[52]

We refer again to Mr. Thomas, who says that only one side of the picture in the Bosnian conflict is being presented, while the interests of many nations and the strong influence of various religions are involved. According to Thomas, the Serbs do not maintain concentration camps, as has been

asserted by Simon Wiesenthal, the International Red Cross, and UN officials. There have been some massacres and ethnic cleansing committed by
some irregular paramilitary units acting on their own, as well as by other
non-Serbs. Crimes are committed by all three sides involved in the conflict.
The only question is to what degree each side is involved. Thomas continues
that Bosnia is not the first case of "ethnic cleansing" in the world.

Should the United States Play the Role of World Policeman?

American politicians should be extremely careful when they deal with
the complexities of the Yugoslav problems. President Wilson was the main
impetus behind forming the Yugoslav state in 1919; in 1991 the United
States should not have promoted the disintegration of the judicial state of
Yugoslavia.

At the heart of recent conflicts were internal borders established in Jajce
by AVNOY in 1943. The congress's decision on the proposed borders
among the Yugoslav republics was made according to party and military
lines and in collusion with the Soviet secret police. Says David Martin,
Yugoslavia's internal borders are a recent invention of the Communist dictator Josip Broz Tito and have no historical validity. The current leadership
of Croatia and Bosnia-Hercegovina recognize only those borders drawn at
the AVNOY congress. They will accept nothing less. Those borders were
not drawn according to the ethnic majority of Yugoslavia's population.

The EC and the United States recognized the rights of Slovenia, Croatia,
and Bosnia-Hercegovina as independent and sovereign states, but without
changing Tito's borders. They had the might but not the legal and moral right
to disintegrate Yugoslavia without consulting the main interested party—the
Serbs, who together with the Allied forces formed Yugoslavia in 1919 and
defended it against German aggression in 1941. Serbs ask only for the same
self-determination the other republics received.

Was the recognition a double standard or a reaffirmation of the social
decisions made by the villain Tito? This tragic circumstance is reminiscent
of the 1937-38 episode when Chamberlain of Britain and Daladier of France
demonized the Czechs and justified Hitler's claims to the Sudetenland. Was
it the aim of Western policy and the U.S. media to dismember Serbia and
liquidate its influence in the Balkans? If Tito's Yugoslavia is dead, as we
strongly believe, at least in spirit and principle, then Tito's 1943 borders
should be negated and changed according to existing ethnic majorities in
that region. How can those borders be considered valid for all time when
they violate the concept of ethnic frontiers? The internal borders of Yugoslavia were the legacy of the Croatian Communist Tito and were arbitrarily
drawn by Tito, who was half Croat and half Slovenian. Even though Serbs

were the majority group in the country no Serbian politicians were present when those artificial administrative borders were drawn. If the United States and the EC really want to solve Yugoslavia's conflicts, they should change Tito's borders. Otherwise, they will be confronted with ominous perpetuation of violence and instability with no end in sight.

Orrin Hatch, a U.S. senator, says the United States is seeking stability in Europe. Yugoslavia can only be built on the foundation of a new political order that allows democratic self-determination for all the constituent republics. That is all that the Serbs are asking for.

Less than ten years after Tito's death his Yugoslav state was polarized; the federal republics had veto power. So Tito's deeds, his ideology, the social and governmental system and his internal and foreign policies, were eclipsed. Not surprisingly, Ljubljana and Zagreb were the first to use the veto to realize their dream of sovereignty and independence from Yugoslavia.[53]

The tragic current plight of Yugoslavia, torn apart by political, cultural, and, paramountly, by religious hatred and intolerance, came about in part because Yugoslavia was considered as "terra mission." Complete cohesion and harmony never existed between Croats and Serbs in Yugoslavia. How could it, when Croats and their church secretly leaned toward a separate Croatian state, or at least one with a dominant role in Yugoslav matters.

Since then, Serbs in Croatia, Bosnia, and Hercegovina have lost all trust in a common state with the Croats, fearful of genocide being repeated against them. Tito as dictator and absolute ruler in Yugoslavia kept them together under his iron fist and the brutal secret police.

Unfortunately, the Serbs were right. In the fatal year 1991 the bloodshed started again. The new Croatian president, Dr. Franjo Tudjman, was elected on a platform of making Croatia a "pure" state. Does "pure" mean the continuation of "ethnic cleansing," or something else?

Bonar's law in 1922 clearly stated that Britain could no longer play the role of world policeman. Can the United States afford to attempt such a role today? Hans van den Brock, the Dutch foreign minister, did exactly the opposite. Could any other means be used to avoid inter-religious warfare in the former Yugoslavia?

The Yugoslav crisis needs patience and time to transfer into "Scandinavization" instead of "Balkanization" (Yugoslav disintegration on the principle of self-determination). Furthermore, the situation in Bosnia is a complex problem that cannot be justly solved by signatures on a document. Rather, its solution requires a solid knowledge of the historic, ethnic, religious, traditional, and cultural elements of the region to comprehend the political/ antagonisms of the groups involved. Knowledgeable people realize that a fair and long-term solution will require the free political will of all the concerned people—Muslims, Serbs, and Croats—and guarantees of equality.

Civil war is always the bloodiest kind of a war because the polarized parties know each other. The most barbaric of all wars is a religious war, because its fanaticism has neither limits nor control nor ethical behavior. A rational thinker would realize logically that religious fanaticism undermines the prestige of the entity involved rather than augmenting it!

The news media have not grasped the real causes of the volcanic eruption of violence, and they are turning a deaf ear to reality and truth. Indeed, as her antagonists have claimed, Yugoslavia proved to be an artificial state. The unification was not fundamentally based, as it should have been, on mutual understanding and reciprocal respect. Rather, it promoted hatred, intolerance, and mistrust. Such a Yugoslavia was doomed to be short-lived. Even though the Serbs paid dearly with over two million dead for Yugoslav unity and her defense in 1941, her end was inevitable. Nothing based on hatred and racism that lead to genocide can live long.

Finally, as Kardelj told Cosich, the Yugoslav "marriage" is over, regardless of the consequences. Therefore, Serbs should not shed any tears over the disappearance of Yugoslavia from the world political scene.

Someone asked the Greek philosopher Socrates what was the best in life. His reply was first, never to be born and, second best, to die young. That thought of Socrates could be applied as a tragic truth to Yugoslavia!

Latest Misrepresentations of Events in Bosnia

During Yugoslavia's factual disintegration, the EC designated a prominent French jurist, the president of the Constitutional Court Board, to lead a commission investigating Yugoslav matters. Orchestrated by the world media, Serbs were immediately demonized. In fact, the media's duty is not only to gather news but also to verify the news. Did the media perform their duty responsibly?

However, there are prominent intellectuals and newspeople as well who took the moral high ground in regard to Yugoslav events, historic and current. Among these was Simon Wiesenthal, a Jewish leader whose work serves as a beacon to enlighten others to follow a moral and ethical path.

The octogenerian Wiesenthal is known to the world as a hunter of Nazi criminals. He has succeeded in locating over 1,100 Nazi leaders around the world, and most of them have been brought to justice for committing crimes against humanity. Wiesenthal also succeeded in putting the Austrian president and former General Secretary of the UN, Kurt Waldheim, on the Nazi list. In 1942, during the Nazi invasion against Serbs in the Kozara area, Waldheim as a German officer captured over 11,000 Serbian children, who later either died or were placed in convents, where they were converted to the Catholic faith. For that accomplishment, Waldheim was decorated by the Croatian Nazi leader Ante Pavelich. According to Mark Aarons and John Loftus in their book *Unholy Trinity*, over 30,000 Nazi criminals escaped justice through the Ratline intelligence services of Britain, France, and the United States and the smuggling efforts of the Vatican.

Wiesenthal reminded the world who "hates Belgrade"— how the horror in Yugoslavia had begun and by whom it was started. Then he appraised the situation in Croatia, where there has been a revival of Ustashe fascism. Such scrutiny caused consternation and pandemonium among Croatian media circles.

Wiesenthal believes it would be catastrophic if the United States and Europe involved themselves militarily in the Bosnian conflict. They could have the same experience Nazi Germany did in World War II. The people in Bosnia know the terrain extremely well, are trained in guerrilla warfare, and are in general well armed. Against the Serbs alone it would be necessary to deploy 250,000 NATO or UN soldiers. This, therefore, would not be the best solution, says Wiesenthal.

Mistakes have been made, particularly the recognition of the sovereignty of Slovenia and Croatia by Germany, Austria, and the Vatican that caused the war. The recognition caused the breakdown of negotiations during a Yugoslav dialogue for the peaceful division of Yugoslavia from one entity.

People don't remember the Serbs were the first refugees in this war. Forty thousand of them were forced to leave Croatia when that country decided to proclaim Serbs a minority on September 22, 1990. Even before Serbia had shown symptoms of extreme nationalism, Croatia was burning Orthodox churches and synagogues and desecrating Jewish cemeteries. Wiesenthal continues, Serbs also did not forget the death camp Jasenovac, where Croatian Ustashe with Nazi solidarity liquidated 700,000 Serbs, Jews, and Gypsies. With the entrance on the Croatian political scene of Tito's general Franjo Tudjman and returning Croatian Ustashe, Serbs were reminded of the traumatic events of World War II.

Therefore, Israel's refusal to recognize Croatia as a sovereign state as long as Tudjman remains the top Croatian leader was no accident. Regarding a Nuremberg-type tribunal to investigate war crimes committed on the territory of the former Yugoslavia, Wiesenthal believes it could have only symbolic meaning, with the culprits' names on vacant chairs. However, he thinks Miloshevich is responsible for the paramilitary group of Vojislav Sheshelj and Zeljko Radznatovich, while Croatian president Tudjman would be responsible for the Paraga Ustashe. According to Wiesenthal, Radovan Karadzich neither committed crimes nor ordered them, though he is a guarantor of his generals.

In an interview with the Italian news media *Corriere della Sera* and *Republic*, Wiesenthal showed an aversion toward Croats and the Croatian state. Croatia could be categorized as a fascist nation if someone wants to read the "anti-Semetic prayers of President Tudjman," he stated. The Tudjman regime is again directed against Serbs and Jews, as the Pavelich regime was. He emphasized that Pavelich's Croatia was a state that condoned hitherto unknown bestialities. That was the main reason for his conflict with the current Croatian president. Wiesenthal also came in conflict with the Austrian diplomatic chief Alois Mock, whom he accused of being anti-Semetic. Wiesenthal does not have much trust in the Vaticans attitude toward Croatians and the Croatian church. For him, the Catholic church has not changed in her relationship with Jews and Jewish problems.

Because of Wiesenthal's fame in bringing Nazi criminals to justice, many Italian publications generously opened their columns to him. However, Croation newspapers were not always complimentary. According to the Croatian newspaper *Free Dalmatia*, Wiesenthal collaborated with the Yugoslav secret police UDBA and KOS to get help hunting Nazi criminals. Also, the Croatian newspaper *The Evening News* was critical about Wiesenthal's objectivity and his ability to look beyond narrow ethnic lines.

It is a paradox that in general the Italians are far more objective and democratically oriented toward the Vatican than Croats are, even though the majority of both people is Catholic. During World War II the Italians as occupier saved more than 200,000 Serbs from being slaughtered by the Croatian Ustashe!

Chichak is the president of the Croatian Helsinki Watch, a committee for human rights, part of the international Helsinki organization. He has voiced astonishment at the extent of the disregard for human rights, the savagery, and the barbarism that are spreading all over Croatia. Allegedly all troubles are begun by Serbs. So, police and others can freely loot Serbs, dynamite their homes, dismiss them from their jobs, et cetera. Over 100,000 homes were dynamited. Because Croatia has no freedom of the press, there is a vital need for outside monitoring, says Chichak.

History Repeats Itself

Since civil war broke out in the western part of Yugoslavia in 1991 (in Slovenia and Croatia) and later in Boxnia and Hercegovina, the international news has concentrated on the former Yugoslav republics. The media were mostly occupied with atrocities, refugees, or the world's inactivity in response to Yugoslav events. During the war in Croatia the stories that reached the world talked only of Serb abuses. The first 60,000 refugees from Croatia were Serbs, although the media did not mention it at all or very shyly.

The villain was an aggressive Serbia or, later, Bosnian Serbs. By any democratic standard, Serbs in the Krajina region of Croatia and Bosnia and Hercegovina have a right to self-determination. In practice, this means the right to govern and protect themselves or to be forcibly integrated into either Franjo Tudjman's racist Croatia or Alija Izetbegovich's Muslim-led Bosnia. In 1941, on the ashes of the former Yugoslavia, Hitler formed the puppet state called the Independent State of Croatia (ISC), which during World War II remained under the auspices of fascist Italy and Nazi Germany. In

1991, history repeated itself! Germany again supported "democratic" Croatia under Tito's general Tudjman (a commissar of the Partisan division Tenth Corps under the command of Shabl). The Germans pulled along other Western nations. Germany and Austria were close with Croatia and Slovenia historically, culturally, religiously, and economically.

During the election campaign in 1990, Tudjman stated, "I am happy my wife is neither Serbian nor Jewish."

Ivo Banac, a Croat, is a professor of southeast European history at Yale University. In an article titled "Misreading the Balkans," he comments on the book *The Fall of Yugoslavia,* by the British writer Misha Glenny. In Glenny's book, says Banac, we "have a set of opinions, the two most important being that (1) Tudjman is responsible for the outbreak of the war (only relatively true and not for the reasons outlined by Glenny) and that (2) Germany's recognition of Slovenia and Croatia was disastrous and widened the conflict (by now an accepted myth, but untrue even in terms of Glenny's own definition.)"

Furthermore, Banac states: "There has not been a single serious study of the Ustashe regime in Coratia in any language." Indeed, if Prof. Banac has not yet had an opportunity to read any serious book about Ustashe criminal activities during World War II, we'll just submit a few titles here:

Documentation of Activities and Crimes Against the People on the Part of Some Catholic Clergy, Zagreb, 1946, Victor Novak, professor first at Zagreb and then Belgrade universities, *Magnum Crimen,* Zagreb: TNZ Hrvatske, 1948 (a scholarly book with outstanding documentation); Anton Miletich, a Croat, *Concentration Camp Jasenovac, 1941–1945,* Belgrade: People's Books, 1986 (vol. 1 and 2) and 1987 (vol. 3); Edmond Paris, *Genocide in Satellite Croatia, 1941–1945,* Chicago: American Institute for Balkan Affairs, 1961; Dedijer Vladimir, *The Vatican and Jasenovac,* Belgrade: Rad, 1987; Vasa Kazimirovich, *The Independent State of Croatia in the Light of German Documents and the Diary of Glaise von Horstenau, 1941–1944,* Belgrade: New Books, 1981; Milan Bulajich, *Ustashe Genocidal Crimes and the Trial of Andrija Artukovich,* Belgrade: Works, 1988 (vol. 1 and 2) and 1989 (vol. 3 and 4); Milan Bulajich, *Mission of the Vatican in the ISC* (vol. 1 and 2), Belgrade: Politika, 1992; et cetera.

The present-day symbols of Croatia are identical with the emblems of Nazi Croatia with her currency kuna. In the Croatian parliament only a few former leading Croatian Communists like the former Yugoslav premier, Mate Mesich, voted against the kuna currency. Mesich reacted negatively to choosing the kuna because the world would identify present Croatia with the fascist Ustashe state.

Lipson's Reaction to Mandich's Defense of Ustashe

Alfred Lipson, a senior researcher, sent a letter in the spring of 1994 to the *New York Times* in reply to Joseph Mandich's continued defense of the

Ustashe cause. *The Protocols of the Elders of Zion,* edited by Tudjman, said, "A Jew is still a Jew . . . even in the [Nazi] camp, and they retained their bad characteristics: selfishness, perfidy, meanness, slyness and treacherousness." Tudjman in his book *Westlands of Historical Reality* tries to prove that genocide is only "human" and should not be condemned. He minimized the Holocaust as a "few" Jews and Serbs who perished during the world war, "killed by Jewish capos." Mandich as an Ustasha apologist, like many of his compatriots, has been trying to turn history upside down.

De facto, "the Ustashe genocide in Croatia during World War II is the root of the present civil war in the Balkans," states Lipson. The perfidious Tito, with his cohorts, ruled Yugoslavia as an iron-handed dictator. They invented the slogan "Brotherhood and Unity" in order to hide the heinous crimes committed by the Coratian Ustashe. Tito, himself a Croat, was the most responsible for saving the Ustashe from paying for all the crimes they had committed. As Dr. Mladen Ivekovich, former inmate of the Jasenovac camp, stated, "There is not a pen capable of describing the horror and terror of the atmosphere of Jasenovac . . . ."

In 1941 there were 1,850,000 Serbs with 800 churches in Croatia. In 1991 and in the years after, many Serbs were persecuted or perished, so in Croatia today there are fewer than a half million Serbs. Also, in 1991 there were nearly 100 Serbian churches razed of the remaining 156! Mandich calls those Ustashe "patriotic" Croats who helped the Nazis defeat Yugoslavia. Historians refer to the Ustashe chapter as "one of the most gruesome in the history of World War II."

C. L. Sulzberger, prominent historian, says, "Yugoslavia was riddled with fifth-column movements among its Croatian, Albanian and German Volksdeutsch minorities. Defections among the non-Serbs were manifold, and the Yugoslav armies were torn apart before they had even been deployed."

Mandich is on friendly terms with Croatian president Tudjman, claiming that he "promotes Western-style democracy for Croatia with full rights for all minorities." He explains why Nazi symbols are being used in Tudjman's government—"to increase Croatian patriotism." What kind of democratic Croatia, as Tudjman and his cohorts call it, is it when today the criminals of yesterday, like Pavelich, Artukovich, and many others including Archbishop Stepinac, are symbols of national heroism and their Ustashe are synonymous with the Nazi SS and are celebrated and praised with highest honors!

In Croatia there is "repression of domestic media, resurrection of the Communist-era law that threatens five years' imprisonment for anyone in the media, domestic or foreign, who criticizes the government." Joel Barromi, former Israeli diplomat at the U.N., is a leading student on the subject of anti-Semitism. His book shows examples from the record of the powerful segment of Croatian society, while nothing in his dossiers shows anything comparable among the Serbs. In the bombing of the main synagogue in

Zagreb it was predictable that Tudjman and his adherents would blame Serbs.

Neo-Nazis in the Croatian Army

Correspondent Eric Gelger in the *San Francisco Chronicle* of April 5, 1994, told a story of hundreds of Austrian and German neo-Nazi mercenaries in Bosnia who were incorporated into the Croatian army—HOV. The tragic events in Bosnia have brought diversified ethnic, religious, and ideological entities into furious conflicts. Croatia hires many mercenaries of various nationalities, including Austrian and German neo-Fascists, while the Bosnian government is getting mujahideen from the Arab countries. Even if the war in Bosnia is over soon, the foreigners' legacy of brutalities will not be forgotten by many on the opposite side of the military spectrum, especially by civilians unable to escape the draconian measures imposed on them by their enemies.

German-speaking far-rightists began to fight in Bosnia in early 1992, when Croats and Slavic Muslims voted to be separated from Yugoslavia where the Serbs were dominant. There were reports of harsh punishments, including Mafia-style killings by neo-Nazis of two defectors in 1993. Underground neo-Nazi publications in Germany and Austria appeal for volunteers "to help our Croatian comrades in defense of the white race." Many of those neo-Nazi volunteers joined the rightist Croatian militia HOS led by Dobroslav Paraga. "Croatian authorities reportedly turned a blind eye toward the growing influx of mercenaries from Austria and Germany. Volunteers were enthusiastically accepted in Bosnia by their comrades in arms of the HOS with "Heil Hitler" salutes and waving of Swastika flags."

Mercenaries were paid $60.00 a month, and they were often assigned to "ethnic cleansing operations" against Muslims. "After regular Croatian militiamen capture a village," a young man said, "they earmark houses of Serbs and Muslims for us so we can loot and destroy them." Those mercenaries have the image among Bosnian Croats as "a sort of new German SS." For that very reason they often were assigned dirty and dangerous jobs. According to the German newsmagazine *Der Spiegel*, these volunteers usually served with the 108th Brigade of the paramilitary HOV, known for its ruthlessness.

Muslims Were in Hitler's SS Division

Dr. Ivan Avakumovich, a professor of history at the University of British Columbia, states: Heinrich Himmler raised two SS divisions [the 13th and the 23rd] among Bosnian Muslims eager to fight "Serb aggressors," while the Luftwaffe strafed Serb guerrilla positions across Bosnia for almost four years. In spite of their overwhelming superiority in the air and on the ground, the invaders and their local accomplices suffered a crushing defeat.

Michael Mennard, a former Foreign Service officer whose letter was published in *Foreign Policy,* no. 93, winter 1993–94, states: If Alija Izetbegovich accepted the European Community-sponsored agreement on March 18, 1992 in Lisbon to turn Bosnia-Hercegovina into a confederation, it could have saved many lives. He reneged on his word under pressure of numerous Muslim states and the U.S. Department of State. The agreement was not good enough for Izetbegovich and his militant fundamentalists. He is still a protagonist of a unified Bosnia, hoping "the Islamic movement will be strong enough morally and numerically to overturn the existing non-Islamic movement." He appears a martyr in the eyes of some media in this tragic Bosnian conflict. Unfortunately, the U.S. Department of State did not learn enough from the experiences of Vietnam, Lebanon, Somalia, or Haiti to allow the formation of a confederated Bosnian state on ethnic principle as the only positive and durable solution.

On January 10, 1994, at a conference in Switzerland, Izetbegovich demanded that the Bosnian Serbs return all territory that Muslims held before the conflict. Why didn't he go a little further to demand that Serbs retain the territories held before Alija's compatriots were joined to Nazi SS divisions?! In Bosnia, what kind of peace does the U.S. prefer!

"What Is So Astonishing?"

Joseph Lapid wrote in the Spring 1994 *Newsletter* that "the Islamic Declaration, a Program for the Islamization of the Moslem Peoples, is a tract of which Khomeini could have been proud." Lapid states: The Bosnians did not anticipate the violent reaction of the Serbs. They should have known better; they should have taken into account the collective memory of horrors the Serbs suffered at the hands of Croats and Muslims in Nazi times. "We Jews identify with people who share our fate. We understand their motivations and their fears, without condoning their misdeeds." Referring to Merlino's book (discussed below), Lapid said it should be clear "for all observers of the conflict to seek hard evidence before assuming Serbian blame."

In Searching for Truth, He Journeyed from Paris to Washington

The author Jacques Merlino is a respected associate editor of French TV's Channel Two who will publish a book in the UK and USA next year. He is very frustrated by the Balkan situation, where the facts are distorted, resulting in confusing pictures emerging from all parties involved in the conflict. Merlino came to Washington to meet with James Harff, director of the American firm Rider Finn and Hill and Knowlton, Inc., which had for several years represented agencies in the former republics of Yugoslavia before her disintegration.

Harff explained to Merlino that he took any rumor, true or false, that could serve his clients by demonizing the Serbs. Then "everything depended on distribution of the story to the appropriate people or organization. All that was needed was a card index, a computer, and a FAX machine. It did not matter if the story was later disproved. By that time, it would have inserted itself as a fact in the recipient's mind.''

Between August 2 and 5, 1992, the New York paper *Newsday* led with a story on Serbian camps. Elie Wiesel told Merlino that ''no comparison could be made between the Nazi slaughterhouse and the prison camp, which Wiesel visited when Serbs incarcerated Muslims and Croats.'' How then were Jewish intellectuals and organizations persuaded? Harff replied, ''We jumped on it and convened three major Jewish organizations: B'nai B'rith's Anti-Defamation League, the American Jewish Committee, and the American Jewish Congress. We suggested to them that they print an insert in the *New York Times* and organize a protest in front of the U.N. building. This really worked: The engagement of Jewish organizations on the side of the Bosnians was a super ploy.''

The story on Serbian camps ''led to associating Serbs with Nazis in public opinion. The dossier was a complex one. Nobody could understand what was going on in former Yugoslavia. To be frank, I can tell you that the vast majority of Americans wondered in which African country they would find Bosnia. In a single shot, we were able to offer a simple story, a history of the good and the bad guys, a concentration camp evoking Nazi Germany and the gas chambers at Auschwitz,'' says Harff to Merlino.

Media Over and Over Again Distorting Facts

There are responsible journalists who are conscientious and dignify their profession and endeavor to break through the walls of mystery, injustice and unscrupulous lies. One of them is Peter Brock, the editor of the *El Paso Herald-Post*. He has written about Yugoslavia and eastern Europe including Russia since 1976.

However, in the Yugoslav civil war the press was a large part of the bad news. Media techniques show vivid reports of cruelty, tragedy, and barbarism. So the media became co-belligerents, no longer disguised as noncombatants and nonpartisan.

The writer Slavko Curuvija pointed out the role played by Western journalists who ''possessed minimal capabilities for covering a vexing civil war. The greatest difficulties for European politicians and commentators in dealing with the Yugoslav crisis was that they knew next to nothing about the country when they first delved into its crisis.''

Following are some of the blatant news errors and imsrepresentations:
1. August 17, 1992, *Time* cover photo, ''Muslim prisoners in a Serbian detention camp.'' However, the man was a Serb, Slobodan Konjevich, 37.
2. In 1992 the BBC filmed an ailing ''Bosnian Muslim prisoner-of-war in a Serb concentration camp.'' Later identification showed that he was retired Yugoslav army officer Branko Velec, a Bosnian Serb held in a Muslim detention camp.

3. August 1992, "Muslim toddlers and infants." A Sarajevo bus was hit by sniper fire. It was identified at the funeral as Muslim by television reporters. However, a Serbian Orthodox funeral ritual was held, which told a different story.

4. January 4, 1993, *Newsweek* published a photo of several bodies. The story began, "Is there any way to stop Serbian atrocities in Bosnia?" Again, the photo was actually of Serbian victims.

5. CNN aired reports in March 1994 from the scene of massacres of fourteen and then ten Muslims who were supposedly killed by Serbs. The victims turned out to be Serbs.

6. August 1993, a *New York Times* photo described a Croat woman from Posusje grieving for her son killed in the recent Serb attacks. In fact, in the Croatian village of Posusje, in Bosnia near the Dalmatian coast, was a bloody scene between Muslims and Croats where thirty-four Bosnian Croats were killed.

More than 1,000 Serb civilians were imprisoned in the Bosnian town of Bradina by Muslims and Croats in the tunnel Konjic near Sarajevo, but this was not reported.

There are many credible reports about Bosnian government forces frequently firing on their own positions and people in Sarajevo for public relations firms and other purposes.

In May 1993, U.N. Secretary General Boutros-Boutros Ghali chided the media for breaking the first commandment of objectivity as he addressed CNN's Fourth World Report. "The American press had become very partisan and anti-Serb. They are very selective and manipulative with the information they use," said one U.N. official. "The reporters here have had their own wars with their editors. It was so disturbing to one reporter that she demanded to be transferred."

"I've worked with the press for a long time, and I have never seen so much lack of professionalism and ethics in the press," said another. "Especially by the American press, there is an extremely hostile style of reporting." "A kind of nihilism has been established," said another U.N. official.

In June 1993 at the Vienna Conference on Human Rights, Bosnian Muslim clients dominated that gathering. Steve Cranshaw reported in the *London Independent,* "The *London Times* noted on November 18, 1991, that 'Clarity was an early victim of the war in Yugoslavia and reality has become progressively enveloped in a blanket of fog. As the desperate attempts to win the hearts and minds of Europe grow, the claims become wilder, the proof skimpier. But the [government-controlled] Croatian media are convinced that officials in London and Washington can be outraged into submission, so the assault continues unabated.' "

A March 15, 1993, *Time* cover story: In the article, Sadako Ogata, U.N. High Commissioner for Refugees, told the U.N. Security Council that "civilians—women, children and old people—are being killed, usually by having their throats cut.'' She continues, ''That information was derived from uncorroborated broadcasts by unidentified [Muslim] ham radio operators in eastern Bosnia.'' *Time* concluded: ''In fact Ogata, like other U.N. officials and foreign journalists, had no firsthand knowledge of what was happening.''

Time repeated that there are still 70,000 ''detention camp inmates.'' That was publicized by the *New York Times* in January 1993. The State Department estimates that there are less than 7,000 in detention camps.

News reports showed that Bosnian Serbs were unusually cooperative in allowing international inspection of their camps, while Bosnian Muslims and Croats either refused or obstructed inspection of their camps. The media did not pay much attention to this.

The *Washington Post* said that France's *L'Observateur* showed paramilitary forces, ''describing them as Serb though their insignia identified them as [Croat] Ustashe.''

Nikolaos Stavron, a Howard University professor, remarked on ''a disturbing pattern in news coverage.''

Did Burns and Gutman Represent Events Scrupulously?

John Burns, correspondent for the *New York Times,* received an award primarily for seven hours of interviews with captured Serbian soldier Borislav Herak. According to the *Washington Post,* the story about Herak ''knocked everyone over.''

In May 1993 the *American Journalism Review* noted that the *Times* used curious wording to describe Burns's achievement: He ''has written of the destruction of a major European city and the dispossession of the Sarajevo people.''

A year after the ''bread line massacre'' happened, U.N. officials acknowledged that ''Muslims, not Bosnian Serbs, had set off explosives that killed 22 civilians outside a Sarajevo bakery.'' Burns and the *Times* still blame Serb mortars for that tragedy. It happened when Bosnian Muslims had pressured the U.N. Security Council to vote for sanctions against Serbia.

Roy Gutman was a winner of the Pulitzer for his scoop in August 1992 about two Serb-run ''death camps.'' British journalist Joan Phillips has pointed out: ''The death camp stories are very thinly sourced. They are based on the very few accounts from alleged survivors. They rely on hearsay and double hearsay. They are given the stamp of authority by speculation and surmise from officials. Gutman is not guilty of lying. [He] did not try to hide the fact his stories were thinly sourced. [However] those stories were the principal basis for the world's belief that the Serbs were not simply holding Muslim prisoners but were operating a death camp in Bosnia.''

In September 1992, Gutman visited the ''scene of a massacre of 17 Serbs near Banja Luka but it was reported three months later, on December 13.'' In July 1993 in the *American Journalism Review* he explained that he ''had abandoned strict objectivity in his coverage in order to pressure governments to act.''

Documented Report

A document submitted to the European Parliament and the U.N. by Bosnian Serbs included some horrible claims:
1. In late March 1992, Serb females imprisoned at Breza were raped and then murdered by Muslims.
2. July 26, 1992, an escapee from Gorazde reported that Muslims forced Serb fathers to rape their own daughters before both were murdered.
3. December 10, 1992, Serbian Orthodox patriarch Pavle in Belgrade told officials of the Swiss federal parliament and representatives of the European ecumenical movement that ''800 Serb women were documented as repeated rape victims in 20 camps operated by Muslims and Croats.''

The lengthy report (S24991) by the U.N. Security Council to the General Assembly was the first report with depositions by Serb rape victims of the incident above. That report received minimal circulation in the United States. However, the Bosnian government's claims that Serb soldiers had raped 60,000 Muslim women were undocumented claims. Meanwhile, Dame Anne Warburton, the head of the European Community delegation, accepted the report of ''the number of victims at around 20,000'' at a hearing of the U.N. War Crimes Commission.

Also, Amnesty International and the International Committee of the Red Cross concurrently declared that ''all sides were committing atrocities and rape.''

French journalist Jerome Bony on February 4, 1993, on a French television program called ''His Trek to Tuzla'' (a concentration of raped Muslim women) said: ''When I was at 50 kilometers from Tuzla I was told, 'Go to Tuzla high school grounds, [where] there are 4,000 raped women.' At 20 kilometers this figure dropped to 400. At 10 kilometers only 40 were left. Once at the site, I found only four women willing to testify.''

In July 1992, senior Western diplomats stated publicly that ''Bosnian Muslim forces in Sarajevo were repeatedly provoking Serb shelling of the city to trigger Western military intervention.'' Kosevo Hospital in Sarajevo was the most attractive backdrop for television journalists to show the public the shelling and killing of children, sick and wounded, the cutting of necessary utilities, and that sources of supply were controlled by Serb forces.

There were many statements from U.N. officials that Bosnian Muslim units initiated their own shelling of Muslim quarters in order that the world would pressure for intervention in Bosnia by leading U.N. nations.

In June 1993, French general Phillipe Morillon blamed the Bosnian Muslim government for failing to lift the seige of Sarajevo.

Mary Hueniken in the *London Free Press* said, ''Sanctions slapped on Serbia prevented it from hiring a PR firm to help it put its two cents in. . . .

The U.S. public won't get a clear picture of what is really happening in the Balkans until Serbia is allowed to present its case through PR.''

In the British *Sunday Telegraph* of February 13, 1994, columnist Boris Johnson says that CNN, with steady exposure of the explosion at the Sarajevo market, brought the Bosnian crisis to a culmination and put Western nations in a warring posture.

Therefore, a proper question to ask is: Who is handling U.S. foreign policy—the U.S. government and Congress or the U.S. media?

Buchanan's Calculations

Pat Buchanan in his article "Russia vs. America in the Balkans" of February 22, 1994 *(Hammond Times)* says: "The triggering event for U.S. intervention was the massacre in Sarajevo that killed 68 Bosnians, the 'bloodiest day' in what the *New Republic* calls a 'war of genocide' in which '200,000 people have been killed . . . and two million people have been made refugees.' ''

Further, Buchanan calculated that if 68 Bosnians were killed every day of a two-year war, the total deaths would be 49,500. For the Serbs to have killed 200,000, they would have had to kill 275 a day, or 2,000 every week. Has that really happened?

Twenty Thousand Cases of Raping the Truth

The agency Srna of the Bosnian Serb republic reported that many thousands of Serbs were imprisoned in Croatia and in Muslim prison camps. They were killed, and their bodies torn apart to free organs that were shipped to German hospitals. Srna also said Serbian children were thrown into the jaws of lions and bears in the Sarajevo zoo.

The Bosnian Muslim radio states that Serbian salt mines were full of Croatian and Muslim prisoners. Muslims accused General Lewis MacKenzie, one of the UN generals in Bosnia, of raping many young Muslim girls! MacKenzie was objective in his account, stating that "each side fires on their own people in order to later accuse the enemy." For that very reason, Muslims tried to discredit him.

On January 27, 1993, HINA, an influential Croatian agency, said the Croatian army had attacked Serbs from Krajina in the region of Zadar. However, the UN was informed the fighting was furious, while HINA made little mention of it. According to HINA's director, Mirko Bolfek, the "fighting ended." Bolfek was following the line defined by the Croatian minister of foreign affairs: "The massive offensive of Zagreb does not mean an offensive, but a police back-up of workers who were in charge of reconstruction of the Maslenica bridge." Such irony!

Such disinformations sent from the former Yugoslavia was taken at face value without any inquiries as to its truthfulness. In the disintegrated Yugoslavia the names of Serbs, Croats, and Muslims were replaced by the names "Chetniks," "Ustashe," and "mudzahedini," respectively.

Publications in Croatian in particular, were censored. The weekly journal *Today's News* was forbidden, while the newspaper *Free Dalmatia* was under strict control from Zagreb. Croatian ministers have interfered with the kind of information HINA could release. Furthermore, when conflict erupted between Croats and Muslims, the Croatian *Globus* carried the headline "Zagreb Becomes Muslimville," referring to the arrival of Bosnian Muslim refugees.

Sarajevo's *Liberation* maintains some degree of truth. Miloshevich controls the state media in Belgrade. There are various free publications in Serbia. In fact, all sides have been distorting the truth to some degree, while in the West the truth is distorted in accounts against Serbs. Serbs are today still demonized in world public opinion. The news reporters are mostly located either in Zagreb or Sarajevo. They gather information from strictly controlled government sources, either from Izetbegovich or Tudjman. Also, reporters are stationed on the territories that are controlled either by Croats or Muslims. Serbs are stamped as "aggressors" with all kinds of brutalities attributed to them, while Muslims and Croats are portrayed as victims and heroes.

The Belgrade *Politika* announced that fourteen Czecheslovakian women parachutists disguised in NATO uniforms fought alongside Croatian armed forces. Later they were captured by Serbian forces.

Says Nenad Shebek, some newspaper editors should be investigated for their instigations in their papers and tried as war criminals. Some mentioned "crimes" that people never heard of before that had happened during World War II!

At the beginning of the war, Reuters agency reported the slaughter of forty-one Serbian children, which later was denied. Did it really occur?

On January 12, 1993, the Associated French Press (AFP) received a telegram from HINA saying Serbian airplanes had attacked Srebrnica, killing nine and wounding twenty. However, the AFP did not verify that Serbian airplanes were forbidden to fly over Bosnia. Three days later the AFP denied the story, saying, "Contrary to Croatian information, there was no attack on Srebrnica."

The ABC World Service informed about 300 million listeners that Serbian snipers were paid 2,700 francs for each child killed. Along with the news came statistics of 400 children killed and 11,000 wounded. The reporter was Steve Watt. He received that information from a Muslim newsman, Irce Zortic, who was employed by a Croatian newspaper. That news was widely publicized over the Croatian radio. Unfortunately, the Western media did not do their duty to verify whether such news was correct or not!

After a German Transall plane was hit by Serbs, flights from Zagreb were suspended. But when Croatians hit UN pilots as well as three helicopters carrying medical supplies on January 25, 1993, silence prevailed. Also, no one mentioned the killing of the Bosnian minister of Croatian heritage, Josip Gogel! However, the killing by Serbs of the vice-president of the Bosnian government, Hakija Turajlica, was widely publicized, with some sarcastic comments. Unfortunately newsmen forgot to mention the reason for that incident: Serbs are in a war with Bosnian Muslims. Turajlica was involved in secret negotiations with Turkish representatives to smuggle weapons and soldiers to Bosnian Muslims.

One Croatian cargo ship was caught at the Adriatic Sea loaded with 150 tons of TNT. Another ship was discovered attempting to deliver side rockets to the Muslims—high-caliber, ground-to-air weapons. Was there any reaction to their breaking the arms embargo?

Why did only *La Croit* investigate the "ethnic cleansings" executed by Croats and Muslims against Serbs? The ethnic cleansings were also in predominantly Croat and Muslim areas. The horrors allegedly committed by Serbs were widely publicized by CNN television, without mention of crimes executed by either Croats or Muslims.

The human drama becomes a political weapon that some media use to try to influence the West to intervene militarily against Serbia. That was asserted by Hose Maria Mendiluce, director of the High Commission for Refugees looking into problems in the former Yugoslavia.

Former U.S. Senator Birch Bayh and the John Kennedy agency located in London defend the Serbian cause. While they have been less successful than public relations firms like Ruder and Finn in Washington and Hill and Knowlton, Bayh and the Kennedy agency are passing correct information to the media hoping to influence political leaders in both houses of Congress, asserts Jim Bankoff, member of the team for Yugoslav study. The Foundation for Human Rights of the American Congress directly financed Croatian propaganda activities, according to the *National Journal*.

The Organization of United Nations Associates for Bosnia and Hercegovina is under the direction of an attache of the Bosnian embassy in Zagreb. The UN war crimes commission estimates that about 3,000 rape cases have been reported, of whom only about 800 victims were identified by the UN panel. In July 1993 the UN Security Council investigated a doctors' report that confirmed 2,400 rape victims and 502 resulting births.

American publications like *The New York Times* publish inflated numbers, as in the case of reported prisoners. On January 24, 1993, the *Times* reported that since the attack in the Zadar region, 70,000 prisoners had been in 135 various camps. The majority of prisoners were under Serbian control. However, the International Red Cross registered only 10,800 prisoners in 52 camps from July to December of 1992. On January 14, 1993, there were 2,757 prisoners in 18 camps, of which 1,333 prisoners were held by Serbs while 1,424 were held by Muslims and Croats. The Red Cross partially supervised 75 percent of the Bosnian territory.

Negative reports about Serbs are due in some degree to poor Serbian communications. They have no "public relations" programs because they believe in God, truth, and justice that must prevail at the end. The consequences of this naive belief have been staggering.

Evidence Refutes Claims of Massive Serb Rapes

Tanjug accused Roy Gutman of being a CIA agent. Gutman in *Newsday* accused Serbian forces of rape. Gutman allegedly collaborated with one Robert Lofthouse, a mercenary of the Croatian-Muslim army. Lofthouse was captured and allegedly admitted his guilt.

The German newspaper *Bild am Sonntag* publicized a list of Serbian crimes perpetrated in concentration camps. They were said to have done horrible experiments on Bosnian Muslim women involving "transplants" of dog fetuses. That information was taken by the Italian journal *Corriere della Sera*. Allegedly the story began with a German congressman of the CDU, C. Schwarz, who gave the information to the *Bild*. He had personally received it from the office of human rights under Bosnian control during Schwarz's journey to Sarajevo!

Rape is one of the most serious crimes. It could be called "the crime against body and soul." Regardless of the weight of responsibility of such a crime, there are too many occurring even in peace time in the United States. In practice, criminal law experts and medical experts, especially gynecologists, not politicians, discover and investigate rape. The discovery of sperm in the vagina of a woman who says she was raped does not always prove it.

The government of Bosnia states that an estimated 50,000 Muslim women were raped. The number was lowered to 38,000, and then 30,000. The EC estimates 20,000 rape victims.

A women's group from Zagreb-Treshnjevik estimates 35,000 rape cases. However, the director of this group, Nini Kadic, possesses "fewer than a hundred" witnesses.

Investigators talked to 300 pregnant women in a Zagreb mosque who said they had been raped. During the rape, the soldiers may have disguised themselves in uniforms of another army. This is easy to do when people speak the same language and have the same complexion and mentality. It was said the Americans became the authors of the various stories by buying services with money. Simon Veil stated that their group was concerned about the enormity of the rapings. They went into the mosque in Zagreb, but they could not find even one translator there.

A Sarajevo branch of the AFP said on February 2, 1993, that Bosnian investigators knew of only one woman who delivered a baby as a result of a rape. Professor Walter Kaelin, of the University of Bern, Switzerland, says the Security Council can see that its project is not feasible. The reputation of the United Nations can be ruined regarding its defense of human rights.

Amnesty International was the first organization to state the facts: All sides in the Bosnian conflict committed rape, though Muslim women were the main victims. Amnesty has not yet succeeded in talking with even one woman who is pregnant as the result of rape.

There is an estimated number of 1,000 pregnancies as a result of rape, according to Irmet Grego, Bosnian representative for refugees. In England, one TV newswoman totally neglected the physiological necessity of a nine-month gestation period for human mothers. The delivery dates of her reported rape victims did not fit chronologically with the alleged assaults.

Paul Miller was in charge of the investigation into rape in former Yugoslavia. The information about rape is not unlike other reports from the area, disinformation about the conflict intended for political purposes. The reality in the West was distortion only about Serbs.

Philip Mizeres, an International Red Cross representative, says the maximum number of POWs in Bosnia held by all three sides (Muslims, Serbs, and Croats) was 10,000 in July 1992. There was no evidence that "rape camps" existed then or ever existed.

Dr. Ljubica Toholj, a medical specialist from Belgrade University, said homesexual rapes of Serbian prisoners were unreported. On March 31, 1993, Jane Olson of Helsinki Watch reported "Serb prisoners were forced to castrate their fellow Serb prisoners. Circumcision was also used as a form of torture." According to Urs Bolgli and Carlo von Fluc, representatives of the International Red Cross in Zagreb, each side broke a majority of the stipulations of the Geneva Convention. Each side is targeting the civilian population.

In fact, "massive rapings" of Muslim women in Bosnia resulted in some black babies delivered in England and Switzerland. This obvious evidence refuting alleged Serbian crimes must worry architects of the journalistic profession. A black baby is a most effective proof of the unscrupulous manipulations of the Western media.

Therefore, it is hoped that the powerful professional media will stop further degrading Serbs, distorting the truth, and twisting the facts. Reporting from the Bosnian quagmire has been extremely biased. Muslim atrocities, rapes, and ethnic cleansings are mostly unreported, while Serbs are castigated on the front pages of many publications! In France some voices are already calling for the formation of media committees, as well as in some American universities. It is hoped this idea will be adopted so journalism can return to its old, traditional moral principles. The media currently is like a cancer that metastically journeys from New York, Paris, and London to Belgrade, Zagreb, and Sarajevo. Men of conscience and rational minds say, "Enough is enough."

The following are some samples of investigations of raped women who delivered dark brown or black babies.[54]

Enisa: She worked in Zagreb. After the Christmas Croatian Constitution of 1990, Serbs were fired in large numbers from their jobs. Later, Muslims met the same fate. Enisa was arrested by Croatian soldiers and taken to a large building that was used as a barracks for mercenaries from abroad (Pakistanis, Kurds, Bangladesh) who fought in the Croatian army. None of them was light skinned.

It was horrible! Humiliating! One raped you while two others with their guns stood by to prevent any resistance. She was given to dirty Pakistanis who used her one after another. Horror! After she became pregnant she went to a clinic for an abortion. The doctor asked her to pay him 3,000 German marks. She was penniless. The Red Cross moved her to a hotel at the Adriatic. Later she was moved to Switzerland, where abortion was forbidden. She was there with some other unfortunate women with the same destiny. They were unable to have abortions. The girl Smilja from Plitvice helped her deliver the baby, a dark-skinned child she did not want. That was her humiliating fate.

Vahida: At the beginning of 1992 she was in Zagreb with her relatives. In Zrinjevac she met a group of dark-skinned youth in the uniform of UNPROFOR. They conversed in English. The boys were from France, although they had originally come from the former French colonies of North Africa. One evening the police raided and took women to the barracks for prostitution. She was protected by one of her UNPROFOR lovers. Later the young men from UNPROFOR were transferred to the Adriatic region. Vahida was pregnant. She made the journey to Switzerland by convoy with some Bosnians. She told Swiss journalists she had been raped by Serbs from Bosnia. In fact, the baby's father was from Morocco!

Sadeta: In spring of 1991, Sadeta lived and worked in Bosanski Brod. When the war broke out, she was caught by Croatian terrorists and brought to a bordello. She serviced Croatians and foreign mercenaries, among them Pakistanis, Tamylians, Kurds, and Bangladesh. She finally succeeded in reaching Switzerland. She registered there as a refugee, receiving thirteen francs a day. She delivered a dark-skinned baby. She heard that some women were forced to say they had been raped by Serbs.

Fatima: She lived in Sarajevo until the summer of 1992. When she found out that some Jews had left Sarajevo, she decided to flee to Belgrade. From Belgrade she moved to Switzerland via Austria. There was a presentation of raped Muslim women from Sarajevo. Fatima tearfully told journalists she had been raped by Serbs. She was rewarded by a few thousand francs. Fatima gave birth to a healthy boy. Her lover, the baby's father, was a citizen of an Arabic country...

Croatia Defies the United Nations Stationed There

The UN Protection Force described the Croatian slaughter of Serbs in the Medac region that began September 9, 1993. According to UN eyewitnesses, Croatian army troops used "scorched earth" tactics, to kill at least seventy Serbian civilians and raze 500 buildings in Serbian villages.

A Peacekeepers' Report said that "evidence indicates the intentional killing of Serb civilians who were unable to escape the attack, regardless of age, sex or status." Croatian soldiers also poisoned wells, stole horses, and slaughtered livestock.

The UN forces' deputy chief, Cedric Thornberry, who toured the Medac region, said nothing larger than "a good-sized brick is left in those villages. You can see how they wanted to obliterate all traces of human settlement."

Tadeusz Mazowiecki, who is a politician as well as a UN human rights investigator, protested to Croatian government officials about the brutal "executions" by the Croatian army. How could it happen in the "most democratic country in Europe," as President Franjo Tudjman has said many times? Croatian authorities would naturally investigate these charges with gloves on, if at all.

After that attack in three Serbian villages, Divoselo, Chitluk, and Pocitelj, nothing survived. There was an "intentional and well-planned Croatian attack against Serbs."

Some brief statistics from Divoselo: In 1857 there were 1,844 Serbian inhabitants. Before 1941 there were 2,216 Serbs. During World War II, 849 Serbs from Divoselo were killed by Croatian Ustashe. In 1991 there were 404 Serbs; since the September 9, 1993 raid there are zero Serbs there and the village is totally razed.

Also, in Sarajevo, Roy Wilkinson, High Commissioner for Refugees, stated; "Bosnian Croats evicted more than 530 Muslim civilians from the Croatian western sector of Mostar on September 29, 1993."

In an article titled "Croats Blamed for Massacre in Bosnia" in the *San Francisco Chronicle* and the *San Jose Mercury News*, it is stated that masked Croatian soldiers killed at least 80 Muslim civilians in cross-fire. A Danish UN truck driver was also slain and nine others were wounded. That happened in the Muslim village Stupni Do, where it was believed there were more Muslims missing.

A Muslim woman, Zinata Likic, hid with her younger daughters in the nearby forest for two days. She described a horrible scene of the Ustashe setting everything on fire and throwing bodies into the flames. "The Croatian Ustashe wore black masks with white ribbons over them." Likic with fifteen other survivors was picked up by UN forces south of Croat-held Vares, in central Bosnia. Stupni Do had an all-Muslim population of about 260, with only 39 armed defenders.

Says Bill Aikman, spokesman in Sarajevo for the UN protection forces, what happened in Stupni Do is of great concern. The Nordic peacekeeper is also concerned about the welfare of several hundred Muslims who have been detained by Croats in the school in the center of Vares. Swedish major Daniel Ekberg worries about the Muslims' safety because HVO (Croat Defense Council forces) are holding 230 Muslims and denying access to UN forces. Croatian troops denied any massacre, though they also forbade UN peacekeepers from entering the village, where they had laid mines.

Another UN High Commissioner for Refugees, Sadako Ogata, condemned the brutal killings of Muslim civilians and tragic loss of UN peacekeepers who had come to the former Yugoslavia on a humanitarian mission. Instead of appreciating their effort and sacrifices, some local megalomaniacs, here and there, play barbarian politics with the peacekeepers' lives.

Why don't Germany and the Vatican attempt to stop the killings, when they are both most responsible for the current Yugoslav tragedy? Could anyone call Croatia civilized and protect her, whether the defender is the strongest economic European country or the largest and most powerful faith in Europe or on the globe? Today we should ask ourselves, does any fairness and justice exist in this world?

Solutions of Serbs Today

After the Serbs can recover they must rid themselves of all the Communist inheritance and change their policies, because their policy—diplomatic, economic, and cultural—has brought the Serbs to a dead end. The old Serbian friends became enemies, while their old enemies became murderers!

The leadership of Serbia and Montenegro as staunch internationalists or Yugoslavs are out of touch with the reality of rescuing people from a sinking boat in troubled waters. The days of the nation are numbered if her leadership loses sight of the future.

At a meeting of members of the Serbian Academy of Science and Art, academic-peasant Radomir Lucich advised how Serbia could survive imposed sactions. Return to the village. Then nobody can harm us because then Serbia would not need petroleum or high technology. During the occupation, he went on, Serbia fed four armies—German, Nedich, Ljotich, and Partisan. In 1944 a kilogram of tomatoes sold for thirty dinars. Wagons were pulled by horses, not tractors, because tractors needed gasoline. What now? There are no more horses in the villages. They all went to the city, and they don't call them horses anymore. However, some of them today sit down in Parliament, so you can see what they are when they speak up there....

Serbs have been pronounced guilty when in fact there is not one side without guilt. According to the media, Serbs have no right to defend themselves against religious fanaticism and political chauvinism. Klara Mandich says you can count on the fingers of one hand people like Serbs who don't know how to hate.

Dr. Klara Mandich is Jewish. Her father was Mordekai Drapinger and her mother Sara Eshkenazi. She compares two chosen people, Jews in the Old Testament and Serbs in the New Testament. Only nations that have survived the same kind of injustice, persecution, and despotism can truly have sensitivity for others who have suffered and still suffer from the world's prejudices.

She continues by saying that many Israelis have chosen to stay in Serbia because of Serbs' warmth, sincere friendship, hospitality, good-heartedness, and, above all, religious tolerance. She greatly appreciates the deeds of the Serbian Orthodox church, which is not a militant church but a true Christian one. Through the centuries this church has taught love, tolerance, and respect regardless of race, color, or religious affiliation. The church still retains these qualities despite the unbearable pressure on her by either the East (Islam) or the West (the Vatican) or by both during the long centuries of her slavery.

Serbs in their historical determination endeavored to be part of Europe, which they defended against the barbaric Ottoman Empire for over five centuries.

In this century the Serbs have been exposed three times to genocide, a threat that continues today in Croatia and Bosnia-Hercegovina through religious and ethnic fanaticism. In this fanatical civil war, some Serbian extremists have taken revenge against Muslim culprits. The absolute majority of the Serbian people disagree with any kind of misdeeds no matter who commits them. The Serbian epos created in the period of Ottoman slavery taught the Serbs that every person, regardless of creed, race, or nationality, should be treated with respect and dignity from the cradle to the grave.

Serbs should debate their problems. At a time crucial for their national survival they should all be aligned together behind their flag to defend their very existence. Otherwise they shall pay dearly, with their lives, properties, and above all their national pride and dignity.

The new Serbian Parliament should pronounce a Declaration of Nullification of all decisions made by the second session of AVNOY in 1943 because Serbs were not represented by their political parties, as were Croats and Slovenes.

All Serbs must be considered as one ethos from the same roots, which is contrary to the policy of "divide and rule" advocated and adopted by the Comintern, Vatican, and the Austrian villain Josip Broz Tito from Kumrovac, Croatia. Tragically, the Yugoslav conglomerate formed in 1918 created great mistrust and hatred, with calamitous experiences and consequences.

In order to survive all Serbs should put aside all idealism, romanticism, and even ideological fanaticism and become pragmatic about protecting their own interests and paving the way to a brighter future. If anyone is still infected with Yugoslavism, let him contact his brother Croats and feel their love and brotherhood on his own skin! Put oneself in the position of Serbs in Croatia or elsewhere outside of Serbia and Montenegro.

Serbs must get along with each other. They need to roll up their sleeves and gather arguments (facts) pro and con and then appeal to the world to hear their voice of truth. Serbs should care for their friends while saying nothing but the truth about their adversaries, which would be detrimental to them; print a white paper about their adversaries and about their own performances; finally, let them run through the world with gas and matches in their hands.

In the final analysis, Serbs strongly believe that truth and justice should prevail and that they will triumph someday. For that very reason the Serbs were totally unprepared for the unscrupulous propaganda that indecently demonized them and stripped them of dignity. In short, the Serbs believed in moral postulates that led them to feel they could defend themselves indirectly by moral strength. Unfortunately, they were mistaken.

If the Serbs temporarily remain alone, they can learn from Israel how she struggled through the centuries and finally survived, standing proudly on her own feet today. Historical principles and the ideas of liberty, truth, and justice with pride and dignity should remain forever the fundamental characteristics of the Serbian nation.

Notes

1. Victor Novak, *Croat, Vatican, and Yugoslav People Before World War II* (Belgrade, 1973), cited in Bulajich, *Mission of the Vatican in the ISC* (Belgrade: Politika, 1992).

2. Bulajich, *op. cit.*, p. 132.

3. General Velimir Terzich (an assistant chief of staff in Tito's army), *Yugoslavia in the April War, 1941* (Podgorica: Graphic Institute, 1963).

4. R. Ambasciata d'Italio presso la Santa Sede, telepresso no. 303206 Rome August 12, 1944, cited in Bulajich, *op. cit.*, p. 815.

5. R. Ambasciata d'Italia presso la Santa Sede, telepresso no. 654534, Rome, September 29, 1944, cited in Bulajich, *op. cit.*, p. 815.

6. Arso Milatovich, "What Actually Happened in Rome," *Nin* (Belgrade), no. 1539, June 24, 1980.

7. Bulajich, *op. cit.*, p. 856.

8. Jelena Lovric, "Drawing in Gloves," *Monitor* (Podgorica), no. 123, February 26, 1993, pp. 36-37.

9. This section draws on newly published material about the role of the Catholic church and the Vatican in Bulajich's book *The Mission of the Vatican in the ISC*, volumes 1 & 2, *op. cit.*

10. Victor Novak, "Principium et Finis—Veritas, Regarding the Case of Archbishop Stepinac," *International Politics* (Belgrade), no. 2026, 1951, p. 7.

11. Bulajich, *op. cit.*, p. 75.

12. *Croatian People* (Zagreb), July 23, 1944.

13. Ivan Cvitkovich, *Who Was Alojzije Stepinac,* (Sarajevo: Liberation, 1986), p. 173.

14. *Ibid.*, p. 171.

15. Bulajich, *op. cit.*, p. 1018.

16. *Ibid.*, p. 338.

17. *Ibid.*, p. 339.

18. La Secretairerie d'Etat a la Legation de Yugoslavie, A.E.S. 6442, Vatican, 25 janvier 1942, *Actes et Documents...* vol. 5, doc. 224, p. 393.

19. American Counterintelligence Corps, Rome, September 6, 1988, U.S. Army, 1947, case no 5650-A.

20. Bulajich, *op. cit.*, p. 69.

21. Bulajich, *The Bishopric Herald of Krizevac*, no. 2, 1941, pp. 10-11.

22. Bulajich, *Mission of the Vatican in the ISC, op cit.*

23. Stepinac's diary, vol. 4, p. 324, cited in Bulajich, *op. cit.*, p. 575.

24. *Catholic Weekly* (Sarajevo), June 5, 1942.

25. SURSR Croatia, Archive UDB-A, Slavko Odic., p. 209.

26. Archbishops Convention, AS no. 31 ap.76.

27. Jakov Blazevich, a Croat, in his book *Sword, Not Peace*, p. 237.

28. American television reporters are trying to be experts all over the world. For them the Cold War is history, and World War II is ancient history. That is an incorrect judgment because of long-existing problems that exist in the foothills of Krajina, the area of Croatia where Serbs are in a majority. In the fifteenth century their forefathers moved there from the Serbian areas, retreating in front of Ottoman aggression and expansion. Then the Austro-Hungarian Empire succeeded in turning Serbian Krajina into a military camp to fight and restrain the Turks from their ambition of taking over all of Europe. The Serbs in Krajina played a tremendous role in preserving Christianity and freedom at the border of Austria-Hungary.

Andrew Roberts thus reminds CNN broadcasters that they forgot the way Franciscan friars slaughtered the Serbs in Croatia and Bosnia in 1941. Many Serbs were slaughtered after converting, even though they had been promised their lives would be spared. Undoubtedly those who do not know the fundamental differences of the people in that particular part of Yugoslavia will not be able to grasp the current tragedy there.

29. In 1945, after World War II, there was in Kosovo a population ratio of 46.16% Serbs and 53.64% Albanians. [V. Djuretich, *The Destruction of Serbs in the Twentieth Century*, Belgrade: 1992, pp. 102-103.] Tito forbade any Serbian refugees who had been expelled by the occupiers during the war from returning to Kosovo. Why then did Tito not forbid Slovenian refugees who had stayed in occupied Serbia during the war to return? They were also expelled by the German occupier! Tito also allowed Bakali, the head of the Albanian Communists in Kosovo, to expel over 100,000 Serbs in 1968-69. The current ratio between Serbs and Albanians is 10% Serbs and 90% Albanians. Who is most responsible for this? The injustice and the atrocities did not begin in 1991 but in 1941, starting with Yugoslav quislings and continuing under Tito's Communist government.

30. OSS officers Weil Farish and MacLean (British SOE), who were attached to Tito's headquarters, stated in their reports to their respective governments (U.S. and British) that the Yugoslav Partisan force had a strength of between 250,000 and 300,000 soldiers. General N. V. Korneyev, the head of the Soviet mission to Tito's headquarters, had estimated Partisan strength at only about 18,000. On June 26, 1944, the Military Intelligence Division (MID) put Partisan strength at 15,000. Lt. Colonel McDowell, also an OSS officer, says the assessment had been made from unsubstantiated claims of the Partisans themselves. Western liberals and most of the media accepted the claim of 300,000 Partisans without question. [Kirk Ford, Jr., *The OSS and the Yugoslav Resistance, 1943-1945*, Texas: A & M University Press, 1992, p. 68.]

31. "Croatian Acts Nexus—New Arms and Trade," *Defense Foreign Affairs and Strategic Policy* (London), September 31, 1992, vol. 20, no. 12.

32. Bulajich, *Mission of the Vatican in the ISC, op. cit.*, p. 974.

33. *Politika* (Belgrade), March 12, 1992, p. 7.

34. Victor Novak, *Magnum Crimen* (Zagreb: New Books, 1948), pp. 714-717.

35. Rastislav Petrovich, *Conspiracy Against Serbs* (Belgrade: Dositej, 1990), pp. 13-14.

36. *Daily Telegraph*, January 19, 1993.

37. *Helsinki Watch*, April 6, 1993.

38. Amphilohije Radovich, "Christ's Victory Would Be Victory for All of Us," interviewed by Jovan Plamenac and Z. Ostojich, *Victory (Pobjeda)*, April 12, 1993, p. 7.

39. Nenad Stefanovich, "Visconti and Schiffer in Country of Wonders," *Duga* (Belgrade), no. 493, January 16-29, 1993, pp. 76-77.

40. *Ibid.*

41. *Northern California Jewish Bulletin*, Feb. 26, 1993.

42. *Duga*, no. 393, March 18-31, 1989.

43. In 1940, at the age of 16, the current Bosnian president, Alija Izetbegovich, founded a religious-political organization called the Young Muslims. During World War II the group collaborated with the Ustashe and killed more than 300,000 Bosnian Serbs alone.

The diverse population in Bosnia-Hercegovina enabled Tehran and its allies to use violence there as a springboard to launch a *jihad* in Europe. Thus, Muslims in Bosnia-Hercegovina have been considered vehicles for Islamic expansion in Europe. Additionally, Tito's pro-Arab policy in 1970 even allowed recruitment of volunteers from his soil to join a terrorist organization like the PLO. Yugoslavia has provided extensive military assistance to the Arab world, sending them experts and technicians, many of whom were Muslims. During the Israel-Egypt war Yugoslav airfields (such as Podgorica) were used to fly war material to the Arabs in the Middle East.

During Tito's dictatorial rule there was an unexpected renaissance for Yugoslav Muslims. Many mosques were erected in Bosnia. From Bosnia alone, about 250 students were sent each year to be educated in the Middle East (notably in Iran) to become radical mullas (Islamic clergy).

In 1984 the Yugoslav security apparatus was complaining of illegal immigration into their country, especially Muslims from Albania and the Middle East, in Kosovo and Metohia in particular.

Under such favorable political circumstances the activities of Izetbegovich are important to mention. In 1949 the Young Muslims had staged an open revolt, for which Izetbegovich was sentenced to four years for crimes committed against Serbs in Sarajevo. Also, in 1983 he was very active within the Young Muslim organization, and again he was charged with crimes against Serbs and the state. He was sentenced to sixteen years in prison, of which he served only six.

In May 1991 Izetbegovich officially visited Tehran. At that time he stated that Islam had very deep roots in Bosnia-Hercegovina. He asked for Iranian help to invest in Bosnia-Hercegovina, to increase the number of Yugoslav Muslim trainees in Iranian schools, to absorb Islamic culture. In the summer of 1991 Izetbegovich also visited Libya, seeking financial and political support. For Muslim countries, judging especially by Iran, the situation in Bosnia-Hercegovina is seen as a red microcosm, resulting in a promising situation for Islam in Europe. Under Iran's guidance the Muslim world must mobilize a volunteer mujahideen Muslim army to defend their brothers in Bosnia-Hercegovina, under the slogan "Allah-o-Akbar" (God is greatest). Those mujahideen were willing to fight the Jihad, to become martyrs for the victory of the Islamic world!

Weapons for Bosnian Muslims were shipped from Iran, Turkey, and Pakistan, mainly through the Croatian ports of Split and Rijeka and through Ploce as well. The Croats agreed to "close their eyes" to the weapon smuggling through their territory.

When Izetbegovich complained of more frequent Croatian attacks on their old Muslim ally, Zagreb reminded him of an agreement to surrender to them seventeen high-ranking Muslim officers who had committed crimes in Croatia as former Yugoslav officers. Those officers held top positions in the Bosnian Muslim army.

"The Islamic Tide Brigade in Europe" is training Islamic terrorists to target some European countries, primarily France, Belgium, Holland, and the UK. They have large caches of weapons and explosives safely hidden all over Europe.

The Islamic top leadership believes nothing less than a strong campaign waged by Western governments will destroy Muslim communities in Europe and prevent their triumph. The greatest carnage in Bosnia-Hercegovina was caused by the foreign mujahideen and by numerous local Muslims who have been highly trained in the Middle East for such operations.

44. Laza Kostich, *Holocaust*, Chicago: Liberty, 1981.

45. Letter of Vuk Drashkovich to Israel.

46. Joseph Gottfried replied to Drashkovich.

47. Bulajich, *Mission of the Vatican in the ISC, op. cit.*, p. 90.

48. Volume 39, No. 1, January 1993.

49. Proclamation by the top party leaders, *Proleter*, organ of the CCCPY, no. 28, December 1932, cited in Djuretich, *op. cit.*

50. Ford, *op. cit.*, p. 157.

51. Deane, "Redwood Mission," Jan. 31, 1945, RG 226, E. 154, B. 25, F. 354, cited in Ford, *op. cit.*, p. 129.

52. Report of American Consul General, Istanbul, Turkey, No. 183.

53. Djuretich, *op. cit.*

54. Published in English, German, French, and Serbo-Croatian with pictures of dark-skinned babies. *New Word*, no. 58-59, April 1993.

A Final Word from the Author

The material gathered for this book, with all its questions, confusions, and contradictions, is offered with one aim—to expose "the truth through the facts," to counter naivety, lies, and false propaganda. When lies are repeated over and over while the truth is hermetically locked up, lies can seem to be true.

The period in which dictator Josip Broz Tito from Kumrovac, Croatia ruled Yugoslavia, as either secretary of the CPY or as untouchable dictator, left its permanent stamp on the psyche of most Yugoslav citizens to the present day. It is important to remember that Tito was installed on the Yugoslav "throne" by Stalin's tanks and Churchill's bombers. When he did not appreciate later what both had done for him, Churchill called him a "snake in the grass." During his entire political career he was never chosen by democratic processes or by a true referendum of the Yugoslav people. It is well known that in Marxist countries, elections were a farce, "a race with one horse."

During Tito's supreme rule there were three kinds of armed conflict: ideological confrontation, a liberation struggle, and ethnic-religious persecutions. The ideological opposition of democracy versus communism and fascism caused civil war within the country; in the struggle against the various occupiers of the country, "national liberation and social justice" was the motto of the Communist propaganda apparatus; the effects of the ethnic-religious fanaticism were truly a holocaust. The most devastating conflict was the fratricidal, because all parties involved knew each other (as in the current conflict in Bosnia).

Using every means available, Tito shaped Yugoslav national policy for nearly fifty years by steering his ship in whatever direction he thought would be most advantageous for him personally. He held all the strings in his hands because he had unbounded power. In return for doing his will his cohorts received princely privileges and benefits even though they lived in a country of "working people and peasants," as they loudly proclaimed. Tito was the undisputed ringmaster, the central player in the theater of all Yugoslav events, a pharoah who lived in unparalled luxury. In consequence of his political career the Yugoslav people went out of the proverbial frying pan into the fire.

Tito, an agent of various foreign intelligence services, succeeded in penetrating into others. Then he was extravagantly praised as a champion of liberty and equality. Senator Pepper proclaimed, "Tito is the Yugoslav Washington, the unifier and liberator of his people."[1]

It is worth mentioning that during World War II there were two resistance movements in Yugoslavia—one led by Gen. Draza Mihailovich, which was made up mostly of Serbs; and the Partisan movement led by the Communist Tito, which was also 95 percent Serb until the Italian capitulation in September 1943. Then the Croatian Fascist Ustashe and other pro-Fascist groups realized Nazi Germany would be defeated. So they began to align themselves with the Partisan movement in order to save their lives and properties. In 1944 Tito extended a deadline for the Ustashe to join the Partisan ranks to fight against Chetniks. He offered them double pension benefits if they would join his movement.

Tito's main adversary in the Yugoslav civil war was Gen. Mihailovich, the first guerrilla leader in occupied Europe. Mihailovich was minister of war in the Yugoslav government-in-exile in London. According to German documents, the general never collaborated with the Germans, although he was shot by Tito's Communists as a collaborator in 1946. Such irony!

In February 1943 the German general Reihard Gehlen, head of military intelligence for eastern Europe, stated that in his opinion the Mihailovich movement was the best organized and had the support of 80 percent of the Serbian people. Mihailovich's men were fighting against the alien yoke for better economic and social conditions.[2]

Let's see how Marshal Tito behaved during World War II with the German occupier. (He was arm in arm with Austria-Hungary and Germany in World War I.) In March 1943 in Zagreb, Tito sent his emissaries to the German command to negotiate. According to German documents,[3] Tito wanted a nonaggression pact with Nazi Germany. The memorandum of the meeting noted: They don't want to fight against either the Croatian Ustashe (similar to German SS) or against the Germans, but exclusively against the Chetniks (Mihailovich's movement). They are armed and ready to resist any enemy that we (the Germans) point out to them, including the British.[4] Also, Ilija Jukich, a Croat, excerpted some German reports that referred to the negotiations with Tito's Partisans. And Tito's biographer, Vladimir Dedijer, wrote about the negotiations and the German documentation.

The historic AVNOY convention was held in Jajce in the fall of 1943. No representatives from Serbia were present, although Serbia was the most populous republic. Serbia played a subordinate role in the federation and was under Tito's thumb under the pretext "Smaller Serbia, greater Yugoslavia." That was a fatal wrong for the survival of Yugoslavia as an entity. At the AVNOY convention Yugoslavia was officially divided into six republics and two autonomous provinces (Kosovo and Vojvodina). The newly organized nation was built on sand, so that even a slight breeze could rock her to her foundation. The republics' boundaries were not established according to ethnic demarcations but according to Tito's whims, which later caused frictions and finally the eruption of armed conflict among the republics in 1991.

Tito secretly abetted all separatist tendencies among the republics, leading to events such as the party convention in 1966, Maspok in 1971 in Croatia, the Muslim renaissance in 1971, the new constitution in 1974, et cetera. The new constitution allowed the formation of independent territorial military units for each republic. This later proved to be a time bomb that with German and Vatican direction and help would cause Yugoslav disintegration.

During and after the Yugoslav calamity of World War II, Tito deceived the West and fell short in bringing peace, freedom, stability, and justice to the people who most deserved it but were least rewarded—the Serbs. He refused to bring the culprits who had committed crimes during the war to trial. If there was any justice, Tito himself would be the first to be tried for committing and hiding unprecedented crimes in that unfortunate country. Instead Tito and his Croatian extremists and Serbian marionettes invented the slogan "Brotherhood and Unity" to cover up the crimes of genocide committed by the extremist right wing, the Croatian Ustashe. Furthermore, Tito also ordered some of his generals ("people's heroes") to cover up all the pits in Croatia, Bosnia, and Hercegovina with armored concrete. Into those pits had been thrown innocent Serbian victims, mostly old men, women, and children, who were the least able to escape the Ustashe hunts. Their only sin was being Serbs of the Orthodox faith. If anybody dared to mention those innocent victims, he or she would be mercilessly persecuted. Thus, "justice" in Tito's "democratic" Yugoslavia closed its eyes to the grisly deeds of murderers and made criminals of those who sought to disclose the wrongdoings.

Even more pathetically and incredulously, the current Croatian authority still denies the magnitude of the Ustashe crimes of genocide. However, documentary evidence from the German and Italian occupiers and even from some prominent Croatians of Yugoslav orientation makes it clear. Germany long since apologized to the world for what Nazi Germany did in the Jewish genocide, and Japan recently admitted wrongdoings in its past subjugation of Korea, but has any apology or understanding been forthcoming from leaders in Yugoslavia about the unthinkable deeds of their past? On the contrary, Tito's General Tudjman, currently Croatian president, has vehemently denied that crimes were committed by the Ustashe. Furthermore, he accuses the British of genocide because British troops stationed in Austria repatriated the Ustashe and their families back to Yugoslavia in May 1945. The Allies had decided before the war was over that the Ustashe should be returned as war criminals.

History denied is history that can return with a vengeance. Here is an example of history repeating itself. One of the thousands of cases of genocide happened on August 4, 1941, in Prebilovci. After fifty years, the Serbs' remains were dug up from the Golubinska pit (jama) and were finally interred with Christian rites and respect. In 1992 the Ustashe came back and took over that region. They blew up the crypt, sending human remains flying into the air. The current Serbian authority refused to show on television two films about the tragic destiny of those Serbs who were twice victimized in Prebilovci.

Also, Dr. Medakovich, a professor at Belgrade University, complained that the Ministry of Information in Belgrade refused to publish accounts of genocide against Serbs. The same ministry also failed to inform its own citizens or the world community that Banski Dvori was targeted in Zagreb by Tudjman's officers, not by Yugoslav army officers as the world media claimed.

Tito's dossier would not be complete without mention of what happened in 1948, when Tito split with Stalin, and how he and his cohorts subsequently behaved. The split came as a surprise to the West. Such a rift was hitherto unknown in the monolithic Marxist ideology. But Tito had been trained to play any political card that would be advantageous to himself. By breaking off relations with the Soviet Union he could let the Yugoslav secret police proceed with their barbaric treatment of Stalin adherents and political opponents, just as they had done before with Mihailovich's adherents. Those pro-Stalin Communists were called Cominformists or Informbureau. Until then they had been close to Tito's political philosophy. Now they faced unspeakable brutalities and tortures. By such treatment of his ideological and wartime comrades, Tito showed his real face. He was ready to change his shirt whenever it was to his personal advantage. Therefore, he lost much respect from his countrymen. Tito's ideology-of-the-moment and his deceitfulness were springboards to gain prestige and personal rewards, in his megalomaniacal ambition and selfishness.

Those Cominformists/political opponents who survived the tortures and humiliations of the secret police became Tito's bitter enemies. The Montenegrin authority has to deal with those surviving prisoners, many of whom were physically and mentally maimed.

The rift between Tito and Stalin was wholeheartedly embraced by all pro-Fascist elements in Yugoslavia, especially by the Croatian Ustashe, who were a bulwark of right extremism. They began to revenge themselves against those they called ''Serbo Communists.'' It is a paradox that those who deserved the most credit for helping Tito grab power were those who suffered the most! The split among Communist rivals was enthusiastically embraced by the West, too, in the hope that other Communist countries would follow Tito's example. Thus, doors were open for Tito in any European capital, as well as in the United States.

Tito's Yugoslavia received billions of dollars of financial and military aid and loans, putting a heavy mortage on the future of younger Yugoslav generations. However, the slogan ''Tito after Tito'' changed the economic picture and increased the political instabilities. The Yugoslav secret police are not as powerful now as they were in Tito's time.

In 1990 discord and separatism among the republics reached a breaking point, and the Yugoslav people were thrown into an abyss from which they cannot yet get out. Late in June 1993 the popular German newspaper *Die Zeit* passed a humiliating judgment on Tudjman's regime, saying that Bonn was the political godfather to the Croatian state. Thus Germany has exposed itself to international pressure. *Die Zeit* says that Tudjman and his clique were the beneficiaries of a generous godfather whose recognition of Croatia was misused; instead of forming a democratic, pluralistic European state they created a neofascist "creature led by a comic dictator." Croatia is currently disappointing Germany, which not only recognized her but also supplied her with large amounts of weapons to "establish democracy" in the Balkans.

Finally, Yugoslavia, after the failure of two Titoist revolutions, proletarian and economic, needs a spiritual renaissance. All the vices inherited from Titoism and its successors should be replaced as soon as possible by the time-honored virtues—love, ethics, morality, dignity, tolerance, mutual understanding, and respect. The sooner these human virtues prevail, the sooner the tragedy in Bosnia and all other territories of the former Yugoslavia will heal, with less pain and fewer fatal consequences. Therefore, all people of good will should help build that unfortunate country, so her people may come to their senses rather than compete to destroy themselves. The Yugoslav disintegration was a problem for the community itself, and the people of Yugoslavia alone should resolve it by themselves.

Notes

1. Radoje Vukcevich, *General Mihailovich, the Trial and Great Injustice* (Chicago: Serbian Historical and Cultural Society, 1984), p. 149.
2. *The Record* (Philadelphia), April 1946, cited in Bosko Vukcevich, *Diverse Forces in Yugoslavia, 1941-1945* (Los Angeles: Authors Unlimited, 1990), p. 114.
3. German military report T-501-265-00128.
4. Misha Lekovich, *The Negotiations of March 1943* (Belgrade: People's Books, 1985), pp. 74, 90, 137.

Bibliography

Aarons, Mark, and John Loftus. *Unholy Trinity*. New York: St. Martin's Press, 1992.

Abramov, Smilja. *Genocide in Yugoslavia*. Belgrade: Politika, 1992.

Avakumovich, Ivan. *Documents of German Foreign Policy, 1918-1945* (Series D, vol. xiii). Washington, D.C., 1964.

Avakumovich, Ivan. *Mihailovich According to German Sources*. London: Liberation, 1969.

Avakumovich, Ivan. *New Stories*. Chicago: Herald-Njegosh Society, n. 50, pp. 81-82.

Barker, Elisabeth. *British Policy in the Balkans During World War II*. Zagreb: Globus, 1978.

Basta, Milan. *The Agony and Collapse of the Independent State of Croatia*. Belgrade: Rad, 1971.

Basta, Milan. *The War Ended Seven Days Later*. Kocevje: Kocevski Tisk, 1980.

Bekich, T. "One Unknown Article about Njegosh." Novi Sad: Collection of the *Serbian Register*, 1968.

Belich, Alex. *1848 of Our Culture*. Belgrade: Our Literature, 1947.

Beljakovich, Miodrag. *Yugoslavia at the Crossroads*. Chicago: Serbian National Defense, 1983.

Beloff, Nora. *Tito's Flawed Legacy*. London: Golloncz, 1985.

Bernstein, Carl. "Holy Alliance." *Time Magazine, 139*(8), February 29, 1942, pp. 28-35.

Boban, Ljubo. "Britain, Croatia and the Croatian Peasant Party, 1941-1945." *Magazine for Contemporary History, 3*, 1978.

Bulajich, Milan. *Ustashe Genocidal Crimes and the Trial of Andrija Artukovich, 1986.* Belgrade: Work, 1988 (vol. 1 & 2), 1989 (vol. 3 & 4).

Bulajich, Milan. *Mission of the Vatican in the Independent State of Croatia* (vol. 1 & 2). Belgrade: Politika, 1992.

Butler, J. R. *History of the Second World War. Grand Strategy* (vol. 3). 1957.

Carroll, Peter. *It Seemed Like Nothing Happened*. New York: Holt, Rinehart & Winston, 1982.

Churchill, Winston. *Closing the Ring*. Cambridge, Mass.: Houghton Mifflin, 1951.

Churchill, Winston. *Triumph and Tragedy*. Boston: Houghton Mifflin, 1953.

Clissold, Stephen. *A Short Story of Yugoslavia*. Cambridge, England: Cambridge University Press, 1986.

Clissold, Stephen. *Whirlwind. An Account of Marshal Tito's Rise to Power*. London, 1947.

Copulos, Nicholas. "Dezinformatsia." *Soldier of Fortune, 1*(11, November 1986.

Corovich, Vladimir. *Black Book: The Sufferings of Serbs in Bosnia and Hercegovina During 1914-1918*. Belgrade, 1989.

Culinovich, Ferdo. *Documents of Yugoslavia*. Zagreb: School Books, 1968.

Curuvija, Slavko. *Ibeovac I, Vlado Dapcevich*. Belgrade: Filip Vishnjic, 1990.

Deakin, F. W. D. *The Brutal Friendship*. New York: Harper & Row, 1962.

Deakin, F. W. D. *The Embattled Mountain*. London: Oxford University Press, 1971.

Dedijer, Vladimir. *New Contributions to the Biography of Josip Broz Tito* (vol. 2). Rijeka: Libernija, 1981.

Dedijer, Vladmir. *New Contributions to the Biography of Josip Broz Tito* (vol. 3). Belgrade: Prosveta, 1984.
Dedijer, Vladimir. *Vatican and Jasenovac*. Belgrade: Rad, 1987.
De Gaulle, Charles. *War Memoirs* (vol. 1). London, 1955.
Djilas, Milovan. *Anatomy of a Moral*. New York: Harcourt Brace Jovanovich, 1959.
Djilas, Milovan. *Legend about Njegosh*. Belgrade: Culture, 1952.
Djilas, Milovan. *Montenegro*. New York: Harcourt Brace Jovanovich, 1963.
Djilas, Milovan. *Njegosh: Poet, Prince, Bishop*. New York: Harcourt Brace Jovanovich, 1966.
Djilas, Milovan. *The New Class*. New York: Praeger, 1957.
Djilas, Milovan. *Wartime*. New York and London: Harcourt Brace Jovanovich, 1977.
Djukich, Slavoljub. *The Collapse of Serbian Liberals*. Belgrade: Filip Vishnjice, 1990.
Djuretich, Veselin. *The Destruction of Serbs in the Twentieth Century*. Belgrade: SANUBI, 1992.
Djurich, Ljubo. *Memories of Personalities and Events*. Belgrade, 1989.
Dragicevich, Risto. *Articles about Njegosh*. Cetinje: People's Books, 1949.
Dragnich, Alex. *The First Yugoslavia*. Stanford, Calif.: Hoover Institute, 1983.
Dragnich, Alex. "The Tragedy of Yugoslavia." *Vanderbilt Magazine, 75*(4), Winter 1992.
Dzadzich, Petar. *New Ustasha's State*. Belgrade: Politika, 1991.
Eden, Anthony. *The Reckoning*. Boston: Houghton Mifflin, 1962.
Fodor, Eugene. *Fodor's Yugoslavia*. New York: McKay, 1969.
Ford, Kirk, Jr. *OSS and the Yugoslav Resistance 1943-1945*. Texas A & M University Press, 1992.
"Genocide and Mass Destruction: Doing Harm to Others as a Missing Dimension in Psychopathology." *Journal of the Washington School of Psychiatry, 49*(2), 1986.
Grcich, Marko. *Bleiburg*. Zagreb: Start, 1990.
Hehn, Paul. *The German Struggle Against Yugoslav Guerrillas in World War II, 1941-1945*. Ohio: Columbus University Press, 1979.
History of the United Nations War Crimes Commission. London: His Majesty's Stationary Office, 1948.
Hopter, B. Jakob. *Yugoslavia in Crises, 1934-1941*. New York and London: Columbus University Press, 1962.
Horvat, Jasha-Shtabuk Zdenko. *Documents of Anti-People Activities and Crimes of Part of the Catholic Clergy*. Zagreb, 1946.
Horvat, Josip. *Ante Starcevich*. Zagreb, 1940.
Huot, Louis. *Guns for Tito*. New York: Fischer, 1945.
Ivanovich, Vane. *Memoirs of a Yugoslav*. New York: Harcourt Brace Jovanovich, 1977.
Jocov, Marko. "The Struggle for Dominance in the Balkans at the End of the XVIth and the Beginning of the XVIIth Century." *Historical Magazine of the Eastern Institute of the Serbian Academy of Science and Art, 34*, 1987, p. 133.
Jasper, Karl. *The Future of Mankind*. Chicago, 1961.
Jelich-Britich, Friketa. *Chetniks in Croatia, 1941-1945*. Zagreb: Globus, 1986.
Jelich, Ivan. *Communist Party of Croatia, 1937-1945* (vol. 2). Zagreb, 1981.
Jelich, Ivan. *Croatia in War and Revolution, 1941-1945*. Zagreb: School Books, 1978.
Jelich, Ivan. *Tragedy in Kerestinac*. Ljubljana: CL. GP Delo, 1986.
Jevtich, Atanasije. *From Jadovno to Kosovo*. Belgrade, 1985.
Jovanovich, Batric. *Montenegrins about Themselves*. Belgrade: People's Books, 1986.
Jukich, Ilija. *The Fall of Yugoslavia*. New York and London: Harcourt Brace Jovanovich, 1974.

Karapandzich, Bora. *Kochevye*. Munich: Iskra, 1945-1970.

Kazimirovich, Vasa. *The ISC in the Light of German Documents and the Diary of Glaise von Horstenau, 1941-1944*. Belgrade: New Books, 1987.

Kljakich, Slobodan. *A Conspiracy of Silence*. Belgrade: Serbian Press Publishing, 1991.

Korach, Stanko. *Between Two Wars, 1918-1941*. Belgrade: Nolit, 1982.

Kordich, Mile. *General*. Belgrade: Professional Books, 1988.

Kordich, Mile. *Goli Otok*. Belgrade: Professional Books, 1990.

Kordich, Mile. *Prophet of Evil*. Belgrade: Professional Books, 1981.

Kordich, Mile. *Schism*. Belgrade: Professional Books, 1991.

Kostich, Lazo. *Holocaust in the ISC*. Chicago: Liberty, 1981.

Krestich, Vasilije. *Serbo-Croatian Relationship and the Yugoslav Idea*. Belgrade: People's Books, 1983.

Krizman, Bogdan. *Ante Pavelich and the Ustashe*. Zagreb: Globus, 1978.

Krizman, Bogdan. *Pavelich Between Hitler and Mussolini*. Zagreb, 1980.

Krsmanovich, Momir. *Running of Bloody Drina* (vol. 1 & 2). Belgrade: Yugoslav Estrado, 1989.

Kuper, Leo. *Genocide: Its Political Use in the Twentieth Century*. New Haven, Conn., 1971.

Lafran, R. G. D. *The Serbs*. New York: Dorset Press, 1989.

Lakich, Mihailo. *War Fortune*. Belgrade: Nolit, 1973.

Letkovich, Misho. *The Negotiations of March 1943*. Belgrade: People's Books, 1985.

Latkovich, Vido. *Petar Petrovich-Njegosh*. Belgrade: Nolit, 1963.

Lee, Michael. *The Rape of Serbia*. San Diego, Calif.: Harcourt Brace Jovanovich, 1990.

Library, Litera. *Kosovo Struggle: Myth, Legend and Reality*. Belgrade: Kosmos, 1989.

Liberal Magazine, Cetinje, 1990, 1991, 1992.

Lukich, Dragoje. *The War and the Children of Kozara*. Belgrade, 1984.

Ljvovic, Nemirovski Evgenij. *Octoich, First Herald of Djuradj Crnojevich, 1494*. Cetinje: Library of Montenegro, 1987.

Maclean, Fitzroy. *Eastern Approaches*. London: Lowe and Brydone, 1949.

Maclean, Fitzroy. *Tito*. New York: McGraw-Hill, 1980.

Macmillan, Harold. *The Blast of War, 1939-1945*. New York: Harper & Row, 1967.

Manhattan, Avro. *Terror and Yugoslavia*. London, 1953.

Manhattan, Avro. *The Vatican's Holocaust*. Springfield, Mo.: Ozark Books, 1988.

Manning, Clarence A. (Trans.). *The Ray of Microcosm by P. P. Njegosh*. Munich: Library Svechanik, 1953.

Marjanovich, Jovan, Moraca Pero. *Our War of Liberation and People's Revolution, 1941-1945*. Belgrade: Prosveta, 1958.

Marquette, Sandy. *Serbia: A Thousand Points of Light, A Report*. Chicago, 1992.

Martin, David. *Patriot or Traitor*. Stanford, Calif.: Hoover Institute Press, 1978.

Mihailovich, B. *Njegosh*. Cetinje: Obod, 1966.

Mihailovich, Dragoslav. *Goli Otok*. Belgrade: Politika, 1990.

Miletich, Antun. *Concentration Camp Jasenovac, 1941-1945*. Belgrade: People's Books, 1986 (vol. 1 & 2), 1987 (vol. 3).

Mitrovich, Jeremije. *Serbophobia: Who Hates Serbs and Why*. Belgrade, 1991.

Morfill, W. *Slavonic Literature*. New York: E. & J. Young, 1883.

Nenadovich, Ljubo. *A Letter about a Montenegrin*. Zagreb: Government Printing Office, 1950.

Nenadovich, Ljubo. *Letters from Italy*. Zagreb: Government Printing Office, 1950.

Nikolich, Nikola. *Jasenovac Camp*. Zagreb: TNZ Hrvatska, 1948.

Novak, Victor. *Magnum Crimen*. Zagreb: TNZ Hrvatska, 1948.
Pantich, Tihomir. *Two Decades under Communism*. Chicago: Pantich, 1965.
The Persecution of Serbs in Croatia, 1990-1991, Documents.
Pershen, Mirko. *Ustashe Camps*. Zagreb, 1966.
Pesut, Mane. *Revolution in Lici, 1941-1945*. Pesut, 1966.
Petranovich, Branko. *Revolution and Counterrevolution* (vol. 1 & 2). Belgrade: Rad, 1983.
Petrovich, Nicholas. *Memoirs*. Cetinje: Obod, 1988.
Petrovich, Petar-Njegosh. *Collected Works* (7 volumes). Belgrade: Graphic Institute, 1967.
Petrovich, Petar-Njegosh. *Mountain Wreath*. Belgrade: Serbian Literary Cooperative, 1983.
Petrovich, Rastislav. *The Conspiracy Against Serbs*. Belgrade: Dositej, 1990.
Petrovich, Rastislav. "Declaration of Montenegrin Parliament." *Politika* interview, February 12, 1988.
Petrovich, Rastislav. *The Extermination of Serbs on the Territory of the Independent State of Croatia*. Belgrade: Serbian Press, 1991.
Plecash, Nikola. *"Nitonja." Conflagration in Krajina*. Chicago: Plecash, 1975.
Popovich, Pavle. *The Life of Petar II Petrovich-Njegosh*. Cetinje: Obod, 1966.
Potkozarac, Jovan. *Serbs of the Past*. Belgrade: Dimitrije Davidovich, 1969.
Radulovich, Filip. *The Love of Josip Broz*. Belgrade: Grafos, 1990.
Radusinovich, Pavle. *Settlements of Old Montenegro*. Belgrade: People's Books, 1985.
Rastoder, Rifat, and Branimir Kovacevich. *Red Stain*. Podgorica: Victory, 1990.
Roberts, Walter R. *Tito, Mihailovich, and the Allies. 1941-1945*. New Brunswick, N.Y.: Rutgers University Press, 1969.
Rootham, Jasper. *Misfire*. London: Chatts and Winders, 1946.
Rovinskij, P. *Montenegro in the Past and Present*. Petrograd: Tipografija Imperatorskoj Akademija Narek, 1915.
Seitz, Albert. *Mihailovich—Hoax or Hero*. Columbus, Ohio: Leigh House, 1953.
Sekulich, Isidora. *Comments on Njegosh*. Novi Sad: Serbian Chronicles, 1960.
Sekulich, Isidora. *To Njegosh*. Sarajevo: Light Publishing, 1968.
Sekulich, Isidora. *To Njegosh: A Book of Great Gratitude*. Belgrade: Culture, 1953.
Seton Watson, Loffan, and Stephen Clissold. *A Short History of Yugoslavia*. Cambridge University Press, 1966.
Seton Watson, R. W. *Yugoslavs—Correspondence, 1918-1941*. Zagreb and London: University of Zagreb, Institute for Croatian History, Britannic Academy, 1976.
Simich, Mihailo. *Roman Catholic Church and Serbs*. Belgrade, Simax, 1991.
Simich, Simo. *Hercegovina's Bishops During Yugoslav Occupation*. Belgrade: Culture, 1990.
Simich, Simo. *Serbs Proselytism During World War II*. Belgrade: Culture, 1990.
Simich, Simo. *Vatican Against Yugoslavia*. Belgrade: Culture, 1990.
Skoko, Savo. *The Slaughters of Hercegovina Serbs 1941*. Belgrade, 1991.
Slijepcevich, Pero. *Some Thoughts about Njegosh*. Novi Sad: Future Printing Press, 1963.
Spasojevich, Svetislav. *The Communists and I*. Grayslake: Free Serbian Diocese for America and Canada, 1991.
Stankovich, Slobodan. *The End of the Tito Era*. Stanford, Calif.: Hoover Institute Press, 1981.
Stanojevich, Branimir. *Alojzije Stepinac: Criminal or Saint?* Belgrade, 1985.
Stojanovich, B. Milinko. *Goli Otok*. Belgrade: Professional Books, 1991.
Sulzberger, C. L. *The American Heritage Picture History of World War II*. New York: American Heritage, 1966.
Sulzberger, C. L. *A Long Row of Candles*. Ontario, Canada: Macmillan, 1969.

Taylor, A. F. P. *From Sarajevo to Potsdam*. London: Harcourt Brace Jovanovich, 1966.

Tepavcevich, Aleksa. *The Struggle for Freedom*. Ontario, Canada: Sinclair Smith Press, 1987.

Terzich, Velimir. *Yugoslavia in the April War, 1941*. Podgorica: Graphic Institute, 1963.

Treshnich, Milan. *From Tudjman to Broz*. Belgrade: Literary Newspapers, 1991.

Tito, Josip Broz. *Zbornik* (Collection, April 2, 1951; January 4, 1954; January 7, 1954; April 16, 1956; February 6, 1957; February 7, 1957; January 20, 1961; February 10, 1962; May 10, 1962; February 2, 1963.

Truman, Harry S. *Memoirs: Years of Decision*. Garden City, N.Y.: Doubleday, 1955.

Victory (main Montenegrin daily newspaper), 1990, 1991, 1992, 1993.

Velimirovich, Nikolaj. *Svecanik*. 1954.

Vojnovich, Novica. *Serbian Pits in Prebilovci*. Podgorica, 1991.

Vucetich, Stevan. *The Civil War in Montenegro, 1941-1945*. Detroit, Mich.: Montenegrin Education Club, 1947.

Vujovich, Djuro. *Lovcenski National Liberation Movement*. Cetinje: Obod, 1976.

Vukcevich, Bosko S. *Diverse Forces in Yugoslavia, 1941-1945*. Los Angeles: Authors Unlimited, 1990.

Vukcevich, Nikola. *A Contribution to the Tradition of Montenegro*. Belgrade: Serbian Enterprises, 1971.

Vukcevich, Nikola. *The Ethnic Origins of Montenegrins*. Belgrade, 1981.

Vukcevich, Nikola. *A Review of Some Questions from Montenegrin History*. Belgrade: Sava Mihich, 1981.

Vukcevich, P. Blagota. "Communist Culprits and the Sufferings of Ljeshnjani Chetniks in Slovenia." *Mirror* (*Ogledalo*) (Podgorica), no. 7, November 28, 1991.

Vukcevich, Radoje. "Blindness of British Diplomacy." *Herald* (Chicago), December 1965.

Vukcevich, Radoje. *General Mihailovich: The Trial and Great Injustice*. Chicago: Serbian Historical and Cultural Society, 1984.

Vukcevich, Radoje. "Three Horrible Crimes Toward Serbian People." *Herald* (Chicago), June 1975.

Vukmanovich, Tempo-Svetozar. *The Revolution Is Continuing (Memoirs)* (vol. 1-3). Belgrade: Communist, 1971.

Vuksan, Dushan. *In Memory of Petar II Petrovich-Njegosh*. Cetinje: Government Printing Press, 1926.

Waugh, Evelyn. *The End of the Battle*. Boston and Toronto, 1961.

Wiles, James W. (Trans.). *The Mountain Wreath by P. P. Njegosh*. London: Allen and Unwin, 1930.

Woodward, Llewellyn. *British Foreign Policy in the Second World War*. London: His Majesty's Stationary Office, 1962.

Wright, Peter. *Spycatcher*. New York: Viking Penguin, 1987.

Zivojinovich, Dragoljub, and Lucich Dejan. *Barbarism in Christ's Name. Contributions for Magnum Crimen*. Belgrade, 1988.

ABBREVIATIONS

NKVD—*Narodni komesarijat vnutrenjih djela* (Soviet secret police)
OSS—Office of Strategic Services (British)
OWI—Office of War Information (U.S.)

OZNA—''Party Organization for the Protection of the People'' (Yugoslav secret police, later called UDBA)

PC—Provincial Committee

PCCCPC—Provincial Central Committee of the Communist Party of Croatia

PCCCPM—Provincial Central Committee of the Communist Party of Montenegro

PCCCPY—Provincial Central Committee of the Communist Party of Yugoslavia

Ratlines—Pope's channels for smuggling Nazi war criminals

SOE—Special Operational Executive (British)

Tito—Secret international terrorist organization (*Tajna Internacionalna Teroristicka Organizacija*)

UDBA—Yugoslav secret police; *see* OZNA

ZAVNOH—Provincial Anti-Fascist Council National Liberation of Croatia

Index